GW00835938

RITCHIE OLD TESTAMENT COMMENTARIES

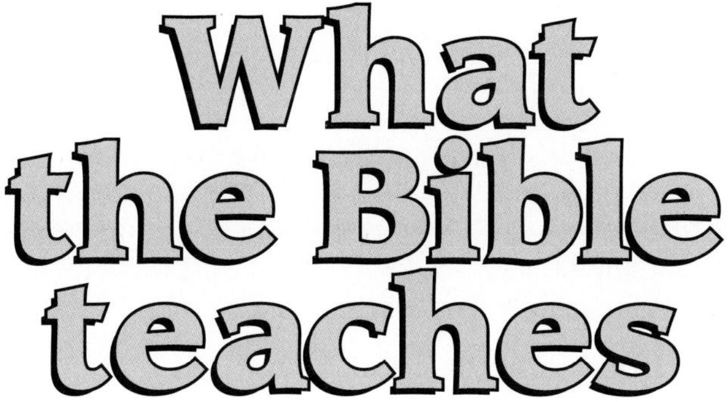

1 CHRONICLES

J. Hay

EDITOR **W. S. STEVELY**

2 CHRONICLES

W. Gustafson

EDITOR **W. S. STEVELY**

SERIES EDITORS

W. S. STEVELY **D. E. WEST**

ISBN-13: 978 1 907731 86 0

WHAT THE BIBLE TEACHES

40 Beansburn, Kilmarnock, Scotland

www.ritchiechristianmedia.co.uk

Typeset by John Ritchie Ltd.
Printed in China.

PREFACE

The publishers have commissioned this Old Testament series of commentaries to complement the completed set of New Testament commentaries issued under the general title "What the Bible Teaches". Together they seek to provide an accessible and useful tool for the study of, and meditation on, Scripture.

While there is no shortage of commentaries currently available on the various books of the Old Testament it was felt that there was no complete series that sought simply to apply the message of Genesis through to Malachi to the concerns of believers today.

The authors of these volumes are not scholars of the original languages and rely on others for guidance on the best modern views of word meanings and similar matters. However, all the authors share the conviction that the Bible in its entirety is the Word of God. They believe it to be reliable, accurate, and intended "for our learning" (Rom 15.4). This view has been explained further by Mr Stevely in a short series of articles that appeared in "The Believer's Magazine", also published by John Ritchie Ltd., in 1999.

The two Testaments fit together so that principles and illustrations from the Old are brought to bear on issues that arise on nearly every page of the New. Knowledge of the Old is therefore an indispensable aid to the proper understanding of the New. In particular the Lord Jesus can be seen in prophecy and picture again and again. He, Himself, as described in the Gospels, is an exemplar of this approach to the Old Testament through His constant reference to people and incidents whose histories are recorded for us, and to those prophetic statements that applied to Him.

Given this understanding of the nature and purpose of the Scriptures, the main lessons of the books are considered and applied to our circumstances today by authors experienced in preaching and teaching the Word of God.

Since no attempt is being made to produce an academic series the technical apparatus has been kept to a minimum. Where authors have judged it of value attention is drawn to linguistic and other issues. Transliteration, where appropriate, is accompanied by reference to the numerical system devised by Strong to allow the reader without knowledge of the original languages to gain access to the various lexical aids which have adopted this system. For clarity, numerical references to New Testament words only are given in italics, following the practice used in Strong's Concordance.

The system of transliteration generally used is that adopted by the *Theological Wordbook of the Old Testament* (TWOT), edited by Harris, Archer & Waltke, and published by Moody Press, Chicago, 1980. However, there are occasions when account has been taken of the commonly recognised English spelling of some Hebrew words.

References to Scripture without attribution are taken from the Authorised (King James) Version. Where other translations are quoted the source is indicated.

Biblical measurements are usually given in cubits. For ease of calculation the general assumption has been adopted that 1 cubit = 18 inches/46cms.

Since the commentaries do not necessarily follow a verse-by-verse approach, and to save space and cost, in general the text of Scripture is not included. It is assumed that all readers have available a copy of the Bible.

The complete Old Testament is expected to be covered in around fifteen to eighteen volumes. These will not appear in the order in which they are found in the Scriptures but simply in order of completion by the authors commissioned for the series.

W. S. STEVELY
D. E. WEST

CONTRIBUTORS

JACK HAY – 1 Chronicles

Jack Hay was brought up in Ayrshire and was saved as a boy, baptised at fourteen, and received into the assembly in Prestwick. In 1972 he was commended to the Lord's work in a full-time way, and at that time relocated to Perthshire. Over the years he has been involved in work with children, gospel preaching, and teaching the Word. His labours have taken him to foreign parts, particularly to places where there is a need for the simple teaching of Scripture. His writings have been mainly in the form of magazine articles, booklets, and tracts.

WALTER GUSTAFSON – 2 Chronicles

Walter Gustafson was born in Massachusetts to immigrant Swedish parents. In his late teens he thought he would like to take up a career as a preacher. His problem was that he was not sure that he himself was right with God. How then could he tell others what to do?

Shortly before turning twenty years of age he attended gospel meetings in Cliff Street Gospel Hall in Boston, Massachusetts. On the third occasion that he did so, on 2nd November, 1941, he was saved. Later that year he was baptized and was received into assembly fellowship early in 1942.

He was commended to the work of the Lord in January, 1954 and laboured in the gospel and in ministry. He spent much time in the state of Vermont, especially over the first ten years, but has preached in all of the Canadian provinces and in many areas of the USA.

More recently he has been occupied with writing while continuing his service in conversational Bible studies, teaching the Word of God in various assemblies and conferences, as well as preaching the gospel.

When writing this commentary he recalled that on the first occasion he spoke at the Toronto conference in 1962 he took up as his subject "Revival in Hezekiah's Day". Chronicles has been a source of enjoyment through the years.

ABBREVIATIONS

Amplified	The Amplified Bible
ASV	American Standard Version (the American variant of the RV).
AV	Authorised Version (known in USA as the King James Version).
ESV	English Standard Version
GNB	Good News Bible, 1976
JND	New Translation by J. N. Darby.
LXX	The Septuagint: the ancient translation of the Old Testament into Greek. Often quoted in the New Testament. (See SEPTUAGINT below.)
NEB	New English Bible, 1970
Newberry	The AV as edited by Thomas Newberry; also known as "The Englishman's Bible.
NIV	New International Version.
NKJV	New King James Version
NT	New Testament
OT	Old Testament

REB	Revised English Bible, 1989
RV	Revised Version, 1885 (published in England; a revision of the AV).
RSV	Revised Standard Version (revision of the ASV).
SEPTUAGINT	The Septuagint: the ancient translation of the Old Testament into Greek. Often quoted in the New Testament. (See LXX above.)
SPURRELL	A translation of the unpointed Hebrew Old Testament Scriptures by Helen Spurrell.
TWOT	*Theological Word Book of the Old Testament*, edited by Harris, Archer & Waltke.
Vulgate	A Latin translation of the Bible by Jerome c. 405 AD, the 1592 revision of which is the official Latin text of the Roman Catholic Church.
YLT	Young's Literal Translation

1 CHRONICLES

J. Hay

CONTENTS

BIBLIOGRAPHY

Allen, Leslie C. *Mastering the Old Testament: 1 & 2 Chronicles.* (General Editor: Lloyd J. Ogilvie.) Word Publishing, 1987.
Interesting practical lessons.

Corduan, Winfried. *Holman Old Testament Commentary: 1 & 2 Chronicles.* (General Editor: Max Anders.) Broadman & Holman, 2004.
Unusual layout but interesting applications.

Ellison, H. L. *The New Bible Commentary Revised.* (Edited by D. Guthrie, J. A. Motyer, A. M. Stibbs, and D. J. Wiseman.) Inter-Varsity Press, 1970.
Helpful despite the limitations of a one-volume commentary.

Ewan, I. Y. *The Caravanserai.* E. A. Ewan, 1980.
A collection of poems, some of which have been quoted in the commentary. A delightful volume of Scripture-based poetry.

Heading, John. *Understanding 1 & 2 Chronicles. The House of God and its Service.* Walterick Publishers, 1980.
As the sub-title suggests, the book majors on house of God teaching from these Old Testament books. Profitable applications.

Howard, J. K. *The International Bible Commentary.* (General Editor: F. F. Bruce.) Zondervan, 1986.
Again, there are interesting things here despite the limited space of a one-volume commentary.

Keller, W. Phillip. *David, The Shepherd King.* Word Publishing, 1987.
With its companion volume, "David, The Time of Saul's Tyranny", it is informative, practical, sometimes imaginative, but very readable.

Ratcliffe, Tom H. *Bible Plants, Fruits & Products.* Christian Year Publications, 2002.
An exceptional Christ-honouring study of the many plants of Scripture.

Rawlinson, George. *Holy Bible with Commentary.* (Editor: F. C. Cook.) John Murray, 1873.
Old fashioned but good. Helps to elucidate some points.

Roberts, Don. *God's Diary: Notes on 1 & 2 Chronicles.* Gospel Tract Publications, 1989.
As the title suggests, the book consists of "Notes" so, inevitably, it is brief, but helpful comments can be lifted.

Selman, Martin J. *Tyndale Old Testament Commentaries: 1 Chronicles.* (General Editor: D. J. Wiseman.) Inter-Varsity Press, 1994.
A very lengthy introduction. Perhaps a little heavy.

Thompson, J. A. *The New American Commentary: 1 & 2 Chronicles.* (General Editor: E. Ray Clendenen.) Broadman & Holman, 1994.
Based on the NIV. Some interesting touches.

Weirsbe, Warren W. *The Bible Exposition Commentary.* Victor, 2003.
As usual, Weirsbe is lucid and helpful, but as far as a study of 1 Chronicles is concerned, it suffers from its merger with 2 Samuel.

Wilcock, Michael. *The Bible Speaks Today: The Message of Chronicles.* (Old Testament Editor: J. A. Motyer.) Inter-Varsity Press, 1987.
Reasonably helpful.

Much help is to be derived from Commentaries incorporated in the ***Online Bible****. Most of these are well-tried older commentaries such as Clarke, Gill, Jamieson Fausset & Brown, Matthew Henry, Poole, and Trapp. Obviously they are not of equal value, and there is a certain duplication, but on the whole these old writers have been helpful.*

INTRODUCTION

Authorship

The author of this book remains anonymous, although both Jewish and Christian traditions attribute it to Ezra. Scholars see his literary style in its pages. "There is not a garment in all Ezra's wardrobe that does not fit the Chronicler exactly" (C. C. Torrey). It may have been that Ezra was the man who penned its pages, but keep in mind that, whoever the scribe, he was "moved by the Holy Ghost" (2 Pet 1.21). Some commentators like to discuss sources of information, but in a sense that is an irrelevance in light of divine inspiration. We do know that the writer lived after the Babylonian captivity, for in the latter part of chapter 3 he traces the descendants of David right through that period of Judah's history. Later in the book there is a reference to the fact that "Judah was carried away captive to Babylon for their transgression" (9.1, RV).

In the Hebrew Scriptures, the two books of Chronicles comprised one volume, and 2 Chronicles ends with a brief account of Cyrus encouraging a return to Judah. This section is replicated in the first few verses of Ezra, another pointer to the fact that he may have been the author.

We are accustomed to thinking in terms of Malachi being the last book of the Old Testament, but in the Hebrew Scriptures, the combined book of Chronicles was placed at the end. Thus the Lord's reference to Abel and Zacharias (Mt 23.35) encompasses the whole of what we call the Old Testament, Genesis to Chronicles in their case. It is interesting that this last book of the Hebrew Scriptures and the first book of the New Testament both contain significant genealogies of David's line, the latter tracing it right to "Jesus, who is called Christ" (Mt 1.16).

First Readers

Whoever the Chronicler, the people who read the book first were people who, although back in their own land, were dominated by a foreign power, and were under threat from unsympathetic neighbours. Their social conditions were dire. It was a far cry from the military supremacy and national prosperity described in this history of their nation. They were now being pointed back to the pristine days of David's kingdom, and the establishing of the God-ordained form of worship at Jerusalem. The implied challenge was to replicate that in days of recovery when Temple worship was being re-established, and to throw off the lethargy that at times left that recovery becalmed. The implied warning was to avoid a repeat of the circumstances that had given rise to the destruction of the first house with all its glory, the insidious advance of idolatry, a trend which had ousted Jehovah and incurred His wrath.

Title

The original Hebrew title of the combined books of Chronicles was "The word of the day", or "The annals of the days". The united book was divided at the time of the Greek translation, the Septuagint, and with the translation, there was a change of title to "Things omitted". The inference was that in these two books fresh material was being supplied, facts that were not divulged in earlier writings. Some take exception to this particular title, but there is no real problem provided that we keep in mind that things included or omitted in any of these books was by divine decree, and not at the whim of a particular writer pursuing his own agenda. The narratives of 2 Samuel and 1 Chronicles are complementary.

The English title "Chronicles" had its origins with Jerome's Latin Vulgate translation. Scripture uses the phrases, "the chronicles (1697/3117) of the kings of Israel", and "the chronicles of the kings of Judah" (e.g. 1 Kings 14.19,29), but these should not be confused with the inspired accounts of 1 and 2 Chronicles. This is evident from the fact that in the Chronicles we are studying there are few references to "the kings of Israel". Allusions to the kings of the ten northern tribes are minimal, and only as they relate to the kings of Judah. These chronicles were just a daily log of events in the two kingdoms, and not an inspired record.

Main Character

The leading figure in the book is David. Obviously, there is a duplication of material found in 2 Samuel, but the repetition of facts and doctrine is a feature of the Word of God; it is a valuable tool in effective teaching. Paul told the saints things "often" (Phil 3.18). Peter put them "in remembrance" of things that they already knew (2 Pet 1.12). 1 Chronicles is not "vain repetition". The focus in both books is on the years of David's reign over Israel.

In 2 Samuel, the emphasis seems to be on David's military conquests, territorial expansion, and political intrigue, whereas in 1 Chronicles the spotlight is on his relationship to the Temple, the house of God. 2 Samuel tends to be political and civil, whereas the tone of 1 Chronicles is spiritual and religious. Significantly, there is no repetition of the record of David's dreadful moral collapse "in the matter of Uriah the Hittite" (1 Kings 15.5).

The first nine chapters of the book consist of genealogies, and, according to Ussher, the historical events thereafter cover a period of about forty-one years. This ties in with the fact that the duration of David's reign was just in excess of forty years (2 Sam 5.4; 1 Kings 2.11; 1 Chr 3.4; 29.27).

Leading Theme

In particular, there is a great emphasis on David's concern to build the temple of God. From chapter 13, he exhibits a deep desire to "bring up" the ark of God, and by chapter 17 he has aspired to providing permanent quarters for it. God postpones David's plans till the next generation, but the latter part of the book is taken up with his supplying a location for the house, gathering materials for it, instructing Solomon to build it, and ensuring that the priesthood was in place to serve it.

Spiritual Value of the Book

Coming to 1 Chronicles, the reader of the Bible might find that the recitation of so many names in the first nine chapters is rather off-putting, and then, just when he thinks that the story is moving on, there is an interruption for more names! Before he reaches the end, he again faces another considerable section comprising mainly of names. The temptation is to ignore the book altogether. However, in common with the other historical Old Testament books, there is at least a threefold benefit from studying its contents.

1. The Lord Jesus said of the Scriptures, "they are they which testify of me" (Jn 5.39), and so you look for Christ in the book. In the New Testament there are few references to the two books of Chronicles, but there is a significant quotation from 1 Chronicles 17.13: "I will be his father, and he shall be my son" (see also 2 Samuel 7.14). In context, the reference is to Solomon, but in Hebrews 1.5 the verse is cited as an indication of the Sonship of Christ, a relationship with the Father that gives evidence that He is superior to angels. So Christ is seen in prophecy in this book. He is also seen in picture. Undoubtedly, the fact that David was now reigning after so many years of rejection and exile foreshadows the experience of the Lord Jesus. He was the One whose "own received him not" (Jn 1.11), and yet one day He will "reign in righteousness" (Is 32.1). The words of a parable expressed their attitude: "We will not have this man to reign over us" (Lk 19.14). By military power, that despised and rejected monarch will become "KING OF KINGS, AND LORD OF LORDS" (Rev 19.16).

2. Another reason for giving attention to these historical records is in this: "all these things happened unto them for ensamples: and they are written for our admonition" (1 Cor 10.11). The quotation refers to a previous generation of Israelites, but it is certainly a general principle of Biblical interpretation. As we read, we observe failures that we should avoid lest we come under divine discipline. Saul's disobedience and his dalliance with spiritism invited the judgment of God (10.13). David ignored divine order, and allied with Uzza's lack of reverence, it stirred the anger of the Lord (ch.13). By allowing Satan to provoke him to number Israel, David was subject to divine retribution (ch.21). Perusing the history then, we ask, "Are there lessons to be learned, and are there pitfalls to avoid?".

3. As explained in the general preface to this series, another benefit of Old Testament history is in this: "whatsoever things were written aforetime were written for our learning, that we through patience and comfort of the scriptures might have hope" (Rom 15.4). We can glean much of a positive nature by being acquainted with these inspired historical accounts. One of the main lessons from this book relates to our attitude to the house of God. As previously noted, a major section of the book is taken up with David's desire to build a dwelling place for God. In that connection, statements and actions can be applied to present circumstances. It should be understood that in this present age God "dwelleth not in temples made with hands" (Acts 17.24). However, "the church of the living God" is said to be "the house of God" (1 Tim 3.15). We will see in David's staunch commitment to his cause a pattern for us, an example of the loyalty that should characterise us in our devotion to the assembly of which we form a part.

Summary

Note some of the salient features of the twenty-nine chapters.

Chapters 1-9: Genealogies, with particular reference to the royal line, and the priestly line.
Chapter 10: The Death of Saul.
Chapters 11-12: David's Men.
Chapter 13: The Tragedy of Uzza.
Chapter 14: David Confirmed as King.
Chapters 15-16: Bringing the Ark.
Chapter 17: The Promise of a Dynasty.
Chapters 18-20: Various Military Victories.
Chapter 21: Numbering the People.
Chapter 22: Preparation for the House (Preparing the Materials and Preparing the Man).
Chapters 23-27: Levites, Priests, Singers, Doorkeepers, Captains, and Rulers.
Chapters 28-29: David's Last Appeal to His Subjects.

1 CHRONICLES 1

Genealogies were always of interest to the people of Israel. At Ephesus, even in New Testament times, some from a Jewish background were so preoccupied with genealogies and the "fables" surrounding those named, that they were a disturbing influence in the assembly (1 Tim 1.4). They were more taken up with that than with "godly edifying".

The first readers of 1 Chronicles knew the value of being able to trace their pedigree, for some who had returned from Babylon were unable to produce documentary evidence of their ancestry, and were, "as polluted, put from the priesthood" (Ezra 2.62). Thus to the Jew the early chapters of 1 Chronicles held a strange fascination while his Gentile counterpart may have seen them as somewhat irrelevant.

A general observation is that God does take note of names, as He does also of the circumstances and location of His people. The words of the Lord Jesus should be such an encouragement to us all: "he calleth his own sheep *by name*" (Jn 10.3).

The purpose of these genealogies is to recount the ancestry of David, and his subsequent progeny, for the family tree of a king is of great significance. This particular king developed a great longing to provide a sanctuary for God, with a functioning priesthood, so the lineage of the priests is also of major importance in the book. Others of the tribes of Israel feature as branches of the family tree.

This first chapter traces the line right back to Adam, and records sundry offshoots, some of which had a relationship with the nation of Israel as neighbours; often that relationship was hostile. The chapter takes us from Adam to Jacob and Esau, leaving us ready to pursue the tribes of Israel from the beginning of chapter 2, commencing with the kingly tribe of Judah. It is significant that in the genealogies Jacob is always referred to by his God-given name of Israel. The Chronicler is keen to remind his oppressed generation of the honour conferred upon their progenitor and of the dignity of their history. He wants to lift up their heads in difficult days.

Our chapter largely follows the genealogies contained in the book of Genesis. Obviously, there are variants of the names, but that factor will not concern us. Commentaries that are more technical and scholarly provide explanations of these differences.

Verses 1-4: Adam to Noah and his Sons

Adam is the fountainhead of all humanity, and, as the head, his one act of disobedience had tremendous implications for all who came under his headship; "many were made sinners" (Rom 5.19). Indeed, sin leapt full-grown into the world when the first man to be born became a murderer. However, there is no mention of Cain and Abel here. There is no need to mention them for there is no one left in the world descended from either of these brothers. There is no record that Abel was ever a father, and all Cain's descendants were wiped out at the flood, as were those of all of Adam's sons with the exception of Seth. Everyone in the world is descended from Adam through Seth and Noah. The deluge brought every other birth line to an end.

The writer assumes our knowledge of Genesis for there is no explanation that Shem, Ham and Japheth are the three sons of Noah rather than son, grandson, and great-grandson respectively. In going on to list their descendants, he does so in the order of Japheth, Ham and Shem, the order in which they are detailed in Genesis 10. In each case, it would appear that Shem is reserved till the end because that is the line that is pursued in the developing history of both books. In this chapter, a similar pattern is adopted for Abraham's sons and Isaac's sons. The son of greatest significance is always held till last. This literary style allows a smooth transition, as we are then given the ongoing generations connected with each of them.

Verses 5-7: The Sons of Japheth

It is generally believed that from Japheth stemmed the Gentile nations whose geographical location was more remote from Israel than that of the Hamites. There is nothing specifically noted about them here, but it is interesting that some of these nations will still be in existence in the end times. During the Tribulation, Israel will experience an invasion from the north, and among their attackers will be those drawn from the sons of Japheth (Ezek 38 & 39). More than a thousand years later, they will again feature in the final rebellion against divine authority at the end of the Millennium (Rev 20.7-10).

Verses 8-16: The Sons of Ham

Ham is said to have four sons, although, for no reason that is apparent to us, descendants of Put (6316) are not listed. "Put" is translated "Libya" or "Libyans" on occasions, e.g. Jeremiah 46.9, so it may be that this man's descendants settled in North Africa.

The most notable of the family of Cush was the infamous Nimrod. His biography is less detailed here than in Genesis 10, but we are again left with the impression of a self-seeking, dominant, aggressive individual, one who did all in his power to resurrect the rebellious inventive character of the Cain line that had been destroyed so comprehensively at the flood.

Mizraim's son Casluhim gets special mention. He was the father of the Philistines who from the days of the Judges were the main protagonists of the nation of Israel, a constant irritant to the people of God. The historical section of 1 Chronicles commences with them defeating and killing King Saul. David, the hero of the book, was in constant conflict with them. They had migrated from North Africa through Egypt to the south-west corner of the land. Typically, they picture mere professors among God's people, for they were in the land without experiencing redemption by the blood of the lamb, or separation from Egypt by the Red Sea. In later years, as a result of their influence and dominance, the land took its name from them and became known as Palestine. What they were to Israel by way of disruption and aggression, professing infiltrators are to the assembly today.

Canaan was the man whose name was linked with the land from the days when Abraham left Ur in response to God's call (Gen 11.31). The names of some of his descendants are familiar as those tribes conquered by Israel when they invaded the Promised Land.

Verses 17-23: The Sons of Shem (1)

Following the pattern of the genealogies of Genesis 10 and 11, these few verses give a preliminary record of Shem's descendants, with one or two digressions, before the straight line from Shem to Abraham is traced in vv.24-27. It is worth noting that Eber (5677) is the name from which the familiar word "Hebrew" (5680) is derived. One of his sons was Peleg (6389) meaning "division". He was so called because "in his days the earth was divided". This seems to be a reference to the confusing of the languages at Babel, and the subsequent scattering of humanity (Gen 11.1-9). That event falls into the time frame of Peleg's life, so the allusion is to that rather than thinking in terms of the movement of land masses, and the formation of continents.

Verses 24-28: The Sons of Shem (2)

As suggested above, these verses review earlier statements, but now give the direct link from Shem to Abram, a name meaning "exalted father" (87). There is a reminder here of his name being changed to Abraham, "father of a multitude" (85). The following chapters help demonstrate the justification for the name change, as his descendants flourish and, as promised by God, become as sand, stars, and dust for multitude.

Abraham's two sons, Isaac and Ishmael, are now introduced. First mentioned is Isaac, the son of promise, offspring of the beloved Sarah. His uniqueness among the sons of Abraham is underlined in that he is described as "his only begotten son" (Heb 11.17). As such, despite being younger than Ishmael, he gets first mention, although as already observed, in keeping with the pattern of the chapter, details of Ishmael's family line feature before his.

These two brothers were literal characters, but they and their circumstances are seen in Scripture as being allegorical. The contrast is between the flesh and the Spirit, between the law and grace, between bondage and freedom (Gal 4.21-31).

Verses 29-31: The Sons of Ishmael

Ishmael's descendants are not traced beyond his immediate sons, of whom there were twelve. However, the fact that he did have twelve sons gives us confidence that God's promise to Hagar was fulfilled: "I will make him a great nation" (Gen 21.18), and the similar promise to Abraham, "I… will make him fruitful, and will multiply him exceedingly" (Gen 17.20).

Verses 32-33: The Sons of Keturah

In Genesis 25.1, the reading of the AV gives Keturah the status of a wife, but here she is described as "Abraham's concubine". This is more likely the case, as Isaac is seen as unique, and in contrast to "the sons of the concubines, which Abraham had" (Gen 25.6), the immediate context having just mentioned Keturah's sons. When Genesis 25.1 says, "Abraham took a wife" (802), the word "wife" is a general word for a female person, woman or wife, and in fact is translated "woman" over 320 times in the AV.

The only familiar name among Keturah's sons is that of Midian. His descendants were another nation who on occasions harassed the people of God. They were instrumental in escorting Joseph to slavery in Egypt (Gen 37.36). They collaborated with Moab to hire Balaam to curse Israel (Num 22.7). Subsequently, they were instrumental in corrupting God's people (Num 25). In Gideon's day they marshalled massive armies to destroy and impoverish Israel (Judg 6-8). Basically, Midian (4080) means "strife", and their activities hold challenging warnings of the effects of strife and unrest among the saints.

Verse 34: Abraham and Isaac; Esau and Israel

"Abraham begat Isaac." The bald statement conceals the drama of the event, as, after years of waiting and frustration, the son of promise was born. It tells nothing of the faith of a man whose body was "as good as dead" (Rom 4.19, RV). There is no reference to the faith of a woman who "received power to conceive seed when she was past age" (Heb 11.11, RV). But it happened: "Abraham begat Isaac".

These same words introduce the genealogy of another King, "Jesus, who is called Christ" (Mt 1.16): "The book of the generation of Jesus Christ, the son of David, the son of Abraham" (Mt 1.1-2). A supernatural birth heads the list; a more remarkable birth concludes it. Mary the mother of Jesus had been "found with child of the Holy Ghost" (Mt 1.18), so Joseph did not beget Jesus; Joseph was "the husband of Mary, of whom was born Jesus, who is called Christ" (Mt 1.16). After many years of barrenness, Sarah had miraculously given birth to a son in her old age, but the child was conceived by the normal process of generation. Mary gave birth to her Son without the instrumentality of a human father at all.

Although Abraham is regarded as the father of the nation, he does not really take centre stage in this genealogy. Like so many others he is seen as a link in the chain that would bring in the king.

Isaac's twin boys now feature, and, as already observed, in these genealogies Jacob is always designated "Israel".

Verses 35-42: The Sons of Esau and Seir

These are named without comment, except that there is a reference to one woman, Timna, "Lotan's sister" (v.39). It would appear that being Lotan's sister she was a daughter of Seir (v.38), a man who had no blood relationship with Esau at all. Esau had migrated to territory that had been occupied by the Seirites and the names Seir and Edom became interchangeable in describing that whole area (Gen 32.3). Obviously, there was intermarriage between the families, and Timna became the concubine of Esau's son Eliphaz (Gen 36.12). Amalek was the fruit of that relationship. Perhaps that is the reason for the mention of Timna here, for more than any others, the Amalekites outraged God by being the first to mount an offensive against His people as they journeyed from Egypt to Canaan (Ex 17.8-16). "If the Midianites were the traders, the Amalekites were the raiders" (Roberts). God pledged to "have war with Amalek from generation to generation" (Ex 17.16). In the days of Saul he ordered their complete extermination (1 Sam 15.1-3) and Saul's non-compliance was the catalyst for his final rejection. It is generally accepted that, illustratively, Amalek is a picture of the flesh, the sinful nature that is within us all. It is incorrigibly evil and can never be improved (Rom 8.7). Both Peter and Paul testify to the perpetual conflict that it promotes (1 Pet 2.11; Gal 5.17). Our only recourse is to be dependent on the Holy Spirit of God; "through the Spirit...mortify the deeds of the body" (Rom 8.13).

Verses 43-50: The Kings of Edom

Esau and Edom are synonymous terms (Gen 25.30; 36.1,8,19), and so we now turn to consider kings who ruled over the descendants of Esau. A monarchy was in place there before ever there was a king in Israel (v.43). God's ideal form of government for His own people was theocracy, and it was only when there was a clamour for a king to make them "like all the nations" that He gave them Saul (1 Sam 8-10). The Gentile nations had long been ruled by kings.

It is of interest that God notes the names of these kings of Edom. The world would regard them as big fish in a very small pond, but God had installed every one of them - "the powers that be are ordained of God" (Rom 13.1). Thus it is still: hence the responsibility of believers to "be subject unto the higher powers". Civil disobedience is not an option except in situations where the law of the land and divine decrees are in direct conflict. Only then does the principle come into play, "We ought to obey God rather than men" (Acts 5.29).

It appears that there was no established dynasty in Edom. However, there is no suggestion that kings were ousted by military coups as became the norm among the northern tribes of Israel. It was only after they had died that others reigned in their place, but there was no tradition of heredity; rather, a strong character emerged to take control. Successive kings had their seat of administration in different places. Only one military conquest is recorded (v.46), and the suggestion is that it was this victory that brought Hadad to the fore and gave him credibility. The haphazard transition of power that obtained in Edom provides the Chronicler with a backcloth that enhances the orderly character of the Davidic dynasty. The word to

David would be, "the Lord will build thee an house" (17.10). David rejoiced in that promise: "thou hast also spoken of thy servant's house for a great while to come" (v.17).

The wife and mother-in-law of another Hadad warrant a reference by the inspired Chronicler (v.50). Perhaps it is conjecture, but the fact that no other women are mentioned suggests that these two made a positive impact on the royal court. The same conclusion can be drawn from allusions to the names of some of the mothers of the kings of Judah in 2 Chronicles. A notable exception is Athaliah, whose influence was totally disastrous (22.2-3).

Verses 51-54: The Dukes of Edom

From a UK perspective, the word "duke" (441) is perhaps too grand a word to describe these men. Most translations use the word "chief", so these were the men who were clan chieftains among the Edomites. Their authority may not have been as extensive as the kings, but they too were in place by divine appointment. "There is no power but of God" (Rom 13.1). Every strata of government, national or local, is of His making, and requires the loyalty of its Christian subjects.

Etymologically, the word translated "duke" holds some lessons for leaders among the people of God. Among other things, it carries with it the thought of being a guide, a friend, and of being gentle. You can read these into the qualifications of an overseer (1 Tim 3.1-7). A guide: "apt to teach". A friend: "given to hospitality". Gentle: many translations substitute that word for "patient" in v.3. It is a far cry from the high-handed way in which men like Saul and Rehoboam dealt with the people of God. A different spirit is called for by Peter: "neither as being lords over God's heritage, but being ensamples to the flock" (1 Pet 5.3). Let the dignity and tenderness implied in the word "duke" feature in the lives of those who guide the people of God today. The word "shepherd" encapsulates these leadership qualities (Eph 4.11, JND).

With many of the offshoots of the family tree explored, the Chronicler is now ready to introduce the sons of Israel, and, in particular, within a few verses take us to the man who will be at the centre of his narrative, David the king (2.15).

1 CHRONICLES 2

From chapter 2 the Chronicler focuses on the descendants of Jacob. Initially, he lists the names of Israel's twelve sons before devoting considerable space to the progeny of Judah. As has been suggested already, this gives priority to the kingly line, a line that would ultimately extend beyond David to Him "who was born of the seed of David according to the flesh" (Rom 1.3, RV). Jacob had predicted that the sceptre would "not depart from Judah" (Gen 49.10), an early indication that royalty would feature in that tribe. In His sovereignty, God "chose the tribe of Judah"; "He chose David also his servant" (Ps 78.68,70). "Judah prevailed above his brethren, and of him came the chief ruler" (1 Chr 5.2).

The creature that is linked symbolically with Judah is the lion (Gen 49.9), an apt emblem of power and regality. Men regard it as the king of beasts, a concept that has some foundation in Scripture, for it is said to be the "strongest among beasts, and turneth not away for any" (Prov 30.30). Our Saviour is "the Lion of the tribe of Juda" (Rev 5.5), a fitting metaphor of His regal majesty. Thus here the kingly tribe has precedence among the other tribes.

Particulars of the tribe of Judah extend right to 4.23, with special reference to "the sons of David" in chapter 3, a record that carries the monarch's line right through the period of the Babylonian captivity.

The genealogies present difficulties from time to time, in that sometimes the names and circumstances of individuals seem to differ from records elsewhere in Scripture. A variety of reasons can account for this. Some people had more than one name, as is the case today. On occasions, people with the same name feature in extended families. There were times when a man fathered a child to perpetuate the line of his deceased childless brother in a situation that we call levirate marriage. Sometimes the word "son" means descendant rather than a literal son. In a few situations the verb "to beget" simply means that the aforementioned person was an ancestor. Attention will be drawn to these situations when they arise.

Verses 1-2: The Sons of Israel

Jacob's twelve sons are not listed according to age, and the reason for the order is unclear. Leah's six sons appear first, then Dan, the first son by Rachel's handmaid Bilhah. Next in the record are Joseph and Benjamin, the sons of Rachel herself, followed by Naphthali, Bilhah's second son. Bringing up the rear are the two sons of Leah's maid Zilpah. Reading the names of these patriarchs, one cannot help but be impressed by the grace of God in establishing that men of their character should form the foundation of such a favoured nation. With the exception of Joseph, they were all seriously flawed, and each one of them had descendants who surpassed them morally, or whose impact for God far outshone that of the father of their tribe. It is all evidence of the Scriptural principle, "not of works, but of him that calleth" (Rom 9.11).

Verses 3-4: The Sons of Judah

Judah fathered five sons, the first three by Shua his Canaanite wife. His story is a sorry illustration of the consequences of backsliding. He "went down from his brethren", and in turning from fellowship with his brethren, befriended "a certain Adullamite, whose name was Hirah". This in turn brought him into contact with the young Canaanite woman who was to become his wife (Gen 38.1-2). Clearly it was an unequal yoke. His sister Dinah encountered the same temptations when she "went out to see the daughters of the land" (34.1). Let the reader apply the lessons.

Er and Onan were the two elder sons of Judah and both came under the judgment of God (Gen 38.7-10). Here there is reference only to the untimely death of Er - he "was evil in the sight of the Lord; and he slew him" (v.3). This is the first reference to Jehovah in 1 Chronicles. Normally that name of God is a reminder that He is the covenant keeping God (Ex 6.2-9), but here we are learning that His faithfulness is balanced by His intolerance of wicked behaviour; Er's persistent rebellion incurred His judgment.

The young man's widow Tamar now enters the picture, for she became the mother of Judah's illegitimate twins Pharez and Zerah. It is a sordid tale of betrayal, resentment, trickery, and lust (Gen 38.11-30). Tamar is the first of four women to feature in the genealogy of the Messiah in Matthew 1. Another two of the four share her immoral character, and then there was Ruth the Moabitess, a young woman from an alien idolatrous background. "Who can bring a clean thing out of an unclean? not one" (Job 14.4). And yet from such a polluted stream came the One who is "holy, harmless, undefiled, separate from sinners" (Heb 7.26).

The line that would lead to David was through Pharez.

Verse 5: The Sons of Pharez

As in Genesis 46.12, two sons are mentioned, Hezron and Hamul. The royal line was though Hezron.

Verses 6-8: The Sons of Zerah

Judah's second twin had five sons. The first is Zimri, or Zabdi (Josh 7.1). One of the tragedies of Israel's history is attributed to this strain of the family. The event is so familiar that the Chronicler assumes that we know the details, even the fact that Carmi (v.7) was the son of Zimri. His son Achar (Achan) was a troubler and a transgressor. Achan's transgression made him responsible for the defeat at Ai, and that event had the effect of troubling Israel. Thirty-six fighting men were lost, the people were terrified, and the invasion was stalled (Josh 7). The incident demonstrates the terrible effects of one miscreant among the people of God.

There is the possibility that Ethan, Heman, Calcol, and Dara were not literal sons of Zerah but rather sons in the sense of descendants, the sons of one Mahol. They are mentioned in 1 Kings 4.31 as being brothers who were famed for great wisdom, a wisdom eclipsed only by that of Solomon. The word Ezrahite is used in that verse, meaning "of the family of Zerah".

Verses 9-13: The Sons of Hezron

Three are cited, and then there is quick transition to Jesse without exploring the offshoots of the family tree at this stage. Familiar names are now mentioned. Nahshon features as the prince of Judah when the tribes were numbered in the wilderness (Num 1.7). His son Salma (Salmon) married Rahab the harlot, and became the father of Boaz, the male hero of the book of Ruth. That little book ends with the birth of Obed, and so to Jesse.

Verses 14-17: The Sons and Daughters of Jesse

Of the Lord Jesus it was said, "And there shall come forth a rod out of the stem of Jesse, and a Branch shall grow out of his roots" (Is 11.1). Isaiah links God's King with Jesse.

At this point in the genealogy we are faced with a difficulty. In 1 Samuel, Jesse is said to have eight sons, with David the youngest of the eight (1 Sam 16.10-11; 17.12-14). Here, David is said to be the youngest of seven. It has been suggested that one of the eight may have been an adopted son, but it is more likely that the seven who are mentioned here are seven out of eight survivors of that family, one having died without children and before David came to prominence. The Chronicler is looking back from the vantage point of centuries, and records only what is of significance for his own era. A deceased son with no progeny was of no consequence to the purpose of his writings.

David's sisters were Zeruiah and Abigail. Zeruiah's three sons, David's nephews, were notable warriors in his army. Abishai and Asahel featured among his mighty men (2 Sam 23.18,24), although the latter was killed by Abner while still in his prime (2 Sam 2.18-32). Joab's military prowess, and his fierce loyalty to David were beyond question, but his ruthlessness and guile robbed him of true greatness. A final act of treachery proved to be his undoing, and, primed by David, Solomon ordered his execution (1 Kings 2.5-6, 28-34).

Abigail's son was Amasa, who briefly commanded the rebel army of his cousin Absalom. As an act of conciliation, David appointed him head of his forces, but Amasa was one of the victims of Joab's brutality (2 Sam 17.25; 19.13; 20.4-13). Joab would brook no rival.

In 2 Samuel 17.25, Abigail is said to be the daughter of Nahash. Most scholars feel that "Nahash" is an alias for Jesse. Others suggest that it is a woman's name, and that Nahash was Abigail's mother, Zeruiah being the daughter of Jesse by another wife. The first suggestion seems more tenable, for in Scripture it is not uncommon for people to have more than one name, just as today most have a family name and a given name.

In that same verse Amasa is seen as the son of "Ithra an Israelite", while here his father is "Jether the Ishmeelite". There is no problem with the two names; they are variations of the same name. The possibility is that Jether was an Ishmaelite by birth, but then was absorbed into the nation as a proselyte, and he is described as "an Israelite" because in the long running rivalry between Judah and the other tribes his allegiance was with the segment that was consistently described as "Israel".

Verses 18-20: The Sons of Caleb

The Chronicler now reverts to some of the offshoots of the family tree, and we are thrown back to v.9 where Caleb is called "Chelubai". (This Caleb should not be confused with his more famous namesake although some commentators take them to be the same person.) Of note is that one of Caleb's descendants was Bezaleel, who with Aholiab was commissioned by God to superintend the building of the Tabernacle (Ex 31.1-11). It is significant that in a book that majors on building a sanctuary for God, there is mention here of a man who was prominent in building the former sanctuary.

Verses 21-24: The Sons of Hezron

We are still backtracking to pick up other strands, and thus we have further details of Hezron. Attention is drawn to the links that he and his family had with the Transjordan tribes in Gilead, and then his death is recorded. Scholars differ as to the location of the place of his decease. What is of significance is that at sixty years of age he had taken a wife, and at the time of his death she was pregnant. We must never lose sight of the fact that in the midst of all these lists of names human tragedies are concealed such as the one that we have here. In every generation life is a patchwork quilt of heartbreaks and disappointments.

Verses 25-41: Various Offshoots from Jerahmeel

Jerahmeel was Hezron's firstborn, and again this line of the family had its own griefs. Some died without children (v.30,32), a bitter sorrow in these ancient times. The barren Hannah described herself as "a woman of a sorrowful spirit" (1 Sam 1.15). Childlessness was a talking point in society, for Elisabeth was described as "her, who was called barren" (Lk 1.36), and she herself spoke of "my reproach among men" (v.25).

While not childless, another in this branch of the family had only daughters and had to revert to giving one of them to his Egyptian servant as a wife, to keep his line going, and to be an inheritor of his wealth (vv.34-35). A similar prospect had faced Abraham before the birth of Isaac (Gen 15.2-4).

It appears that Ahlai (v.31) was a daughter, the word "son" being a generic term.

Verses 42-55: Various Offshoots from Caleb

Once more we take a backward step to explore some other branches of the family tree connected with Caleb. This is the Chelubai of v.9, and the Caleb whose name already features in the chapter. It has already been suggested that he is not Caleb the son of Jephunneh, although respected commentators differ from that view. Each did have a daughter named Achsah (Josh 15.16; 1 Chr 2.49), but it is not unusual even today for the same name to be used for several individuals in an extended family. Jacob had a son called Joseph. Another Jacob had a son called Joseph (Mt 1.16), so it is not unimaginable that two Calebs had daughters called Achsah.

Towards the end of the chapter the list of names is mingled with place names, so it is extremely likely that places derived their names from the men associated with them. Of most significance is the fact that there were scribes at a place called Jabez (v.55). If the place takes its name from the man who bears that name (4.9-10), it would appear that he made an impact on others so that some in his sphere of influence were encouraged to take an interest in the scriptures too. The power of a godly example cannot be overstated.

A man called Ephratah features, as does one Bethlehem (vv.50-51), and inevitably our thoughts go to the prediction of the birthplace of Messiah, "Beth-lehem Ephratah" (Micah 5.2). Bethlehem, of course, was the "the city of David" (Lk 2.4), and in 1 Chronicles 2 the mention of the two men who gave their names to the place is another small step in preparing us for the emergence of David the king.

Sub-divisions of the tribe also feature by name, and of particular interest is the mention of the house of Rechab. Just prior to the captivity, Jeremiah had involved these nomads in an action parable to expose the rank disobedience of the people of Judah (Jer 35). The Rechabites were men of great character. Their forefather Jonadab had commanded a nomadic and abstentious lifestyle and under no circumstances would they deviate from it. By contrast, the men of Judah had no compunction about rejecting God's commands.

1 CHRONICLES 3

The descendants of Judah still feature in chapter 3, but with particular reference to the family of David. His own sons are mentioned, and then those men whose biographies are recorded in 2 Chronicles as the kings of Judah. Reference is made to the various kings at the time of the Babylonian invasion, and then through Jeconiah the line continues beyond the captivity. At that stage, attention is drawn to various branches of the tree, and some of these names would have been familiar to the original readers as being contemporaries.

Verses 1-4: Sons who were Born at Hebron

Prior to being a fugitive, David had been married to Michal. He had also taken wives during his exile (1 Sam 25.40-44), but he does not appear to have had children until after he was king. His adverse circumstances were certainly not conducive to family life. Perhaps that is the thought in Paul's mind when he sees singleness as a preference at the time of writing to the Corinthians: "by reason of the present distress" (1 Cor 7.26, RV).

Hebron was David's seat of authority while he administered the tribe of Judah. Like Abraham, Caleb, and others, for him there was a special attraction about Hebron. Its name means "association" or "fellowship", and it pictures the importance of living in fellowship with God. "He that ruleth over men must be just, ruling in the fear of God" (2 Sam 23.3). Leaders among God's people should keep that in mind. Living close to God is essential for their function, for they are taking care of "the church *of God*" (1 Tim 3.5). They are "steward(s) of God" (Titus 1.7), administering His house, and as such must make constant reference to Him. Spiritually, they must dwell at Hebron.

Some of these sons of David were a grave disappointment to him, and if what was true of Adonijah was true of the rest it is little wonder, for "his father had not displeased him at any time in saying, Why hast thou done so?" (1 Kings 1.6). There was a serious lack of discipline in David's household. Not least of David's heartbreaks was the atrocious behaviour of his firstborn Amnon, an appalling crime that invited vengeance at the hands of his brother Absalom (2 Sam 13).

In 2 Samuel 3.3 David's second son Daniel is called "Chileab".

Absalom and Adonijah were rebels who aspired to David's throne. Both insurgencies were thwarted, because by divine decree Solomon was destined to rule.

Of Shephatiah and Ithream we know nothing. It is suggested by some that Ithream's mother Eglah was Michal, who gave birth to him between being reinstated as David's wife and being punished for her cynicism, resulting in her having "no child unto the day of her death" (2 Sam 6.23). Of such an assertion we cannot be sure.

Six sons, six mothers; it is a sad commentary on a serious flaw in David's character. At a practical level, how could such a household live harmoniously? Is it any wonder that with the passing of the years relationships in the family were strained to breaking point? Whenever God's ideal of a one-man one-woman relationship is violated, an intolerable psychological burden is placed on those who may be the innocent victims of the entanglements - the families involved.

Verses 5-9: Sons who were Born at Jerusalem

Bath-shua (Bath-sheba) was the mother of four of David's sons. Both her father and her first husband were among his mighty men (2 Sam 23.34,39). Ammiel here is "Eliam" in 2 Samuel 11.3; 23.34. Both names have to do with God being a kinsman. If Eliam was her father, then Ahithophel was her grandfather (2 Sam 23.34). Perhaps this goes some way to explaining the treachery of this trusted friend and advisor at the time of Absalom's rebellion. It appears that secretly he had harboured a smouldering grudge against David for the way in which he had treated his granddaughter.

Although Solomon was the first of Bath-shua's surviving sons, he is mentioned last because, as in ch.1, the line that will be developed is reserved till the end. It may be that Nathan was so named in honour of the prophet who had dealt so faithfully and yet so graciously with his father David. Mary the mother of Jesus was descended from David through Nathan (Lk 3.31).

Another nine sons are mentioned without reference to mothers. None of them had the notoriety of Absalom, nor yet the fame of Solomon, but still they are noted by God as the sons of a king. Perhaps the majority of God's people attract no attention either by infamous exploits or heroic deeds, yet heaven notes their relationship to the King, and in that they can rejoice.

The sons of concubines remain unnamed, but mention is made of Tamar, the wretched girl who was tricked and abused by her brother Amnon (2 Sam 13). Sexual abuse within a family is not a modern phenomenon. It existed in ancient times, and in the highest of circles.

The mention of so many wives and concubines exposes a blemish in David's character. Israel's kings were prohibited from multiplying horses, wives, or silver and gold (Deut 17.16-17). As far as wealth was concerned, David was indifferent. This book will show that he willingly devoted his accumulated riches to the house of God. As far as horses were concerned, he hamstrung captured chariot steeds, lest he be tempted to rely on them rather than on God (2 Sam 8.4). As far as wives were concerned, he ignored the divine command. Two out of three is insufficient when it comes to complying with the Word of God!

Verses 10-16: Solomon and the Kings of Judah

In the kingdom of Judah authority passed from father to son right down to the years prior to the Babylonian invasion except for an interlude of almost seven years when the usurper "Athaliah reigned over the land" (2 Chr 22.12). She had led a satanic plot to exterminate the line through which the Messiah would come. A baby boy was rescued from the carnage, and even although David's line appeared to be hanging by a thread, by divine superintendence it held, and in process of time Joash the survivor was installed as king (2 Chr 23). There are no references to Athaliah either here or in the birth line of the Messiah in Matthew 1.

From this point, things moved on uninterruptedly until Babylon was emerging as the superpower of the day. Then circumstances arose that disturbed the smooth transition of power from father to son. Around that time Josiah insisted on attacking Egyptian forces, and it resulted in his death. The people of the land made Jehoahaz (Shallum, Jer 22.11-12) their king, but why they should have chosen the fourth son is unclear. After three months he was deposed by the king of Egypt and removed to that land where he died. His brother Eliakim was installed as a puppet king, and given the name Jehoiakim. After eleven years he was led off in fetters to Babylon, and his son Jehoiachin (Jeconiah, Coniah) reigned briefly. He in turn was transported, and his uncle Zedekiah then ruled for eleven years. (He is described as his "brother" (2 Chr 36.10), but only in the general sense of being in the same family. 2 Kings 24.17 is more precise in describing him as "his father's brother".)

From a human point of view Zedekiah's rebellion against Nebuchadnezzar brought the kingdom of Judah to an end, but in reality it was occasioned by divine intervention on account of the sins of the nation and its rulers. The foregoing history is found in 2 Chronicles 35 and 36.

Perhaps it should be noted that Jeremiah said of Coniah (Jeconiah, Jehoiachin), "no man of his seed shall prosper, sitting upon the throne of David, and ruling any more in Judah" (Jer 22.30). None of his descendants ever did sit on the throne, but it is through him that the royal line passed on down to Joseph the carpenter (Mt 1.12-16). Through Joseph, the Lord Jesus has the right to that throne, but keep in mind that while Joseph was the legal father of the Lord, he was not His literal father. Jeremiah's prophecy holds good even although one day the Lord Jesus will be given "the throne of his father David" (Lk 1.32). The Lord is not of the seed of Coniah, but is descended from David through Mary by a different route (Lk 3.23-38).

Verses 17-24: Beyond the Captivity

Strangely, after years of incarceration in Babylon, Jehoiachin (Jeconiah) was released, and enjoyed special eminence at the king's court (2 Kings 25.27-30). Divine providence is seen in all of these affairs, because his high profile would give status to his descendant Zerubbabel, one of those in the forefront of the return to Judah and the rebuilding of the Temple.

Jeconiah's imprisonment is reflected in the name of one of his sons. "Assir" means "captive", so that some have translated, "Jeconiah, the captive", rather than regarding Assir as a person at all, thus making Salathiel (Shealtiel) Jeconiah's son (Mt 1.12).

Zerubbabel is spoken of consistently as "the son of Shealtiel" (e.g. Ezra 3.2), and yet here he is seen as one of the sons of Pedaiah. Numerous explanations of the difficulty have been given, including the fact that in the transition from v.17 to v.18, another generation is being introduced making Pedaiah the son of Salathiel, in which case Salathiel (Shealtiel) was the grandfather of Zerubbabel. If that it so, it would not be unusual for him to be called his father, and Zerubbabel his son; see, for example Daniel 5.18, where Nebuchadnezzar is seen as the father of Belshazzar, when in actual fact he was his grandfather. Against this explanation is the fact that "Salathiel begat Zorobabel" (Mt 1.12), but then the same chapter says "Joram begat Ozias" (v.8), which he did not do literally. Generations are skipped at that point in the genealogy. "Begetting" in Matthew 1 is not always to be taken literally.

Less complicated is the explanation that likely Shealtiel had died childless, and in accordance with the law of levirate marriage, his brother Pedaiah had taken his widow, the resulting offspring being regarded as Shealtiel's (Deut 25.5-6).

Beyond Zerubbabel, there is not a name that we recognise. From a human perspective, they were nonentities, so much so that by New Testament times the rightful heir to David's throne was Joseph the carpenter of Nazareth. While Heaven recognised him as "son of David" (Mt 1.20), to all intents and purposes the dynasty had gone into oblivion. It is the fulfilment of the picture that Isaiah paints of David's family line as a tree cut down to the very roots (Is 11.1). Out of these roots there emerged a strong vigorous shoot, the One who is called "The Branch", "and the spirit of the Lord shall rest upon him" (Is 11.2).

The length to which the genealogy stretches at this point suggests that its latter stages have been added by a hand other than Ezra's and this may be the case.

1 CHRONICLES 4

The descendants of Judah continue to occupy the first section of chapter 4. They are designated "The sons of Judah", with "The sons of Simeon" featuring from v.24. The territory occupied by the tribe of Simeon was really an enclave in Judah's inheritance (Josh 19.1-9), so there was an affinity between the tribes. As early as the conquest of the land the two had co-operated (Judg 1.3), and so they are brought together here. As these verses show, the tribe of Simeon was feeble numerically, and maintained an almost itinerant lifestyle. As late as Hezekiah's day they were marauders who annexed the territory of neighbouring nomadic tribes (v.41). Simeon was almost absorbed into Judah, being the first of the tribes to virtually lose its identity in the land. Next in line to go into obscurity were the Transjordan tribes (ch.5) who were the first to be carried off to captivity.

In chapter 4, the monotony of the lists of names is lightened by the inclusion of points of human interest, little details about a few of the people who are mentioned, especially Jabez, the man who "was more honourable than his brethren" (vv.9-10).

Verses 1-8: Sons of Judah

Details are again given of descendants of Judah through Pharez, and it appears that notable families are being highlighted. There is a slight variation from the record of chapter 2, but it is evident that the emphasis remains on this tribe because it was the one that outlasted the others as far as its visible presence was concerned. It had survived captivity, and its people were re-established in the land at the time of writing.

Verses 9-10: Jabez

His name appears without introduction, but it is generally thought that he was a son of Coz who is mentioned in the previous verse. While there is no definite mention of his father, specific reference is made to his mother: she was the one who gave him his name, a name that means "sorrowful" or "pain". Obviously, there are similarities between his birth and the birth of Benjamin, first named "Benoni" by Rachel his dying mother. "The son of my sorrow" is the meaning of Benoni, but his father changed it to Benjamin, "the son of the right hand" (Gen 35.16-19). We must not assume that, like Rachel, the mother of Jabez died while giving birth, and any suggestion as to why he was thus named enters the realm of speculation. There is no record of the prevailing circumstances in the nation of Israel at the time of his birth, so we are in the dark about why he should have been given such a disagreeable name, except his mothers own words: "I bare him with sorrow". Such sorrow is common to childbirth, a consequence of the advent of sin: "in sorrow thou shalt bring forth children" (Gen 3.16); "A woman when she is in travail hath sorrow" (Jn 16.21). The simple reason for his name is that the memory of her labour was so vivid that she wanted it perpetuated in the name of the son she bore. Mercifully, he was one of those people in Scripture who rose above the connotations of his name. He certainly had no desire for the grief that sin would bring (v.10). In contrast to Jabez, the name Felix means "happy", but he was a man who, by rejecting Christ, forfeited true happiness and invited eternal misery (Acts 24.24-27).

Jabez was "*more honourable* (3513) than his brethren". The word appears frequently in the Old Testament and is translated in a variety of ways. However, the translation here is exactly the same as in the reference to a young man called Shechem: "he was more honourable than all the house of his father" (Gen 34.19). Tragically, his honour had been tarnished by scandalous behaviour. As revealed by his prayer, this was the very thing that Jabez was anxious to avoid.

On occasions the word carries the idea of wealth, as when "Abram was very *rich* (3513) in cattle, in silver, and in gold" (Gen 13.2). If that is the thought here, and if it was in wealth that Jabez surpassed his brethren, take note that material prosperity did not dull his sense of dependence on God. The fact that he prayed gave evidence of that.

However, it does seem more likely that the mention of honour refers to his character, and that morally and spiritually he outstripped his brothers. Despite this, his prayer indicates that he was neither complacent, nor content with his spiritual condition. He craved further blessing from God and constant shelter from evil. The lesson for us is that we should never be self-satisfied; there is always potential for progress - "abound more and more"; "increase more and more" (1 Thess 4.1,10).

The prayer of Jabez is instructive. It was addressed to "the God of Israel", and there is a throwback to the time the name of Israel is first mentioned in Scripture. At the end of his nocturnal encounter with God, Jacob's name was changed to Israel (Gen 32.22-32). While it was God who initiated the wrestling, Jacob's tenacity is seen in his clinging, and insisting, "I will not let thee go, except thou bless me". Jabez appears to have had the same determination, and the same aspiration: "Oh that thou wouldest bless me indeed". Thus he prayed to the God of *Israel*. He drew courage from the record of Scripture, as we all may do.

The language used to describe the appeal of Jabez is that he "*called* (7121) on the God of Israel". The first mention of men calling on God is in Genesis 4.26 at the birth of Enos. His name means "frail mortal man". When men began to understand that they were fragile and mortal, they realised their need of God and began "to call upon the name of the Lord". Jabez had that same spirit of dependence upon his God.

Even the casual reader will see that this was a short prayer, in contrast to those who "for a pretence make long prayer" (Mt 23.14). Despite its brevity, every word counted. His earnestness is evidenced in the opening words, "*Oh* that thou wouldest bless me indeed". It is what James would call "effectual fervent prayer" (5.16). He was very specific in his request. It was the blessing of *God* that he wanted: "Oh that *thou* wouldest bless me indeed". Esau was concerned about receiving a blessing from his father: "Bless me, even me also, *O my father*" (Gen 27.34). Jabez wanted "The blessing of the Lord, it maketh rich, *and he addeth no sorrow with it*" (Prov 10.22). Remember, Jabez means "sorrowful"; the blessing of the Lord would replace his sorrows.

He wanted to be blessed personally: "O that thou wouldest bless *me*". He was aware that Jacob had been blessed by the God of Israel, but he coveted the blessing of God in his own life. It is worth reminding ourselves that one of the prerequisites for enjoying divine blessing is to bring "all the tithes into the storehouse" (Mal 3.10). Giving God His portion makes us candidates for His blessing.

Part of the blessing he craved was an increase of his territory; "enlarge my coast (border)". God always encouraged expansion: "Enlarge the place of thy tent, and let them stretch forth the curtains of thine habitations: spare not, lengthen thy cords, and strengthen thy stakes" (Is 54.2). As has been said, we are unaware of where Jabez featured as far the history of Israel is concerned, but it appears that he was well settled into his inheritance, and yet he had ambitions to extend his sphere of influence. What was true of him in a material way should be true of us spiritually. We should be ambitious to break new ground with the gospel of the Lord Jesus Christ, and increase our sphere of influence in divine things. The Thessalonian believers were exemplary in this: "from you sounded out the word of the Lord…in every place your faith to God-ward is spread abroad" (1 Thess 1.8). The original disciples were instructed to extend their activities from the centre at Jerusalem to "the uttermost part of the earth" (Acts 1.8). There is always the need for fresh initiatives in the service of God, but we should ever keep in mind that we are dependent on Him to enlarge our borders.

In the Scriptures, reference to the Lord's hand is metaphorical for His power - see, for example, Numbers 11.23; Isaiah 50.2; 59.1. Evidently, Jabez wanted evidence of divine power in his life, protecting, enabling, directing. That same divine power is necessary for the service of God in this age, as when believers pioneered with the gospel at Antioch - "And *the hand of the Lord was with them*: and a great number believed, and turned unto the Lord" (Acts 11.21).

The climax to his prayer was the request that he be kept from evil, a priority prayer that should be on the lips of every believer: "Lead us not into temptation, but deliver us from evil" (Mt 6.13). He knew that evil inevitably brings grief. As suggested earlier, although his name means "sorrowful" he had no desire for the misery that is caused by sin. Any kind of sin creates heartache, but in the Word of God specific sins are said to promote sorrow. Those who have been covetous have "pierced themselves through with many sorrows" (1 Tim 6.10). Drunkenness brings despair: "Who hath woe? who hath sorrow? who hath contentions? who hath babbling? who hath wounds without cause? who hath redness of eyes? They that tarry long at the wine; They that go to seek mixed wine" (Prov 23.29-30). Envy is another of the evils that saps a man's joy, for it is "the rottenness of the bones" (Prov 14.30). Little wonder that Jabez appealed for preservation from evil.

He was not disappointed, for "God granted him that which he requested". Not for him the frustration of unanswered prayer. "Thy prayer is heard" was the word to Zacharias (Lk 1.13). Let every believer know what it is to be "praying in the Holy Ghost" (Jude v.20), and asking "according to his will" (1 Jn 5.14), so that it may be said of us that "God granted him that which he requested".

Verses 12-23: Further Families of Judah

The remaining references to the family of Judah throw up the names of some who are familiar to us, people like Othniel the judge, and Caleb the spy. Of interest are some little details about other people who seem to be insignificant, but from fragments of information are seen to be playing a crucial role in the life of the tribe.

Joab (v.14) must not be confused with his namesake David's general, being a man of an earlier generation. He is said to be "the father of the valley of Charashim", Charashim meaning "craftsmen". Some translations supply the words, *the inhabitants of* the valley of Charashim. What is being said is that Joab was the man who had pioneered these skills, just as the descendants of Cain pioneered pastoral activity, entertainment, and industry (Gen 4.20-22). Some were said to be "the father" of those who were involved in these activities.

It seems that there was harmony among these "craftsmen" to the extent that they banded together in the same area, a valley that appears to be in proximity to Jerusalem (Neh 11.35). In the east it was customary for men of a like trade to group together in one neighbourhood. For example, a street in Jerusalem was known as "the bakers' street" (Jer 37.21). Trade secrets could be maintained if there was solidarity on the part of the trade or guild.

It is unclear why the craftsmen are mentioned in particular unless it be that with the narrative eventually leading to the construction of the Temple the need for such men becomes apparent.

Translations of v.18 are unclear as to the meaning, but some leave the impression that Mered had two wives, one a Jewess, translated "Jehudijah" (AV), and the other a daughter of Pharaoh. Marriage liaisons with Egypt were not uncommon, and even at a much later date Solomon married a daughter of the Pharaoh of the day (1 Kings 3.1). Some see the phrase "daughter of Pharaoh" as merely a figure of speech for an Egyptian woman.

Reference is made to those whose families specialised in "fine linen" (v.21). Again, the likely reason for the mention is the fact that the story will lead on to a Temple with an active priesthood, fine linen being an essential requirement for priestly activity. One can hardly read the words "wrought fine linen" without being transported in mind to the last book of the Bible. The Lamb's wife is seen to "be arrayed in fine linen, clean and white" (Rev

19.8). John explains the significance: "the fine linen is the righteous acts of the saints" (RV). In this sense, may God help us all to be numbered among those of whom it is said, "they wrought fine linen", our actions marked by righteousness, honesty and integrity.

There is reference here to those "who had the dominion in Moab" (v.22), but from the Chronicler's generation, this was perceived as an ancient record, and it is difficult to establish to which period it belongs. Perhaps the reference is to those of Judah who administered Moab during David's reign, for he had conquered and subjugated that land (2 Sam 8.2).

Translators are divided as to how to render v.23, with some making "plants and hedges" place names - "Netaim and Gederah". Perhaps this alternative is more reasonable, for it is hardly to be supposed that the king would dwell among plants and hedges, except it be figurative language for delightful rural surroundings. However, whatever the correct translation, these potters were on hand and available for the king's work, and therein there lies a spiritual lesson. To work for the King demands dwelling with Him. When the Lord Jesus called His disciples His purpose was two-fold - first "that they should be with him", and then "that he might send them forth to preach" (Mk 3.14). Effective service requires the two to be held in balance. Dwelling with the Lord, that is, living in communion with Him, is a precondition for any work for Him. May we like the potters dwell with the king for his work.

Verses 24-38: The Sons of Simeon

As stated earlier, the tribe of Simeon was associated with Judah, and so it features next in the list of genealogies. The fact that they occupied certain cities "unto the reign of David" (v.31) is perhaps an indication that at that point, being disaffected, they relocated. They withdrew from their association with Judah, affiliating with the northern territory of Israel which eventually seceded from the dynasty of David. Evidently, some of the tribe remained loyal, for mention is made of their exploits as late as the days of "Hezekiah king of Judah" (v.41). Alternatively, the reference to "the reign of David" may pinpoint the time when the tribe of Simeon became so integrated with Judah as to become almost unrecognisable.

In this chapter, the names of Simeon's descendants do not coincide exactly with lists elsewhere in Scripture (e.g. Gen 46.10; Num 26.12-14), but the differences can generally be accounted for by the fact that it was common enough for people to have a number of names.

Attention is drawn to the fact that, in the main, this tribe did not experience the growth that Judah had known (v.27), but there were exceptions in some families (v.38) - they "increased greatly". A lesson for our own lives is that, while there may be a lack of spiritual growth on the part of believers around us, there is no need for us to be underdeveloped. Spiritual growth can be experienced in our personal lives, fostered of course by feeding on the Word of God (1 Pet 2.1-2). Congregationally, we should look for growth even although in the Western world shrinkage is the trend of our age.

Verses 39-43: Territorial Expansion

The growth of the families that are mentioned in the previous verses necessitated migration to sustain their burgeoning flocks. Gedor proved to be an excellent location. Two men of Judah had borne that name (vv.4,18), and perhaps the place took its name from them. Its whereabouts is uncertain though generally reckoned to be in the south-west of the land, Philistine territory, a buffer zone between Egypt and Israel. Some take it to be synonymous with Gerar.

The description of the area is graphic. As to its fertility, it was "fat pasture and good", productive and pleasant. As to its dimensions, it was "wide", the kind of place of which Isaac might have said, "the Lord hath made room for us" (Gen 26.22), or of which David might have said, "He brought me forth also into a large place" (Ps 18.19). This was expansive territory. As to its atmosphere, it was "quiet, and peaceable", almost reminiscent of Laish, where the people "dwelt careless...quiet and secure" before they were destroyed by the invading Danites (Judg 18.7). It is remarkable that in Hezekiah's reign, when the military might of the Assyrians was so pervasive, this fertile valley should be free of the ravages of war. This was a pastoral paradise.

Believers will be blessed if their spiritual environment is as favourable, with these three features in place - pastureland, elbowroom, and tranquillity. Rich spiritual feeding is provided by the Shepherd who makes us "to lie down in green pastures" (Ps 23.2). Under-shepherds should be as earnest as the Simeonites as they seek out suitable pasture for the little flock of God. It takes diligent study of the Word, so that, as "apt to teach" (1 Tim 3.2), they can impart the varied spiritual diet that their sheep require.

Space is another necessity for the sheep, and the New Testament pattern for gathering leaves room for every spiritual gift to function, in contrast to the restrictive effects of the clerical system.

A harmonious atmosphere in the assembly is conducive to spiritual progress and effective outreach. Remember the debilitating consequences of commotion caused by party spirit at Corinth, or the damaging effects of the estrangement of the two sisters at Philippi.

The princes of the Simeonites were able to expel the former occupants of the territory, descendants of Ham, and they remained in place until the time of writing, "unto this day". There is a less happy "unto this day" at the end of ch.5. At the time of writing the Transjordan tribes were still held captive by the Assyrians.

A further 500 Simeonites forged eastwards into the Edomite territory of Mount Seir, and annexed the lands of refugee Amalekites who were there, those "that were escaped". Saul had been less ruthless with the Amalekites than ordered (1 Sam 15). Four hundred of them had escaped David's clutches after the sack of Ziklag (1 Sam 30.17), but now, centuries later, the descendants of these fugitives were "smitten" by the men of Simeon who settled in their lands.

These few verses see the fulfilment of a number of Bible predictions. God had cursed the descendants of Ham (Gen 9.25). He had promised to wage war on Amalek (Ex 17.16). Through Jacob, He had predicted that the tribe of Simeon would be scattered (Gen 49.5-7). In measure, all three predictions merge in these obscure verses at the end of 1 Chronicles 4.

1 CHRONICLES 5

This chapter contains the genealogies of the Transjordan tribes, Reuben, Gad and half the tribe of Manasseh. In preference to entering the land of Canaan, these two and a half tribes had settled on the east side of the river Jordan (Num 32). We have details here of their push further eastward in quest of fresh pastureland, and so their expansionist ambitions and some of their military exploits are recorded. The danger of being on the fringe is also made clear; they were the first of the tribes to be targeted by the Assyrians and deported into permanent exile, "unto this day" (vv.25-26). To be spiritually off centre rather than at the heart of things has its perils. This is illustrated again when those who were "the hindmost" fell foul of Amalek (Deut 25.18), or when those "in the uttermost parts of the camp" experienced divine retribution (Num 11.1), or when the young man sitting in the window fell to his death (Acts 20.9).

Verses 1-10: The Sons of Reuben

Before "the sons of Reuben" are listed, an explanation is given about why this tribe did not occupy first place in these genealogical records. It is acknowledged that Reuben was "the firstborn of Israel", but he had been responsible for a shameful family scandal. At a time when Jacob was still smarting from the sudden loss of his beloved Rachel, Reuben "lay with Bilhah his father's concubine: and Israel heard it" (Gen 35.22). There is no record of a blazing row, but Jacob never forgot the outrage. It irritated him till his dying day, and so as he lay on his deathbed, the whole issue was resurrected. He addressed the offender: "Unstable as water, thou shalt not have the excellency" (Gen 49.4, RV). Because of his moral instability, Reuben forfeited the rights of the firstborn. Excellency was never connected with the tribe of Reuben. There is no record of it ever producing any eminent person, either judge, prophet or king.

Under the law, the firstborn was to inherit "a double portion" even though he may have been the offspring of a "hated" wife as Reuben was (Deut 21.15-17). That tradition must have been in place even before the age of law. Because of his disgraceful conduct, Reuben's "double portion" passed to Joseph by his father's sovereign decree, and the patriarch regarded Joseph's *two* sons as his: "as Reuben and Simeon, they shall be mine" (Gen 48.5). The importance of that event is evident, for a whole chapter of Scripture is devoted to it. Thus the descendants of Ephraim and Manasseh were to occupy large areas of the land, particularly the tribe of Ephraim, a tribe that became so dominant that by Hosea's day the name Ephraim was synonymous with the ten northern tribes of Israel.

Because the birthright passed to Joseph, we may have expected that in these lists of genealogies Ephraim and Manasseh would appear first, but a further explanation is given: "the genealogy is not to be reckoned after the birthright". The reason for Judah's inclusion at the head of the tribes is independent of birthright; it was because "Judah *prevailed above his brethren*, and of him came the chief ruler". Judah always had leadership qualities. He took the lead in selling Joseph into slavery (Gen 37.26-27), but he really rose in stature when he was willing to stand guarantor for Benjamin; in the hour of crisis he made a genuine offer to take his brother's place in servitude (Gen 44.18-34). He was also the man whom his father delegated to pave the way when the whole family came into Egypt (Gen 46.28). Thus, when Jacob was blessing his sons and anticipating future days, he predicted that Judah would be the royal tribe: "The sceptre shall not depart from Judah" (Gen 49.10). "Judah is my lawgiver", said God (Ps 60.7). That is the main emphasis in 1 Chronicles. Among all the secondary genealogical roads that are mapped, the main road leads to David the king.

Judah as a tribe "prevailed above his brethren", for that tribe became the most numerous and most influential in the nation, and of course, "of him came the chief ruler" or "prince" (RV; 5057). In the context of 1 Chronicles, David is the chief ruler, but we detect a prophetic statement regarding the Lord Jesus, who "sprang out of Juda" (Heb 7.14).

Brief comments about Reuben's descendants are of interest. Beerah, who was one of their princes, was "carried away captive" by "Tilgath-pilneser king of Assyria" (v.6). This was the fate of the whole tribe and its associates (v.26), but the mention of this particular man must have significance. His name (880) means "a well", and, if true to his name, he ought to have been a source of refreshment for the people of God. However, it appears that his leadership of the tribe had no positive impact. He had done nothing to stem the flood of idolatry that swamped it, and thus when "the God of Israel stirred up" the Assyrians to discipline His people (v.26), Beerah was among those who were marched off to exile. Let leaders avoid his failure, and exert a godly refreshing influence over their people. Said Paul to Philemon, "the bowels of the saints are refreshed by thee, brother" (v.7).

Branches of Reuben's family had expanded eastward. As already noted they had settled originally in Gilead because they "had a very great multitude of cattle", and Gilead "was a place for cattle" (Num 32.1). The lush pasture land was ideal for their needs. They must have been expert stockmen, for here "their cattle were multiplied" (v.9), and so there was need for new grazing. Thus they pushed eastward, not to the river Euphrates itself, but to the edge of a wilderness that extended westward from the river, a wilderness so extensive that it took Ezra almost four months to traverse it (Ezra 7.9). It is of interest that David's authority took in all that territory right to the river Euphrates, as did that of Solomon (2 Sam 8.3; 1 Kings 4.21).

There is a lesson to be learned from the Reubenites. In a spiritual sense numerical increase of flocks and herds should be our constant ambition, accomplished in this age by energetic gospel activity, but providing for the feeding of these increased flocks and herds has to be a priority. Both concepts are brought together near the end of Paul's first missionary journey: "they...preached the gospel to that city, and...taught many" (Acts

14.21). Teaching is essential for those who believe the preaching. The effects of both preaching and teaching are seen at the start of the second journey: "And so were the churches established in the faith, and increased in number daily" (Acts 16.5). In local assemblies, let gospel activity and Bible teaching be held in balance as they were right to the end of the Acts of the Apostles: "Preaching the kingdom of God, and teaching the things which concern the Lord Jesus Christ" (Acts 28.31).

Reuben's movement eastward took place in the days of Saul when they annexed the territory of the Hagarites, nomadic tribesmen descended from Hagar, Sarah's maid (v.10). Historically, these people were confederate with the enemies of Israel (Ps 83.1-8). As with the modern Arab world, their ambition was to "cut them off from being a nation; that the name of Israel may be no more in remembrance" (v.4). Their defeat in the days of Saul is recorded in more detail in vv.19-22 of our chapter. Saul's first military victory was at the relief of Jabesh-Gilead (1 Sam 11). No doubt the Transjordan tribes were emboldened by that event in their own district, so they penetrated Hagarite country, and occupied "their tents throughout all the land east of Gilead" (RV). Saul's determination and valour encouraged them. In the same way, Paul's fortitude in the face of adversity instilled confidence into others to preach the gospel "without fear" (Phil 1.14); the power of example is compelling.

Verses 11-17: The Sons of Gad

Reuben's neighbours were the descendants of Gad, fellow occupants of Bashan and Gilead, the districts east of Jordan. Here, little is said of their exploits, and it is rather sad that there was nothing significant to record about them either good or bad. To their credit, subsequent verses reveal that they did have valiant men who were able to co-operate with the neighbouring tribes in the conflict with the Hagarites, but, generally, there seemed to be a paltriness about the tribe of Gad. There is always the danger of settling down to be ordinary. Spiritual ambitions and aspirations to be holy are to be commended, rather than contentment with blameless mediocrity.

Gad's territory (v.16) included a place called Sharon, and it should not be confused with the plain that borders the Mediterranean. Obviously, this location was east of Jordan and it gets a mention on the Moabite Stone (line 13), unearthed in 1868 but dating from around 850 BC.

Gad's genealogy was compiled over a period of years (v.17), with the initial recording in the days of Jeroboam II of Israel, a time of great prosperity. An updating was conducted in the reign of Jotham, king of Judah, by which time things had deteriorated and the Assyrians were a real threat (2 Kings 14.23; 15.32). At a time when their captivity was pending, they seemed more taken up with their past history than with present dangers. Our Lord's generation had a similar outlook: "We be Abraham's seed, and were never in bondage to any man"; "Abraham is our father" (Jn 8.33,39). Glorying in their past history and in their privileged position as a covenant people, they were ignoring present reality, the need for a right relationship with God through Him whom the Father had sent. A glorious history is no substitute for present spiritual prosperity.

Verses 18-22: War with the Hagarites

We are now given a more detailed account of the invasion of the land of the Hagarites. Verse 10 left us with the impression that the conflict had involved the Reubenites alone, but now we learn that the two and a half tribes were all committed to the offensive. As in Numbers 1, the precise number of warriors is mentioned, in this case 44,760. God notes the number of warriors in His armies; are you counted in? To win the victory, co-operation on the part of the tribes was essential. Paul refers to Epaphroditus and Archippus as his *fellow* soldiers (Phil 2.25; Philem v.2), an indication that in fighting "the good fight" (2 Tim 4.7, RV), there has to be team work on the part of the combatants. Disunity spells defeat.

The courage of these warriors is noted: they were "valiant men". They were not the kind who would have to be sent home because they were "fearful and fainthearted". Such men were discharged because their anxieties were infectious (Deut 20.8). The men here were courageous. "In nothing (be) terrified by your adversaries" (Phil 1.28).

They were skilled in both defence and attack, hence the mention of the "buckler" (shield - 4043) for protection, and the "sword" for the offensive. The Christian soldier has been furnished with both. "The shield of faith" and "the sword of the Spirit" are both part of his armoury in the conflict with infernal powers (Eph 6.16-17). Let the believer avail himself of divine provision, so that "having done all" he may "stand" (v.13). These valiant men could not only engage effectively in hand-to-hand conflict, but they had an ability to wage war at a distance - they were expert archers. The first known archer in Scripture is Ishmael (Gen 21.20), and if the Hagarites took after their progenitor they were beaten by men who outclassed them in their own field of expertise. In spiritual conflict, we can expect "the fiery darts of the wicked" to rain upon us. These can be quenched by the shield of faith (Eph 6.16). In returning fire we are dependent on Him whose "arrows are sharp in the heart of the king's enemies" (Ps 45.5). "If God be for us, who can be against us?" (Rom 8.31).

These men were also "skilful in war". As in every other field of human activity, the ability to fight is an acquired skill. Scripture speaks of "learn(ing) war" (Is 2.4). Men of the world speak about martial *arts*, techniques that have been developed for combat and defence. These men here had trained and practised; they had studied strategy and honed their skills as warriors so that in the hour of conflict they emerged as victors. Spiritual warfare demands knowledge of enemy strategy: such knowledge can be derived only from the Scriptures. "We are not ignorant of his devices" (2 Cor 2.11). It requires a dedication to discipline and duty that involves us in being disentangled from the legitimate affairs of this life (2 Tim 2.3-4). To "war a good warfare" means "Holding faith, and a good conscience" (1 Tim 1.18-19), that is, combining commitment to the truth of God with personal integrity. To engage effectively in a spiritual military campaign, we dare not submit to the innate desire to pamper ourselves, but rather to "abstain from fleshly lusts, which war against the soul" (1 Pet 2.11). Metaphorically, may it be said of us as believers, "skilful in war".

"If it had not been the Lord who was on our side, when men rose up against us: Then they had swallowed us up alive" (Ps 124.2-3, RV). The Lord *was* on their side here, and hence the conquest. Training and equipment in themselves are no guarantee of victory; "The children of Ephraim, being armed, and carrying bows, turned back in the day of battle" (Ps 78.9). Here "they were helped", for the two and a half tribes had gone into the fray with a sense of dependence on God. "They put their trust in him", and so "they cried to God in the battle", and thus "the Hagarites were delivered into their hand". Godly kings of Judah had the same experience. In the heat of the battle Asa exclaimed, "help us, O Lord our God; for we rest on thee, and in thy name we go against this multitude" (2 Chr 14.11). Trapped, and in danger, Jehoshaphat "cried out, and the Lord helped him" (2 Chr 18.31). Again, prior to a battle that in the end he had no need to fight, Jehoshaphat expressed his total dependence upon his God; "we have no might against this great company that cometh against us; neither know we what to do: but our eyes are upon thee" (2 Chr 20.12). That same spirit of dependence should characterise the Christian soldier. Self-confidence means certain defeat, but it is a great encouragement that alongside the provision of our spiritual armaments there is a facility to express our total reliance on our God: "Praying always with all prayer and supplication in the Spirit" (Eph 6.18).

Not only did this battle give them increased territory, but the spoils of battle were huge. Unspecified numbers of cattle were taken, and then the precise amount of camels, asses and sheep are mentioned, together with human captives who presumably were pressed into slavery (v.21). The mention of 100,000 captives in addition to "many slain" (v.22) is staggering, remembering that the victors had an army of 44,760 warriors. Little wonder the Chronicler is at pains to stress the role that God played in the proceedings, with His people left simply to "trust in him". "Greater is he that is in you, than he that is in the world" (1 Jn 4.4).

"The war was of God" (v.22). In His sovereignty He initiated it. He used His people to wage it, and delivered their enemies into their hands. If all that we do is by divine direction and in accordance with the will of God, inevitably we will be the victors. In this case, God's hostility towards the Hagarites was undoubtedly on account of their idolatry and its attendance vices. Their gods are mentioned in v.25, so, as in every other case, there was no injustice in divine dealings. In an earlier generation the inhabitants of Canaan were routed and expelled by Israel because they had reached a limit of iniquity beyond which God would not allow them to pass (Ex 15.16). Here again, God's people were used as instruments of judgment upon the idolatrous Hagarites. "Is there unrighteousness with God? God forbid" (Rom 9.14).

It is rather sad that this paragraph ends on a sour note; "they dwelt in their steads *until the captivity*" (v.22). Territory gained was lost as the Assyrians removed them from the land they had taken from the Hagarites. In spiritual things there is always the danger of forfeiting territorial gains. The Hebrews had "*become* such as (had) need of milk, and not of strong meat" (Heb 5.12). The inference is that they had once had a capacity for strong meat, but they had lost ground. The Galatians were also in reverse gear; "Ye did run well; who did hinder you?" (Gal 5.7). Spiritual progress should never be allowed to stall. Truth gained should never be relinquished. Moral integrity should never be compromised. Be as firm about spiritual things as Naboth was about his inheritance. Neither the demands of a bullying king or the lure of money or the prospect of bigger and better things could persuade him to surrender his God-given inheritance (1 Kings 21.1-3). If by divine grace you have created a bridgehead in enemy territory, hold your ground, and advance even further.

Verses 23-24: The Half Tribe of Manasseh

A handful of men are mentioned in connection with this segment of the tribe of Manasseh, men who are described in a three-fold way: "mighty men of valour, famous men, and heads of the house of their fathers". Paul refers to spiritual leaders at Thessalonica in a similar way (1 Thess 5.12-13). They are "heads" inasmuch as they are "over you in the Lord". They are "famous" in the sense that the saints have to be familiar with them, and to "know them" and "esteem them very highly in love". They are "men of valour" in that they must have the spiritual courage to "admonish" the saints when such action is required. Let today's leaders exhibit these same qualities as with tenderness, and yet with divine authority, they shepherd the little flock of God.

Verses 25-26: The Assyrian Captivity

The reason for the two and a half tribes being carried into captivity is explained: "they transgressed against the God of their fathers". Although the Chronicler had been speaking of Manasseh, it is clear that the "they" of v.25 includes all three tribes (v.26). Living in proximity to the heathen, they had observed their practices, and had fallen into their idolatrous ways. Violating commandments one and two was transgression against God, wilful rebellion against His revealed will. Sin being always against God (Ps 51.4) makes it so very serious.

God is described here as "the God of their fathers". Abraham and Isaac and Jacob all had their failings, but as far as idolatry was concerned, there was never a suspicion of it with any of them. God was "not ashamed to be called their God" (Heb 11.16). Now, the godly faithful example of the fathers was being ignored. Their descendants had not been so loyal, and their sin is regarded as spiritual fornication. They "went a whoring after the gods of the people of the land". God always abhors divided loyalties, and even in this Christian era it is possible to live in such a way as to resemble a woman disloyal to her marriage vows. "Ye adulteresses, know ye not that the friendship of the world is enmity with God?" (James 4.4, RV). May we be preserved from the kind of divided affections that characterised the people who were installed in Samaria by the Assyrians; they "feared the Lord, and served their own gods" (2 Kings 17.33). God demands one hundred per cent allegiance.

Amazingly, the gods to which the two and a half tribes were drawn were the "gods of the people of the land, whom God destroyed before them". In the immediate context, the reference is very likely to the gods of the Hagarites rather than the gods of the original inhabitants of Canaan. The transcendence of the living God had been demonstrated in the conquest of the Hagarites, and yet they abandoned Him in favour of these vanities. They were no gods at all, and had been proved impotent when it came to assisting even their own devotees! Equally ludicrous was the behaviour of King Amaziah when he bowed down to the gods of his defeated foe (2 Chr 25.14). There is something bizarre and illogical about these situations, but it is all a solemn reminder of the blinded perverted nature of the human heart. Is there a lesson in it for us? Is it possible that any one of us could see God at work in our lives, giving us victory over hostile forces, only for us to drift, and to be allured by the pastimes and habits that feature in the lives of those who have opposed our Christian principles and practices?

God now moves in judgment against His disloyal people. "The God of their fathers" of v.25 is described as "the God of Israel" in v.26. He was still the God of the nation even though they had proved rebellious. When Jonah cried to God from the belly of the fish, Scripture records that he "prayed unto the Lord *his* God" (Jonah 2.1). God was still "his God" despite his previous disobedience. Applied in the light of New Testament teaching, we have the doctrine of the eternal security of every genuine believer in Christ. A true believer may sin, but to him God is still "the Father" (1 Jn 2.1).

Although Jehovah is "the God of Israel", His sphere of influence is not confined to one nation. "The king's heart is in the hand of the Lord, as the rivers of water: he turneth it whithersoever he will" (Prov 21.1). Thus He "stirred up the spirit of Pul…and the spirit of Tilgath-pilneser". Most translations and commentators regard Pul and Tilgath-pilneser as being two names for the same person, Tiglath-pileser III. Pul was his personal name, and the other the throne name in Assyria. God was using this Assyrian monarch to discipline His people. He first advanced on Israel in a threatening way and was bought off with 1,000 talents of silver (2 Kings 15.19). Subsequently he was used by God to carry the two and a half tribes away and the Chronicler records their locations "unto this day". Shalmaneser finished the job as far as the remainder of the nation was concerned (2 Kings 17.23). At a time when Judah had been exiled and then reinstated in their land, the northern tribes were still captives, and far from home. Even yet they have not returned to the land en masse, so that they are commonly known as "the ten lost tribes". You can be sure that they are not lost as far as God is concerned, and the day is coming when the twelve apostles will "sit upon twelve thrones, judging *the twelve tribes of Israel*" (Mt 19.28; Lk 22.29-30). The Lord Jesus is not merely King of the Jews; He is "King of Israel" (Jn 1.49), that is, monarch of the reunited realm of Israel and Judah.

The chapter has ended on a sobering note, in sharp contrast to the earlier section in which there is so much to encourage. The very obvious lesson is that devotion to God and dependence on Him will bring victory (vv.18-22), whereas disloyalty and disobedience will inevitably spell defeat (vv.25-26).

1 CHRONICLES 6

This large chapter is devoted to the tribe of Levi, and is of major significance within the framework of the book. As already suggested, the key theme of the narrative is the life of David, with particular reference to his desire to build the house of God. Priests were necessary for that temple to function, and so there is here a record of the priesthood, and details of the three divisions of the tribe of Levi, each of which had its own specific sphere of activity in the conduct of temple worship. Under the tabernacle system, the three branches of the Levitical family had detailed tasks in moving it from place to place (Num 3-4), but their precise remit for temple activity is not so clear. However, in order to function, both priests and Levites did require a credible pedigree. It has already been observed that in the generation that would have first read 1 Chronicles, some were, "as polluted, put from the priesthood". They were unable to find their register (Ezra 2.62): hence the importance of Levi's genealogy in this chapter of Scripture.

In tabernacle days, the order of the camp of Israel was divinely organised, with all the tribes pitching "by his own standard" (Num 2.2). The family of Levi comprised an inner circle in proximity to the sanctuary, with the priests and Moses located at the east end, Kohath to the south, Gershon at the west, and Merari on the north. From earliest days then, it was obvious that Levi occupied the central place in Israel's relationship with their God. This chapter reflects that fact.

The tribe of Levi had no territorial inheritance in the land, but were scattered throughout the other tribes. "Their dwelling places" are listed in the latter part of the chapter.

Verses 1-15: The Priests

These first fifteen verses focus mainly on the sons of Aaron, those who should have followed in his steps as high priests in Israel. Somewhere along the line the succession strayed, and the opening chapters of 1 Samuel see Eli functioning as high priest, a man who according to secular accounts was descended from Ithamar and not Eleazar. Abiathar was in Eli's line but was deposed by Solomon because of his treachery. It was all in accordance with the sentence of judgment that was passed on Eli's wayward household (1 Kings 2.27).

As in other genealogies, there can be variants of the names, or the use of alternative names for the same person. For example, Amminadab (v.22) is very evidently Izhar (vv.2,18,38). It seems clear too that the list of priests is not complete, another common feature of recorded genealogies.

Just as the kingly line of Judah is traced from David to the captivity (3.1-24), so this priestly line is traced from Aaron to the captivity, because the sons of Aaron and the sons of David were both vital factors in the restoration of the nation to its former status.

The fact that numerous names are mentioned is proof of the assertion of Scripture: "they truly were many priests, because they were not suffered to continue by reason of death" (Heb 7.23). By contrast, our Great High Priest lives in "the power of an endless life"; He "continueth ever"; "he ever liveth" (vv.16,24,25). Thus He is "a priest for ever". He has "an unchangeable priesthood". "He is able also to save them *to the uttermost*" (vv.17,24,25). There is continuity with Him. Fugitives in the cities of refuge welcomed the death of the high priest in Israel, for it signalled the end of their confinement (Num 35.25). We rejoice in the permanence of our High Priest, for it spells uninterrupted sympathy and succour.

> Their priesthood ran through several hands,
> For mortal was their race;
> Thy never-changing office stands
> Eternal as Thy days.
>
> (Isaac Watts)

The priests were descended from Levi through Kohath and then Amram, the father of Aaron, Moses and Miriam. Of Kohath himself we know nothing, but we are indebted to Stephen and the Hebrew writer for telling us that Amram was at one with his wife Jochebed in preserving and nourishing Moses (Acts 7.20; Heb 11.23). He was a man of faith and courage. In a Christian marriage, the same spiritual compatibility is crucial.

Aaron himself had a chequered history, at times showing solidarity with Moses and on other occasions proving to be unreliable. In the outrageous episode of the golden calf he was unquestionably culpable; his defence was totally unconvincing (Ex 32).

Nadab and Abihu were his two elder sons, and on offering "strange fire before the Lord" they were devoured by "fire from the Lord" (Lev 10.1-2); the priesthood had a shaky start! The lesson is that God's work must always be done in God's way.

The high priesthood passed to Eleazar of whom we know little. However, a reading of the book of Numbers reveals that even when his father was alive, certain responsibilities devolved upon him (e.g. 3.32; 4.16). He is one of a number who bore the name Eleazar (NT equivalent, Lazarus). Its meaning is encouraging: "God has helped". An awareness of divine help should be an antidote to covetousness and a stimulus to contentment. "Let your conversation be without covetousness; and be content with such things as ye have: for he hath said, I will never leave thee, nor forsake thee. So that we may boldly say, The Lord is my helper, and I will not fear what man shall do unto me" (Heb 13.5-6).

Phinehas was a notable character who featured prominently at some critical points in Israel's history. It was he who acted decisively when a prince of the Simeonites flaunted his adulterous relationship with a socialite from Midian. Their brazen behaviour cost them their lives, the victims of Phinehas' javelin (Num 25). His uncompromising action elicited unqualified commendation from God (vv.10-13), and was celebrated by the Psalmist centuries later (Ps 106.30-31).

In the subsequent offensive against Midian, Phinehas accompanied the armies of Israel, directing operations with the blast of a trumpet (Num 31.6).

There came a time when the two and a half tribes were under suspicion - were they in the process of creating a rival form of worship? Phinehas was dispatched as the major investigator and negotiator. Knowing his track record as a no nonsense uncompromising individual we might have been nervous about the outcome. Would he inflame the situation? Would the emergency escalate into civil war? In the event, the man who traditionally was so firm, acted with the utmost wisdom and tact, and cool heads prevailed. The crisis passed, with the integrity of both sides intact (Josh 22).

The final incident in which he was involved was the occasion of the strife between the tribe of Benjamin and the other tribes. Phinehas was the man who was able to discern the Lord's mind as he directed the military campaign against Benjamin (Judg 20.27-28). It is evident that he was a very notable character. All in all, we see him as a man of courage and unswerving loyalty to Jehovah. He did not shirk the dangers of battle, and yet there was a tenderness about him, a willingness to understand. He was a man in touch with God. Such qualities were so fitting for a priest.

After Phinehas, none of the names are recognisable until we arrive at David's generation, and the familiar names of Zadok and Ahimaaz appear (v.8). They were men who risked their lives by remaining loyal to David at Absalom's rebellion and during Adonijah's failed coup (2 Sam 15-18; 1 Kings 1). In particular, the young Ahimaaz exhibited daring and courage in David's intelligence service, acting as a crucial channel of information for the beleaguered king (2 Sam 17.15-21). Zadok's loyalty was rewarded by Solomon when he was installed as the rightful high priest in place of Abiathar (1 Kings 2.35). The high priestly line had again moved rightfully to the descendants of Eleazar.

Some scholars suggest that Johanan (v.9) is an alias for Jehoiada, the man responsible for rescuing young King Joash when Athaliah "destroyed all the seed royal" (2 Kings 11.1,4). There is no definite proof of this, or that the Azariah of v.10 is the man who so nobly confronted King Uzziah when he attempted to combine priestly activity with his role as a king (2 Chr 26.16-23). However, based on the fact that special mention is made of him here, the possibility is that this is the same Azariah. If not, it seems superfluous to say that he "executed the priest's office", for every priest did that! The point seems to be, that he *legitimately* "executed the priest's office" in contrast to the king, who had ambitions for that function, endeavouring to take to himself an honour that God had reserved for His Son, the only true King-Priest.

Azariah's sphere of operation is said to be "the temple that Solomon built in Jerusalem", a reminder of the former glory of the house. No doubt this would encourage the first readers, those now toiling to rebuild the sanctuary in these days of recovery.

Hilkiah (v.13) was the high priest who featured in King Josiah's reign. He superintended funds to finance the refurbishing of the temple. He was also responsible for discovering the lost book of the law, the reading of which effected such deep repentance on the part of the young king. Another of his functions was to play a major role in organising the celebration of the Passover that was such a vital factor in the brief recovery of that era (2 Chr 34-35).

Seraiah (v.14) was priest at the time of the Babylonian invasion, and lost his life at the hands of Nebuchadnezzar (2 Kings 25.18-22). The influence of the priests over the people was well known, and so the enemy perceived him as a danger and eliminated him. Even in our Lord's day, it is evident that the priests exerted considerable control over the common people.

Jehozadak (v.15) is the last mentioned priest in this line, and was carried into captivity. It is rather sad that while Aaron, the first priest in the line, was released from captivity in Egypt, the last to be mentioned was carried into captivity in Babylon, and all because of the rebellion and idolatry of the nation. The story is not told here, but while in captivity this priest fathered a son called Joshua, one of those who pioneered the return to Jerusalem, and was a major participant in the rebuilding of the temple.

Verses 16-30: The Sons of Levi

Verse 16 gives details of Levi's immediate family, his three sons being Gershom, Kohath and Merari. These three branches of the family held responsibility for the tabernacle as decreed by God in Numbers 3-4. The sons of Gershom(n) took charge of the coverings and hangings. The Kohathites had responsibility for the Ark of the Covenant and all the other vessels. Merari's descendants looked after the heavy items such as the boards and sockets.

There are one or two notable names in this section. Korah (v.22), a grandson of Kohath, was responsible for spearheading a rebellion against Moses that ended in the rebels and their property being swallowed up as "the earth opened her mouth" (Num 16.32). It appears that their grievance stemmed from discontentment with their God-appointed task. Korah had ambitions to be a priest! (v.10). His mind-set is replicated in the New Testament when a man called Diotrephes aspired to be dominant in the assembly and exclude gifted teachers whom he perceived as rivals (3 Jn vv.9-11). Sadly, these ancient attitudes have not gone away. Mercifully, Korah's descendants rose above their tragic family history, and some of the delightful Psalms are attributed to the sons of Korah, e.g. Psalm 45. Let us apply the lessons. In the context of New Testament assemblies, the function of spiritual gift is likened to the various activities of the human body (1 Cor 12.14-19). The foot has a function distinct from the hand; the ear has a function distinct from the eye. Neither should covet the role of the other, the attitude that proved to be the downfall of Korah. Be content to exercise your own God-given gift.

If there has been breakdown, either in the family or in the assembly, be like the sons of Korah and rise above it. A disappointing family history never excludes anyone from effective participation in the work and worship of God.

Elkanah is another recognisable name in this section (v.23), with the assumption that we already know that he was the father of Samuel (v.28). When we are first introduced to him in Scripture, he is described as "an Ephrathite" (1 Sam 1.1). We now learn that he was a Levite, so the term "Ephrathite" has no tribal connotation but is a geographical term, Ephrath being an alternative name for Bethlehem (Gen 35.19). People who originated in Bethlehem were Ephrathites - for example, Jesse of the tribe of Judah (1 Sam 17.12).

Now that we have come to understand that Samuel was a Levite, we can see why he was so much at home in tabernacle service, and not, as may have been supposed, an intruder from an alien tribe. There was added to him the further honour of being a prophet of God.

As far as Samuel's sons are concerned, there is a difference between v.28, and the record of 1 Samuel 8.2 where the firstborn is said to be Joel, and the second Abiah. Here the firstborn is said to be Vashni. Some translations substitute Joel for Vashni in this verse, e.g. ESV, RSV, and NKJV. Other scholars tell us that "Vashni" is not really a name at all, but rather a word meaning "the second" - hence a rendering, "the firstborn (without naming him), and the second Abiah". Whatever the exact situation may be, the conduct of these two men was the catalyst that created the clamour for a king in Israel. Despite Samuel's undoubted qualities, he had a flaw that clouded his latter years - he was guilty of nepotism. It is a fault that has blighted many lives: the ability to turn a blind eye to the waywardness of family members, and to advance them regardless of their obvious failures (1 Sam 8.1-5).

Verses 31-48: The Singers

Still concentrating on the descendants of Levi, the Chronicler gives us details of those who were involved in superintending "the service in song" in the interim period between the ark being brought to Jerusalem and the construction of Solomon's temple. Singers were drawn from all three branches of the Levitical family, so this function was not the sole responsibility of any one group. Although David was denied the privilege of building the temple, his zeal was such that he was keen to have everything in place in preparation for temple service to function. He was determined that there would be a smooth transition from tabernacle to temple. Among other things, that involved the songsters being in readiness. The record of the commencement of their ministry is found in ch.16, with a man called Asaph overseeing the proceedings.

The phrase "after that the ark had rest" (v.31) anticipates the end of ch.15; it is a delightful expression. In the wilderness, there was an occasion when the ark went before the people "to search out a resting place for them" (Num 10.33). Now there would come a time when it in turn would have "rest". In addition to its forty years of wilderness journeys, it had been captured by the Philistines, and had been located in different places with various tragic circumstances surrounding it. Finally it would have "rest", and there would be those who would "minister before the ark of the Lord, and to celebrate, and to thank and praise the Lord, the God of Israel" (1 Chr 16.4, RV). If we see the ark as a type of the Lord Jesus, it is perhaps a pointer to the day of His being seated at God's right hand. The One who in death passed through the turbulent judgment waters of the river Jordan in spate (Josh 3.11-17), now has "rest".

Jesus, in His heav'nly temple,
Sits with God upon the throne;
Now no more to be forsaken,
His humiliation gone.

Never more shall God, Jehovah,
Smite the Shepherd with the sword;
Ne'er again shall cruel sinners
Set at nought our glorious Lord.
(Robert C. Chapman)

None of the features of tabernacle and temple worship were carried over into Christianity. This includes the "service in song"; it was never an official activity of New Testament churches. However, joyous, melodious, hearty singing will be a feature of Spirit-filled believers as they are "Giving thanks always for all things unto God and the Father in the name of our Lord Jesus Christ" (Eph 5.19-20). Again, seeing the ark as a type of the Lord Jesus, the lesson is that it is only when He is in His rightful place in the sanctuary of our hearts and in the sanctuary of our assemblies, that the note of praise will sound, and God receive the worship that is His due.

The location of the singers' ministry is said to be "before the dwelling place of the tabernacle of the congregation" (v.32). Two words are used to describe the venue, both of which are frequently employed in reference to the tabernacle. "Dwelling place" (4908) is first used by the Spirit in Exodus 25.9, translated there and extensively by the word "tabernacle" itself. The usage of this word is a reminder that it was the divine residence: "let them make me a sanctuary; that I may dwell (7931, related to 4908) among them" (Ex 25.8). Thus the singers' praise was directed to the One who resided in the tent. The New Testament equivalent is "singing with grace in your hearts *to the Lord*" (Col 3.16).

The second word that is used is "tabernacle" (168), another word that is frequently translated in that way to describe God's sanctuary. However, it is commonly employed for the ordinary tent of the nomad such as in its first usage: "the father of such as dwell in tents" (168) (Gen 4.20). This word is perhaps a reminder of the passing nature of the structure. In our context it is contrasted with a more permanent construction, "the *house* of the Lord in Jerusalem". It brings to mind Paul's teaching regarding the contrast between our present mortal bodies, and the resurrection body. The one is said to be "earthly" and the other "in the heavens". The one is a "tabernacle", and the other a "house". The one will be "dissolved" and the other is "eternal" (2 Cor 5.1).

The service of these singers was according to divine instructions. "They waited on their office according to their order." A more modern translation elucidates: "they performed their service according to their order" (ESV). The word "order" (4941) should not be interpreted as a "course" similar to that of the priests when their numbers necessitated a shift system, but rather the fact that these men were under instructions. It is getting back to the fact that God's work must be done in God's way. The danger of ignoring "the due order" (4941) of things is highlighted in 15.13. A pattern for "all the work of the service of the house of the Lord" had been committed to David (1 Chr 28.13), and even in the interim period before the house was built David had things operating according to that pattern. Thus the singers functioned "according to their order". The ancient injunction still holds good today: "See...that thou make all things according to the pattern" (Heb 8.5). In relation to "the house of God, which is the church of the living God" (1 Tim 3.15), we dare not deviate from the divine ideal.

The first mentioned major participant in the singing was a Kohathite named Heman (v.33). Heman was Samuel's grandson. His father was the infamous Joel who was guilty of taking bribes and of gross injustice (1 Sam 8.1-3). It is another reminder that a father's sins should never preclude a son from making his mark for God. Standing at Heman's right hand would be "his brother Asaph" (v.39), a brother only in the wider sense of being a relative, for Asaph was descended from Gershom (v.43). To their left hand were representatives of Merari, in particular a man called Ethan (v.44). All three were prominent when the ark was being transported to Jerusalem (ch.15).

Heman had the added honour and responsibility of being "the king's seer in the words of God" (25.5). Clearly, he was a man in touch with heaven, not only addressing praise Godward, but also communicating prophecy manward.

Asaph was a psalmist, credited with Psalms 50 and 73-83, either as author or compiler. It appears that which of these functions he fulfilled "is not clear, and neither can be proved or disproved" (J. Flanigan; *What The Bible Teaches: Psalms*; p.223).

Ethan is also called Jeduthun (e.g. 16.41; 25.1). He is designated "the chief musician" in Psalms 39, 62 and 77. Jeduthun (3038) means "praising", an appropriate name for the function he fulfilled.

Singing was not the only function of the Levites, for v.48 indicates that they had responsibility for "*all* manner of service of the tabernacle of the house of God". Not all of them were capable singers, but all had some role, with diverse tasks to perform. For this they were "appointed" (5414; "given", JND). God uses the word when the Levites were first commissioned to serve: "I have given (5414) the Levites as a gift to Aaron and to his sons" (Num 8.19). These men were God's gift to the priestly family, men whose assistance was vital to the effective conduct of the service of God. It would be good if we could see ourselves in that light. The ascended Christ still gives men as "gifts unto men" (Eph 4.8-16). In serving Him by assisting others, we fulfil the function for which we have been given. As in these ancient times when the Levites were responsible for "all manner of service", so today there is a great variety of work to be done, and each believer is suitably endowed by God for the task that He has in mind for them: "to every man his work" (Mk 13.34).

Verses 49-53: Aaron and His Sons

The Chronicler now reverts to the priestly family, but this time he traces the line from Aaron to Ahimaaz without deviation (vv.50-53). On this occasion, he prefaces the genealogy with their job description. He is drawing the distinction between tasks allotted to the Levites and what was peculiarly priestly. The priest's first area of activity was in connection with "the altar of the burnt offering". In offering a burnt offering, the offerer himself had certain responsibilities, but he was dependent on the priest to "sprinkle the blood", to attend to the fire, and to arrange the parts of the offering on the altar (Lev 1.3-9). The "holy priesthood" of New Testament times offers up "spiritual sacrifices, acceptable to God by Jesus Christ" (1 Pet 2.5).

The priest's second function related to "the altar of incense", details of which are found in Exodus 30.1-10. In the Holy Scriptures, incense is linked with prayer (Ps 141.2; Lk 1.9-10; Rev 8.3-4), and the lesson from the ancient priests is that, as "a holy priesthood", part of our responsibility is to be intercessors.

The Aaronic priest was also entrusted with "all the work of the place most holy, and to make an atonement for Israel". It would appear that these two phrases should be taken together, for, in reality, activity in the most holy place was confined to the one day in the year when atonement was made for the nation, the Day of Atonement, the record of which is in Leviticus 16. Meticulous detail was given for the ritual of that day, and yet the point that is made in the New Testament is that its repetitive nature exposed the inadequacy of it all. It is superseded now by something grander, something effective, something lasting - the work of the Lord Jesus upon the cross (Heb 9-10).

Even although Israel's priests were mortal, and all the ritual was inadequate and passing, it had still to be done "according to all that Moses the servant of God had commanded", for he in turn had received his instructions from heaven. Mention has already been made of the folly of Nadab and Abihu acting independently of divine instructions, and of David removing the ark in an unscriptural fashion (ch.13). It should be a salutary lesson to us all that we dare not trifle with a holy God, and that His principles must be upheld without deviation, whether they relate to our personal lives or to corporate activity as an assembly. "Our God is a consuming fire" (Heb 12.29).

Moses is here designated, "the servant of God". God Himself was happy to acknowledge him as such: "Moses my servant" (Josh 1.2). Caleb described him as "the servant of the Lord" (Josh 14.7), but not before he had first called him "Moses the man of God" (v.6). It would be good for us all to be servants of God in reality, but we can only function adequately as His servants if we have the moral and spiritual qualities of a man of God.

Having given us details of the work of the priests, the Chronicler then restates the identity of these men who were so privileged to minister for God (vv.50-53).

Verses 54-81: The Dwelling Places of the Levites

Simeon and Levi had exhibited great fury and cruelty in their treatment of the men of Shechem, and as a result Jacob decreed that they would be divided, and scattered throughout Israel (Gen 49.7). God saw to it that the prediction came to pass, but with Levi He operated in a different way. We have already seen how the Simeonites were scattered as a result of their territorial ambitions, but the Levites were dispersed by another method. They had no inheritance allotted to them, but they were to settle throughout all the land, with each of the tribes having responsibility to afford them sanctuary within its borders. The last section of the chapter records the whereabouts of these descendants of Levi.

Their position was decided "by lot" just as Canaan itself was divided by lot (e.g. Num 26.55). Keep in mind that "The lot is cast into the lap; but the whole disposing thereof is of the Lord" (Prov 16.33). Thus, whether it be the position of the tribes in the land, or the location of the Levitical family, it was God who directed where each should be placed.

The family of Aaron, that is, the priestly family, is the first to be mentioned (vv.54-60). The tribes of Judah and Benjamin played host to them, so they were most conveniently placed for the time when the temple would be built and Jerusalem would become "the place which the Lord (their) God (would choose) out of all (their) tribes to put his name there" (Deut 12.5).

The word "castles" (2918) is perhaps more appropriately rendered "encampments" (RV, JND) or "settlements" (ESV), although it does convey some idea of fortification. God does take an interest in the safety of His priests. Hebron is the first mentioned location of these men of God. As noted formerly in connection with David's administration, the name conveys the idea of "fellowship". Not only is it essential for a ruler among God's people to live in fellowship with Him, but those who act as priests must also enjoy communion with Him. We will never worship adequately if we are out of touch with Him.

Hebron had been promised to Caleb as an inheritance, and lest we should think that he had been ousted from that cherished environment to accommodate the priests, there is the reminder that "the fields of the city, and the villages thereof" had been given to him (v.56). Hebron had been virtually the first place that he had surveyed as a spy (Num 13.22), and more than forty years had failed to erase the memory of its delights. "Give me this mountain" was his earnest appeal to Joshua (Josh 14.12). It would be wonderful if we were all as earnest in our desire to enjoy fellowship with our God.

There is a reminder that this notable place was also a city of refuge for the manslayer (v.57). If the priests were as compassionate as they were expected to be (Heb 5.2), their company should have made the irksome confinement of the manslayer a little easier to bear. God is wonderfully kind.

Debir (v.58) was another city with links to Caleb, and Othniel was the man who captured it for him (Judg 1.11-13). Its former name was Kirjath-sepher. Debir (1688) means "oracle", and Kirjath-sepher (7158), "the city of the book". Both names are a reminder of the important place that the Word of God should play in the lives of God's people, those who are His holy priesthood. "The priest's lips should keep knowledge, and they should seek the law at his mouth: for he is the messenger of the Lord of hosts" (Mal 2.7). To instruct others effectively, we must dwell at Debir ourselves.

Beth-shemesh (v.59) is another city that features elsewhere in Scripture, particularly on the tragic occasion when 50,070 men perished there (1 Sam 6.19). Impiously, men from the district had looked into the ark, and their curiosity cost many lives. We are surprised to learn now that the place was one of the "dwelling places" of the priests. Obviously, the priests had never promoted any spirit of reverence in the area.

Anathoth (v.60) was home to Jeremiah the prophet, so as late as the days prior to Judah's captivity the priests were still domiciled there, for Jeremiah was "of the priests that were in Anathoth" (Jer 1.1).

The balance of the chapter tells us the whereabouts of the three sections of the tribe of Levi. There is a summary in vv.61-65, and then more precise details of the sons of Kohath (vv.66-70), and of the sons of Gershom (vv.71-76), and finally, of the sons of Merari (vv.77-81).

Throughout the section, the word "suburbs" (4054) should be interpreted as the open pastureland around the cities, in some instances common ground.

Thus the tribes of Israel played host to the Levitical family. There is no mention of their being located anywhere in Dan, although back in Joshua 21.5, 23-24, Dan had contributed cities to accommodate Kohathites. The tribe of Dan became the first tribe to fall into idolatry (Judg 18), so possibly such an environment was no longer deemed suitable for men so closely linked to the house of God, for our associates can have a real impact upon our lives. Dan gets no mention in the list of tribes in Revelation 7 either. It may well be that being the frontrunner in idolatry has debarred him from representing God even to the last days. However, it is delightful to note that the tribe will have its place in the nation in millennial days (Ezek 48.1). Little wonder Frederick Faber wrote:

> For the love of God is broader
> Than the measure of man's mind;
> And the heart of the Eternal
> Is most wonderfully kind.

1 CHRONICLES 7

Having given the genealogies of Judah, Simeon, the Transjordan tribes and the Levitical family, the Chronicler now turns his attention to most of the remaining tribes of Israel. Brief details of these are given in chapter 7, and then a fuller record of the line of Benjamin is outlined in chapter 8. Doubtless this gives due respect to the tribe from which Israel's first king had come.

There is no mention of the tribes of Dan and Zebulun. Reference has already been made to the fact that the Danites had pioneered idolatry in Israel and that they had forged into territory far to the north (Judg 18). Zebulun did feature honourably in David's day, particularly in respect of their discipline and loyalty. They "could keep rank: they were not of double heart" (12.33), but again, they occupied land that was out of the way, described by Isaiah as "Galilee of the nations" (9.1). Perhaps by post-exilic times both of these tribes had become so obscure and absorbed that they warranted no mention.

It should be stated that a small number of commentators see a reference to Dan at the end of v.12, but this is dependent on tinkering with the text! The alteration does not seem to have general acceptance among scholars. A quotation from The New American Commentary, page 93, may suffice to show this. "We noted earlier that Dan seems to be missing. One commentator (Williamson) has proposed an emendation at the end of v.12 to give a reading 'the sons of Dan: Hushim, his son, one'. This is rejected by other commentators".

Verses 1-5: The Sons of Issachar

Jacob used a variety of creatures to illustrate characteristics of his sons (Gen 49). It would please Judah and Naphtali to be likened to a lion and a hind respectively. Less flattering were the references to Dan and Benjamin - the one compared to a serpent, and the other to a wolf. Issachar would hardly have been enamoured to hear his father refer to him as "a strong ass" (v.14). Strength he had, but the tribe seemed content just to plod on in a rustic environment, avoiding anything that would disturb their easy-going life-style, even to the extent of being willing to accept peace at any price (v.15). There were occasions when the tribe rose above this relaxed attitude, as when they responded to Barak's call to arms, and were mentioned in dispatches (Judg 5.15). Of more relevance to the present narrative was their commitment "in the days of David" (v.2). To their credit, they were willing to acknowledge David's claim to the throne, for they "had understanding of the times, to know what Israel ought to do" (1 Chr 12.32). Known for their prudence, they were persuaded that the time had come for the ten tribes to throw in their lot with David.

Here, emphasis is placed on their military prowess. The strain of the tribe that came through Tola was able to muster 22,600 fighting men "in the days of David" (v.2). In fact the total number of warriors coming from Issachar was 87,000 (v.5). It appears that Issachar shook off the lethargy of former days, and became a burgeoning tribe with expertise and valour in warfare. Like them, let us throw off a laid-back attitude to life, and be militant in pursuing the Lord's interests. "Let us not sleep, as do others; but let us watch and be sober" (1 Thess 5.6).

A remark is needed regarding the sons of Izrahiah (v.3). Four are listed, and then the comment, "five: all of them chief men". Alternative renderings make it clearer that their father made up the number of the five who were "chief men". For example, the ESV translates, "all five of them were chief men". Young's Literal Translation suggests an alternative explanation by making the number five a proper name, "Hamishah".

Verses 6-12: The Sons of Benjamin

Of Benjamin's ten sons (Gen 46.21), only three are mentioned here, with five being listed in 8.1-2. The now familiar variation of names is in evidence again. The tribe came close to extinction when many were slaughtered in the circumstances recorded towards the end of the book of Judges, so perhaps some elements of the family were totally wiped out.

The main talking point in Benjamin's line is that the heads of various branches of the family were all "mighty men of valour" (vv.7,9,11). Now, as then, it is important for leaders to give a lead, to be exemplary, to be courageous. Weak leadership leaves people drifting. A shepherd is a man who cares, but he is also a man of courage. By contrast, the hireling when faced with danger "leaveth the sheep and fleeth" (Jn 10.12). "Be thou an ensample to them that believe" (1 Tim 4.12, RV); "Neither as being lords over God's heritage, but being ensamples to the flock" (1 Pet 5.3).

Verse 13: The Sons of Naphtali

Only Naphtali's immediate family members are mentioned, corresponding exactly to the record of Numbers 26.48-50 but with a slight variation in the spelling of two of the names. There is a reminder that they were descended from Bilhah, Jacob's concubine, their paternal grandmother.

In a chapter where so many are described as "mighty men of valour" none are mentioned in connection with Naphtali. His father had said of him; "a hind let loose: he giveth goodly words" (Gen 49.21). Perhaps he had the timid temperament of the hind as well as the grace of its movements. He was better known for counsel than for combat: he was a man of words and not a man of war. The attitude of the Psalmist was shared by Naphtali; "I am for peace: but when I speak, they are for war" (Ps 120.7). Even when they rallied to David's banner, there is only the record of the numbers who supported, and the fact that they had the necessary arms (12.34). Once more, in that chapter it is noted that many were "men of valour" or "expert in war"; the men of Naphtali had no such military credentials. However, it is to their credit that despite being naturally timorous and disinclined for warfare, they *did* rise above their innate feelings, and in the hour of crisis they supported David when the time came to "turn the kingdom of Saul to him" (12.23). When reading of Timothy, we get the impression that he too was naturally timid as many of us are. Let us pay heed to the exhortations to him: "God hath not given us the spirit of fear…Be not thou therefore ashamed…(2 Tim 1.7-8); "Endure hardness, as a good soldier of Jesus Christ" (2.3); "endure afflictions" (4.5). Let us be like the men of Naphtali, and when occasion demands, suppress our natural reticence and fears to take a stand, and do what is right.

Verses 14-19: The Sons of Manasseh

Space is now devoted to the portion of the tribe of Manasseh that had its inheritance in the land of Canaan. Ashriel's mother, described as "she" (v.14), is presumably Manasseh's wife as suggested by the italicised "his wife" of the Revised Version. By contrast Machir was the son of a concubine, and through this line we arrive at Zelophehad whose name features in the earlier history of Israel. Surrounding him there was a legal issue occasioned by his having fathered only daughters, and dying without a son and heir. As here, whenever Zelophehad is mentioned, attention is drawn to the fact that his family consisted exclusively of girls. These five daughters had concerns that they would have no inheritance in the land. Their father had died in the wilderness, so all hope of their having a brother to occupy what was due as an inheritance had gone forever (Num 27.1-11). Were they to be left with nowhere that they could really call home? Evidently, personal sin had been the cause of their father's death (v.3) although in fact, with two notable exceptions, no one who left Egypt aged twenty and upwards survived the wilderness. So these five young women petitioned Moses, who, faced with a new set of circumstances, referred the matter to the Lord (v.5). He acted similarly in the case of the man who "blasphemed the Name" (Lev 24.11, RV), and in the situation of the man who gathered sticks on the sabbath day (Num 15.32-36). Like David, he frequently "enquired of the Lord". There is a salutary lesson there for us all. So often we are like Joshua, who "asked not counsel at the mouth of the Lord" (Josh 9.14), a blunder he had made earlier in the debacle at Ai (ch.7). We need to seek divine guidance for all the decisions of life. It is imperative that we lay to heart the instructions of the wise man: "In all thy ways acknowledge him, and he shall direct thy paths" (Prov 3.6).

In the case of Zelophehad's daughters, God gave a landmark decision, a legal precedent that affected similar cases - in the absence of sons, daughters would be the beneficiaries of their late father's estate. A proviso was added at a later stage. The Lord gave a directive insisting that these five girls marry into families of their own tribe (Num 36). This was to avoid Manasseh's territory being ceded to another tribe. When the time came for allotting the land, the daughters of Zelophehad had not forgotten the promises made, and appealed to Eleazar and Joshua for the territory due to them

(Josh 17.3-6). Their tenacity and courage in a male-dominated society is to be admired, and God rewarded their aspiration to possess a little part of Canaan. Let Christian women have the same ambition when it comes to their spiritual inheritance. The enjoyment of rich spiritual provision in Christ is not the exclusive domain of the males. It is open to all, brothers and sisters, to revel in the wealth of the spiritual inheritance attaching to those who have been "blessed…with all spiritual blessings in heavenly places in Christ" (Eph 1.3).

An unusual situation warrants a passing mention. "Maachah the wife of Machir bare a son, and she called his name Peresh" (v.16). It was not unusual for a mother to name her child, for we have observed already that it was the mother of Jabez who gave him his unfortunate name, "Sorrowful" (4.9). Rachel named her infant "Benoni", "the son of my sorrow", although her choice of name was overturned (Gen 35.18). What is unusual is the disgusting name that this woman gave her boy, for Peresh means "dung" (6570). There is no hint of why he was given such a disagreeable name, except it be found in the meaning of his mother's name. According to Strong, Maachah means "depression", and if her temperament was reflected in her name, then she may have been acting irrationally when naming the child. If so she was to be pitied, as so many are when a dark cloud of depression settles over them. It can trigger actions and talk that are completely out of character, as when Elijah "went for his life" and then promptly "requested for himself that he might die" (1 Kings 19.3-4). Did he want to live or die? Did he really think that he was no better than his half-hearted forefathers in Gilead? Was he serious when he said, "I only am left"? Sadly, depression can rob its victims of the ability to think and act logically.

Verses 20-29: The Sons of Ephraim

This little section divides in two, with references to Ephraim's family down to Joshua (v.27), and then allusions to some of the places where members of the tribe were located. In vv.20-21, a pattern is set as the descendants of Ephraim's son Shuthelah are traced. In each case, the name is followed by the words "his son". That pattern is abandoned when mention is made of Ezer and Elead. The Chronicler is backtracking to introduce another two of Ephraim's immediate family as is seen from the reference to "Ephraim their father" (v.22). Joseph had survived to see these grandsons (Gen 50.23). Could he ever have anticipated the catastrophe that would come their way? Thomas Gray had observed the boys of Eton College and pondered their unknown future with the sorrows it would hold:

Alas, regardless of their doom,
The little victims play!
No sense have they of ills to come,
Nor care beyond today.

He concluded his ode with the famous lines:

> Yet ah! why should they know their fate?
> Since sorrow never comes too late,
> And happiness too swiftly flies.
> Thought would destroy their paradise.
> No more; where ignorance is bliss,
> 'Tis folly to be wise.

Joseph would never have imagined that these little grandsons who played at his feet would meet such an untimely death, but such are the twists and turns of life.

The sad little story about these two men is the background to Beriah being burdened with such an unusual name. It means "in trouble", or "misfortune", or "in tragedy", depending on which lexicon you consult, but each conveying the same basic idea. He was a late child whose name perpetuated the memory of the earlier family disaster that left Ephraim feeling as desolate as his grandfather Jacob had been at the loss of his beloved Joseph (Gen 37.34). Beriah was one of the forebears of the illustrious Joshua, hence the inclusion of these points of interest.

Opinion is divided regarding Ezer and Elead. Generally, older commentaries see them as being victims, killed when defending their herds from Philistine marauders. More modern commentators regard them as the aggressors, pursued and slain while attempting to rustle the cattle of these men of Gath. Without being dogmatic, perhaps the first is more tenable when taking all the facts into account. This incident took place when the children of Israel were still in Egypt for it was many generations after Ephraim's day before they were liberated from slavery (Gen 15.13). The Israelites were located in Goshen in the north-east of Egypt, and Gath was not too far round the corner in the south-west corner of Canaan. The phrase "they came down" seems more appropriate to a Philistine incursion, unless you regard Ezer and Elead as having circled Gath, to descend upon it from a vantage point. Again, the Philistines were naturally belligerent. They were hostile to Isaac (Gen 26.12-33), and at the time of the exodus God deliberately led Israel by a circuitous route to avoid their attentions (Ex 13.17-18). The city of Gath was among those that were home to men of great stature up to and long after the occupation of the land (Josh 11.22; 1 Sam 17.4). Whether they were the assailants or the defenders, Ezer and Elead were no match for these tough men of Gath they were slain.

Their killers are here said to have been "born in that land" (v.21). The Philistines had migrated from north Africa and had settled in that south-west corner of Canaan. They had come from Egypt without experiencing redemption by the blood of the lamb, or separation from Egypt by the Red Sea. They stand as an illustration of those who merely profess to be saved, without reality, and yet they are present among the Lord's own people. Their offspring, those "born in that land", can perpetuate hostility to genuine believers, and hate them, and thus become their "murderers" (1 Jn 3.15). It is a fact that those who are Christians in name only create considerable unrest among the saints. They are intolerant of those who are godly, as illustrated in the aggressive cynicism of Judas when confronted with the devotion of Mary of Bethany (Jn 12.1-8).

Ephraim was inconsolable at the death of his two sons (v.22). It is not the norm for a son to predecease his father but there are numerous examples of it in Scripture. The very first father lost one of his sons when Cain murdered his brother (Gen 4.8). Like Ephraim, David lost more than one of his sons, and, again like Ephraim, was overwhelmed by grief (2 Sam 18.33). Ephraim's "brethren", that is the extended family, rallied to his support. Their efforts to soothe the troubled mind and heal the broken heart seemed futile, but it is to their credit that they tried. Whether in a family or in an assembly, it is important to show solidarity with those who experience deep trial. Job's friends rallied around him, but sadly their foolish attitude aggravated his distress. They were more helpful when they sat for a week and said nothing (Job 2.13). Here, Ephraim, like the mothers in Ramah "refused to be comforted" (Jer 31.15). He was determined to keep the tragedy at the forefront of his mind, and so the late addition to his family had to bear a name that made that obvious to all. Ephraim never wanted to forget that "it went evil with his house". It is not unspiritual to grieve, but we should seek God's help to avoid Ephraim's unhealthy preoccupation with grief and tragedy.

It appears that there is a considerable time lapse between verses 23 and 24, for circumstances are mentioned now that could relate only to the land of Canaan. If that is so, Sherah must be a "daughter" of Beriah in the sense of a descendant. She built Beth-horon, which is mentioned for the first time in Joshua 10.10-11, and also Uzzen-sherah, presumably named after her, but the location of which has never been identified. It is hardly to be supposed that she herself was involved in digging foundations and laying bricks, but she must have been a planner and motivator. Building is used illustratively in the Scriptures, for example in 1 Corinthians 3 in respect of our input into the local assembly. Like Sherah, Christian women can be influential in encouraging the builders to see a spiritual edifice rise to the glory of God.

If Sherah is to be regarded as a literal daughter of Beriah or alternatively, Ephraim, then it must be her descendants who were responsible for building the aforementioned cities. She is perceived as a vital player in their ancestry, just as it was said of faithful midwifes that God "made them houses" (Ex 1.21).

Ephraim's genealogy comes down now to his most distinguished son, Joshua the son of Nun (v.27), a man whose history is traced in Scripture from being "a young man" (Ex 33.11) to being "old and stricken in years" (Josh 13.1). Like Daniel and the Apostle John, a lifetime of commitment to

God is chronicled in the sacred writings. It is wonderful when believers in old age have the same conviction and devotion that were the hallmarks of their youth, "still bring(ing) forth fruit in old age" (Ps 92.14).

The rest of the Ephraim section details some of the locations at which the tribe settled.

Verses 30-40: The Sons of Asher

The people that we encounter here are unknowns to us, but, as in Numbers 26.46, Serah (Sarah, Num 26.46) the daughter of Asher warrants a mention among so many males. Perhaps she is of note because she bore a name akin to her renowned ancestor, the wife of Abraham, Sarah's name meaning "princess". Possibly she bore it with royal dignity, just as every Christian woman by her charm and decorum can reflect the regal majesty of the royal family to which she belongs.

As with other tribes, the heads of Asher are described as "mighty men of valour" (v.40), but with this addition - "choice" (1305), a word that on five occasions in the AV is translated "pure". Mighty men of valour can be aggressive, and it is a well-known fact that war brutalises men. It is delightful then that when necessary these men of Asher were able to commit themselves to warfare without compromising integrity and morality. It would be good to capture that balance. Jude urges believers to "earnestly contend for the faith" (v.3), but before he is through he appeals, "of some have compassion" (v.22). Paul speaks to Timothy about "war(ring) a good warfare", but alongside that, "Holding faith and *a good conscience*" (1 Tim 1.18-19). When contending for what is right and Scriptural, we should never allow the fray to embitter us, or destroy our courtesy, or make us stoop to unethical behaviour. Men of valour should also be "choice" men.

Asher's fighting forces had seriously diminished since the days of the wilderness (Num 1.41; 26.47). Perhaps this was due to a period of their history when they had no stomach for warfare. Deborah's song highlights their inertia at that time: "Asher sat still at the haven of the sea, and abode by his creeks" (Judg 5.17, RV). Lack of commitment will inevitably impact upon effectiveness in the long term, and so the lesson is that, in the great conflict between good and evil, the members of the believer's body should be yielded "as instruments (weapons, 3696) of righteousness unto God" (Rom 6.13). Let us never allow the number of enlisted men to be diminished through non-involvement.

1 CHRONICLES 8

With the conclusion of the genealogies of the tribes at the end of chapter 7, further space is now devoted to Benjamin, with particular reference to the tribe producing the first king of Israel, Saul the son of Kish (v.33). Doubtless, one of the reasons for revisiting Benjamin is to give due acknowledgment of that fact. The details of chapter 8 differ from those of the previous chapter. There, the focus is on Benjamin's fighting forces; it is a military census. Here, to a large extent the emphasis is on the location of many of the people of Benjamin; it is geographical.

Earlier in the book, the tribe of Judah had double exposure, for it was the royal tribe, David's tribe. Politically, Benjamin was linked with Judah after the division of the nation, combining to form the kingdom of Judah. There, David's dynasty was in place until the captivity. Here in Chronicles, then, both tribes are granted what might be regarded as a disproportionate amount of space, but it is *their* history that is being recounted in the ongoing narrative right through to the end of the second book.

In this chapter there is no clear transition from generation to generation. For example, the sons of Ehud are mentioned in v.6 without Ehud himself having featured previously. A NIV footnote does say in v.3, "Gera the father of Ehud", but no other translations go down that route. Comments on this chapter will be scanty then, focusing on one or two individuals or places, with reference to some of the circumstances that feature.

Verses 1-2: The Sons of Benjamin

As mentioned formerly, three sons are referred to in 7.6, whereas there are five here. Ten receive mention in Genesis 46.21. It was suggested earlier that large parts of the tribe were wiped out subsequent to the sordid affair of Judges 19 leaving some of Benjamin's ten sons with no descendants beyond that: hence there was no need to trace their lineage down to that point.

Verses 3-5: The Sons of Bela

It appears that two of Bela's sons had the same name, Gera. Every other translation stands with the KJV without amending the text in any way. Some commentators with hard-to-follow arguments and a little manipulation do try to make a case for the first Gera being the father of Ehud, and the second his son. They follow the NIV footnote ruling out Abihud (end of v.3) as a name, and substituting the translation, "the father of Ehud". In favour of the first part of their argument is the fact that the father of the Benjamite judge who bore that name was a man called Gera (Judg 3.15). Adding weight to the case is the fact that it is unusual for two sons in the same family to bear the same name, but then, the first Gera is among the elder boys in the family whereas the second appears among the younger members. Perhaps the first had died before the birth of the second! Pure conjecture, but at this distance, who knows?

Verse 6: Ehud

There is no absolute certainty that this Ehud was the distinguished judge who delivered Israel from Moabite domination (Judg 3.12-30), but it does seem likely. We do know that he was a Benjamite (v.15), and like so many of his tribe he was left handed (Judg 20.16) while others were ambidextrous (1 Chr 12.2). A slight doubt is cast upon this Ehud being the judge because the Hebrew name here is Echuwd (261) whereas the judge is consistently called Ehuwd (164). However, the difference does not seem to be a deterrent to many commentators who are expert in Hebrew; they seem content that both words relate to the same man.

Verses 6-7: "Removed"

Some elements of the family experienced removal, being uprooted and transplanted elsewhere. The "they" who did the removing in v.6 is uncertain; there is no antecedent. In v.7, it appears that Gera did the removing for he is the last antecedent to the pronoun "he". Whatever the circumstances or the perpetrators, people were moved around against their will. In a past generation, there were those who were described euphemistically as "displaced persons". They were the victims of war and oppression. In more recent times the term "ethnic cleansing" has leapt to prominence. Again, people have been moved on. It happened frequently in Bible times, and there were some who used these unwelcome circumstances of upheaval and relocation to further the work of God. "They which were scattered abroad upon the persecution that arose about Stephen" saw their enforced dispersion as an opportunity to preach the gospel wherever they went (Acts 11.19). Anti-Semitism drove Aquila and Priscilla to Corinth, but there they became central figures in the commencement of a work for God in that sordid city (Acts 18.1-3). It would be good for us all if we could see necessary adjustments or unexpected developments in our lives as opportunities in the service of God.

Verses 8-11: Shaharaim

If in vv.6-7 people were "removed", in v.8 two women were "sent…away". They were the two wives of Shaharaim. Most translations make that clear; for example, JND speaks of him fathering sons "after he had sent away Hushim and Baara his wives". ESV and others concur. Very evidently Shaharaim had divorced these two women, and then had married the Hodesh of v.9.

All that we learn about this man shows him in a poor light. First, he should never have had two wives. At the dawn of creation God made it clear that as far as marriage is concerned the divine ideal is for a one man one woman relationship. That ideal was infringed as early as Genesis 4 when "Lamech took unto him two wives" (v.19). Lamech came in the line of Cain, and may be regarded as worldly and ungodly. Sadly, it is often the case that, given time, what is acceptable among such people can be tolerated among the people of God. Thus, even as early as the days of the patriarchs, Abraham and Jacob abandoned monogamy. The one man one woman relationship is still the divine ideal and to violate it in any way permanently disqualifies a man from overseership and deacon service. The elder and the deacon must be "the husband of one wife", literally, "a one woman man" (1 Tim 3.2,12).

Shaharaim then compounded his sin by divorcing these wives. Even in an age when God allowed a certain latitude about divorce (Deut 24.1-4), a latitude that He did not extend to the Christian era (Mt 5.31-32), He did declare His opposition to it. "For the Lord, the God of Israel, saith that he hateth putting away" (Mal 2.16).

Having dispatched these two wives, he took a new wife Hodesh, and fathered sons by her. By this time he was resident in Moab (v.8), and so another failure comes to light. Whatever was he doing in Moab? Moab had held Israel in thraldom for eighteen years (Judg 3.14) and its citizens were no friends of the people of God. Ehud had ended that servitude. Like Elimelech (Ruth 1.2), this man thought that he could fraternise with a defeated foe and remain unscathed. Let us be warned. By virtue of its origins (Gen 19.30-38), and the proportions of Eglon its king (Judg 3.17), Moab stands as a picture of "the flesh" to which frequent reference is made in the New Testament. "The flesh" can be adequately defined as the old sinful nature within us. As believers we "have crucified the flesh" (Gal 5.24). We cannot indulge it any more - "make not provision for the flesh" (Rom 13.14). Connected with it are lust (1 Jn 2.16) and defilement (Jude v.23), so Moab is no place for a child of God!

Prior to his divorce, Shaharaim had had sons by his wife Hushim (v.11) including Elpaal whose line is now followed.

Verse 12: Ono and Lod

Elpaal's sons were responsible for building Ono and Lod, places that were familiar to the postexilic people who first read this narrative. Ono was the place where Nehemiah's enemies set a trap for him (Neh 6.1-9). He was not taken in by their duplicity: "they thought to do me mischief" (v.2). Neither was he worn down by their persistence in coming back at him on four occasions (v.4). Nor did their threats do anything to intimidate him, as with confidence he left the whole issue with his God: "Now therefore, O God, strengthen my hands" (v.9). May God help us to be as discerning and determined and dependent as he was.

Verse 13: Beriah and Shema

These sons of Elpaal recorded a remarkable military victory over "the inhabitants of Gath". Much has been said of the military prowess of the Philistines, and of the physique of the men of Gath including Goliath, its most famous son. Their deadly skirmish with the sons of Ephraim had been noted in 7.21, but at some unknown point in their history they experienced bitter defeat at the hands of these Benjamites. Frequently in the Word of

God there is the reminder that insurmountable problems can be handled when God is brought into the equation. The first readers of this book had been taught through Zechariah that a "great mountain" would become "a plain" by the power of the Holy Spirit, symbolised then as oil (Zech 4). Let us all be encouraged that the antagonistic plans of the enemies of God and His people can be thwarted, for, "If God be for us, who can be against us?" (Rom 8.31).

Verses 14-28: Sundry Unknowns

I call them unknowns, but every one of them spent their allotted time on the planet, and would have made their contribution to their locality. Some would be known for their interest in the welfare of their society; others would be anti-social, but all were known to God as evidenced in the recording of their names. There is no such thing as a nonentity as far as He is concerned.

Those mentioned last were residents of Jerusalem (v.28; see also 9.3).

Verses 29-40: Saul's Line

Gibeon (v.29) was not so very far from Jerusalem and was another Benjamite city. It was rich in history, not least because its original residents conceived a sophisticated plan to deceive Joshua in order to avoid certain death at the hands of Israel (Josh 9). Their capitulation raised the ire of their former allies, and so Gibeon came under attack, only to be rescued by Joshua's forces on an occasion that was unique in human history. The sun stood still for about a whole day ensuring complete victory (Josh 10.1-15). In a later generation, in the ongoing civil war between Saul's supporters and David's, a grisly contest was fought at Gibeon followed by a battle that did end at sun down with Abner appealing for restraint (2 Sam 2.12-32).

Saul's forebears originated at Gibeon. As in other lists of names, some mentioned here had alternative names if compared with other records. For example, Meri-baal the son of Jonathan would be more familiar to us as Mephibosheth because of his interesting history in 2 Samuel. A few like him have "baal" incorporated into their names, and indeed in one case Baal itself was the man's name (v.30). We should not read anything sinister into this, because "baal" (1168) simply means "lord", and these men were given their names long before Baal worship became a regular feature of the religious life of Israel. After Ahab established Baal worship as the religion of the nation it would have been an affront to Jehovah for anyone to incorporate "baal" when naming a child.

An innocuous little thing is said of some of the Benjamites in v.32: "these also dwelt with their brethren in Jerusalem". However, one can hardly read it without remembering Psalm 133.1 with its reference to brethren dwelling together. There, stress is laid on the need for "unity" in such circumstances. Happy were these Benjamites if they were able to coexist harmoniously, reflecting something of the meaning of the "salem" part of

Jerusalem - "peace". "How good and how pleasant" it would have been. Let us be those who are able to "dwell" with our brethren, without animosities and jealousies bubbling to the surface to disturb the peace.

Saul's sons are mentioned at v.33, the three eldest perishing with their father on Mount Gilboa (10.2). The survivor, Esh-baal, is very evidently Ish-bosheth, the spineless individual who was installed as king by Abner, his late father's general (2 Sam 2.8-11). His tenure was brief before he was assassinated by disloyal captains (2 Sam 4).

The Chronicler will return to Saul's line at the end of ch.9, as a precursor to the sad record of his demise in ch.10.

1 CHRONICLES 9

It is important to remember that the books of Chronicles were written after the Babylonian exile, with the strong possibility that Ezra was the inspired penman. This chapter gives details of the people who returned from Babylon, and the functions that they fulfilled in relation to the sanctuary that rose from the rubble and ruin of Solomon's temple. Keep in mind that the core of the book relates to the reign of David with particular emphasis on his desire to build a house for God. That dream was never realised in his lifetime, but the second book records the construction of a magnificent edifice in the days of Solomon his son. Recalling such history would be for the encouragement of these returning exiles whose remit from Cyrus had been to "build the house of the Lord God of Israel…which is in Jerusalem" (Ezra 1.3), with the added concession from Artaxerxes to "beautify the house" (Ezra 7.27).

So, this chapter incorporates not only the names of those who returned, but in particular, their various tasks in maintaining the service of the house of God. Priests were needed (v.10), and Levites too (v.14), men who were involved in a great range of activities including door-keeping, superintending the storehouses, and singing.

The chapter ends (vv.35-44) with a restatement of Saul's genealogy as a lead-in to the sad record of his passing in ch.10.

Verse 1: A Summary

The Chronicler gives a brief word of summary before passing on to speak of his own generation as of v.2. A wide range of genealogies has been covered in the first eight chapters, and now he gives us a hint of his "sources". Never forget, though, that inspired writers did not really require "sources"! However, he had dredged the records of the "kings of Israel", and from them he recorded such details as were relevant to his purpose as decreed by the Spirit of God. The reference to "the book of the kings" does not relate to any inspired volume of Scripture, but rather to logs or journals maintained by the monarch of the day. It is evident that the writer was selective in the material that he copied; he speaks here of "all Israel" being "reckoned by genealogies" in this book of the kings. Our Chronicler has certainly not recorded the details of "all Israel". In fact, as we observed formerly, some tribes receive no mention at all.

Most translations make some kind of a break after the words "kings of Israel", excluding Judah from the reference to "the book". For example the RV reads like this - "they are written in the book of the kings of Israel: and Judah was carried away captive to Babylon for their transgression". To the repatriated men of Judah the last statement is a solemn reminder of the reason for their enforced exile in Babylon; their fathers had been guilty of "transgression" (4604). The word enshrines the concept of unfaithfulness. By espousing idolatry, they had become like an unfaithful wife to Jehovah, with the grim consequence of seventy years of captivity in Babylon. That area of the world was the very cradle of idolatry, and there they would observe the excesses that went hand in glove with such an iniquitous religious system. The experience so sickened the nation that to this very day the Jews have steered well clear of idolatry and will never revert to it until the days of the man of sin (2 Thess 2.3-5).

There is a warning to us that any unfaithfulness on our part could invite divine discipline. Out of affection for us, the Almighty can employ means to restore loyalty. To an assembly that had left its first love, the Lord Jesus said, "Remember…repent…or else…" (Rev 2.5). Apparently the stern ultimatum went unheeded for there has been nothing for God at Ephesus for many centuries. Let us shun unfaithfulness and aspire to the divine accolade, "Well done, thou good and faithful servant" (Mt 25.21).

Verses 2-9: The First Inhabitants

As suggested earlier, when these verses allude to "the first inhabitants" the reference is to those who returned after the captivity. Before any specific names are recorded, four groups receive mention. "The Israelites" were the general populace, because not everyone had particular tasks in connection with the temple. The other three groups did have special responsibilities, and attention has already been drawn to the different functions of priests and Levites. However, for the first time in Scripture we are introduced to the Nethinims. It is generally accepted that they were the descendants of the Gibeonites whom Joshua condemned to be "hewers of wood and drawers of water for the house of my God" (Josh 9.23). Joshua regarded his pronouncement as a curse, but maybe some of the Gibeonites felt honoured to be assigned to serve God, albeit in a lowly servile way! Wood was in constant demand to feed the altar, and the temple lavers required a steady supply of water. The Nethinims' task may have appeared menial, but it was a vital part of the function of the house of God.

In assembly life today, there are many practical matters that need attention, and there are those who happily sacrifice time and energy to deal with what may appear to be the less glamorous aspects of the service of God. Very often their diligence to duty frees up those who have been gifted differently, allowing them in an unhindered way to attend to their own responsibilities. For example, in Acts 6 men were appointed to superintend serving tables to allow the apostles to give themselves "continually to prayer, and to the ministry of the word" (v.4). The Nethinims were as necessary as the priests and Levites.

It is of interest that some from the tribes of Ephraim and Manasseh settled among the people of Judah and Benjamin at Jerusalem (v.3). Obviously they were a minority group as there is no further record of their names and numbers, but it is significant that they were there. Possibly they had heard of the grace that had been shown to Judah, and had made the trek from their own place of exile in Assyria to share in the blessing, and settle at

Jerusalem. We will never know how many from the ten tribes were involved, but as late as our Lord's day, Anna, a descendant of Asher, an aged woman who was in constant attendance at the temple (Lk 2.36-37), was domiciled at Jerusalem.

When God is blessing it should have a magnetic effect on others. It was when Naomi heard "how that the Lord had visited his people in giving them bread" that she resolved to return to Bethlehem (Ruth 1.6). During Asa's reign Scripture records that "they fell to him out of Israel in abundance, when they saw that the Lord his God was with him" (2 Chr 15.9). Paul made clear that when godly order obtains in an assembly unbelievers and unlearned folks who are present have to acknowledge, "God is among you indeed" (1 Cor 14.25, RV). There is something appealing about a situation in which God is present and granting blessing. In modern times it would be wonderful if we could create circumstances that would allow God to dwell among us happily, and work among us effectively, so that the assembly would attract others.

Verses 10-13: The Priests

Again, sundry names are mentioned, names that mean nothing to us, but God has noted the status of these dear priestly men. One was designated, "the ruler of the house of God" (v.11). As late as Acts 4.1 it was still the custom to have such a man in place, described there as "the captain of the temple". No doubt by that time the job was a very formal affair, with more attention being given to satisfying the whims of the chief priests than maintaining the honour of God. In earlier days, things were different; the house was His, and yet He used men to maintain its order, and superintend its affairs. The same is true of the present day "house of God, which is the church of the living God" (1 Tim 3.15). There are those connected with it who have responsibility to rule, and such elders have to be "counted worthy of double honour, especially they who labour in the word and doctrine" (5.17). A New Testament assembly is not a democracy, and its elders are divinely appointed (Acts 20.28). That makes them accountable to God as "steward(s) of God" (Titus 1.7); the word "steward" (*3623*) indicates a household manager, the house in question being God's house. It is a grave responsibility to rule in such a way as to maintain the holiness of the house, its dignity and its order, while at the same time displaying a deep affection and care for those connected with that household.

Another group is described as "heads of the house of their fathers…very able men for the work of the service of the house of God" (v.13). There is a wealth of instruction in these few words. These priests were heads of family groups, and as such had responsibility for order and discipline within these families. That gave training for their duties in connection with the house of God. Similarly, one of the qualifications of the New Testament elder is that he is "one that ruleth well his own house, having his children in subjection with all gravity; (For if a man know not how to rule his own house, how shall he take care of the church of God?)" (1 Tim 3.4-5). The verse does not exclude a bachelor or childless husband from overseership. Scripture always looks at things as they are generally: i.e. the majority of men are married and rear a family, or the majority of people are right handed (Mt 5.30; 6.3), or the majority of Christian women have a believing husband to whom they can address their difficult theological questions (1 Cor 14.35): but not all have. Thus in 1 Timothy 3 Paul is stating that those brethren who have a wife and family must order their households in such a way as to qualify for overseership. The family unit is an excellent training ground for caring for the church of God.

These priests are further described as "very able men"; they had the ability for the task on hand. Again, it is a Biblical principle that God equips people for the task to which He assigns them. A phrase from the parable of the talents explains why there was no uniform distribution of the talents: "he gave…to every man according to his several ability" (Mt 25.15). It is a fact of life that not everyone has the same capabilities, and God tailors a person's work to their ability. He gives different gifts to different people, and whatever our gift it is our responsibility to "minister *the same* one to another, as good stewards of the manifold grace of God" (1 Pet 4.10). We should never be tempted to intrude on someone else's field of expertise. God has made us "able" for our own sphere of service. "If any man minister, let him do it as of *the ability which God giveth*" (v.11).

The duties of the priests are described as "*the work* of the service of the house of God". It was work! It demanded time. It sapped energy. It required commitment. Similarly the various duties of New Testament servants of God are described as work. Overseership is "a good *work*" (1 Tim 3.1). The Bible teacher who diligently explores the Scriptures is described as a *workman* (2 Tim 2.15). Spreading the gospel is "the *work* of an evangelist" (4.5). In whatever area of service we may be involved, let us remember that it is a work that demands application on our part. Never have to be asked, "Why stand ye here all the day idle?" (Mt 20.6). Rather, "Be ye strong, and let not your hands be slack: for your work shall be rewarded" (2 Chr 15.7, RV).

The work of these priests is also described as "the service of the house of God", just a reminder that all that was being done was in God's interests; it was service to Him. This elevates everything that we do as far as "the work of the Lord" is concerned. As we preach the gospel and endeavour to reach out to needy humanity, often uppermost in our minds is their need of salvation. Paul's outlook was different; he regarded his efforts as being a Godward ministry: "ministering the gospel of God, that the offering up of the Gentiles might be acceptable, being sanctified by the Holy Ghost" (Rom 15.16); "we are unto God a sweet savour of Christ, in them that are saved, and in them that perish" (2 Cor 2.15). If we only realised that everything we do is for Him and for His honour, it would add dignity and diligence to our efforts. Paul encouraged slaves to understand that even the drudgery of their daily grind was an opportunity to serve Him: "ye serve the Lord Christ" (Col 3.24). This raises the most menial task to a wonderfully high level.

Emphasis is laid on the focus of their labours; it was "the service of *the house of God*". These men were not dissipating their strength; their energies were being poure d into a specific task, the service of the house of God. Similarly, the church of God at Corinth required committed people who would build on the foundation that Paul had laid (1 Cor 3.10-15). There is still the need for that loyalty to the assembly. There is the danger of dividing our time, resources, energies and interest by supporting interdenominational activity or committing to parachurch organisations. Our remit is to build on the foundation of the assembly to further the work of the house of God.

Verses 14-16: The Levites

Obviously, not all the returning Levites are mentioned here as is indicated in the phrase "of the Levites", similar to v.10, "of the priests". Lists akin to these are contained in Nehemiah 11, where details are given of the duties of some of these men. Here, all that we learn is that some of them "dwelt in the villages of the Netophathites". This district of Judah features a number of times in Scripture, and had the honour of producing two of David's mighty men (2 Sam 23.28-29), both of whom were appointed as monthly captains over his host (1 Chr 27.13,15).

Verses 17-25: The Porters

The porters were Levites, but Levites assigned to the specific task of superintending activity and ensuring security at the gates of the house of God. (The word "porter" is used in its old fashioned sense of a door-keeper.) They would screen those who entered the temple precincts, excluding undesirables, and admitting those whose presence was legitimate. It is clear that by the time the Lord Jesus was here, porters had become redundant, for at the start of His ministry His Father's house had become "an house of merchandise" (Jn 2.16), deteriorating into "a den of thieves" by the time of His last visit to Jerusalem (Mt 21.13). There was a great need for "porters" in the days of New Testament churches for not everyone who came to them came with a true motive. In Jude's day, "certain men (had) crept in unawares" (v.4). At Ephesus, the porters were more vigilant, for they had "tried them which say they are apostles, and are not, and (had) found them liars" (Rev 2.2). There is the same need for caution today. The assembly should be satisfied that those who want to link with the saints are genuine believers, baptised as such, and subscribing to the "apostles' doctrine" as it affects every area of their lives, personal and ecclesiastical (Acts 2.42). While exercising caution, it should be kept in mind that no one with the necessary credentials should be denied acceptance by the assembly as is illustrated in our chapter. The function of certain porters was "the opening" of the house of God (v.27); the house was opened each morning to admit the people. Applying the illustration, we should understand that when people come to us seeking fellowship, the hope and expectation should be that the doors be open to them, although there will be occasions when an interview will expose either behavioural or doctrinal issues that would of necessity debar.

It is very evident that to some extent the post-exilic temple had been patterned on Solomon's temple. Historically, the east gate had been the gate through which the kings of Judah had passed (v.18). During the millennium, the east gate of the temple will be open only on the sabbaths, but again it will be the gate through which "the prince shall enter" (Ezek 46.1-2). Here, porters were stationed at the east gate. They were "in the companies of the children of Levi", that is, Levites who operated on a rota system in taking responsibility for that particular gate.

Those with overall responsibility for the porters are mentioned in v.19. There had been a family history of such activity as indicated by most translations. For example, the RV reads, "their fathers had been over the camp of the Lord, keepers of the entry". It is so good when a noble family tradition is kept alive. This is not to imply that overseership is a family right, or that the gift of the evangelist or teacher runs in the blood, but a tradition of godliness and spirituality in a family is worth preserving and perpetuating. It is so commendable when succeeding generations maintain a high level of commitment to the things of God.

In the past, the most eminent man with responsibility for the porters had been Phinehas (v.20). Much was said about him in the comments on 6.4, and it would appear that he was functioning in his role as a door-keeper when he slew the prince of Simeon (Num 25.6-15). Certainly, the sorry episode took place in the precincts of the tabernacle, for the offender was parading his pagan lady friend "in the sight of all the congregation of the children of Israel, who were weeping before the door of the tabernacle of the congregation" (v.6). What an example Phinehas left for the new generation of porters!

On this occasion, all that the inspired Chronicler records of Phinehas is that "the Lord was with him". No matter the task, the paramount need is for the presence of God. In this very book, the reason for David's increasing greatness is said to be the presence of God (11.9). The secret of Joseph's prosperity both in the house of Potiphar and in the prison was the fact that "the Lord was with Joseph" (Gen 39.2,21). Much has been said and written about the Lord's promise to those who spread His evangel, "lo, I am with you alway" (Mt 28.20), so His power and presence are indispensable for effective gospel activity. Here, the experience of Phinehas demonstrates that porters as well as preachers need His presence. Divine guidance is so necessary for those who have responsibility to interview prospective assembly members. The task has to be undertaken in dependence upon God, and without allowing any judgment to be clouded by the status of the individual concerned, whether socially or in respect of family connections.

So, then, the present supervisors among the porters were pointed back to Phinehas as a worthy role model. He was the yardstick, just as David as a king became the yardstick for the kings of Judah - their performance was matched against the pattern he had set (e.g. 2 Chr 17.3). What kind of an example do we leave for the generations who come on behind us?

Another former porter had been Zechariah the son of Meshelemiah, a contemporary of David (26.2). In fact David and Samuel had established the routine by which the porters operated (v.22), a system that was still in place after the captivity. Such had been the wisdom of these two men of God, that succeeding generations saw no need to tinker with their methods. A roster had been established which ensured constant supervision at the gates at each point of the compass (vv.24-25).

The phrase "in their set office" (530) is of interest (vv.22,26,31). The word conveys the idea of faithfulness, or a trust. In other words, the task of these doorkeepers was a solemn trust, a duty to be discharged with a deep sense of responsibility. The sanctity of the house of God had to be preserved. Today, the task of the door-keeper is equally demanding, requiring wisdom from above to maintain the purity of the assembly morally and doctrinally, while at the same time ensuring wholehearted reception of those who are eligible to take their place among the Lord's people. The charge is a trust that must be undertaken in the fear of God.

Verses 26-27: The Four Chief Porters

The responsibilities of these four men extended to overseeing chambers, probably storage areas for firstfruits and tithes of produce. The treasuries also came under their supervision. As late as Hezekiah's day porters still had an involvement in these matters (2 Chr 31.14). They had the duty of ensuring that priests and Levites were provided for in accordance with the original pattern.

In modern times, there is the idea that responsibility for money matters lies with deacons. In fact, according to the New Testament pattern, ensuring the wise distribution of funds is one of the functions of elders. When Barnabas and Saul carried a monetary gift from Antioch to Judæa it was placed in the custody of "the elders" (Acts 11.29-30), the first usage of the word "elder" in connection with New Testament assemblies.

Another issue that emerges is that no one man had the job of handling these financial matters; four porters were involved. That principle is carried over to the New Testament. For example, when a collection for needy saints was being carried to Jerusalem, a number of reputable brethren were involved. The explanation for this course of action is given: "Avoiding this, that no man should blame us in this abundance which is administered by us: Providing for honest things, not only in the sight of the Lord, but also in the sight of men" (2 Cor 8.20-21). Things had to be done honestly, but it was vital that they were seen to be done honestly.

To be on hand to discharge their responsibilities, the four chief porters "lodged round about the house of God" (v.27). They did not commute from the villages as did their subordinates who were on the shift system (v.25). Among their duties was the opening of the doors each morning, a seemingly insignificant chore that a boy could do (1 Sam 3.15). Before long though, the boy Samuel who opened the doors "was established to be a prophet of the Lord" (v.20). Opening doors was all part of his training to be something outstanding for God. Opening the house of God was a major responsibility then, and these four men had to be in proximity to their charge.

Generally, Levites did live in a place convenient for their work. During the wilderness journeys, with the priests and Moses they were the inner circle that surrounded the tabernacle (Num 3.23,29,35,38). The tribes encamped under their banners a little further out. During the rebuilding of the walls of Jerusalem, it is recorded of the priests that "From above the horse gate repaired the priests, every one over against his house" (Neh 3.28). Where they lived, there they laboured. Again, there is a simple practical lesson in all of this. God expects His people to be busy for Him wherever they are situated at any given time. It is true that some of His servants are like Paul, "and have no certain dwellingplace" (1 Cor 4.11), and are "In journeyings often" (2 Cor 11.26), but for the more part, people are in a fixed location, and that location becomes their sphere of service. Geographically it is not always possible to be in close proximity to the centre of operations, but ensure that from a spiritual standpoint life is lived "round about the house of God".

Verses 28-34: Sundry Duties

Various duties are now described, the first being responsibility for "the ministering vessels". Meticulous care had to be taken that every vessel that was counted out for use was then counted back in again; they were to "bring them in and out by tale". It is almost reminiscent of the weighing of the vessels that Ezra brought out of Babylon, and their subsequent reweighing in the sanctuary at Jerusalem (Ezra 8.24-34). The lesson is one of accountability. What God has apportioned to us, whether of a spiritual or material nature, is in trust, and, to lift a phrase from context, one day He will say to us, "give an account of thy stewardship" (Lk 16.2). It would be wonderful if in every case the inventory were complete with nothing missing and nothing underweight. Let us guard against squandering, misusing or under employing any thing He has given us, for we are all accountable.

It would appear that others had the care of the vessels when they were actually in use (v.29). The word "instruments" (3627) is exactly the same as that translated "vessels" in the immediate context. Probably these vessels differed in shape and size, each suitable for its own specific task. For example, mention is made of fine flour, wine, oil, frankincense, and spices, so different vessels would be needed for different commodities. The fine flour was necessary for the meat offering, a reminder that none of His delightful moral features eclipsed another.

In smooth and silken whiteness,
Without a rough'ning grain,
In clear, unbroken brightness,
Without a speck or stain,
The fine flour in its beauty
The perfect man portrays
In all His path of duty,
In all His heavenly ways.
(I. Y. Ewan)

The wine was required for the drink offering, the pouring out of which prefigured Him who "poured out his soul unto death" (Is 53.12). Oil, an emblem of the Holy Spirit whose power is essential for effective testimony (Zech 4), was needed for the lamps. Among other things, the frankincense was a necessary addendum to the shewbread which receives mention at v.32. Doubtless it illustrates the fragrance of the life of Him who was "the bread which came down from heaven" (Jn 6.41). The pleasure that He brought to His Father is incalculable.

The spices were stacte, onycha, and galbanum, and together with pure frankincense they were blended in equal proportions to create the incense for the golden altar of incense (Ex 30.34-38). The sweet scent of the incense was dependent on it's being beaten "very small", and being burned (Ex 30.1), another picture of the self-humiliation and sufferings of our beloved Lord. From these experiences there flowed a delightful fragrance to His Father God. The offering of the incense is also linked with the prayers of the people of God (Ps 141.2; Lk 1.10; Rev 8.3-4).

The recipe for the incense was in the public domain, but there was a stern warning against its general use. It was exclusively for use in the sanctuary (Ex 30.37-38), and so here priests had the responsibility of blending the spices to create that incense (v.30). No doubt the aroma would linger on their persons just as those who live in company with Christ and are occupied with Him inevitably display something of the beauty of His character.

Applying the lessons from all of this, each one of us has responsibility for maintaining a spirit of worship in the assembly, whereby the Lord is given His rightful place, and the fragrance of His person is evident. The incense of prayer should be a major feature, its priority being seen in the fact that Paul placed it top of his agenda when speaking about behaviour in the house of God (1 Tim 3.15). Of the prayer meeting he said, *"first of all"* (2.1); it took precedence in his thinking. Ensuring the free flow of the oil of the Spirit by allowing Him, ungrieved, to operate among us is another essential if witness is to be effective.

Mattithiah (v.31) had the trust "over the things that were made in the pans" ensuring that priests shared what was their due from, for example, the meat offering (Lev 2.3,10). A weekly task for some of the Kohathites was to prepare the shewbread (v.32). Normally the word "shewbread" is a combination of two Hebrew words. The first (3899) signifies "bread", and the second (6440) means "before", i.e. in the presence of. So sometimes the shewbread is described as the "Presence-bread" (Ex 25.30, RV margin). These loaves were on the table before the face of God. Here the word linked with bread is a word meaning "row" or "line" (4635), and thus the emphasis here is on the orderliness of the twelve loaves on the table.

The overall impression that we are left with is that even although the age of law was well advanced, God still demanded meticulous attention to detail, especially in these things that foreshadowed the beauties and worth of His own dear Son. Food for the priests was a priority, and what nourished them physically pointed forward to Him who is the sustenance of His believing people in this church age.

We taste Thee, O Thou living bread!
And long to feast upon Thee still;
We drink of Thee, the fountain-head,
And thirst our souls from Thee to fill.
(Bernard: Palmer)

The last group of specialists among the Levites were the singers (v.33). They were free from all other duties to concentrate exclusively on the various aspects of their task. No doubt it involved composing and practising as well as performing. Again there is the lesson that the men who were expert in that field were to be left to do it, without expecting them to be committed to other aspects of service. It is "to every man his work" (Mk 13.34). Perhaps some of their brethren regarded them as having an easier life than most and begrudged them their sinecure, but we are told that "they were employed *in that work* day and night" It was work, and it demanded constant attention. The praise of God must be perpetual, as seen in the activity of the living creatures around His throne: "they rest not day and night, saying, Holy, holy, holy, Lord God Almighty" (Rev 4.8). Just as angels rest not day and night in heaven, so these temple musicians were employed day and night in their ministry on earth. God must be honoured and praised continually. In a day when His people Israel were robbing Him, He declared, "from the rising of the sun even unto the going down of the same my name shall be great among the Gentiles" (Mal 1.11).

As o'er each continent and island
The dawn leads on another day,
The voice of prayer is never silent,
Nor dies the strain of praise away.

The sun that bids us rest is waking
Our brethren 'neath the western sky;
And hour by hour fresh lips are making
Thy wondrous doings heard on high.
(John Ellerton)

It has already been observed that trained singers and instrumentalists never featured in the assemblies of the New Testament, but Spirit-filled believers will be "speaking one to another in psalms and hymns and spiritual songs, singing and making melody with (their) heart to the Lord" (Eph 5.19, RV). Their singing will be intelligent and hearty: "I will sing with the spirit, and I will sing with the understanding also" (1 Cor 14.15). Singing in the gatherings is not a time wasting appendix, it is a spiritual exercise to be undertaken in a spiritual way for the glory of God. Some hymns are particularly fitting for the remembrance of the Lord at the Lord's Supper. Others may be more appropriate for a prayer meeting or a teaching meeting. Some are never suitable - they contain sentiments that are totally unscriptural. This may be in contrast to a minor inaccuracy that could be regarded as poetic licence for the sake of rhyme or rhythm! The lesson from the singers is that God never regards singing His praise as a mere time-filler.

Verses 35-44: The Genealogy of Saul

It was suggested formerly that in all likelihood, the return to Saul's genealogy here is to prepare us for the record of his death in the next chapter. When 8.29-40 records the details of these individuals it is as a finale to Benjamin's genealogy. Here the record is the run-in to the narrative of Saul's final battle, when he and his sons were slain, making way for God's anointed king, David the son of Jesse.

1 CHRONICLES 10

With the lengthy genealogies at an end, the Chronicler now turns his attention to the narrative. The main story-line starts in chapter 11 with David being anointed king over all Israel. Chapter 10 paves the way for that as it recounts the details of the tragic death of his predecessor King Saul. As so often happens in Scripture, one man is removed to make way for another. Ishmael was expelled to make way for Isaac (Gen 21.10). Esau had to give place to Jacob (Gen 25.23). Most importantly, Adam was superseded by Christ (Rom 5.12-21; 1 Cor 15.21-22, 45-49). Here, Saul the man after the flesh is cut off to usher in the "man after (God's) own heart" (1 Sam 13.14). Paul made reference to it in his preaching at Antioch in Pisidia; "when (God) had removed him, he raised up unto them David to be their king" (Acts 13.22).

1 Samuel provides an extensive coverage of Saul's history that is not repeated in 1 Chronicles. As has been stated formerly, the Chronicler's purpose is to focus on the life of David with particular reference to his desire to build a house for God. The life of Saul has no bearing on that, but the concise account of the sin that occasioned his death throws into relief the faithfulness of the man who succeeded him. Once again in Scripture, a jewel sparkles against a dark background.

The short chapter divides into four small sections. Verses 1-7 record the details of Saul's death followed by the triumphalism of the Philistines in vv.8-10. His burial by the men of Jabesh-gilead is the subject of vv.11-12, and the reason for his death is explained in the last section (vv.13-14).

Verses 1-7: The Death of Saul

Saul's death can be viewed in various ways. We might regard him as a victim of warfare, cut down by his enemies the Philistines. His passing could be perceived as a suicide for he fell on his own sword. Whatever the physical circumstances, v.14 pinpoints the underlying cause of death; "he (the Lord) slew him". (The Amalekite's account of the event (2 Sam 1.1-16) is to be discounted as an unsuccessful ploy to curry favour with David.) The death of Saul was by divine decree for reasons explained at the end of the chapter, but God engaged human instruments to accomplish His plan. He is never dependent on human agents to effect His purpose, but He does frequently employ them. This is seen particularly in the circumstances surrounding the crucifixion (Acts 4.27-28).

"The Philistines fought against Israel" (v.1). As noted formerly, from the time of Isaac the Philistines had been hostile to the people of God; motivated by envy they had stopped up wells that had been used by the family for many years. When Isaac reopened these wells they were confiscated (Gen 26). In the days of the exodus, God led His people out of Egypt by a circuitous route to avoid these aggressive warmongers (Ex 13.17-18). They were the main opponents of Israel in the land, and Samson the last of the judges died in their custody (Judg 16). Now the first of the kings would also fall at their hands.

(Reviewing the comments on 1.12 regarding the spiritual significance of the Philistines, it will be seen why we judge them to be illustrative of mere professing believers among the people of God.) Here, they are acting true to form in attacking God's people just as their present day counterparts criticise and undermine the genuine saints of God.

This battle proved to be a rout, with the men of Israel fleeing and falling before the Philistines. In any situation, individuals who are bereft of the presence and power of God face abject defeat.

It is clear on this occasion that it was no mere marauding band that had invaded Israel's territory. The Philistines had marshalled their forces in strength with the intention of crushing Saul's regime once and for all (1 Sam 28.1; 29.1). They were determined to apprehend their quarry and so they pursued him relentlessly; they "followed hard after Saul" (1 Chr 10.2). Three of his sons fell in the fray, including Jonathan the natural successor to his throne. It appears that Jonathan's genuine affection for David and his sympathies with him were outweighed by loyalty to his father. There were two separate incidents in which he could have associated with David the fugitive, but Scripture records that "Jonathan went into the city", and "Jonathan went to his house" (1 Sam 20.42; 23.18). On the second occasion David and Jonathan had made a pact that in David's administration Jonathan would be his right hand man (v.17). However, his fondness for David never extended to him associating with him in exile so he never did become his deputy. He died here on the same day as his father. David lamented that fact, but his comments betrayed no sense of resentment or bitterness. "Saul and Jonathan were lovely and pleasant in their lives, and in their death they were not divided" (2 Sam 1.23). Having never suffered with David, he never reigned with him (2 Tim 2.12). Let us learn the lesson. If we sidestep the stigma and sacrifice of being associated with the rejected Christ, we deprive ourselves of reward in a coming day.

Eventually it was the archers who brought Saul's flight to an end (v.3). He was one of a few in Scripture who were brought down by the bow. In each case it was the sovereign will of God that brought about the removal of these individuals. It appears that Ahab's predicted death (1 Kings 21.17-29) had been deferred because of his change of heart, but it was inevitable, and it came at the hands of a man who "drew a bow at a venture" (22.34). God had promised good King Josiah that necessary judgment would not take place in his day and age (2 Chr 34.24-28). He had to be removed so that the judgment could fall, and once more the archers did the damage (35.23-27). It appears that in any ancient theatre of war, the bow and arrow were the most lethal of all the armaments.

An effective weapon in the hands of our enemy is described as "the fiery darts of the evil one" (Eph 6.16, RV). He rains these missiles of doubt upon the people of God from various sources: militant atheism; dead formal religion; cynical satire and comedy. There is a great need to take "the shield of faith", to say, "I believe God" (Acts 27.25), lest the enemy's flaming arrows set our minds ablaze with scepticism and unbelief.

It cannot be certain that Saul was fatally wounded, but his injuries rendered him immobile; he was at the mercy of the pursuing enemy. He knew that they were ruthless and they would not be content just to arrest him or to kill him immediately. He was in dread of them "abusing" (5953) him. Gathering up various translations of the word, he had reasonable fears of their torturing him, making sport of him, mistreating him. Perhaps he remembered the way in which Samson had been abused when he was taken at the last (Judg 16.21); he had been blinded and baited, and Saul had no desire to share his fate.

The treatment of Saul's remains demonstrates that his fears were justified. Thus he appealed to his armourbearer, "thrust me through" (v.4). Fear paralysed the young man. Was it a fear similar to that of David when he said, "who can stretch forth his hand against the Lord's anointed, and be guiltless?" (1 Sam 26.9). Or was it the fear of being misunderstood and held culpable as with the man who discovered the helpless Absalom and refused to dispatch him from this life (2 Sam 18.13)? Or was it the kind of fear that prevented Gideon's son from slaying the kings of Midian? He was so young to be responsible for killing men of royal blood (Judg 8.20)! Whatever the reason, the man refused to comply with the wishes of his lord. Rightly, he would not be party to what the modern world describes as "assisted suicide".

Saul, the first king, then resorted to suicide at the point of his sword. Samson, the last judge had brought about an end to his own life, but it was with the objective of achieving his greatest victory over the Philistines, so we might be inclined to defend his actions. There is no way in which we could justify Saul's suicide.

Other cases of suicide among the people of Israel were Ahithophel and Judas both of whom hanged themselves (2 Sam 17.23; Mt 27.5), and Zimri the seven-day king who set fire to his palace and died in the blaze (1 Kings 16.18).

The power of example is evident for Saul's armourbearer followed his lead and he too fell on his sword (v.5). There is no record of his being wounded, and there is the possibility that he could have made good his escape as Abner, Saul's general, had done, but he chose to die with his master. Some may commend his loyalty, but loyalty that extends to self-harm and suicide must be questioned. The example and counsel of leaders should be followed if it is right and good as when the Thessalonians made Paul and his companions their role models and they in turn became exemplary (1 Thess 1.6-7). A bad example on the part of leadership should always be ignored.

There is a little summary of events in v.6. The phrase "all his house" cannot mean Saul's whole family for we know that his son Ish-bosheth was installed as king albeit briefly (2 Sam 2.8-10). Those referred to are obviously additional to the family, the phrase being an advance on the other one - "his three sons". The equivalent phrase in the record of 1 Samuel is "all his men" (31.6), so clearly it is a reference to his close associates, his bodyguard and household attendants who were present on that fateful day. It does appear though that there was a near extermination of Saul's household.

News of the rout and of Saul's death spread from the heights of Gilboa to the valley below. There was a panic-stricken evacuation of locations in the valley, and the Philistines settled themselves in these vacated cities (v.7). The solemn lesson is that defeat at the hands of the enemy inevitably means the loss of territory and it is never easy to retake lost ground. Hence the importance of Paul's exhortations to the Ephesians: "Neither give place to the devil", and "stand against the wiles of the devil" (Eph 4.27; 6.11). Both James and Peter insist that he should be "resisted" (James 4.7; 1 Pet 5.9). To retreat in the face of his aggression means that we deprive ourselves of part of our spiritual heritage, or at least we lose the enjoyment of it, just as surely as these people yielded their inheritance in the land.

Verses 8-10: The Aftermath of Battle

There are a few features of these verses that require comment. As was customary, the victorious army scoured the battlefield to retrieve anything of worth and involved in that was stripping enemy corpses of any valuables they may have been wearing. Paul alludes to this practice by way of illustration when referring to the Lord's victory at the cross (Col 2.15). His battle was with "principalities and powers", and the conquest was so comprehensive that He "spoiled" them. Figuratively, He carried off the spoils of battle, and as an extension to that, figuratively again, He headed the prisoners of war in a triumphal parade as "he led captivity captive, and gave gifts unto men" (Eph 4.8).

Another point of interest is the way in which the language of the Spirit of God exposes the inanimate nature of the gods of the heathen and hence their absolute impotence. The Philistines had to "carry tidings" of their victory not only to their people but to their idols! By contrast the living God is omniscient, and no one has to alert Him to breaking news. "God is greater than our heart, *and knoweth all things*" (1 Jn 3.20). The prophecy of Isaiah is at pains to demonstrate the superiority of "the living and true God" over the idols of heathendom, not least in 46.1-7. The prophet's major point is that the heathen have to "carry" their idols and put them in their place (v.7). How different from our God. We do not have to carry Him but He carries us, and He carries us for a lifetime: "carried from the womb" (v.3); "to hoar hairs will I carry you" (v.4). Philistine idols would be told of the exploits of their worshippers, but they would not hear - "They have ears, but they hear not" (Ps 115.6). In a very few years these very idols would be burned to a cinder at the orders of David (1 Chr 14.12). No wonder the gods of the heathen are called "vanities" (e.g. Jer 8.19).

As suggested earlier, Saul's fear of abuse was well founded when we see how the Philistines treated his body. He was decapitated and his head was placed in the house of Dagon their god (v.10). Perhaps they felt well pleased that the carrying of Goliath's head to Jerusalem had been avenged at last (1 Sam 17.54). At that time, Goliath's armour had been a prize just as Saul's was here.

Impaling Saul's head in the house of Dagon did not have the same effect as placing the ark of God there in an earlier generation (1 Sam 5.1-5). Then, in the company of what was a symbol of both the presence of God and the Christ of God, the idol fell on its face. In fact, on that occasion its head was severed from its "stump" whereas here it was the king of Israel's head that was the token of defeat. A disobedient, defeated, and now dead man could make no impact on idolatry.

Verses 11-12: Saul's Burial

News of the desecration of Saul's body reached the ears of the men of Jabesh-gilead and to their credit they intervened. It is assumed that the first readers of 1 Chronicles would have been acquainted with the fact that his body had been "fastened" to the wall of Beth-shan and that it was incinerated before his bones were buried (1 Sam 31.10-13). Here, details are more limited. However, the main factor is that it was courageous men from Jabesh-gilead who performed this service for their deceased sovereign. It was probably gratitude that motivated them. Forty years earlier their city had been under threat from the Ammonites. The terms of surrender involved all the men of Jabesh having their right eyes put out. Saul was the man who came to their rescue in what was really his first military campaign as Israel's king (1 Sam 11). They never forgot his efforts and this generation knew that their fathers would have lived out their lives half blind had he not taken up their cause. Now they had opportunity to repay their debt. Others were content to let things be, and avoid the risk involved in stealing the bodies and attending to the funeral rites, but the men of Jabesh-Gilead rose to the occasion in an expression of appreciation.

Gratitude is a noble virtue just as ingratitude is a shameful disgrace as is illustrated in the following. When Athaliah massacred "the seed royal", Jehoshabeath, the wife of Jehoiada the priest rescued the infant Joash (2 Chr 22.10-12). In course of time, Jehoiada was instrumental in installing the young lad as king (ch.23). At a later date, when reproved by Jehoiada's son, Joash was responsible for having the prophet stoned. The commentary of Scripture is, "Thus Joash the king remembered not the kindness which Jehoiada his father had done to him, but slew his son" (2 Chr 24.22). What base ingratitude! It is serious enough to "render evil for evil" (1 Thess 5.15), but to forget a kindness, and repay it with evil is inexcusable. David had experienced the bitterness of that: "they have rewarded me evil for good, and hatred for my love" (Ps 109.5). On another occasion, his sincere condolences to the bereaved king of Ammon were rebuffed and his servants were treated shamefully (2 Sam 10.1-4). David was so careful to avoid treating others in the same way. Among his final words to Solomon were these: "But shew kindness unto the sons of Barzillai the Gileadite, and let them be of those that eat at thy table: for so they came to me when I fled because of Absalom thy brother" (1 Kings 2.7). David never forgot the timely intervention of Barzillai and his friends (2 Sam 17.27-29), and was desperately keen for it to be reciprocated. Here, the men of Jabesh-gilead are to be commended for their long memories and their willingness to settle a debt of love. Let us take note of the example they set.

The period of fasting for Saul was seven days. It seems limited compared to the seventy days of mourning for Jacob (Gen 50.3), or the thirty days for Aaron and Moses (Num 20.29; Deut 34.8). The lesson is that expressions of grief should be in keeping with the character and worth of the person being mourned, with tributes avoiding unnecessary platitudes and exaggeration. One of the saddest comments in Scripture relates to Jehoram of whom it was said, he "departed without being desired" (2 Chr 21.20). "Live to be missed" is a familiar maxim. Obviously Stephen did, for at his burial they "made great lamentation over him" (Acts 8.2) as did the whole nation at the death of King Josiah (2 Chr 35.24-25).

Verses 13-14: Reasons for Saul's Death

Having recorded the details of Saul's death and burial, the Chronicler now supplies the reasons for his death and they were two-fold. The first was disobedience: "his transgression" which is said to be the fact that "he kept not" "the word of the Lord". The reference is to 1 Samuel 15 where he was under orders to wipe out the Amalekites completely (v.3). Their fate had been settled from the time that they craftily attacked Israel in the early days of the wilderness journey (v.2); Saul was the chosen instrument of God's vengeance against Amalek. Rather than following his instructions to the letter, Saul spared Agag the king, and "the best of" the livestock (v.9), announcing to Samuel the prophet, "I have performed the commandment of the Lord" (v.13), and insisting again, "I have obeyed the voice of the Lord" (v.20). By contrast, God's assessment of the situation was, "he is turned back from following me, and hath not performed my commandments" (v.11), and Samuel's charge against him was, "thou hast rejected the word of the Lord" (v.23). The simple lesson is that partial obedience is really no obedience at all. Indeed it is described as "rebellion" and "stubbornness" (v.23), sin that was on a par with the witchcraft and idolatry against which Saul had waged war (1 Sam 28.3). There is no value in giving precise and passionate attention to some of God's commands while being careless about others. We can know His approval if like Zacharias and Elisabeth we are "walking in *all* the commandments and ordinances of the Lord blameless" (Lk 1.6). This is His longing for us: "O that there were such a heart in them, that they would fear me, and keep *all* my commandments *always*, that it might be well with them, and with their children for ever!" (Deut 5.29). In the end, Saul's partial obedience cost him his life.

The word "transgression" (4604) has already received comment (9.1). Numerous translations (e.g. NKJV, RSV) render it "unfaithfulness". The verbal form of the word is used in 5.25. There, it was unfaithfulness that occasioned the captivity of the Transjordan tribes. In 9.1 it was unfaithfulness that brought about the removal of Judah to Babylon. Here, it was unfaithfulness that brought Saul under judgment, unfaithfulness expressed in his disobedience to the voice of God. Let us emulate our beloved Lord of whom it was said, He "was faithful to him that appointed him" (Heb 3.2).

The second reason for Saul's decease was his folly in consulting "one that had a familiar spirit" on the very eve of his death (1 Sam 28). During his reign he had mounted a crusade to rid his kingdom of these agents of the devil, and now, at the end, he arranged a consultation with one of them. What a solemn lesson here for us all. There is a danger in becoming obsessed with some particular vice or error, marshalling facts and Scriptures to oppose it, and then at the last performing an about-turn to embrace it. This tendency has been observed in believers from time to time. It was right that Saul should take the Word of God seriously when it said, for example, "Thou shalt not suffer a witch to live" (Ex 22.18), or "A man also or woman that hath a familiar spirit, or that is a wizard, shall surely be put to death" (Lev 20.27). His mistake was in majoring on that to the neglect of other issues, an imbalance that is so often in evidence in our own lives. Now his folly was being compounded by him "build(ing) again the things which (he) destroyed", if we may venture to lift a Scripture from context (Gal 2.18). Consistency of belief and behaviour is vital. We dare not change our ground if our persuasions are based firmly on the teaching of the Word of God. There is something illogical about allowing firm convictions to be abandoned as when King Jehoshaphat "strengthened himself against Israel", and then subsequently "joined affinity with Ahab" (2 Chr 17.1; 18.1). Here, in consequence of being deprived of divine guidance, Saul discarded his former "Bible–based" prejudice against witchcraft, and as a final act of folly and rebellion asked "counsel of one that had a familiar spirit, to inquire of it".

There is no doubt that in modern times there are many charlatans purporting to be spiritist mediums. The gullible are relieved of their cash as these impostors ply their trade. However, the Scriptures never conceal the fact that there are those who in reality are in touch with the world of evil spirits, and are able to effect the miraculous by the devil's power. As early as the book of Exodus, we encounter people with such capabilities, described there as "the magicians of Egypt" (7.11). The book of Revelation indicates that their like will still be around in the latter stages of earth's history (9.21), and will be among those who will occupy "the lake which burneth with fire and brimstone: which is the second death" (21.8). Presently, their power is real, though limited as compared to divine power.

We should never be tempted to think that the paranormal is proof of God at work. Again, Saul's experience should be a beacon of warning against ever being persuaded in any way to become involved with those who practise spiritism and witchcraft.

How do we interpret v.14 when it tells us that Saul "inquired not of the Lord" when 1 Samuel 28.6 says this: "when Saul inquired of the Lord, the Lord answered him not, neither by dreams, nor by Urim, nor by prophets". The narrative in 1 Samuel leaves us with the impression that it was only as a last resort, when his back was to the wall, that Saul "inquired of the Lord", and by then it was too late. Possibly it was done in such a shallow half-hearted careless way as to justify the comment here that he "inquired not of the Lord". How could a mind tormented by an evil spirit (1 Sam 16.14) be given a dream that would give him guidance? How could he expect God to answer him by Urim when he had slaughtered His priests (1 Sam 22.6-23)? How could he hope for a prophetic word when he had threatened and persecuted the prophets of God (1 Sam 16.2; 19.16,18-24)? Thus a man completely bereft of divine counsel and comfort resorted to seeking advice from the woman whom we call the witch of En-dor. The message he received was chilling, an accurate prediction of imminent death, and it took place on the very next day when the Lord "slew him, and turned the kingdom unto David the son of Jesse".

These closing verses are the sad obituary on a wretched life, a life that had held so much promise but had deteriorated so badly. By contrast, Jacob's last days were his best; "By faith Jacob, when he was a dying… worshipped, leaning upon the top of his staff" (Heb 11.21). Never let it be said of us, "Ye did run well; who did hinder you that ye should not obey the truth?" (Gal 5.7).

The final statement of the chapter is a brief account of the divine activity that transferred power to David, the details of which appear in subsequent verses.

1 CHRONICLES 11

With the death of Saul, the reins of regal authority passed into the hands of David. The last verse of chapter 10 indicates that it was all by divine arrangement. This chapter outlines how it transpired practically, with "all Israel" (v.1) anointing David king at Hebron (v.3). Many years earlier, Samuel had anointed the shepherd boy as Israel's prospective sovereign (1 Sam 16.1-13), but the intervening period had been strewn with privations and close encounters with death. All credit to him, David was not like the impatient Abraham and Sarah (Gen 16). He was willing to wait God's time, and refused to do anything to precipitate his ascension to the throne. God had preserved him throughout these days of crisis, and the divine purpose was now being brought to fruition.

As has been stated at regular intervals, one of the main objects of 1 Chronicles is to describe David's reign with an emphasis on what is spiritual and religious rather than on what is secular and social. Foremost in the narrative is his desire to build a house for God. By chapter 13 there are hints of this, with his determination to bring the ark of the covenant to Jerusalem. Chapters 11 and 12 form a distinct segment of the book, a section that sets the stage for the unfolding of this spiritual aspiration. They give an account of David establishing a firm power base that allowed him to pursue his goal. They also tell of those who had been loyal to him when in exile, men whose efforts had been contributory to his eventual supremacy. Chapter 12 is particularly concerned with the record of those who defected to him in the latter stages of his banishment, and of those who came to install him as king in Hebron. It has been said that in chapter 11 we have the heroes, and in chapter 12 we have the helpers, help being a recurring word in that chapter. "There are far more helpers than heroes!" (D. Gilliland). Even now, perhaps only a few can be designated heroes but it is open to us all to be helpers. The gift of "helps" is of significance in the lists of 1 Corinthians 12 (v.28), and there are many among the people of God who fall into that category, folks who are expert in playing a supportive role. For example, Peter enjoyed the backing of his fellow apostles when he stood up "with the eleven" (Acts 2.14). Let us all be an encouragement to those who are in the vanguard.

Chapter 11 divides as follows. Verses 1-3 tell of David's enthronement at Hebron. In verses 4-9 Jerusalem is captured to become his seat of administration. This took place seven and a half years after he began his reign in Hebron (3.4). The balance of the chapter is taken up with the names of his associates in government, and of the exploits of some of these "mighty men" (v.10), men who must have been tough and fit, but, above all, loyal to David.

Here, the names of these men appear at the beginning of David's reign whereas in 2 Samuel they are listed subsequent to what are described as "the last words of David" (ch.23). There, we are left with the impression that David was conducting a review at the end of his days, and saluting the memory of those who had been so dedicated and dependable. It is almost a picture of "the judgment seat of Christ" (2 Cor 5.10), at which there will be an assessment of our lives and service, and of which Scripture says, "then shall every man have praise of God" (1 Cor 4.5). In light of that day Paul writes, "Wherefore also we make it our aim…to be well-pleasing unto him" (2 Cor 5.9, RV). Do we have the same kind of ambition? In this setting we are introduced to David's mighty men at the inauguration of his kingdom in what is a show of strength that underscores the positive aspects of his reign. This is a feature of this book, in which there is no record of many of the negative factors that blighted his later life. For example, there is no mention of the sad episode of Bathsheba and Uriah or of Absalom's rebellion.

Verses 1-3: David Anointed at Hebron

Hebron was a city that was rich in history, but frequently it had been a place of tears and mourning, for the patriarchs and their wives were buried there (Gen 49.31). (Mamre is Hebron, Gen 13.18). Now it was a place of coronation, and it would ring with shouts of joy.

"All Israel gathered" (v.1), in contrast to the tribe of Judah over which David had already reigned. That was during a period when Abner had endeavoured to shore up Saul's dynasty under Ishbosheth (2 Sam 2-3). For a considerable time then many had opposed David's claim to the throne, but God's purposes can never be thwarted. Now the whole nation acknowledged him, with the phrase "all Israel" repeated in v.4, where all twelve tribes were solidly behind him in his attempt to make Jerusalem his seat of power. His former antagonists advanced three reasons for their capitulation. First, there was the matter of kinship; "we are thy bone and thy flesh". Of necessity, Israel's king must be one of their own people. "One from among thy brethren shalt thou set king over thee" (Deut 17.15). David was no illegitimate pretender as was Abimelech whom the men of Shechem installed as a king (Judg 9.6). Abimelech was an opportunist who ranked as a bramble in comparison to fruitful trees such as the olive, the fig or the vine (v.14). Neither was David an Edomite stranger like Herod, a puppet king set up by Rome. In chapter 2 the genealogy of the tribe of Judah established his credentials as a son of that royal tribe, and so on the basis of relationship the nation now acknowledged him as king. Their words must have sounded rather hollow even to themselves, for in reality this was a surrender!

The second reason for their about turn was his previous experience in affairs of state. They acknowledged that under Saul, David "leddest out and broughtest in Israel" (v.2). He was no novice as far as matters of administration and leadership were concerned. They could have been more generous in acknowledging that his former responsibilities under Saul had been discharged wisely and successfully (1 Sam 18.5) despite behind the scenes plotting for his downfall; however, they did acknowledge his past performance in the previous administration. In New Testament assemblies, one of the qualifications for elderhood is experience in divine things; "Not a novice", says Paul (1 Tim 3.6). The verse shows that leadership responsibility for the immature could result in the kind of pride that condemned the devil.

There was a third reason for "all Israel" acknowledging David as king, and they seemed to be very reluctant to submit to it. "*The Lord thy God said unto thee*, thou shalt feed my people Israel, and thou shalt be ruler over my people Israel". David was king by divine decree; he had a mandate from heaven. Israel had known this and yet they were so slow to comply with the command of God. David's responsibilities are summarised in two statements. He was to "feed" and to be "ruler". The word "feed" (7462) carries the thought of feeding as does a shepherd. David's previous experience on the hills of Bethlehem was an excellent training ground for his new sphere of activity. Governing the nation would demand firm rule, the maintenance of justice, even-handed administration, zero tolerance of corruption, and so on, but it also required the care and compassion that befits a shepherd. It is to David's credit that for a lifetime he admirably fulfilled that dual role: "So he fed them according to the integrity of his heart; and guided them by the skilfulness of his hands" (Ps 78.72). This balance of things will be a feature of our Lord's reign. "He shall rule (*4165*) them with a rod of iron" (Rev 19.15); the "rod of iron" is indicative of His intolerance of rebellion, but married to it is the concept of shepherding, enshrined in the word "rule". He will be firm but fair; He will be just but compassionate.

The same qualities should be features of the elders of local assemblies. They have a responsibility to "rule well" (1 Tim 5.17), but allied to that they are to "feed (as a shepherd - *4165*) the flock of God" (1 Pet 5.2). Godly rule and tender care must go hand in hand.

Observe that in v.2 the phrase "my people" features twice. It is as if God emphasises that they belong to Him, and that they are extremely precious to Him, but to men He gives the charge of feeding them and ruling them. Their preciousness is such that God wants only the choicest of men to fulfil that function: hence His appointment of a man like David. Again, we can apply that principle to present conditions. The assembly is "the flock *of God*" (1 Pet 5.2) and every believer is dear to Him, purchased by precious blood (Acts 20.28). They have to be shepherded and He still requires the highest standards of integrity, morality and spirituality on the part of those who have that responsibility (1 Tim 3.1-7).

The location of David's enthronement was Hebron and already attention has been drawn to the Biblical significance of Hebron, carrying as it does the concept of "fellowship". It is crucial for those in leadership to live their lives in fellowship with God and, indeed, in fellowship with those for whom they have a care. They have to be "among" their people, and their people are "among" them (1 Pet 5.1-2). A true shepherd will never be the equivalent of an absentee landlord, and it would be very difficult to combine the role of an overseer with that of an itinerant preacher.

Notice that "the elders of Israel" took a lead in anointing David as king (v.3). It would seem, then, that when v.1 speaks of "all Israel", it does not mean that every last man in the country came to Hebron, but that they were all represented there by the attendance of their elders. The elders took the initiative in this. In Deborah's time, there were leaders of the same calibre: "the governors of Israel...offered themselves willingly among the people" (Judg 5.9). Is it any wonder that, having that example, "the people willingly offered themselves" (v.2). There is a simple lesson lying on the surface, and it is that those in leadership should give a lead! Inertia among God's people can often result from those in leadership just allowing circumstances to take their course rather than being proactive in new initiatives.

From a geographical standpoint, the agreement into which David entered with the elders of Israel was made in the city of Hebron, but more significantly it was "before the Lord" (v.3). God was the unseen observer of all that transpired, and the silent listener to every pledge that was made. That concept is challenging, and necessitates caution on our part. "Be not rash with thy mouth, and let not thine heart be hasty to utter any thing before God: for God is in heaven, and thou upon earth: therefore let thy words be few" (Eccl 5.2). It is better never to vow "than that thou shouldest vow and not pay" (v.5).

Anointing David as king had been predicted and promised by God through Samuel the prophet. God had indicated to Samuel, "I have provided me a king among (Jesse's) sons" (1 Sam 16.1). An unlikely candidate was the youngest, the shepherd boy on the hillside, but he was God's choice, and after the passage of many years, and following many close encounters with death, "the word of the Lord by Samuel" was now fulfilled, and "they anointed David king over Israel". It is a fresh reminder that God's Word is unassailable, and His promises are unfailing. Let us take cheer from these glorious truths.

Anointing and kingship are linked with David's great descendant, the Lord Jesus Christ. He is God's "anointed", He is God's King (Ps 2.2,6).

Verses 4-9: The Capture of Jerusalem

This military campaign was a vital link in the chain of events leading to the building of the temple. God had promised that there would be a site where He would "choose to place his name in" (Deut 16.6): Jerusalem would be that place. Up until this point the Jebusites had been well entrenched there - a defiant Gentile enclave in the midst of the nation of Israel. In ousting them, David not only established a new seat of administration for himself in Zion, but cleared the way for the building of the temple at Moriah.

Jerusalem (Salem) had its first mention in Scripture in connection with its then king, Melchizedek, "the priest of the most high God" (Gen 14.18). As far back as that, kingship and priesthood were combined in a man who was linked with Jerusalem. Melchizedek foreshadowed the Lord Jesus (Heb 7), who will combine kingship and priesthood when He ascends "into the hill of the Lord", Zion, and stands "in his holy place", the temple (Ps 24.3). "He shall be a priest upon his throne" (Zech 6.13). Our verses record an incident that was paving the way for what were then distant future events.

In the conquest of the land, Jerusalem came within territory assigned to the tribe of Judah, but they never quite rid the city of its former inhabitants the Jebusites (Josh 15.63). For generations both had coexisted within the boundaries of that favoured city. David had been brought up in close proximity to it, and when he came to prominence in his duel with Goliath he carried the giant's head to Jerusalem; for David, Jerusalem had a magnetic appeal. Now he was determined to expel its Gentile inhabitants and make it his royal city. From a practical point of view, Hebron was too far south to be an effective capital from which to govern the whole nation; Jerusalem was much more central.

It is clear from 2 Samuel 5, that the Jebusites were confident of their security to the extent of being boldly insolent (v.6). Their bravado did not match their military prowess, and our verses simply record, "Nevertheless David took the strong hold of Zion" (v.5, RV). "All Israel" had supported David in this assault, and the lesson is that if we expect victory there has to be solidarity on the part of the people of God. A kingdom divided against itself is no threat to the enemy.

The city was formerly named Jebus after its previous residents the Jebusites. It would now be known as "the city of David" on the basis that David took up residence there in Zion (v.7). Consistently the city bore that name throughout the historical books of the Old Testament, and, in particular, "the city of David" became the burying place of many of the kings of Judah. Interestingly, when Luke uses the phrase "the city of David" on two occasions he is referring not to Zion but to Bethlehem the place of David's nativity (Lk 2.4,11). Significantly, his narrative relates to another birth, the birth of the One who was "of the seed of David according to the flesh" (Rom 1.3), the Lord Jesus. When the Lord referred to Jerusalem, He linked it to a greater King than David, and called it "the city of the great King" (Mt 5.35). He was quoting from Psalm 48, where "The city of the great King" is said to be "the city of our God" (vv.1-2).

In Bible days, incentives were offered to those who would be bold and daring. Caleb promised his daughter as a bride for the man who would secure Kirjath-sepher (Judg 1.12-13). Saul offered wealth, his daughter as a wife, and a tax-free existence to the man who would kill Goliath (1 Sam 17.25). Here, David offered promotion to the man who would spearhead the attack on the Jebusites. The intrepid Joab rose to the challenge and became David's commander-in-chief. The possibility is that he achieved his victory by climbing up the city's water channels (2 Sam 5.8). One wonders if David regretted his rash promise, for while there was a fierce loyalty about Joab, and while his ability as a strategist could never be questioned, his cunning and cruelty made him a very unsavoury character. It is significant that while he features here as being the man who won the top job, there is no mention of him subsequently among "the chief of the mighty men". His brothers and his armour bearer are listed, but of him we read nothing. In fact, later events prompted David to order his execution despite his advanced years (1 Kings 2.5-6). There is an obvious lesson here and it is that ability and drive are no substitutes for integrity and spirituality. In New Testament times, the believers in Corinth "(came) behind in no gift" (1 Cor 1.7), and yet they were "carnal" (3.1). Just as Joab was an expert in his field but devoid of moral character, so a believer could exercise a spiritual gift with style, and yet be sadly lacking in moral and spiritual qualities.

With the Jebusites expelled, David turned his attention to a reconstruction job; he "built", and Joab "repaired". Possibly Joab was assigned to repair areas of the city that his assault had destroyed. David took personal responsibility for building "Millo round about". "Millo" (4407) means "rampart" or "mound", and in all likelihood it was a strategic part of the city's defences. The men who had breached these defences knew best how to make the area more secure. In every administration the defence of the nation is a major priority, so David superintended this project personally. Even today, leaders have a responsibility to guard their flock, and the injunction is to "watch" (Acts 20.31).

The section ends with a statement of David's increasing power and influence; he "waxed greater and greater", a phrase that is used of Mordecai at a later date (Esth 9.4). Here there is a reminder of the reason for his success; "the Lord of hosts was with him" (v.9). Many years earlier, as he was about to run out to engage Goliath, Saul's words of encouragement rang in his ears, "Go, and the Lord be with thee" (1 Sam 17.37). The Lord *had* been with him, and His presence had extended to this time when David's authority in the nation was now unquestioned, and his military power was subduing the nations around. In any activity for God, there is no substitute for His presence and power. Joseph's prosperity and effectiveness both in the house of Potiphar and in the prison was on account of this: "the Lord was with Joseph" (Gen 39.2,21).

We can apply this principle to the present gospel age. As the Lord Jesus commissioned His apostles, He promised His presence to be with them: "lo, I am with you alway" (Mt 28.20). That promise was fulfilled, for "they went forth, and preached every where, the Lord working with them" (Mk 16.20). This age has almost run its course, and we still lay hold on His promise. We know that we are so very weak, as fragile as "earthen vessels" (2 Cor 4.7). We know too that the minds of unbelieving men have been blinded by "the god of this world" (v.4), and nothing can effect blessing but God's own presence and power. May we share the experience of the preachers at Antioch in ancient times, when "the hand of the Lord was with them: and a great number believed, and turned unto the Lord" (Acts 11.21).

Verse 10: David's Mighty Men

Details are now given of the great warriors who were loyal to David, and supportive of his fledgling administration. As in the genealogies of the former chapters, there are variations in the spelling of names as compared with the list of 2 Samuel 23, but there is no need to draw attention to that every time it occurs.

Once more there is the use of the phrase "all Israel", but "the chief of the mighty men" stand in contrast to the run-of-the mill characters who were encompassed in the "all Israel". It would appear that the mention of "*the chief* of the mighty men" implies that some were superior to those who may have been regarded as ordinary mighty men! In fact as the narrative proceeds we read of some who "attained not to the first three" (vv.21,25), so there were categories of loyalty, courage, commitment and effectiveness. Applying this to our relationship with the Lord, we might well ask ourselves where we fit in. Are we content to be average, or do our spiritual ambitions rise higher than that? Elisha had no desire to be ordinary for he requested that "a double portion" of Elijah's spirit be upon him (2 Kings 2.9). Among Paul's priorities was to "press toward the mark for the prize of the high calling of God in Christ Jesus" (Phil 3.14). In a spiritual sense these men rose above the mundane and ranked among the "chief mighty men". What about us?

These mighty men "shewed themselves strong with him" (RV). All their energies were being devoted to establishing David's kingdom. They were focused, and allowed nothing to divert them from this major issue. Are we as committed to the cause of Christ or have we been distracted in any way?

Despite their long-standing association with the harried fugitive, they were willing to co-operate with "all Israel", many of whom had but lately formed their convictions about David's legitimate claim to the throne. The overriding motivating factor was this: all that was being done was "according to the word of the Lord concerning Israel". If it was God's will, that was good enough for them. Perhaps there is a lesson there for us. It is possible to work with people who are willing to abandon entrenched positions to adopt what is according to the Word of God.

Verse 11: Jashobeam

Only two of those designated "the first three" are mentioned in this record, and the first is Jashobeam who was also called Adino the Eznite (2 Sam 23.8). What is meant by "a Hachmonite" (2453) or "the Eznite" (6112) is unclear, except that in the only other usage of "Hachmonite" it is the proper name Hachmoni, whose son Jehiel appears to have been a tutor to David's sons (1 Chr 27.32). In fact, an alternative translation of our verse is "Jashobeam, the son of Hachmoni" (JND). If both Jashobeam and Jehiel were sons of the same man, or even sons in the sense of descendants, it is interesting that despite common ancestry, in very diverse ways they were able to be of service to David, the one a soldier, and the other a scholar. "Hachmoni" means "wise", and his sons lived up to the father's name; wisdom would be needed for the top-flight warrior as well as for the schoolmaster. "Wisdom is the principal thing; therefore get wisdom: and with all thy getting get understanding" (Prov 4.7). In every sphere of life, interaction with others requires wisdom, whether it be with our fellowbelievers or those who are not connected to the assembly at all. Of the one Paul says to the Colossians, "in all wisdom teaching and admonishing one another" (Col 3.16, JND), and of the other he says, "Walk in wisdom toward them that are without" (4.5).

The word "Eznite" means "sharp" or "strong", perhaps a fitting description of Jashobeam's characteristics, considering that "he lifted up his spear against three hundred slain by him at one time". It cannot go without comment that the number in 2 Samuel 23.8 is said to be 800. Some have suggested that the references are to two separate battles. Others feel that in a certain battle, he personally slew 300, with another 500 falling at the hands of his men, with the whole 800 being attributed to him as the general. Whatever the answer, it is clear that he was a man of considerable ability and strength, not unlike the fearless Shamgar, "which slew of the Philistines six hundred men with an ox goad" (Judg 3.31). "If God be for us, who can be against us?" (Rom 8.31).

Verses 12-14: Eleazar

The second of "the first three" to be mentioned is Eleazar (499), a name that enshrines the concept of help from God, and he certainly experienced the divine help that his name implies. This is the only recorded exploit in which he and David were involved and our verses tell us that "The Lord saved them by a great deliverance". Courage and strength they had, but in the face of such odds only the power of God could leave them standing. Christian service requires that same divine assistance. Nearing the end of a very fruitful life of service, Paul attributed his continued labours and fidelity to "the help that is from God" (Acts 26.22, RV). "Having therefore obtained help of God, I continue unto this day, witnessing both to small and great…" (AV). If anything is going to be done for God, will-power and dogged determination will never accomplish it. In the sphere of Christian activity, the man who is nerveless and pushy is at no advantage over those who are shy and reticent. Help from God is what is required.

The incident for which Eleazar was famed involved "a parcel of ground full of barley". The marauding Philistines had designs on that field, either to appropriate its harvest for themselves, or at least to raze it and deprive the people of God of their food supply. David and Eleazar were shoulder to shoulder in the defence of the barley. Others had fled in the face of the aggressors, but these two men stood their ground and with divine help not only beat off the attack but slaughtered the attackers.

The Philistines always had their eye on the food of the people of God as when they robbed the threshingfloors at Keilah (1 Sam 23.1). We have been suggesting that they illustrate a professing element among God's people, and such mere professors have the same mind-set as these ancient Philistines. They have no appetite for spiritual food themselves, and want to deprive believers of their nourishment, squeezing the time devoted to Bible teaching by substituting the entertaining for the edifying. Just as David and Eleazar resisted the Philistines and stood in the midst of the barley field to defend it, so today, the spiritual food of the people of God has to be defended. Are we going to be like "the people who fled from before the Philistines", or will we be like the heroes of the hour and resist the evil one's designs to make us as "ill favoured and leanfleshed" as Pharaoh's cattle (Gen 41.3)?

There is no obvious reason for the omission of the name of Shammah in this record (2 Sam 23.11), but the Chronicler moves on to deal with the heroics of the three who made the incursion on Bethlehem.

Verses 15-19: Three of the Captains

These three heroes remain unnamed for the moment, but it appears that one of them was Abishai (v.20), and another was Benaiah (v.24). Of the third we have no knowledge.

This venture took place when David was hiding at Adullam, so these men had been associated with the rejected king. "They went down to the rock to David" (v.15). It is interesting that his place of shelter is described as a "rock", and his poetic instinct was impressed with that; frequently he sees his spiritual preservation being dependent on One whom he calls not only "*a* rock" (Ps 18.31), but also "*my* rock" (vv.2,46). The introduction to Psalm 18 indicates that it was penned at a time when David was delivered "from the hand of all his enemies, and from the hand of Saul". Adullam itself would never have been an adequate refuge for him were it not for the fact that "The Lord (was his) rock, and (his) fortress, and (his) deliverer" (v.2). David was constantly aware of his need of this divine shelter. "Be thou my strong rock, for an house of defence to save me" (Ps 31.2); "lead me to the rock that is higher than I" (Ps 61.2). Let this be an encouragement to us all. What the Lord was to David He will be to His subjects when He reigns in righteousness in His millennial Kingdom, for "a man shall be…as the shadow of a great rock in a weary land" (Is 32.1-2). In a spiritual sense we experience that here and now as Elizabeth C. Clephane expressed in her hymn:

Beneath the Cross of Jesus
I fain would take my stand,
The shadow of a mighty Rock
Within a weary land;
A home within the wilderness,
A rest upon the way,
From the burning of the noontide heat
And the burden of the day.

When David was in hiding at Adullam, the main fighting force of the Philistines was concentrated in the valley of Rephaim, but some were garrisoned at Bethlehem (vv.15-16). Bethlehem (1035) means "house of bread". It is another evidence of Philistine efforts to interfere with the food supply of the people of God. They were hindering the cultivation of an area that was a bread basket of the nation. The spiritual lesson has been drawn at vv.13-14.

Adullam was one of the most inhospitable areas of the land, situated as it was in the vicinity of the Dead Sea. The torrid atmosphere of that barren landscape sapped David's energy, and made him think of boyhood days when water from the well at the gate of Bethlehem slaked the thirst of playful lads, and satisfied them as they developed into young men with responsibility for caring for sheep beneath the blistering eastern sun. And so David "longed" for "water of the well of Beth-lehem" (v.17). The three mighties were not under orders to fetch it, but they heard his expressed desire, and at great personal risk accomplished the task. What they did might illustrate the subtle difference between keeping "his commandments" and keeping "his word" (1 Jn 2.3-5). David's men were not commanded to do what they did, but their affinity with David was such that they knew the longings of his heart and were quick to act upon that. It would be wonderful if we were living so close to the Lord that we too were able to discern His will in any situation and had the desire to act so as to bring refreshment to Him. The Apostle John occupied that position of nearness (Jn 13.23).

The fact that these loyal souls "put their lives in jeopardy" (v.19) moved David, and his sensitive nature regarded the precious liquid as "the blood of these men". They had risked their lives for him, but that spirit was in evidence in the Christian era too. There were those who "hazarded their lives for the name of our Lord Jesus Christ" (Acts 15.26). "For the work of Christ", Epaphroditus was "nigh unto death" (Phil 2.30). He gambled with his life to ensure that the gift from the Philippian assembly was safely delivered to Paul at Rome. Aquila and Priscilla "laid down their own necks" in his interests (Rom 16.3-4). Loyalty in the face of danger was the hallmark of these dear believers. One of the demands of discipleship is to hate "(our) own life also" (Lk 14.26). With shame we have to acknowledge that we sidestep risk-taking in the interests of Christ in preference to a comfortable secure lifestyle.

David was willing to forego the luxury of the refreshment from Bethlehem and he devoted it to God: what he had longed for, he dedicated to the Lord. In its strictest sense, this was not a drink offering, but it borrows the character of the drink offering, in that, with deliberation, David poured it out "to the Lord". Throughout his life he had an awareness that only what was precious and personal was suitable to give to God. At a later date he said, "neither will I offer burnt offerings unto the Lord my God of that which doth cost me nothing" (2 Sam 24.24). There is an important principle here. There are times when God calls upon us to relinquish what is most precious to us, as when He called upon Abraham to offer his "only son Isaac, whom (he loved)" (Gen 22.2). God was demanding what was closest to his heart, the treasure for which he had longed for so many years. Abraham rose to the challenge. Hannah was in a similar position and she willingly implemented her promise to give to God the boy she had so earnestly anticipated (1 Sam 1). Paul was willing to "count all things but loss" in the pursuit of spiritual advancement (Phil 3.8). In fact, on two occasions he regarded himself as being poured out as a drink offering (Phil 2.17; 2 Tim 4.6). Even life itself was not to be prized but held subservient to the will of God. Applying the lesson, let us all regard long cherished ambitions and precious possessions as being dispensable. They should be as things that can be "poured out" in a spontaneous act of devotion to the Lord, or in response to a command from Him. Both of these are illustrated in the men named by David.

There is just the hint that David was appalled at the ramifications of his desire for the water from Bethlehem. As things turned out, all was well and the incident had given opportunity for heroism and devotion to be expressed, but it could have been so different. David quaked as he thought of what might have been and seemed to discern divine disapproval. "My God forbid it me, that I should do this thing." Let us all take into account the consequences for others of any word or action on our part.

Verses 20-21: Abishai

"The three" that are mentioned in these verses are evidently the three heroes of Bethlehem that have already been cited. We learn now that Abishai was one of the three, and indeed was "chief of the three". In rank he was ahead of the other two, but was junior to "the first three". He is described here as "the brother of Joab", one of three mentions of Joab in relation to others. These serve to underline the fact that the general himself received no acclaim; his mean ruthless spirit had discredited him.

Abishai's leadership of the three was on account of his "lifting up his spear against three hundred". Promotion was on the basis of merit; it was not a case of nepotism on account of his family relationship with David. That was the blunder that Samuel made, advancing his sons even although they were lacking in moral fibre and financial integrity (1 Sam 8.1-3). In an assembly situation, family relationship should never be the criterion when encouraging others to take responsibility.

Another reason for Abishai's promotion is said to be the fact that "he was more honourable (3513) than the two". We have encountered the phrase already in connection with Jabez who "was more honourable than his brethren" (4.9). It was suggested there that while this word has a variety of meanings and is translated in numerous ways, the likelihood is that it has to do with the character of these men, the fact that they were morally and spiritually ahead of their peers. No doubt Joab could have matched his brother in courage and martial skills, but honour is not a word that we would ever associate with him. Let us be among those who "seek…the honour that cometh from God" (Jn 5.44). So Abishai was the captain of the three for these two reasons - first, his undoubted courage and military competence, but allied with that, an honourable character. Leadership today should embrace these same features - ability for the task and an irreproachable character.

Although not mentioned here, it should be noted that David owed his life to Abishai. In his final military campaign, when his strength was on the wane, Abishai came to his rescue when he was facing certain death (2 Sam 21.15-17).

Verses 22-25: Benaiah

It would appear that Benaiah had also been involved in the audacious raid on Bethlehem, for he is said to be "among the three mighties" (v.24). While he did not match the standing of Abishai, he "had a name among the three mighty men" (v.24, RV); i.e. his reputation exceeded that of the unnamed third warrior, and he certainly had a higher status than that of "the thirty" while not attaining to "the first three" (v.25). Spiritual life should never be lived in a spirit of competition, and Christian service has no place for rivalry, but having said that, mediocrity in divine things is not an option. In contrast to the wayward majority at Thyatira there were "the rest" (Rev 2.24). At Sardis there were "a few names" which had not defiled their garments (3.4). Let us all aspire to be at the top level as far as spirituality, godliness and effectiveness are concerned, and never be content to be part of the crowd for whom the things of God have become a lesser priority. Let us have "a name" among others and be known for all the right reasons.

Benaiah was in a line of men of courage, and was perpetuating an honourable family trait (v.22). He was not a disappointment to his forebears, and would have lived up to their expectations for him. It is evident that we know only a fraction of his exploits for he "had done many acts", and examples are given. In a feeble way what is said here foreshadows what was said by John about the Lord Jesus - "many other signs truly did Jesus in the presence of his disciples, which are not written in this book: But these are written…" (Jn 20.30-31). "There are also many other things which Jesus did" (Jn 21.25).

Among Benaiah's victims were "two lionlike men (739) of Moab". Numerous translations are happy with the AV rendering, so it appears that these were renowned heroes of Moab who had all the strength and ferocity of a lion. Their combined efforts were no match for this courageous warrior. The next of his exploits involved him killing "a lion in a pit in a snowy day". The Word of God often notes not only what men did, but the circumstances in which they did it, for often the circumstances and timing of events make ordinary things extraordinary. Giving "a cup of cold water" is an everyday thing and not worthy of any great reward, but if it is done in the circumstances of hostility described in earlier verses, the giver "shall in no wise lose his reward" (Mt 10.34-42). Threshing wheat was a common activity, but to do it by a winepress when the Midianites were in the land made it worthy of note (Judg 6.11). Killing a lion is certainly more adventurous than any of these other actions, but Samson had done it (Judg 14.5-6), and David had done it (1 Sam 17.34-37). The location and the timing of Benaiah's contest made it more dramatic and special. In the confined space of a pit, and on a snowy day when underfoot conditions were treacherous, he slew the majestic beast. Let us be encouraged that when God assesses our actions, He will take into account the circumstances and the timing of what is done, and will reward appropriately.

The third recorded feat was the slaying of an Egyptian of immense proportions. Benaiah appears to have been at a serious disadvantage as far as weaponry was concerned, but he skilfully disarmed his opponent, and "slew him with his own spear", an act that was reminiscent of David's killing of Goliath with the giant's own sword (1 Sam 17.51).

These three incidents illustrate the conflict that believers have with three distinct foes. Because of that tribe's origins we regard Moab as a picture of the flesh, our fallen sinful nature (Gen 19.34-37). "Fleshly lusts... *war* against the soul" (1 Pet 2.11), so there is the need to "mortify the deeds of the body" (Rom 8.13). The lion illustrates the devil: "your adversary the devil, as a roaring lion, walketh about, seeking whom he may devour" (1 Pet 5.8). He has to be resisted (v.9). Egypt seems to be an apt illustration of the world, in particular the world with its sinful pleasures (Heb 11.25). It has to be overcome (1 Jn 5.4). It would be wonderful if we were spiritual Benaiahs, accomplishing figuratively what he achieved physically.

Benaiah was loyal to David till his dying day, and had the honour of heading the king's bodyguard - "David set him over his guard" (4928). Basic to the word "guard" is the idea of listening and being obedient. These were men who could be relied on to listen to orders and act upon them: hence their suitability to be in proximity to David as bodyguards. It hardly needs saying that the same kind of attention and obedience should be given to the Word of God and it is that which will mark us out as those that are as faithful to our Lord as these men were to their sovereign.

Benaiah's loyalty to the regime extended into Solomon's reign and he became executioner-in-chief to the young king (1 Kings 2.12-46) as he "gather(ed) out of his kingdom all things that offend" (Mt 13.41).

Verses 26-47: The Valiant Men of the Armies

The rest of the chapter lists the names of others who may not have achieved the fame of those formerly mentioned, but whose loyalty to David was unquestioned. Most of them were unknowns as far as we are concerned, but acknowledged by David and noted by God. This must be an encouragement for those who may never have sought the limelight, but whose quiet consistent service for their Lord has not gone unnoticed in heaven. As Thomas Gray reflected on life's illustrious nonentities, he wrote his oft-quoted words:

Full many a gem of purest ray serene
The dark unfathom'd caves of ocean bear:
Full many a flower is born to blush unseen,
And waste its sweetness on the desert air.

Taking God into account, these sentiments can never be true. His all-seeing eye appreciates the sterling character and noble deeds of those who are devoted to Him, and "a book of remembrance (is) written before him" (Mal 3.16).

A few comments on some of these heroes will suffice.

Asahel (v.26) was the youngest of Zeruiah's three sons, a man whose life came to an untimely end at the hands of Saul's wily old general Abner (2 Sam 2.17-23). Unlike his brother Abishai, his days of service were few. There is a similar situation in the New Testament, where martyrdom ended James' life of service (Acts 12.1-2). By contrast, his brother John lived on to be an elderly man who in old age was still in active service despite banishment to Patmos (Rev 1.9). Whether life is long or short, it is quality that counts and not quantity. The men who served for an hour received a penny as did those who had "borne the burden and heat of the day" (Mt 20.1-16). Asahel was honoured for what he had packed into his short life in terms of valiance, and devotion to David.

Naharai was Joab's armourbearer (v.39). The exclusion of Naharai's master and his inclusion in the list is a reminder that when it comes to the day of review there could be some big surprises. Some who have had a high profile in Christian service may be eclipsed by those who have played the supportive role of the armourbearer. That is why Paul encouraged the Corinthians to "judge nothing before the time, until the Lord come, who both will bring to light the hidden things of darkness, and will make manifest the counsels of the hearts: and then shall every man have praise of God" (1 Cor 4.5). Faithfulness and not fame will be the benchmark on that coming day (v.2).

Not surprisingly, Uriah the Hittite features in the list (v.41). What little we know about him leaves us with the impression that here was a man whose commitment to God and to his commander and fellow-soldiers was his top priority (2 Sam 11.11). Personal comforts and enjoyments took a backseat to his sense of calling as a military man. Paul presses home the challenge of that attitude when writing to Timothy: "No man that warreth entangleth himself with the affairs of this life; that he may please him who hath chosen him to be a soldier" (2 Tim 2.4). For the believer, active service in the Lord's army demands a lifestyle that is untrammelled by side issues. Very legitimate affairs such as family obligations, emotional concerns, and business commitments must be subservient to our major focus in life, because "the time is short" (1 Cor 7.29-31).

Thus our chapter concludes, and in the next the emphasis shifts from those who had supported David from the earliest days of his exile, to those who defected to him in its latter stages, and whose help was instrumental in establishing him as king over Israel.

1 CHRONICLES 12

In the introduction to chapter 11, it was mentioned that these two chapters form a distinct section of the book. They are taken up with military matters as David consolidated his power base in the nation before embarking on his plan to bring the ark of the covenant to Jerusalem; his fond hope was that in course of time a permanent home would be provided for it. It was suggested formerly that chapter11 lists the heroes, David's mighty men, but this chapter is taken up with the helpers, a word that appears in various verses (vv.1,17,18,19,21,22). One of these verses uses the word in a negative way, v.19, and another refers to divine help, v.18, but the rest of the references are to people who gave help to David in his time of danger. In addition to the obvious references to helping, the idea lies hidden in the names of some who feature in the chapter - Ahiezer (v.3), Joezer (v.6), and Ezer (v.9). So then, the main theme of the chapter is David's helpers.

For the more part, chapter 12 speaks of those who defected to David towards the end of his days as an outlaw, men who subsequently were involved in installing him as king in Hebron.

Broadly speaking, the chapter divides into three sections. Verses 1-7 deal with those who came to him when he was resident at Ziklag, verses 8-22 speak of some who came to "the hold", and the rest of the chapter records details of those who arrived at Hebron to ensure the transition of power (v.23). The narrative moves from location to location as credit is given to the various individuals and groups who rallied to his cause.

Verse 1: Ziklag

The full story of David's time at Ziklag is recorded in 1 Samuel. He had come to a stage where he felt that there was no longer a safe haven in Israel; amazingly, the Philistine king of Gath gave him asylum. The city of Ziklag was allocated to him, and for the last sixteen months of his exile he and his men were in occupation of that area (1 Sam 27.1-7). Our chapter reveals that during his residency support for Saul ebbed away, and the trickle of defectors became a torrent. The first reference to them being helpers is found in this verse: "his helpers in war" (RV). In the introduction to the previous chapter, attention was drawn to the significant gift of "helps" in 1 Corinthians 12.28. We amplify the importance of being a helper by appealing to the example of Priscilla and Aquila, "my *helpers* in Christ Jesus" (Rom 16.3), or to Apollos, who "*helped* them much which had believed through grace" (Acts 18.27). In the first case, Aquila and Priscilla had assisted Paul in a material and physical way by providing employment and lodgings (Acts 18.1-3). In the second, Apollos gave help in a spiritual way by his preaching, as the subsequent verse explains (v.28). People need support in both of these spheres, and to be a "help" is a most noble activity. It is good to "assist (them) in whatsoever matter (they) may have need of you" (Rom 16.2, RV), whether secular or spiritual.

Here, those who "came to David" helped him militarily, and in Christian experience we have the need of fellow combatants. Paul described both Epaphroditus and Archippus as being "a fellowsoldier" (Phil 2.25; Philem v.2). In the previous chapter it was noted that David was dependent on his fellowsoldier Abishai for defence and rescue. Jonathan was dependent on his fellowsoldier for an assault against the enemy (1 Sam 14.1-14). In Christian warfare believers have to stand shoulder to shoulder when under attack. When advancing into the Evil One's territory there has to be solidarity. Unitedly, we all have to be "helpers of the war".

Those who came to David did so at a time "while he yet kept himself close because of Saul". In other words his activities were very restricted, as emphasised by both AV and RV marginal readings, "being yet shut up" (6113). In linking themselves with David, these men were accepting certain limitations as far as their movements were concerned, and yet the magnetism of the man made the sacrifice worthwhile. For us, the personal acknowledgement of Christ's Lordship, and our commitment to an assembly that gathers to His name means that our movements and behaviour become as restricted as the Word of God demands. The Scriptures set out parameters for our conduct, personally and congregationally. Loyalty to Christ is exhibited by a willingness to accept any limitations that the Word may place upon us, just as loyalty to David made these men happily accept the restriction on their freedom.

Verses 2-7: Saul's Brethren of Benjamin

The first group that came to him was from the tribe of Benjamin, Saul's brethren. Their family relationship with Saul did not impede their conviction that they should now ally themselves with David. Too often family ties can hinder devotion to Christ: hence the stringent demand of discipleship that prospective followers "hate" various family members (Lk 14.26). It appears that the family relationship clouded Barnabas' judgment about John Mark (Acts 15.36-41; Col 4.10). Family affection was almost a hindrance to Elisha following Elijah (1 Kings 19.20), a situation that was replicated in a potential follower of Christ (Lk 9.61). We should never allow the tender ties of our natural relationships to impede commitment to the Lord Jesus. Kinship to Saul was no hindrance to these men of Benjamin making the right choice in rallying to David's standard.

These warriors came equipped with their weaponry, but mention is also made of their skill in handling both sling and bow. They were ambidextrous, which is an advance on the abilities of their left-handed forebears (Judg 3.15; 20.16), though that former generation could hit the target! Applying the lesson, let us all be equipped with "the weapons of our warfare" (2 Cor 10.4), and, just as these men devoted both hands to fighting for David, yield "your members as weapons (*3696*) of righteousness unto God" (Rom 6.13, RV margin). Our whole being can be enlisted on the side of right, in the perennial conflict between good and evil.

The first two men to be mentioned were brothers whose father Shemaah was a Gibeathite, that is, a citizen of Gibeah the hometown of Saul (1 Sam 10.26). Here were people who were not only related to Saul, but had lived in proximity to him. They abandoned Saul and Gibeah for David and Ziklag just as throughout the years many have switched allegiance, and relocated in the interests of Christ. The name of Ahiezer (295) means "my brother is help", perhaps a significant pointer to the fact that these men were an encouragement to each other in their momentous decision to forsake what was familiar and comfortable for what was risky and uncertain. Brotherly support is always a big factor when facing the major issues of life. "Lay(ing) down our lives for the brethren", that is, living in their interests by lending them support, is seen as the true evidence of our affection for them (1 Jn 3.16-18). Let us all assist our brethren and encourage them in making the right choices in life.

Ahiezer is said to be "The chief", but there is no suggestion of annoyance on the part of his brother Joash. The same could not be said of Aaron. Smouldering resentment against Moses erupted when Aaron and Miriam made a complaint against their brother (Num 12.1). Their charge was only a smokescreen, for, in reality, they felt peeved that he had special status. "Hath the Lord indeed spoken only by Moses? Hath he not spoken also by us?" (v.2). A God-given position should never be eyed with jealousy.

Joezer's name means "Jehovah is help" (3134), and the references to divine help in Scripture are so numerous that it would be impossible to range over them. For our encouragement let us simply recollect the words of Samuel when in the wake of victory over the Philistines he set up the stone which he named Ebenezer, the stone of help, adding, "Hitherto hath the Lord helped us" (1 Sam 7.12). Samuel's experience can be the experience of believers today, as we say with the writer to the Hebrews, "The Lord is my helper, and I will not fear what man shall do unto me" (13.6).

Verses 8-15: The Gadites

The writer now turns the clock back to speak of men who were drawn to David when he was still in "the hold in the wilderness" (RV), presumably a reference to the cave of Adullam. The first mentioned are "of the Gadites". These verses are fulsome in describing their character, conduct and commitment, and this is particularly pleasing when it is remembered that the fathers of this tribe had been reluctant to enter their inheritance in Canaan, preferring to settle on the east side of Jordan. This generation was rising above a chequered tribal history to support the claims of the Lord's anointed king. It is wonderful when new generations can reverse the trend of family indifference and shallowness, and emerge as stalwarts for God and His interests. In modern times, speaking generally, the future of the testimony depends on the present generation being better men than their fathers ever were.

Note that they "separated themselves unto David". The positive aspect of their separation is stressed in that it was "unto David", just as the Christian believer is called upon to "go forth therefore *unto him* without the camp, bearing his reproach" (Heb 13.13). But allegiance to David necessitated separation from what they had formerly supported, the decadent administration of Saul; it was impossible to be loyal to both. Doubtless there was an attraction about David that tipped the scales and encouraged fidelity to him, just as the appearing of "the God of glory" was the factor that drew Abraham from Mesopotamia with its idols (Acts 7.2). Turning "to God" was the positive cause for the Thessalonians turning "from idols", for that God was "the living and true God" (1 Thess 1.9). In every case, the appeal and attractiveness of the positive occasioned the abandonment of the negative. The heart that is enraptured with Christ and is separated to Him will inevitably discard all that is inconsistent with being associated with Him, morally, socially or ecclesiastically. A person who has presented his body as a living sacrifice will have no problem in avoiding conformity to the world (Rom 12.1-2). "Come out from among them, and be ye separate" (2 Cor 6.17).

Their separation to David involved sacrifice, for it was "to the hold in the wilderness" (v.8, RV). They were not opting for a comfortable lifestyle in associating with David. All he could promise them was danger and privation, and yet they made the sacrifice. Similarly, the Nazarene never guaranteed ease and prosperity for those who would be separated to Him. He did insist that any potential follower "deny himself, and take up his cross, and follow me" (Mk 8.34). Paul was never guilty of painting a rosy picture of the Christian life, warning young converts of inevitable persecution: "For verily, when we were with you, we told you before that we should suffer tribulation; even as it came to pass, and ye know" (1 Thess 3.4). Peter was equally forthright, speaking of the God "who hath called us unto his eternal glory by Christ Jesus, after that ye have suffered a while" (1 Pet 5.10). Let us be prepared for the cost of being separated to Christ. In recent generations believers in the western world have been spared from the worst excesses of persecution, but being true to Him and His Word often brings misunderstanding and criticism. We should be like the Gadites and be willing for any sacrifice involved in making the right choices in life.

The Chronicler draws attention to their "might", so all their energies were now to be poured into their support for David. Scripture encourages us to love the Lord "with all thy strength" (Mk 12.30). The believers at Philadelphia had only "a little strength", but what little they had was channelled into keeping His Word and not denying His name (Rev 3.8).

Evidently these men of Gad were skilled warriors, for they were "men of war fit for the battle", or "men trained for war" (RV). Mention is made of their expertise in handling their weaponry. Again, all these acquired skills were now at David's disposal. Believers also have acquired skills and perhaps natural abilities that can be used for God. These are to be distinguished from their spiritual gift, but are nevertheless invaluable when it comes to necessary tasks in connection with the service of God. There is no point in having an assembly secretary who is not methodical and has no communication skills. A treasurer would have to be able to count. Those who have these acquired skills can use them profitably for God, and certain aspects of secular training can be used for Him.

The faces of these Gadites "were like the faces of lions", probably conveying to us a certain fierceness that marked them, with possibly a hint of the majesty of the king of beasts. They were not the kind of men to meddle with, but now all that pent up aggression was to be unleashed in promoting the cause of David. Saul of Tarsus was not so much lion-like, but he had displayed the wolf-like features of Benjamin when he was "breathing out threatenings and slaughter against the disciples of the Lord" (Acts 9.1). However, that same determined proactive attitude was channelled into the service of His new-found Lord and Saviour, when "straightway he preached Christ in the synagogues, that he is the Son of God" (v.20). As unsaved people, many believers have had a passion for sports, pastimes or secular activities. It would be hoped that the same kind of zeal could now be ploughed into the service of God.

The next simile that is used to describe these men of Gad likens them to "the roes upon the mountains". If the lion depicts them as being severe, the roe indicates that they were "swift". Despite their strength and determination, they were nimble and surefooted. Once more, these are physical qualities that can be mirrored in spiritual life. There is the danger that strength and determination could give way to impetuosity, with a wrong move leading to a slip and disaster. Joseph the husband of Mary was a man who had strength of character, but he was surefooted in the way he handled matters. In dealing with big issues he was never impetuous, but gave serious thought before acting. This is illustrated in the phrase, "while he thought on these things" (Mt 1.20). In all of our lives let the strength and courage of the lion be married to the speed and the caution of the roe.

It should be observed that the roe is used illustratively of Asahel (2 Sam 2.18), and of the bridegroom of the Song of Solomon, a picture of our beloved Lord (e.g. Song 2.9).

Thirteen names are now mentioned, the first being that of Ezer (5829), the third man in the chapter to have the thought of "help" in his name. In fact, this word is cognate with the word "help" as it is first mentioned in the Bible when God said of Adam, "I will make him an help meet (5828) for him" (Gen 2.18). It would appear that this man Ezer would be of tremendous assistance to David, for being first mentioned, he is likely among the "greatest" of v.14.

These warriors are placed in a specific order, first, second, third, and so on. Again, as far as the divine record goes, there is no murmur of disapproval on the part of those further down the list. They all seemed to be happy to be slotted in just where they were. In this vein it is interesting that when the evangelists list the names of the apostles, Mark and Luke both speak of one of the pairs as Matthew and Thomas (Mk 3.18; Lk 6.15), whereas Matthew himself reversed the order and spoke of Thomas and Matthew (Mt 10.3). Obviously it was all under divine inspiration, but it does appear to be a delightful touch of humility on the part of Matthew. It is the principle of "esteem(ing) other better than themselves" (Phil 2.3). Joseph's descendants always had an inflated notion of their own importance, and consistently felt aggrieved when they were not given their "rightful" place. "I am a great people", they said to Joshua (Josh 17.14). They complained to Gideon, "Why hast thou served us thus, that thou calledst us not, when thou wentest to fight with the Midianites?" (Judg 8.1). Joshua and Gideon handled them with kid gloves but Jephthah treated them far differently when they adopted the same pretentious attitude with him (Judg 12.1-6). Self promotion was far from the thoughts of the Gadites; there was not a murmur of complaint at the order in which they appeared.

However, the men who had no thought of promoting self were in fact promoted, some of them captains over 100, and some of them over 1,000 (v.14). It is the principle of Luke 14.11: "he that humbleth himself shall be exalted". These were humble men, but men who could shoulder responsibility.

Some versions have a different slant on this verse that magnifies the worth of these men. For example, the RV says, "he that was least was equal to an hundred, and the greatest to a thousand". It is almost an echo of a conditional promise made by God back in Leviticus 26.8: "five of you shall chase an hundred, and an hundred of you shall put ten thousand to flight". At the time of Absalom's rebellion, David was told by his men, "thou art worth ten thousand of us" (2 Sam 18.3). Even allowing for hyperbole, a literary device that is used extensively in inspired writings, it is evident that some of these warriors were more than a match for superior numbers, and many times the value of most of their peers.

One of their military ventures is mentioned at v.15. The circumstances are unknown, but it was a campaign that straddled both sides of the River Jordan. "All them of the valleys, both toward the east, and toward the west" were "put to flight". The Gadites were resident on the east of Jordan, and this enterprise involved them going "over Jordan", presumably following the footsteps of those who were first to enter the land. Circumstances were akin to those early days, for again the Jordan was in spate (Josh 3.15). It is a little reminder of the value of doing things as they were done at the beginning. Of Jehoshaphat it was said that "he walked in the *first* ways of his father David" (2 Chr 17.3). The church at Ephesus was told to "do the first works" (Rev 2.5). Solomon gave his son a sound piece of advice when he told him, "meddle not with them that are given to change" (Prov 24.21). As Christian believers, we regard the record of early church history in the Acts of the Apostles as a pattern for our belief and behaviour just as surely as these men of Gad saw in the people of Joshua's generation an example for them to follow.

The fact that they were willing to hazard the crossing of the fast flowing river is an evidence of their determination. It was a major obstacle, but they did not allow it to deter their campaign. A "great mountain" can "become a plain" when the Spirit of God is at work (Zech 4.7). Let us be encouraged that seemingly huge barriers can be overcome.

Such was the calibre of the Gadites who came to David when he was still "in the hold".

Verses 16-18: The Children of Benjamin and Judah

In the early verses of the chapter, mention was made of Benjamites who came to David when he was in Ziklag, men who were closely related to Saul. These verses now demonstrate that others of the tribe of Benjamin had deserted the king at an earlier stage when David was still in "the hold". With them were some from the tribe of Judah. It is interesting that David waylaid these prospective supporters and challenged them regarding their intentions (v.17). At a time when, from the point of view of logic, he should have been glad of any support he could get, he was wary of these new arrivals. He interrogated them and probed their motives. When an atmosphere of intrigue prevails it is hard to be unsuspicious. He had already witnessed treachery on the part of Doeg (1 Sam 22.9), and had experienced it at the hands of the men of Keilah and Ziph (1 Sam 23.12,19); is it any wonder that he was cautious? In later days he was in the same frame of mind when faced with the dilemma of whether to believe Ziba or Mephibosheth (2 Sam 19.24-30).

Putting people to the test was not an uncommon occurrence in the Word of God. Naomi put her daughters-in-law to the test; one failed, and the other passed with flying colours (Ruth 1.6-18). The Lord Jesus put the rich young ruler to the test, and he shrank back from commitment to Christ (Mk 10.17-22). The church at Ephesus "tried them which (said) they (were) apostles and (were) not" and exposed them as frauds (Rev 2.2). Kindly caution is never out of place when either counselling people regarding salvation, or interviewing them as prospective assembly members. Genuine people will never resent being checked out, provided that the questioning is not conducted in a suspicious and abrasive manner. In this case, "David received them" (v.18), the probing having elicited a wonderful declaration of appreciation for David, and a wholehearted commitment to his cause. As far as assembly matters are concerned, some may feel that such is the paucity of numbers in some places that we should be happy to receive anyone who comes our way, with few questions asked. But to be careless about reception or to ignore a dubious track record would be to invite trouble a little further down the road. David's policy was to test wisely to prove that all the parties were the genuine article.

To David's mind, these men had come either to help him or to betray him to his enemies. If the first was the case, then his heart would "be knit" (3162) to them (v.17). The word "knit" is very expressive, but that translation of the Hebrew word is unique to this verse. Most frequently it is translated "together" and has to do with union. If these men had come with a genuine desire to support him, they had David's wholehearted affection and appreciation. On the other hand, if they had come with the hostile intention of infiltrating his forces, he called on God to intervene and deal with them. He was able to do this with the absolute confidence that betrayal was totally unwarranted because of his moral character: "seeing there is no wrong in mine hands". One who was more righteous than David ever was experienced cruel betrayal, but the arch-traitor was compelled to confess, "I have betrayed the innocent blood" (Mt 27.4). In this case, if treachery was afoot, David was prepared to leave recriminations in the hands of God just as the Lord Jesus "committed himself to him that judgeth righteously" (1 Pet 2.23).

The spokesman for this band of men was Amasai and he is regarded by many as being the same person as Amasa, a nephew of David. Here he appears in a good light, though many years later he headed the forces of Absalom. After the rebellion, David had plans to build bridges by appointing him as his new general, but Amasa was brutally slaughtered by his cunning cousin Joab (2 Sam 17.24-26; 19.13; 20.8-10).

Amasai was "chief of the captains (7970)", or as some translations say, "of the thirty". The reason for his acting as spokesman is not attributed to his rank, but to the fact that "the spirit came upon Amasai". The Newberry Bible rightly capitalises the word "spirit", for the reference is evidently to the Holy Spirit of God. In these Old Testament days He frequently "came upon" (3847 "clothed", margin) individuals, either empowering them in what they did, or as here directing them in what they said. These references are most frequent in the books of Judges and 1 Samuel. In the Christian era, He indwells believers, the transition being intimated by the Lord Jesus in the upper room; "he dwelleth with you (presently), *and shall be in you*" (as of Pentecost) (Jn 14.17).

Amasai's Spirit-led statement is replete with devotion and commitment. "Thine are we"; he acknowledged that they belonged to David, vassals who were at his disposal and subject to his commands and we do well to apply these same principles to our relationship with Christ. "And on thy side"; now that they were committed to him, all their energies would be channelled into defending his person and promoting his interests. The two statements run parallel to Paul's reference to his God as he stood on the heaving deck of a ship: "whose I am" (thine we are), "and whom I serve" (and on thy side) (Acts 27.23). The Scriptures say to us, "ye are not your own"; we belong to God, and being on His side demands that we "glorify God in (our) body" (1 Cor 6.19-20).

Spirit-led, Amasai, in referring to David as "son of Jesse", was paying tribute to David's auspicious background. By contrast, Saul used the phrase in a cynical manner, (e.g. 1 Sam 20.27,30,31), and Nabal was guilty of using it in a very caustic manner: "Who is David? and who is the son of

Jesse?" (1 Sam 25.10). David himself never forgot his humble yet honoured background, for even in his "last words" he referred to himself as "David the son of Jesse" (2 Sam 23.1). Let that be an example to younger believers; they should never forget the parents who perhaps scrimped and saved to bring them up. In some cases that may have involved expensive further education in an endeavour to give the family advantages the parents did not have. There is the danger that the humble parents can be sidelined when the younger generation "makes good" socially and financially. There are some who regard the modest family background as an embarrassment! David never forgot that he was "the son of Jesse".

"Peace"; it may seem a strange greeting from men who were armed to the teeth to those in a similar position, but Amasai's wish for David and his helpers was that soon the conflict would be over and that peace would prevail. He had confidence that this would be a reality, because "thy God helpeth thee". As has already been noted, help from God is crucial in every area of our lives, and only the God of peace can create tranquil conditions out of turmoil and chaos. "A great calm" can emerge from "a great storm" at the bidding of Him who says, "Peace, be still" (Mk 4.35-41).

The double Shalom Shalom (7965) is translated "perfect peace" in Isaiah 26.3, and is enjoyed by those "whose mind is stayed on thee: because he trusteth in thee". No doubt David fell into that category and so, even in the midst of severe pressure, this was no mere platitude on the lips of Amasai; "shalom shalom be unto thee" was a genuine greeting and a realistic appraisal of his seemingly chaotic situation.

This brief speech, delivered in such earnest tones and in the power of the Spirit was enough to convince David that these men were authentic, and so he not only "received them", but gave them responsibility as "captains of the band".

Verses 19-22: Some of Manasseh

There is now the record of some from the tribe of Manasseh joining forces with David. This particular incident is pinpointed precisely, in that it took place right at the end of David's time on the run, when he was forbidden to join forces with the Philistines in what was Saul's last stand. Mention is also made of "the band of the rovers", the Amalekites who raided Ziklag in his absence. Full details are found in 1 Samuel 30.

It appears that the intention of these men of Manasseh was to support David's battalion in the army that was about to attack Saul. Doubtless a divine hand intervened to prevent this, but from a human standpoint their non-involvement was attributed to Philistine prudence (v.19). They had enough sense to realise that it was a highly dangerous strategy to have such unproven recruits among their forces. At any time these men could change sides to ingratiate themselves with King Saul.

David was making the trek back to Ziklag when a number of named captains of Manasseh fell in behind him (v.20). Their services were of great value in tracking and overcoming the Amalekites (v.21). Let it be remembered that this was at a time when David's original supporters were greatly discouraged and mutinous (1 Sam 30.6). Some of them are described as "wicked men and men of Belial" (v.22), so it must never be thought that everyone in David's paramilitary organisation was a man of integrity, and as loyal as those of whom comment has been made in the previous verses. As in every military group, some of them were just brutalised men of war, villains who saw in the present unrest an opportunity for personal enrichment. Many of the distressed and the debtors and the discontented who gravitated to the cave of Adullam (1 Sam 22.2) would have been unwholesome characters. In circumstances like that, the new recruits from Manasseh were invaluable.

Which segment of the tribe of Manasseh did they come from - east or west? Obviously we cannot be certain, but the previous mention of the Gadites may suggest that these men of Manasseh were their neighbours, those who were located on the far side of Jordan. If that is the case, what about the other Transjordan tribe, the tribe of Reuben? Is it possible that the present generation was as indifferent as those of Deborah's generation? At Barak's call to arms, despite all the debate and soul-searching Reuben did nothing but abide "among the sheepfolds" (Judg 5.16). The instability of their progenitor seemed a permanent feature of the tribe. They were fence-sitters who only threw in their lot with David when it was evident that his was the winning side (v.37). Let us be less timid in our commitment to the Lord Jesus.

The men of Manasseh were late arrivals as were the men hired at the eleventh hour (Mt 20.6-7), but in both cases, their contribution was very useful. Their arrival was the signal for backing for David to reach immense proportions, and as day followed day that flow of support deepened and widened until his forces amounted to "a great host, like the host of God" (v.22). The phrase "day by day" has its New Testament counterpart when after Pentecost "the Lord added to them day by day those that were being saved" (Acts 2.47, RV). It would be wonderful if even at this late stage in the church age we could see that daily increase being effected in our own districts as the gospel goes out.

Verse 23: Hebron

The narrative now reverts to the occasion of David's enthronement at Hebron of which there was coverage in ch.11. The scene is revisited to give details of the number of fighting men mustered by the various tribes to ensure a smooth transition of power: "these are the numbers…" (v.23). The verse again stresses that what was transpiring was "according to the word of the Lord". To David and many others, the fulfilment of His promise may have appeared long in coming, but the hour had now arrived. David, like ourselves, had to learn patience, and perhaps the Lord's word to Habakkuk has relevance for us all: "For the vision is yet for an appointed time, but at the end it shall speak, and not lie: though it tarry, wait for it" (Hab 2.3). But then, no one likes to be kept waiting! "Ye have need of patience…" (Heb 10.36). Longfellow translated an ancient proverb like this:

> Though the mills of God grind slowly, yet they grind exceeding small;
> Though with patience He stands waiting, with exactness grinds He all.

The mills of God seemed to be grinding slowly as far as the sidelining of Saul was concerned, but His word was brought to fruition and the kingdom was turned to David.

Verse 24: Judah

Nothing is reported of David's native tribe of Judah except their numbers and the fact that they were "armed for war" (RV). It is good to be in state of readiness. "Be ready always…" (1 Pet 3.15). The number from Judah may appear small, but it has to be remembered that Judah had already avowed allegiance to him.

Verse 25: Simeon

The recruits from Simeon are said to be "mighty men of valour" which would appear to be an advance on the previous verse. Here were men of outstanding courage, and the reminder to our own hearts is that "God hath not given us the spirit of fear; but of power, and of love, and of a sound mind" (2 Tim 1.7). "Be thou strong and very courageous" (Josh 1.7). Spiritually, let us be mighty men of valour.

Verses 26-28: Levi

It seems a strange thing that the Levites, including the priestly family, were willing to take up arms in support of David. They were combining the roles of worshippers and warriors. Two men are mentioned specifically: Jehoiada who was a leader, and Zadok a young priest. As well as being noted for his courage, Zadok is described as "a young man", a term that is sprinkled extensively throughout Scripture. Another notable "young man" is Joshua, thus described at a time of crisis when it is recorded that "Joshua, the son of Nun, a young man, departed not out of the tabernacle" (Ex 33.11). Let the example of these young men impact on the lives of young believers today. Zadok was devoting his young life to promoting the interests of David, and in later life in the days of Solomon he functioned as the high priest (1 Kings 2.35); he was the man honoured to be the first high priest in the newly built house of God. Let the youthful reader resolve to be as committed to Christ as Zadok was to David, and doubtless further down the road of life He will impart honoured responsibility in His service.

Verse 29: Benjamin

For many of the men of Benjamin, enthroning David was a massive about turn. The vast majority of these men had "kept their allegiance to the house of Saul" (RV), for in every age, sadly, blood is thicker than water. Even after the death of their kinsman, they had supported the shaky administration of his son Ishbosheth. With hopes of a dynasty now shattered, they at last threw in their lot with David. It does take courage to confess, "We got it wrong". These men were willing to admit that, and, though their numbers may appear small in comparison to others, keep in mind that this was a tribe that was few in number as it had been almost wiped out a few generations earlier (Judg 19-21).

Verse 30: Ephraim

A unique comment is made about those who came from Ephraim. They were "famous throughout the house of their fathers". These were the well-known men of a proud and sizeable tribe, and yet they were rallying to David. Sometimes those who are prominent have no desire for Christ. "Not many wise men after the flesh, not many mighty, not many noble, are called" (1 Cor 1.26). However, some such do experience salvation, and have opportunity as "famous" people to be very effective devoted servants of the Lord. Manaen had been brought up with Herod the tetrarch (Acts 13.1). Erastus was the chamberlain of the city (Rom 16.23). At Corinth, both Crispus and Sosthenes had been chief rulers of the synagogue (Acts 18.8,17). Luke was a respected doctor (Col 4.14). Each of these men of comparative fame made their mark for God.

Verse 31: Manasseh

The half tribe of Manasseh that was on the west of Jordan (see v.37) mustered 18,000 men, said to be "expressed by name". This would indicate that of all those who may have been suitable to come or may have wished to come, these were the men chosen to be the delegates of the tribe. Thus they could hold their heads high as honoured representatives of Manasseh. They had a precise remit, "to make David king", and every ounce of energy and valour had to be devoted to that goal. They now had a responsibility to prove themselves worthy of the confidence that had been placed in them. The familiar maxim should be heeded: "Privilege brings responsibility, and responsibility accountability". There is a sense in which every servant of the Lord is responsible to Him alone, but to balance that servants should feel a sense of responsibility to those who have shown confidence in them. That is why Paul and Barnabas returned to their commending assembly and "rehearsed all that God had done with them" (Acts 14.27).

Verse 32: Issachar

Now the spotlight falls on the tribe of Issachar. We are not told how many troops they marshalled, only that over them were 200 "heads". These 200 commanded the respect and obedience of all; "all their brethren were at their commandment". Insubordination was unheard of among this regiment. Thus it should be in a New Testament assembly. "Obey them that have the rule over you, and submit yourselves" (Heb 13.17). The guidance and instruction of godly elders should never be trodden underfoot as in the fear of God they endeavour to steer the company in the right ways of the Lord.

These men of Issachar had "understanding of the times, to know what Israel ought to do". A similar phrase is used in Esther 1.13 in relation to the "wise men" of the court of King Ahasuerus. In that context we could be tempted to relate it to their commitment to astrology or similar activities, but knowing the times seems to be equated with knowing "law and judgment". In other words, they had the ability to suggest the right and honourable course of action in any given circumstance. That seems to be the state of affairs in our present verse. Civil commotion prevailed, and these men of Issachar assessed the situation and knew that the only right and proper course of action for Israel was to make David king, and so they supported the cause wholeheartedly.

Being able to read a situation and act appropriately is a great talent. Paul encouraged it in Romans 13.11: "knowing the time, that now it is high time to awake out of sleep: for now is our salvation nearer than when we believed". A proper appraisal of prevailing circumstances is that we are living in a time of dense moral and spiritual darkness, with the coming of the Lord imminent, for "The night is far spent" (v.12). That assessment demands a course of action: awaking, casting off the works of darkness, walking honestly, putting on the Lord Jesus Christ. Let us be like the men of Issachar and have understanding of the times, and act appropriately.

Verse 33: Zebulun

Zebulun features next. As an advance on characteristics that have appeared in previous verses and have already been considered, it is said of these men that "they could keep rank: they were not of double heart". Once more, there are simple lessons to be applied. God always desires order - "Let all things be done decently and in order" (1 Cor 14.40). When His people came out of Egypt it is said that "the children of Israel went up in orderly ranks out of the land of Egypt" (Ex 13.18, NKJV). Breaking rank not only spoils the appearance of an army on the march, but destroys its effectiveness, and, in the context of the New Testament church, those who break rank have to be admonished. "Warn them that are unruly" (1 Thess 5.14). The word "unruly" (*813*) holds in it the concept of breaking rank, and its cognate word is used twice in the second epistle translated there "disorderly" (2 Thess 3.6,11). Evidently some at Thessalonica were breaking rank by being idle and interfering in other people's affairs. It blighted the testimony in the city and impaired their effectiveness in service. Let us be like the men of Zebulun and have the ability to keep rank. There is nothing wrong with conformity if it is conformity to what is Biblical. Unorthodox activity, either personally or congregationally, may appeal to the independent spirit, but what does it do for the testimony of God? Paul was a man who kept rank: "we behaved not ourselves disorderly among you", and thus he said, "ye ought to imitate us" (2 Thess 3.7, RV).

"Not of double (3280) heart (3280)" is another wonderful commendation. A literal translation is, "without a heart and a heart" (AV margin). Single-minded loyalty and devotion was their hallmark. "Flattering lips" are the stock in trade of the double hearted (Ps 12.2). These men had made no attempt to flatter Saul to ingratiate themselves with him, then cosy up to David to elicit his favour. Sitting on the fence was not their way. Keeping their options open was never a consideration. They had no plan B; they were totally committed to David.

In a similar way, God also demands the undivided affection of His people: "Thou shalt have no other gods before me" (Ex 20.3). The Samaritans who were installed in the land attempted to show deference to every deity when "They feared the Lord, and served their own gods" (2 Kings 17.33). That kind of arrangement will never satisfy God. God and mammon are incompatible (Mt 6.24). Christ and Belial can never agree (2 Cor 6.15). "Friendship of the world is enmity with God" (James 4.4). God demands 100% allegiance. He asks us, as Jehu asked Jehonadab, "Is thine heart right, as my heart is with thy heart?" (2 Kings 10.15). Let it be true of us, "not of double heart"; "Let us draw near *with a true heart*" (Heb 10.22).

Is there a thing beneath the sun
That strives with Thee my heart to share?
O tear it thence, and reign alone
The Lord of every motion there!
(Gerhard Tersteegen)

Verse 34: Naphtali

The tribe of Naphtali appears to have been well supplied with men with leadership qualities, for 1,000 captains arrived with 37,000 men. Like others, it is recorded that they came "with shield and spear". They had the sense to know that David could hardly be expected to supply the military hardware for so many recruits, and so they came armed with their own weapons. As far as the believer is concerned, we are not expected to supply our own resources for spiritual conflict, for God has an arsenal in readiness for us, described in Scripture as "the whole armour *of God*" (Eph 6.13). It is for us simply to "take" it.

Verse 35: Dan

Nothing is recorded of this tribe except the substantial force that was sent and that they were expert in war, and already the lesson has been drawn regarding the necessity for believers to be trained and disciplined in the matter of spiritual conflict.

Verse 36: Asher

With so little said about this tribe, it may be an opportunity to draw attention to the Revised Version translation of the repeated phrase "expert in war". Consistently in this chapter, it renders the expression, "that could set the battle in array". In an endeavour to outmanoeuvre the enemy, these men knew how to deploy their resources to best advantage. Today, the Spirit of God in His sovereignty not only imparts spiritual gift (1 Cor 12.11), but directs its deployment (Acts 13.1-3). It is for us to be sensitive to His guidance, and to know best how to set the battle in array. Ben-hadad the king of Syria abdicated his responsibility in this respect, and was more interested in feasting than in fighting, leaving it to others to "Set (them) selves in array" (1 Kings 20.12-21). Is it any wonder that he lost the day? Let us be more vigilant, and employ Scriptural strategies that are calculated to make inroads into enemy territory.

Verse 37: The Transjordan Tribes

It is good that the two and a half tribes rallied to David as well, for Ishbosheth's regime had been so marginalised that it had been centred on their side of Jordan. Now the last vestiges of opposition were dispelled, with every tribe acknowledging David's right to the throne.

Verses 38-40: Celebrations at Hebron

The occasion was one of great joy, not least because of the attitude of those involved. These "men of war" who assembled at Hebron "came with a perfect heart", and those who had been left at home, "all the rest also of Israel", are said to have been "of one heart". How important is the attitude of the heart! In the first case, the perfect heart indicates that they were solidly behind David - they had no reservations, they were completely transparent in their motives in making him king. The "one heart" indicates a unity of purpose on the part of the whole nation. No one was heard to demur, no one had difficulty in accepting the situation, no one had an alternative suggestion; the people had spoken and David was now their king.

"A perfect heart"; it is a phrase unique to the Old Testament. Hezekiah professed to have it (2 Kings 20.3), David aspired to have it (Ps 101.2), and Solomon was encouraged to have it (1 Chr 28.9). While the phrase is never found in the New Testament, the concept is undoubtedly there. Paul spoke of the Romans having "obeyed *from the heart* that form of doctrine which was delivered (them)" (Rom 6.17). He encouraged servants to be "doing the will of God *from the heart*" (Eph 6.6). For a believer, to have a perfect heart means unswerving loyalty to God and wholehearted obedience to His Word. Let us all aspire to that, and never let it be said of us as of Amaziah, that "he did that which was right in the sight of the Lord, *but not with a perfect heart*" (2 Chr 25.2).

The single-mindedness of the "one heart" is enjoined when Paul wrote to the Philippians: "stand fast in one spirit, with one mind striving together for the faith of the gospel" (Phil 1.27). Just as there was a united heart to make David king, so in every assembly, forces should be combined with the common aim of bringing the gospel to a needy world.

A three-day period of feasting was an indication of the nation's delight at David's accession to the throne. Seven days of fasting had attended the passing of Saul (10.12), but fasting and gloom were now changed to feasting and gladness as the new era dawned.

In the Scriptures, eating and drinking together was often a token of friendship and fellowship, and so this new relationship between David and Israel was being cemented during these three days of feasting. There is an emphasis on the fact that "there they were *with David*".

The massed armies would require substantial provisions for three days of eating and drinking, and the people of the neighbourhood, those who are described here as "their brethren" (v.39), rallied to provide what was necessary. Brotherly love provides for the needs of others in the family, and would never stifle any feelings of compassion (1 Jn 3.17). It would never be content to love "in word, (or) in tongue; but in deed and in truth" (v.18). Genuine faith would never make the careless remark, "be ye warmed and filled", without taking steps to meet the need (James 2.16). Thus with so many mouths to feed, the brethren rose to the challenge, and indeed, from as far away as the northern territories rations were dispatched post haste.

A variety of beasts of burden were used: asses, camels, mules and oxen. In fact, whatever men had, they were willing to contribute to the service of God. The Samaritan made his beast available to the wounded traveller on the Jericho road (Lk 10.34). Unnamed disciples donated their colt to Christ when they heard, "The Lord hath need of him" (Lk 19.29-34). Are modern day means of transport so readily available for the needs of the saints and for the work of the Lord?

A great variety of provisions were sent, something to satisfy every taste with no possibility of the menu becoming boring. Barzillai was equally thoughtful when he brought relief to David as he fled from the rebellious Absalom (2 Sam 17.27-29). Spiritual feeding should be as varied and appetising. The Shepherd provides "green pastures" (Ps 23.2), tender, wholesome, satisfying, but He also "feedeth his flock among the lilies" (Song 2.16, RV), that is, in an environment that is pleasant and appealing. Let us imitate Him. It is possible to impart "Sound speech, that cannot be condemned" (Titus 2.8) in such an unappealing way as to make it counterproductive. Those who feed the saints should see that every need is catered for and that every subject is handled, for the people of God need a healthy, balanced, varied, spiritual diet.

The reason for the feasting is explained in the last phrase of the chapter: "for there was much joy in Israel". It seems that the flames of delight had sped on their way across the whole country. The pall of gloom that had hung over Saul's oppressive regime had at last been lifted, and ecstasy filled every heart at the thought of a new tomorrow with God's anointed king now wielding a sceptre of righteousness.

The chapter's end finds a New Testament counterpart in Acts 8 which concludes on virtually the same note: "he went on his way rejoicing" (v.39). The circumstances are so different, and yet the underlying cause of the joy is the same. Israel's obedience in turning the kingdom to David "according to the word of the Lord" resulted in universal joy in the land. The Ethiopian's obedience in the matter of believers' baptism brought to him a joy that was in addition to the joy of salvation. Obedience spells happiness; rebellion spells misery. "If ye know these things, happy are ye if ye do them" (Jn 13.17).

1 CHRONICLES 13

After the ecstatic joy of chapter 12, this chapter strikes a jarring note, with the statement that "David was displeased" (v.11). This was a "displeasure" that he brought upon himself because of his careless attitude to the things of God. It is a solemn reminder to us all that a casual approach to divine things invites unhappiness. The plan was to bring the ark of God to the "city of David" (v.13), so the events of this chapter took place some time after the happenings of chapter 12. There, the narrative centred on Hebron, but by now David's seat of administration was Zion. Despite this time gap, the fact that the events are placed in juxtaposition demonstrates that if carelessness creeps up on us, then tragedy can follow triumph and grief can follow glory.

Constant reference has been made to the main theme of 1 Chronicles, namely David's desire to build a house for God. It was suggested that chapters 11 and 12 pave the way for that main theme to be developed. It will not be pursued without interruption, but here, for the first time, we are given an insight into the trend of David's thinking as he expressed his desire to "bring again the ark of God" (v.3). In Psalm 132 he indicated that he had always had an interest in the ark and in the house of God. He had made a vow to the Lord: "Surely I will not come into the tabernacle of my house, nor go up into my bed; I will not give sleep to mine eyes, or slumber to mine eyelids, Until I find out a place for the Lord, an habitation for the mighty God of Jacob" (vv.2-5). From his infancy in Bethlehem Ephratah he had "heard of it" (the ark) (v.6) and it appears that from earliest days he harboured ambitions to provide this "habitation for the mighty God of Jacob". It is such a pity that his first attempt to bring the ark brought catastrophe because he did not go about things "after the due order" (15.13).

After the ark had been returned by the Philistines it had been situated at Kirjath-jearim in the house of Abinadab (1 Sam 7.1-2). Its location was so rural as to be described as "the fields of the wood" (Ps 132.6). Subsequently there is only one fleeting reference to it in the whole of 1 Samuel when Saul called for it in days prior to his final rejection by God (1 Sam 14.18). It was from Kirjath-jearim that David intended to bring the ark; there he had "found it" (Ps 132.6).

It is instructive that here in 1 Chronicles his interest in the ark takes precedence over the building of his own house (14.1-2). It was a top priority to which personal comforts became subservient. He was not like the people of Haggai's generation who dwelt in their "ceiled houses" while the house of God was lying waste (Hag 1.4). Rather, his attitude to the things of God was as urgent as Hezekiah's when he, "in the *first* year of his reign, in the *first* month, opened the doors of the house of the Lord, and repaired them" (2 Chr 29.3). David was making the ark and the house of God his main concern in life. It need hardly be said that believers should have the same outlook, seeking "*first* the kingdom of God, and his righteousness" (Mt 6.33).

The chapter is short with a single story-line running throughout it, so perhaps it is unnecessary to give a precise division, but it might be helpful to summarise it like this: verses 1-4 give details of David consulting the nation to express what was in his heart. In verses 5-8 they congregate at Kirjath-jearim and commence the journey with the ark. The next section (verses 9-12) records the appalling incident of the death of Uzza, and the rest of the chapter (verses 13-14) tells of the procession being diverted to the house of Obed-edom where the ark was left for three months.

Verses 1-4: Consultation and Agreement

As was observed in the previous chapter, David's position as monarch had universal acceptance and was completely unrivalled, and yet he did not adopt the stance of a dictator. Wisely, he wanted to carry the people with him in his project, and so there was consultation; he did want popular support. This was the man who understood the danger of bad advice and warned about the "counsel of the ungodly" (Ps 1.1), but he was not averse to seeking guidance from others. Indeed there were those who were designated his counsellors (27.32-33). It is good when leaders realise that they do not have a monopoly on wisdom, and that it is important to encourage others to have an input into any debate. On this occasion, David wisely consulted the leaders of the people (v.1) before he put the matter to "all the congregation of Israel" (v.2). It is never prudent to go over the heads of leaders to appeal to their people, so David acted intelligently in the way he handled things. By contrast, his son Absalom shrewdly undermined the leadership of the nation when he fawned over the common people and stole their hearts (2 Sam 15.1-6).

While neither dictatorship nor democracy should feature in New Testament churches, consultation is not unscriptural as observed in Acts 6.5 when apostolic proposals "pleased the whole multitude".

In David's thinking, two criteria had to be satisfied before he would ever embark on this venture of bringing back the ark. First, it would have to be the mind of the people: "if it seem good unto you". More importantly, it had to "be of the Lord our God" (v.2). So he wanted to be confident that he had unanimous support, and the assurance that it was all in the mind of God. On occasions it is possible to have the one without the other. In Acts 16 Paul and his companions were at one in their attempts to go into Bithynia with the gospel, but it was not the will of God (v.7). In 2 Corinthians 2 it was evidently God's will for Paul to preach at Troas for "a door was opened unto (him) of the Lord", but because of the weight of circumstances he did not enter that open door and "(took his) leave of them" (vv.12-13). However, when the will of committed people coincides with the will of God great things can be accomplished for Him. Another reference to Acts 16 illustrates this well. Luke gives details of the triumphs of the gospel at Philippi, and prefaces the record by telling us that following Paul's vision "immediately we endeavoured to go into

Macedonia, assuredly gathering that the Lord had called us for to preach the gospel unto them" (v.10).

There is great stress on the need for unity and co-operation in this enterprise. Observe David's language when he spoke of "the Lord *our* God": "let *us*"; "*our* brethren *every where*"; "*all* the land of Israel". He was keen to capture collective enthusiasm for the venture, the kind of enthusiasm that was in evidence centuries later when after the captivity "the people gathered themselves together *as one man* to Jerusalem" (Ezra 3.1). If Christ is ever to have the central place among His people as illustrated in the bringing up of the ark, and if the assembly is ever going to be edified as illustrated in the building of the temple, then there has to be a common goal and collective zeal among the believers.

In David's address to the congregation he made particular mention of the priests and the Levites. He knew right well that they would be crucial to this project (15.2), but on the day he foolishly dispensed with their services with disastrous results. His conduct was not that of someone acting in ignorance; willingly he allowed a procedure that was far removed from the revealed will of God (Num 4.15; Deut 10.8). To allow things that are unscriptural on the grounds of convenience or modernity leaves us as culpable as David.

In v.3 David indicated that for all of his lifetime the ark had never been central to the life of the nation. Although there was that one reference to Saul requesting its presence (1 Sam 14.18), in all David's associations with him this was the situation: "we inquired not at it in the days of Saul". (It should be noted that a few translations refer to the ephod rather than the ark in 1 Samuel 14.18.) Even before the days of Saul, for the first twenty years of its location at Kirjath-jearim it was virtually ignored until Samuel encouraged the nation to "return unto the Lord" (1 Sam 7.1-3). Of these twenty years Scripture records that "the time was long". The phrase conjures in the mind the impression of people who were drained and desolate because they had abandoned their God. There is the danger of that weariness of life surfacing in our own day; the time will be long if God is left out of the equation.

For more than a generation then, the ark had been forgotten, a token of the fact that God had been displaced, but now was the time for that omission to be corrected. God must become central to the lives of His people again. No longer must the symbol of His presence remain distant. "Let us bring again the ark of our God *to us*". In modern times we too must place God at the centre of our lives. If there has been slippage on our part, there is the need to reinstate Him to His proper place in our hearts and homes. Let the words of Israel after Absalom's rebellion be a challenge to us all: "why speak ye not a word of bringing the king back?" (2 Sam 19.10).

There was solid support for David's plan (v.4) as stressed by the repetition of the word "all": "*all* the congregation"; "*all* the people". First there had been an appreciation that "the thing was right". Then there had been a verbal commitment to the cause - "the congregation said that they would do so" -

but within a few verses, thought and word had become action, and that is to their credit. Too often good intentions fall back dead or are deferred, as when the Corinthians debated for a year about ministering to needy saints. Paul had to encourage them: "Now therefore perform the doing of it" (2 Cor 8.10-11). By contrast, the disciples at Antioch "determined" on a course of action, "Which also they did" (Acts 11.29-30). Let pledges of support for a divinely directed work be translated into concrete activity.

Verses 5-6: Kirjath-jearim; The Journey Begins

They journeyed from the extremities of the land for this historic event, from as far afield as Shihor near Egypt in the south and Hemath near Syria in the north. The venue was the city of Kirjath-jearim; for many a year its precincts had played host to this symbol of the divine presence. The place name means "city of forests", which gives us a clue as to why David made reference to finding the ark "in the fields of the wood" (Ps 132.6). The repetition of the phrase "all Israel" in vv.5 and 6 again demonstrates the unity of purpose that was exhibited on the part of the nation.

The dignity of this vessel of the sanctuary is emphasised at v.6; it was "the ark of God, the Lord, that dwelleth between the cherubims, whose name is called on it". This God (430), to whom we are introduced as the great God of creation in the first sentence of the Bible, dwelt between the cherubims of the mercy seat. This Lord (3068, Jehovah), who was the covenant keeping God of Israel (Ex 6.2-9), was resident there. When God gave instructions for the construction of the ark with its mercy seat, He made promise to Moses: "And there I will meet with thee, and I will commune with thee from above the mercy seat, from between the two cherubims which are upon the ark of the testimony" (Ex 25.22). This promise was fulfilled, as indicated in Numbers 7.89: "And when Moses was gone into the tabernacle of the congregation to speak with him, then he heard the voice of one speaking unto him from off the mercy seat that was upon the ark of the testimony, from between the two cherubims". The Psalmist spoke to the Shepherd of Israel as "thou that dwellest between the cherubims" (Ps 80.1). These, with other Scriptures, show us that the ark was seen as the location of God's presence, and so reference had been made to it as the symbol of the divine presence.

It was also the place where the name of God was invoked; this seems to be the best way to understand the phrase "whose name is called on it". The two words "on it" are italicised in the AV indicating their non-inclusion in the original Hebrew. Young's Literal Translation puts the phrase like this: "where the Name is called on". That is why, after the disaster at Ai, Joshua prostrated himself "before the ark" (Josh 7.6). Also, the phrase helps to explain David's statement in v.3: "we *inquired not* at it in the days of Saul". So the ark was a place where God was enthroned and from which He spoke to men, and it was also a place where men spoke to Him. With that in mind, we can well understand David's earnest desire to "bring again the ark". He had a longing to be the recipient of divine communications, and to have the privilege of calling on the name of God there, so keeping the circle of fellowship with His God intact. For us, that circle of communication remains unbroken as long as we listen to His voice through the Word, and invoke His name in prayer. Peter emphasises both when he tells us, "Ye call on him as Father", and, "desire the sincere milk of the word" (1 Pet 1.17, RV; 2.2).

These statements regarding the majesty of the ark make the next verse all the more shocking when we come to read it. How could they treat this magnificent symbol of God's presence in such an undignified way?

Verses 7-8: The New Cart

Transporting the tabernacle was facilitated by the provision of six covered wagons (Num 7.3). Two of these were given to the sons of Gershon, and four to the sons of Merari (vv.7-8). The Kohathites received none, for their responsibility was to carry the vessels of the sanctuary which "they should bear upon their shoulders" (v.9). In our chapter, the use of a cart violated that ordinance. Even the Kohathites were forbidden to "touch any holy thing" under penalty of death (Num 4.15). In our chapter that prohibition was ignored and the sentence fell. The lesson that lies on the surface is that it is not only foolish but perilous to ignore divine procedures. Enthusiasm can sometimes make us careless; using a cart would be faster than shouldering the heavy burden! Using a *new* cart would show necessary respect for this vessel of the sanctuary! A cart that was begrimed with constant use in the fields would be totally inappropriate! Trying to avoid damage to the holy chest seemed so logical. But all of these weighty arguments fell down in light of the fact that the whole process was "not after the due order" (15.13), and in a dramatic and unexpected way God intervened in judgment.

The Philistines had used a new cart when they returned the ark to Israel (1 Sam 6). They were pagans who knew no better, and for them the journey passed without incident even although the cart was without a driver. It seems that God was prompting and directing the cattle that were drawing it. In that case catastrophe occurred at journey's end when the men of Beth-shemesh looked into the ark occasioning the "great slaughter" of 50,070 men (v.19). That part of the episode should have been a warning to David that God is not to be trifled with, but he ignored the lessons of history with disastrous consequences.

Accordingly, he adopted a Philistine method of transporting the ark. Maybe he felt that because it worked for them it would work for him, but he should have known better than they did, and so he was more responsible. It is an important principle in the Word that enlightenment makes people more accountable, as the Lord Jesus made clear to the citizens of Chorazin, Bethsaida, and Capernaum. They were more responsible than those of Tyre and Sidon because they had the privilege of His presence among them (Lk 10.13-16).

Throughout the commentary it has been suggested that the Philistines illustrate professing Christians. In the world of Christendom many who bear the name "Christian" use unbiblical methods to boost membership, or to increase funds, or to create goodwill in the community. People who know their Bibles should never be tempted to argue that if it works for them it could work for us, with the subsequent abandonment of Scriptural principles. Unscriptural "new carts" produce spiritual casualties just as surely as this situation proved disastrous for Uzza.

In a sense we have been pointing the finger of blame at David for this deviation from the divine pattern. We cannot be certain that he initiated the proceedings, but as leader he condoned what was taking place. Leaders do have responsibility for what happens under their management. The Lord Jesus charged "the angel of the church in Thyatira", "thou sufferest that woman Jezebel..." (Rev 2.20); sin was being tolerated.

Again, the king's failure had ramifications for others. In the ultimate it was Uzza who suffered as a consequence of David's actions, another solemn lesson for our own lives. "No man is an island", said John Donne. What happens to us inevitably impacts on others and vice versa, and David's displeasure with God would have been better directed at himself; he was the cause of the poor man's death. Achan's family suffered because of his greed (Josh 7.24-26) as did Gehazi's because of his (2 Kings 5.27). Let us beware lest failure on our part should have a negative impact on family, friends, workmates or fellow-believers.

The drivers of the cart were Uzza and Ahio (v.7). They were part of the family that had been the custodians of the ark for the many years of its exile (2 Sam 6.3). Both were very familiar with the sacred chest. Was it familiarity that made Uzza careless? And is it possible that we too could become over-familiar with holy things? Could we become so used to attending meetings, and remembering the Lord, and engaging in service, that we lose an appreciation of the holiness of the God whom we worship and serve? Is it possible that irreverence could creep into our activities? "Let us have grace, whereby we may serve God acceptably with reverence and godly fear: For our God is a consuming fire" (Heb 12.28-29).

The procession was accompanied by fanfare and noise (v.8), and of course this was replicated when the proper procedures were adopted in ch.15. Nothing negative is said about it, but one wonders if all the noise contributed to the oxen stumbling. Certainly, the din and the music were no substitute for the smile of divine approval and did nothing to disguise the fact that from God's standpoint all was not well.

The people could not be faulted for lack of enthusiasm, for what they did was "with all their might", so it is possible to be zealous in a situation that has no Scriptural authority. Although this whole scenario was far from the mind of God, He was there, for all that they did was "before God" (v.8); it was because He was there that Uzza died, for, says v.10, "he died *before God*". The whole situation is a solemn warning to us all, lest we should abandon Scriptural procedures. If what is being done is ostensibly in His name it means that He does take an interest, and there could be consequences if a certain line is crossed.

The singing was accompanied by an orchestra with its various sections - strings, wind, and percussion (v.8). It need hardly be remarked that while singing featured in New Testament assemblies, there is no record of any instrumental accompaniment such as obtained in many of these Old Testament incidents.

Verses 9-10: The Death of Uzza

The fatal incident took place at the threshingfloor of Chidon, an alias for a man called Nachon (2 Sam 6.6). (Three threshingfloor scenes feature in the life of David: the threshingfloors of Keilah (1 Sam 23.1), this threshingfloor, and then the threshingfloor of Ornan the Jebusite (1 Chr 21.15ff) which will be considered later in the book.) At the threshingfloor of Chidon the oxen became restive and were in danger of toppling their precious cargo. Instinctively, but irreverently, "Uzza put forth his hand to hold the ark". He presumed to do that which was forbidden even to the Levites. To him it may have seemed the right action to take, but it was a clear breach of the Lord's command, and he perished under divine judgment. "Good ideas" that seem to be tenable can never prosper if they displease a holy God.

Uzza's irreverence invoked the Lord's anger, resulting in summary judgment: "he died *before God*". A similar act of irreverence was answered in the same way when Nadab and Abihu "offered strange fire before the Lord" and "died before the Lord" (Lev 10.1-2). These are sombre incidents that surely instil a sense of fear into our hearts, lest we also should treat divine things lightly, and forget that the God "with whom we have to do" (Heb 4.13) is "the high and lofty One that inhabiteth eternity, whose name is Holy" (Is 57.15). We could be particularly susceptible to irreverent talk or behaviour when in a state of high excitement as were the people here. It is false consolation to presume that the God of the New Testament is a different Being from Him who acted so severely in Old Testament days. At Corinth, impiety was expressed by many of the believers adopting an off-hand attitude to the Lord's Supper, relegating the occasion to one of feasting and revelry. The sad commentary of Scripture is this: "For this cause many are weak and sickly among you, and many sleep" (1 Cor 11.30).

Verses 11-12: David's Displeasure and Fear

It appears that David's displeasure and frustration were directed against God, "because the Lord had broken forth upon Uzza" (v.11, RV). According to some translations (e.g. RV and JND) it was he who gave the place the name that kept the incident in mind, and this is in agreement with the record of 2 Samuel 6.8. The word "displeased" (2734) is the word translated "kindled" in the previous verse, and it almost indicates an outburst of indignation on the part of David. JND translates, "And David was indignant". As suggested earlier, his outburst would have better directed against himself, and his own folly, but God was to blame! Blaming God has been the thing to do right from the Fall when Adam made the thinly veiled suggestion that it was all His fault: "the woman *whom thou gavest to be with me*..." (Gen 3.12).

How swiftly circumstances can change! In a moment of time, the orchestra had become silent, the singers had become mute, the shouts of joy had become cries of indignation, and all because God had responded in judgment to carelessness and disobedience.

It seems that David sensed that he was courting danger, and his indignation gave way to fear: "And David was afraid of God that day" (v.12). We suggest that this was a feeling of real terror rather than the reverential fear of God of which Scripture speaks so frequently. When Adam sinned he said, "I was afraid...I hid" (Gen 3.10). He wanted no contact with a holy God. David's fear of God invoked the same reaction so now he tried to keep God at a distance: hence his reluctance to "bring the ark of God home to me". He would have felt so uncomfortable to have that symbol of the divine presence anywhere near his residence in the city of David.

Consistently in Scripture manifestations of divine power or discipline made people want to distance themselves from deity. Said Peter, "Depart from me; for I am a sinful man, O Lord" (Lk 5.8). After the judgment on Ananias and Sapphira the record is that "of the rest durst no man join himself to them" (Acts 5.13). In the same way, on this occasion David had the inclination to isolate himself from God.

May God preserve us from acting in any way that would debar us from experiencing the presence of the Lord in every area of life. The two who journeyed to Emmaus welcomed Christ into the home (Lk 24.29). Boaz brought God into the workplace (Ruth 2.4). The divine presence can be enjoyed in the assembly (1 Cor 14.25). Let us do all in our power to create conditions that make it possible to enjoy the warmth of His presence in each of these spheres.

The fact that the site of the tragedy was called Perez-uzza, *the breach of Uzza*, "unto this day" would be a perpetual reminder to succeeding generations of the holiness of God and the danger of being reckless in their dealings with Him. Similarly, a pile of stones in the valley of Achor was a permanent monument to the sin of Achan with its sad implications for the whole nation of Israel (Josh 7.26). Today, there is no need for place names and monuments to provide solemn reminders for us. We have in print the inspired history of divine dealings with men, with the general principle that "these things happened unto them by way of example; and they were written for our admonition, upon whom the ends of the ages are come" (1 Cor 10.11, RV). Let us all be warned.

Verses 13-14: The House of Obed-edom

Divine intervention now changed the plans. The procession had been heading for "the city of David" but was immediately redirected to the "house of Obed-edom the Gittite". Presumably when David "carried it aside" it was now done in the proper manner. The possibility is that this man was a Gentile immigrant from Gath of the Philistines, and it is wonderful to think that he was honoured to be the guardian of that sacred vessel. He had drawn nigh to God; now God was drawing nigh to him (James 4.8). However, some commentators regard him as a Levite from the Levitical city of Gath-rimmon (Josh 21.24-25), and, if that be so, then he was very suitable to be the custodian of the ark in this situation, and for his subsequent duties in connection with it. Whatever the case, we salute the man's courage in being willing to give the ark sanctuary under his roof. He knew how the Lord had plagued the Philistines because of it, and of the tragedy at Beth-shemesh. He had likely witnessed the sudden collapse of Uzza, and had watched David shrink back from further involvement with it. Yet such was his loyalty to his God that he made room for Him, with the full knowledge that the presence of the ark demanded moral and spiritual suitability on his part. Little wonder he was subsequently blessed.

Mention is made of the Gittite's family, and it is clear that the man's willingness to accommodate the ark brought blessing to the whole household, for "the Lord blessed the house of Obed-edom". Previous paragraphs have shown that sin can have disastrous consequences for a whole family as illustrated in Achan and Gehazi, but here we discover that a man's willingness to give God His place can mean blessing for the family.

We are not told the precise nature of this blessing, but it took in "all that he had". The assumption is that in terms of health, material prosperity, and productive fields, it was soon evident that for this family, the graph of their circumstances was on a steep upward curve.

Welcoming God and giving Him His place in our lives spells inevitable blessing. In this present age there is no guarantee of the physical and financial benefits that were the product of obedience in Old Testament times. The exponents of the so called "prosperity gospel" ignore the fact that early Christians had to "(take) joyfully the spoiling of (their) goods" (Heb 10.34), or that even such well-used men of God as Timothy and Trophimus experienced sickness (1 Tim 5.23; 2 Tim 4.20). God's blessings for us are primarily spiritual and we have been endowed with every one of them (Eph 1.3). The enjoyment of these blessings will be in the measure in which we give God His place in our lives as Obed-edom did here.

Having given place to the ark, and having enjoyed subsequent blessing, Obed-edom had no desire to be separated from it again. The day would come when they would remove it from the precincts of his home, but he travelled with it, and became one of the "doorkeepers for the ark" (15.24). The blessing that he had experienced was maintained, for as late as 26.4-5 we are told of his extensive family, "for God blessed him". For Obed-edom, permanent devotion and commitment to the ark meant the permanent blessing of God on his life.

The ark was in the home of Obed-edom for "three months". That meant blessing for him, but it also meant that three months were lost as far as progress towards the ultimate goal of a house for God was concerned. Sin and disobedience always hinder progress. When Miriam sinned she was put out of the camp for seven days, and the record of Scripture is, "and the people journeyed not till Miriam was brought in again" (Num 12.15): her sin impeded the onward march of the people. In this passage, David's blunder threw the project back for three months.

Evidently, the three months gave him time to reflect, and when he heard of Obed-edom's blessing (2 Sam 6.12), he was emboldened to revive his plan to bring the ark to Jerusalem, the record of which is found in ch.15.

1 CHRONICLES 14

As far as chronology is concerned, it would appear that the events of chapter 14 precede those of chapter 13. Indeed the account of 2 Samuel 5-6 outlines the sequence of things in chronological order. It was suggested previously, that in 1 Chronicles the order is to emphasise the priority that David gave to the ark and the temple. In chapter 13 mention is made of his desire to bring up the ark to Jerusalem before there is any talk about his own house in this chapter; he was putting God's interests first.

After the disastrous attempt to bring up the ark in chapter 13, there is an interlude before the successful operation of chapter 15. This chapter deals with domestic issues, and matters relating to defence. In verses 1-7 there are details of David's house and family; the story of the first attack of the Philistines occupies verses 8-12; and the rest of the chapter (verses 13-17) tells of them regrouping and making a fresh assault.

Verses 1-2: David's House

The chapter shows that while David had bitter enemies to the south, on his northern border he had a staunch ally in Hiram king of Tyre. As king of a very minor state he may have lacked military power, but his expertise in other matters made him an invaluable supporter of both David and Solomon. The man's consistency is to be commended, for Scripture records that "Hiram was ever a lover of David" (1 Kings 5.1). Loyalty that spans the years is so valuable, whether it is faithful commitment to a friend or consistent fidelity to the Lord. The shifting circumstances of life will never affect that kind of devotion.

It was in the providence of God that a bond was created between the two men, for Hiram's resources and skills were priceless when it came to the building of the temple. God is always a step in front, so, a generation ahead of time, he promoted a friendship which would facilitate the construction of His sanctuary.

Hiram's (2438) name means "noble", and he was one of those persons in Scripture who lived up to his name, for not only was he noble as to his status in life but he was also noble in his character.

It appears that Hiram took the initiative in providing a residence for David. Unsolicited, he sent materials and workmen to undertake the task. We know nothing of David's accommodation at that time, but happily the cave and the hideouts were all a thing of the past. The long period of rejection had given way to glory and kingship: Adullam had receded, and the palace beckoned. It is to David's credit that he had no grandiose notions of splendour, but had to be encouraged to embark on this venture to provide a home that was consistent with his new station in life - he saw the hand of God in it all (v.2).

The timber that Hiram sent was "timber of cedars" for only the very best would do for a king. In 1 Kings 4.33, a reference to Solomon's writings leaves us with the impression that the cedar tree was the most magnificent specimen of the flora of the district, with hyssop the most insignificant. So then, David's majestic edifice was constructed of the very best material: "I dwell in an house of cedars", he said (17.1). The great Sovereign of the universe also demands the best. "Cursed be the deceiver, which hath in his flock a male, and voweth, and sacrificeth unto the Lord a corrupt thing: *for I am a great King*, saith the Lord of hosts" (Mal 1.14). May we all be preserved from offering Him anything that is cheap or inferior.

As well as materials, Hiram sent men who were masons and carpenters. Among the Sidonians there were skilled craftsmen (1 Kings 5.6; 2 Chr 2.7-8), and their know-how was to be employed in building this house for David. The men who were qualified for the job were the men who did it. There is a lesson in that for assembly life. Materials and men have been provided for building a house for God. By that is meant that God has gifted men in various ways to accomplish His work. Spiritually speaking, the carpenter should not be doing the mason's job and vice versa. "As every man hath received the gift, even so minister *the same* one to another, as good stewards of the manifold grace of God" (1 Pet 4.10). Let us never encroach on anyone else's sphere of activity but exercise the gift that God has given us.

Hiram's initiative provided David with circumstantial evidence that his enthronement was of the Lord, for "David perceived that the Lord had confirmed him king over Israel" (v.2). Sometimes the Lord does use developing circumstances to give His people the assurance that they are being carried along in the stream of His will for their lives. David had the same kind of confidence as the missionary band of Acts 16.10 who went into Macedonia, "assuredly gathering that the Lord had called us for to preach the gospel unto them". They, like David, had had their ups and downs, their disappointments and their thwarted plans, but now there was a happy contentment that God was directing their course. The quiet satisfaction of being assured of the will of God for our lives is something that is to be coveted. "Live the rest of your time…to the will of God" (1 Pet 4.2, RV).

In v.2 we are given an insight into one of the reasons for God's choice of David as king: it was "because of his people Israel", or "for his people Israel's sake" (RV). Under David's wise patronage the kingdom would be "lifted up on high" and all for the benefit of its subjects. During Saul's tenure, the kingdom had been greatly diminished as the affairs of state became secondary to his obsession to eliminate David. As a result of his maladministration, the Philistines were the winners and his people were the losers. Now, with David at the helm, the power and prestige of the kingdom was on the ascendancy, and the fear and impoverishment that had been endemic under the previous government had melted away.

God always wants the very best for His people, and with that in view, He installed David as king. His mandate from God was clear: "He that ruleth over men must be just, ruling in the fear of God" (2 Sam 23.3). If God's people were to be happy and prosperous, justice and equity were to be the order of the day, and so God appointed a God-fearing man, a man of great integrity. God still wants the best for His people, and so His ideal is that in the assembly there will be leaders who will "take care of the church of God" (1 Tim 3.5). For the good of their people, let these men be firm but fair, true but tender.

Verses 3-7: David's Family

In eastern lands it was customary for the ruling monarch to have his harem, but the practice was never the mind of God for the king of Israel. God's ideal was always a one-man one-woman relationship. As noted earlier in the commentary, in Deuteronomy 17.16-17 Israel's king was forbidden to "multiply" horses, wives, or silver and gold. David got two out of three right. Captured horses were hamstrung (18.4), acquired wealth was devoted to God (29.16), but sadly he was fatally flawed when it came to his relationships with the opposite sex - he multiplied wives. When it comes to obedience, God will never be satisfied with a ratio of two out of three. "O that there were such an heart in them, that they would fear me, and keep *all* my commandments always" (Deut 5.29). He longs for the wholehearted obedience of His people even from the point of view of their own good. "O that thou hadst hearkened to my commandments! then had thy peace been as a river, and thy righteousness as the waves of the sea" (Is 48.18).

Comments were made regarding David's sons when they featured in the genealogical section of the book (3.1-9).

Verses 8-9: The Philistines' First Assault

Having dealt effectively with Saul, the Philistines now intended to crush David's fledging regime. The plan was to strike swiftly in the early stages of his administration to take advantage of a novice king. There was a massive show of strength; "*all* the Philistines went up to seek David" (v.8); they would take no chances, for no doubt they had memories of defeat at his hands. This was no marauding band of plunderers, but every brigade was marshalled with the ambition of smashing David's power. What they had "heard" about him being accorded his rightful place in the nation provoked their attack. Of course, their assault was unsuccessful, for "*the Lord* had established him king over Israel" (v.2, RV).

One or two practical issues emerge from this. First, when Christ is given His rightful place in the hearts of His people as individuals, or among them collectively, it will not go unnoticed; the enemy is sure to "hear". His irritation will be such that it will incite him to attack. For example, when Peter was used by the Father to accord to the Saviour His proper position as "the Christ, the Son of the living God", the devil was soon on the scene to attack him and to use him in an attempt to sidetrack the Lord Jesus (Mt 16.13-23). In days of devoted fervour then, let us be vigilant, in the expectation of an imminent attack.

Second, let us understand that our enemy is unprincipled, and will make every attempt to take advantage of a new situation or of inexperience. No sooner had the Lord Jesus left Nazareth to embark on a new sphere of ministry than there was the temptation in the wilderness. No sooner had He stepped out of the boat into new territory than "*immediately* there met him out of the tombs a man with an unclean spirit" (Mk 5.2). No sooner is good seed sown than "Satan cometh *immediately*, and taketh away the word that was sown in their hearts" (Mk 4.15). No sooner had Paul arrived in Philippi with the gospel than he had the unwelcome attention of the "damsel possessed with a spirit of divination" (Acts 16.16). Let us be aware of the devil's designs on new converts, new assemblies, new ventures, new overseers or whatever. While people are trying to find their feet, he wants to knock them off their feet. He attempts to take advantage of inexperience.

Third, if God has established a servant or a work, the enemy's attacks will be frustrated. "If God be for us, who can be against us?" (Rom 8.31). "Greater is he that is in you, than he that is in the world" (1 Jn 4.4). When the Lord opens, "no man shutteth" (Rev 3.7). At Dothan the immature young man failed to see "the mountain…full of horses and chariots of fire" and had to be informed that "they that be with us are more than they that be with them" (2 Kings 6.15-17). The enlightened man of God enjoyed these glorious truths. Let us be encouraged that, despite enemy activity, there will not fail "ought of any good thing which the Lord (hath) spoken" (Josh 21.45).

With news of the Philistine advance David "went out against them" (v.8); he was never one for retreat. When he was a youth he "hasted, and ran toward the army to meet the Philistine" (1 Sam 17.48), so here he marched to confront the invaders. Despite his courage, he was not incautious. Perhaps in the emergency he had set out instinctively without any reference to heaven, but that was soon rectified when "David inquired of God" (v.10). Jacob's situation was similar. He was so excited when he heard of the glory of Joseph that he reacted immediately; "I will go and see him before I die" (Gen 45.28), and so he set out. But then he too realised his omission and the procession stopped at Beersheba to seek divine sanction (46.1-7). Even if we have embarked on some course of action without seeking the mind of God, when the oversight has come to light, it would be well to pause to "inquire of God".

The valley of Rephaim was familiar territory for the Philistines for they had encamped there during David's days at Adullam (11.15). It seems to have been a very productive area of the land (Is 17.5), so perhaps they saw in it a source of sustenance and hence they gravitated there and "spread themselves" (6584) amidst its fertile fields. Possibly they saw in their familiarity with the surroundings a strategic factor in the battle.

Some translations prefer the phrase which indicates that they "made a raid in the valley of Rephaim". If acceptable, it suggests perhaps that in the course of their invasion they had their eye on plunder, and halted to take advantage of the prosperous nature of the district before throwing themselves upon David and his forces.

Verses 10-12: Victory

"David inquired of God" (v.10). It is to his credit that he did so on numerous occasions, although towards the end of his reign he allowed a problem to persist for three years before he "inquired of the Lord" (2 Sam 21.1). It is better to do as he did here, and seek God's face at the start. David was not guilty of Joshua's blunder when he and his fellow-leaders "asked not counsel at the mouth of the Lord" (Josh 9.14). Let us be like David rather than Joshua and be among those who are "continuing instant in prayer" (Rom 12.12).

David had two questions for God, and the assumption is that he received the answer to these questions by means of the Urim which God used to communicate His mind (Num 27.21). When Saul's administration was in its death throes, "the Lord answered him not…by Urim" (1 Sam 28.6). The answer to David's first question was, "Go up", and the answer to his second was, "I will deliver them into thine hand". The promise of v.10 was fulfilled in v.11. "It is impossible for God to lie" (Heb 6.18, RV).

Encouraged by a green light from heaven, David attacked, and won the day. It is always best to wait for a response to a request for guidance before actually advancing. In the Garden of Gethsemane the disciples asked the Lord Jesus, "Lord, shall we smite with the sword?". Before there was time for a response, "one of them smote the servant of the high priest" (Lk 22.49-50). Peter did not wait for divine approval, so what he did was without divine sanction.

As in ch.13, a locality was named as a consequence of an event that took place there, but this time the circumstances were much happier (v.11). Baal-perazim (1188), "the place of breakings forth", was named thus because David's victory under the hand of God was so comprehensive that he likened it to the unleashing of a great torrent that swept his enemies to the side. That is how it appealed to his poetic temperament.

It is significant that David attributed the triumph to God; "*God* hath broken in upon mine enemies by mine hand". It was his hand - that is, he was the human instrument, but it was a work of God. The reason why God whittled down Gideon's army was because, with a larger force, they could not be relied upon to ascribe the victory to Him: "lest Israel vaunt themselves against me, saying, Mine own hand hath saved me" (Judg 7.2). God could trust David to give Him the credit. When Paul and Barnabas returned to Antioch at the end of a very encouraging missionary tour, they were quick to pinpoint the source of their success; "they rehearsed all that *God* had done with them, and how *he* had opened the door of faith unto the Gentiles" (Acts 14.27). Let us all adopt the attitude of the ancient Psalmist, "Not unto us, O Lord, not unto us, but unto thy name give glory" (Ps 115.1).

Very evidently, the Philistines had brought their idols into the fray, and in the wake of defeat they were strewn across the battlefield (v.12). David's wisdom is again in evidence in that he "gave a commandment, and they were burned with fire". These were the gods to whom the news of Saul's defeat had been carried in 10.9. See what had become of them now! In the circumstances, David's commandment was very appropriate. Human nature is so fickle and perverse that the idols of a defeated foe could easily become a potential spiritual hazard. When Amaziah king of Judah conquered the forces of Seir, Scripture records that "he brought the gods of the children of Seir, and set them up to be his gods, and bowed down himself before them, and burned incense unto them" (2 Chr 25.14). The whole situation defied logic. These so called gods were impotent to help and protect their own people and now Amaziah had become one of their devotees. Understanding the dangers, David dealt with the Philistine idols decisively. He was not alone in the effective way he treated false gods. Moses "burnt (the golden calf) in the fire, and ground it to powder" (Ex 32.20). In the days of Joash, Baal's altars and images were broken in pieces "thoroughly" (2 Kings 11.18). Hezekiah "brake in pieces the brasen serpent" that had become an object of worship (2 Kings 18.4). Jacob was less dramatic in the way he disposed of the idols and earrings - he "hid them under the oak which was by Shechem" (Gen 35.4). There is no record of them ever being retrieved, but the possibility was there, particularly when there was such an obvious landmark to pinpoint their position. David and these others dealt with the idols far more determinedly.

"Little children, keep yourselves from idols" (1 Jn 5.21) was a word to believers. If there is an idol that gives trouble, reducing the time that we allocate to it is not sufficient, or trimming the budget that we devote to it is not the answer. Figuratively, or perhaps even literally, we must burn it with fire and thus put it beyond recall. "If thy right hand offend thee, cut it off, *and cast it from thee*" (Mt 5.30). We need to be as decisive as that.

Verses 13-17: The Second Attack

Winning the battle did not end the war, and the Philistines regrouped and came at David again. (v.13). The enemies of God's people are always very persistent as is the arch-enemy, the devil himself. Scripture records that, having been defeated by the Lord Jesus in the wilderness, Satan "departed from him *for a season*" (Lk 4.13), with the inference that he would be back. Potiphar's wife "spake to Joseph *day by day*" (Gen 39.10); she never acknowledged defeat. The Pharisees were unrelenting in their harassment of the man who had been born blind: "Then *again* the Pharisees also asked him…" (Jn 9.15); "They say unto the blind man *again*" (v.17); "Then *again* called they the man that was blind" (v.24); "Then said they to him *again*…" (v.26). Let it be a warning to us all lest we ever become complacent, for as surely as we lower our guard, the enemy will come back at us with fresh resolve.

"David inquired again of God" (v.14). The natural thing to do would have been to attack immediately. It was the same enemy, it was the same terrain, the previous tactics had been so very successful, why delay? But the man who was in touch with his God took time to seek His guidance, and he was instructed in a new strategy. There is a valuable lesson in that. Previous success does not mean that it would be the mind of God to do the same thing in exactly the same way the next time round. For example, after a fruitful series of gospel meetings it is a temptation to say, "Same time again next year, same venue, same preacher", but do we "inquire of God"? The "streets and lanes of the city" proved to be a successful source of guests in the parable of the great supper. Another incursion into these areas may have been thought wise, but the servant's energies were channelled in a different direction when he was sent to "the highways and hedges" (Lk 14.21-23). It is always best to "inquire *again* of God".

On this occasion the line of attack was to be somewhat different and there had to be no frontal assault. David's forces were to veer away from the Philistines towards some mulberry trees and attack from a different angle (vv.14-15). They had to hold their fire until they heard "a sound of going in the tops of the mulberry trees" and then "go out to battle". Presumably they were to await the rising wind rustling the leaves of the trees. The sound was an indication that God was at work, that He "had gone forth before (them) to smite the host of the Philistines". Even the nature of the sound should have encouraged them. The word "going" (6807) is translated "marching" in various translations (for example, RV, JND, ESV), and it leaves the impression of God stepping out ahead of them to confront the foe, which indeed He did. "The Lord your God which goeth before you, he shall fight for you" (Deut 1.30).

Again, there is surely instruction in all of that. In the Word of God, the wind is illustrative of the Holy Spirit of God (Jn 3.8). In every initiative for God we need to wait His guidance (Acts 13.2) and depend on His power (1 Cor 2.4; 1 Thess 1.5). Regeneration with its cleansing effect is by His divine activity (Titus 3.5). In our passage, the wind was indicative of the divine presence, and to operate independent of the wind of the Spirit is to be bereft of the presence and power of God.

The idea of God marching ahead of His people was seized on by abolitionists in the US and enshrined in The Battle Hymn of the Republic: "Our God is marching on". Let the concept be a stimulus to us in our Christian service, encouraged by the awareness that He controls and paves the way as when Paul expressed his desire: "Now God himself and our Father, and our Lord Jesus Christ, direct our way unto you" (1 Thess 3.11).

"David therefore did as God commanded him" (v.16). The statement is brief and simple, but how telling! It is what God wants of every one of us, simple obedience. The Lord Jesus instructed the servants in John 2 to "Fill the waterpots with water". Their obedience was swift, unqualified, and wholehearted: "they filled them up to the brim" (v.7). Obedience was maintained when He said, "bear unto the governor of the feast. And they bear it" (v.8). Obedience is a feature of every genuine believer in Christ; "hereby we do know that we know him, if we keep his commandments" (1 Jn 2.3).

Obedience brought victory, for "they smote the host of the Philistines from Gibeon even to Gazer". The mention of these geographical locations indicates a complete rout of the enemy.

When we walk with the Lord,
In the light of His Word,
What a glory He sheds on our way!
While we do His good will
He abides with us still,
And with all who will trust and *obey*.

Trust and obey; for there's no other way
To be happy in Jesus, but to trust and obey.
(John H. Sammis)

Suppressing the Philistines brought David universal fame (v.17). At v.8 when the Philistines "heard" of him, it provoked them to attack. When the nations heard about him now it struck terror into their hearts, a fear that was divinely induced. It was the kind of fear that gripped the people of the region when Israel first invaded (Deut 2.25), a fear that was acknowledged by such as Rahab the harlot (Josh 2.9-11). Throughout the times of the Judges and in the days of Saul no one need really have feared them, for as a nation they were often demoralised as they suffered under the discipline of their God. Now, with the ascendancy of David, that fear had been reinstated. In 13.12, "David was afraid of God". Here, the nations were afraid of David.

One can hardly read this verse without being reminded of Luke's record of the Lord Jesus: "there went out a fame of him through all the region round about"; "the fame of him went out into every place of the country round about" (Lk 4.14,37). There is one major difference between the two contexts. David was famed for warfare, bloodshed, and military supremacy. The Lord Jesus was famed for kindness, healing and tender compassion. "Hallelujah, what a Saviour"!

Believers will be famed and respected if they follow the pattern of the Thessalonians: "in every place your faith to God-ward is spread abroad" (1 Thess 1.8). The Romans had a similar reputation: "you faith is spoken of throughout the whole world"; "your obedience is come abroad unto all men" (Rom 1.8; 16.19). Let news of our faith and obedience fan out, just as surely as "the fame of David went out into all lands".

1 CHRONICLES 15

This chapter resumes the narrative of the journey of the ark to Jerusalem. The story had been suspended at the end of chapter 13, but is now picked up, and arrives at a happy conclusion. Transporting the ark by an illegitimate means had proved disastrous, but by resorting to "the due order" (v.13) the task was accomplished with much joy. The experience of chapter 13 had left David reluctant to proceed (13.12), but on hearing of the blessing that the presence of the ark had brought to Obed-edom, his desire was rekindled (2 Sam 6.12).

The chapter could be summarised as follows. Verses 1-2 record details of the preparation for bringing the ark by providing "a place" for it and stipulating the means of transport. In verses 3-11 the people are regathered for the event, and particular reference is made to those of the Levitical family who were to be involved. They receive their instructions in verses 12-13, and comply with these instructions in verses 14-15. Singers, instrumentalists and doorkeepers are listed in verses 16-24. The ark's journey is recorded in the rest of the chapter (verses 17-29) and includes David's ecstatic behaviour which stirred scorn in the heart of Michal.

Verse 1: A Place for the Ark

Before the record of the bringing of the ark to Jerusalem, there is a brief statement regarding David's own houses in the city. The mention of "houses" in the plural is most likely a reference to the fact that his various wives with their offspring would be accommodated in different locations, in the sense that they would each have their own apartments. The point is disposed of briefly because the focus is still on the religious aspect of David's life rather than the domestic. He was not negligent of his family responsibilities, but the overriding concern of his life was the ark of God.

It appears that, in every way, David was now exercising much greater care than formerly. On the previous occasion he was in such an enthusiastic rush that no thought had been given even to where to locate the ark at Jerusalem. This time, he "prepared a place" for it. (A surface thought is that here we have a child of God preparing a place for something that typifies Christ, but in John 14.2 we have Christ preparing a place for the child of God. Here we have a man of Israel preparing a place for God, but in Revelation 12.6 we have God preparing a place for persecuted Israel.)

The word "prepared" (3559) is used frequently in the book, particularly in relation to David's groundwork for the building of the temple. As the narrative proceeds we will be told of the things that he prepared, with this phrase summarising it all: "David prepared abundantly before his death" (22.5). The word is also used for the site that he provided for the temple: "mount Moriah…the place that David had prepared in the threshingfloor of Ornan the Jebusite" (2 Chr 3.1). So he prepared a place for the ark and he prepared both the materials and the site for the temple. His experience should be a lesson to us lest we should be either haphazard or lackadaisical in our approach to the things of God. Thought and preparation must precede any activity, to say nothing of the constant need for prayer and divine guidance.

In the previous chapter this word (3559) is used of God, there translated "confirmed" (v.2) as when "David perceived that the Lord had *confirmed* him king over Israel". On a number of occasions it is translated "established" (e.g. 17.11) in reference to God establishing either David or Solomon's throne or house. There is reciprocation here. God was preparing things for David, and David was preparing things for God.

At the time when David pitched this "tent" for the ark, the tabernacle was still at Gibeon (2 Chr 1.3-4). It appears that David had an insight into the fact that Jerusalem was the place where the divine presence was to dwell and hence the provision of the tent as an interim measure. The Lord had chosen "the mount Zion which he loved" (Ps 78.68). It would not be long before David felt the tent to be inadequate (17.1), but in the meantime it became the temporary shelter for the ark.

Verse 2: The Due Order

We learn here that the method of transport adopted in ch.13 had not been employed inadvertently. David had known that only the Levites should "carry the ark" (Num 4.15). Sadly, even although he had been familiar with the divine order, he deviated from it with the terrible results that have already received comment. He knew what had been written and had ignored it. To violate divine commands knowingly is to risk retribution.

The Levites had been "chosen" to carry the ark, just as in every generation a sovereign God makes choice of His servants. In the context of service, the Lord Jesus said to His disciples, "Ye have not chosen me, but I have chosen you, and ordained you, that ye should go and bring forth fruit, and that your fruit should remain" (Jn 15.16). Paul had been separated from his mother's womb for a ministry to "preach (Christ) among the heathen" (Gal 1.15-16). God still appoints His people their tasks, and it is important for us all to have a sense of calling as far as our own sphere of activity is concerned, for with it will come a corresponding sense of responsibility.

Responsibility for the ark would rest with the Levites "for ever", that is, as long as the Levitical order of things was in place. A notable exception to this was in Joshua 3-4, and again in ch.6 in the circumstances of the crossing of Jordan and the fall of Jericho. On these occasions, the priests carried the ark, but then, they were Kohathites, and what they did was with a divine mandate.

Verse 3: All Israel Gathered

As in 13.5, "all Israel" assembled to escort the ark to Jerusalem, by which we understand that representatives of every tribe were present. It is commendable that despite the previous catastrophe, there was still the will to co-operate with David's exercise to give God His place among His people. In the verse, emphasis is again laid on the fact that on this occasion everything was properly in place, for the enjoyment of God's presence demands necessary preparation on the part of His people. The tent was in readiness to receive the sacred chest.

Verses 4-11: The Levites

Once more, David called for the priests and the Levites, and these verses focus particularly on the names of some Levites who were present, together with the numbers of those associated with them. All three branches of the Levitical family were present, although on this occasion only the Kohathites were involved in the main function of carrying the ark. Others had ancillary duties.

In these verses, a recurring phrase is of interest: "the chief, and his brethren". Those connected to the chiefs are said to be their brethren, and not their subordinates. Perhaps it is a reminder to those in leadership among God's people, that those whom they shepherd are their brethren and are to be treated as such and not with the overbearing attitude that Peter described as "lording it over the charge allotted to you" (1 Pet 5.3, RV).

Verses 12-13: Instructions for the Journey

On this occasion, before setting out with the ark, David held a conference with the priests and Levites to ensure that they were all familiar with their responsibilities. There were positive instructions, and then a solemn reminder of the tragic incident of ch.13 to reinforce the importance of carrying out proceedings "after the due order". This time, the lesson of history had been learned.

Those addressed were the priests and those designated as "the chief of the fathers of the Levites". They were instructed to sanctify themselves, which in the history of Israel had involved physical washing and avoidance of the marriage bed (Ex 19.14-15). "Be ye clean, that bear the vessels of the Lord" (Is 52.11). Applied spiritually, there has to be moral and spiritual suitability for involvement in divine things, "a vessel unto honour, sanctified, and meet for the master's use" (2 Tim 2.21).

David gave these leaders the responsibility of ensuring that their "brethren" were also sanctified, and the simple lesson is that those who have the rule over the people of God "watch for (their) souls" (Heb 13.17). Paul's message to the elders at Ephesus was, "Take heed therefore unto yourselves, and to all the flock, over the which the Holy Ghost hath made you overseers" (Acts 20.28). It is an echo of what we have here - "sanctify yourselves, both ye *and your brethren*".

The reminder of the previous sad episode was a salutary warning to them: "*ye* did it not at the first". Is there the suggestion that there had been reluctance on their part? Had the new cart been their brainchild? Was it a scheme to avoid the backbreaking task of carrying that weighty vessel?

Even if they were culpable, David acknowledged his part in the sorry affair when he said, "*we* sought him not after the due order". As observed in the comments on ch.13, leaders have to take responsibility for what happens under their superintendence.

Here, David acknowledged that for the carrying of the ark, there was a "due order", a Biblical way of doing things. There is a Biblical way of behaving in the home and in the workplace, and in the assembly. Deviation from Scriptural standards inevitably displeases God, so if there are matters that need to be "set in order" (1 Cor 11.34), let us give diligence to make the necessary adjustments.

Verses 14-15: Preparation and Performance

Complying with David's commands, these Levites "sanctified themselves to bring up the ark...". Whatever was involved in their preparing for the task, they did it. In a very special way, the Lord Jesus, for our sakes, sanctified Himself. He set Himself apart with a view to the work of the cross (Jn 17.19). In His case, no moral preparation was required for the work, but in a definite way He consecrated Himself to undertake it. There is our pattern. Let us set ourselves apart to do what has to be done in a focused committed way making any preparation that is necessary for the task in hand.

This time "the Levites bare the ark of God upon their shoulders". They were doing it under command from David, but our verse stresses that what was being done had been commanded by Moses, and he in turn had given instructions by "the word of the Lord". The Lord, Moses, David, the Levites - truth that had God as its source was being communicated from one to another. It is a Biblical principle. "The things that thou hast heard of me among many witnesses, the same commit thou unto faithful men, who shall be able to teach others also" (2 Tim 2.2). It is the duty of each generation to relay the truth of God to the next, so that Scriptural practices can be maintained over the passing years.

As has already been suggested, the proceedings here were based on such passages as Numbers 4.15 and 7.9. When the pattern of the ark was first given, the staves received a mention as being an integral part of the vessel, "that the ark may be borne with them" (Ex 25.13-15). They were not to be taken from their rings, and indeed were only removed when eventually the ark had its permanent resting place in the temple when its journeys were finally over (2 Chr 5.9).

Verses 16-24: Singers and Doorkeepers

As in ch.13, transporting the ark was accompanied by singing and music, and this time singers and instrumentalists were provided from the ranks of the Levites. The choice of participants seems to have been more selective than on the previous occasion when "David and all Israel played before God with all their might" (13.8). It is another indication of the increased thought and care that David had put into this fresh venture.

Despite the previous disaster, the keynote here was to be joy; note the recurring phrase, "with joy" (vv.16,25). This had to be a joyous occasion and contributing to the joy were the vocal expressions of praise - "lifting up the voice with joy". There was an awareness that doing things carefully and reverently and "after the due order" meant that all could be accomplished "with joy". We apply two lessons. First, in the life of the New Testament church, when divine order is observed joy will ensue. Second, expressions of praise can be "with joy" if they are articulating Biblical truths and not mere sentiment, allied with singing "with (the) heart" (Eph 5.19, RV), or as here, "by lifting up the voice". Muttering hymns and spiritual songs almost inaudibly does not portray any concept of joy!

Some of the participating Levites were named in ch.6, and observations regarding them were made in that section of the commentary.

In v.18 some are said to be "of the second degree". The word "degree" is not in the original Hebrew, but translators feel the need for some word to follow "second" and most choose the words "rank" or "order". Here were men who, like the military men of a previous chapter, "attained not to the first three", but whose contribution was invaluable. It is another lesson for us that in every sphere of Christian activity those who appear to be in the "second rank" as opposed to those who are in the limelight have a very necessary part to play, not only for the good of the work, but for the glory of God as is the case in this context.

Some of those in "the second degree" were doorkeepers (v.18), so they were being asked to fulfil a double role, and indeed some of them as players of stringed instruments were to "excel" (v.21) or "lead" (RV). It is unclear whether it is the men or the instruments to which the idea of leading refers, but the two are hardly divisible. The point is that it was men of the second degree who were appointed to give the lead, in that their stringed instruments took precedence over the percussion section of the orchestra. Let any who think themselves inferior see themselves as having tremendous potential for God. Like some of these men they may be asked to be involved in more than one sphere of activity, or on occasions their duties may incorporate a leading role.

Chenaniah was the man who directed the proceedings of the day (v.22). The phrase "chief of the Levites, was for song" conveys the fact that he was in charge of musical affairs on that auspicious occasion. He was qualified for such an assignment "because he was skilful", and we have been learning frequently in this book that God uses those who are equipped for the job on hand. Jael used a tent peg and hammer to strike a blow for God. These were things with which she was familiar as a nomad (Judg 4.21). When Peter, a fisherman and untrained in martial skills, used a sword in the defence of his Master, it was to no effect (Jn 18.10). Let us be involved in what we are gifted for and leave other things to those who have been fitted for them.

Chenaniah imparted his knowledge to others for "he instructed about the song", and although this is in reference to the particular occasion, it illustrates a general principle that knowledge should be passed on to others. The knowledge that the Colossians had of spiritual truth had been "learned" from Epaphras (Col 1.7). From their experience of life, older Christian women should be able to "train" the younger women in matters of homecare and family duty (Titus 2.4, RV). King Lemuel was the beneficiary of his mother's knowledge (Prov 31.1). These illustrations all demonstrate the importance of being a channel of knowledge rather than a reservoir.

The fact that there were to be "doorkeepers for the ark" (vv.23,24) is an indication that it was still necessary to guard it from inquisitive eyes as in the case of the men of Beth-shemesh (1 Sam 6.19), or from the impious hand as in the case of Uzza (1 Chr 13.9). Doorkeeping was important. It was among the young Samuel's first duties in the service of God (1 Sam 3.15), and the sons of Korah esteemed the task as being a great honour: "I had rather be a doorkeeper in the house of my God, than to dwell in the tents of wickedness" (Ps 84.10). Amidst all the excitement of the ark being brought then, the religious euphoria that had characterised the previous attempt was now being tempered by the caution and respect that the occasion demanded.

It is interesting that Obed-edom was ranked among the doorkeepers of the ark (v.24). No doubt his appointment was in recognition of the sterling work he had done as its temporary custodian, preserving it as he did from any damage or any unwelcome intrusion. His acceptance of the appointment is an indication of his attachment to the ark. Its presence had brought blessing to his household, and he had no desire for his connection with it to be severed. Again, two lessons can be applied. First, we have to prove ourselves worthy for any service for God as when it is said of the deacon, "let these also first be proved" (1 Tim 3.10). Second, let our attachment to Christ be as strong and enduring as was Obed-edom's commitment to the ark.

Verses 25-28: All Israel Brought Up the Ark

The ark's journey is not as detailed here as in the parallel passage in 2 Samuel 6, but there is duplication of the major facts. The start of the journey is recorded as they brought it "out of the house of Obed-edom with joy" (v.25), and there was still "shouting" at journey's end (v.28). This time, nothing had happened to mar the occasion and inhibit the joy.

It is delightful that v.26 records that "God helped the Levites that bare the ark of the covenant". The nature of the help is not specified, but after the previous incident one can imagine the terror that filled every heart as their hands were put to the staves of the ark. God gave help to overcome these fears. Again, the ark was an extremely heavy vessel, overlaid as it was with gold. The Lord gave help by granting the physical strength for the journey. For all of these Levites, shouldering the ark was a new experience, and the Lord gave help to cope. Help from God is so necessary for every aspect and phase of life. Let us all appreciate it and never arrive at a point where we feel independent as did King Uzziah who "was marvellously helped, till he was strong" (2 Chr 26.15). Like Paul, believers who have weathered the storms of life and are still standing attribute it all to divine help rather than to their own grit and determination. "Having therefore obtained help of God, I continue unto this day…" (Acts 26.22).

The gratitude of the Levites for this divine help was expressed in their offering seven bullocks and seven rams. "What shall I render unto the Lord for all his benefits toward me?" (Ps 116.12). The question begs the thought that divine providence necessitates a response from the beneficiary. "The mercies of God" demand the logical response of a presented body (Rom 12.1). "The love of Christ" requires that its recipients should not "live unto themselves, but unto him which died for them, and rose again" (2 Cor 5.14-15). Here, grateful Levites presented their offerings.

In v.27 attention is drawn to the clothing of the participants. David and all his associates were "clothed (with robes) of fine linen" with David having added "an ephod of linen". "Vestures of fine linen" were deemed suitable attire for Joseph as he entered the employment of a king (Gen 41.42). Here, in the presence of a superior authority, a king sees the linen garment as appropriate dress for himself, as a token of his respect for divine majesty and holiness. We give him credit for that, but may question how appropriate it was for a king to wear an ephod which was connected more with priesthood. It should be said though that there was no thought of him acting in a priestly way by offering sacrifices or burning incense, but rather his participation was only in song. He had not fallen into the sin of which Uzziah was guilty, attempting to combine kingship and priesthood, an honour that God has reserved for His Son (2 Chr 26.16-23). For some strange reason, Gideon had a strong desire for an elaborate ephod and it became "a snare" to him and his family (Judg 8.24-28). However, we apply the lesson that if David felt it necessary to be suitably dressed for involvement in the things of God, a dress code should be in place today as we engage in worship and service. Where there is no "thus saith the Lord" we dare not legislate, but there is a danger of appearing so casual and slovenly as to bring into question one's respect for God. At the other extreme it is possible to be so overdressed that people may wonder about our motive, and judge the whole appearance to be ostentatious and out of keeping with the character of the lowly Nazarene whom we profess to serve. Surely there is a level of smartness that denotes a reverence for the presence of God without in any way attracting attention to ourselves.

Verse 29: Michal

Consistently, Scripture calls Michal "the daughter of Saul". It seems that after her initial infatuation with David she cooled, and her sympathies lay with her father who hated him so bitterly. True, there was an occasion when she saved his life, but even then an element of the story reveals that David and Michal were never really spiritually compatible. She used an image, a household god, to give the impression that David was still asleep in his bed (1 Sam 19.11-17). Whatever was such a large idol doing in David's home? It can only be assumed that Michal was the culprit, but in this passage too their incompatibility is obvious. She did not share David's enthusiasm for the ark of God, and when confronted with his exuberance "she despised him in her heart". Of course, according to the record of 2 Samuel 6.20, what was in her heart was expressed in biting sarcasm, "for out of the abundance of the heart the mouth speaketh" (Mt 12.34). The importance of both parties in a Christian marriage being spiritually compatible cannot be stressed enough, for if one is less enthusiastic than the other, it will certainly impair the spiritual partner's effectiveness in the service of God. Aquila and Priscilla serve as a noble example of what a Christian marriage should be. It has often been pointed out that you never read of the one without the other. They were at one in their commitment to the work of the Lord.

Another general lesson is that the enthusiastic committed Christian can expect criticism from those who are worldly and carnal as when the Corinthians "judged" Paul and had to be told that he was unfazed by their criticism for "he that judgeth me is the Lord" (1 Cor 4.1-5).

The reader could profitably explore the occasions in Scripture where windows feature, and among them a number where individuals were looking out of windows as did Michal here. Another line that could be followed is the number of people in the Word who were despised as was David in this passage. Most notable of course was He who was "despised and rejected of men" (Is 53.3), epitomised on an occasion when "they laughed him to scorn" (Mk 5.40). It was bad enough for God's anointed king to be despised, but for men and women to despise the Son of God is beyond comprehension.

Thus the chapter ends on a sour note, but the unpleasantness did not derail the great project that was on hand, for the next chapter commences with the ark being installed in the tent that David had prepared for it.

1 CHRONICLES 16

Subsequent to the harmonious music of chapter 15, metaphorically, Michal's intrusion had created a discordant note. Now there is a resumption of the happy atmosphere that attended the ark's journey from the house of Obed-edom to the city of David. In verses 1-3 there are celebrations associated with the ark being set in its tent. The appointment of Levites to "minister before the ark" is the theme of verses 4-6. The major section of the chapter is from verse 7 to verse 36 where there is the record of a psalm that David put into the hand of Asaph as being a suitable song of praise for the occasion. The psalm is comprised of sections of three psalms from the inspired psalter, though not quoted verbatim. The quotations are as follows: verses 8-22 - Psalm 105.1-15; verses 23-33 - Psalm 96.1-13; verse 34 - Psalm 106.1; verses 35-36 - Psalm 106.47-48.

Verses 37-38 summarise the details of the attendants of the ark, while verses 39-42 take us to Gibeon, the location of the tabernacle, where the priests still had daily responsibilities. Verse 43 records the dispersal of the people after the ark was settled in its place.

Verse 1: The Ark in the Midst

For the Kohathites, the end of their journey had come when they "set (the ark) in the midst of the tent that David had pitched for it". If the ark in Jordan (Josh 3-4) is a picture of the Lord Jesus in His baptism of suffering (Lk 12.50), the ark in Zion prefigures His glorious ascension, exaltation, and session at God's right hand.

"In the midst" seems such an appropriate phrase for a vessel that speaks so eloquently of Christ, for frequently that very phrase is used of the Lord Jesus, not least to describe the central place that He occupies in heaven itself (Rev 5.6). The One who was "in the midst" when impaled to the cross (Jn 19.18) is now the focus of heaven's interest and worship, and yet such is His omnipresence as a divine person that He is also in the midst of His gathered people below (Mt 18.20).

Installing the ark was the signal for offering "burnt sacrifices and peace offerings before God". The burnt offering was exclusively for God and for His pleasure. By contrast, God, the priest, and the offerer all had their portion of the peace offering. Possibly these peace offerings provided at least some of the flesh that David distributed to the people (v.3). The peace offering could be offered as an expression of thanksgiving, and also to accomplish a vow (Lev 7.12,16; 22.21). Both of these concepts seem appropriate here. The safe arrival of the ark after the ill-fated first attempt must have occasioned great thanksgiving, and so the peace offerings were presented. The pledge that David had made in his heart had now been fulfilled, and so there were the accompanying peace offerings.

Verses 2-3: He Blessed the People

Having given God first place, David turned his attention to the people who were in attendance and "he blessed the people in the name of the Lord". The fact that the blessing was pronounced "in the name of the Lord" is an indication that David regarded himself as a representative of God with some authority to pronounce such a blessing. The benediction was accompanied by tangible expressions of blessing as he distributed these various items of foodstuffs to all the people. Most translations render "a flagon of wine" as "a cake of raisins".

As was frequently the case in Scripture, David had both a God-ward function, and a man-ward function. Melchizedec blessed both God and Abram (Gen 14.19-20). Simeon blessed God, and Joseph and Mary (Lk 2.28,34). The Aaronic priest "offered" God-ward, and had "compassion" man-ward (Heb 5.1-2). This concept is still in place in the Christian era. Believers constitute a "holy priesthood" that has a responsibility to "offer up spiritual sacrifices", a God-ward ministry, but they are also a "royal priesthood" with the duty to "shew forth the praises of him who hath called (them) out of darkness into his marvellous light", a man-ward ministry (1 Pet 2.5,9). This dual responsibility is underlined in Hebrews 13.15-16, where we are encouraged to "offer the sacrifice of praise to God continually" and then "to do good and to communicate". Both the God-ward and man-ward activities are regarded as pleasurable to God, "for with such sacrifices God is well pleased". Thus here David offered his sacrifices to God and "did good" by bestowing these gifts upon his people.

Verses 4-6: Ministering Before the Ark

Despite being remote from the tabernacle, there was still a desire for religious activity to surround the ark in its new location, and to this end David appointed Levites "to minister before the ark of the Lord". That ministry was mainly in the nature of praise and thanksgiving. Ministering to the Lord is not exclusive to the Old Testament, for in the church at Antioch there were those who "ministered to the Lord, and fasted" (Acts 13.2). It should always be borne in mind that amidst the various activities of the local church God's interests should never be neglected, and that He should have His portion from His people in terms of worship and thanksgiving.

Before the Levites are named, their function is explained to us: "to record, and to thank and to praise the Lord God of Israel" (v.4). The words "to record" (2142) are translated "to celebrate" by the RV and JND, and "to commemorate" by the NKJV. Basic to the expression is the idea of remembering, and that comes out in the psalm in the later part of the chapter: "Remember" (v.12), "Be ye mindful" (v.15), with much of the psalm being reminiscences of God's dealings with Israel. Based on their reflections on God's dealings with them, then, thanks and praise ascended to Him. In the New Testament none of the gatherings of the assembly were designated by the terms "praise gathering" or "worship meeting", but there was a meeting to which the idea of remembrance was foundational. The Lord Jesus said of the breaking of bread, "this do in remembrance of me" (1 Cor 11.24). On such occasions hymns that would be suitable on other occasions are inappropriate, and the supplications and intercessions of the prayer meeting are out of place. Based on the idea of remembrance, appropriate hymns would be those that focus on Christ, and suitable expressions of worship would be those that reflect on His person and work. Thus while the Lord's Supper is never called the worship meeting in the Word of God, it is a fitting occasion for expressing our worship. It is possible to worship God without remembering the Lord Jesus, but one can hardly remember the Lord Jesus without worshipping God.

The men selected for this ministry before the ark were led by Asaph (v.5). As noted earlier in the commentary, he was either a composer or compiler of a number of the psalms. He was responsible for the percussion that complemented the stringed instruments and trumpets of the orchestra, "with cymbals, sounding aloud" (RV). It would appear that with the volume of his contribution he was giving a lead to the praise and thanksgiving.

Two priests were to be trumpeters, with the word "continually" describing the consistency of their activity. Presumably "continually" means regularly at stated times. It is hard to suppose that they could be engaged in playing such instruments every moment of the day!

This remembering and thanking and praising was something that was to be perpetuated "before the ark of the covenant of God". The same consistent spirit of gratitude and praise should be a feature of the believer's life today: "In every thing give thanks" (1 Thess 5.18); "Giving thanks *always* for all things unto God and the Father in the name of our Lord Jesus Christ" (Eph 5.20). "Neither were (they) thankful", says Paul of the pagan world (Rom 1.21), and "In the last days...men shall be...unthankful" (2 Tim 3.1-2). We should never allow the spirit of ingratitude that is a feature of both heathendom and the last days to become characteristic of our lives as believers. We have so much for which to thank our God, even at times when we might be tempted to be over anxious about adverse circumstances (Phil 4.6).

Verse 7: Introduction to the Psalm

With the ark in place, David committed to Asaph and his brethren a composition that could be performed appropriately on such an occasion. The word "first" could convey different meanings. The AV leaves the impression that this psalm was first among others that were entrusted to Asaph and that is a possibility, for his name is linked with numerous psalms. However, the words "this psalm" are in italics as not being part of the original Hebrew. The RV renders thus: "on that day did David first ordain to give thanks unto the Lord, by the hand of Asaph and his brethren". The ESV says, "on that day David first appointed that thanksgiving be sung to the Lord by Asaph and his brothers". These and other renderings leave us with two possibilities. We could take out of what is said the fact that thanksgiving was a priority, "first", or we could come to the conclusion that this was the first time that Asaph and his fellow-choristers had responsibility in this way. Despite these considerations prompted by alternative translations, it seems likely that this was the first psalm ever to be entrusted to Asaph, compiled specially for the occasion by "the sweet psalmist of Israel" (2 Sam 23.1).

Verses 8-12: Imperative Verbs

The first stanzas of the psalm contain a number of imperative verbs, by which the people are encouraged to give to God the praise that is His due, and to render to Him the honour that is rightfully His.

"*Give thanks*" (v.8). No doubt, in this particular setting it would be specific thanksgiving for the safe arrival of the ark, but we have been observing the need for this spirit of gratitude to be a permanent feature of our lives.

"*Call* upon his name" (v.8). If we follow what Bible students have called the law of first mention, we get an inkling in Genesis 4.26 into what is enshrined in the concept of calling upon His name: "then began men to call upon the name of the Lord". Why then? A little child had been born and he was given the name of Enos. The naming of the boy gives us the clue as to why at that point in history they began to call upon the name of the Lord. The name means "frail mortal man", and it was when people were beginning to realise just how frail and vulnerable and mortal they were, that they turned their eyes heavenward to seek divine help. Calling upon the name of the Lord denotes an attitude of reliance upon God. In our own experience it started with an understanding of our dependence on Him for salvation, "For whosoever shall call upon the name of the Lord shall be saved" (Rom 10.13). Our subsequent Christian lives have been lived with a sense of our constant need of Him, and so we call upon His name, or as Peter puts it, we "call on the Father" (1 Pet 1.17).

"*Make known* his deeds" (v.8). Having encouraged thanksgiving and the prayer of dependence God-ward, the psalmist now underscores their responsibility man-ward. God's "deeds" would have included His superintendence of the return of the ark, but surely the thought must be widened. As a nation, they had experienced His constant intervention both in blessing and judgment, and on many occasions these interventions had been miraculous. The knowledge of God's dealings with them was not to be kept secret, but had to be made known "among the peoples" (RV). In our own age, news of "his deeds" must be publicised among men, for the gospel is the only hope for needy humanity. At its launch, men of various tongues heard in their own language "the wonderful works of God" (Acts 2.11). Let us not be negligent in making known His deeds, for "how shall they believe in him of whom they have not heard? and how shall they hear without a preacher?" (Rom 10.14).

"*Sing* unto him" (v.9). He is the object of praise, and indeed the subject of praise. "Sing psalms" is translated by most, "sing praises" and we mention that fact just as a word of caution lest any should feel that the only legitimate ascriptions of praise to God are from the book of Psalms.

"*Talk*" (v.9). The "deeds" of v.8, are the "wondrous works" of v.9, for a feature of Hebrew poetry is not so much rhyme and rhythm, but repetition. They had a duty to converse about these things. The word "talk" (7878) is translated to "meditate" on five occasions in Psalm 119, and so there is a dual thought here. God's wondrous works deserve careful consideration, and ought also to be the subject of conversation. David spoke about "the words of my mouth, and the meditation of my heart" (Ps 19.14); the two go in tandem. Never let us be slow to talk of all He has done. The man of Gadara was told to "Go…and tell", and Mark records that "he departed, and began to publish in Decapolis *how great things* Jesus had done for him" (Mk 5.19-20). What had transpired was certainly among the Lord's "marvellous works" as the RV translates our verse, for "all men did marvel" (Mk 5.20).

"*Glory*" (v.10). Although this word "Glory" (1984) is most frequently rendered "praise", translators seem agreed that here it is best understood as meaning to glory or honour. The people were being encouraged to honour God on account of the wonderful works already mentioned, but also on account of the holiness of His character as expressed in the phrase, "his holy name". As we ponder the majesty of His power and holiness, we fall down and say, "How great thou art".

"*Seek*" (v.11). The previous verse had indicated that the hearts of those who seek the Lord can rejoice. Isaiah shows that for those who do so there is rich blessing: "he will have mercy upon him…he will abundantly pardon" (Is 55.6-7). Well might the hearts of the seekers rejoice.

In our psalm, the injunction is to "Seek the Lord and his strength". To live for Him, divine strength is required. To serve Him, His power is essential. In this Christian era, the Holy Spirit is seen as both the power for Christian living and the energy for Christian service (Rom 8.4; 1 Thess 1.5). Let us seek the Lord and His strength, for in ourselves we are as weak and fragile as earthen vessels (2 Cor 4.7).

"Seek his face evermore" (RV), is a reminder that we ought never to become complacent or self-sufficient. As long as we are in this world we will be dependent on the divine strength that can be tapped by means of prayer. In that vein, the Lord Jesus said, "Ask…*seek*…knock" (Mt 7.7). Let us be like those in the days of King Asa who "sought him with their whole desire" (2 Chr 15.15).

"*Remember*" (v.12). The faculty of memory is a great blessing, and so often in the Word of God we are encouraged to reflect on God's ways. His deeds are again described here as "marvellous works" and "wonders", for this nation had a rich history of divine intervention. There is also the plea to remember "the judgments of his mouth". Neither what He has done nor what He has said should ever be forgotten. "Forget not all his benefits" (Ps 103.2). The same is true about our Lord Jesus. His works and words should always be in mind. "Remember that Jesus Christ of the seed of David was raised from the dead" (2 Tim 2.8). "Remember the words of the Lord Jesus" (Acts 20.35). Peter never forgot His words: "Then remembered I the word of the Lord" (Acts 11.16). Luke's Gospel was written to give exposure to both the works and words of the Saviour: "all that Jesus began both to *do* and *teach*" (Acts 1.1). Let us "Remember his marvellous works…and the judgments of his mouth".

Verses 13-22: The Covenant which He Made with Abraham

There is now a section of the psalm that reflects on Israel's right to the land, by virtue of a sovereign God apportioning it to Abraham and his descendants. The people were encouraged to be "mindful always of his covenant" (v.15). The "token of the covenant" was the rite of circumcision (Gen 17.8-14). When Hebrew boys were left uncircumcised, it was indicative of a spirit of unbelief that called in question God's ability to give them the land: hence God's displeasure with Moses at his failure to circumcise his son (Ex 4.24-26). This spirit of unbelief was manifested right through the wilderness journey, for not one child born in the wilderness had been circumcised (Josh 5.5).

The way the psalm addresses the people is delightful (v.13). They are first described as the "seed of Israel his servant". To Israel (Jacob) there is given this dignified designation, "his servant". Despite Jacob's somewhat chequered history, God was "not ashamed to be called (his) God" (Heb 11.16). How often He is described as "the God of Jacob", so, says God, he is "my servant" (e.g. Is 44.1-2). David's subjects were Jacob's seed.

As linked with Jacob, they were also God's "chosen ones". In this context they were chosen particularly to be the rightful inhabitants of the land of promise, for they were being called upon to remember the covenant whereby God granted them tenure of that delightful part of the world. By contrast, God's choice of us had in view "spiritual blessings" rather than an earthly inheritance (Eph 1.3-4), our inheritance being "reserved *in heaven* for us" (1 Pet 1.4, AV margin).

In v.14, there is a reminder that although Israel enjoyed a special relationship with God as His people, His sphere of jurisdiction extends universally: "His judgments are in all the earth". He superintends the affairs of the nations, and, as individuals, men everywhere are accountable to Him. Only the favoured nation had the commandments written on the tables of stone, but men worldwide had them "written in their hearts" (Rom 2.15). Divine justice extends to every corner of the earth.

Keep in mind that the covenant that is being considered here is the promise of "the land of Canaan, The lot of your inheritance" (v.18). The word "lot" (2256) is the same word as is translated "lines" in Psalm 16.6 - "The lines are fallen unto me in pleasant places". It is metaphorical language based on the use of measuring cords in staking out each portion of inheritance. God had staked out the territory to be apportioned to this privileged nation and had promised that territory to Abraham their great progenitor.

At v.15, we are told *for whom* that covenant had relevance - "a thousand generations". In other words the land was to belong to Israel perpetually. There have been times in history when the nation has been displaced, but end time prophecies anticipate her being located in the land. In fairly recent history, after years of dispersal, many Jews returned to the land, and in course of time the State of Israel was established in that territory. This continuing association with the land is evidence of God's ultimate intention whether it be fulfilled soon or well into the future.

The word "commanded" is important for it is a reminder that God's covenant to give the land to Abraham's descendants is non-negotiable, and will never be rescinded. The promise of the land must not be spiritualised.

In vv.16-17 we are told *with whom* the covenant was made - Abraham, Isaac and Jacob. Scriptures that record these promises are as follows: Genesis 15.18-21; 26.3; 35.12, and that list is not exhaustive.

In v.18 we are told *what* was promised - the land; and in vv.19-20 we are told *when* the covenant was made - it was when they were "very few" (RV), stateless nomads among peoples who were long established nations. In other words, from a human perspective the likelihood of the promise being fulfilled was remote, just as the likelihood of a childless old man becoming "a father of many nations" (Gen 17.4) seemed very farfetched. God specialises in accomplishing the improbable and even the impossible, such is His divine power and wisdom. This must have been a great encouragement to the first readers of the book, people who like their forefathers were relatively very few, and living in "the day of small things" (Zech 4.10). Let it be an encouragement to us too, when faced with circumstances to which there may be no apparent solution.

The section concludes by telling of *how* this covenant was kept, in that God shielded those to whom the undertaking was made, and preserved them to enter into the enjoyment of the promise (vv.20-21). "He suffered no man to do them wrong", and this included the vengeful Laban (Gen 31.22-55) who had watched his substantial flocks and herds being relentlessly transferred to Jacob's ownership. But God not only controlled a rogue cattleman, "he reproved kings for their sakes", by plaguing Pharaoh and appearing to Abimelech in a dream (Gen 12.10-20; 20.1-18). Our verse makes particular reference to the second of these incidents, in which Abraham is designated "a prophet" (Gen 20.7). Sometimes he is regarded as a pilgrim (Heb 11.13), sometimes as a prince (Gen 23.6), but here it is as a prophet. Again, these facts regarding divine protection must have cheered the post-exilic readers, harassed as they were by belligerent neighbours intent on hindering the building of both the temple and the walls of Jerusalem.

God is no less protective of His people today, and while we are never guaranteed safety from physical violence or harm, nothing that earth or hell can contrive will ever rob us of the spiritual blessings that are promised us, or deprive us of the ultimate blessing of entering our heavenly inheritance.

"Who shall separate us from the love of Christ?" Nothing in heaven, earth or hell "shall be able to separate us from the love of God, which is in Christ Jesus our Lord" (Rom 8.35-39). Let us be encouraged.

Verses 23-27: Sing unto the Lord

It is at this point that the celebratory psalm moves to the quotation from Psalm 96. In quoting from Psalm 105, the focus had been mainly on God's dealings with the nation of Israel. Now there is an emphasis on the whole world: "all the earth" (v.23); "the heathen", "all nations" (v.24); "the peoples" (v.26, RV); "kindreds of the people" (v.28); "all the earth" (v.30); "the earth", "the nations" (v.31); "the earth" (v.33). The end of the quotation anticipates the Lord's coming to inaugurate His universal reign (vv.31-33). Keep in mind that this ascription of praise was in connection with the return of the ark, described on an occasion as "the ark of the covenant of *the Lord of all the earth*" (Josh 3.11).

The whole universe of men is now called upon to "Sing unto the Lord", and to "shew forth...his salvation" (v.23). The two functions are not unrelated, for an appreciation of "his salvation" will inevitably give rise to praise. This has to be done on a daily basis, "day by day", as exemplified by Anna whose devotion was so constant as to be described as "night and day" (Lk 2.37).

Israel is now placed under responsibility to "Declare his glory among the nations" (v.24, RV). With evangelical zeal they should have spread abroad the truth of the majesty and honour of their God. It is a sad indictment that rather than magnifying God, their behaviour left a warped impression in the minds of the Gentile peoples; "the name of God is blasphemed among the Gentiles through you" (Rom 2.24). We may well ask ourselves if our own conduct among the people of the world enhances God's testimony or detracts from it.

In v.12, the people were called upon to "Remember his marvellous works". Now they are enjoined to "Declare" them "among all nations". It is only as we reflect on God's doings, and the wonders of His dealings with us, that we will have any desire to disseminate the news of this to others.

The constant reference to divine operations as "*marvellous* works" has a counterpart in the New Testament, for one aspect of the miracles of the Lord Jesus was the effect that they had on those who witnessed them. They caused them to marvel, and so they were designated "wonders" (Acts 2.22). A few quotations will demonstrate the point. "The men marvelled" (Mt 8.27). "The multitudes...marvelled" (9.8,33). "The disciples...marvelled" (21.20). The God who had operated so dramatically in Old Testament days was now "in the world" (Jn 1.10). He "was manifest in the flesh" (1 Tim 3.16), and the continued demonstration of divine power in the life of a man in the world created utter astonishment in the minds of observers.

At v.25 a reason is advanced as to why the people of Israel were under obligation to spread the fame of their God among the nations; "great is the Lord". His greatness was evidenced in the work of creation for "the Lord made the heavens" (v.26). Other so-called deities were but idols (457), "things of nought" (RV margin). The root of the word lends some weight to that translation, and indeed the AV gives it that rendering in Jeremiah 14.14. It is a clear indication that idols were worthless, helpless, and good-for-nothing in contrast to the living God whose power was demonstrated so majestically when "he made the stars also" (Gen 1.16). The fact that He made the heavens enthralled David as he scanned the night sky. The majestic sight made him feel like a tiny speck in the vast universe: "When I consider thy heavens, the work of thy fingers, the moon and the stars, which thou hast ordained; What is man, that thou art mindful of him? And the son of man, that thou visitest him?" (Ps 8.3-4). His greatness demands our praise and His transcendence over "the gods of the people" demands our fear. Let us give Him the worship and reverence that is His due.

It is interesting that among the other attributes connected with God as being "in his presence" and "in his place" in v.27 is "gladness"; Paul described Him as "the blessed God" (1 Tim 1.11). We are to understand that there is inherent joy in deity that does not in any way impair the holiness of the divine character or impinge on divine power. That "gladness…in his place" is communicated to those who share that place. Very likely the primary interpretation of "the place" is the earthly sanctuary, as indicated in the rendering of the verse in Psalm 96.6: "Honour and majesty are before him: strength and beauty are in his sanctuary". Pilgrims who visited that place shared the joy of deity - "How amiable are thy tabernacles, O Lord of hosts" (Ps 84.1). "I was glad when they said unto me, Let us go into the house of the Lord" (Ps 122.1). Even yet, when the Lord is present among His people there is a pleasure in that which stirs redeemed hearts and is an encouragement to us to be there.

Widening the thought of the "gladness" connected with God and His presence, we can apply the reference to "the place" to His immediate dwelling place in heaven. "In thy presence is fullness of joy; at thy right hand there are pleasures for evermore" (Ps 16.11). The psalm had spoken of the multiplied sorrows of those that "hasten after another god" (v.4), but in contrast to the multiplied sorrows of the unregenerate, those who will share the divine dwelling place will have a full cup of joy, and a pleasure that eternal years will never dampen. Little wonder the author Henry Durbanville entitled his book on future blessing, *The Best Is Yet To Be*.

If fellowship here with my Lord can be
So inexpressibly sweet,
O what will it be when His face we see,
When round His bright throne we meet!
(Mrs. C. H. Morris)

Verses 28-29: Worship the Lord

Before the celebratory psalm concludes its extract from Psalm 96 by anticipating divine rule in the world, there is a further call to worship. We are told *who* were to worship: "ye kindreds of the people". The whole of humanity is under obligation to give "glory and strength" to the God of the universe.

We are told *why* they had to worship: it is "due unto his name". While the word "due" is italicised in some publications of the AV, most translations retain it as being necessary for the understanding of the text. The majesty, supremacy, and authority of deity demands submissive and hearty recognition on the part of frail creatures who are but "dust and ashes" (Gen 18.27). It is His due.

We are told *how* they were to worship: sacrificially and "in the beauty of holiness". In Scripture the two go together, for to "bring an offering" without moral suitability never satisfied God. "Will the Lord be pleased with thousands of rams...what doth the Lord require of thee, but to do justly, and to love mercy, and to walk humbly with thy God?" (Mic 6.7-8). "To what purpose is the multitude of your sacrifices unto me?...Wash you, make you clean; put away the evil of your doings from before mine eyes; cease to do evil; Learn to do well; seek judgment, relieved the oppressed, judge the fatherless, plead for the widow" (Is 1.11, 16-17). God always set a great premium on holy living and moral integrity, and it was always a necessary prerequisite for "bring(ing) an offering". "The beauty of holiness" has at all times held an appeal for a holy God, and such is still the case. "Bring an offering", was the appeal then, and so to believers now the demand is made: "present your bodies a living sacrifice" (Rom 12.1). But true consecration demands that the living sacrifice be "holy". A life that is tainted by iniquity will never be acceptable to God, even though it is ostensibly dedicated to Him. "The beauty of holiness" is an essential precondition for bringing an offering whatever that offering may be. Men may regard holiness as austere and dull; God considers it to be beautiful.

Some translations (e.g. RSV) substitute "the beauty of holiness" with "holy array", but even if accepted it does not destroy the practical application of the verse. Frequently in the Scriptures garments are illustrative of character and behaviour, as when we "put on" (as a garment) the new man at conversion, and are still called upon to "Put on...bowels of mercies, kindness, humbleness of mind, meekness, longsuffering" (Col 3.10,12). Let such holy array adorn us as we worship Him.

Verses 30-33: The Lord Reigneth

With the ark in its rightful place among the people, it seemed appropriate to David to anticipate the day when the Lord Himself would have His rightful place as "the Lord of all the earth" (Josh 3.11; Ps 97.5). In light of His creatorial power and His impending visible rule over His universe, "all the earth" is called upon to "Tremble before him" (RV).

His power and authority should invoke a reverential fear that might well be expressed in a physical trembling which will give way to the earth rejoicing when it is said among the nations, "The Lord reigneth". He has the right to reign because He is the Creator. "The world also is stablished that it cannot be moved" (v.30, RV). Although He hung the earth "upon nothing" (Job 26.7), there is a stability about it that will persist until such times as He chooses to fold up His whole creation like a vesture (Heb 1.12). Before that day arrives, God the Son will come to "judge the earth" (v.33), that is, He will establish a visible administration over the world, and it will be said, "The Lord reigneth". It is for that day that creation longs. Presently it is in the "bondage of corruption" from which it will be "delivered" when the Lord Jesus is manifested with "the sons of God" (Rom 8.19-23). In poetic language, our verses anticipate the excitement that will grip creation as that final era in human history arrives. There will be joy in both the celestial and terrestrial spheres (v.31). The seas that are teeming with marine life will "roar" (v.32). Fields will "rejoice" and trees will "sing" (vv.32-33). All nature will be attuned to the fact that in a very obvious way the Creator will have taken control of His universe, and harmony will be sounding where once the discordant notes of a groaning creation had grated on the ear.

Then the heavens, and the earth, and the sea shall rejoice;
The field and the forest shall lift the glad voice;
The sand of the desert shall flourish in green,
And Lebanon's glory be shed o'er the scene.

Her bridal attire and her festal array
All nature shall wear on that glorious day;
For her King cometh down with His people to reign,
And His presence shall bless her with Eden again.
(Horatius Bonar)

Verses 34-36: Give Thanks unto the Lord

The thought of Christ's benign rule stirred David to appeal again for the spirit of thanksgiving, and v.34 corresponds with Psalm 106.1, while vv.35-36 are drawn from vv.47-48 of the same psalm. It is cause for gratitude that because God "is good" and "his mercy endureth for ever" He will usher in the last stage of human history during which the effects of curses upon the earth and its creatures will be suspended (Gen 3.14,17-19). "The wilderness and the solitary place shall be glad; and the desert shall rejoice, and blossom as the rose" (Is 35.1, RV). "Instead of the thorn shall come up the fir tree, and instead of the brier shall come up the myrtle tree" (55.13). Wild animals will lose their ferocity, and predators will become vegetarian in that final phase of God's dealings with the earth (11.6-9). To add to the bliss of that era, man's propensity for warfare will have gone (2.4), and the devil will be exiled from the earth for 1,000 years (Rev 20.1-3). Little wonder the call goes out, "O give thanks unto the Lord; for he is good".

However, as yet that day of earthly paradise had never dawned, and David and his people had still to face the harsh realities of the present, including the likelihood of enemy activity. Thus there is an appeal to the God of their salvation, "Save us, O God" (v.35). Perhaps there is even a future aspect to these words, for over the centuries Israel has been scattered, and before the Millennium arrives, the nation will have to be gathered together and delivered from "the nations" (v.35, RV). That in turn will result in further thanksgivings. Deliverance should always be acknowledged with praise. The note of praise sounded when Israel was emancipated from Egyptian bondage: "Then sang Moses and the children of Israel this song unto the Lord..." (Ex 15). It rung out when Paul contemplated the liberty that the Roman Christians enjoyed: "God be thanked...ye were the servants of sin... Being then made free from sin, ye became the servants of righteousness" (Rom 6.17-18).

Thus this psalm that celebrated the settling of the ark at Jerusalem ends on a note of triumph, with the words of Asaph and his brethren exploding in exultant worship, "Blessed be the Lord God of Israel for ever and ever". The multitudes concurred with these sentiments and added their "Amen", and joined their voices in praising the Lord.

At a practical level, a hearty congregational "Amen" at the end of expressions of worship and praise is Biblical, based on the practice of New Testament assemblies. At Corinth there was the "amen at thy giving of thanks" (1 Cor 14.16). In heaven, as the worth of the Lamb is proclaimed, majestic spirit beings instinctively say "Amen" (Rev 5.14). Surely there is a pattern there. When Christ has been honoured and His Father worshipped, an enthusiastic "Amen" is far more appropriate than a stony silence.

Verses 37-38: The Ark at Jerusalem

Verse 37 picks up the threads of the narrative from v.6 after the record of the inaugural psalm. Asaph had had the responsibility of celebrating the arrival of the ark, but that duty was not to be a one-off event. His attendance upon it was to be permanent, "continually, as every day's work required". There was to be no let up in the stream of adoration that would ascend to the Lord, for God's desire is for a constant flow of praise to His name. It is thus in heaven for there are mighty living creatures who "rest not day and night, saying, Holy, holy, holy, Lord God Almighty, which was, and is, and is to come" (Rev 4.8). It will be so on earth, "For from the rising of the sun even unto the going down of the same my name shall be great among the Gentiles" (Mal 1.11). Let that constant spirit of appreciation be a feature of our own lives, for the Spirit-filled believer will be "Giving thanks *always* for all things" (Eph 5.20).

Among the songsters, Obed-edom and Hosah doubled as "porters" in the old-fashioned sense of that word: they were doorkeepers. There was need for security to be in place, for the ark would have to be guarded from prying inquisitive eyes. The incident at Beth-shemesh had demonstrated the dangers for the curious and impious (1 Sam.6.19), but the lessons of history are often ignored. Hence the doorkeepers were in place; undesirables would be excluded, and genuine worshippers admitted.

Verses 39-42: The Altar at Gibeon

During this brief period in Israel's history, an unusual situation obtained. The tabernacle was in one location and the ark was in another. For many years the ark had been absent from the tabernacle as a result of the folly of Eli's generation (1 Sam 4.3), but now there had been opportunity to reposition it in the Holy of Holies. That option had been ignored in favour of locating it at Jerusalem. As was suggested formerly, it appears that David had insight into God's intention to place His name at Jerusalem, so until such time as the temple was built, this temporary situation existed, with ark and altar separated.

As has been observed, provision was made for constant worship to ascend in proximity to the ark. Before all those who had accompanied it on its journey dispersed, David also made certain that everything was in place for the continuation of the sacrificial system at the tabernacle at Gibeon. To satisfy the instructions of Leviticus, sacrifices were offered under priestly supervision, so "Zadok the priest, and his brethren the priests" were left "before the tabernacle of the Lord". As with Asaph at Jerusalem, they too had daily duties, theirs being the offering of "burnt offerings...continually morning and evening". A perpetual savour of Christ had to ascend for the pleasure of God.

Although the situation was abnormal, every attempt was being made to adhere to divine instructions. What was being done was "according to all that is written in the law of the Lord, which he commanded Israel" (v.40). Perhaps the lesson is that even in circumstances that may be unusual and far from ideal, we should give diligence to operate in conjunction with the revealed will of God insofar as we are able.

As at Jerusalem, singers, instrumentalists, and porters were all in place at Gibeon (vv.41-42). The participants were not volunteers, but "chosen, who were expressed by name", a reminder that God sovereignly appoints His people to their tasks, the Spirit of God endowing them with a gift "as he will" (1 Cor 12.11), and the Son of God choosing them for their sphere of service, and appointing them "that (they) should go and bring forth fruit, and that (their) fruit should remain" (Jn 15.16). Let us be content with our remit, and labour earnestly in the sphere to which we have been assigned.

Verse 43: The Homecoming

With the ark in place in its tent, and the celebration and feasting at an end, "all the people departed every man to his house". David made the short journey to his own home with the intention of blessing "his house". While domestic responsibilities are subservient to spiritual duties, they cannot be ignored, and the king had an interest in bringing blessing to his own household. Though her thoughts had been disclosed at the end of the previous chapter, this chapter says nothing of the biting sarcasm that awaited him on his encounter with Michal, a sour end to a happy day (2 Sam 6.20-23), for, as so often, the Chronicler assumes our knowledge of events and has the tendency to omit matters that are irrelevant to his main theme.

Centuries after this event, at the end of another joyous religious festival, another crowd dispersed from Jerusalem and "every man went unto his own house" (Jn 7.53). A solitary figure peeled off from the throng, and, unlike David, Jesus did not return to His house, but "went unto the mount of Olives" (Jn 8.1). His father David had his opulent cedar mansion with its comforts and luxury. Servants stood in attendance to cater for his every need. The great Creator "(had) not where to lay his head" (Lk 9.58). Although so rich, "for (our) sakes he became poor" (2 Cor 8.9). When others were abandoning the makeshift booths of the Feast of Tabernacles to return to their home comforts, He set out for the hillside.

> The foxes found rest, and the birds their nest
> In the shade of the forest tree;
> But Thy couch was the sod, O Thou Son of God,
> In the deserts of Galilee.
>
> (Emily E. S. Elliott)

It bows our hearts in worship.

1 CHRONICLES 17

With the ark installed in its new location, David turned his attention to providing more permanent quarters for it. We have arrived at a point in the book where this major theme is developed; the Chronicler will go on to provide details of various events that climax in Solomon constructing the house of God, the record of which is in the second book. Some of these proceedings demonstrate God's ability to turn evil circumstances to good account. In this chapter Nathan's presumption gave God opportunity to divulge His own plan for the building of the temple. In chapter 21 David sinned in numbering the people. The ensuing threat of judgment gave an opening for the purchase of a site upon which to build the holy edifice. God's "ways (are) past finding out" (Rom 11.33).

The drift of the chapter is as follows. In verses 1-2 David expressed his desire to provide a permanent structure in which to house the ark, to which Nathan gave his agreement. Verses 3-15 record God's intervention in which He disclosed two very important items of information. First, David would not build the temple but his son would. Second, God would establish a dynasty for David. Clearly, to head the dynasty was a far greater honour than to build the house. The chapter will show that God had never requested a permanent residence on earth, but He had purposed to establish His kingdom in this world. Nebuchadnezzar would destroy the temple, but the kingdom would be forever. God's king will be "his Son Jesus Christ our Lord, which was made *of the seed of David* according to the flesh" (Rom 1.3). For David, to head the Messiah's line was an inestimable privilege.

The rest of the chapter tells of David's reaction to the two items of news. In general terms his response was a credit to him. Nathan had unwisely and inadvertently raised his hopes, so it must have been a bitter blow to hear of the revised arrangement. His immediate reaction was to pray, and in his prayer there is no hint of a grudging acceptance of the divine plan. The attitude he exhibited was commendable, focusing as it did on the positive aspect of God's message to him. He was absolutely thrilled to think that God had honoured him, a man of such humble origins, to head up a royal dynasty. "Do as thou hast said", was his happy response to the Almighty (v.23).

The unconditional promises made to David in this chapter constitute what has been called the Davidic Covenant. The parallel passage in 2 Samuel 7 is relevant to this as is Psalm 89. In his celebrated treatment of prophetic themes, *Things to Come*, J. Dwight Pentecost quotes comments by John Walvoord as he summarised the provisions of that covenant (pp.101-102).

"The provisions of the Davidic covenant include, then, the following items: (1) David is to have a child, yet to be born, who shall succeed him and establish his kingdom. (2) This son (Solomon) shall build the temple instead of David. (3) The throne of his kingdom shall be established forever. (4) The throne shall not be taken away from him (Solomon) even though his sins justify chastisement. (5) David's house, throne, and kingdom shall be established forever".

At this point it would be worthwhile commenting on the kindness of God. He gave David an encouraging promise that would more than compensate for the crushing disappointment of being denied the distinction of building the temple. That is typical of God. Doubtless, the drudgery of Joseph's years of servitude and imprisonment were lightened by the memory of God-given dreams that foretold his supremacy and glory. John's distress at being exiled on the rocky outcrop that was Patmos would be more than balanced by the fact that he was privileged to be the recipient of "The Revelation of Jesus Christ" (Rev 1.1). God's dealings with His people are so gracious.

It is also worth noting that in David's subsequent history there was never a hint of resentment at this apparent rebuff. In fact, the remainder of this book of 1 Chronicles depicts a man dedicated to doing all in his power to facilitate the building of the house of God though it would never be a reality in his lifetime (vv.11-12). His attitude is a condemnation of those who do nothing because their personal ambitions have been thwarted: the foot saying, "Because I am not the hand, I am not of the body", or the ear saying, "Because I am not the eye, I am not of the body" (1 Cor 12.15-16). David gave unstinting support to a project in which he was not the key player; his name would never be associated with the temple; it would be known for ever as "the temple that *Solomon* built in Jerusalem" (1 Chr 6.10). Salome was another who may have felt snubbed as she made representations in the interest of her sons (Mt 20.20-23). That apparent rejection did nothing to embitter her or dull her affection for Christ. She was with the loyal group of women at both the cross and the tomb (Mk 15.40; 16.1). We salute the generous spirit of these individuals.

Verses 1-2: David's Plan

Nathan the prophet was one of three men who had close spiritual links with David. The others were Samuel and Gad (29.29) and all three wrote biographies of his life. David was the most renowned of all the kings of Israel. He dominated the Middle East of his day, and yet only three volumes were needed to record his life-story! By contrast, John said of the "things which Jesus did", "I suppose that even the world itself could not contain the books that should be written" (Jn 21.25). The most illustrious of earth pale when contrasted with Him who has "the preeminence" (Col 1.18).

Nathan featured on a number of occasions in David's life. With courage, he confronted him with his guilt after the sordid business of Bathsheba and Uriah: "Thou art the man" (2 Sam 12.7). He was also used by the Lord to confer an alternative name on Solomon, Jedidiah, beloved of the Lord (v.25). He was a key figure in thwarting Adonijah's rebellion, and having Solomon anointed as king (1 Kings 1). On this occasion he was a somewhat rash, but was big enough to rectify his mistake immediately. This incident predates any of the others that have been mentioned (2 Sam 7).

Attention has already been drawn to the magnificence of David's house (14.1-2). Creditably, he did not regard it as being for his own exclusive use. Nathan was there as a guest, a lesson in "Us(ing) hospitality...without grudging" (1 Pet 4.9).

Having Nathan in the home is an indication that David enjoyed the company of the right kind of people. "I am a companion of all them that fear thee" (Ps 119.63). Spurgeon attributes that psalm and that statement to David on the basis of literary style and spiritual content. If his deduction is correct, David gave evidence of his claim, for his companion was a God-fearing man. There is a lesson here regarding the importance of cultivating spiritual companionship, and being careful about the company that we keep. It is a pity that David's son Amnon did not have the same discernment as his father when it came to the choice of friends. He "had a friend...Jonadab...a very subtil man" (2 Sam 13.3). The advice of that "friend" was repulsive and it led to Amnon's ruin. "Evil company doth corrupt good manners" (1 Cor 15.33, RV). David was able to share with his companion his spiritual aspirations for they were kindred spirits.

It seemed a source of embarrassment to David that, while he was settled in his palatial home, the ark was still "under curtains". What he had in mind remained unspoken, but it appears that Nathan read his thoughts, and assumed that the king's ambition was a noble objective; he was quick to give the go-ahead (v.2). It sounded good, and God was with David (v.2), so it must be right! It is true that God was with David (v.8), but His presence did not mean that David was the man chosen to build the temple. God calls David "my servant" (vv.4,7), but, again, that did not mean that he was the servant chosen to construct God's house. Being in God's service and experiencing the divine presence does not mean that the man in question is necessarily God's choice for a particular task. As in everything else, the will of God must be ascertained. We would have supposed that Elijah would be the man to foretell Ahab's death at Ramoth-gilead, for he was still around, but God chose the unheralded Micaiah (1 Kings 22). We may have expected Paul to carry the gospel to Colosse, but God used Epaphras (Col 1.7). He is not restricted to one channel of ministry.

Nathan was too impulsive on this occasion, and he made the mistake of failing to "inquire of the Lord", a phrase that we have encountered before in our studies. His rash response, "Do all that is in thine heart", reinforces the lesson of how important it is to seek God's mind in prayer before taking action in any matter. The same lesson can be learned from Samuel's visit to Bethlehem in 1 Samuel 16. Without consulting heaven, whenever he saw Eliab Samuel said, "Surely the Lord's anointed is before him" (v.6). It may be that the sudden about-turn accounts for Eliab's resentment of David in the next chapter (v.28), an attitude that happily did not fester, for Eliab (Elihu) became one of David's trusted administrators with responsibility for the tribe of Judah (1 Chr 27.18). It does appear though that Samuel's hasty pronouncement caused some damage.

Verses 3-6: Thou Shalt not Build Me an House

God's intervention was immediate, "the same night", another evidence of His kindness. He did not allow David's expectations to be heightened before they were dashed. He did not wait until plans for the project had taken hold in his mind before uprooting them. He moved immediately to limit the damage of Nathan's misjudgment. The phrase "the same night" features also in the story of Gideon, again underscoring the kindness of God. Just when God had reduced his army to 300 men, and before he had time to feel apprehensive, "the same night" God allowed him to hear the Midianite's dream and dispel his fears. No wonder "he worshipped" (Judg 7.9-15).

"Thou shalt not build me an house." When the message was relayed to David he must have been numb with disbelief. It does not take much imagination to think that his excitement had been at fever pitch and that sleep had been elusive. The sight of a magnificent building and priestly activity would have been tumbling around in his mind; the sounds and smells of the court and its altar would have been vivid in his imagination. But now the early morning knock at the door turned these dreams to ashes. In the introduction to this chapter we observed how David was able to overcome the disappointment, but he never forgot it. When addressing Solomon in first charging him to build the house, he said, "the word of the Lord came to me, saying…thou shalt not build an house unto my name" (22.8). At the end of his days, when encouraging the heads of the nation to take the project seriously, he said again, "God said unto me, Thou shalt not build an house for my name" (28.3). This incident was never erased from his mind, but God gave him grace to live with the memory of the disappointment, and rise above it.

Forgetfulness is a human failing, but it is a strange anomaly that we find it impossible to expel certain memories. Joseph thought that his new circumstances had erased the memories of home, and so he called his firstborn, Manasseh, that is, "forgetting" (Gen 41.51). He discovered that it is not so easy to forget, for in the very next chapter, with the unexpected appearance of his ten older brothers the memories came flooding back. Like David and Joseph, we need divine grace to cope happily with the might-have-beens of life.

In verses 5 and 6 God protests that in all His dealings with Israel He had never made any request for a "house of cedars". He had gone "from tent to tent, and from one tabernacle to another". The language used does not signify that the ark had been housed in many tents, but rather that the tabernacle had been located in various places. During its time in the wilderness there had been numerous sites as the journey had progressed. In the land, we know of different locations: Gilgal, Shiloh, Nob, and Gibeon.

God had been mobile, and had never indicated a desire to be perceived as static in an elaborate edifice. David's desire to build Him a house was not in any way a response to a divine directive; it had come from his own heart. These verses contain an implied commendation of this.

That God is not confined to one place is an encouraging thought, or, to put it more plainly, the omnipresence that allows Him to be with His people wherever they be, and to be in attendance in any crisis. In the complicated vision of Ezekiel 1 the mention of wheels may be another indication of this concept of a mobile God. His executors can move to where they are required at any given time in working out His great purpose.

There are phrases in these verses that are of interest, although not crucial to the main thrust of the passage. For example, God speaks of having "brought up Israel", doubtless a reference to their emancipation from slavery in Egypt. In the historical books there are constant allusions to that great event. It ought to have regulated their relationship with their God when they remembered His intervention in redemption. Similarly, the memory of "Christ our passover" should be a powerful stimulant to the purging of all kinds of leaven from our lives (1 Cor 5.7-8).

Another telling phrase is this: "I have walked with all Israel". In their journeys He was their constant companion. This is another factor that demanded a response in holy living. "The Lord thy God walketh in the midst of thy camp...therefore shall thy camp (in the context, a military camp) be holy" (Deut 23.14). God walked with them; in v.8 David is said to have been walking, and he had walked with the enjoyment of the divine presence: "I have been with thee whithersoever thou hast walked". Happy is that people with whom God walks, and who in turn walk with God. However, there is this caveat, quoted perhaps a little out of context: "Can two walk together, except they be agreed?" (Amos 3.3). Walking with God and enjoying His presence demands acceptance of His terms for the journey. He never lowers His standards to accommodate us.

A third phrase has reference to the "judges of Israel" and relates to their responsibility "to feed my people". One would judge that this was a literal command. We tend to spiritualise such statements, but it must be remembered that the leaders of the nation were political figures with responsibilities for defence, education, housing and every other social need. That included superintending the nation's diet, and ensuring that there were no empty stomachs. Of course, we must apply it in a spiritual way. One feature of elders in a New Testament assembly is that they be "apt to teach" (1 Tim 3.2). The same book shows that it is the teaching of the Word of God that provides necessary nourishment for the child of God: "nourished in the words of the faith, and of the good doctrine which thou hast followed until now" (4.6, RV). Spiritual leaders are under obligation to ensure that their people are provided with a healthy balanced spiritual diet. In our verse the judges were "*commanded*" to feed the people. In the context, that took priority over their building a temple for God. Elders are under instructions to "Feed the flock of God" (1 Pet 5.2).

Verses 7-8: I Took Thee from the Sheepcote

These two verses contain a synopsis of God's dealings with David. Despite the king's humble origins God had destined him for power and greatness. God describes Himself here as "the Lord of hosts", and yet, from all the "hosts" under His control He made choice of David, an act of divine sovereignty. Similarly, from the great array of names in Genesis 10 and 11 He chose Abram. He is never under obligation to explain His selection for He is God.

Caring for sheep was a very humble occupation, and yet a responsible task. As with Joseph and Moses, this was a training ground for future responsibilities in caring for people. Disdainfully, Eliab referred to David's charge as "those few sheep in the wilderness" (1 Sam 17.28). David displayed a greater appreciation of that little flock when he said to Saul, "Thy servant kept *his father's* sheep" (v.34). Reliably looking after someone else's sheep equipped him for looking after Someone else's people, for God calls the nation here, "*my* people Israel". David never forgot his pastoral origins or the parallel between that and his responsibilities as "ruler" over Israel. When the people were under threat of judgment because of his folly, he said to the Lord, "as for these sheep, what have they done?" (21.17).

There is the New Testament equivalent of all this. Assemblies are designated "the flock of God" (1 Pet 5.2); they belong to God. However, just as He raised up David to be a ruler over His people Israel, so He has decreed that His flock today should be tended by human carers. In His sovereignty the Holy Spirit has appointed overseers, and they have the responsibility to take heed to themselves "and to all the flock, over the which the Holy Ghost hath made (them) overseers, to feed the church of God" (Acts 20.28). It would be wonderful if they were able to display the same care that David showed for literal sheep, and subsequently for "my people Israel".

God now assures David that "I have been with thee". From the day that he was taken from the pastures (sheepcote) of Bethlehem God's presence had been a reality, a truth that should encourage us all. David's experience can be enjoyed by each of us, "for he hath said, I will never leave thee, nor forsake thee" (Heb 13.5). For David, the divine presence extended to "*whithersoever* thou hast walked". That "whithersoever" included the valley when he faced up to the giant. It took in the brief days of popularity as a member of Saul's royal court. It embraced his days as an outlaw, hiding in the wilderness or in the woods. The "whithersoever" incorporated days of exile in the land of the Philistines and latterly his days of kingship in Hebron and Jerusalem. His life had been a patchwork quilt of experiences, but in them all he had this assurance, "I have been with thee". Let that encourage us, and whether we are at Marah or Elim in our Christian pathway, let the assurance of the divine presence enable us to be buoyant even in the face of adversity.

God had also "cut off all (David's) enemies". No doubt David was a mighty warrior and an expert strategist, but his supremacy was on account of divine activity. Preservation from Saul, and victory over the Philistines and other foes were dependent on the fact that God was on his side. We will see in the next chapter that "*the Lord* gave victory to David whithersoever he went (18.6,13, RV). In the same way, in the face of relentless hardship, believers are "more than conquerors *through him that loved us*" (Rom 8.37), and then, when the last triumph has been achieved, our note of praise will be, "thanks be *to God*, which giveth us the victory *through our Lord Jesus Christ*" (1 Cor 15.57). Our dependence on God and His gracious Spirit is summed up in a verse of Harriet Auber's hymn:

And every virtue we possess,
And every victory won,
And every thought of holiness
Are His alone.

At the end of ch.14 we observed that "the fame of David went out into all lands" (v.17). Who made him famous? God says here, "(I) have made thee a name like the name of the great men that are in the earth". In ancient times, proud men announced their lofty ambitions: "let us make us a name" (Gen 11.4). God frustrated their pretentious plans by confounding their languages. It illustrates the Biblical principle that "whosoever exalteth himself shall be abased" (Lk 14.11). David exemplified the converse principle that "he that humbleth himself shall be exalted". As a young man his attitude was, "Who am I"? (1 Sam 18.18), and again, "I am a poor man and lightly esteemed" (v.23). Of that self-effacing young man God now says, "I have made thee a name". Let us all be persuaded that "promotion cometh neither from the east, nor from the west, nor from the south. But God is the judge: He putteth down one, and setteth up another" (Ps 75.6-7). "He hath put down the mighty from their seats, and exalted them of low degree" (Lk 1.52). Let these principles regulate our thinking. If we are happy to allow God to bring us to the fore in His own time and if it be His will, that will preserve us from the damaging effects of conceit and pretension in our lives.

Verses 9-10a: Precious Promises

Having given a brief account of His dealings with David in the past, God now turns to the future. He first makes promises relating to the nation as a whole, and then more specifically to David and his family. He draws attention to two particular periods of their history when "the children of wickedness (had wasted) them", and He pledges that there would be no repeat of that. The first was "at the beginning", that is, when Israel was enslaved in Egypt and at the mercy of Pharaoh and his forces. The second was during the time of the judges when there were constant attacks from a variety of oppressors. God gives the assurance that they would not experience the likes again. The scattering and harassment of these eras would give way to a settled existence free of the threat of displacement. Some may argue that these promises were broken, because in course of time both Israel and Judah experienced banishment and exile. Scripture must be interpreted in context, and the context here is a divine communication to David relating to him and his successor, and as far as they were concerned, under their administration settled conditions obtained. "I will subdue all thine enemies", says the Lord, and before too long we are told that "David smote the Philistines, and *subdued* them" (18.1). Divine promises, made by a God who "cannot lie" (Titus 1.2), will never fail. Let that be an encouragement to us all.

Verses 10b-11: The Lord will Build thee an House

Turning from predictions regarding the general wellbeing of the nation, this fresh promise relates to David personally, and has to do with his "house". Obviously, on this occasion the word "house" does not relate to a material structure, for the first few verses of ch.14 recount details of the building of his home, and the opening verse of the present chapter finds him comfortably settled there. Our English word "dynasty" conveys the sense of what is being promised here; David would head a dynasty that would run forever, for the One who "shall reign over the house of Jacob for ever" (Lk 1.33) is "of the seed of David according to the flesh" (Rom 1.3). This usage of the word "house" to mean family or household is fairly common in the Bible, and indeed there was another occasion when God granted a family line by way of reward. Of faithful midwives Scripture says, "(God) made them houses" (Ex 1.21).

A continuing family line was big in the thinking of the people of those ancient times. This is evidenced in the fact that Jonathan elicited a promise from David, under oath, that even after his decease David would continue to show kindness to his family (1 Sam 20.14-17). David was careful to keep that promise right to the end of his reign (2 Sam 21.7).

In the present context, the promise of "an house" for David extends no further than the next generation: "I will raise up thy seed after thee". The promise is extended at vv.12 and 14 - "his throne shall be established for evermore". Hence David's response to the Lord: "thou hast also spoken of thy servant's house for a great while to come" (v.17). The emphasis is on David's immediate successor, for the main theme of the whole book is the building of the house of God, and David's successor Solomon was to be responsible for that great venture.

Obviously, the successor would not be in place until after David had died, and the description of David's passing in v.11 enshrines fundamental Bible facts about death. First, there is a reference to David's days being "expired" or "fulfilled" (RV). The inference is that we all have what we call euphemistically "an allotted span", and God is the One who dictates every man's life span: "Seeing his days are determined, the number of his months are with thee, thou hast appointed his bounds that he cannot pass" (Job 14.5). The Lord Jesus is said to have "the keys of death and Hades" (Rev 1.18, RV). He is the One who unlocks the door that separates this life from the next; it is at His command that each will pass through that door or exit it in resurrection. In the face of the divine decree, everyone is helpless: "There is no man that hath power over the spirit to retain the spirit; neither hath he power in the day of death" (Eccl 8.8). When the same book says that there is "a time to die" (3.2), it means, at *God's* time.

Second, the inevitability of death is stressed: "thou *must* go to be with thy fathers". It was to David that a wise woman said, "we *must* needs die" (2 Sam 14.14). In New Testament doctrine the statement is made, "death passed upon *all men*" (Rom 5.12). A statistic against which there is no argument is that 100% of people die. (Of course, at the rapture there will be a small exception to that general rule. A tiny proportion of the billions who have inhabited the planet will go to heaven without dying; according to 1 Corinthians 15.51: "We shall not all sleep, but we shall all be changed".)

Third, there is an allusion to the afterward, to life, in the reference to David going "to be with (his) fathers". Every Bible-believing person accepts that there is life after death and it would be inappropriate in this volume to launch upon a discourse on that theme. All that is being said here is that, in what might seem an incidental reference to David's death, the assumption is that his demise did not signal the end of his existence but rather his removal to another sphere, a fact consistent with detailed Bible teaching on life after death.

God now makes the promise that, after David's death, from the ranks of his sons He would "raise up" one, unnamed as yet, and would "establish his kingdom". The God-ordered settled conditions of that kingdom would be conducive to the building of the house of God. This thought is introduced in the following verse.

Verses 12-14: He shall Build Me an House

"Thou shalt not build me an house" (v.4). "He shall build me an house" (v.12). God is sovereign in the choice of His servants not only as to personnel but also as to the deployment of His men, and thus here Solomon and not David is chosen for the task. Elsewhere, reasons are given for David's exclusion from this enterprise and these will receive comment in due course (e.g. 22.7-8), but here the emphasis is on the positive side - that Solomon would build the house. In one of the very few references to Solomon in the New Testament, Stephen said, "Solomon built him an house" (Acts 7.47).

Our verse speaks of something that Solomon would do for God, and something that God would do for Solomon: "He shall...and I will". As explained to Eli, God always richly recompenses what is done in His interests: "them that honour me I will honour" (1 Sam 2.30). In this case, Solomon's commitment draws out the promise of God, "I will stablish his throne for ever". That promise was never revoked. Solomon's failure at the end of his days can not be overstated. His dreadful lapse warranted the kingdom being taken from him. God was true to His promise here. In mercy the judgment that was pronounced was deferred until the next generation (1 Kings 11.11-13). However, God's unconditional promises are always irreversible and so the Lord Jesus will be the final fulfilment of the promise.

If v.12 speaks of Solomon as a sovereign with a throne, v.13 refers to him as a son with a Father. As stated in the introduction to the commentary, while we see pictures of the Lord Jesus in 1 Chronicles, perhaps this is the only direct reference to Him in the book, for the Spirit of God applies this verse to the Saviour (Heb 1.5). The Spirit as the divine Author of the Scriptures has the right to apply them as He will. We would never have seen Christ in Hosea 11.1 for in its context the reference to God's son is a clear allusion to the nation of Israel, but, guided by the Spirit, Matthew applies it to the Lord Jesus and His sojourn as a child in Egypt (Mt 2.15). Similarly, we would hardly have applied this verse and its parallel in 2 Samuel 7.14 to the Son of God in His unique relationship with the Father, but the Spirit of God does, as a proof text of the superiority of the Lord Jesus over angels: such a thing was never said of them.

The truth of the fatherhood of God is more readily found in the New Testament, but it is not altogether absent from the Old. As far back as the time of the exodus God said to Moses, "Israel is my son, even my firstborn" (Ex 4.22), and as late as Malachi's day He threw out the challenge to a careless people: "...if then I be a father, where is mine honour?" (Mal 1.6). The fact that He is father-like was a great source of encouragement to the psalmist: "Like as a father pitieth his children, so the Lord pitieth them that fear him. For he knoweth our frame; he remembereth that we are dust" (Ps 103.13-14). Let us as believers rejoice in the intimacy of the relationship that we have with the Almighty. We have been honoured to be able to address Him as "Abba, Father" and His Spirit gives us confidence to do so (Rom 8.15-16). Of course, that relationship means that it is legitimate for Him to administer chastening if need be, as He deals with us "as with sons" (Heb 12.7). God makes that point when speaking of His relationship with Solomon (2 Sam 7.14, the parallel passage to the one we are studying now).

Possibly David had vivid memories of the failures of his predecessor Saul, failures that resulted in God discarding him altogether. To allay any fears that such a thing could be replicated in the life of Solomon, God promised David, "I will not take my mercy away from him, as I took it from him that was before thee". The mention of mercy implies that there would be lapses necessitating divine forbearance, and so there were, but true to His word God never abandoned Solomon even in the extreme folly of his latter days. Of necessity Saul's tenure as king was terminated without the reins of government being passed to the next generation, for Judah was the royal tribe and not Benjamin (Gen 49.10). Despite failure, that would never happen to Solomon or by implication to any of his successors, for the Messiah would come in that line of David.

How do we interpret this statement about Solomon: "I will settle him in mine house and in my kingdom for ever" (v.14)? Do we regard God's house here as being Israel with Solomon installed as its sovereign, or is His house the house that features so much in the context, the temple that Solomon would build? Giving consideration to the equivalent passage in 2 Samuel perhaps neither of these is the answer. There the Lord says to David, "Thine house and thy kingdom shall be established for ever before thee" (7.16). In that passage the house and the kingdom are David's; here they are said to be God's. David's dynasty was God's in that He initiated it and would maintain it. David's kingdom was God's in that, in the final analysis, David and his successors were acting only as viceroys in the interests of God; they were "over *my* people Israel" (v.7). Solomon then would be "settled" as an integral part of the dynasty, and as a major figure in the kingdom, but it would always be kept in mind that the kingdom was the Lord's. In ch.28 these facts are aired again. In v.5 Solomon is said to "sit upon the throne of the kingdom *of the Lord*". In v.7 the kingdom is said to be Solomon's but, in the final analysis, "The Lord reigneth" (16.31).

The words "for ever" (5769) and "for evermore" (5769) take the prophecy beyond the days of Solomon and have definite Messianic undertones. Solomon would occupy the throne for as long as he lived, but the One whom James Montgomery described as "the Lord's Anointed, Great David's greater Son" will never vacate His throne either by death or abdication. Insurrection will never oust Him. "Of the increase of his government and peace there shall be no end, upon the throne of David, and upon his kingdom, to order it, and to establish it with judgment and with justice from henceforth even for ever" (Is 9.7).

The repetition of the word "establish" or "stablish" (3559) (vv.11,12,14) referring to Solomon's kingdom and throne is an indication of the stability of his administration, and the certainty of the succession that would pass on down to Messiah.

Verse 15: The Faithful Prophet

Nathan was under instructions from God: "Go and tell David" (v.4). With the minimum of words our verse sees him discharge that responsibility. Despite the fact that he would have anticipated unpleasantness, he went. For him, there was loss of face and the need to acknowledge, "David, I got it wrong; I misled you". For David there would be the demolition of a cherished ambition, and who could predict the reaction? The anticipated encounter was intimidating but Nathan went. Centuries later a young woman called Esther was faced with another daunting encounter, "go in unto the king" (Esth 4.8); she went. Fast forward another few centuries, and "a certain disciple …named Ananias" was told by the Lord, "go into the street which is called Straight…" (Acts 9.10-11). Fear almost choked him but he went. These people teach us that if we are under orders to undertake something for God it is well to seek His help to suppress natural anxieties and fulfil our mandate rather than to be like Jonah and attempt to run from our responsibilities (Jonah 1.1-3).

Nathan was careful to convey to David exactly what had been communicated to him. Notice the phrases, "*all* these words" and "*all* this vision". He told David what he would have been delighted to hear; he also rehearsed the unpalatable side of the message. Like Nathan, servants of God have a responsibility to give a well-rounded presentation of the truth of God. Paul said to the Ephesian elders, "I shrank not from declaring unto you the whole counsel of God" (Acts 20.27, RV). "I kept back nothing that was profitable unto you" (v.20). Audiences have a responsibility to welcome each aspect of truth. "Now therefore are we all here present before God, to hear *all things that are commanded thee of God*" (Acts 10.33). Samuel's first commission was as difficult as it was possible to be. The message committed to him was loaded with predictions of judgment for his old mentor Eli, but it is recorded that "Samuel told him every whit, and hid nothing from him" (1 Sam 3.18). Let us be as faithful. Whether it is the preaching of the gospel or the teaching of the Word of God, our remit is to proclaim the truth without embellishment, and without subtraction. "The things that thou hast heard of me among many witnesses, *the same* commit thou to faithful men, who shall be able to teach others also" (2 Tim 2.2).

Verses 16-19: David's Humility

We have arrived at a pivotal point in the book. David's concern for the ark has already been noted and it had now been located at Jerusalem. From here on there will be ceaseless activity on his part, with each stage of the unfolding story having a bearing on the ultimate goal of preparing for the temple that his eyes would never see. The disappointment of being denied the privilege of building it will be superseded by relentless action summarised in a later statement, "David prepared abundantly before his death" (22.5). But before all the bustle of activity, "David...sat before the Lord". At v.1 he sat in his house with a man of God; here he sits before the Lord Himself. He spent time in the Lord's presence before he embarked on the unrelenting activity that dominated his latter days. The lesson is that service must be preceded by supplication. A frequently noted illustration of this is the fact that the Lord Jesus called His disciples to be "with him" before He sent "them forth to preach" (Mk 3.14). Three succeeding chapters of Luke's writings reinforce the point. In Luke 24, the disciples were worshipping (v.52). In Acts 1 they were waiting (v.4). In Acts 2 they were witnessing. Getting the order right is of paramount importance. To work without waiting will prove sterile. To preach without praying will be futile. Toil without the tears of intercession will produce nothing for God, and so David "sat before the Lord". Presumably the venue for this encounter with God was before the ark in its new location.

His posture is of interest. On occasions, people in Scripture knelt to pray as did Solomon at the dedication of the temple (2 Chr 6.13). Daniel followed that pattern in his private devotions three times every day (Dan 6.10). The custom was maintained in the New Testament when Paul publicly and privately knelt before God (Acts 20.36; Eph 3.14). Kneeling is indicative of respect for God and is an acknowledgement of His supremacy. Believers who are able to do so should endeavour to replicate these Biblical precedents. There were others who stood to pray as when Abraham "stood yet before the Lord" (Gen 18.22). His standing seemed to indicate an urgency about his appeal as when Moses "stood before him in the breach" (Ps 106.23). But here David sits, and in doing so indicates his quiet contentment with the Lord's will, and his simple enjoyment of the Lord's presence. The language he employs in his prayer makes clear that the fact that he sat did not betray a casual attitude to God. He had the utmost respect for the Almighty, but he settled himself in the tranquillity of devotion to delight himself in the presence of God. There is perhaps a case for that kind of thing when anticipating longer periods of communion in the presence of the Lord as when the bride of the Song of Songs declared, "I *sat down* under his shadow with great delight" (Song 2.3). Zealously she *ran after* him in 1.4. Now she is content to *sit* in his presence and enjoy communion with him.

David's humility is evidenced in his exclamation, "Who am I" (v.16). He had articulated these sentiments when he was a nobody (1 Sam 18.18), but our verse describes the speaker here as "David *the king*". It is wonderful to see that fame and power had not spoiled him. Saul had been a reticent young man (1 Sam 10.21-22), but the prestige of kingship transformed him into an egotistical tyrant. David never allowed his position of authority to mar his sense of modesty and dependence upon God. There are many who have allowed increased wealth or fame to turn them into intolerable snobs. With some, seeming success in the service of God has left them with an inflated sense of self-importance. In a sphere of unprecedented blessing at Ephesus that could easily have engendered pride, Paul was "Serving the Lord with all humility of mind" (Acts 20.19). Let "lowliness of mind" feature in all of our lives - that mind "which was also in Christ Jesus" (Phil 2.3,5).

David realised that the position of favour that he enjoyed and the promises made to him were neither the result of personal merit nor that of his "house", past or present. His family history was humble and his own family left much to be desired. He knew what an ideal ruling family should be but had to admit, "my house be not so with God; yet he hath made with me an everlasting covenant" (2 Sam 23.5). It was divine grace that had conferred on David the honour of being the head of a dynasty; it was not on account of his personal worth or that of his family. He acknowledged, "*Thou* hast brought me hitherto". As quoted earlier, he realised that promotion comes from God (Ps 75.6-7).

At v.17 David regards what he had experienced from God up till that point as being a "small thing" in God's estimation compared to what had now been promised - a royal blood line that would extend "for a great while to come". To him it was staggering that God should place a man of such humble origins on a par with "a man of high degree". This phrase contains an interesting paradox for the word "man" (120) is the word "adam", a word with a reminder that man originated from the red dust of the ground. Even the most noble of earth consist of dust, and to the dust they will return. The elite are as vulnerable as everyone else. Death is the great leveller, and whether a man is placed in a pauper's grave or is accorded a state funeral is of no consequence in the final analysis.

Considering the great honour that had been conferred upon him, David was left speechless (v.18). There are some things that defy description and that beggar language. Paul refers to the Lord Jesus as God's "*unspeakable* gift" (2 Cor 9.15). In the same epistle he records an experience when he heard "*unspeakable* words" impossible to communicate (12.4). Peter refers to a "joy *unspeakable* and full of glory" (1 Pet.1.8). Here, although not altogether at a loss for words, David, a great poet and lucid communicator felt tongue-tied as he pondered the immensity of what he had been promised.

It should be noted that frequently in this short section David refers to himself as "thy servant". Twice in the chapter God called him "my servant" (vv.4,7), and David was happy to take the position he had been accorded. He carried out his task for God with the dignity that befitted his station as the king of Israel, but he never forgot that, exalted though he was, he was only a servant administering in the interests of God. Some aspects of the service of God may *appear* to be more prestigious than others, but we should never forget that at the best we are all servants. "Who then is Apollos, and who Paul? Ministering servants, through whom ye have believed" (1 Cor 3.5, JND).

"For thy servant's sake" (v.19). Here David is happy to acknowledge that one of the main reasons for God divulging His purpose for the future was for his advantage. True, the plan for a dynasty for David was itself for his sake, but predicting it was also for his benefit. The great promise would help alleviate the frustration of being denied the privilege of building the temple. As noted in the introduction to the chapter, God is so kind and His interventions are so timely. This information about the future could have been divulged at any point in David's reign, but God chose to make it known here as a positive sweetener at a time of crushing disappointment.

There is another indication of God's sovereignty in all this when David declares that it is all "according to thine own heart". It is encouraging that the word "heart" is used rather than "mind", because it is an indication of divine affection. It was because God loved David that these wonderful blessings were in store for him. For us, future blessing flows from the love of God. "In love he predestined us for adoption" (Eph 1.4-5, ESV).

Verses 20-22: David's Worship

"Faith cometh by hearing" (Rom 10.17). Thus it was with Rahab - "we have heard..." (Josh 2.10) - and what she heard promoted faith in the living God.

And thus it was with David. He speaks here of "all that we have heard with our ears", and what he had heard had convinced him of the uniqueness of God - "there is none like thee". Added to that he had come to appreciate the solitary nature of his God - "neither is there any God beside thee". These expressions of worship on the part of an Old Testament saint are mirrored in New Testament doctrine. "There is one God" (1 Tim 2.5). "There is none other God but one", and while there are "gods many" that are "called gods", "to us there is but one God, the Father" (1 Cor 8.4-6). The unique solitary nature of God was one of the factors that moved the hearts of Moses and the children of Israel to worship in the wilderness: "Who is like unto thee, O Lord, among the gods? who is like thee, glorious in holiness, fearful in praises, doing wonders?" (Ex 15.11). We too worship in the presence of One who is transcendent.

If in v.20 David is taken up with the uniqueness of God, at v.21 he focuses on the uniqueness of Israel. "What one nation in the earth is like thy people Israel?" First, he cites their redemption experience as being a main feature of their distinctiveness. Redemption is mentioned twice in the verse, but in the first reference the emphasis is on its effects from God's viewpoint; they were redeemed "to be *his* own people". The second reference highlights the benefits for them as being "redeemed *out of Egypt*". These two elements of redemption are true in our own experience. In writing to Titus Paul speaks of "our great God and Saviour Jesus Christ; who gave himself for us, that he might redeem us from all iniquity, and purify unto himself a people for his own possession, zealous of good works" (Titus 2.13-14, RV). Redemption has not only delivered us from the tyranny of sin, but has made us special, the unique people of God among the billions on the planet. That carries with it the responsibility of reflecting this high honour by living a life that is manifestly different from those around. Belonging to God necessitates our glorifying Him in our bodies (1 Cor 6.20).

Being redeemed was not the only mark of distinction that Israel had. He granted them further fame and prestige by "driving out nations from before thy people", but in reality the expulsion of the nations of the land, with Israel's subsequent supremacy, was "to make (Him) a name". It was all for His own honour and to heighten His own reputation among the nations of men, but Israel was the favoured instrument for the enhancement of God's glory. Similarly, in dealing with us He has made us the beneficiaries of a raft of spiritual blessings, but it is all "to the praise of the glory of his grace", "to the praise of his glory", and "unto the praise of his glory" (Eph 1.6,12,14). Everything He has done magnifies His own glory, including the exaltation and universal acknowledgement of the Lord Jesus, which is all "to the glory of God the Father" (Phil 2.11).

It would be easy to miss the two words "for ever" in v.22, but they are very significant. "The gifts and calling of God are without repentance" (Rom 11.29). The people whom God redeemed from Egypt are His special people "for ever". "Hath God cast away his people? God forbid...God hath not cast away his people which he foreknew" (Rom 11.1-2). It is true "that blindness in part is happened to Israel", but it is only "until the fulness of the Gentiles be come in" (v.25). The promises to the patriarchs and to the nation will be fulfilled and must never be explained away as being only illustrative of the spiritual blessings of the church. In the divine plan there is still a remarkable future for Israel.

Just as Israel's position is secure because *God* made them "(his) own people for ever", so the believer in Christ can never be lost. The blessings we enjoy are said to be "eternal": "eternal salvation" (Heb 5.9), "eternal redemption" (9.12), "eternal life", and reception of that eternal life includes the fact that we shall "*never* perish" (Jn 10.28). These blessings could never be described as "eternal" if they are revocable. The cliché, "once saved always saved", attracts some criticism, but the eternal security of the believer is clearly taught in the Word of God.

Verses 23-27: Do as Thou hast Said

In the balance of the chapter David continues to speak to God, but the tone changes from worship to one of supplication. It is not that he has any major request to make, except that God simply put into effect what He had promised. The supplicant is a man well satisfied with the will of God and compliant with the divine plan. His own scheme had been far different, but now that the divine strategy was revealed he would doubtless acknowledge that He is "able to do exceeding abundantly above all that we ask or think" (Eph 3.20). Like Mary the mother of Jesus, he says in effect, "be it unto me according to thy word" (Lk 1.38); or like Paul's companions, "The will of the Lord be done" (Acts 21.14); in his own words, "do as thou hast said". Nathan had said to him at the start of the incident, "Do all that is in thy heart" (v.2). Submissively, David says to God about the revised plan, "do as *thou* hast said".

Although for David the promise of a dynasty was a great honour, an honour that he appreciated, he rather sees it is a further opportunity for God to be esteemed, "that thy name be magnified for ever" (v.24). In v.21 divine activity in the past brought glory to God; here His activity in the future in establishing stable government in the line of David would be another source of honour, for that line would culminate in Messiah.

In part, the glory that would be ascribed to God would be on account of the fact that He would be seen to be not only "the God *of* Israel" but "a God *to* Israel". As the God *of* Israel they were His devotees, and it would be a great source of encouragement to them that their God was "The Lord of hosts", majestic and supreme. As a God *to* Israel He was responsible for them and available to them, and His care for them was going to be evidenced in His establishing this royal line of David.

Transfer these thoughts to our own situation. Believers who comprise "the temple of the living God" can claim the divine promise, "I will be their God" (2 Cor 6.16). They can also enjoy the fact that He is a God *to* them;

"(I) will be a Father unto you, And ye shall be my sons and daughters, saith the Lord Almighty" (v.18). In taking responsibility for us, He combines the power of the Almighty with the tenderness of a Father. Truly, as His people we are well catered for.

Having rejoiced in the fact that God is the God of Israel, David now addresses Him in a more intimate way as he calls Him "my God" (v.25) and repeats the frequent expression, "thy servant". There is no substitute for a personal relationship with Him.

It was David who had said, "The secret of the Lord is with them that fear him; and he will shew them his covenant" (Ps 25.14). That truth is expressed right here: "Thou, O my God, hast told thy servant that thou wilt build him an house". The man who was living in fellowship with his God, was the one to whom these divine "secrets" were divulged. In modern times, God's "secrets" are in a sense open secrets, available to all who are willing to explore the Word of God. As we read and meditate, the secrets are unlocked to us, and we can "rejoice …as one that findeth great spoil" (Ps 119.162).

Another practical point that emerges from v.25 is this: it was the promise of God that had stirred David to pray, for note the "therefore" of the verse. In his prayer David was simply expressing his willingness to lay hold on the promise of God. Some of his successors in the line of faith would do the same. Undoubtedly, Elijah believed the promise of God when he prayed that it would not rain (1 Kings 17). Daniel's prayer of ch.9 was based on the promise of God through Jeremiah the prophet. Faith accepts divine promises, and prays accordingly.

David rounds off his prayer by simply reiterating his request for God to bless as He had promised. His lineage would be the object of blessing "for ever", for, as we have noted constantly, the dynasty would continue right through until the days when the Messiah would "reign over the house of Jacob for ever" (Lk 1.33). Psalm 72 is the kingdom psalm, and at the end we are told, "The prayers of David the son of Jesse are ended". It was not that he never prayed again, but a man whose hopes were of earthly blessing and earthly glory could ask for no more as he anticipated that day when the Messiah would occupy the throne and reign universally and without interruption. The father of English hymn-writers, Isaac Watts, wrote a well loved hymn based on the Psalm:

> Jesus shall reign where'er the sun
> Doth his successive journeys run;
> His kingdom stretch from shore to shore
> Till moons shall wax and wane no more.

We echo the words at the conclusion of the psalm, "Amen, and Amen".

1 CHRONICLES 18

Chapters 18-20 form a section of the book that records David's military triumphs. This may appear irrelevant to the main theme, the building of a house for God, but in fact these exploits were crucial to that project. First, in stamping Israel's supremacy on the whole restless region David created the conditions of peace that were necessary for the construction of the temple. Second, the spoils of these wars were the main source of the materials that were necessary for the building. The spoils of Egypt had provided constituents for the tabernacle; these spoils of battle were the resources for the temple. So what may appear to be a hiatus in the main story-line is in fact an integral part of the narrative.

Chapters 17 and 18 provide an illustration of the teaching of the Lord Jesus in the Sermon on the Mount: "seek ye first the kingdom of God, and his righteousness; and all these things shall be added unto you" (Mt 6.33). In ch.17, by his desire to build the house of God, and by his spirit of devotion as he sat before the Lord, David showed that he was making the things of God his top priority. As recompense, in ch.18 material things were "added unto" him. It is wonderful to observe that subsequently he donated to God what God had given to him.

We lose what on ourselves we spend;
We have as treasure without end
Whatever, Lord, to thee we lend,
Who givest all.
(Christopher Wordsworth)

Verse 1: The Philistines

"After this." In Scripture, time pointers are very important, and such phrases as "in these days" or "after these things" should be taken into account when considering the significance of any event. The timing of incidents often holds a lesson for us. The "after this" here obviously relates to the events of ch.17. God had made promise of a settled existence for Israel and the destruction of David's enemies (vv.9-10). In fulfilment of the promise, the Philistines and other enemies were now subdued. Lesson one is that God is always true to His word. In v.16 David had "sat before the Lord", but "after this" he was in conflict with enemies. Lesson two is that life is not one long period of uninterrupted communion with God. There are enemies to be faced and battles to be fought, but time in the presence of the Lord fortifies us for the spiritual conflict. In ch.17 David was worshipping; here he is warring.

The Philistines were the inveterate enemies of the people of God. They constantly tormented Israel and frequently conquered them. At last their power was broken. What had commenced in the days of Samson (Judg 13.5) and was achieved temporarily in the days of Samuel (1 Sam 7.13) was now a *fait accompli* under David. Hereafter, Scripture references to the Philistines are sparse, and their troubling of Israel minimal.

Comments have been made previously as to the typical significance of the Philistines. They represent unregenerate men who masquerade as believers among the people of God. It is not sufficient to curtail their influence; they must be repulsed and banished.

So great was David's victory that he displaced them from the city that had reared their champions for "Gath and her towns" were taken out of their hands. God's promise of 17.10 was not fulfilled in half measure.

Verse 2: Moab

If a spiritual lesson is to be learned from Moab we could regard that nation as being an illustration of the flesh. We arrive at that conclusion as we take into account its sordid origins (Gen 19.37). The word "subdued" is not employed here as in v.1, but rather that "David *smote* Moab". The flesh will never be totally subdued but will always try to assert itself. "Fleshly lusts...*war* against the soul" (1 Pet 2.11). In his first epistle John speaks of the Christian's three enemies: the world, the flesh and the devil. He says that the young men had "overcome the wicked one" (2.14). He teaches too that the world can be overcome (5.4-5). There is no reference to the flesh being overcome for the conflict with it seems to be constant; "the flesh lusteth against the Spirit, and the Spirit against the flesh" (Gal 5.17). However, we can "Walk in the Spirit", and "be led of the Spirit", and bear "the fruit of the Spirit", and "live in the Spirit" (vv.16,18,22,25). Submitting to the Holy Spirit limits the damaging effects of the flesh in our lives.

Keeping in mind what was said in the introduction to the chapter, it is significant that the Moabites "brought gifts" to David, the tribute due by a subservient nation. These events are recorded as having a bearing on the main theme of the book - building a house for God. These "gifts" from Moab would be among the materials dedicated to that project.

Verse 3-4: Hadarezer, King of Zobah

Zobah was to the north-east of Israel, and its defeat was an absolute rout, to the extent that its forces were pursued to Hammath far to the north. King Hadarezer had expansionist ambitions with plans to retake annexed territory as far east as the Euphrates (2 Sam 8.3). David punctured that dream and no doubt took control of that region himself, bringing the boundaries of his kingdom closer to the bounds of the land that had been promised to Abraham (Gen 15.18).

Hadarezer had a massive military machine (v.4) but David stripped him of every resource. It should be noted that whereas 2 Samuel 8.4 indicates that 700 horsemen were captured, the number here is said to be 7,000. An added complication is that some translations of 2 Samuel 8.4 omit the word "chariots" and speak of 1,700 horsemen, so translations give us no help in accounting for the apparent discrepancy, but the general feeling among commentators is that the 700 refers to the captains, each of them being responsible for a band of ten. Here is a quotation from the commentary on 2 Samuel 8.4 from *John Gill's Expositor*:

"'Chariots' are not in the text here, it is only 1,700 'horsemen'; but it is supplied from 1 Chronicles 18.4; where the word is expressly mentioned, and there the horsemen are said to be seven thousand as in the Septuagint version here, and in Josephus; which may be reconciled by observing, with Kimchi and Abarbinel, that here the chief officers are meant, there all the chariots and horsemen that were under their command are mentioned, which together made up that large number; or else here are meant the ranks and companies of horse David took, which were seven hundred; and these having ten in a company or rank, made seven thousand; and there the complement of soldiers in those companies and ranks are intended".

Other commentators prefer to speak of an apparent copyist's error at 2 Samuel 8.4 - for example, J. A. Thompson in *The New American Commentary*.

David's dependence upon God is evidenced in that he "houghed (hamstrung, ESV) all the chariot horses" rendering them useless for military purposes. Some may be outraged at the cruelty to the animals, but this was ancient arms control, pure and simple. These horses could have been a great asset to his own army but he himself had written, "Some trust in chariots, and some in horses: but we will remember the name of the Lord our God" (Ps 20.7). It is good when a man's practices and pronouncements agree. The Lord's indictment of the Pharisees was this: "they say, and do not" (Mt 23.3).

God had warned Israel's kings against "multiply(ing) horses" (Deut 17.16), and at a later date Judah was told by Isaiah, "Woe to them that go down to Egypt for help; and stay on horses, and trust in chariots, because they are many; and in horsemen, because they are very strong; but they look not unto the Holy One of Israel, neither seek the Lord!" (Is 31.1). Reliance upon chariots and horses was an indication that dependence on God had been abandoned, and David did not make that blunder. Human logic would have dictated that cavalry and chariot divisions among his forces would have increased the likelihood of victory, but, rather than leaning "unto (his) own understanding", he trusted "in the Lord with all (his) heart" (Prov 3.5). Let us all challenge our hearts about this. In the emergencies of life, is our trust in the Lord, or do we have our own well thought out schemes to resolve the crisis? Do we resort to the logical and the obvious or do we depend on God in prayer?

Why David should have spared a hundred chariots is not clear. It has been suggested that they were reserved for a triumphal parade then dealt with as the others. Or perhaps they were to be used as wagons to transport the spoils of battle. We have entered the realm of speculation!

Verses 5-6: Syria

Damascus was quick to come to the aid of Zobah, an ill-fated campaign which left 22,000 of its warriors slain. The attack and the defeat of the Syrians meant that it was unnecessary for David's army to advance en masse as far north as Damascus. However, as in v.13, garrisons were placed in the vanquished territory. The simple lesson is that in spiritual things, ground gained has to be defended. If not kept in check, every defeated foe will regroup and make fresh assaults. It is important never to yield an inch of the ground that we have taken; we need to consolidate any progress that has been made. Syria too was placed under tribute. More materials for the house of God!

We are now informed of the secret of David's success. "The Lord gave victory to David whithersoever he went" (RV; see also v.13). Once more we are learning that God is always true to His word. As promised in 17.10, "all" David's enemies were subdued. Because God was on his side, no weapon formed against him prospered (Is 54.17). We have been taught this lesson throughout the book, but let it be an encouragement once more. "If God be for us, who can be against us?" (Rom 8.31). With John E. Bode we sing,

> I shall not fear the battle
> If Thou art by my side,
> Nor wander from the pathway
> If Thou wilt be my guide.

Verses 7-8: Plunder

The victory over Hadarezer and his confederates yielded great plunder, and we are told specifically that in time this was utilised by Solomon in connection with the temple. The mention of this confirms what has been said about this chapter being an integral part of the main theme of the book and not a mere interlude.

Reference is made to shields of gold. While these were taken to Jerusalem, they must not be confused with those that Solomon had; Solomon's were purpose made (1 Kings 10.17). Sadly, they were confiscated by the king of Egypt in Rehoboam's day and substituted by "brasen shields" (14.25-28). It is a little insight into how there can be deterioration from one generation to the next, of how we can become content with brass instead of gold.

The tonnage of brass that was removed from Hadarezer was well used by Solomon for various items of the temple, including the sea, a thick elaborate receptacle that rested on twelve oxen (1 Kings 7.23-26).

Verses 9-11a: Tou, King of Hamath

Hadarezer's retreating army had been pursued as far north as Hamath (v.3), and it appears that Tou, king of that area, saw himself as David's next target. He had no stomach for conflict and endeavoured to pre-empt an attack. The conquest of Hadarezer had pleased him since they were long standing rivals, so he sent his son to placate David. It appears to have been an ancient custom to send a son as a representative of the highest honour. In one of the Lord's parables, after servants had been assaulted, stoned and slain, it was anticipated that a son would be treated with dignity; "They will reverence my son" (Mk 12.6). That would have been the norm. In a future day it will be said to the rulers of the nations, "Kiss the Son, lest he be angry, and ye perish from the way, when his wrath is kindled but a little. Blessed are all they that put their trust in him" (Ps 2.12).

In his endeavour to appease David, both greetings and gifts were sent. The tenor of the greetings is interesting. First, he "inquire(d) of his *welfare*" (7965), the very familiar word SHALOM, peace. Care was taken to observe customary protocol. Then, he "congratulate(d) (1288) him" as the AV says, and it almost smacks of flattery, a real attempt to ingratiate himself with the conqueror. Many translations are happy to retain the word "congratulate" although the word is translated extensively "to bless" throughout the Old Testament. "Congratulate" does seem to fit the context here, for Tou appears pleased and grateful that an old opponent had been vanquished, and so he applauds the victor.

Gifts were also sent, "all manner of vessels of gold and silver and brass", and so on this occasion David had his spoils without conflict. Whether it was the plaudits or the donations that carried weight with David is unclear, but he seems content to see Tou as an ally rather than a threat.

The materials sent by Tou were "dedicated unto the Lord". The chapter has shown David's obedience to the command of Deuteronomy 17.16, the ban on a king multiplying horses. There is now compliance with the terms of the following verse: "neither shall he greatly multiply to himself silver and gold" (v.17). There was potential for David to amass phenomenal amounts of wealth and material resources. He had no such ambitions, but rather what had been committed to him was held in trust for God and dedicated to Him. For David, material things were a matter of disinterest. Apply the lesson as you consider the New Testament truth of stewardship. "Lay not up for yourselves treasures upon earth" (Mt 6.19). "Make to yourselves friends by means of the mammon of unrighteousness" (Lk 16.9, RV). "Let every one of you lay by him in store, as God hath prospered him" (1 Cor 16.2). "Let him labour, working with his hands the thing which is good, that he may have to give to him that needeth" (Eph 4.28). These are sample quotations that show us that we ought to be the channels rather than the reservoirs of material resources. As with David, whatever comes our way is held in trust for God to be used wisely and well. One day we will hear the summons, "give an account of thy stewardship" (Lk 16.2).

The chapter commenced with conquests in the south-west, as far south as Gath. Then we were taken to the east with the defeat of the Moabites. These latest verses have seen triumphs in the north. Of course there was no danger from the west, because Israel's territory extended right to the Mediterranean Sea, so really, every point of the compass was accounted for as David imposed his authority on the whole region. Eliminating the possibility of assault created security for his land so that the temple could be constructed in an atmosphere of peace.

Verses 11b-13: Further Conquests

Evidently other nations had been conquered, and again, the spoils of battle had been "dedicated unto the Lord". The dedication of plunder from the north was not a one-off occurrence; it had become the usual procedure. This house of God was going to be "exceeding magnifical" (22.5) so it demanded exceptional resources. There was absolute consistency in the way David handled these material resources. God's interests always came first. When Jonah "paid the fare" for his boat trip to Tarshish, he was using the Lord's money to pursue a pathway of disobedience (Jonah 1.3). Are we like David, making sure that the Lord always has His portion, or like Jonah, misusing what God has given us in the pursuit of something unsanctioned by heaven?

At v.12 the spotlight falls on one of Abishai's exploits. 2 Samuel 8.13 attributes this resounding victory over Edom to David. Evidently Abishai was delegated the task and commanded the forces and won the victory, but it was David who "gat him a name". What was done in David's name reflected on him and the lesson is that what is accomplished for Christ by His servants is for His glory, rather than for the honour of the servant.

There is just the possibility that the Edomites had tried to take advantage of David's absence on his northern campaigns to mount an attack against Judah. When dealing with subtle enemies we must always watch our backs!

In the wake of victory, garrisons were established in the occupied territory, with the fresh reminder that defeated foes must be kept in check. The spiritual lesson has been applied in the comments on v.6.

The statement is repeated that "the Lord preserved David *whithersoever he went*". As we have noticed, the "whithersoever he went" encompassed areas to the north, south, and east. Divine preservation was enjoyed in every sphere and it was the Lord who gave the victory every time. Successive victories and universal success never inflated David's ego or robbed him of his sense of reliance upon God. The consistency of his attitude and behaviour is most commendable, a model for us all as we move from project to project in the service of God, or to use the language of our verse, "whithersoever" we go.

Verses 14-17: David's Administration

This short paragraph gives some details of David's administration of which further information will be released in ch.27. There, the names of his officials and civil servants are recorded, as well as those of the members of his cabinet (vv.32-34). What little we learn here gives us an insight into the character of David's regime. First, his kingdom was a united kingdom - he "reigned over *all* Israel". The civil war that had followed Saul's death was a thing of the past and the whole nation had rallied under David's banner. Happy is that kingdom that is not "divided against itself" for if it is, it will be "brought to desolation" (Mt 12.25). This kingdom's battles had been against foes outwith its borders as the chapter has shown; it had not been torn apart by internal strife. Let us learn the lesson. Of our relationship with each other Peter says, "be subject one to another". Of our attitude to the enemy he says, "Whom resist" (1 Pet 5.5,9). On the eve of the Battle of Trafalgar, Lord Nelson confronted two squabbling officers, pointed to the French fleet, and said, "Yonder, gentlemen, is the enemy".

In this kingdom, David "executed judgment and justice". There was no injustice, and no exploitation. The judicial system was unimpeachable and there was a policy of zero tolerance towards corruption. David ruled in the fear of God. Thus it will be under the administration of the KING OF KINGS; "Behold, a king shall reign in righteousness" (Is 32.1). "With righteousness shall he judge the poor, and reprove with equity for the meek of the earth" (Is 11.4). "A sceptre of righteousness is the sceptre of thy kingdom" (Heb 1.8).

This justice extended to "*all* his people" so there was no discrimination. In the days of Amos, the poor were exploited, and had no recourse to the legal system. "They afflict the just, they take a bribe, and they turn aside the poor in the gate from their right" (5.12). David operated an even-handed system of justice that was not influenced by a man's wealth or status. He dealt with things in a non-partisan manner and did not pander to any special interest groups. Such would bring pleasure to God, for there are constant warnings in both Testaments regarding the mistreatment of the poor and underprivileged. "My brethren, have not the faith of our Lord Jesus Christ, the Lord of glory, with respect of persons" (James 2.1). Let that principle govern every department of our lives, avoiding prejudice in the business world, in family life, and in assembly matters.

Perhaps the reason for David's impartiality was that he regarded all the people as "*his* people". He felt responsible for them all. Although they were God's people, they were his people in that he was accountable for them all as "ruler over my people Israel" (17.7). These people as his people were dear to him, and hence his concern that in matters of "judgment and justice" there was equal opportunity for all. If we regard every believer as being dear to us, a brother "for whom Christ died" (1 Cor 8.11), that attitude will regulate our behaviour towards them and enable us to treat them all in a fair-minded way.

David was not only concerned about a fair, judicial system for his people, but the defence and security of the nation was a top priority. Hence, "Joab the son of Zeruiah was over the host" (v.15). Comments were made earlier about Joab's lack of integrity. Undoubtedly he was greatly deficient in the finer points of life, but he was an expert military man. Under his command wars were won and the security of the nation preserved, and despite his obvious shortcomings, he did display a fierce loyalty to David. Spiritual leaders should be as concerned as David for the defence of their people. Paul warned the Ephesian elders of danger from "grievous wolves", who would "enter in...not sparing the flock" (Acts 20.29). A true shepherd will do all in his power to protect the flock rather than being like a hireling who flees when the wolf approaches (Jn 10.12-13). It is important to have a good defence policy in place.

Recording the nation's history was also of interest to David, and so Jehoshaphat was employed as a "recorder", a chronicler; a record was being maintained. We often have to remind ourselves that our individual lives are like a story that is unfolding, a story that is being recorded by a divine Chronicler. "We spend our years as a tale that is told" (Ps 90.9). The details of every human life are maintained in a database in heaven. This has particular relevance for the lost, for they will be "judged out of those things...written in the books, according to their works" (Rev 20.12). For the believer, "the things done in his body" will be recompensed at "the judgment seat of Christ" (2 Cor 5.10). For us, too, the story of life has been well documented.

The spiritual health of the nation was also of great concern to David, and so mention is made in v.16 of the priests. At this point, there appears to have been an unorthodox arrangement, with two men functioning as high priests, Zadok and Abimelech. Zadok was the legitimate incumbent in the line of Aaron's son Eleazar (6.4-8). At some point there had been an unauthorised transfer of the high priesthood to the line of Ithamar, and Eli was of that stock. However, the judgment on his family resulted in the eventual displacement of his descendant Abimelech. He had taken sides with Adonijah in his rebellion, and consequently was expelled by Solomon (1 Kings 2.27), and from then on Zadok functioned alone. The descendants of this noble man will feature in the priesthood in the days of the Millennium (Ezek 40.46; 43.19; 44.15; 48.11). It is wonderful to think that throughout many generations God has had His eye on this priestly line; Zadok's descendants will survive right through the last phase of human history until time is no more.

Shavsha was David's "secretary" (RV margin), no doubt attending to his correspondence and his diary. The passing allusion to a seemingly minor function is an indication of the orderly way in which David attended to the affairs of state, with the reminder to us that in the things of God we ought to "Let all things be done decently and in order" (1 Cor 14.40).

It is generally agreed that the Cherethites and the Pelethites were David's personal bodyguard, supervised by Benaiah, a man whose responsibilities extended into the reign of Solomon. Indeed, he acted for Solomon as an executioner (1 Kings 2) as every rebel and rival were put to the sword. Kings' bodyguards feature here and there in Scripture, as for example, the sixty valiant men who protected Solomon, each with their sword at the ready. (Song 3.7-8). At his coronation, the young king Joash was surrounded by protectors, "every man with weapons in his hand" (2 Kings 11.8). Let us apply a practical lesson. Our blessed Lord is under attack. The great truths of His deity, His virgin birth, His bodily resurrection and other major doctrines are being assailed. In the face of increasing atheism, cult activity, and the damaging pronouncements of apostate Christendom, His people, with the "sword of the Spirit...the word of God" (Eph 6.17) in their hands, should militantly promote these glorious truths. Let us be spiritual Cherethites and Pelethites and defend the King.

The last clause of the chapter indicates that David involved his sons in his administration. Perhaps this was a weak point in his arrangements. They had no job description, were ministers without portfolio, and yet they were part of the decision making process. At least some of these young men were ill fitted for the task, having neither spiritual desires, natural wisdom, nor complete loyalty to their father. David should have remembered the problems created by Samuel's sons (1 Sam 8.1-5). Sadly, Samuel was blinkered to their failings as can so often be the case when a family is involved. There is no sphere of life where nepotism can be justified, and it is most certainly out of place in the spiritual realm.

Military conquests, and stable government - our chapter has taken us a stage nearer the goal of "an house for the Lord God of Israel" (22.6).

1 CHRONICLES 19

Keep in mind that chapters 18-20 form a section of the book in which there are the records of David's military triumphs. These were victories that created the conditions of peace necessary for building the house of God and for providing the resources for the project.

Various campaigns were recounted in ch.18, but now the focus is on one particular war, the details of which extend to 20.3. If the Nahash of our chapter is the same king as was defeated by Saul in his first military triumph (1 Sam 11), he must have been an extremely old man. It is more likely that Nahash was a common name among Ammonite kings and that the references are to two different men. Insulting behaviour on the part of his son was the catalyst for this conflict, and it all ended in disaster for him and his people.

It was during the latter stages of this episode that there was the dreadful incident of David's adultery (2 Sam 11), but the Chronicler leaves that unmentioned, obscured in the mists of history; it has no bearing on his main theme, the building of a house for God. In the context of 2 Samuel, it was necessary that the whole situation be exposed, for it served as a background for narratives recounting the disintegration of family life in the royal court; in the behaviour of his family, David was reaping what he had sown.

Verses 1-2: David's Kindness

Undoubtedly David had a combative and courageous approach to life, but there was a warmth about his personality that was admirable. The mean-spirited would benefit from a study of his character. "I will shew kindness" (v.2). It was not the first time that his benevolence had been expressed. Mephibosheth, a crippled fugitive and a potential rival had experienced "the kindness of God" courtesy of David (2 Sam 9.3). The eighty-year-old Barzillai could have been another beneficiary of David's largesse had he responded to the invitation to be one of the royal court (2 Sam 19.31-39). Now the bereaved Hanun is the object of David's kindly interest.

> Be kind; in this cold, callous world be kind.
> A lovely ornament for souls to wear
> Is that warm gem of kindliness of mind,
> That touch of human sympathy so rare;
> Be kind.
>
> (I. Y. Ewan)

Some have found fault with David for having any contact at all with the people of Ammon, but the reason for his interest is explained. In some circumstance of which we know nothing, the deceased king had shown consideration to David, and David's wish was to reciprocate that favour by at least expressing his condolences to the bereaved family. It is shameful to be unappreciative and there can come the moment when it is pay-back time. Paul made that point in connection with the responsibility of a family to its widowed mother. The word he used was "requite" (287), translated "repay" in the NKJV (1 Tim 5.4). A mother's expenditure of care, affection, energy and finance on a growing family should be reciprocated by that family in her old age. In the general round of life that feeling of responsibility towards a benefactor is not always in evidence, as is seen in various Scriptures. Jehoiada the priest saved the life of the infant Joash and guided him wisely as long as he lived. After Jehoiada's decease, Joash was responsible for slaying his son, and Scripture records: "Thus Joash the king remembered not the kindness which Jehoiada his father had done to him, but slew his son" (2 Chr 24.22). Converts in Asia had forgotten the rigours and hazards that Paul had encountered in bringing them the life-changing gospel so that in his old age Paul wrote of their disloyalty: "all they which are in Asia be turned away from me" (2 Tim 1.15). Nine cleansed lepers appear to have been so euphoric about their healing that they forgot the Healer. "Where are the nine?", was the Lord's enquiry (Lk 17.17). David's heart was bigger than that so his desire was to return the courtesy that had been shown to him.

Generally speaking, visiting the bereaved is a comfort to them. On the death of Lazarus, "the Jews" visited the home at Bethany, and John tells us plainly that they "comforted" the sorrowing sisters (Jn 11.19,31). On occasions, "comforters" can be less than adequate as in the case of Job's friends who "made an appointment together to come to mourn with him and to comfort him" (Job 2.11). The visitors to the home of Jairus were very superficial and intrusive (Mk 5.38-40). Wisdom is needed in such distressing circumstances. Most of us feel inadequate and tongue-tied, but there are occasions when just a brief visit indicates enough interest and concern to encourage the desolate mourner. Thus with a genuine motive and a desire to be helpful, David sent his representatives to "Hanun the son of Nahash".

It may be worth mentioning that the name Hanun means gracious, and Nahash means serpent. Taking the present narrative into account, it appears that Hanun rose above the connotations of his name, and that the behaviour of Nahash gave the lie to the meaning of his!

Verses 3-4: Hanun's Folly

Every government has its advisors, and it is to be expected that inexperienced leaders lean heavily on their counsellors. However, on more than one occasion in Scripture novice kings accepted unsound advice. Rehoboam solicited guidance, and in acting upon it he divided the nation (1 Kings 12.1-20). Ahaziah's mother and "the house of Ahab" were his counsellors and it was "to his destruction" (2 Chr 22.1-5). Here, "the princes of the children of Ammon" filled Hanun's ear with falsehood and suspicion and set him on a route that led to disaster. Advice can be helpful, particularly if taken from Him who is called "Wonderful, Counseller" (Is 9.6), but we all need to be wary about walking "in the counsel of the ungodly" (Ps 1.1). Unhelpful advice from unsaved people can place us on a pathway to ruin.

Perhaps the people of Ammon had reason to fear David, for they were among his conquests (18.11), but to question his motives so seriously was completely unjustified. The mission of mercy was portrayed as a military ploy. We need to be constantly reminded that we are not in a position to judge motives. The Corinthians ran a critical eye over Paul, and he was "judged" by them. He indicated to them that a true assessment awaits the coming of the Lord for He alone fully understands our motives, and in that day of review He "will make manifest the counsels of the hearts" (1 Cor 4.1-5). No doubt there are occasions when it is obvious that a man's activities place a question mark over his motives as when Absalom's smooth ingratiating manner was calculated to "(steal) the hearts of the men of Israel" (2 Sam 15.1-6), but here there was nothing in David's manner to suggest that his men were on a spying mission; the insinuation was a slander.

David's representatives were subjected to a double insult. Their beards were shaved and the Chronicler assumes that his readers are familiar with the cynical way in which this was done; it added significantly to the indignity (2 Sam 10.4). In these ancient times, to be clean-shaven was deemed a disgrace. They interfered with their garments in such a way as to ensure that they were humiliated. Their feelings are summarised at v.5: "the men were greatly ashamed". Perhaps it gives us an insight into the feelings of our beloved Lord in the events surrounding His trial and crucifixion for He was not insensitive to the cruel mockery of His creatures. "Thou knowest my reproach, and my shame, and my dishonour" (Ps 69.19, RV). "I am worm, and no man; a reproach of men, and despised of the people" (Ps 22.6). His beard was not shaved but rather they "plucked off the hair" from His face (Is 50.6). For Him, there was stinging pain as they tugged handfuls of hair from His cheeks. The removal of His garments is also well documented in the Gospel records. They became perquisites for the soldiers, so try to imagine His sense of disgrace at being stripped and left exposed on a tree in sight of a vulgar gaping mob.

Bearing shame and scoffing rude
In my place condemned He stood;
Sealed my pardon with His blood;
Hallelujah! what a Saviour!
(Philip P. Bliss)

Verse 5: David's Concern

On hearing of the outrage, David was gripped by a sense of indignation, and it became evident to all that matters would not rest there; there would be reprisals. However, it is to his credit that his first concern was for his abused and embarrassed servants. No sooner had they re-crossed Jordan and arrived at Jericho than he had the message delivered, "Tarry at Jericho until your beards be grown". They were given leave of absence until their dignity was restored. There is a lesson there in industrial relations. The servant/master relationship not only demands loyalty on the part of the servant, but consideration on the part of the master; there has to be mutual respect. It was so with the centurion and his servant in Luke 7. The servant was obedient to his master; "I say…to my servant, Do this, and he doeth it" (v.8). The master was fond of his servant; he was "dear unto him" (v.2). There was a similar rapport between Boaz and his workforce. He said to them, "The Lord be with you", and they responded, "The Lord bless thee" (Ruth 2.4). Let Christian employees be diligent and loyal, and let Christian employers or managers be as considerate as David was here.

Verses 6-7: Hanun Mobilises

Whether David was already gathering his army, or Ammonite intelligence had uncovered his intentions, they now knew that they would be targeted as a result of the disgraceful episode; they "saw that they had made themselves odious to David". The word "odious" (887) is the same word that Jacob used after the genocide at Shechem. He said to his sons Simeon and Levi, "Ye have troubled me to make me to *stink* among the inhabitants of the land" (Gen 34.30). The word is very expressive of the utter disgust that David felt in consequence of the shabby treatment of his envoys. Of course, it had also been a slap in the face for him, questioning his integrity and his compassion, and thus military retaliation was inevitable. Under threat, Hanun marshalled his forces and hired mercenaries from three different sources at a cost of 1,000 talents of silver. Sin is always costly, and the price of sin seems to escalate. No doubt the chief priests thought that they were rid of the Nazarene cheaply at a cost of thirty pieces of silver. Soon afterwards they were paying "large money" to bribe the guards to spread a falsehood about the empty tomb (Mt 28.12). Sadly for him, Hanun's outlay was going to be money misspent.

Verses 8-9: Preparation for Battle

Hanun's choice of battleground was Medeba (v.7), a frontier town on the river Arnon, and there Joab was "sent"; David delegated this campaign to his general. He did not underestimate the enemy for with Joab he sent "all the host of the mighty men", but it appears that he saw no need for the supreme commander to be present! Is there a hint of complacency here? Has David settled down? Have the flames of militarism been doused? Has he forsaken the trenches for the comfort of the palace? Whatever the reasons for his non-involvement, it had disastrous results. As stated in the introduction to the chapter, it was at this period that he got involved with Bath-sheba, an unfortunate watershed in his life with things never being the same again. His experience should be a beacon of warning. Complacently delegating responsibility in favour of ease and comfort leaves us vulnerable. To go for the soft options in life can be to invite trouble. To abandon the spiritual fray by entangling ourselves "with the affairs of this life" brings displeasure to "him who hath chosen (us) to be a soldier" (2 Tim 2.4). Never let your guard down as David appeared to do here.

The enemy divided his forces, the Ammonite regiment being "before the gate of the city" and the mercenaries "in the field". As subsequent verses will show, in plotting his strategy Joab took these circumstances into account. The way the enemy deploys will dictate how we should face him. There is no standard approach when it comes to spiritual conflict, for sometimes the devil can display the cruelty that his title "the dragon" implies, and on other occasions he can be as subtle as his title "that old serpent" suggests (Rev 20.2). Hence Peter's call to "be vigilant" (1 Pet 5.8), alert, in the face of his subtlety, but also to "resist" him, firm in the face of his cruelty (v.9). Here, Joab's tactics gave appropriate consideration to the battle-lines that had been drawn up.

Verses 10-12: Joab's Strategy

Whatever may be said about Joab's moral character, he was undoubtedly a master of his art; his expertise as a military man was beyond question. The Syrian mercenaries with their chariot divisions were deemed to be the main threat and so he selected "the choice of Israel" to handle that side of the battle. As a leader, he knew his men and their capabilities, and deployed them appropriately. Spiritual leaders today should ensure that those under their care are used to maximum advantage in the sphere for which God has gifted them, recognising that not everyone has the same capabilities. Shepherds, know your sheep.

By way of making a practical point, it should be stated again that Joab did have a strategy in all this. He was not haphazard in his approach to the battle, simply reacting to circumstances as they emerged. Similarly, leaders today should be pro-active in taking appropriate initiatives in the things of God; there is no virtue in just waiting for circumstances and reacting to them.

The Ammonites were seen as the enemy's weak flank and "the rest of the people" under Abishai's command were assigned to that area of the battlefield. However, the two brothers agreed to be supportive of each other should one or other come under pressure from the enemy. Again, there is a lesson in that for us. Hypocritically, the wicked Cain renounced all responsibility for his brother - "Am I my brother's keeper?" (Gen 4.9) - but as believers we do have a responsibility for our brethren. When the Lord Jesus saw Peter under attack from Satan He said to him, "I have prayed for thee" (Lk 22.32); we have a responsibility to pray. We all need each other, for "Two are better than one…if they fall, the one will lift up his fellow: but woe to him that is alone when he falleth; for he hath not another to help him up" (Eccl 4.9-10).

Verse 13: Words of Encouragement

Man-management seemed to be another of Joab's leadership qualities, and so, prior to engaging the enemy, there was the pep talk, the morale booster, the words of encouragement. "Be of good courage, and let us behave ourselves valiantly." No doubt the bulk of his forces were seasoned campaigners, veterans of many a conflict, but perhaps never before had they seen such a formidable force of chariots, and hence the need for encouragement. God graciously encouraged Joshua using similar language. Moses was a hard act to follow and Joshua was about to enter uncharted territory and face ferocious resistance, but the word from God was this, "Be strong and of a good courage" (Josh 1.6,7,9). From the unlikely source of the trans-Jordan tribes there were similar words of support (v.18). In the lives of the disciples there were numerous incidents in which fear gripped them, and almost unconsciously we raise our eyebrows in disapproval. We forget that so often we ourselves have been paralysed by fear, and what should have been done was left undone, and what should have been said was left unsaid. Let us take courage: "God gave us not a spirit of fearfulness; but of power and love and discipline" (2 Tim 1.7, RV); "Let not your heart be troubled, neither let it be afraid" (Jn 14.27).

In his speech Joab provided a stimulant for courage. This conflict was for "our people, and for the cities of our God". Enemy aggression was directed at the people of God and so in the ultimate at God Himself. Israel's cities were *His* cities. The needs of the people of God, and the interests of God Himself should motivate us to be valiant in living for God, serving Him, and fighting His battles. In the face of opposition let us keep in mind the words of Nehemiah, "Be not ye afraid of them: remember the Lord, which is great and terrible, and fight for your brethren" (Neh 4.14).

Joab's short word of encouragement concluded with an expression of reliance on God, and submission to His will: "let the Lord do that which is good in his sight". An expert battle-plan and courageous warriors would be of no avail if the Lord were not at work on their behalf. The same is true in a New Testament context as regards the work of the gospel. Paul was "bold" (1 Thess 2.2), and his integrity as the Lord's servant was beyond question (vv.3-12), but the crucial element for success at Thessalonica was the fact that the word came "in power, and in the Holy Ghost" (1.5). On our part, then, there has to be planning and effort, integrity and conviction, but we are totally dependent on divine activity if anything at all is to be accomplished for eternity.

Verses 14-15: Victory

Joab took the battle to the enemy and the might of Syria turned tail. Observing this, the Ammonites fled and were holed up in the city, their final defeat being effected in ch.20. There is a simple lesson here on the power of influence. Fear, discouragement and cowardice can be infectious. That is why the commanders of Israel were told to discharge "the fearful and fainthearted", "lest his brethren's heart faint as well as his heart" (Deut 20.8). Let us beware lest our pessimism should have a negative impact upon our fellow-believers. The adverse effects of influence are illustrated in John 21 when Peter declared, "I go a fishing" (v.3). There was an immediate response from another six disciples, "We also go with thee". If we do carry weight with other people, let us induce them to do what is right rather than wrong; "be thou an example of the believers" (1 Tim 4.12). In our present passage, the Syrian retreat demoralised the Ammonites and they followed suit.

This initial victory was the signal for Joab to report to Jerusalem, and it appears that David involved himself in the next phase of the campaign (v.17).

Verse 16: Reinforcements

Syrian pride was hurt, and so they sent for reinforcements to exact revenge. Normally "the river" signifies the great river Euphrates, so the extra forces were being drawn from afar. The name, Hadarezer, has already featured in the previous chapter when "David smote Hadarezer" (v.3). It appears that the reference is to his forces being conquered though the man himself survived. On this occasion his commander Shophach was "at their head" (RV). One can almost picture him proudly striding ahead of his troops in support of his fellow-countrymen, but he was leading them to their destruction. The Syrians had regrouped, and the lesson is that the enemies of the people of God never lie down despite being defeated. Further attacks can be expected. After his encounter with the Lord Jesus in the wilderness, the devil "departed from him *for a season*" (Lk 4.13), the implication being that he would be back! Nehemiah's opponents had a plan to ambush him, and to that end they tried to entice him to leave his labours to attend a conference of peace and reconciliation! They were so persistent that "they sent unto (him) four times after this sort" (Neh 6.4), and then "the fifth time" (v.5). He was wise to their "mischief" and resisted every time. It never pays to be complacent in the wake of victory for sometimes victory can be the back door to defeat.

Verses 17-19: David Takes Control

Had Joab withdrawn too soon? Could he have finished the task as far as the Syrian threat was concerned? Whatever, David assumed control, amassed his entire army, "all Israel", and took the fight to the strengthened enemy. He faced them on a battlefield on the other side of Jordan. Again, there is maybe the lesson that as believers we need to be as positive as he was when it comes to the battles of life. We should heed the exhortation of Jude and be no mere "defenders of the faith", but "*earnestly contend* for the faith which was once delivered unto the saints" (v.3).

Carnage among the Syrians was extensive, and the numbers slain are cited (v.18). Comparing this list with 2 Samuel 10.18, it appears that ten men had been assigned to each chariot. Among David's victims was "the captain of the host" himself. Perhaps there is the reminder that in the great conflict at the cross not only were "principalities and powers" "spoiled" (Col 2.15), but the Lord Jesus dealt with their captain; He destroyed "him that had the power of death, that is, the devil" (Heb 2.14).

> He subdued the powers of hell;
> In the fight He stood alone;
> All His foes before Him fell,
> By His single arm o'erthrown.
> They have fall'n to rise no more;
> Final is the foe's defeat;
> Jesus triumphed by His power,
> And His triumph is complete.
> (Thomas Kelly)

Having suffered such a comprehensive defeat, the Syrians sued for peace and withdrew their support for the Ammonites. The Ammonites themselves were intransigent, and dug in to withstand a siege. The final outcome was never in doubt, the story of which will unfold in the next chapter.

1 CHRONICLES 20

It is clear that chapter 20 divides into two distinct sections. In vv.1-3 there is the final episode of the story that commenced in the previous chapter with the Ammonites now being crushed. They had been holed up in "the city" (19.15), presumably the city of Medeba the site of the battle. With a lull in hostilities over the winter period, it appears that the main fighting force had relocated to Rabbah the capital, and, bereft of Syrian support, they had settled down to withstand the inevitable siege. From the account of 2 Samuel 11, it seems that they had put up stout resistance, but the outcome was predictable.

The rest of the chapter is devoted to details of battles with the Philistines, recounting the slaying of remnants of Goliath's family circle. In the parallel passage in 2 Samuel 21.15-22, there is an account of David's having a brush with death. Ishbi-benob had ambitions to make him the first victim of his new sword, and had it not been for the intervention of Abishai, David would have died; that incident was the finale to David's military career. There is no record of it here, for, as noted in other incidents, the Chronicler, guided by the Spirit, tends to omit things that are detrimental to David, assuming that his readers are familiar with the circumstances, and feeling no need to cover the ground again. "He that repeateth a matter separateth very friends" (Prov 17.9). In a poem, Henry Durbanville urged caution when you are tempted to circulate information that has come your way. Make it pass through what he called, "three gates of gold".

> Three narrow gates: first, Is it true?
> Then, Is it needful? In your mind
> Give truthful answer. And the next
> Is last and narrowest – Is it kind?

Verse 1: Unfinished Business

"To every thing there is a season, and a time to every purpose under the heaven…a time for war" (Eccl 3.1-8, RV). With the winter season over it was now time to resume hostilities with Ammon and deal with some unfinished business. It was a "time that *kings* go out to battle", but significantly, "David tarried at Jerusalem". As was noted in the previous chapter, in failing to lead his troops he placed himself in grave spiritual danger. In the first phase of this campaign he had delegated responsibility to Joab; afterwards, he took control personally; here he reverted to the previous arrangement. There is no way in which reneging on our responsibilities could ever be to our benefit as David discovered to his cost.

The fact that Joab "led forth *the power* of the army" is an indication that this whole enterprise was being taken seriously. There was no hint that Joab underestimated the might and resolve of his enemies and so he marched against them at full strength. By contrast, Joshua sent a nominal force against the little city of Ai with disastrous consequences (Josh 7.2-5). There is the danger that we could miscalculate the power of our spiritual foes, and become complacent to the point of defeat. Joab meant business; Ammon must be crushed.

As he advanced on Rabbah Joab adopted a scorched earth policy, for he "wasted the country of the children of Ammon". Who could have anticipated the ramifications of Hanun's insults? His people were paying dearly for his rash behaviour. It would be good for us all just to think through the possible outcome of our actions, not only from our own point of view, but as to how these actions might impact on those around us. We do not have to go further than the next chapter to see this illustrated again when David brought pestilence on his subjects by his determination to number the people. No one lives unto himself.

Rabbah was now a beleaguered city, and such well fortified places were never easy to penetrate in the short term. Solomon used this kind of situation as an illustration by saying that "A brother offended is harder to be won than a strong city" (Prov 18.19). Let us do all in our power to avoid giving offence, for the aggrieved party could become as entrenched in his resentment as a city under siege. It could demand endless patience if he is ever to be won round.

Using the minimum of words, the Chronicler tells of the fall of Rabbah with the full story recorded in 2 Samuel 11-12. There, casualties are mentioned including Uriah, the progress of the war is charted, with David ultimately being summoned to administer the coup-de-grace.

Verse 2: The Crown of the King of Ammon

Again, the Chronicler assumes our knowledge of the history of the war with Ammon, and the summons that David had received to put a final end to the resistance. Joab had taken the part of the city called "the royal city" and "the city of waters", and he seemed confident that cut off from its water supply, the citadel would soon fall, and so David was called. In our chapter he is at Jerusalem in v.1 and at Rabbah in v.2 with no explanation of the transfer. Joab had called him to Rabbah to ensure that the king was credited with the victory and not he himself (2 Sam 12.26-29), for there was the possibility that the conquered city would be renamed after him. In both ancient and modern times, cities have been named or renamed after illustrious individuals as for example Alexandria, Constantinople, and Leningrad. Joab ensured that that would never happen at Rabbah; it would never bear his name. By acting as he did, he demonstrated again that despite his other deficiencies he was fiercely loyal to David.

Part of the victor's honour was the placing of the vanquished king's crown upon his head. This crown was a unique work of art, weighing a talent of gold, and encrusted with "precious stones". It was good for David that he had shaken himself out of his lethargy to be there for that prestigious event, rather than hearing of Joab being thus honoured. Is there a hint of this occasion when the Lord Jesus addressed the assembly at Philadelphia: "hold that fast which thou hast, that no man take thy crown" (Rev 3.11)? Potential reward could be forfeited as suggested in 1 Corinthians 3.15: "If any man's work shall be burned, he shall suffer loss".

The weight of gold in this crown was the same as that devoted to the golden candlestick of the tabernacle (Ex 25.39). A significant contrast is the fact that the gold for the candlestick was designated "*pure* gold", as befitting Him of whom that holy vessel speaks. However, the fact that it took a talent of gold to construct such as a candlestick gives some idea of the weight of Hanun's crown. How sad that a man who appears to have been so honoured should have behaved in such an unbecoming way. He seems to have had no regard to the dignity of his kingly office, and the elaborate crown that had adorned his brow was just an external display of pomp that shrouded a mean, suspicious, belligerent disposition.

The "exceeding much spoil" that was taken from the city would add to the stockpile of materials to be devoted to the house of God.

Verse 3: Retribution

Commentators are divided about the meaning of this verse, and such as Matthew Henry see David as being guilty of what we would now call serious war crimes. Did he torture the people of Ammon by ripping them and hacking them with the implements mentioned? It would seem to be out of keeping with his character. It is true that he was intensely angry about the way his ambassadors had been treated, but it hardly warranted torturing the general populace. Justice would have been served if the villains of the piece had been punished. It is also true that he would still be smarting, and ashamed of his own recent conduct in relation to Uriah and Bath-sheba, but he would hardly vent his frustrations on foreigners who had nothing to do with his misdemeanours. It seems better to interpret the verse as suggested by its counterpart in 2 Samuel 12.31, that he subjected his vanquished foes to hard labour, with the implements mentioned being the tools of their toil.

Verse 4: War with the Philistines

Back in 18.1 "David smote the Philistines, and subdued them". The comment was made there that Philistine power was broken at last, with very few mentions of them troubling the people of God thereafter. These verses contain one of those few mentions. The equivalent passage in 2 Samuel is 21.15-22. There, it seems evident that a considerable period of time had elapsed between the Ammonite campaign and the events of our present verses. All the circumstances surrounding Absalom and his rebellion had intervened, and so the "after this" of our verse is not an immediate "after this" but allows for quite a time lag.

It also appears clear from 2 Samuel that the Philistines had taken the initiative as far as this series of battles was concerned. Throughout this book there has been the constant lesson that the enemies of the people of God will never lie down. If they have been "subdued" they will do all in their power to regroup and revive their power to make fresh assaults on their conquerors. As God's people we can never afford to let our guard down or relax our vigilance. Even within these few verses there is an illustration of this. Notice the words "war again" in v.5 and "yet again there was war" in v.6. Philistine professors among God's people will never be content or passive and we have to be constantly alert to their activities.

Gezer and Gob (2 Sam 21.18) seem to be alternative names for the same location. Some of the personalities of these verses also have more than one name. There will be no need to make further comment about this because, as observed formerly, it is a regular feature of 1 Chronicles.

Men of unusual physique feature from time to time throughout the Word of God. In Noah's day "There were giants in the earth" (Gen 6.4). Their stature and renown did nothing to preserve them from divine wrath when the deluge came. The spies who reconnoitred Canaan reported, "there we saw the giants, the sons of Anak, which come of the giants" (Num 13.33). The three gigantic sons of Anak were no match for Caleb, for the man who had "wholly followed the Lord" had the Lord on his side (Josh 14.9-15; 15.13-19). The formidable Goliath who terrorised the armies of Israel fell victim to the shepherd boy who came to him "in the name of the Lord of hosts" (1 Sam 17.45). Here, his family members fell before David's men. These Philistines were endowed with the same physical attributes as Goliath but their opponents could rely on divine support. As quoted frequently in this commentary on military campaigns, "If God be for us, who can be against us?" (Rom 8.31).

The first victor was Sibbechai, who was mentioned among David's mighty men (11.29), and who ultimately had charge of the 24,000 troops that had responsibility for security during the eighth month of each year (27.11). His name means "A Weaver", so if he had plied his trade in such an everyday situation, it is to his credit that he made such a success of his career change!

Verse 5: There was War Again

During this second battle, there was another duel, with Elhanan emerging the victor. His opponent had superior weaponry, but Elhanan's name means "God has been gracious", and this occasion was one during which he proved the reality of that name. To accomplish anything for God requires His grace as mentioned so often in Scripture. In particular, Paul was aware that it was only "by the grace of God" that he was what he was, and that he could take no credit for his abundant labours, for it was "the grace of God which was with (him)" (1 Cor 15.10). The founding of the Corinthian assembly to which he was writing proves this very point. "According to the grace of God which is given unto me, as a wise masterbuilder, I have laid the foundation" (3.10). Divine grace accounted for the effectiveness of his labours just as divine grace secured Elhanan's victory here. In spiritual walk, work, and warfare, let us all realise that our major need is for divine favour, rather than natural ability, charisma, or initiative.

Verses 6-7: Yet Again There was War

During this third encounter the hero was a man called Jonathan, David's nephew, the son of Jesse's third son Shimea or Shammah (1 Sam 16.9). There is emphasis again on his opponent's stature and on his abnormalities, but extra height and extra digits are no match for a man with God on his side. "Like father, like son", the world says, and this giant was as brash and self-confident as his father for the same word is used of both: "he *defied* Israel" (1 Sam 17). Had he forgotten the story of his father's fall, a story that has been immortalised as the ultimate illustration of the triumph of the underdog? Did he think that he could succeed where his father failed? Did he suppose that since he was on his home ground of Gath, the outcome was a foregone conclusion? What a rude awakening he had! He stands as another monument to the truth of Scripture: "Pride goeth before destruction, and an haughty spirit before a fall" (Prov 16.18). "Let him that thinketh he standeth take heed lest he fall" (1 Cor 10.12). His experience stands as a beacon of warning, lest we too become as brazen, opinionated or self-assured as he was. It would be the inevitable precursor to spiritual disaster; ask Simon Peter about that (Mt 26.31-35).

In normal family life, appearance and temperament are often reproduced in the next generation as in the case of Goliath and his unnamed son; we often speak of "family features". It is a pity when disagreeable traits such as pride or self-interest or temper are replicated in the offspring. At a spiritual level, people take character from their parentage. The Lord Jesus said to the people of His day, "Ye are of your father the devil, and the lusts of your father ye will do" (Jn 8.44). Of Cain it was said that he "was of that wicked one, and slew his brother" (1 Jn 3.12). Unsaved people exhibit their spiritual parentage. Similarly, by their character and behaviour the children of God should display the features of their Father. "If ye know that he is righteous, ye know that every one that doeth righteousness is born of him" (1 Jn 2.29). "Whosoever is born of God doth not commit sin; for his seed remaineth in him: and he cannot sin, because he is born of God" (1 Jn 3.9). In both of these verses, the verb tense indicates an ongoing activity, so really John is saying that people who have been born of God will make a habit of doing righteousness as does their Father, and they will not habitually practise sin. Are the family features of the divine being produced in our lives? "Let the beauty of the Lord our God be upon us" (Ps 90.17).

Some have wondered if the victim of this verse was a literal son of Goliath, or if the term "son of the giant" is a generic term describing all the monstrosities connected to this nest of giants located at Gath? Even if this is the case, it does not altogether destroy the practical lessons that have been gleaned regarding "family features".

Jonathan's name means "The Lord has given", and his involvement here is just a reminder that in any crisis the Lord always has His man on hand, and provides the appropriate personnel for the job. If Goliath's son was a replica of his father, by contrast Jonathan was so different from his father Shimea. Shimea had been one of the army whom Goliath had defied, and of whom Scripture records, "they were dismayed, and greatly afraid" (1 Sam 17.11). With his fellow-soldiers he had quailed at the sight of the champion of the Philistines. Courage did not rise within his heart; trust in God to give victory was absent; his inclination was to flee rather than fight (v.24). His son Jonathan proved to be a better man than he ever was. If the shrinkage of assembly testimony in the western world is ever to be reversed, it will mean that sons will have to be better men than their fathers ever were. There will have to be courage in the face of adversity, commitment instead of complacency, and devotion in place of lukewarmness. Will new generations rise to the challenge?

Verse 8: A Summary

"These were born…they fell." There is the reminder that death is inevitable for all, even the tallest, strongest, most muscular of men. These men lived and died in the dangerous environment of warfare, but even in the safest of surroundings there is no hiding place from the grim reaper, "so death passed unto all men, for that all sinned" (Rom 5.12, RV). Only a minority of the world's population die as the result of "accidents" or violence as in the case of these men, but the relentless ageing process takes its toll. In the ultimate, physical fitness and bodily strength will fall victim to the insidious effects of sin in the body. In ancient times, this process took hundreds of years, but the outcome was inevitable. "And he died" is the repeated climax to the brief biographies of Genesis 5.

David is credited with contributing to the fall of these giants, and, while in the passage there is no record of his participation, no doubt he was involved strategically in these battles with the Philistines. The co-operation between him and his men is implied, a very necessary feature of any activity for God, even in modern times. Leaders must give a lead, and others must be willing to be led.

1 CHRONICLES 21

Constant reference has been made to the major theme of the book - the preparation for building the house of God. To set the stage, the ark had been brought to Jerusalem (chs.15-16), Solomon had been designated as the temple builder (ch.17), and wars had been fought to provide the necessary materials and to create conditions of peace for the project (chs.18-20).

Now ch.21 records one of the great failures of David's life - he numbered the people. It has been observed that his shortcomings are generally overlooked in 1 Chronicles, so why is this incident included? The reason is that it is a vital event in the overall picture, an integral part of the whole story, the episode that led to the purchase of a site for the building of the temple; it cannot be ignored.

As was noted in the introduction to ch.17, it is one of those incidents in the Scriptures that demonstrate God's ability to turn evil circumstances to His own advantage. "His ways (are) past finding out" (Rom 11.33). To cite but a few examples: jealousy exiled Joseph to Egypt, and God used the circumstance to preserve His people (Gen 50.20); persecution scattered the early church, and God used it for the furtherance of the gospel (Acts 8.4); anti-Semitism took Aquila to Corinth and God used him in His work there (Acts 18.1-3). Examples could be multiplied, but let it encourage our own hearts. When caught up in adverse circumstances, let us trust our God to work out His own purpose, for "Surely the wrath of man shall praise thee" (Ps 76.10). While possibly lifting this statement from its context, let us rejoice in the truth of it, that "all things work together for good to them that love God" (Rom 8.28). Despite all of that, we should never adopt the attitude, "Let us do evil, that good may come" (Rom 3.8). In spiritual things, the end does not necessarily justify the means.

Another general observation that is worth making is the significance of the timing of this event. It was just when final victory over ancient foes had been effected (ch.20) that the calamity took place. It is one of those occurrences in Scripture that highlights the danger of success, for it can spawn complacency, and, as has often been said, victory can be the backdoor to defeat. For Joshua, the humiliation of Ai followed the triumph of Jericho (Josh 7). For Elijah, the depression of Horeb followed the elation of Carmel (1 Kings 19). Let us all be vigilant lest being lulled into a smug frame of mind we become an easy target for the one who is described in our chapter as "Satan".

Another similar lesson emerges. This satanic attack on David took place when he was an aging man. He was the veteran of many military campaigns but was now approaching the last lap of the marathon of life. Such is the pitiless nature of the devil that neither age nor infirmity softens his approach. The weak and vulnerable can expect his merciless attention. That is why Paul instructed Titus to tell the "aged men" to be "sober" (*3524*) (Titus 2.2). The word carries the combined thought of sobriety and vigilance. There is the need to be spiritually alert right to the end of the journey. Noah was the first in a long line of Bible characters whose latter days were blighted (Gen 9.20-21). Preachers often highlight lessons for those who are young in the faith. This is a lesson for the elderly and mature. Let the devil's assault on the aged David be a salutary warning to us all. We will never be free of his unwanted attention.

Verse 1: Satan

In the parallel passage in 2 Samuel 24, it appears that it was the Lord who "moved David" to number the people because of His displeasure with the nation for an unspecified reason (v.1). There need be no major problem here, for God is in overall control of His universe, and nothing happens apart from divine permission. Here, He allowed Satan to be the agent to instigate these events, culminating in Him bringing judgment upon the people. The situation in Job's experience was not dissimilar although there is no thought of divine judgment there. Satan was permitted to introduce one catastrophe after another, but God was superintending the whole situation (Job 1-2).

For the first time in the Bible, the devil is given this personal name, Satan, which conveys the idea of an adversary. This is not the place for an in-depth commentary on his various names and titles, but there is a little cluster of descriptions of him in Revelation 20.2. He is "the dragon", a suggestion of his cruelty as depicted especially in Revelation 12. He is "that old serpent", an indication of his subtlety, in which character we first encounter him in Holy Scripture (Gen 3.1). He is "the Devil", which has the basic meaning of a slanderer, for he is "the accuser of our brethren…which accused them before our God day and night" (Rev 12.10). He is "Satan" the adversary, for his history has been one of permanent opposition to God and His people.

Here, he "*stood up* against Israel". Elsewhere, he is seen as being restless, "going to and fro in the earth, and…*walking* up and down in it" (Job 1.7). Relentlessly, he stalks the earth like a predator, "a roaring lion…seeking whom he may devour" (1 Pet 5.8). He has a throne that at one stage in history was sited at Pergamos (Rev 2.13). We have no idea where it is located now, but wherever it is, he is seated on that throne, administering his nefarious activities and directing his demon hosts. In our verse, he rises from his throne, not to prowl the earth but to stand up against the hated people of God. He is intent on doing them mischief and focuses his malevolent eye upon them.

Around the time of the writing of 1 Chronicles, the prophet Zechariah had had a vision of Joshua the high priest "standing before the angel of the Lord, and Satan standing at his right hand to resist him" (3.1). There, a courtroom scene is depicted, with Satan standing as prosecuting counsel. He endeavoured to strike at the nation through its religious leader, the high priest. Here, the attack on the nation is through its political leader,

King David. Centuries divide the incidents, but the passing of time shows the evil one to be incorrigible. Beware; his persistence survives until this present age.

As has already been noted, it was "against Israel" that Satan stood up, but the nation's leader was to be the channel through whom the satanic assault would be made. The challenge for leaders is that failure on their part impacts on those for whom they are responsible. 2 Chronicles demonstrates that the level of Judah's spiritual health was often dependent on the spiritual condition of the king on the throne. If he drifted into idolatry, he took his people with him with disastrous consequences for all and sundry. On a more positive note, a godly example on the part of leaders influences their people. After a lapse in the rebuilding of the post-exilic temple, Zerubbabel and Jeshua responded to the challenging preaching of Haggai and Zechariah and "began to build", aided by the very men who had done the preaching (Ezra 5.1-2). Let leaders remember then that they can be such an influence for good, but they can also be special targets for the enemy in his attempts to injure the people of God as a whole.

Note that Satan "provoked David". The powers of the evil one are amazing. He has the ability to remove from human hearts the memory of what has been conveyed to them from the Word of God, as depicted by birds devouring seed (Mt 13.4,19). He also has the ability to implant suggestions in the hearts of men as when he "put into the heart of Judas Iscariot" to betray the Lord Jesus (Jn 13.2), and as when he "filled" the heart of Ananias to act deceitfully (Acts 5.3). Here, he was the one who inserted in David's mind the notion to number the people. In light of that, let us resort to the Scriptures to test the "good ideas" that come into our minds, for their origin could be devilish rather than divine.

The sin here was that David wanted "to number Israel". On former occasions, the people had been numbered as in the book of Numbers, and doubtless a half shekel "atonement money" had been paid in accordance with the instructions of Exodus 30.11-16. There is no mention of the atonement money here, and undoubtedly failure to collect it contributed to the transgression of the incident. The denial of the need for atonement would have delighted Satan, and of course the original atonement money was appointed "for the service of the tabernacle". Here, a new structure was about to be built for God, and He was denied the half-shekel contribution from the military men who were numbered on this occasion.

It is of interest that in Exodus 30 there was the threat of a plague if the half shekel was not taken (v.12). As a result of David's numbering the people here, a "pestilence" swept the land (vv.12,14). God's warnings are ignored at our peril.

It appears, though, that David's major sin was either his desire to glory in his massive war machine, or to place reliance on that rather than on the living God, for the census that was taken was of the military men, "men that drew sword" (v.5). It seems that there was no immediate danger from enemy action necessitating an appraisal of his military strength, but it appears that David just wanted a sense of security from any possible danger, the cosy feeling that he was impregnable. Rather than relying on God for his security, he drew succour from what was visible and tangible; he wanted to enjoy what modern politicians call the feel-good factor. It seems then, that his sin was that of a diminished trust in God. We could be guilty of a similar attitude, not in the sense of relying on military might rather than God, but of wanting to feel the warm glow that financial security brings rather than being content to have our trust in God to supply our recurring needs. A diminishing trust in God is seen in the desire to accumulate rather than to distribute, to be acquisitive rather than generous. The person who "lays up" and who is anxious about material things is said to be "of little faith" (Mt 6.19-34). It appears that it is David's lack of faith that comes in for censure here.

Verses 2-4: Joab

The man delegated with the task of numbering the people was David's wily old general Joab. A thorough job had to be done, for the king demanded that every last man be accounted for, "from Beer-sheba even to Dan", the southern and northern extremities of the land respectively. Strangely, on this occasion Joab appears to have had a greater insight into the dangers of the project than David had, so opposition to David's plan came from an unlikely source. Joab was never noted for being spiritual or sensitive to divine leading, but here he got it right. In a recent chapter it was noted that for Joshua, encouragement came from an unlikely source as the Transjordan tribes pledged their unwavering support for the new leader (Josh 1.12-18). For the Lord Jesus, criticism came from the strangest of sources when "*Peter* took him, and began to rebuke him" (Mt 16.22). At times, life throws up some surprises!

It is unusual that we should be learning positive lessons from Joab, but another emerges. He was taking a different point of view from David, and his point of view was right, but while arguing his case he was still respectful; three times over he refers to David as "my lord". In debate and argument there is always the danger of raised voices and extravagant language as when "the words of the men of Judah were fiercer than the words of the men of Israel" (2 Sam 19.43). Cool heads and measured tones are much to be preferred, "For the wrath of man worketh not the righteousness of God" (James 1.20). Joab showed respect.

He had three main objections as to why David had no need to "require this thing". First, the Lord was in control of the demographics of the nation. What need was there to know the precise number of men available for the armed forces? Had not the Lord on numerous occasions promised a nation as populous as stars or dust or sand? "The Lord make his people an hundred times so many more as they be." Could God not be trusted to provide manpower where and when necessary?

Second, Joab argued that all David's subjects were loyal, so why take the trouble to trawl the land to list trusty warriors? Absalom's rebellion was history, and the fractious northern tribes seemed content for the moment; "are they not all my lord's servants?". The whole exercise was pointless! It was the old problem of wanting to fix something that was not broken; there are restless spirits who always want to be tinkering.

Joab's third argument was the most compelling. David's actions would be "a cause of trespass to Israel". The whole nation would be accountable for his sin, as when "the children of Israel committed a trespass in the accursed thing" when in fact the offender was one man, Achan (Josh 7.1). This principle persists even in the Christian era. The whole assembly at Corinth was "leavened" as a consequence of one man's misbehaviour (1 Cor 5.6). This is a solemn warning to us all that our conduct has a bearing on everyone connected with us, and for them there is guilt by association, or at least defilement by association. Joab had assessed the situation rightly, and the whole nation did suffer as a result of David's decision to conduct this census; he was the "cause" of the calamity that came upon the land, to use the word of v.3. Sin is never a private thing.

Twice over in the verses we read of "the king's word": "the king's word prevailed" (v.4); "the king's word was abominable to Joab" (v.6). The fact that "the king's word prevailed" leaves David branded in this incident as unreasonable, opinionated, intransigent, and determined. Joab's well-constructed and well-articulated arguments carried no weight with him. He was the king and it was *the king's* word that prevailed! There were others in Scripture who were unwilling to listen to reason. Uzziah paid no heed to the pleadings of Azariah the priest. He was determined to function in the priestly office (2 Chr 26.16-23). Balaam ignored the warnings of both God and the angel of the Lord and was unwavering in his resolve to take advantage of Balak's lucrative offer (Num 22). There are times when to be strong-minded is a virtue, but when determination flies in the face of divine commands, and defies sound counsel, it becomes a vice.

It is little wonder that Joab felt aggrieved and regarded the king's word as being "abominable". He was being ordered to undertake something that was palpably wrong. This was not the first time that David had asked someone to do something unethical. He encouraged Jonathan to tell lies for him which Jonathan did with some enthusiasm, adding his own embellishments to David's story and almost paying for it with his life (1 Sam 20.6,28-34). Joab himself had been a willing collaborator in the cover up of David's affair with Bathsheba (2 Sam 11.14-25). For some reason, on this occasion he was more scrupulous and resented being involved in a project that was so obviously contrary to the command of God. There is a lesson here for us all. We should never, out of self-interest, encourage others to do what is wrong, nor allow them to influence us to behave incorrectly on their behalf. It becomes all the more difficult, as in this incident, when the command to do wrong comes from a superior. On occasions secretaries are asked to tell lies for their bosses, or accountants are told to massage the figures, or the sales staff are instructed to short-change the customer. For a Christian, it takes courage and risks future discrimination to do what is right in such circumstances. "Provide things honest in the sight of all men" (Rom 12.17); "walk honestly toward them that are without" (1 Thess 4.12).

Joab's reluctance was evident in that while he "went throughout all Israel" as commanded, he was less than diligent in fulfilling his commission, and tendered figures that were less than accurate. Perhaps we see his old subtlety surfacing again. No one would be able to report him for failing to show up in their district, but he certainly had no stomach for the task on hand.

Verses 5-6: The Figures

Without a blush, Joab "gave the sum of the number of the people unto David". He had made no attempt to number the warriors precisely as in the early chapters of the book of Numbers. There, in the case of some tribes, the number was to the nearest fifty. Here, the ten tribes were lumped together, and Judah was quoted separately to the nearest 10,000! The tribe of Levi was not enlisted as might be expected, but it seems that Joab had no desire to antagonise Benjamin, and they were omitted from the total as well. They were the tribesmen of the old regime. What was the point of irritating them and perhaps opening old sores? Thus, because "the king's word was abominable to Joab", he had no heart for taking any risks and treated the whole business in a resentful, lackadaisical way.

Verses 7-8: God was Displeased

"And God was displeased with this thing." The words are almost reminiscent of the ominous statement at the end of 2 Samuel 11: "But the thing that David had done displeased the Lord" (v.27). As believers we should have the ambition "to be well-pleasing unto him" (2 Cor 5.9, RV), but as it was with ancient Israel, so it could be true of us - "with many of them God was not well pleased" (1 Cor 10.5). Let us aspire to the tribute that Enoch received: "he had this testimony, that he pleased God" (Heb 11.5).

The "therefore" of our verse shows that God's displeasure with that whole incident was the reason for His smiting Israel. David's sin had ramifications for the whole nation as we have already observed. It would appear that this "smiting" was independent of the punishment that would yet be inflicted when David chose from the three alternatives. Its exact nature is not specified, but it was sufficient to alert David to his guilt, and draw from him a genuine confession and true regret.

In his confession (v.8), David accepted personal responsibility for the sin: "*I* have sinned". There were no excuses and no attempt to blame anyone else, not even the devil, as when Eve declared, "The serpent beguiled me" (Gen 3.13). Nor did he try to water down the enormity of his guilt: "I have sinned *greatly*"; "I have done *very* foolishly". There was also the entreaty that God would "put away...the iniquity of thy servant" (RV). He made similar appeals in his great penitential psalm: "blot out my transgressions" (Ps 51.1); "blot out all mine iniquities" (v.9). "Wash me", "cleanse me", "purge me", were the pleas that were wrung from his tortured soul. David was no stranger to confession and contrition.

Amidst all his distress and the awareness of his folly, David still had the knowledge that while the enjoyment of his relationship with God had been disturbed the relationship itself had not been broken; he speaks of "the iniquity of *thy servant*"; he was still the servant of the Lord.

David's experience here illustrates the Bible's teaching regarding the steps a believer should take when he sins against God. There is the need for confession. "If we confess our sins, he is faithful and just to forgive us our sins, and to cleanse us from all unrighteousness" (1 Jn 1.9). Like David's, the confession should be frank and fulsome, with no attempt to water down our guilt. Allied with confession should be the determination that with divine help there will be no repeat of the misdemeanour. "He that covereth his sins shall not prosper: but whoso confesseth and forsaketh them shall have mercy" (Prov 28.13). There have been many who confessed their sins without forsaking them. Balaam acknowledged, "I have sinned" (Num 22.34), but he persisted in pursuing his sinful course for he "loved the wages of unrighteousness" (2 Pet 2.15). King Saul admitted, "I have sinned…I have played the fool, and have erred exceedingly" (1 Sam 26.21), but he went on to play the fool to an even greater extent when he consulted the medium at Endor (1 Sam 28). Genuine, heartfelt confession involves the repentance factor.

Like David, believers can lose the sweetness of their relationship with God because of sin, but that does not interfere with the relationship itself. "If any man sin, we have an advocate with *the Father*, Jesus Christ the righteous" (1 Jn 2.1). God is still said to be the sinning believer's Father. His position in Christ is secure.

Another of David's concerns was for the removal of his sin, and again allowance is made for this in the realm of New Testament doctrine, and it is "the blood of Jesus Christ his Son (which) cleanseth us from all sin" (1 Jn 1.7). When confession is made, God is "faithful" to the blood, and "just" because of the blood, enabling Him "to forgive" and "to cleanse" (v.9).

Verses 9-12: David's Seer

It appears that Gad had a special relationship with David in that he is designated "David's seer". He was one of David's biographers, the other two being Samuel and Nathan (29.29). There is only one other incident in which Gad features in Scripture, and that is in 1 Samuel 22, when he encouraged David to abandon "the hold", Adullam, and move back to Judah (v.5). Around forty years passed between that event and this present situation. Gad had a long life of service for God, even though most of it was spent away from the limelight. His experience may be that of many. There may be highlights in their lives that are fairly common knowledge, but for the more part they have been working quietly, away from the public eye, and yet of all they have done it can be said, "thy Father which seeth in secret himself shall reward thee openly" (Mt 6.4).

It seems that, with Nathan, Gad was responsible for assisting David in organising the Levites as far as their musical contribution to temple service was concerned. In fact, these men were the channels of divine instruction on these issues (2 Chr 29.25). There is no record of his involvement in this as the history of this 1st book of Chronicles unfolds. We are left with the impression that every such initiative originated with David himself, but 2 Chronicles 29.25 makes clear that David was acting with a divine mandate with Gad and Nathan being God's spokesmen.

Gad's implicit prompt obedience is worthy of note: "Go and tell David" (v.10); "So Gad came to David" (v.11). Like Nathan in ch.17, the message he brought would be unwelcome, and yet he simply obeyed the voice of God. Philip the evangelist is a New Testament example of the same submissive spirit: "Arise, and go"; "And he arose and went" (Acts 8.26-27). May we exhibit the same ready obedience.

Gad's message for David was unique in the Word of God, in that a choice of punishment was on offer! There were three alternatives - three years of famine, three months of relentless defeat at the hands of their enemies, or three days of "the sword of the Lord", here an idiom for a ravaging lethal epidemic. "The sword of the Lord" receives mention in connection with Gideon's exploits, the instrument of divine judgment against the Midianites (Judg 7.20). The first mention of the sword in Scripture is in connection with God's judgment when "he placed at the east of the garden of Eden Cherubims, and a flaming sword which turned every way, to keep the way of the tree of life" (Gen 3.24). It is seen again at the cross, an emblem of the judgment that fell on the Lord Jesus: "Awake, O sword, against my shepherd, and against the man that is my fellow, saith the Lord of hosts: smite the shepherd…" (Zech 13.7).

Verses 13-14: David's Choice

Prior to this, David had experienced three years of famine, a lingering legacy of one of Saul's misdemeanours (2 Sam 21.1). David's mistake at that time was to be slow in "inquir(ing) of the Lord" as to the cause of the dearth, but it seems that he had no desire to renew the experience of such a protracted discipline. That reduced his choices to two. He calculated that, knowing both the character of God and that of his enemies, it would be prudent to cast himself on God's mercy and "fall now into the hand of the Lord", although let it be said, that "It is a fearful thing to fall into the hands of the living God" (Heb 10.31). David had a different estimate of the divine character from that of the man who said in the parable, "thou art an austere man" (Lk 19.21). From long experience he concluded that he was more likely to receive mercy at the hand of God than at the hands of men. His reasoning was sound, for there were occasions when God used human instruments to effect His judgment and they went beyond what was justified. In Ahaz' day He used the ten tribes to chasten Judah, but they slew them "in a rage", and in turn came under divine censure (2 Chr 28.5-12). Regarding the way the Babylonians had treated Judah God said, "I am very sore displeased with the heathen that are at ease: for I was but a little displeased, and they helped forward the affliction" (Zech 1.15).

The strain on David seemed intolerable. The word "strait" (6887) is translated in most versions by the word "distressed", but, distressing though it was, the decision had to be made and David elected to fall into the hand of the Lord.

These events had been taken up with David's concern about population size; no sooner had his choice of punishment been recorded than the "pestilence" reduced the population by 70,000, and the work of judgment was still unfinished. What a price to pay for his determination to ignore a divine decree!

Verse 15: God Sent an Angel

Fairly frequently in the Word of God, angels were the executors of God's judgment, as when the firstborn in Egypt were smitten by "the destroyer", presumably an angel (Ex 12.23), or when "the angel of the Lord went out, and smote in the camp of the Assyrians an hundred fourscore and five thousand" (2 Kings 19.35). Here, an angel was sent to "destroy" Jerusalem. Translators are divided as to whether this angel "was destroying" or "was about to destroy". Perhaps the latter is to be preferred since the angel is depicted as "having a drawn sword in his hand stretched out over Jerusalem", as if the sword had not yet fallen (v.16). It is at this point that the wisdom of David's choice is seen, and his assessment of God's character (v.13) is justified; "the Lord beheld, and he repented him of the evil". The fact that "the Lord beheld" indicates that all that was being done was under divine supervision; the angel was not acting on his own initiative.

The Lord not only beheld, but He spoke: "It is enough, stay now thine hand". The precise location of this incident is said to be Moriah (2 Chr 3.1), and centuries earlier at exactly the same spot, a similar command was given: "Lay not thine hand upon the lad", and Isaac's life was spared (Gen 22.12). On both occasions, by divine command the sharp instruments of judgment were lowered. The centuries rolled by and at another outcrop of Mount Moriah a blessed Man was impaled to a cross. The sword of justice awoke against Him (Zech 13.7). This time there was no pitying eye. This time there was no divine intervention. This time there was no lowering of the sword. This time the full price was exacted.

The angel of the Lord had taken up his position by "the threshingfloor of Ornan the Jebusite", also called Araunah (2 Sam 24.16). This is one of three threshingfloor scenes in David's history, the others being the threshingfloors of Keilah, (1 Sam 23.1), and the threshingfloor of Chidon, the scene of the death of Uzza to which reference has already been made in the commentary (13.9). Here, the angel was poised to strike a deadly blow against Jerusalem.

Verses 16-17: David's Appeal

In v.15, the "Lord beheld", and here "David lifted up his eyes, and saw". As the Lord beheld, He was in control, whereas David was a helpless spectator. What David saw was the angel standing "between the earth and the heaven", an indication that for angels there is movement, and communication between earth and heaven as when Jacob saw the staircase "set up on the earth, and the top of it reached to heaven" (Gen 28.12). On this occasion the judgment was descending from above. What David saw moved him and his elders to repentance, a repentance that was evident both in their clothing and their posture, for "clothed in sackcloth, (they) fell upon their faces". Genuine repentance will manifest itself in one form or another, as, for example, when the publican "would not lift up so much as his eyes unto heaven, but smote upon his breast" (Lk 18.13). True repentance never holds its head high; a chastened spirit bows low in the presence of God.

This visible demonstration of contrition was no charade, for his appeal to God matched the stance he had adopted. The man who had been a shepherd from earliest days was still a shepherd at heart, and he was stirred at the plight of "these sheep" when he saw them under the threat of judgment. David would fain have shouldered the full weight of the judgment personally; "even I it is that have sinned". He absolved the people from blame - "what have they done?". His shepherdly care is most commendable. He was no hireling who treated his position in government as a source of personal gain or a platform for self-aggrandisement. He never forgot that those under his charge were God's people, "thy people", and he always had their best interests at heart. Just as he had risked his life when defending his flock from the lion and the bear (1 Sam 17.34-36), so here he willingly appealed to God to concentrate His judgment on him rather than on His people. The spirit of Moses was being replicated in David (Ex 32.31-32). The same attitude was seen in Paul as he thought upon "(his) brethren, (his) kinsmen according to the flesh" (Rom 9.1-3). Let such be a pattern for those who shepherd God's flock today. These men saw themselves as dispensable; they were willing to be sacrificed in the interest of those for whom they had a care.

Verses 18-19: The Saying of Gad

As stated formerly, we know very little about Gad, but it is evident that he was in attendance at the threshingfloor on this occasion. He had not abandoned the wayward king in his time of great need, and he was a man who was available when needed. Elisha was another who was on hand when a word from God was required (2 Kings 3.11-19). He marched with the troops, and when necessary, he brought a timely word from God. Let us all be ambitious to be as available as these men, to be on the spot when required, to bring a communication from God.

The message through Gad was that David should rear an altar in Ornan's threshingfloor. This was not the first altar at Moriah; as noted earlier, "Abraham built an altar there" (Gen 22.9). In raising an altar on Moriah, David was taking the first step that would result in temple worship being established there; hence his words in 22.1, "This is the house of the Lord God, and this is the altar of the burnt offering for Israel". It is evident that the sacrifices here satisfied divine justice and appeased divine wrath, for it was only after the offerings were made that the angel was finally instructed to sheath his sword (v.27).

Verses 19-21: Ornan and His Sons

Just as Gad had been prompt in His obedience to the Lord in v.11, so David was quick to obey the word through Gad here: "And David went up at the saying of Gad". That word had been spoken "in the name of the Lord", and, detecting the authority by which Gad had spoken, David's response was immediate. It is another lesson in the importance of swiftly responding to God's voice, whether we hear it as we read the Word personally, or through His servants as they expound its truth to us. May God preserve us from a dilatory response to His commands.

We are introduced to Ornan himself at v.20. His day had started like any other day in harvest-time. No doubt he was begrimed with chaff as he attended to the tedious task of circling the floor with his threshing-sledge. Little did he realise that that day he would have a visit from both an angel and a king! Out of the blue it was a life-changing day for Ornan when, without warning, he would vacate the land that he had farmed for years. Life-changing circumstances can materialise so unexpectedly.

With his four sons, Ornan was "threshing wheat", wheat that would be offered for a meat offering (v.23). What was a very ordinary task was suddenly transformed into something of great moment, a crucial requirement for the ritual of that momentous day. The wheat that Gideon had been threshing "to hide it from the Midianites" (Judg 6.11) became a necessary ingredient for the "unleavened cakes" that were offered to the Lord (v.19). We all need to understand that the mundane and ordinary can be transformed into something for God. The routine toils of life provide us with something that can be offered to our God. The fishing skills of Peter and Andrew were commandeered by the Lord as they were transformed into "fishers of men" (Mk 1.17). A pen was the tool of Matthew's trade. He had used it in the employ of Caesar, but then it was requisitioned by the Spirit to write about "another king, one Jesus" (Acts 17.7). God lays claim to His people's goods and talents.

The appearance of the angel was a distraction for Ornan, and, understandably, his first reaction was to hide. The sight of the approaching king seemed to give him courage to emerge from his bolt-hole. It is interesting that he recognised David, dressed as he was in attire that was so unsuitable for a king. It leaves the impression that David was well known to his subjects and the unusual clothing did not disguise him. He was no stranger to them and certainly not aloof or distant. Again, there is a lesson here for spiritual leaders. Elders should be "*among*" their people (1 Pet 5.1). They "labour *among* you" said Paul (1 Thess 5.12). There should be rapport, warmth, closeness between shepherds and the flock.

Although a Jebusite, with the majority of his race vanquished by David and displaced from Jerusalem (11.4-9), Ornan held no grudges, and showed the utmost respect for the king. Thus he "bowed himself to David with his face to the ground". Be like him, and never allow resentment to sour your relationship with any.

Verses 22-25: Purchasing the Temple Site

As stated in the introduction to the chapter, David's sin is recorded because flowing out of the whole incident is the purchase of the plot of land upon which Solomon would build the temple. We have now arrived at that critical part of the narrative. David made representations for the site, for the initial purpose of building an altar "that the plague may be stayed from the people". Only sacrifice would satisfy God and move Him to withdraw the threat of further judgment.

The fact that Ornan was a Jebusite meant that David could happily relieve him of his property, whereas if it had belonged to a man of Israel, it would have been an inheritance that he could not concede (Lev 25.23; Num 36.7). When King Ahab tempted Naboth to relinquish his inheritance he met with stout resistance from one who would in no way contravene divine commands (1 Kings 21). David was dealing with a Jebusite and so he need have no scruples about concluding a deal to secure the property.

From the word go, David made clear to Ornan that he was not looking for a bargain, or discount: "thou shalt grant it me for the full price". There is a real lesson in that. Although everyone likes a good deal, there is a danger of expecting concessions when we are dealing with fellow-believers. The Christian tradesman, mechanic, or professional man is under no obligation to give discount to his fellow-Christian, and the person using his services or buying his goods should not feel aggrieved if the normal price is charged. Of course, it would be hoped that he would never create disappointment by over-charging! However, David did not belong to the culture that was always looking for something cut-price.

Ornan's generosity is in evidence in v.23 - "I give it all". This may have been the kind of protocol that was current in the east as when Abraham was bargaining for a burying place for Sarah (Gen 23), the first piece of property that he ever owned in the land. However, it is admirable that Ornan was genuinely open-handed. He covered every contingency in his offer to David - oxen, wheat, and wood. He was not the type of man who was impulsive, allowing his heart to rule his head. He had thought the matter through, and deliberately he made offer to David of everything he needed: "I give it all". Let it impact upon us all, as expressed in Isaac Watt's hymn,

Love so amazing, so divine,
Demands my heart, my life, my all!

Many a man would immediately have taken advantage of such generosity, but David was adamant. "I will verily buy it for the full price" (v.24). The reason for his insistence was that this was something for God: "I will not take that which is thine for the Lord, nor offer burnt offerings without cost". This was the tragedy of Malachi's day. Most of his first chapter is taken up with the fact that the people were offering inferior animals in sacrifice. They were worthless blemished creatures, just left-overs, things that they would never have dreamed of gifting to their civil governor (v.8). We have to challenge ourselves about this. When it comes to giving to God, are we like the people of Malachi's generation, or is the sacrificial spirit of David in evidence in our lives? To be acceptable, worship has to be a sacrifice (1 Pet 2.5). To please God, our giving has to be sacrificial (Heb 13.16). Rich men donated to the temple treasury "of their abundance"; the widow woman "cast in all that she had" (Mk 12.44). She was the one who attracted divine approval. When it comes to consecration, the body has to be offered as a "living sacrifice" (Rom 12.1). Only then will it be "acceptable unto God". We need to be preserved from offering to God what is merely the excess of our time, our energy, our affection and our resources, in other words, offering "burnt offerings without cost".

When the bargain was struck, David paid Ornan "six hundred shekels of gold". This is a figure that is substantially at variance with the sum mentioned in 2 Samuel 24.24, "fifty shekels of silver". There, the silver was paid for "the threshingfloor and the oxen". Here, the gold was handed over for "the place". It is evident that the higher price was the cost of the whole area of ground that was under Ornan's ownership, the full extent of which would be needed to accommodate the temple of God.

Verses 26-27: The Altar

On the newly acquired property, David "built…an altar". He did it in obedience to God's command, and his obedience was precise in that it was reared in the place of God's choice (v.18). There is another lesson here in the matter of obedience, that is the importance of following divine instructions to the letter without allowing for flexibility.

Both burnt offerings and peace offerings were offered on that altar, so first and foremost God received His portion, and yet there was provision for the offerer and those who were with him. David also "called upon the Lord" which from the days of Genesis 4 was an indication of an awareness of personal frailty and a sense of dependence on God (Gen 4.26).

God demonstrated His acceptance of the offerings by "answer(ing) him from heaven by fire". This was not unique, the most notable instance being the time when Elijah confronted the prophets of Baal at Carmel (1 Kings 18). On that occasion, when "the fire of the Lord fell" (v.38), the intense heat was such that not only was the drenched sacrifice consumed, but the very altar stones disintegrated, and the water in the trench vaporised. Baal was exposed comprehensively for what he was, a dead idol with no ability to respond in any way to the anguished appeals of his devotees. By contrast, He who is frequently called "the living God" can answer by fire, and in doing so at Ornan's threshingfloor He showed that sacrifice had stayed the judgment, and so "the Lord commanded the angel; and he put up his sword again into the sheath thereof". There was no such suspension of the judgment at the cross. The sword that awoke against Him (Zech 13.7) remained unsheathed and the full penalty was exacted. The Lamb was not "sodden at all with water, but *roast with fire*" (Ex 12.9). There was no clemency on that dark day.

Jehovah bade His sword awake;
O Christ, it woke 'gainst Thee!
Thy blood the flaming blade must slake,
Thy heart its sheath must be;
All for my sake my peace to make,
Now sleeps that sword for me.
(Anne Ross Cousin)

Verses 28-30: A New Centre of Worship

The fact that the Lord had "answered" him, and had heard his appeal for his endangered people stirred David to express his appreciation and worship, and so "he sacrificed there". A simple lesson is that God's responses to our supplications and intercessions should promote worship in our hearts. On his arrival in Mesopotamia, Abraham's servant immediately appealed for divine help and guidance (Gen 24.12). When his prayer was answered "the man bowed down his head, and worshipped the Lord" (v.26). Answered prayer demands a response of gratitude.

Although the ark of the covenant had been relocated to Jerusalem, the tabernacle with its altar of burnt offering was still standing at Gibeon. The whole situation was unorthodox and temporary, but was it legitimate for David to sacrifice at Ornan's threshingfloor when the tabernacle was still standing? It was, for he was doing it by divine mandate (v.18), and indeed David perceived these instructions to be sanction for transferring the whole sacrificial system to this new venue (22.1, a verse which really belongs to the section under consideration now). To his thinking, there was now divine authority for this new site to be deemed "the house of the Lord God" with the altar, "the altar of the burnt offering for Israel". With the purchase of the location, and the rearing of the altar, the building of a house for God had come a step nearer.

It is possible that v.30 is giving a late explanation of why David had not scurried to Gibeon to make an appeal to God when he first saw the angel with the drawn sword. The matter was too urgent, just as in Numbers 16 when Aaron had to run with his censer to make atonement for the people, and stood between the dead and the living to stay the plague (vv.47-48). In both instances speed was of the essence, and so here, in accord with the divine command, the altar was raised on the spot.

It could be, though, that the verse is indicating that after his recent experience of God's chastisement David was left with a fear of God that made him reluctant to make any approach to the Almighty at the tabernacle at Gibeon; he "could not go before it to inquire of God". It is rather sad that the man of whom Scripture says so frequently, "David inquired of the Lord", was now in a position where he was paralysed by fear, and could not bring himself to make representations to his God. The same fear had gripped him on the occasion of Uzza's death, when "David was afraid of God that day" (13.12). Let us all learn the solemn lesson, already noted in relation to v.13 and underlined again here, that "It is a *fearful* thing to fall into the hands of the living God" (Heb 10.31). We cannot be certain of how long that fear persisted, but by the next chapter his zeal for God had revived, and further plans for the house of God were set in motion.

1 CHRONICLES 22

With the temple site purchased, it was all systems go in preparation for building the house, and this chapter records David's endeavours to muster men and materials for the task. In subsequent chapters he turns his mind to arranging the various orders of Levites, priests and singers in readiness for the day when temple service would begin.

Mention was made formerly that v.1 properly belongs to the narrative of ch.21. In vv.2-5 there is the record of David gathering labourers and masons for the stonework, collecting metal and timber for the structure, and pledging his backing for the son who would oversee the project - the youthful and inexperienced Solomon.

The core of the chapter is taken up with his charge to Solomon to superintend the building of the house (vv.6-16), with the final section being a command to the princes of Israel to give unstinting support to Solomon as the undertaking proceeds (vv.17-19).

Verse 1: The Site

David understood that the implications of the Lord's command to build an altar on Ornan's threshingfloor extended beyond the present. On ascending the throne, he would have been obedient to the divine command to write out personally "a copy of this law in a book", and "all the days of his life" he would have been reading God's law in his own handwriting (Deut 17.18-19). Frequently, then, he would have read of a place where the Lord would choose "to put his name there", "his habitation", the place to which the people of Israel would bring their burnt offerings and sacrifices (Deut 12.5-6). As David surveyed that threshingfloor, now bereft of the accoutrements of agriculture, with the smoke and smell of sacrifice filling the air, he said in effect, "The day has arrived; the Lord has chosen this unlikely place to put His name here; the location is fixed". "This is the house of the Lord God, and this is the altar of burnt offering for Israel" (RV). Not one stone had been laid, not one workman had appeared on site, no priest had been relocated from Gibeon, and yet David saw it all as an accomplished fact. It is almost reminiscent of Jacob looking across a barren rock-strewn tract of land, and saying, "this is none other but the house of God" (Gen 28.17). The divine presence made it such (v.16). Similarly, this site had special status because it was the place where "the Lord appeared unto David" (2 Chr 3.1).

(It would have to be said that not all expositors endorse David's pronouncement here. John Heading writes: "...it was a hasty, unpondered decision, based on relief, fear, confusion, agitation". Professor Heading contends that God's choice was Mount Zion rather than Mount Moriah. To him, Moriah destroys a spiritual lesson that could have been made had it been Zion, "As we suggest elsewhere", but unfortunately, the "elsewhere" is not divulged, so that the thrust of the argument is lost.)

Verse 2: The Workforce

In many societies there is an underclass of foreigners who are prepared to carry out the tasks that the indigenous people avoid. It appears that this was the case in David's kingdom. There was a residue of the conquered tribes of Canaan still in the land, "not of the children of Israel" (1 Kings 9.20-21), and these "strangers" were press ganged into service. 153,600 were mustered, and they were detailed to be "bearers of burdens", and "hewers in the mountain" (2 Chr 2.17-18). Perhaps some were aggrieved at being coerced into menial backbreaking work, but doubtless there were others who felt privileged to play even a minor role in such a prestigious activity. It was for God. It was to promote His honour. It was with a view to perpetuating His worship; anyone who had any regard for Him would be pleased to participate. Similarly, any Gibeonites with reverence for God would have welcomed the "curse" of being "hewers of wood and drawers of water for the house of my God" (Josh 9.23) as already noted at 9.2 of the commentary. Sometimes we sidestep necessary but unglamorous aspects of the work of God. There was nothing spectacular about what Epaphroditus did for God, trekking hundreds of miles through inhospitable terrain and bandit country as a courier for the assembly at Philippi, and yet it immortalised him in Holy Scripture (Phil 2.25-30). If the grind of labour is necessary, "Whatsoever thy hand findeth to do, do it with thy might" (Eccl 9.10).

Another group of workers was essential, men with a little more expertise, the masons who would "hew wrought stones". The word "wrought" (1496) is normally translated "hewn", so the stones for the temple had already been hewn from a quarry. The mason's job was to hew (2672) them further, to cut them to size, or sculpt them to shape, to make them suitable for the house of God. Perhaps there is a picture here of those who are called by Peter "living stones" (1 Pet 2.5, RV). For us all, there was the initial experience of being hewn from the quarry of nature at conversion. That was only the beginning of a divine work, and God used those with the gift of the evangelist to see that start made. But since then there has been an on-going work of God in our lives, as He has been shaping us morally and spiritually according to His own purpose, and for that, among other things, He uses those with the gift of teaching.

While on the subject of David and stones, it will be remembered that when he was younger he had the need for another kind of stone, and so he "chose him five smooth stones out of the brook" (1 Sam 17.40). God uses smooth stones, stones with abrasions removed by the constant flow of the stream. "The waters wear the stones" (Job 14.19). On occasions, He allows circumstances to be like the agitation of a torrent to remove disagreeable traits from our lives and make us smooth stones that are usable in His hands.

As far as the temple was concerned, the work of the masons was not on-site. "And the house, when it was in building, was built of stone made ready before it was brought thither: so that there was neither hammer nor axe nor any tool of iron heard in the house, while it was in building" (1 Kings 6.7). As far as possible, noise and dust and rubble were distanced from the building site. Dignity and decorum were features of the whole enterprise, and they should be a characteristic of any activity for God.

(Some have seen in the involvement of the Gentiles a picture of the fact that in New Testament times God would "take out of them a people for his name" (Acts 15.14), but the connection seems a little forced.)

Verses 3-4: The Materials

"David prepared", with the addition of the English adverb "abundantly" at v.5. Some of the materials that he prepared are mentioned, but they had to be prepared! Groundwork has to be done to serve God acceptably. Engage in His service with forethought rather than as an afterthought. Abraham had to make preparation before he could adequately entertain the Lord; "Make ready..." (Gen 18.6). To present a meat offering demanded preparation at home, with attention to detail (Lev 2). The women who anticipated embalming "the body of Jesus" engaged in necessary preparation; "they returned, and prepared spices and ointments" (Lk 23.56). Let us avoid being haphazard, or ill prepared for any activity for God. While organizational skills are not the key to success in divine things, every aspect of service will suffer from the chaos that disorganization brings. Open-air meetings, children's work, preaching and teaching all require prayerful planning. Here, before the building, there had to be the preparing.

The "abundantly" of v.5 is a summary of the repeated phrase here, "in abundance". The attitude of Ornan, "I give it all" (21.23), was mirrored in David's generosity. Our God is a God "that giveth to all men *liberally*" (James 1.5) and many of His people want to be as open-handed as He is; David was one of those. This was the man who called upon his own soul to "Bless the Lord...and forget not all his benefits" (Ps 103.2). The recipient of divine bounty never forgot it, and was now proving to be a liberal benefactor himself, and thus it should always be. The word to Abram was, "I will bless thee...be thou a blessing" (Gen 12.2, RV). To be mean and grudging ill befits the children of "the Father of mercies" (2 Cor 1.3).

A multitude of "nails for the doors of the gates" necessitated vast amounts of iron. It is amazing that mention is made of something that seems as trivial as a nail, but God always gives attention to detail. Pins and hooks and fillets all get a mention in connection with the building of the tabernacle. Perhaps there is an underlying warning for us here that such is the precision of divine arrangements we should avoid the temptation to make what would be regarded as even minor adjustments to any pattern that He gives for our lives, whether at a personal level, or in the family, or in the assembly.

Every nail in the doors added strength to them, and each nail contributed to the solidity of the whole. Even people in general understand the knock-on effect of failure to attend to the little things. An ancient proverbial rhyme puts it this way:

For want of a nail the shoe was lost.
For want of a shoe the horse was lost.
For want of a horse the rider was lost.
For want of a rider the battle was lost.
For want of a battle the kingdom was lost
And all for the want of a horseshoe nail.

Give attention to detail then, for the God whom we love and serve is exact in all His arrangements.

It is significant that even at this early stage, mention is made of the doors and gates of the temple, for they will feature in subsequent chapters. Space will be devoted to "the porters", that is, the doorkeepers, the men with the responsible task of admitting legitimate worshippers, and excluding the undesirable.

The phrase "in abundance" (369; 4557) in relation to the cedar trees is a different expression from "in abundance" (7230) used twice in v.3 and also in v.5, translated there "abundantly". However, the term (7230) is used in v.4, translated there by the word "much". "In abundance" in the AV of v.4 is a combination of two words, translated by the RV as "without number". Thus innumerable trees were provided, but there is an emphasis not only on quantity but also on quality; these were cedars, the most desirable growing things in the Middle East (1 Kings 4.33). Only the best would do, for it was for God. Are we building the very best of materials into the local assembly, or are we content with what is bulky but inferior (1 Cor 3.12-15)?

Not only was an abundance of materials provided, and that of the very best, but men with the ability to handle them were employed - "the Zidonians and they of Tyre". Local men did not have the expertise, as expressed in Solomon's words to Hiram: "thou knowest that there is not among us any that can skill to hew timber like unto the Sidonians" (1 Kings 5.6). So not only were the very best of materials used, but the best of workmanship was employed; this was for God! Why is it that when it comes to His work, we scrimp, and cut corners, and content ourselves with a shoddy job when He really deserves the very best that we can do?

Verse 5: The Builder

By divine decree, Solomon would be the builder of the house, but David was conscious of the overwhelming responsibility that this would be. He was also aware of Solomon's inexperience of life in general; he was not only "young", but also "tender". Warfare brutalises men; Solomon had no experience of that. Business dealings and negotiations can make men hard-nosed, and in that realm Solomon was unschooled. "The children of this world are in their generation wiser than the children of light" (Lk 16.8). It appears that David feared that Solomon's youthful naïvety could have been a hindrance to what he saw as the drive and vision that was necessary for such a major project, or perhaps he feared that the follies and distractions of youth could hinder; hence the "therefore" of the verse: "I will *therefore* now make preparation for it". David was determined to give a lead, to provide practical backing, to show solidarity, even although he would never see even the first stone laid. There is a major lesson there for us all. There are aspects of service in which we will never be directly involved, but it is so important to support those who are. Paul referred to Priscilla and Aquila as "my helpers in Christ Jesus" (Rom 16.3). So many of God's people function as "helps" (1 Cor 12.28).

In the case of David there is an added dimension. David himself was a great man. This was not a case of a novice assisting a veteran. David was the veteran and Solomon was the novice, and as far as the house of God was concerned the novice would eclipse the veteran. It is a testimony then to David's large-heartedness that without a shred of jealousy he was determined to do the maximum to help the project forward. The same spirit was seen in Barnabas. In advancing Paul he would have to live in his shadow, and yet for the good of the believers he was willing for that to be the case (Acts 11.25-26).

Another element that motivated David was the fact that the temple was "for the Lord" and hence "*must* be exceeding magnifical". Such would be the majesty of this building that it would be spoken of universally, "of fame and of glory throughout all countries". David's ambition was to make his contribution towards the splendour of such an edifice. It would be wonderful if we too could grasp the majesty of the work with which we are associated. It too is "for the Lord", and there is a grandeur about the gospel that we endeavour to promote, and a dignity about the saints whom we try to help. The whole scheme is so splendid that we should feel privileged to be involved, and excited about having such an honour conferred upon us.

> View the vast building, see it rise;
> The work, how great! the plan, how wise!
> O wondrous fabric! power unknown,
> That rests it on the "Living Stone".
> (Samuel Medley)

It should be noted that the nations around would hear about the temple, and hence the need to make it as striking as it could possibly be. David was determined to pour his energies into this project not only to support Solomon, and not only because it was "for the Lord", but, to use one of our clichés, "for the sake of the testimony". May our contribution to the work of God in our neighbourhoods have the effect of enhancing His reputation in the community, for people do hear and observe.

Our verse concludes with the statement, "So David prepared abundantly before his death". Comment has been made on the fact that he prepared "abundantly", but we are now told, significantly, that this was all "before his death". Very likely, what is being said is that the last days of his life were devoted to this task; he gave it his undivided attention. For him, there was no retirement in the things of God. "Paul the aged" (Philem v.9) was the same, and his voice and pen were available to God until the day when he said, "I am now ready to be offered" (2 Tim 4.6). Though age and infirmity bring increasing restriction, let us all be determined to continue to use whatever strength and ability we have in the interests of God. It may be prudent to shed certain responsibilities if necessary faculties are impaired, but "early retirement" is not an option for the servant of God.

In the phrase "before his death" there is an underlying reminder that our period of service is limited. "I must work the works of him that sent me, while it is day: the night cometh, when no man can work" (Jn 9.4). Our service for God will extend into eternity (Rev 22.3), but reward-earning service relates only to "the things done in the body" (2 Cor 5.10, RV). Let us all be as diligent as David was, and, until death or the Lord's coming, let us be committed to the work of our God.

Verse 6: The Charge

As indicated in the introduction to the chapter, the major part of it is devoted to David's charge to Solomon to undertake the project of building the house of God, so from here to v.16 we have a personal address to Solomon, with the solemn charge to "build an house for the Lord God of Israel". The word "charged" (6680) is translated "command" over 500 times in the Old Testament. This was a binding command from a father to his son, a command that was based on what God had decreed as will be seen in the subsequent verses. It is so good that the charge was heeded. In one of the few references to Solomon in the New Testament there is the simple statement, "Solomon built him an house" (Acts 7.47). Neither his youthfulness nor the scale of the task proved to be any impediment; there was implicit obedience to the divine commission. This was a house for Jehovah (3068) Elohim (430) of Israel: what an honour to be involved in its construction!

Verses 7-8: Why not David?

Before formally charging Solomon, David recounted a little bit of personal history. He bared his soul, and told of his own dream of building the house, but life has its disappointments. Paul had an ambition to visit Spain via Rome, but was it ever realised (Rom 15.22-29)? David was denied the privilege of being the temple-builder because, as a general rule, he was connected more with warfare than worship; the word from the Lord was, "thou hast shed much blood upon the earth in my sight". The temple would never be a monument to a great warrior. It was inconsistent that a man whose whole life had been linked with conflict and violence should at the end of his days be engaged in such a holy exercise as building the house of God; his previous life impacted on his suitability for the task. In

New Testament times, there was always stress on qualifications for service. The seven deacons of Acts 6 had to be "men of honest report, full of the Holy Ghost and wisdom" (v.3). Elders and deacons all had to meet certain criteria to fit them for their sphere of service (1 Tim 3.1-13). Let us all beware lest our actions or attitudes should preclude us from certain aspects of the service of God.

It seems that Solomon put a different gloss on what David told him here. When speaking to Hiram, his words were these: "Thou knowest how that David my father could not build an house unto the name of the Lord his God for the wars which were about him on every side, until the Lord put them under the soles of his feet" (1 Kings 5.3). No doubt what he said what true, but the phrasing puts David in a slightly better light that what we have in our passage. It is a very common human ploy. When writing to Felix, and in describing Paul's rescue, Claudius Lysias readjusted the chronology of events just a little to show himself in a good light: "having understood that he was a Roman" (Acts 23.27, but see 22.25-29). Wrong impressions can be left by omitting or embellishing facts, or by the intonation of the voice, or the inclination of the head or the raising of an eyebrow. Transparency is a wonderful quality.

Verses 8-9: He Shall Build an House

The word from the Lord to David had not only been negative, in that it precluded him from being the temple-builder, but it had been positive in that it had indicated who the builder would be. "A son shall be born to thee": so, even before his birth Solomon was earmarked for this task. The anonymous appointee of 17.11-12 is now identified as Solomon. Samson was another whose work for God was intimated before his birth (Judg 13.2-5), as was Jeremiah's ministry - "Before I formed thee…I ordained thee a prophet to the nations" (Jer 1.5). A sovereign omniscient God can choose whom He will, and when He will, at times making His appointments before the birth of the individual in question.

This son would be "a man of rest" in contrast to his warrior father; his very name "Solomon" means "peaceable". God gave promise here that his reign would be characterised by "peace and quietness", and when history was written it was recorded of that period, "And Judah and Israel dwelt safely, every man under his vine and under his fig tree" (1 Kings 4.25); it foreshadowed millennial days (Micah 4.4).

From a typical point of view, it takes both David and Solomon together to illustrate the kingship of Christ. The warrior king points forward to passages like Revelation 19, where the "KING OF KINGS" vanquishes His foes. The "man of rest" prefigures the King of peace, during whose benign reign even animals and reptiles will live together harmoniously (Is 11.6-9).

From a practical point of view there is a clear lesson. The house of God could never be built while there was strife and commotion. It is interesting that in the land initially the tabernacle was located at Shiloh, meaning "tranquillity". The lesson is that for God's assembly to prosper it demands peaceable, tranquil conditions rather than the atmosphere of tension that stems from sour human relationships. "If ye bite and devour one another, take heed that ye be not consumed one of another" (Gal 5.15).

Verse 10: A Greater than Solomon

In the introduction to the commentary, the observation was made that when reading the Old Testament we are looking for Christ. In 1 Chronicles, on occasions we see Him pictured, but our present verse is the only direct reference to Him in the book. Left to ourselves we would never have applied it to the Lord Jesus, but the Spirit of God takes this verse and its counterpart in 2 Samuel 7.14 and relates it to Him (Heb 1.5); it is cited as proof that as Son He is superior to angels. Initially, the application is to Solomon, but there are hints that the teaching of the verse extends beyond him. The "throne of his kingdom" is said to be established *"for ever"*. Obviously, a mortal like Solomon could never reign indefinitely, so the teaching relates to One who lives in "the power of an endless life" (Heb 7.16). "Of the increase of his government and peace there shall be no end…" (Is 9.7).

Verses 11-13: Words of Encouragement

In charging Solomon to undertake this mighty work for God, David had first of all assured him that what he would do was by divine mandate, and that he himself was the man of God's choice (vv.9-10). This would be an incentive. Now David brings a direct message of encouragement prefaced by these words, "my son". He had used the same address at the start of his conversation (v.7), and Solomon himself used that form of words some twenty-seven times in the book of Proverbs when as a father he counselled his own son. The fact of relationship ought to carry weight.

"The Lord be with thee." When David embarked on the first of his own exploits for God, he went with these words ringing in his ears, "Go, and the Lord be with thee" (1 Sam 17.37). He never forgot it. The divine presence was vouchsafed to all whom He commissioned to serve Him: Moses, Joshua, Gideon, and so many others. The promised presence holds good to this present age, so let us be encouraged: "lo, I am with you alway, even unto the end of the world" (Mt 28.20). The only One who did anything for God without the assurance and consolation of God's presence, was He who said, "My God, my God, why hast thou forsaken me?" (Mt 27.46). Let us prize His presence and power; when it comes to His service, nothing else is needed, but nothing less will suffice.

"Prosper thou, and build…". How could it be achieved? The answer is in v.13: "Then shalt thou prosper". But to what does the "then" refer? It involved Solomon putting in place the criteria for success that David demanded here, and only then would the work go on apace and prosper.

What were the necessary prerequisites for a successful work? It would demand "wisdom and understanding" from the Lord. Solomon regarded himself as being in short supply of such wisdom, but it was granted abundantly upon request (1 Kings 3.7-12), and is still available today (James 1.5-8). In the context of 1 Kings 3, and here, the need was for wisdom and understanding to govern the nation, "charge concerning Israel", so that there would be no major political upheaval to impede the building of the house of God.

Obedience was another essential if the work was to prosper. There would have to be obedience to any current commands from the Lord (v.12), but, in particular, to the ancient law that was given through Moses (v.13). A work of God will never prosper in the hands of people who treat His Word carelessly, and who deliberately ignore His commands. There are echoes here from God's message to Joshua when he succeeded Moses as leader of the people of Israel. He was enjoined to meditate on God's word "day and night"; he was instructed to "observe to do according to all that is written therein"; the promise was, "*then* thou shalt make thy way prosperous, and *then* thou shalt have good success" (Josh 1.8). Prosperity and success were dependent on his commitment to the commands of God.

Another crucial factor for success was the need for fortitude and tenacity, and David urged this with four pithy injunctions, two positive, and two negative: "be strong, and of good courage; dread not, nor be dismayed". The work would never prosper if Solomon succumbed to weakness, fear or discouragement. A project that would span a period of years would inevitably have its low points when there was the danger of frustration and disappointment through lack of progress. The halfway point in any activity can have its perils, when the first flush of enthusiasm has waned, and the end is still not in sight. An illustration of this was when they were rebuilding the walls of Jerusalem. When the walls were "joined together unto the half thereof" discouragement set in, and the complaint was, "The strength of the bearers of burdens is decayed" (Neh 4.6-10). There is the constant need for perseverance. The world has a maxim, "When the going gets tough, the tough get going". To be more Biblical, an injunction to New Testament believers is, "be ye stedfast, unmoveable, always abounding in the work of the Lord" (1 Cor 15.58). Let us take note, and rise above the tendency to discouragement and pessimism.

Verse 14: I Have Prepared

Having encouraged Solomon to be committed to his task, David holds himself up as an example of such commitment, a role model worth emulating; "*I* have prepared for the house of the Lord". It is so good when those who are inciting others to action can point to themselves as an example of their demands. For example, when Paul was encouraging the Ephesian elders to care for the disadvantaged, he said, "*I* have shewed you all things, how that *so labouring* ye ought to support the weak" (Acts 20.35). To the Philippians he said, "Those things, which ye have both learned, and received, and heard, and seen in me, do" (Phil 4.9). The power of example is compelling, and so David here drew attention to his own massive input into the project.

It is of interest that he indicated that it was "in (his) trouble" that he prepared for the house. He was not so preoccupied with his own circumstances that he neglected the things of God. It is an echo of the sentiments of Psalm 132 where we learn of David's desire "to find out a place for the Lord, an habitation for the mighty God of Jacob" (v.5). There, too, his commitment to that project was born out of "all his afflictions" (vv.1-2). When faced with trials, we can become introverted, almost filled with self-pity to the extent of resigning responsibilities, and putting our work for God on hold. This man did not allow affliction to deter him, but saw it as an opportunity to further his activity for the house of God. Paul's attitude was the same: "the things which happened unto me have fallen out rather unto the furtherance of the gospel" (Phil 1.12). May we be preserved from being so taken up with personal adversity that we step back from serving God.

Some have thought that the phrase "in my trouble" refers to the personal effort that David made to accumulate the materials. For example, Braun translates the phrase like this: "by my hard work". David was at pains to gather up all that was necessary and put effort into the task. If that is a valid concept, there is a healthy spiritual lesson in it. We cannot expect things just to "happen" without energetic commitment and a willingness to be inconvenienced.

Marginal translations suggest yet another thought. "In my poverty I have prepared" (AV margin). "In my low estate I have prepared" (RV margin). To provide the necessary materials for the house of God, was David willing for a less opulent life-style than his station in life afforded him? Was there a measure of frugality about how he lived? No doubt it was all relative, but perhaps there is the thought that there should be an element of sacrifice about what we give to God. Doing good and communicating material things comes under the umbrella of "sacrifices" in Hebrews 13.16.

Mention has already been made of David's generosity, but once more it is underscored here. An enormous weight of gold and silver is detailed, an indication that David was not haphazard in his giving to God; what he gave was calculated. Passages like Acts 11.29-30, 1 Corinthians 16.1-2, and 2 Corinthians 9.7 all show that as believers we too ought to give consideration to what we give to God, rather than making a random contribution.

There is a massive variation between the weight of gold and silver here, and weights that are mentioned in 29.4. There, the amounts donated were from David's personal fortune, "a treasure of mine own" (v.3, RV). Here, the spoils of war had provided the bounty. War normally depletes a nation's exchequer. In this case, it had enhanced it immensely.

David provided a mass of material, but the concession was given to Solomon, "thou mayest add thereto". There was no thought of David resenting someone else being involved. He encouraged Solomon's practical contribution as well as the administrative skills that would be necessary when the time for building arrived.

Verses 15-16: Arise and Be Doing

The materials had been amassed, the workmen, skilled and unskilled, were in attendance, and all that remained to be done was to commence the task; "Arise therefore, and be doing". As far as we are concerned, all that we need to build for God has been provided. We have His Word in our hands and His Spirit in our hearts. He has gifted men appropriately for every facet of the work. All that remains is for the activity to start; "be doing". "Why stand ye here all the day idle?" (Mt 20.6).

David re-emphasised the need for the divine presence: "Arise therefore, and be doing, and *the Lord be with thee*". Psalm 127.1 is relevant here: "Except the Lord build the house, they labour in vain that build it". The title of the Psalm indicates that it was either "for Solomon" (AV) or "of Solomon" (RV). "It is not clear whether it was actually written by Solomon, or composed by David for Solomon" (J. M. Flanigan; *What the Bible Teaches: Psalms*), but, one way or the other, the psalm is linked clearly with Solomon. The house to be built here was the house of God. Materials and workmen were in readiness. Solomon was poised to initiate proceedings, but the whole project would be futile if devoid of the presence of God. Let us learn that lesson too. A suitable venue, presentable advertising, zealous believers and a gifted preacher are all commendable assets to any work for God, but "Except the Lord build the house, they labour in vain that build it".

Verses 17-19: The Princes of Israel

The final part of the chapter comprises an exhortation to the princes of Israel to support Solomon in his undertaking of building the house of God. We often hear said that one man with God is a majority, and we understand these sentiments, but in reality God seldom used just one man working in isolation. His normal pattern was to use people who were co-operating with each other. True, invariably one man would give a lead, but he would be supported by others as when "Peter (stood) up with the eleven" (Acts 2.14). Thus here, while Solomon would be the main mover in this great project of building the temple, "David also commanded all the princes of Israel to help Solomon". Observe that the command was to "*all* the princes". He expected everyone to become involved. Paul's imprisonment and fortitude emboldened "most of the brethren" but sadly, not all (Phil 1.14, RV). In Christian service, one hundred per cent participation should be a target at which to aim.

Just as the Lord would be with Solomon as an individual in his labours (v.16), so the princes could count on His presence congregationally: "Is not the Lord your God with *you*?" (v.18). If they would but throw their weight behind Solomon, they could rely on divine support themselves. David reminded them of the conditions of peace that existed in the land after so many years of both internal and external strife. The temptation would be for these administrators to capitalise on that by taking life a little bit more easily. There was no longer a red alert as far as national security was concerned, so there would be more time for rest and recreation! In reality, David urged them to see the tranquil conditions as an opportunity to press ahead with this great project that was in hand. "Arise therefore, and build ye the sanctuary of the Lord God" (v.19). For many, employment creates great pressure these days, but to a large extent the present generation has more leisure time than former generations did. In Jim Elliot's biography, *Shadow of the Almighty*, one of the chapters is entitled, "The Test of Free Time". Free time is a test; is it being used to maximum advantage? The Biblical injunction is, "Redeeming the time, because the days are evil" (Eph 5.16). "Where God gives rest, He expects work" (Matthew Henry).

Before they could build, they were to "seek the Lord your God". As ever, prayer and supplication must precede work for God. This whole thing involved setting the heart and soul to seek Him; in other words it commenced internally, and from that individual work within, and internal conviction about personal involvement, the external work would flow. Paul spoke about "serv(ing) *in (his) spirit* in the gospel of his Son" (Rom 1.9, RV; see also JND). The public activity was the product of his internal commitment to the God whom he served.

Thus the princes were commissioned, with the inference that they were to be sure to carry the project through to its conclusion by seeing the ark installed in the completed building. The ark would be brought from the tent that David had pitched for it. The "holy vessels" would be brought from the tabernacle at Gibeon. At this point it all seemed an object on the far horizon, but the day came when it was a reality, and, with the ark installed, "the house was filled with a cloud, even the house of the Lord" (2 Chr 5.7,13). God had come to dwell, not only symbolically as seen in the ark, but in reality as seen in the cloud.

1 CHRONICLES 23

A new section of 1 Chronicles commences here. The ark had been brought to Jerusalem and a site for the temple had been procured. Workmen had been marshalled and materials for the construction had been accumulated. Solomon and the princes of Israel had been commanded to build. Now chapters 23-27 take proceedings a stage further as David anticipates the day when the building will be completed, and when temple service will commence. In preparation for that, he arranges various courses of Levites, priests, singers and doorkeepers who would operate a shift system to ensure the smooth functioning of divine service. Chapter 27 rounds off the section with details of those in the military and in the civil service of the nation. Such particulars may seem superfluous to the overall theme of the book, but the security of the nation and its political stability would facilitate the building of the house of God and the subsequent religious activity connected with it.

Reading these chapters, one gets the impression that David personally initiated this whole rota system, and that it was a scheme that he himself had devised. However, it is clear that he had a divine directive for all that he set in place. A "pattern" had been given to him, not only for the temple structure itself, but "Also for the courses of the priests and the Levites, and for all the work of the service of the house of the Lord, and for all the vessels of service in the house of the Lord" (28.13).

When the temple was built and Solomon adopted the system of courses, the comment is made, "so had David *the man of God* commanded" (2 Chr 8.14). His designation as a man of God would seem to imply that he was the channel of instruction and not the source. Similarly, in Hezekiah's reign there is reference to the way things operated in the temple, and it was "according to the commandment of David, and of Gad the king's seer, and Nathan the prophet: *for so was the commandment of the Lord* by his prophets" (2 Chr 29.25). So, then, the system was not invented by David, but was put in place by divine decree. What David had been given "by the spirit" (1 Chr. 28.12) was what he implemented. It would be good for us all to be equally obedient to what the Spirit of God has dictated. In our case it relates to the pattern for a New Testament church, and the instructions are far less complex than those David was applying here.

Verse 1: David Was Old

It has been noted at regular intervals that 1 Chronicles omits many details about David that are recorded elsewhere in the inspired Scriptures, particularly some negative features. Here we are spared the spectacle of a decrepit old man shivering in his bed (1 Kings 1.1). With the ensuing political intrigue, that incident was relevant to the narrative there, but irrelevant here with the emphasis on the house of God. Even the language of our English Bible seems softer here - "full of days" in contrast to "*stricken* in years" as in the former narrative. Again, there is no retelling of Adonijah's rebellion, for it would have no bearing on the overall theme.

Normally, an eldest son would succeed a deceased father to the throne, but in his old age David installed Solomon as his successor, or at least gave an indication of his choice. This was essential because *God* had commanded that Solomon should be the next monarch (22.9-10), and he was by no means David's eldest surviving son. This whole scenario was re-enacted "a second time" (29.22), for there had to be public declarations of both the divine intention and David's compliance with it. This proved crucial when Adonijah did aspire to the throne, for Solomon's sympathisers were able to point to David's former commitment, and the frail old king was sharp enough to enforce what had been decreed (1 Kings 1.11-40). There is the possibility that in David's closing years, he and Solomon acted as co-regents, with Solomon wielding some power, but with David still perceived as the figure-head in the eyes of the general public.

There is a lesson, lying on the surface, that it is the duty of those who are aged to oversee the transition of responsibility to younger men. As was noted in a former chapter, that should never be done prematurely for the sake of an easier life, but there comes a point when physical powers deteriorate and the mind is no longer agile. (Ecclesiastes 12.1-8 makes touching reading!) In these circumstances obligations become burdensome, and public responsibilities are discharged in a hesitant or bumbling fashion that can be embarrassing for others. A wise old man will know when the time has come for him to pass on the baton and allow others to make the running.

Verse 2: Another Gathering

Throughout the book David made great orations to his subjects. This will not be the last of them, but it is one in a line of messages that aged leaders made to their people before their passing. Moses (Deut 32-33) and Joshua (Josh 23-24) in the Old Testament, and Peter (2 Pet 1.13-14) and Paul (Acts 20) in the New Testament all had weighty issues to raise with the people of God before their call to higher service. Here, much of David's message related to administrative matters, but there is a cutting edge to his appeals in the final chapters of the book; there is gravitas about a man's final pronouncements and pleas.

Verses 3-5: Thirty-Eight Thousand Levites

As in Numbers 4.3, the Levites were numbered from the age of thirty. Temple service would not be as physically exacting as transporting the tabernacle, but the various functions of the Levites still demanded men in their prime. Maturity was required for some of their responsibilities, so the age limit precluded those with little experience of life. No upper limit of the age of fifty is mentioned here, possibly because the new duties were less strenuous than formerly.

Later in the chapter David made a new reckoning of the Levites, and at vv.24 and 27 mention is made of the age of twenty. It seems clear that these younger men were to be working in close co-operation with the priests (v.28), and hence under their supervision. Be like the Levites and be prepared to devote the best years of your life to God.

A large number of Levites were mustered, 38,000 in all. While they had not been numbered when Joab conducted the illegitimate census (21.6), they were counted here. They had a variety of functions, and if we take the summation of the numbers apportioned to each task, it means that every last man had a job to do; no one was redundant. Christian service is no different. Apply the words of a parable to our own situation: "to *every man* his work" (Mk 13.34). In the work of God, no one should feel excluded or unneeded, for we have all been allocated our assignment, a personal commission for which we have been singularly fitted. "Take heed to the ministry which thou hast received in the Lord, that thou fulfil it" (Col 4.17).

The majority of the Levites, 24,000, were to "oversee the work of the house of the Lord" (v.4, RV). There would be an endless stream of sacrifices with which the priests would require assistance, and there would also be the constant business of carrying out dirt, and maintaining the cleanliness of the vessels of the sanctuary.

6,000 were involved in administration as officers and judges, effectively the magistrates of the land. A further 4,000 were doorkeepers of whom more will be said in a later chapter. The final 4,000 were involved in the exercise of praise, using instruments provided by David himself, and this was a new ministry. Formerly, a fanfare of trumpets would have signalled the start of a special day in Israel's calendar (Num 10.10).

Just as there was a variety of function then, so there is still an assortment of tasks in the work of God; "there are diversities of gifts...there are diversities of ministrations...there are diversities of workings" (1 Cor 12.4-6, RV). Let us all be aware of our role and give it our very best.

When it comes to a more detailed account of their functions in the following chapters, the order of their activity is somewhat different. Those who worked closest to the priests are mentioned first, then the singers, then the doorkeepers, and finally those who "were for the outward business over Israel, for officers and judges" (26.29). As in other instances in Scripture, God was working from the inside out. Details for the tabernacle started with the ark and worked out from there. We understood the death of Christ in its sin offering character before we had any appreciation of its burnt offering character, but God started with the burnt offering and worked out (Lev 1). We tend to speak about body, soul and spirit. God speaks of "spirit and soul and body" (1 Thess 5.23).

Verse 6: Courses

The "courses" (4256) or "divisions" (AV margin), were groupings of Levites who operated a shift system, each group functioning for a scheduled period, guaranteeing that there were always enough of them on duty to ensure the smooth functioning of temple service in its various aspects. The courses were divided in keeping with the three branches of the Levitical family.

With such vast numbers available for temple service, it was imperative that they were organised in an orderly fashion, for God never operates in a haphazard way. Each shift would consist of the correct number, without anyone being either overburdened or crowded out. Similarly, a New Testament principle is, "Let all things be done decently and in order" (1 Cor 14.40). When speaking in tongues was legitimate, stringent legislation governed its use (vv.27-28). The gift of prophecy was also strictly regulated (vv.29-33). Chaotic conditions never honour the God of order.

Verses 7-11: The Sons of Gershon

Laadan and Shimei were the immediate sons of Gershon, variations of the names recorded in Exodus 6.17. Thereafter, descendants of Laadan are mentioned, designated "chief of the fathers of Laadan". As far as Shimei was concerned, two branches of his family were numerically weak, and so were combined to make a single family unit (v.11). There is perhaps the lesson there that on occasions there may be a case for smaller entities combining into a single force for some specific project that requires numerical strength.

Verses 12-20: The Sons of Kohath

The four sons of Kohath are named as at Exodus 6.18. Amram was of particular significance for he fathered Aaron and Moses. Prominence is given to Aaron here, for, as in tabernacle service, his descendants would function as the priesthood in the new order of things, "he and his sons for ever".

"Aaron was separated", separated not only from the nation as a whole, and not only from the tribe of Levi as a whole, but even from the Kohathite branch of the family. Aaron was distinct; Aaron was unique; his role and that of his descendants was more prestigious than even that of his favoured Kohathite brethren.

Four priestly duties are mentioned here, three of them Godward and one manward. (It has been said that very often when four things are linked in Scripture, three are similar and one is different. It would take diligent labour to discover whether that general statement can be borne out consistently, but a striking example is the four Gospels, three of them being what we call the Synoptic Gospels with John's Gospel distinct.)

The priest's first duty was to "sanctify the most holy things", that is, to ensure that every accoutrement connected to the service of God was maintained for that purpose. In every respect, priests had to discern how to "put difference between holy and unholy, between unclean and clean" (Lev 10.10). A charge laid against the priests in Ezekiel's day was that "Her priests have violated my law, and have profaned my holy things: they have put no difference between the holy and profane, neither have they shewed difference between the unclean and the clean" (Ezek 22.26). May God enable us all to be discerning, and to ensure that things that are inappropriate never intrude into divine activity even although they may have their place in other spheres of life.

The second function of the priest was "to burn incense before the Lord", and this was what occupied Zacharias when Gabriel appeared to him (Lk 1.8-20). There, the offering of the incense is linked with prayer; "the whole multitude of the people were praying without at the time of incense" (v.10). Similarly, in Revelation 8.3 "there was given unto (an angel) much incense, that he should offer it with the prayers of all saints". Thus the offering of incense pictures our prayers arising to the throne of God. As a "holy priesthood" (1 Pet 2.5), then, let us fulfil the priestly function of offering incense figuratively, that is, let us be involved constantly in the exercise of prayer. Apart from any benefit that we may derive, there is a fragrance as it ascends to God. "Let my prayer be set forth before thee as incense" (Ps 141.2).

The third responsibility of the priest here was to "minister unto him". This would take in his involvement in the sacrificial system. According to Leviticus 1, the offerer had certain responsibilities as far as the burnt offering was concerned, but the priests had their duties too, normally prefaced by the expression, "the priests, Aaron's sons shall...". Apply the lesson again. As a holy priesthood we have the responsibility "to offer up spiritual sacrifices, acceptable to God by Jesus Christ" (1 Pet 2.5). This is a ministry that is "*unto him*", to lift the phrase from our verse. There could be the danger that we are so busy in ministering for Him that we neglect to minister to Him. Never let us ignore the exercise of worship.

The manward side of the priest's activity was "to bless in his name for ever" for every variety of priesthood had this dual function. Melchizedec blessed Abram and blessed God (Gen 14.19-20). The Christian priesthood has a Godward function as we have seen but also a manward function, to "shew forth the praises of him who hath called you out of darkness into his marvellous light" (1 Pet 2.9). The Aaronic priest was no different. His function Godward was to "offer both gifts and sacrifices for sins", but his function manward was to "have compassion on the ignorant, and on them that are out of the way" (Heb 5.1-2).

Aaron's sons were instructed in the language they would use in blessing the people, a most beautiful benediction. "The Lord bless thee, and keep thee: The Lord make his face shine upon thee, and be gracious into thee: The Lord lift up his countenance upon thee, and give thee peace" (Num 6.24-26). May we all be as keen to invoke the wellbeing of others, even those who have expressed hostility towards us. "Bless them which persecute you: bless, and curse not" (Rom 12.14). "Not rendering evil for evil, or railing for railing: but contrariwise blessing" (1 Pet 3.9).

Aaron's posterity was far more privileged than that of his younger brother Moses. Here, the descendants of Moses had no special status among the

Kohathites because of their attachment to "the man of God". It is rather sad that there is no record of any of Moses' descendants making a mark for God. Indeed, if most translations are to be accepted, the idolatrous young Levite, Jonathan, was his grandson (Judg 18.30). Neither spirituality nor responsibility in the things of God runs in the blood; in fact there is no relationship with God that is transferable from one generation to the next. Samuel made the mistake of installing his sons as judges even although they were bereft of moral character and commitment (1 Sam 8.1-3). Let leaders be wary of nepotism. For us all, there could be the danger of claiming privilege because of an attachment to someone who is perceived to be of importance among the people of God!

Not for the first time is Moses described here as "the man of God" (v.14). Another notable occasion when he was thus described was when Caleb was claiming his inheritance. On that occasion he gave Moses two distinct designations, "Moses the man of God", and "Moses the servant of the Lord" (Josh 14.6-7). The order is significant. A man can never adequately be a servant of the Lord unless he is first and foremost a man of God. The phrase is used sparingly in Scripture. It has often been observed that the only man in the New Testament to be designated a "man of God" is Timothy (1 Tim 6.11), but it is evident that the resources are available to make us all fully fledged men and women of God; these resources are contained in the inspired Scriptures (2 Tim 3.14-16). Let us all be ambitious to have this appellation.

Verses 21-23: The Sons of Merari

Merari's immediate family is named as in the RV of Exodus 6.19. One branch of the family produced only daughters, but another strain of the family took them as their wives. This practice was law from the days of the five daughters of Zelophehad (Num 36). In that case it was to safeguard an inheritance from passing from one tribe to another. Obviously from that point of view, the precaution was unnecessary here, for the tribe of Levi had no inheritance in the land.

Verse 24: These...did the Work

The chiefs of the fathers of the three branches of the tribe of Levi have been named, and from these various clans of the tribe the roster for temple service was drawn up with its twenty-four courses in all. Their proposed activity is said to be "the *work* for the service of the house of the Lord". These men were highly honoured to be God's choice for His service, but they were never to forget that it was "work". There was no place for idleness; shirking was out of order; diligence was of paramount importance for it was for God. Even today the service of God in its various aspects is work. Overseership is work (1 Tim 3.1); witnessing is work (2 Tim 4.5); the earnest Bible teacher is a "workman" (2 Tim 2.15). Nothing will ever be accomplished for God without us diligently applying ourselves to the task on hand. Take heed to the words of a parable although taken from context here: "Son, *go work* to day in my vineyard" (Mt 21.28).

As noted before, at this verse the threshold for entering Levitical service is lowered to the age of twenty, and indeed this was still the case as late as the days of Hezekiah (2 Chr 31.17). The first readers of 1 Chronicles would have been familiar with that arrangement too, for the Levites who returned from the Babylonian captivity were appointed "from twenty years old and upward" (Ezra 3.8). The reasons for making younger men eligible to serve as Levites are advanced in subsequent verses, but undoubtedly David anticipated the need for larger numbers.

Verses 25-27: They Shall no More Carry the Tabernacle

The word "For" at the start of the verse indicates that there will now be an explanation for admitting younger men to serve as Levites. The basic reason was the fact that there was no more need for men to transport the tabernacle, a rigorous task that demanded just a little more strength and maturity than might be expected of a twenty year-old. God "knoweth our frame" (Ps 103.14), and so He decreed that only men in the full powers of their manhood would be employed in that demanding activity. With the tabernacle now assigned to history, and the likely need for more helpers for temple service, the twenty year-olds were deemed eligible to serve.

Why did the Levites "no more have need to carry the tabernacle" (v.26, RV)? David supplies two reasons at v.25. First, God had "given rest unto his people". Wilderness wanderings were a distant memory, and for generations they had been resident in the land. Under David's tenure erstwhile foes had been completely vanquished and the ensuing "rest" facilitated the building of the temple which rendered the tabernacle redundant.

The second reason for the tabernacle being phased out was that God had come to reside in Jerusalem, so there was no more need for a moving tent as had been required in the wilderness and in the early days of their occupancy of the land. (Most translations allude to the fact that it was God who was now dwelling in Jerusalem; the reference is not so much to them (the nation) as in the AV, but to Him.) David speaks of God dwelling in Jerusalem "for ever". We know that this was not literally the case. There came a day when the glory departed from "the midst of the city" (Ezek 11.23), for rebellion and idolatry necessitated the withdrawal of the divine presence. However, the point that David is making here is that God's Presence in Jerusalem was "for ever" in that it was domiciled in a permanent structure in contrast to a moveable tent that was relocated many times in the wilderness, and on occasions in the land.

Thus, because of the rest that the people enjoyed, and the fact that God had chosen to place His name in Jerusalem permanently, there was no further need for the tabernacle, and hence no need for the backbreaking task of transporting it. With all that in the past, men of a lesser age and physique could now be helpers in temple service.

This shift of policy was among the last things that David decreed (v.27), but as was stated in the introduction to the chapter, never forget that it was all by divine command.

Verses 28-32: The Functions of the Levites

The latter part of the chapter is devoted to the functions of the Levites, their overall responsibility being described earlier as "to oversee the work of the house of the Lord" (v.4, RV). Now a more detailed description of their activities is provided.

The first thing that is stated is again fairly general, in that "their office was to wait on the sons of Aaron for the service of the house of the Lord", so their initial remit in the book of Numbers was being perpetuated under the new circumstances. As late as New Testament times, priests and Levites were linked, in that case collaborating in the investigation of John the Baptist (Jn 1.19).

God's original intention had been for the firstborn sons of Israel to function in tabernacle service, but that never materialised, and hence He gave the Levites to the priests as their assistants and also compensated the priests in a monetary way on account of a comparatively small shortfall in personnel (Num 3.40-51). For the more part the Levites were content to function in their subsidiary role, but a sad situation arose when Korah and others underestimated their privilege, and aspired to the priesthood (Num 16.8-10). They came under the judgment of God - a salutary lesson for us all, lest we too should cast a greedy eye on someone else's work for God instead of being satisfied to labour at what has been assigned to us. "As every man hath received the gift, even so minister *the same* one to another" (1 Pet 4.10). Exercise the gift that God has given you without attempting to displace someone else.

Thus here, the original Levite/priest relationship was to be maintained under the new order of things in temple worship; they were still to be effectively the priests' assistants, aiding them in the external activities of "the courts", and in the internal activities of "the chambers". Doubtless that involved the very menial tasks of keeping these areas clean, for with so many animals passing through, and such frequent preparation of meat offerings, there was tremendous potential for clutter and mess.

Priority had to be given to maintaining the cleanliness of vessels that were in use for preparing the shewbread and the meat offering with its various recipes. Details of the first are found in Leviticus 24.5-9, while the second is the subject matter of Leviticus 2. The spiritual mind will see much of Christ in aspects of both the shewbread and the meat offering, but that would be for a commentary on the book of Leviticus rather than 1 Chronicles. The Levites were to be involved in the preparation of all these things so that priests would have everything at hand for their constant activity in the service of God.

Weights and measures was another area of responsibility for the Levites:

"all manner of measure and size". So many of the meat and drink offerings had stated weights and measures involving the ephah and the hin. In secular business dealings God demanded transparency and precision. "Just balances, just weights, a just ephah, and a just hin, shall ye have" (Lev 19.36). From God's standpoint, cheating the customer was intolerable. How much more necessary to avoid depriving Him in what was being offered to Him! Levites were under orders then to ensure the precision of temple weights and measures. They were the maintenance men who diligently tested the accuracy of scales, and the measures for liquids.

Another function of the Levites was to render the morning and evening thanksgiving and praise (v.30). Their posture while so doing was "to stand", indicative of the reverence in which they held the God who was the object of their worship. Let us be equally reverential, and as regular in our devotions as these men were. God's "compassions fail not. They are new every morning" (Lam 3.22-23), so it is fitting to acknowledge that in thanksgiving at the break of the day.

When Abraham's servant experienced divine leading throughout the day, in the evening he "bowed down his head, and worshipped the Lord" (Gen 24.11,26-27). Let us be just as grateful to our God as we kneel before Him at the close of the day to reflect on His gracious dealings with us. Of course, men like David and Daniel incorporated another devotional time into their day (Dan 6.10). "Evening, and morning, and at noon, will I pray, and cry aloud" (Ps 55.17). It is always appropriate to express our thanks to a beneficent God, and those who are filled with the Spirit will be "Giving thanks *always* for all things unto God and the Father in the name of our Lord Jesus Christ" (Eph 5.20).

The Levites would also assist with the "burnt offerings" (RV). The reference here is not so much to an individual coming with his offering as in Leviticus 1, but rather to the ritual connected to special days in Israel's calendar. Some were weekly, "the sabbaths". Some were monthly, "the new moons". Some were annually, "the set feasts", and then the word "continually" is used. It is all a reminder of the inadequacy of the Old Testament sacerdotal system in contrast to the sufficiency of the work of Christ. "Every priest standeth daily ministering and offering oftentimes the same sacrifices, which can never take away sins: But this man, after he had offered one sacrifice for sins for ever, sat down on the right hand of God" (Heb 10.11-12). We are indebted to Isaac Watts for expressing in poetic form the teaching of these great chapters of the Epistle to the Hebrews. He does so in his delightful hymn, "Jesus in thee our eyes behold…". One verse encapsulates our present consideration.

> Fresh blood as constant as the day
> Was on their altar spilt;
> But Thy one offering takes away
> For ever all our guilt.

The number of victims for the altar for each of Israel's special days was prescribed, and the Levites had to adhere diligently to divine instructions. It was "by number". Equal care had to be taken to do everything "according to the order commanded unto them". There was no room for flexibility, and personal initiatives were not an option when it came to this. Not for the first time in the book we are learning the lesson that God's work has to be done in God's way, if we may be permitted to borrow sentiments that were immortalised by Hudson Taylor. There is no substitute for strict conformity to God's blueprint for service as contained in the Holy Scriptures.

The final verse of the chapter is a kind of summary of their responsibilities, with the repetition of the word "charge" (4931) to describe their spheres of duty. It is rather strange that this last verse makes mention of the tabernacle. We are left wondering if the previous verses are retrospective rather than prospective but that cannot be because mention is made in v.28 of "the chambers" of which there were none in the tabernacle. The likelihood is that the reference is to the last stages of tabernacle service, the period that was left pending temple worship being instituted. Levites still had duties in connection with that final phase of activity at the tabernacle before the changeover to the temple took place.

Thus the courses and responsibilities of the Levites are delineated, and from there the inspired narrative will move on to the courses of their brethren, the sons of Aaron.

1 CHRONICLES 24

In this chapter, David continues to make the preparations for temple service. In the early verses the spotlight falls on the priests, before the narrative swings back to the Levites at v.20.

Having organised the Levites into four teams for varying tasks, and these teams into different shifts, David now arranges the priests into twenty-four "courses" (v.1, RV). This explains Luke 1.5, where Zacharias is said to be "of the course of Abijah" (RV), a course that features in v.10 of our chapter.

Keep in mind the remarks that were made in the introduction to the previous chapter regarding God being the instigator of the new arrangements. David was implementing divine instructions.

Verses 1-2: The Sons of Aaron

These verses mention Aaron's immediate family without retelling the tragic circumstances of the judgment on Nadab and Abihu. All that is said of them is that they died "before their father, and had no children", explaining why there would be no representatives of that side of the family serving in the temple.

The word "before" (6440) is not so much a time term, but indicates "in the presence of". "Haran died *in the presence of* (6440) his father Terah" (Gen 11.28, RV). Young's Literal Translation uses that same phrase in this verse. However, implied in the statement is that Nadab and Abihu did predecease their father, not an uncommon occurrence in Holy Scripture. In fact, the first human father was predeceased by his son Abel (Gen 4.8). Parents who have experienced the heartbreak of burying their children are in a long line of individuals who have shared that sorrow.

The two surviving sons, Eleazar and Ithamar, are said to have "executed the priest's office", and from these two every priest of David's generation could trace his pedigree.

Verse 3: Consultation

When dividing the manpower, David did not operate in a highhanded way, but co-operated with two of the leading priests of his day, Zadok and Ahimelech, representatives of the two segments of Aaron's family. Most translations make that clear. "With the help of Zadok…and Ahimelech… David organized them…" (ESV). Perhaps there is a lesson there in the need to consult, and to carry people with us when some new undertaking is anticipated.

The mention of Ahimelech is perplexing. Abiathar and not Ahimelech was the man most frequently linked with Zadok. Ahimelech was Abiathar's father, the victim of a deception on the part of David that led to his execution (1 Sam 22). That rules him out of the present consideration. Some commentators (e.g. Clarke) see Ahimelech here as an alternative name for Abiathar himself, although it would be difficult to prove that from Scripture.

Verse 6 indicates that Abiathar had a son called Ahimelech, and there is no reason why he should not have been Zadok's companion.

"Their offices in their service" is elucidated by the NKJV, "the schedule of their service", a reference to the system of shift work for the priests that was being introduced as an innovation at that time.

Verse 4: Chief Men

Aaron's posterity through Eleazar had expanded considerably, much more so than the descendants of Ithamar. There were sixteen family groups connected to it, as opposed to only eight in the line of Ithamar. The heads of these families, the twenty-four "chief men", were to feature prominently in the new arrangements. The inequality of numbers reflects the judgment pronounced on the house of Eli who was on the Ithamar side of the family (1 Sam 2.27-36).

Verses 5-6: Divided by Lot

Everything was done to ensure that the allocation of the twenty-four duty rotas among these twenty-four "chief men" was not only fair, but was seen to be fair. There would be no cause for complaints or squabbles. There could be no accusations of fraudulent activity or favouritism. "The lot causeth contentions to cease" (Prov 18.18), and so the method employed to apportion responsibilities was that of casting lots. From the Christian perspective it seems inappropriate, but let us keep in mind that with the events of the Day of Pentecost the new age of the Spirit of God was introduced. Within almost a generation of that event, the Holy Scriptures were complete. With the Spirit and the Word for guidance we are at a decided advantage over these Old Testament characters. "The lot is cast into the lap; but the whole disposing thereof is of the Lord" (Prov 16.33). In light of that, we judge that a divine hand superintended all these arrangements, and those involved seemed satisfied with the outcome; there were no complaints of bias.

There was another notable occasion when casting lots was used to determine huge issues. That was when the land was divided among the twelve tribes of Israel according to the instructions given to Moses (Num 26.52-56).

In our passage, equity is again in evidence in that both sides of Aaron's family were represented - "sons of Eleazar" and "sons of Ithamar" - no one need feel excluded. We have observed though that the one group did have double the amount of leaders by sheer weight of numbers.

It appears that the allocation of different duties was also decided by the casting of the lots, some to be "princes of the sanctuary", and others "princes of God" (RV). It could be that, as with the Levites, some of these priestly leaders would have duties in relation to the temple, and others as magistrates in the land as seen in the different terms that are used. In the case of the priests, they would have responsibilities of a supervisory nature as "governors" (AV). It should be said that some commentators regard the two terms as being synonymous.

The transparency of this whole procedure is seen again at v.6. The names to go "into the hat", as we would say, were written out by Shemaiah, a scribe from among the Levites. The "draw" was to be observed by a range of very credible witnesses including David himself, and representatives of those who would be affected by the outcome.

While we can hardly imagine any modern circumstance that would approximate to this incident, the general principle of the need for fairness and transparency should be kept in mind: "Providing for honest things, not only in the sight of the Lord, but also in the sight of men" (2 Cor 8.21). That is a New Testament principle, and in its context it has to do with financial issues, but let it be a rule governing all our dealings with others.

Another general principle emerging from this episode is the need for matters to be appropriately witnessed. The Lord Jesus highlighted this when speaking of an aggrieved brother. If he gets no satisfaction when raising his grievance with the offender, he should take "one or two more, that in the mouth of two or three witnesses every word may be established" (Mt 18.16). On occasions there is the need for actions and conversations to be properly attested.

Verses 7-18: The Twenty-four Courses

From a Biblical standpoint, we know nothing more of these twenty-four courses except that the course of Abijah (v.10) is mentioned in connection with Zacharias (Lk 1.5) as noted in the introduction to the chapter.

In the book of Revelation there are "four and twenty elders" around the throne of God (4.4). Some have seen in this an allusion to the twenty-four courses of the priests, with the inference that the four and twenty elders constitute a priestly company in heaven. It is put forward as a major plank in the argument for these twenty-four elders being seen as representative of the church.

Verse 19: As the Lord Commanded

Doubtless the phrase, "the orderings of them in their service", relates to the time for them going on duty and then making way for the new shift, as for example in the days of Jehoiada the priest. On the day that he brought young Joash from hiding, when the new shift of priests arrived, he "dismissed not the courses" in order to augment the numbers of priests who would stand to protect the young child at his coronation (2 Chr 23). The Sabbath day was the day for the changeover (vv.4,8).

Some old commentators see the reference to Aaron as a term relating to any high priest at any given time, the man with overall responsibility for temple activity. They suggest that in calling him "their father" the verse simply indicates the respect in which any high priest was to be held. However, an alternative interpretation should be considered. With the introduction of the system of courses for the priests, something new was emerging. Despite this innovation, the basic form of sanctuary activity would remain unchanged. Practices that had been in place since the days of Aaron were to be maintained, for they had been given to him by divine command, "as the Lord God of Israel had commanded him". As then, so now; while human arrangements can be altered, anything given by the command of the Lord, and incorporated in Holy Scripture, is non-negotiable. Passing centuries with changing culture and styles do not negate the teaching of the inspired Word of God. "Whatsoever he saith unto you, do it" (Jn 2.5).

Verse 20-31: The Rest of the Sons of Levi

Most of the names mentioned in this list have been referred to in the previous chapter, but it seems that the casting of lots is being used here (v.31) to line up courses of priests with courses of Levites as regular partners in the work of the sanctuary. There would appear to have been merit in priest and Levite being familiar with each other and their ways of working. While the Levites were subordinate to the priests, and in effect their helpers, the verse refers to them all as "brethren". The lesson is that in the various aspects of the work of God, despite variety of function and responsibility, those involved are all members of the family of God, and that fact should govern attitudes. No one should ever feel superior because of what may appear to be a leading activity. No one should ever be afflicted by an inferiority complex because his or her service is supportive rather than prominent. We are all brethren in the family, and dependent on each other's co-operation.

On this occasion there is no mention of the Gershonite side of the family having any part to play.

Younger men were to be involved as well, and the outcome of the lot had to be followed whether it was the name of a "principal father" or one of the "younger brethren" that was being aligned with any particular course of priests. Again there is an underlying lesson. In the things of God, young and old should be able to co-operate happily, the energy and enthusiasm of youth being tempered by the wisdom and experience of age. A generation gap should never be regarded as the norm in divine things. Moses had his Joshua. Elijah had his Elisha. Paul had his Timothy. Let young and old be "striving together for the faith of the gospel" (Phil 1.27).

1 CHRONICLES 25

This chapter continues the section of the book in which David is thinking ahead to temple service. He is still putting in place structures that would be necessary for the worship of God under the new order of things. Levites and priests had already been organised into twenty-four manageable groups to function in rota, and now a similar arrangement is made for the singers. Keep in mind that David had a divine mandate for each of these initiatives.

Verse 1: Asaph, Heman and Jeduthun

Allusions have been made to these three men earlier in the book, and they are now being officially installed as superintendents of the instrumental and vocal aspects of temple service. This chapter records the details of those who were assigned to them, those "separated to the service of the sons of Asaph, and of Heman, and of Jeduthun". For the more part, their aides would be family members, but there is the inference in v.7 that others with the necessary skills were also involved.

Various musical instruments would be used in their worship, but the stated function of these men was to "prophesy with harps, with psalteries, and with cymbals". In other words, the emphasis was not on the noise, or the rhythm, or the tune, but rather on the expressions of praise that the music accompanied. One of Moses' last legacies to Israel was "this song" (Deut 31.30), a hymn of instruction for the people of God.

"Prophesying" is explained in v.3 as "giving thanks and praising the Lord" (RV). Thus, the quality of a hymn is not determined by the beat, or the tempo, or the lilt of the tune. The value of the lyrics is crucial, although it should be said that an excellent hymn could be impaired by setting it to an inappropriate tune. Words and melody should be in sympathy, but more importantly, expressions of praise should be Biblically accurate, an accuracy that should never be sacrificed in the interests of poetic embellishment.

The men who were assigned to this ministry of praise are designated here "workmen" (AV), "them that did the work" (RV). Praising God demands energetic involvement, and even today congregational singing should be hearty, "singing and making melody with your heart to the Lord" (Eph 5.19, RV). Casual muted participation neither honours the Lord nor inspires His people. Let us be "workmen" when it comes to praising our God.

Verse 2: The Sons of Asaph

Asaph's sons were appointed as his assistants with this job description: "which prophesied according to the order of the king". It has already been noted that prophesying is explained at v.3, but the fact that this was "according to the order of the king" indicates that David knew the value of wholesome worship. The legacy of ascriptions of praise that he left in his psalms gives testimony to this.

Verse 3: The Sons of Jeduthun

Jeduthun had a total of six sons who shared his responsibilities; five of these are mentioned here. It seems that the Shimei of v.17 is son number six, but there is no apparent reason for his omission here.

As far as the sons of Jeduthun were concerned, their area of expertise was the harp, and so they "prophesied with a harp, to give thanks and to praise the Lord".

There may be a fine distinction between giving thanks and praising. Giving thanks would be expressing appreciation for what God has done; praising would be expressing adoration for who He is. Both should be incorporated in our public and personal acts of devotion.

Verses 4-5: The Sons of Heman

Heman's sons were more numerous than those of his colleagues, fourteen in all. Added to the four sons of Asaph and the six of Jeduthun, this gave the total of twenty-four that was needed to head the twenty-four courses of singers.

Heman is described as "the king's seer in the words of God". It is evident that throughout his life David had kept company with men who were in touch with God. When threatened by Saul he "fled, and escaped, and came to Samuel to Ramah" (1 Sam 19.18). Nathan was a welcome guest in his house (1 Chr 17.1). Like Heman, Gad is spoken of as "David's seer" (21.9). He saw the value of surrounding himself with spiritual men who knew their God. In Psalm 101.6 he wrote, "Mine eyes shall be upon the faithful of the land, that they may dwell with me: he that walketh in a perfect way, he shall serve me". We should be as wise as he was in selecting our company, for, inevitably, our companions colour our attitudes and influence our behaviour.

In describing Heman as "the king's seer in the words of God", the verse is indicating that Heman was a channel of divine communication, conveying messages from the throne of God to David. We have no knowledge of any particular truth that he passed on, or any specific incident in which he was involved, but there must have been occasions when he was at David's side as advisor and confidant. Even a man of David's calibre and standing required the support of another who could counsel him with the "words of God". The Lord Jesus encouraged His disciples to follow "a man...bearing a pitcher of water" (Lk 22.10). Figuratively, we should comply with these instructions. If a man of God is able to refresh you with the water of the Word, it would do no harm to follow him and benefit from his teaching, without in any way idolising the man.

This group seemed to preside over the wind instruments, for their function was "to lift up the horn".

Heman's family is said to be a gift from God. "God gave to Heman fourteen sons...". "Children are an heritage of the Lord: and the fruit of the womb is his reward" (Ps 127.3). God opens wombs, or withholds "the fruit of the womb" (Gen 29.31; 30.2). The fact that children are His gift means that the recipients of these gifts should appreciate the privilege that they have in bringing up these young ones for God; they should be made a top priority in life. A feature of the last days is that people generally are "Without natural affection" (2 Tim 3.3). That involves, among other things, a careless attitude to their children. Christian parents should act more responsibly than that, and while being conscientious about matters relating to health, welfare, and education, the spiritual needs of the family should be the major consideration. "Train up a child in the way he should go: and when he is old, he will not depart from it" (Prov 22.6).

For no apparent reason, mention is made of Heman's three daughters which is unique in this context. We can but speculate that they played some part in the orchestra, as illustrated in David's words in Psalm 68.25: "The singers went before, the players of instruments followed after; among them were the damsels playing with timbrels".

It is rather sad that no one descended from Heman is mentioned among those who returned from the Babylonian exile, an indication that families do not necessarily follow in the footsteps of their forefathers, even although these men may have set a godly example.

Verses 6-7: The Songs of the Lord

The three fathers directed the songs and the music; the families "were under the hands of their father". In the things of God it is important for one generation to instruct and guide the next, provided that the guidance is sourced in God as it was here. All that was being done was "according to the king's order" to the fathers, and as has been stated repeatedly, David's directives came from God. David gave these instructions to Asaph, Heman and Jeduthun. Their sons took directions from them, and they in turn were responsible for courses of singers over whom they presided as the rest of the chapter will show. It is almost reminiscent of Paul's words to Timothy: "the things that thou hast heard of me among many witnesses, the same commit thou to faithful men, who shall be able to teach others also" (2 Tim 2.2). There has to be the constant transmission of God's truth. Asaph himself understood this as expressed in one of his psalms. He saw himself as a link in the chain of communication. Things he had learned from his "fathers" would not be hidden from "their children, shewing to the generation to come the praises of the Lord" (Ps 78.1-6). May we all do our part in passing on the legacy of Biblical tradition.

All this was for the "the service of the house of God", and so the songs of praise had to be appropriate; they are called "the songs of the Lord". Those participating had to be "instructed" in these songs; they had to get it right; this was for God. To be involved they had to be appropriately gifted, "cunning" is the word that the AV uses, that is, "skilful" (RV); I emphasise, this was for God. Perhaps the lesson is that nothing but the very best of effort, content, and skill will suffice in the things of God. A hymn that some of us learned in school days encapsulates this concept. It was penned by Mary Ann Hearn who wrote under the pseudonym of Marianne Farningham.

Just as I am, young, strong and free,
To be the best that I can be
For truth, and righteousness, and Thee,
Lord of my life, I come.

Perhaps some of the first readers of 1 Chronicles were among those who had been encouraged to provide entertainment for the Babylonians; "Sing us one of the songs of Zion". In their grief, the disheartened captives had hung their harps on the willows, and their response was, "How shall we sing the Lord's song in a strange land?" (Ps 137.1-4). "The songs of the Lord" could be sung fittingly in the courts of the Lord's house by Levite singers, but it seemed totally out of place for people enduring exile under the disciplining hand of God to fake the joy and exultation connected with these sacred songs of praise.

Two hundred and eighty-eight musicians are mentioned here, allowing for twelve in each of the twenty-four courses. This figure of 288 is far short of the 4,000 mentioned at 23.5. Presumably the 288 were in a supervisory role, ensuring that the instructions that came down the chain of command were fully implemented.

Verses 8-31: Casting Lots

As with the Levites and the priests, lots were cast to determine at which point of the calendar each group of singers would function. Again, the method adopted obviated partiality and prejudice. No doubt the process was as well supervised and attested as formerly, although there is no repetition of that fact here.

Neither social standing nor intellectual achievement biased the result of this lottery. Small and great, teacher and scholar were all incorporated, and the outcome demonstrates that seniority in the family was not taken into account. The order that emerged spread the three different families through each other, with younger family members preceding their older brothers at times. Matthew Henry provides a helpful list of the names with a reference to where each one fits in to his respective family: for example, Joseph was the second son of Asaph, and Gedaliah was the eldest son of Jeduthun (v.9) and so on.

Perhaps there is a lesson on the surface, that in the things of God, social background, intellect, or family position has little bearing on a man's suitability for the work of God. What is of real consequence is spiritual gift and moral integrity.

As far as the house of God is concerned, it only remained for porters to be appointed and arranged in order, and that matter is addressed in ch.26.

1 CHRONICLES 26

With Levites, priests, and singers in place, it remained for temple doorkeepers to be appointed. Primarily, these men had responsibility for the security of the house of God, guarding it from malicious intruders attracted by its vast wealth. The chapter also records the names of those who had duties relating to various temple treasuries (vv.20-28), and some with wider responsibilities that extended throughout the land (vv.29-32).

We learned in 23.5 that 4,000 Levites were assigned to the doors, but here, we have the names of those who superintended their work.

Doorkeepers were necessary to exclude from the temple those who had no right to enter, and to admit the genuine worshippers. One of Samuel's early duties was to open the doors of the house of God (1 Sam 3.15).

When it came to allocating duties, all four points of the compass had to be covered, north, south, east and west (vv.12-19). Perhaps there is a reminder in this that God's house was to be a "house of prayer *for all the nations*" (Mk 11.17, RV). It catered for "all the ends of the earth". There was a facility there for people from all quarters to petition God, as indicated in Solomon's prayer of dedication: "Moreover concerning the stranger…if they come and pray in this house; Then hear thou from the heavens" (2 Chr 6.32-33). Because people were coming from every direction and background, porters were on duty on every side. Borrowing a New Testament concept, they had to obviate the possibility of people creeping in unawares (Jude v.4).

To make the application to modern times, there still has to be vigilance in the matter of reception to God's assembly. The assembly at Ephesus had good door keepers: "thou hast tried them which say they are apostles, and are not, and hast found them liars" (Rev 2.2). Without being suspicious or unkind in any way, it is still needful to conduct a meaningful interview with prospective assembly members, so that the doctrinal and moral purity of the assembly is maintained; in Scripture, moral and doctrinal evil are both perceived as leaven that "leaveneth the whole lump" (1 Cor 5.6; Gal 5.9). Happily, the vast majority of such interviews prove to be positive, but there is constant need for caution.

Verses 1-3: The Sons of Meshelemiah

The word "divisions" (4256), or "courses" (RV), is a word that we have encountered frequently throughout this large section of 1 Chronicles. It occurs constantly in connection with apportioning temple duties. Although it is not stated specifically, perhaps there is the inference here that as with Levites, priests and singers, there were twenty-four courses of porters; vv.17-18 seem to suggest this.

The first group to be mentioned is Meshelemiah and his sons, descendants of Korah. It is wonderful that the rebellion of Korah did not exclude his descendants from the service of God. A bad family history is no barrier to anyone being useful and effective for God as illustrated in many Bible narratives. To take but one example, Gideon's father was a Baal worshipper, and yet Gideon was chosen to "save Israel from the hand of the Midianites" (Judg 6.14). This could be encouragement for someone with a problem in the family background for which they had no responsibility. They can put that seeming impediment to the side, and be totally committed to the things of God.

It should be noted that the Asaph in the verse is not the notable singer of the previous chapter. That Asaph was a Gershonite (6.39-43); this man, being linked to the Korhites, was of the Kohathite strain of the tribe of Levi (Num 16.1). He is the Ebi*asaph* of 6.37.

Seven sons of Meshelemiah are listed here, whereas eighteen are mentioned at v.9. His "brethren" are included in that number.

Verses 4-8: The Sons of Obed-edom

This interesting character has featured formerly in the book as the man who gave sanctuary to the ark following the disastrous death of Uzza (13.13-14). As ever, God recompensed what had been done in His interests as is substantiated by this comment, "the Lord blessed the house of Obed-edom". One of the ways in which he was blessed was in the gift of eight strapping sons (v.5). God always amply rewards any sacrifice made, or any inconvenience experienced for Him. To cite but one illustration, the use of Peter's boat was repaid by a miraculous draft of fish (Lk 5.1-11). We will never be disadvantaged by putting God's interests first (Mt 6.33).

> We lose what on ourselves we spend;
> We have as treasure without end
> Whatever, Lord, to Thee we lend,
> Who givest all.
>
> (Christopher Wordsworth)

The involvement of Obed-edom as a doorkeeper was a duty that was added to his former appointment as a singer (16.4-5). In the things of God there are some who can play a dual role. Sometimes the question is asked, "In a New Testament context, is it possible for a man to have more than one gift?". Undoubtedly it is. No one would deny that Paul exercised a number of spiritual gifts. Peter was another with multiple tasks. He was a stirring evangelist (Acts 2), and yet later in life he described himself as an elder, a shepherd under orders to feed Christ's flock (1 Pet 5.1; Jn 21.15-17). It may be argued that Peter and Paul were special, being apostles, but Timothy was another whose public ministry was directed towards both believers and unbelievers. Within the compass of a few verses Paul instructs him to "preach the word; be instant in season, out of season; reprove, rebuke, exhort, with all longsuffering and teaching", and then, "do the work of an evangelist" (2 Tim 4.2, RV, 5). There are some, then, to whom God commits more than one responsibility, and to whom He has given the necessary gifts for their various activities.

Obed-edom had previous experience as a doorkeeper at the time when David pitched a tent for the ark. He was one of those who were designated, "doorkeepers for the ark" (15.24). The smaller task was a training ground for the bigger job of being a porter for the house of God. Having proved himself reliable in the very responsible post of a doorkeeper for the ark, he now graduated to this new assignment in connection with the temple of God. There appears to be a Scriptural principle here: "He that is faithful in that which is least is faithful also in much" (Lk 16.10). Deacons must "first be proved; then let them serve as deacons, if they be blameless" (1 Tim 3.10, RV). Obed-edom had been faithful; he had been tested and approved, and thus he was equipped for his new duties. Let us all aspire to the same level of trustworthiness, so that with confidence, we can be entrusted with further responsibilities.

The grandsons of Obed-edom administered family affairs (v.6), men who were up to the task by being "mighty men of valour". Doubtless their family responsibilities stood them in good stead for their duties in connection with the house of God. Even in a modern context, family life is a good training ground for the man who is exercised about serving as an overseer in the assembly (1 Tim 3.4-5). If there is breakdown in family discipline, it does not bode well for his ability to "take care of the church of God".

Between verses 6 and 9, there is a Hebrew word (2428) that is used on four occasions and is translated in three different ways, "valour" (v.6), "strong" (vv.7,9), and "able" (v.8). (The same word is also used in each of the three last verses of the chapter, translated there consistently as "valour".) The usage of this word seems to imply that temple porters were in effect a military guard. Another possible reason for the stress on their physical strength is because, at a very practical level, the temple gates were so heavy that according to Josephus, it took twenty men to open and close them.

The three English words that are used to translate the Hebrew word seem to give us an inkling of the kind of qualities that these men would require if they were to police effectively the gates of the temple. Valour, or courage, would be needed to confront any undesirable would-be visitors to the temple. Possibly, strength would be necessary to debar effectively such as should be excluded. Ability would be essential to handle each situation wisely and well. These same qualities are crucial when it comes to regulating assembly life today. "If any man minister (serve), let him do it as *of the ability which God giveth*" (1 Pet 4.11).

Of the sixty-two members of Obed-edom's family it was said that they were "able men for strength for the service" (v.8). In any aspect of the service of God it is only divine ability that will equip us for the task. For his final assault on the Philistines, Samson prayed, "strengthen me, I pray thee, only this once" (Judg 16.28). In the normal course of things, we need to make that appeal constantly, "Strengthen me, I pray thee". "Vain is the help of man. Through God we shall do valiantly" (Ps 60.11-12; 108.12-13).

Verse 9: Eighteen Valiant Men

Nothing further need be said about Meshelemiah's family save that they too had the necessary physique and courage for their assignment as doorkeepers.

Verses 10-11: The Sons of Hosah

Hosah was of the Merarite branch of the Levitical family, and from his sons and brothers, thirteen men were assigned to door-keeping duties. He had been a companion of Obed-edom, and with him had been privileged to be a guardian of the ark (16.38). He too was a man of previous experience as far as responsibility for holy things was concerned, so he was no novice when assuming his duty as a porter in the house of God.

For an undisclosed reason, Hosah had made his son Simri head of the family in place of his firstborn son. On occasions, failure on the part of firstborn sons necessitated their being side-lined in favour of a brother, as when Judah was made "chief ruler" of Jacob's family in preference to Reuben (5.1-2), or when Solomon was given precedence over older members of David's family. It is assumed then, that because of some misdemeanour Hosah's firstborn was replaced as clan chieftain by his younger brother Simri. (Hopefully that is not a suspicious, unjustified assumption.) There is the simple lesson - that of the need for constant vigilance lest we forfeit privileges on account of some moral or spiritual breakdown.

Perhaps a more charitable way of looking at the situation is to see Hosah's appointment of Simri as "chief" (7218) as solely in connection with door-keeping duties, for the word "chief" is used in that context in v.12. It could be that the firstborn was either deceased or did not have the physical strength for the arduous task of supervising the porters; we have entered the realm of conjecture!

Verses 12-19: The Allocation of Posts

As in previous chapters the casting of lots determined the apportioning of duties, in particular the locating of each family group at the appropriate gates, north, south, east and west.

The ESV translation of v.12 helps to elucidate the meaning of the verse: "These divisions of the gatekeepers, corresponding to their chief men, had duties, just as their brothers did, ministering in the house of the Lord". The inference seems to be that the porters were not one whit inferior to their brethren, although their task may have seemed less prestigious. Like their brethren the priests, the Levites, and the singers, their role was an integral part of the whole temple system; it was a vital function in "ministering in the house of the Lord". We all need to be content with the work that the Lord has allocated to us, rejoicing in this, that whatever it may be it is service rendered to Him and to promote His interests; it is done as a small but crucial part of a vast overall plan, as He brings His great eternal purpose to fruition. Just as the various functionaries at the temple had their part to play, so every believer has been endowed with a spiritual gift that must be employed in co-operation with fellow-saints with the single objective of honouring the Lord and advancing His cause. Gatekeepers had God-given duties, just as their brothers did! It was a great privilege as understood by the writer of Psalm 84: "I had rather be a doorkeeper in the house of my God, than to dwell in the tents of wickedness" (v.10).

As with the singers (25.8), "as well the small as the great" were involved in the doorkeeping. Social standing was neither a qualification nor a barrier for involvement in this work, nor should it be in the work of God today. Believers from every station in life can co-operate happily in the activity of God's assembly. "Erastus the chamberlain of the city" seemed content to be linked with "Quartus a brother", very likely slave number four in some household (Rom 16.23). Both extremities of the social scale had been reached with the gospel, and were now rejoicing in being yoked together in service for God.

Zechariah the son of Shelemiah (Meshelemiah vv.1,2,9) was "a wise counsellor" (v.14). His obvious prudence and the respect in which he was held did not make him eligible for preferential treatment in the allocation of his duties; he had no liberty to select his own position. Like the others who were involved, he had to submit to the casting of lots, and "his lot came out northward". The simple lesson is that in the things of God neither status nor intellectual ability should be allowed to create an elite that has advantages over others who are involved in the same work.

The mention of a wise counsellor should make us halt to ask about the advice that we seek. In the western world, counselling is available for every conceivable condition or circumstance. The believer has to think about whether the guidance on offer is in keeping with the Word of God. Many opinions expressed could be merely the perceived wisdom of the world, a wisdom that is so often at variance with divine ideals. "Blessed is the man that walketh not in the counsel of the ungodly" (Ps 1.1). King Ahaziah started his reign at a serious disadvantage, for "his mother was his counsellor to do wickedly" (2 Chr 22.3). If we do need advice let us be certain that it is offered by someone who in reality is "a wise counsellor", and never let us forget that there is One whose name is "Wonderful, Counseller" (Is 9.6); the advice that He tenders is found in the inspired Scriptures which if followed can never be detrimental.

Obed-edom had charge of the south gate, and to his sons was committed "the house of Asuppim" rendered almost uniformly by other translations as "storehouse" (v.15). Although the Hebrew word is not related to the word for "storehouse" in Malachi 3.10, there is the reminder that connected to the temple there were areas where tithes of grain were stored for the maintenance of those in temple service. To neglect to bring the whole tithe was to invite impoverishment; to give God His portion wholeheartedly was to ensure blessing. The sons of Obed-edom must have been men of integrity to be entrusted with resources that would meet the need of their fellow-servants, just as Barnabas and Saul were deemed trustworthy to carry the bounty of the assembly at Antioch to the needy saints in Judæa (Acts 11.29-30). Let us ask ourselves about our own reliability; would people regard us as being honest enough to have responsibility for material things, "faithful in the unrighteous mammon" (Lk 16.11). Those who were detailed to supervise "the daily ministration" had to be "men of honest report" (Acts 6.2-3).

Perhaps it should be said that a few expositors take the word "Asuppim" to mean "gatherings", and state without real conviction that maybe it was a place where elders gathered to consult.

The "gate Shallecheth" (7996) (v.16) is generally regarded as the point through which temple refuse would be removed. The RV margin translates the word, "Casting forth". The reference to "the causeway of the going up" has been linked with 1 Kings 10.5 where allusion is made to Solomon's "ascent by which he went up unto the house of the Lord". The procession to the temple was part of the pageantry of Solomon's administration that left the Queen of Sheba breathless.

"Ward against ward" would indicate either that the defenders of each area virtually merged so that there was comprehensive cover, or that there was a smooth transition from one shift of porters to the next.

It is generally felt that the appointment of six Levites to the eastern gate rather than the four or two that are mentioned for other quarters is an indication that the east was the direction from which the majority of visitors approached the temple. The summation of the number of guards at the various stations is twenty-four as has been noted formerly.

Verses 20-28: Levites over the Treasuries

The emphasis now shifts to give the names of men with responsibility for the treasures of the house of God, for there was great wealth connected with it. This vast treasure was the result of military conquests, the spoils of battle being dedicated to the Lord as will be seen in vv.26-28. Sadly, in later generations invaders plundered some of these assets, as when in the days of Rehoboam, "Shishak king of Egypt came up against Jerusalem, and took away the treasures of the house of the Lord" (2 Chr 12.9). On other occasions they were used to buy off those who were threatening Judah as when Jehoash (Joash) used resources from the temple to head off an attack by the Syrians, or when Ahaz did the same with the Assyrians (2 Kings 12.17-18; 16.8-9). The men appointed here, then, had tremendous responsibility to see that what was committed to them was used in the divinely directed way.

The mention of "dedicated things" (v.20) is a reminder that God must have His portion from His people. His work requires financial resources.

The Scriptures are very practical, and even in this passage there is mention of at least one avenue of expenditure as far as the temple was concerned. Like every other building it would need maintenance, and some of the capital was used "to maintain (repair, RV) the house of the Lord" (v.27). In the days of Jehoash the structure was in desperate need of repair, and there were no resources available. To finance the refurbishment, a chest with a hole bored in its lid was placed "beside the altar" (2 Kings 12.4-16). A man's estimate of the offering on the altar would determine the extent of his financial commitment to the temple. Perhaps there is the lesson that the depth of our appreciation of the death of Christ will decide the level of our sacrificial giving.

Ahijah (v.20) had prime responsibility for these treasures, with other Levites under his control. It is interesting that some of Moses' descendants receive mention and it is gratifying that at least some of the great man's posterity made a mark for God.

Shelomith (v.26) had particular responsibility for the portion of temple resources that had been the spoils of battle. As early as Abraham's day God had His share of such spoils. On his encounter with Melchizedek, "priest of the most high God", Abraham "gave him tithes of all" (Gen 14.18-20). As far as Jericho was concerned, everything in it was to be dedicated to God: "And the city shall be devoted, even it and all that is therein, to the Lord" (Josh 6.17, RV).

Here, anticipating that a temple would be built, prophets, kings and generals had all devoted at least some of their plunder to the Lord, but the word "whosoever" in v.28 indicates that warriors in general felt a duty to contribute towards His service. In other words, it was not only the wealthy and famous that had responsibility to maintain things, but every last man had the honour of ministering to the Lord in this way. The "whosoever" would take in not only "chief fathers" and "the captains" at the various ranks, but foot soldiers and auxiliaries. That principle extends to the New Testament. Macedonian believers were particularly poor, and yet "their deep poverty abounded unto the riches of their liberality" (2 Cor 8.2). Such sacrificial giving gives immense pleasure to the Lord as seen in His commendation of the widow who donated her two mites to the temple treasury. In His estimate of things, she had "cast in more than they all" (Lk 21.3). Giving to God is not a privilege that is exclusive to affluent believers. "Upon the first day of the week let *every one of you* lay by him in store, as God hath prospered him" (1 Cor 16.2).

The mention of some of the names in v.28 may produce a gasp of surprise! Whoever would have linked "Samuel the seer" with the spoils of battle? Like Elisha after him, he must have marched with the troops and so shared their bounty (2 Kings 3.11). These men did not stand aloof from their people but were willing to share their experiences of life just as did Ezekiel the priest, who "sat where they sat" (Ezek 3.15). As far as Samuel was concerned, we do know that he had promised to be on site for Saul's battle with the

Philistines in an early campaign (1 Sam 13.8-14). So then, from any benefits he had received as a result of warfare, Samuel had dedicated a portion to the house of God. It confirms his defence of his honest unselfish character: "whose ox have I taken? or whose ass have I taken…?" (1 Sam 12.3). This man was not a grasper but a giver.

It seems that even under Saul's regime "Out of the spoils won in battles" a proportion was devoted to God. Again, this may seem surprising given Saul's track record, but Scripture pays tribute to the fact that both he and Abner were among those who "had dedicated". There may be the simple lesson that whatever a man's failings it is well to value anything that may be commendable about him. The same could be said of Joab, at times a most unsavoury character, and yet here he is cited as a donor to the cause.

Shelomith, then, had responsibility for this special fund, being the resources set aside from the spoils of battle, and used as a fabric fund for the maintenance of the building. He would guard it against embezzlers and pilferers, and ensure its proper use in repairing the structure when necessary.

Verses 29-32: The Outward Business

In the generation when 1 Chronicles was first penned, there were those who "had the oversight of the outward business of the house of God" (Neh 11.16). Our writer takes us back to when this institution was first introduced. The men responsible for this "outward business" were the six thousand officers and judges of 23.4. 1,700 of these are said to be of the Hebronites (v.30), with another 2,700 functioning on the east of Jordan (v.32), leaving a balance of 1,600 whom we presume to be those who were "Of the Izharites" (v.29). It appears that the main concept of "outward business" was the maintenance of both civil and religious law throughout the land: "for all the business of the Lord, and for the service of the king" (v.30, RV), and "every matter pertaining to God, and affairs of the king" (v.32). No doubt they supervised the provision of everything necessary to sustain temple service, the provision of wood for the altar for example, and they would see to it that adequate attention was given to the king's interests for the smooth running of his administration. However, in the main these Levites were scattered throughout the land to ensure strict adherence to divine commands and precise subjection to civil authority. Ideally, these two should never be at variance, hence Peter's injunction, "Fear God. Honour the king" (1 Pet 2.17). In the event of them diverging, the same preacher gave liberty for civil disobedience on the part of the believer: "We ought to obey God rather than men" (Acts 5.29).

It is presumed that "over Israel" (v.29) means over the major part of the land, and, as has been suggested, 1,600 Izharites were responsible for that area. Another tract of land was under the superintendence of 1,700 Hebronites. They were accountable for "them of Israel on this side Jordan westward" (v.30). It may seem disproportionate then that 2,700 Levites were assigned to the Trans-jordan tribes! These supervisors were Hebronites but domiciled on the east of Jordan at Jazer of Gilead (v.31). Could it be that the two and a half tribes were perpetually under suspicion as at the start (Josh 22)? Were they deemed less reliable than the rest of the tribes? Is there the thought that because they were remote from Jerusalem they were more likely to abandon the religion of their fathers? Was their loyalty to the king questioned because their territory had been used as a power base by the last vestiges of the previous regime? (2 Sam 2.8-11). Whatever the reason, Reuben, Gad and half of Manasseh were under stricter scrutiny than the nation as a whole.

All these arrangements were finalised in the fortieth year of David's reign (v.31), the last year of David's life. While the reference is to the Trans-jordan Hebronites being "sought for" during that period, it is a fair assumption that, in general, what has been considered throughout this section of 1 Chronicles took place in the dying stages of David's administration. However, perhaps the words "sought for" imply that there was now a certain urgency about proceedings. Possibly David was fast approaching the state of health that found him decrepit and bedridden (1 Kings 1.1); appointments had to be made quickly. For all of us, life is fragile and uncertain, and in light of that, and certainly in light of the Lord's imminent return, let us treat His interests with the urgency that they demand. Procrastination and a lackadaisical attitude should have no place in our thinking. "The night cometh, when no man can work" (Jn 9.4).

The framework for temple service was now in place, with the appointment of Levites, priests, singers, porters and treasurers. All was in readiness, but the building itself awaited construction. It remained for David to make final orations to Solomon and the leaders of the nation, words of instruction, and words of encouragement to launch the project. Before these inspirational speeches, a chapter is devoted to military and civil matters relating to David's kingdom.

1 CHRONICLES 27

This chapter of 1 Chronicles concludes the section of the book that commenced at 23.1. The content here is somewhat different in that it focuses on political matters rather than religious. In fact, God is mentioned only once in the chapter, at v.23. The four preceding chapters were taken up with the appointment of the various functionaries required for temple service. Here the stress is on the organisation of the armed forces and other matters of state. Despite the dramatic shift in emphasis, the subject matter of the chapter is not irrelevant to the overall theme of worship in the house of God. That activity could proceed happily only if state security was adequate and civil government was stable. The provision for such security and stability is explained in the verses before us.

This chapter sets the stage for the events of chapters 28 and 29, for the various leadership groups mentioned here were all summoned to the investiture of Solomon the crown prince when in their hearing, David charged him with the responsibility of building the temple (28.1).

It is evident that the procedures recorded here predate preparations for the temple; it seems that David had organised the affairs of state in this way throughout his reign. For example, there is a mention of Asahel in v.7. He featured in the early stages of David's administration at the point where David's authority extended only to the tribe of Judah. Before David controlled the whole nation Asahel had experienced an untimely death at the hands of Abner at the height of the civil war (2 Sam 2.17-23). He was long gone by the time the building of the temple was anticipated.

The chapter divides as follows.

In vv.1-15 there are details of twelve commanders, each in charge of 24,000 soldiers who would serve on a monthly basis throughout the year.

Verses 16-24 record the names of the leaders of the tribes of Israel. No mention is made of the tribes of Asher and Gad and no reason is advanced for their omission.

The next section is from v.25-v.31 where economic and agricultural responsibilities are highlighted.

The chapter concludes with details of David's cabinet.

Verse 1: Officers that Served the King

A system of "courses" was in operation for the military men as well as for those involved in religious service. Militias of 24,000 men served in rota from month to month throughout the year. No doubt at times of national emergency those who were not on monthly duty would be called up for service. In total then, 288,000 men had links with the armed forces. An agrarian nation could never have sustained that number of people being absent from their fields on a permanent basis, so this scheme was adopted whereby only 24,000 at a time would be committed; no one was overstretched. One cannot help but see the care and kindness of God in all of this. In a previous generation He had shown concern for betrothed men, newly-weds, new homeowners and those who had just planted a vineyard. They were excused military service (Deut 20.1-9; 24.5). Here, He spreads responsibility thinly; a man would never be away from his family and fields for more than a month at a time. "He knoweth our frame; he remembereth that we are dust" (Ps 103.14). God was similarly considerate in the way He structured the timetable for the seven annual feasts of the Lord (Lev 23). Nothing was scheduled for the busy times for the farmers, the sowing and reaping seasons. How good is the God we adore!

Jehoiada the priest took advantage of the course system on the occasion of the overthrow of Athaliah and the coronation of Joash. He timed the coup to coincide with a new group arriving, and before the other was dismissed the whole issue had been settled. He had double the forces and double the attendant Levites that he might have had at any other time (2 Chr 23.1-15)!

A variety of participants are mentioned here in v.1, each at a different rank from the other, but they all had this in common that they "served the king". A lesson that has been learned already from the book is the importance of believers at every stage and at every level and in every sphere being focused on serving the Lord. The blending of varying gifts, responsibilities and levels of experience produces a cohesive endeavour to promote His interests and expand His kingdom. "There are varieties of service, but the same Lord" (1 Cor 12.5, ESV). Let us all give diligence to whatever variety of service has been committed to us, so that as these men did, we, too, may serve "the king".

Verses 2-3: The First Month

Jashobeam was responsible for the first course of 24,000 during the first month of the year. He was the first of David's mighty men to be mentioned in 11.11, one of "the chief of the mighty men whom David had" (v.10), one of "the first three" (v.21). He was a man of outstanding valour, unswerving loyalty, and proven experience. Who better to start the year and set the standard? Who better as a role model for the rest to follow? Men who take a lead should have a healthy track record and be worthy of emulation; Jashobeam was the ideal choice. "Be thou an ensample to them that believe" (1 Tim 4.12, RV).

"He was of the children of Perez" (v.3, RV), that is, a descendant of Judah through his son Pharez (Gen 38.29). Jashobeam was David's fellow-tribesman, perhaps another reason for his being given this major role.

Verse 4: The Second Month

During the second month responsibility was shared between Dodai and Mikloth, an arrangement that is unique in the context. There is no suggestion that Mikloth was a successor to Dodai; successors are mentioned in relation to some of the other months. It does appear that Dodai was the superior and Mikloth his lieutenant, but why was that necessary in month two? Were there enforced absences as far as Dodai was concerned? Had he aged? Had his health failed to the extent that he required assistance? Or was it that Mikloth was named because he was more illustrious than any other deputies that were in place? The possibilities are numerous, but the real reason has been withheld from us.

Dodai is very evidently Eleazer the son of Dodo, another of the "three mighties" (11.12). These men who had shared David's privations, and had been solidly behind him in his rejection, and had endangered their lives in conflict with the Philistines, were now rewarded with positions of responsibility in his administration. The New Testament equivalent is, "if we suffer, we shall also reign with him" (2 Tim 2.12); "...endure hardness, as a good soldier of Jesus Christ" (v.3).

Verses 5-6: The Third Month

Benaiah was another of David's mighty men. Although he "attained not unto the first three", he was "honourable among the thirty", and his exploits are rehearsed in 11.22-25. The AV, followed by most translations, describes him here as "the son of Jehoiada, a chief priest" which would make Benaiah a priest as well. It does seem unlikely that a priestly man would be so fully committed to military service and hold down such a demanding post in that sphere. Most commentators part company with the translators and claim that the word "priest" (3548) can be equally translated "ruler", and it seems to suit the situation rather better. (See 2 Samuel 8.18 where the word is descriptive of David's sons and translated "chief rulers". Being David's sons, obviously they were not priests.)

Of the 24,000 men under Benaiah's command only one name is mentioned, that of his son Ammizabad. It is pleasing that his son followed in his footsteps as a loyal devotee of the king. It is also praiseworthy that the young man appeared happy to serve under the authority of his famous father. In similar situations some young men have hang-ups and grudges that make them resentful of their fathers, and reluctant to co-operate with them - not so Ammizabad.

Verse 7: The Fourth Month

Asahel was commander of the forces who were responsible for the fourth month. As mentioned in the introduction to the chapter, his inclusion shows that this system of security had been in place since the earliest days of David's regime; it was not an innovation in anticipation of the building of the temple. He is described as "the brother of Joab" which made him David's nephew. There is no record that he was ever as subtle or cruel as his older brother, although the circumstances of his death at the hands of Abner depict him as being rather rash and ambitious (2 Sam 2.17-23).

On his premature decease, his son Zebadiah was appointed in his place, a tribute to the calibre and prowess of the young man. Very few would be able to step into the shoes of such a capable father. Younger men should prepare themselves to take responsibility. It could be thrust upon them as suddenly and unexpectedly as was the experience of Zebadiah here.

Verses 8-15: Months Five to Twelve

For the more part, lesser-known characters commanded those on duty in the remaining months though each of them was among David's mighty men. They were drawn from various tribes, and were not exclusively of David's own tribe of Judah.

It may seem inconsistent to make something of Heldai's (2469) name (v.15) while ignoring the others, but it does appear to mean "worldly". Let it be hoped that a man with such a major responsibility among the people of God did not reflect the meaning of his name! His ancestry was good, descended as he was from Othniel the famous judge. "Othniel" means "lion of God" and the fact that Heldai was among the mighty men would encourage us to believe that he displayed the same courage and devotion as his illustrious ancestor. It is wonderful when commendable family features resurface in succeeding generations.

Verses 16-22: Rulers of the Tribes of Israel

We now come to a list of those who headed the tribes of Israel. As usual, twelve tribes are mentioned, but as on other occasions in Scripture there are omissions. Both halves of the tribe of Manasseh are mentioned, as is the tribe of Levi, to the exclusion of Asher and Gad. As a subdivision of Levi, Zadok is included as head of "the Aaronites", the priestly family (v.17). Commentators have speculated about the exclusion of the two tribes, some suggesting the loss of registers, and others some integration of tribes under the one head. It has to be acknowledged that it is all a matter of conjecture, and Poole admits that their omission is for "some other causes now unknown, and not worth our inquiry"!

It appears that these men were not functioning by appointment of the king but by heredity. Obviously they would have his sanction but it was their status as members of their particular tribe that gave them their authority. For example Elihu (Eliab) (v.18), was Jesse's eldest son, and as such was in direct line from Salmon, and thus the rightful head of the tribe. It appears then that there was some measure of devolved government within the kingdom, or a system of local government, as there is in virtually every land. The believer has a responsibility to acknowledge each level of government that exists. "Submit yourselves to every ordinance of man for the Lord's sake: whether it be to the king, as supreme; Or unto governors…" (1 Pet 2.13-14). Countrywide regulations and local byelaws should all be observed; state laws and federal laws must all be adhered to.

Some of the names warrant brief comment. Zadok (v.17) became high priest in the reign of Solomon, in preference to Abiathar who was involved in Adonijah's rebellion (1 Kings 1.7-8; 2.26-27). The shift to Zadok taking the high priestly line back to Eleazar was part of God's judgment on the family of Eli. (We are indebted to secular historians, e.g. Josephus, for informing us that Eli had been descended from Ithamar and not Eleazar.) Following the slaughter of the priests at Nob, Abiathar had been the sole surviving member of Eli's line. With his expulsion in 1 Kings 2.27, the judgment on Eli's family was complete.

As suggested above, Elihu (v.18) is an alternative name for David's oldest brother Eliab. He was the man in whose heart Samuel had raised hopes of kingship; "Surely the Lord's anointed is before him" (1 Sam 16.6). If only Samuel had just thought it and not said it! Instantly, Eliab's hopes were dashed. The disappointment perhaps accounts for his sour attitude to David at the time of the incident with Goliath (1 Sam 17.28-29). Wonderfully, he rose above his frustration, and was happy to serve his younger brother as an administrator over the extensive tribe of Judah. He was one of the men of Scripture who having made a bad start then went on to be useful. Jacob, Joseph of Arimathæa and John Mark were others in the same category. Let that be an encouragement to any who feel that the early stages of Christian experience have been mediocre. It is possible to assign past failure to the dustbin of history and make an impact for God during "the rest of your time" (1 Pet 4.2, RV).

It is to David's credit that he was willing to sanction the appointment of his older brother after the insult he had experienced at his hands. "Be ye kind one to another, tender-hearted, forgiving one another, even as God for Christ's sake hath forgiven you" (Eph 4.32).

Another office-holder with an interesting background was the ruler of the tribe of Benjamin, "Jaasiel the son of Abner" (v.21). Abner had been Saul's loyal general right to the end, and had done all in his power to perpetuate his dynasty in denial of David's divinely decreed right to the throne. It is another evidence of the king's tolerance that he did nothing to block the appointment of Jaasiel as Benjamin's leader. He seemed to have an amazing capacity to rise above resentment and prejudice, a trait that we would do well to emulate. Another lesson is that a father's behaviour should never influence our attitude to his children.

Verses 23-24: The Stars of the Heavens

Having given details of tribal leaders, there is now an explanation for the omission of tribal numbers. Reference is made to the unhappy incident of David's numbering the people (ch.21). From what is said here it is clear that he had no intention of conducting a full census, but only a list of men who were eligible for military service (21.5). It seems that David's sin was to abandon dependence on God. He wanted to feel comfortable in the knowledge that for the security of the realm multitudes of fighting men were at his disposal.

David had seemed happy with God's promise that in terms of the total population "the Lord had said he would increase Israel like to the stars of the heavens" (see Gen 15.5), but somehow he had lost confidence in God as "a shield" for him (Ps 3.3). Let us avoid his mistake, and take God at His word for *every* promise that He makes rather than being selective. "For *all* the promises of God in him are yea, and in him Amen, unto the glory of God by us" (2 Cor 1.20).

It is of interest that the simile of the stars relates to Israel. It has been said that when Scripture speaks of Abraham's seed as being like the stars it refers to his spiritual seed (Gal 3.29) by reason of stars being "of the heavens", whereas dust and sand exist on planet earth. That statement cannot be substantiated in light of this verse, and, for example, Moses' statement in Deuteronomy 1.10: "ye are this day as the stars of heaven for multitude". Like the dust and the grains of sand, the illustration of the stars signals the extensive nature of Abraham's earthly descendants, the nation of Israel.

Our verses remind us of the fact that the census was aborted because of divine wrath "against Israel". It is another solemn reminder that although the king was the guilty party in this venture, his subjects suffered as a consequence. Bad behaviour and errors of judgment on our part can have serious ramifications for others.

"The number" was very imprecise because of Joab's reluctance, and his failure to include Levi and Benjamin, but it seems that because of the expression of divine displeasure David had no heart for any record to be made in the official chronicles of his reign. Perhaps he regarded it as an episode best forgotten, but the whole story is recounted twice over in the inspired Scriptures, and there is another allusion to it here. Failure cannot be camouflaged. Our history cannot be rewritten. There is no way to turn the clock back. God sees things as they are, and tells things as they are and so there is constant need for us to think before acting and to pray before proceeding.

Verses 25-31: The Rulers of David's Substance

It is difficult to decide whether these verses relate to David's personal fortune, or to state finances and state property. Commentators are divided, but one is left with the impression that the references are to David's own business interests (v.31; 28.1). His considerable personal expenses and the upkeep of his court would be financed from his own resources. It could be though that in these ancient times the distinction between a monarch's wealth and state resources was blurred. "Moreover the profit of the earth is for all: the king himself is served by the field" (Eccl 5.9).

The word translated "treasures" (214) is exactly the same Hebrew word as is rendered "storehouses" (v.25). Presumably Azmaveth was responsible for the main treasury at Jerusalem while Jehonathan was accountable for those in provincial areas. It does seem that both material wealth and resources of grain came under their jurisdiction; the mention of "the fields" implies the latter.

These men acted as what are called stewards in other parts of Scripture, men with a responsibility to administer another man's business affairs. In fact, the word "steward" is used to describe them in the AV rendering of 28.1. That concept is applied in a spiritual way to the believer in Christ. In very practical terms we are seen as responsible for the material resources with which God has endowed us (Lk 16.1-13); they belong to Him and we administer them for Him. Paul saw himself as a steward of spiritual truth and a steward of the gospel (1 Cor 4.1-5; 9.16-17; "dispensation" = "stewardship"). He regarded an elder as "the steward of God" (Titus 1.7). Peter looks upon us as being responsible for our spiritual gift "as good stewards of the manifold grace of God" (1 Pet 4.10). In these various ways then let us manage God's business effectively and well. An overriding principle in connection with stewardship is this: "it is required in stewards, that a man be found faithful" (1 Cor 4.2).

Before there could ever be resources of grain, the ground had to be tilled, and Ezri was appointed over those who worked in the fields (v.26). In the spiritual realm as well as in the physical, the sowing of the seed must precede the harvest. "In the morning sow thy seed, and in the evening withhold not thine hand" (Eccl 11.6). "Blessed are ye that sow beside all waters" (Is 32.20). "He that goeth forth and weepeth, bearing precious seed, shall doubtless come again with rejoicing, bringing his sheaves with him" (Ps 126.6). "Behold, a sower went forth to sow" (Mt 13.3). "The seed is the word of God" (Lk 8.11). Let us all be diligent in sowing seed, for there will never be an ingathering if the fields are left unworked.

Shimei had responsibility for the vineyards, with Zabdi as the superintendent for the next stage, "the increase of the vineyards for the wine cellars" (v.27). Again, it is so good to see that there was the anticipation of fruit. A spirit of optimism and expectation prevailed rather than the defeatist attitude that is a feature of so much activity today. In serving God, the Thessalonians were characterised by a "work of faith" (1 Thess 1.3). They really believed that God could work through them. Today, many believers go around with a hangdog expression that betrays a feeling of futility at what is being attempted for God.

These vineyards would need constant attention if the potential that was there was to be realised. "Our vineyards are in blossom" (Song 2.15, RV). Blossom is the promise of fruit, but that potential can be lost on account of the activity of "little foxes". They have to be taken and dealt with. Shimei would see that action was taken with regard to all hindrances to fruit bearing or he would have nothing to commit to Zabdi. If there are any "little foxes" in our lives that we ought to attend to, may God give us grace to deal with them effectively, so that "the fruit of the Spirit" (Gal 5.22) will feature in our lives, including that aspect of which wine speaks, a genuine joy in the soul (Judg 9.13; Ps. 104.15).

The olive and sycomore trees were also expected to be productive, and so there was not only the appointment of Baal-hanan to supervise their cultivation, but that of Joash "over the cellars of oil" (v.28). (In Bible times, the sycomore tree was a type of fig tree, with a fair amount of expertise required to gather its fruit; Amos 7.14.)

It requires just a passing mention that olive oil in Scripture is an emblem of the Holy Spirit of God (Zech 4).

Appropriately, the man who was responsible for the herds in Sharon was from that part of the country, Shitrai the Sharonite. The plain of Sharon extended for many miles up the western edge of the country and was particularly fruitful. Its lush pasturelands were ideal for grazing the king's cattle, but golden opportunities can be squandered if not managed properly, so with his local knowledge and acumen, Shitrai was an ideal man for the task. Even in the things of God, local men with a local knowledge are best placed to adjudicate on local issues, as seen in the assembly at Antioch commending Paul and Silas after the stand-off between Barnabas and Paul (Acts 15.40).

Rearing cattle "in the valleys" may have demanded a different technique from methods that were used in Sharon, so another man had responsibility there, Shaphat the son of Adlai. "To every man his work", said the Lord Jesus in one of His parables (Mk 13.34).

Those who looked after camels, asses and flocks of sheep and goats all had their supervisors (vv.30-31). It is significant that with such a variety of domesticated animals mentioned, there is no reference to horses. David had taken to heart God's command for future kings: "he shall not multiply horses to himself" (Deut 17.16). This was the man who wrote, "Some trust in chariots, and some in horses: but we will remember the name of the Lord our God" (Ps 20.7).

An Ishmaelite and a Hagerite were on David's pay roll. He must have regarded them as being well fitted for their tasks, and employed them without prejudice. Some commentators feel that these men may have been born in Israel, but had spent a considerable time among these other peoples, there learning the skills that equipped them for their appointment by David.

Verses 32-34: David's Privy Council

It was David's son Solomon who wrote on two occasions that in the "multitude of counsellors there is safety" (Prov 11.14; 24.6). It is helpful to have advisors. There are many who feel that to avoid time wasting and endless debate the ideal number on any committee is one! However, David valued advisors and friends as seen in this little section. Let it be said that conflicting advice is never helpful, for it leaves us open to shopping around until we get the advice that we want! That was the problem with Rehoboam; he was unhappy with the advice he received from older and wiser men, and, to his loss, he followed the counsel that was proffered by his youthful contemporaries (1 Kings 12.1-20).

First mentioned is Jonathan, an uncle of David, but his appointment was not on account of the family relationship as is clear from subsequent comments. (Most translators are content to describe Jonathan as David's uncle although, according to 20.7, David had a nephew by that name.) David could never be charged with nepotism. Nehemiah was another who appointed a family member to a responsible post as jointly in charge of Jerusalem. Again, as with David, the inspired writer safeguards Nehemiah's integrity for it is said of his brother that "he was a faithful man, and feared God above many" (Neh 7.1-2). It is not wrong to involve the family in aspects of God's service, provided that they have the necessary spiritual and moral qualifications. The danger is in advancing them when they are patently unsuitable as in the case of Samuel's sons (1 Sam 8.1-3).

Jonathan was "a wise man and a scribe", so his wisdom and secretarial skills would have added much to the smooth running of David's administration. Possibly, the designation, "a scribe", indicates that he was familiar with the law of God, and thus an invaluable man to have at hand. The law of the country and the law of God ought to have been one and the same, so who better to give legal and spiritual advice than someone thoroughly acquainted with divine commands.

Jehiel "was with the king's sons", no doubt with the responsibility of tutoring them and honing their administrative skills, for they too were involved in running the country (2 Sam 8.18).

Ahithophel is described as "*the* king's counsellor" as if to say he was the most prominent among them all. In two of his psalms David alludes to him in terms that indicate that Ahithophel was not merely a government minister but a personal friend: "Mine own familiar friend, in whom I trusted, which did eat of my bread" (Ps 41.9): "A man mine equal, my guide, and mine acquaintance. We took sweet counsel together, and walked unto the house of God in company" (Ps 55.13-14). Like Judas, the man whom he prefigured, Ahithophel was a good actor; David had no hint of the resentment that filled his heart, a resentment that eventually spilled over as he allied himself with Absalom in his rebellion (2 Sam 15.12). We can hardly begin to appreciate how crushed David would have felt when "one told David, saying, Ahithophel is among the conspirators with Absalom" (v.31). *The* king's counsellor had turned traitor.

Hushai was "the king's companion" or "friend" as rendered by the RV. In contrast to Ahithophel, in the circumstances of the revolt he remained true to David while masquerading as an insurgent. As a spy, he endangered his life as he professed allegiance to Absalom and gave faulty advice which, from a human standpoint, jeopardised Absalom's prospects (2 Sam 17.5-14). In actual fact, "the Lord had appointed to defeat the good counsel of Ahithophel, to the intent that the Lord might bring evil upon Absalom" (v.14). Written over Hushai's life could be placed the words of Scripture: "a friend loveth at all times" (Prov 17.17).

Junior to Ahithophel, or perhaps, successors to him, were "Jehoiadah the son of Benaiah, and Abiathar" (v.34). If Benaiah is the famed mighty man, which is not absolutely certain, the situation is interesting. Benaiah was a seasoned warrior and executioner right into the reign of Solomon (1 Kings 2). His son Ammizabad followed in his steps with a career in the army (1 Chr 27.6) but it appears that this other son Jehoiadah was more cerebral in character, hence his role as an advisor to the king. It is interesting that two men from the same household could render David service, but in such diverse ways - the one a tough army man, and the other an intellectual, functioning in an advisory capacity.

Abiathar was the priest and doubtless in matters of religion he was on hand to guide. "For the priest's lips should keep knowledge, and they should seek the law at his mouth: for he is the messenger of the Lord of hosts" (Mal 2.7).

Sadly, Abiathar too had a stain on his record. While remaining loyal during Absalom's rebellion, when David was on his death bed he sided with Adonijah in an effort to install him as David's successor, as did the last mentioned in the chapter, Joab the general (1 Kings 1.7). David and Joab had a rocky relationship throughout the years, but despite the man's dubious character, there is no doubt that he was an extremely competent military commander, making him a hard man to dismiss.

Having given us an insight into the workings of David's administration, all that remains for the inspired Chronicler to do is to record David's final pleas and exhortations in relation to the building of the temple, and these occupy the balance of the book.

1 CHRONICLES 28

We did observe that chapter 27 was a relevant interlude in the overall theme of the book; it dealt with matters of state, military and administrative. A new section begins here which concludes the major topic, David's commitment to building a house for God. This section virtually runs to the end of the book.

His pilgrimage was almost at an end, but, like mighty leaders before him, prior to his departure he took the opportunity to address his people one last time. Moses had done it (Deut 31.30-33.29), and Joshua had followed his example (Josh 24). In that tradition, David now summoned the leaders of the nation for his valediction.

For the greater part these last two chapters are taken up with the convention called to finalise arrangements for the temple. It also served as an opportunity to ensure the smooth transition of power to his son Solomon. He addressed the leaders of the nation and Solomon in turn, and among other things he committed to Solomon the pattern for this house of God with all its accoutrements. Much of what had been said to Solomon privately in 22.6-16 was now repeated in the presence of witnesses.

Pleas were made for commitment to the task, and there was an appeal for further resources that produced a massive response (29.6-9). Interspersed with the exhortations were prayers and praises, and the two chapters make very happy reading as the book approaches its climax.

Chapter 28 divides as follows. In verse 1 we have the record of the attendees at the gathering. Verses 2-7 are a restatement of God's dealings with David in respect of the house of God. In verses 8-10 there are exhortations to the leaders, and to Solomon personally, encouraging them in a general way to be loyal to the Lord, and then, more particularly, to build the house. In the main section of the chapter, verses 11-19, the pattern for the project is committed to Solomon, a pattern that had been written by divine inspiration (v.19). The last two verses comprise a further word of encouragement for Solomon before David addresses "all the congregation" again at the start of chapter 29.

Verse 1: Those who were Summoned to Jerusalem

David summoned the elite of the nation, those who headed the various groups of ch.27. Regional heads were there together with top military men and their subordinates. He called for the managers of his various business interests, and those who acted for his sons. In addition to those groups mentioned in ch.27, "officers" (5631) were called, the eunuchs who functioned as ministers of state or civil servants. Finally, "the mighty men, even all the mighty men of valour" (RV) were there, so, in effect, anyone who was anything was under mandate to attend. David wanted to ensure that anyone in the land with any responsibility or influence, anyone with any kind of power, would hear his final appeals in respect of his successor and take on board what had once been a personal ambition, but was now a national responsibility, to build the temple of God.

If we are ambitious in the things of God, it is vital to transmit to others an enthusiasm for any project, ensuring its support and subsequent implementation. Solomon was young and inexperienced; he was going to need the patronage of the leaders of the nation, those men of influence who could muster backing for his grand venture. Small minds would have thought it an unnecessary and elaborate distraction from the grind of making ends meet, but if the nation's leaders embraced the lofty ambitions of the royal family, then any objections would be overcome.

Verses 2-3: Shattered Dreams

When David was denied the privilege of building the temple, he "*sat* before the Lord" (17.16). On recounting the story here, he "*stood up* upon his feet". Considering just how frail he was soon to be (1 Kings 1), it would have taken considerable effort to rise to address the assembled company. However, he did rise to his feet to show his respect for this illustrious audience.

The manner in which he addressed them is another indicator of his respect: "my brethren, and my people". The order is significant. The man who is here designated "David the king" was not ashamed to refer to his subjects as "my brethren". The relationship that he had with them in the family took precedence over his authority over them. Spiritual leaders should keep that in mind. Every person for whom they have responsibility is described in Scripture as a "*brother*...for whom Christ died" (1 Cor 8.11). This should obviate any sense of superiority on the part of the elder, and keep in focus the value of the people for whom he cares.

David again recounted what has now become a familiar story to us. He never forgot the disappointment of the morning when Nathan arrived at the palace to cancel planning permission (17.15), but he rose above what appeared to be a major setback to his ambition. As in 22.7, he publicly disclosed what had been a cherished aspiration - to build what he called here, "an house of rest for the ark of the covenant of the Lord". How descriptive is the phrase, "an house of rest". For generations the ark had journeyed with the people, and even in the land had been located in various places, but now it was to "rest". Undoubtedly, the ark is a picture of our Lord Jesus Christ, who after dwelling, or literally, tabernacling among us (Jn 1.14), "sat down at the right hand of God" (Mk 16.19, RV). His work was done: now He could "rest".

The temple was to be for "the footstool of our God". "His footstool" is the place of worship (Ps 99.5; 132.7), so David had in mind a venue at which the people could express their homage. The mention of His footstool is also an indication that, like Solomon, he was aware of the truth of the omnipresence of God; "heaven and the heaven of heavens cannot contain thee" (2 Chr 6.18). Such is His majesty that He declared through the prophet

Isaiah, "The heaven is my throne, and the earth is my footstool" (Is 66.1). Here, the mercy seat is perceived as the footstool of Him "which dwelleth between the cherubims" (e.g. 1 Sam 4.4).

What David had planned he had also prepared for - he speaks about having "made ready for the building". It is good when plans are backed by action, although in this case things would not proceed as anticipated. Too often, good intentions fall back dead as a result of an unwillingness to expend energy, spend money, or devote time to the proposal.

The "But God" of v.3 is proof of the old adage that "man proposes but God disposes". The reasons for David's being side-lined have received comment in a previous chapter, but briefly, it was his history as a warrior with blood on his hands that disqualified him. The man who would build the house was Solomon whose very name means "peaceable". The lesson is that peaceable conditions must obtain, and peacemakers must be employed, if we are to build anything for God. Strife and commotion will inevitably wreck any potential blessing. "And be at peace among yourselves" (1 Thess 5.13).

Verses 4-7: God's Choice

Still reflecting on the disappointment of being rejected as a temple-builder, David remembered with joy what God had given as a welcome sweetener that day. God promised that he would head a dynasty, a promise that had undertones of the coming of the Messiah. A key word of this little section is "chosen". David was chosen, Judah had been chosen, Solomon was chosen. God is sovereign in His choice of servants. It is in the context of service that the Lord Jesus said to His disciples, "Ye have not chosen me, but I have chosen you, and ordained you, that ye should go and bring forth fruit, and that your fruit should remain" (Jn 15.16). Here, David is enamoured with the fact that it was the majestic Jehovah Elohim of Israel who had taken an interest in him, and had installed him as king. He remembers vividly the day when the nervous men of Bethlehem had watched Samuel arrive in their village (1 Sam 16). He recalls his summons from the hillside and the sensation of the anointing oil trickling over his head. No doubt he had heard that Samuel had scrutinised and rejected his seven older brothers; "the Lord God of Israel chose me before all the house of my father". Out of all the sons of Jacob, Judah had been chosen as the royal tribe; "the sceptre shall not depart from Judah" (Gen 49.10). Out of all the tribe of Judah, the house of Jesse had been chosen. Out of all the sons of Jesse, David had been chosen, and now out of all his "many sons", Solomon had been chosen. (This lineage was never stated of any subsequent king.) Judah was not the firstborn and yet he was chosen; Jesse was a nonentity who "went among men for an old man in the days of Saul", a man who was the owner of just "those few sheep" (1 Sam 17.12,28), and yet he was chosen. Messiah would "come forth a rod out of the stem *of Jesse*, and a Branch shall grow out of his roots" (Is 11.1). David was the despised youngest son of Jesse, and yet he was chosen; "he took pleasure in me to make me king over all Israel"

(RV). Solomon was the fruit of a union that should never have been and yet he was chosen. No wonder Scripture says of the sovereign God of the universe, "how unsearchable are his judgments, and his ways past finding out!" (Rom 11.33).

One or two other features of this section deserve comment although similar references have been made to these factors in former chapters. David saw his appointment as being "for ever" (v.4). At this point he was approaching the end of life, so he had no illusions of possessing eternal life in some physical sense! However, he had grasped the fact that God had promised him a dynasty that would survive the generations of time, and have as its ultimate head Him of whom the angel Gabriel said, "the Lord God shall give unto him the throne of his father David: And he shall reign over the house of Jacob *for ever*; and of his kingdom *there shall be no end*" (Lk 1.32-33). The angel's message ratified Isaiah's prediction: "Of the increase of his government and peace *there shall be no end*" (Is 9.7). David anticipated Messiah's reign.

David saw his many sons as a gift from God (v.5). "Lo, children are an heritage of the Lord: and the fruit of the womb is his reward" (Ps 127.3). If only the modern world could grasp this it would bring to an end some prevalent social evils in the western world, among them the murder of the unborn child, and the tendency for mothers to put a career before the family.

Here in v.5 David saw Solomon as his successor by divine choice, but the language he used is instructive. Solomon would "sit upon the throne *of the kingdom of the Lord* over Israel". The kingdom was the Lord's and Solomon would administer it in His interests. There is a parallel truth in the New Testament. Every New Testament assembly is a "flock of God", "God's heritage", and elders must keep that in mind as they function as shepherds. They must always remember that they are responsible to Him who is described as "the chief Shepherd". This will preserve them from an overbearing manner and a dictatorial style. They are administering in the interests of Another (1 Pet 5.1-4).

Solomon was not only chosen "to sit upon the throne" (v.5), but he was chosen "to be my son" (v.6). It was because he had been chosen as son that he was selected to build the house. "He shall build my house…*for* I have chosen him to be my son". From a spiritual standpoint, sonship and service go hand in hand, a fact that was not understood by the prodigal son. "I…Am no more worthy to be called thy son: make me as one of thy hired servants" (Lk 15.18-19). Malachi speaks of a man sparing "his own son that serveth him" (Mal 3.17). To be a willing servant of the Most High God one must first have a relationship with Him as a son of God. In the world of Christendom there are multitudes ostensibly serving God, but they have known nothing of the regenerating power of the Holy Spirit in their lives. Of course, there are those who are unwittingly the servants of God such as those who are in positions of authority in the nations, tools in His hand to effect His great purposes (Rom 13.3-4), but as far as spiritual service is concerned sonship is a necessary prerequisite.

God spoke to David of Solomon as "thy son", and yet He now designated him "my son". It would be the prayer of every Christian father that his boys will become the "sons of God, through faith, in Christ Jesus" (Gal 3.26, RV).

The writer to the Hebrews takes the original statement regarding Solomon's sonship, and applies it to the Lord Jesus (Heb 1.5) as part of his argument to demonstrate the superiority of Christ the Son over angels.

"He shall build my house" (v.6); "Solomon determined to build an house" (2 Chr 2.1); "Then Solomon began to build the house" (2 Chr 3.1); "So Solomon built the house, and finished it" (1 Kings 6.14). There is an order there that holds good for every aspect of the work of God. God appoints His servant. That servant resolves to do His bidding. The work commences, and the diligent servant sees it through to its conclusion. Are we all as co-operative and earnest as Solomon was?

According to v.7, the continuity of Solomon's kingdom would be dependent on his resolute commitment to divine commands. As things stood, "as at this day", God gave him credit for being happily compliant with His will, but many others had started out well, but then there had been slippage. God demanded that he be "constant (2388) to do my commandments". The word really means, "to be strong", for it does require strength of resolve to obey God when there are so many pressures to do otherwise. The ESV combines the thoughts of constancy and strength by translating, "if he continues strong…". Let us all be firmly and permanently committed to the precepts of the Word of God, for "If ye know these things, happy are ye if ye do them" (Jn 13.17).

It is a sad fact that Solomon lapsed in the later stages of life, and consequently, in the early days of his son Rehoboam's reign, ten tribes seceded from the kingdom. God's threats of judgment should be taken as seriously as His promises of blessing.

Verse 8: An Exhortation to the People

Here, David addressed the gathered company. His exhortation was not communicated in some furtive way but "in the sight of all Israel the congregation of the Lord". It is only those with a hidden agenda who purvey their teachings secretly, "they which creep into houses" (2 Tim 3.6). Paul taught the truth "among many witnesses" (2 Tim 2.2), and the Lord Jesus said, "I spake openly to the world; I ever taught in the synagogue, and in the temple, whither the Jews always resort; and in secret have I said nothing" (Jn 18.20). It is always suspicious when some unorthodox suggestion is made round a supper table, something that would never be aired in a public meeting. When it comes to the communication of truth, openness is of the essence.

David's message was also "in the audience of... God", a factor that should regulate both the preacher and the congregation. Cornelius seemed to understand that: "Now therefore are we all here present before God, to hear all things that are commanded thee of God" (Acts 10.33). He realised that an awareness of the divine presence would motivate the preacher to tell the message as it had been given him, and would persuade the listeners to receive it as a communication from heaven. Frequently, Paul reminded Timothy that what was being said to him was "before God", or, "in the sight of God" as some translations phrase it (1 Tim 5.21; 6.13; 2 Tim 2.14; 4.1). It would impact on every aspect of our lives if we could only remember that our God is El Roi, the God who sees (Gen 16.13).

David's exhortation to the people related to God's commandments. First, they had to "keep" them; it was an appeal for obedience. Then they had to seek them out (RV). In other words, there was no excuse for ignorance. There was a documentary record of all God's demands, and it was for them to search the Scriptures to find the answer to this crucial question, "What doth the Lord require of thee?" (Micah 6.8; see also Deut 10.12). Next, they had to take into account *every* precept of the law, "*all* the commandments". There was no latitude in selecting which commandments to obey. They would have to be like Zacharias and Elisabeth, who were "walking in *all* the commandments and ordinances of the Lord blameless" (Lk 1.6). The standard was high, but if we credit David with Psalm 119, he had made it his own focus in life: "O how love I thy law! It is my meditation all the day" (v.97). He had proved the value of such an approach to life:s "Great peace have they which love thy law" (v.165). May such a submissive attitude to the Word of God be a feature of all of our lives.

For David's subjects there were great rewards for willing obedience to God's Word. It would ensure their continued possession of the "good land" that God had gifted them, and its transfer to succeeding generations. What an incentive to obedience! By implication, there was the threat that disobedience would entail their removal from their land, "a land which the Lord thy God careth for" (Deut 11.12). Sadly, by the time 1 Chronicles had been written that had been a reality, and the first readers had but recently been repatriated. The rewards for obedience are great; the cost of disobedience is high.

Verses 9-10: Exhortations to Solomon

In an atmosphere that would be highly charged with emotion, David's gaze now fell upon his young son, upon whom such a great weight of responsibility was about to fall: "And thou, Solomon my son…". For himself, David had lived his life in the knowledge of God, and it was his great desire that Solomon should perpetuate this intimate relationship with the Almighty: "know thou the God of thy father". Everyone must have his own experience of God, and neither salvation nor devotion runs in the blood. Thus David made his appeal to his son to get to know God, for "the people that do know their God shall be strong, and do exploits"

(Dan 11.32). For Paul, everything else in life was subservient to "know(ing) him" (Phil 3.10).

Next, David encouraged Solomon to "serve him" and he laid emphasis on the way in which this had to be done, "with a perfect heart and with a willing mind". Service that is mechanical and routine is of little value. David's appeal was for a devoted heart and a zealous spirit, for God's assessment of what is rendered to Him takes into account not only what is done, but also motive and attitude: "the Lord searcheth all hearts, and understandeth all the imaginations of the thoughts". Paul confirmed David's thinking about this when he spoke of the Lord's appraisal of a believer's service at the coming day of review: "who both will bring to light the hidden things of darkness, and will make manifest the counsels of the hearts" (1 Cor 4.5). All this should encourage us constantly to inspect our activity, and probe our motives. Even as believers we are constantly aware of the subtlety of our hearts: "The heart is deceitful above all things" (Jer 17.9). May there be transparency and enthusiasm as we engage in the work of the Lord. When it came to the construction of the tabernacle there was a call for the participants to be "wise hearted" and "willing hearted" (Ex 35.10, 22). "Keep thy heart with all diligence" (Pr 4.23).

"Know God"; "serve God"; now, "seek God". The injunction was echoed by Azariah the son of Oded, when he encountered King Asa and his victorious army. "If ye seek him, he will be found of you; but if ye forsake him, he will forsake you" (2 Chr 15.2). In that generation the appeal was not ignored, for "they entered into a covenant to seek the Lord God of their fathers with all their heart and with all their soul" (v.12). Indeed, they "sought him with their whole desire; and he was found of them" (v.15). Such earnest consecration is rare, but not unique. The sons of Korah expressed it like this: "As the hart panteth after the water brooks, so panteth my soul after thee, O God. My soul thirsteth for God, for the living God: when shall I come and appear before God?" (Ps 42.1-2). May we all have such healthy spiritual desires, responding to the Lord Jesus as did two of His early disciples. When faced with the question, "What seek ye?", their immediate response was, "Rabbi…where dwellest thou?" (Jn 1.38). There is rich reward for those who "diligently seek (God)" (Heb 11.6).

Before giving instructions to Solomon about the temple, David struck a sombre note: "if thou forsake him, he will cast thee off for ever". It was almost prophetic, as if David had some kind of premonition that it might happen. In our English Bible, 1 Kings 11 commences with an ominous "But". Thereafter there is the record of Solomon's latter days, his involvement with foreign women and his devotion to their idols; it was all tantamount to forsaking the Lord. On account of that, the kingdom was divided; "Because that they have *forsaken* me, and have worshipped Ashtoreth…" (v.33). Selman remarks that his divided devotion led to a divided kingdom. If only Solomon had heeded his old father's warnings! Solomon said to his own son, "My son, forget not my law; but let thine heart keep my commandments"

(Pr 3.1). Sadly, he forgot *his* father's laws; he did not keep *his* father's commandments but abandoned them on the last lap. If parental advice has been sound, and if the counsel of elders and Bible teachers has been spiritual, it is good to hold it in mind until the last mile of life's journey has been travelled.

Having given these general injunctions, David became more specific and focused on Solomon's responsibility to build the house of God. For the third time in a few verses, David refers to Solomon as having been chosen. He had been chosen as a sovereign (v.5). He had been chosen as a son (v.6). Now he is chosen as a servant with the specific task of building for God.

Thus David recalled God's sovereignty in the matter, "the Lord hath chosen thee to build an house for the sanctuary", but as ever, allied with divine sovereignty there is the thought of human responsibility. "Be strong, and do it". The Spirit of God dispenses spiritual gifts sovereignly (1 Cor 12.11), but men have a responsibility to desire gifts (v.31). The Spirit appoints elders sovereignly (Acts 20.28), but men have a responsibility to desire overseership (1 Tim 3.1). Thus here, God had chosen, but Solomon must now act. The encouragement to be strong and to act is repeated at v.20. The people who would have first read 1 Chronicles had received a similar word of encouragement when faced with rebuilding the temple. "Be strong…and work" (Hag 2.4); "fear not, but let your hands be strong" (Zech 8.13). In any activity for God, strength of resolve and spiritual might are so necessary. If the Lord has laid something on your heart, "do it". "Whatsoever he saith unto you, do it" (Jn 2.5).

Verses 11-19: The Pattern

Solomon had been commissioned and encouraged to build the house of God, but how should he proceed, and where would the materials come from? These questions are addressed in the remainder of the book. A pattern for the temple is given as to its buildings (vv.11-12), as to its personnel (v.13), and as to its contents (vv.14-18).

Before commenting on specifics, some general factors should be noted. The mention of a pattern is reminiscent of the pattern for the tabernacle that was committed to Moses with this solemn stipulation, "look that thou make them after their pattern, which was shewed thee in the mount" (Ex 25.40). A New Testament preacher and a New Testament writer both appreciated the importance of that injunction because both made reference to it (Acts 7.44; Heb 8.5). God had an inflexible pattern for the tabernacle, and we are now learning that He also had a pattern for the temple, both of them regarded as a house of God. Human design or architecture did not feature in either of these structures. Thus it should be with the modern day "house of God", the local "church of the living God" (1 Tim 3.15). There is a clear pattern in the Acts of the Apostles and in the epistles for the conduct of the local assembly. No one ever tried to tinker with the patterns for tabernacle or temple, but the history of Christendom has been one of constant interference with the divine New Testament pattern to the extent that, in great measure, denominational traditions bear no resemblance to the simplicity of that pattern. From the days of Constantine, so-called Christianity has absorbed Judaistic ritual and pagan practices that see it far removed from the New Testament procedures of apostolic times. It would be easy to insert an excursus at this point to enumerate many areas of deviation from the New Testament blueprint, but we will content ourselves with a plea for faithfulness to the Word of God, and an appeal to reject the "good ideas" of men if they in any way impinge on the divine pattern.

Another general observation is that this pattern had been committed to David, but he now relayed it to the next generation. God has always encouraged the transmission of truth from generation to generation. Thus the law had to be read publicly every seven years, "that their children, which have not known any thing, may hear, and learn to fear the Lord your God" (Deut 31.13). Asaph spoke of things which "our fathers have told us. We will not hide them from their children, shewing to the generation to come the praises of the Lord" (Ps 78.3-4). In the New Testament, both Paul and Peter stressed the importance of the repetition of truth (Phil 3.1,18; 2 Pet 1.12-13; 3.1). Bible teachers should keep this in mind. Every area of doctrine should have exposure on a regular basis, remembering that what is perhaps a refresher course for some is an initiation course for others.

The precision of the pattern should also be noted. Not only did it cover areas of the temple so diverse as "the place of the mercy seat", "upper chambers", "inner parlours" and "courts", but it prescribed the exact weight of vessels and the precise composition of these vessels down to whether it was gold, refined gold, or pure gold. The most expert quantity surveyor, or the most sophisticated computer predictions could never have arrived at such accurate figures for all that was required. God is always precise, and so in His things, attention to detail is important. This is seen in the teaching of the Lord Jesus. He warned against breaking "one of these least commandments" (Mt 5.19), and while He criticised the Pharisees for ignoring massive moral issues while majoring on little things, He did say, "these ought ye to have done, *and not to leave the other undone*" (Mt 23.23). Let us all give attention to detail, whether it is in matters relating to our personal lives, or in corporate assembly activity as illustrated in the pattern for the house of God.

The pattern encompassed the internal areas of the temple, but also the visible external parts of the structure, the "courts of the house of the Lord", and even took in what may have appeared to be the mundane matter of "treasuries". Similarly, in the New Testament there are details of how New Testament assemblies should function Godward, and clear instructions about external visible activity towards needy humanity. Clear teaching is given about money matters there too, as, for example, in 2 Corinthians 8 and 9.

Another factor that should be re-emphasised is that the creation of courses for the priests and Levites was part of the pattern (v.13). If we had only the earlier chapters to go by, we would have surmised that it was an expedient that David had devised personally.

Before leaving this section, allow one or two comments about particular statements. At v.12 there is an indication that as far as the pattern was concerned "all that (David) had" was "by the Spirit". The Newberry Bible with JND and others place a capital letter at the word "Spirit" making it a clear reference to the Holy Spirit of God; this appears to be a correct interpretation. It seems far more feasible than Jamieson, Fausset and Brown's suggestion that the translation should be, "with him in spirit", which they take to mean, "floating in his mind"! In general terms, "holy men of God spake as they were moved by the Holy Ghost" (2 Pet 1.21). David was one of these "holy men" as claimed by himself in 2 Samuel 23.2: "The Spirit of the Lord spake by me". Peter confirmed his claim, for he spoke of a Scripture "which the Holy Ghost by the mouth of David spake" (Acts 1.16). Again, when addressing the Lord, the early disciples referred to Him speaking "by the mouth of thy servant David" (Acts 4.25). Thus David was a channel of divine communication, and it is evident that in the present context the Spirit of God had revealed the pattern to him.

At v.19 there is the further disclosure that the Lord had made the revelation "in writing". Was David himself inspired to write it? Had it been committed to Samuel and passed on to David as some suggest? Did an angel write it? Did God Himself write it as He did the ten commandments, "written with the finger of God" (Ex 31.18)? We are not informed, but the first suggestion seems the most likely.

However it came about, the pattern was not just a series of instructions that David retained in his mind, but by the Spirit they had been committed to paper. Thus it is with the pattern for the present day "house of God". We are not dependent on oral tradition for guidance, but the Spirit of God inspired the apostles to commit to writing all that we need to know, now contained in the volume that we call the New Testament. We all have access to the mind of God about these issues and it is for each of us simply to replicate the New Testament pattern as it is found there. Some are uncomfortable with the word uniformity, but there is a sense in which if everyone is following the same pattern, the same results should ensue. Paul taught the same things "in every church" (1 Cor 4.17). He "ordained" the same "in all churches" (1 Cor 7.17). Never let it be thought that he was promoting his own ideas; he was presenting a pattern that he had received from heaven. "I have received of the Lord that which also I delivered unto you." "If any man think himself to be a prophet, or spiritual, let him acknowledge that the things that I write unto you are the commandments of the Lord." "I delivered unto you first of all that which I also received" (1 Cor 7.17; 11.23; 14.37; 15.3). Like David here, Paul was simply relaying the mind of God. He had done it verbally, and now it is part of the inspired record. Let us all be submissive to the teaching.

Like David in this setting, we too have the capacity to "understand" what is revealed in writing by the Spirit. "Consider what I say; for *the Lord shall give thee understanding* in all things" (2 Tim 2.7, RV).

Here, "*all* the works of this pattern" had been committed to writing as with the New Testament pattern. In other words, we are not at liberty to either add to or take from what has been revealed as is the case with Scripture as a whole (see, for example, Deut 4.2; 12.32; Pr 30.5-6; Rev 22.18-19). There is always the danger of failing to implement divine demands, or, on the other hand, augmenting these demands with human regulations.

Perhaps it should be noted that while there was one table and one lampstand in the tabernacle, there were a number in the temple (vv.15-16). In fact 1 Kings 7.49 speaks of ten lampstands, and 2 Chronicles 4.8 refers to ten tables. Unlike the tabernacle, some of these vessels were of silver, and commentators suggest that silver lampstands would have illuminated priests' quarters, or were perhaps portable lamps, and because of the commodious nature of the new structure, furnishings were necessary in every quarter, not all demanding the gold that was essential for vessels in proximity to the sanctuary. We are in the realm of conjecture again! It should be noted that there remained but one ark and one altar of incense. The essential elements of worship were left unchanged.

"The chariot of the cherubims" (v.18) is described in 1 Kings 6.23-28, thus designated because in the poetry of the Psalms God is perceived as not only sitting "between the cherubims" (Ps 99.1), but riding "upon a cherub" (Ps 18.10; see also Ps 68.17). It is a poetic expression of the mobility of God, as illustrated too in the vision of Ezekiel 1 with its emphasis on wheels. These two large cherubim were another feature of the holy of holies in the temple that was additional to tabernacle conditions. However, we are assured here that there were divine instructions for the change.

Verses 20-21: The Final Charge to Solomon

"Do it" (v.10). These were David's last words to Solomon before he handed over the scrolls with the drawings and directions for the temple. Now he repeated the command - "do it". It would need strength of character and courage to proceed. Obviously, the young man was apprehensive, or why the "fear not"? But he could move forward confidently with this assurance, "the Lord God, even my God, will be with thee". "My God", the God whom David had proved over a lifetime of frequent danger and continual exposure to trial, "my God, will be with thee". From personal experience of the faithfulness of God, David could assure his son of His constant care and interest. God would not fail him. With every twist and turn of the road, with every unexpected crisis, with every apparent impediment to progress, there would be a supply of grace, and direction from heaven. Nor would God weary of supporting the inexperienced monarch. The divine presence was guaranteed till the work was "finished". That promise became a reality, for, as quoted earlier, Scripture records that "Solomon built the house, and *finished* it" (1 Kings 6.14).

David's words of encouragement were almost a replica of God's words to Joshua as he took on the mantle of Moses (Josh 1.5). He was by no means as youthful as Solomon, but he had lived in the shadow of Moses for forty years, and now his mentor was gone, and the burden of leadership had fallen on him. "A word spoken in due season, how good is it!" (Pr 15.23). How timely are God's interventions.

Let us take courage ourselves and be willing to devote ourselves unreservedly to the work of God, with the assurance of the Lord's presence as a stimulus to earnest endeavour. It took seven years to build the temple (1 Kings 6.37-38), and it is hardly to be supposed that in all these seven years everything was plain sailing. Nevertheless, Solomon saw the project through to its completion with divine assistance. In the same way, let us be willing to persevere in our labours despite any obstacles that may be placed in our path, for He has promised, "lo, I am with you alway, even unto the end of the world" (Mt 28.20). Furthermore, let us, like David, be willing to encourage others. Words of appreciation and support go far in spurring others in their endeavours. It is never wise to encourage the egotistical, but on the other hand, such is the human psyche that to be bereft of any appreciation can create discouragement that would make it easy to give up the endeavour.

David's final word of encouragement was to assure Solomon that he had the support of his fellow men. The work was great (29.1), too great for the capabilities of one man, but others would help sustain him in his project. Support would come from a variety of sources. The courses of priests and Levites that David had already set in place were in position to function the moment the house was built; the spiritual side of things took top place in David's thinking so they are mentioned first. The structure itself needed a range of men "for all manner of workmanship". They too were in readiness, both as to their expertise, and their willingness for the task: "willing skilful (men)". Ensure that the exercise of your gift is not hampered by an unwillingness to function. Skill and will must go together.

Finally, "the princes and all the people" were under the authority of Solomon, with the inference that they would happily co-operate as their work was delegated to them. David painted a word portrait of a variety of people with a variety of backgrounds, and a variety of capabilities, but all with a common aim - to build a house for God. With that picture etched firmly on his mind, Solomon was now ready to move forward.

1 CHRONICLES 29

This lengthy final chapter is a splendid top stone to the account of God's dealings with David, an unfolding narrative that has held much interest for us. If viewed in the light of Romans 15.4, the closing stages of the story raise many practical issues for our lives; "whatsoever things were written aforetime were written for our learning". There is also much to be learned about the character of God as we peruse David's ascriptions of praise to Him.

The narrative continues the description of David's last great convention before his death. Statesmen, stewards and soldiers were all arrayed before him, straining to catch every syllable that fell from the old man's lips. He had already enlightened them about his ambition to build a house for God, and had encouraged them to be willing participants as Solomon spearheaded the venture. Then, fixing his eye on Solomon, he had addressed him personally, and, without apparent ceremony, had presented him with the "pattern" for the structure. With the parchments, there were suitable words of encouragement for the young builder.

David now turned from his son and eyed the serried ranks before him. He made one last appeal for co-operation and contributions to facilitate the erection of the building and, happily, the response was overwhelming, giving rise to a wonderful paean of praise. To borrow New Testament language, David was here provoking his people "to good works" (Heb 10.24).

The division of the chapter is as follows. In verses 1-5a, there is the record of David's personal contribution to the building of the temple. From verse 5b to verse 9 he challenges the people to emulate him, and there are the details of their response. The largest section (verses 10-19) notes the content of David's prayer. Verses 20-25 contain the reaction of the people, including their enthronement of Solomon. In the rest of the chapter (verses 26-30) there is a résumé of David's reign followed by the details of his death.

Verse 1: The Work is Great

The inspired Chronicler never allows us to forget that the man who had convened the gathering and was making the oration was "David the king", majestic and dignified in spite of the severe limitations of age and illness. However, despite his status David was at pains to stress to his subjects that the choice of Solomon as temple builder had not been his but God's: "Solomon my son, whom alone God hath chosen". As has been noted frequently, there is no place for nepotism in the things of God. Solomon was the man for the job not because he was the son of David, but because God had declared, "He shall build me an house" (17.12).

It had yet to be written, but in general terms it is true: "Woe to thee, O land, when thy king is a child" (Eccl 10.16). From a human standpoint Solomon seemed unfitted for the task. He was still inexperienced: "young". He had never been tempered by the toughening experiences of life:

"tender". Moreover, the assignment that faced him was immense: "the work is great". Yet because he was the man whom God had chosen, despite these seeming disadvantages the work would proceed, and it did. It seems that Solomon's lack of experience was the express reason for David's own intense involvement (v.2), and his plea for their commitment too (v.5b). Younger believers need the backing of older saints in their labours for the Lord, not only in prayer and by advice, but also in every practical way possible. Remember, though, that if the exercise is theirs, then the involvement of others is mainly supportive. In such circumstance there should never be an attempt to hijack the operation, leaving the younger friend sidelined in any way.

"The work is great." One can hardly read it without remembering Nehemiah's response to those who made subtle attempts to lure him from his task of rebuilding the walls of Jerusalem: "I am doing a great work, so that I cannot come down" (Neh 6.3). It would be wonderful if each of us were to perceive our work for God as being just as important and vital as that. To estimate it aright would promote commitment to it, and a respect for it.

In this context, the work was "great" because "the palace is not for man, but for the Lord God". "The house that is to be builded for the Lord must be exceeding magnifical" (22.5). Only the best will suffice for God. Why is it then that what we render to Him can be so shoddy at times? Why is it that what we build is so often substandard? Why is it that if what we were doing were for "man", the outcome would never be second rate? Like Solomon, let us keep in mind that it is the majestic Jehovah Elohim whom we serve.

The word "palace" (1002) is an unusual description for the temple, and is used again at v.19. Apparently the word was of foreign origin, used frequently in the book of Esther in the phrase "Shushan the palace". Its usage here is just another indication of David's perception of the magnificence of the building.

Verses 2-5a: David's Example

As David surveyed the nation's elite, he proposed to challenge them pointedly about their personal commitment to this undertaking of building a house for God. "Who then is willing to consecrate his service this day unto the Lord?" (v.5b). But first he would tell them of his own personal contribution. He would never be the hypocrite who encouraged others to do something for which he himself was unwilling. That was a major failure in the lives of the Pharisees; "they say, and do not" (Mt 23.3). Paul was like David. When he encouraged the Ephesian elders to give financial support to "the weak", he cited his own personal example as an incentive: "I have shewed you all things, how that so labouring ye ought to support the weak" (Acts 20.34-35). David and Paul were the kind of men who could say like Gideon, "Look on me, and do likewise" (Judg 7.17). They led by example; let us take a leaf out of their book.

Back in 22.5, David had declared his intention of preparing for the house of God: "I will therefore now make preparation for it". The Spirit of God records, "So David prepared abundantly before his death". David's intentions became concrete realities. He now testified himself, "I have prepared *with all my might*". At that stage in life he had had a one-track mind, and his objective had been achieved by dint of sheer determination and commitment. All his energies had been directed into preparing for what he called, "the house of *my* God". This God with whom he had a personal relationship deserved his very best. Let us translate it into modern circumstances, and apply the lesson in the words of the old chorus:

Out there among the hills, my Saviour died.
Pierced by those cruel nails, was crucified.
Lord Jesus, Thou hast done all this for me!
Henceforward I will live, only for Thee!

David's preparation was extensive, taking into account the need for precious metals, gems, timber, and building blocks, many of them marble. He had taken every need into account, and so his groundwork was thorough. Paul was as diligent in his work for God. "From Jerusalem, and round about unto Illyricum, I have fully preached the gospel of Christ" (Rom 15.19). Says God, "Cursed be he that doeth the work of the Lord negligently" (Jer 48.10, RV). In the context of Jeremiah 48, "the work of the Lord" was a work of judgment, but surely there is a general principle there. Negligence in the work of God is never acceptable. May we all be preserved from a lackadaisical approach to His service.

What motivated David to go to so much trouble, to expend so much energy, and to sacrifice so much from his own private purse? Happily, it was not a pharisaical craving "to be seen of men" (Mt 23.5). No, he had "set (his) affection to the house of (his) God" (v.3). David had always had a great love for the house of God. "Lord, I have loved the habitation of thy house, and the place where thine honour dwelleth" (Ps 26.8). "One thing have I desired of the Lord, that will I seek after; that I may dwell in the house of the Lord all the days of my life, to behold the beauty of the Lord, and to inquire in his temple" (Ps 27.4). The sons of Korah had the same kind of feelings for the house of God. "How amiable are thy tabernacles, O Lord of hosts! My soul longeth, yea, even fainteth for the courts of the Lord" (Ps 84.1-2). David's life had centred round the house of God when it was just a flimsy tent, but his affection for all that it stood for was such that he longed to set in motion a chain of events that would see God's dwelling on earth the most exquisite and substantial edifice that could possibly be. His commitment to it is seen in the fact that three times in two verses, he calls it, "the house of my God". It would be a wonderful thing if the same kind of affection was seen in our own lives, an affection for the God of the house, an affection for the people who constitute the assembly, an affection for the activity connected with it, and an affection for the principles that govern it. As in David's case, such love would stimulate us to the heights of commitment and sacrifice that he speaks of here.

Observe that he described the temple not only as "the house of my God", but also as "the holy house" (v.3). It was a building that was set apart for God, and hence a standard of holiness was expected of all who were connected with it. "Holiness becometh thine house, O Lord, for ever" (Ps 93.5). The same is true of the modern equivalent, God's assembly. "The temple of God is holy, which temple ye are" (1 Cor 3.17). Anyone who is linked to a New Testament assembly must keep in mind the need to maintain holy conduct, for if even one life is besmirched, it impacts on the whole company. "A little leaven leaveneth the whole lump" (1 Cor 5.6). In light of that, Peter's appeal is so relevant: "as he which hath called you is holy, so be ye holy in all manner of conversation" (1 Pet 1.15).

The phrase "of mine own proper good" indicates that the contribution to which David referred came from his own personal resources, and were not the spoils of battle to which reference had been made in earlier passages. For example, the Revised Version translates as follows: "because I have set my affection to the house of my God, seeing that I have a treasure of mine own of gold and silver, I give it unto the house of my God, over and above all that I have prepared for the holy house". He had personally paid for the site (21.25); now he contributed lavishly to the construction of the house.

This was a personal sacrifice on the part of David, and, very carefully, he had given thought to what he would donate. Thus he knew precisely the amounts of gold and silver that he had given - 3,000 talents and 7,000 talents respectively; it was an immense contribution. He knew that the gold had been sourced in Ophir; it was superior class (Job 22.24; 28.16; Ps 45.9; Is 13.12). He knew that the silver had been refined. Everything was the very best for it was for God; there was quality as well as quantity. Believers should give the same thought to what they give to God. "Let every one of you lay by him in store, as God hath prospered him" (1 Cor 16.2). Our giving should be calculated and systematic rather than haphazard and last-minute. Of course, this does not rule out impulse giving when an unexpected need arises. "God loveth a cheerful giver" (2 Cor 9.7).

Many in the land could never have come near to matching David's lavish monetary donation to the house of God, but they were able to contribute something that he could never have given - their skills. Thus there is mention of the "hands of the artificers". These working class artisans would devote time, energy, and expertise to the great task of building for God. It is another lesson in the need for blending skills and resources. No one can accomplish single-handedly anything for God in the assembly. We have to make use of the pooled talents of an assorted group of believing people.

Verse 5b: The Challenge

"And who then is willing to consecrate his service this day unto the Lord?" David's challenge to his people has reverberated throughout the generations of Christian testimony, and on hearing it many a man has been brought to a crisis in life and has responded to the call of God for some particular aspect of service. Perhaps he had dithered with indecision for months but that is now left behind and the fears and uncertainties are abandoned. The cost of obedience has been measured and with God's help paid in full. Full and glad surrender has been made.

Let us all face up to the challenge of David's words. "*Who?*" "*Who* is on the Lord's side?" (Ex 32.26). "*Who* will go for us?" (Is 6.8). At the time of President Ronald Reagan's second Inaugural Address on 21st January, 1985, his nation faced huge economic problems; he felt the responsibility of addressing these. He had said to his Cabinet, "If not us, who? And if not now, when?". When confronted with the claims of service and discipleship, we might all ask, "If not us, who?". To be available is a wonderful thing as illustrated in the Lord's dealings with Ananias. He had only to say to him, "Ananias", and there was an immediate reaction, "Behold, I am here, Lord" (Acts 9.10). Ananias was available.

"Who then is *willing?*" As ever, the response is down to willingness. For those whom David confronted, among other things it would mean a considerable sacrifice of their personal means. In the same kind of context Paul emphasised to the Corinthians the need for "a willing mind" (2 Cor 8.12). The same willingness is one of the criteria for discipleship. JND and the NKJV translate Mark 8.34 uniformly: "Whoever *desires* to come after me, let him deny himself...". There has to be the desire. The demands of the elderhood must be embraced "not by constraint, but *willingly*" (1 Pet 5.2). Amasiah was a man "who *willingly* offered himself unto the Lord" (2 Chr 17.16). In Deborah's day "the people *willingly* offered themselves" as did their governors (Judg 5.2,9). These people stand as a condemnation of modern, shallow, half-hearted Christianity.

"To *consecrate*" (4390) means, literally, to fill the hands. The word was used in connection with the high priest and his sons being initiated into their office (e.g. Ex 28.41). Sacrifices that they brought would actually have filled their hands, but it was all part of the ritual whereby the whole man was being set apart for a holy function. Here, too, David was urging hands to be filled with something to offer, but in reality he was appealing for the dedication of the whole man. Most translations phrase David's question like this: "who then is willing to consecrate *himself*...?". In New Testament language, this is presenting the body as "a living sacrifice" (Rom 12.1). If there is a presentation of ourselves, it means that everything connected to us will be yielded as well. This was the case with the Macedonian believers. They "first gave their own selves to the Lord" (2 Cor 8.5). That led to the kind of lives that placed the needs of others ahead of their own. Had they known Miss Havergal's hymn they would have sung it with some feeling:

> Take my life, and let it be
> Consecrated Lord to Thee.

That had led to the next step as with David's willing subjects:

> Take my silver and my gold,
> Not a mite would I withhold.

On occasions, preachers have been criticised for presenting a "crisis ministry", that is, a call for an immediate response, rather than allowing the patient teaching of Scripture over a period of time to have its cumulative effect on the life. However, there are occasions when matters must be brought to a head. It cannot be denied that this was "crisis ministry" from David. "Who then is willing to consecrate his service *this day* unto the Lord?" David was pressing for immediate results. For the people of Joshua's generation it was decision time too. "Choose you *this day* whom ye will serve" (Josh 24.15). At times there is great need for instant action, for an urgent decision, lest, like the Corinthians, we should let a full year drag past without any definitive action (2 Cor 9.2).

Verses 6-9: They Offered Willingly

There are six references in the chapter to the people offering willingly, the first of them here in v.6. Faced with the precedent of David's example, and the fervour of his appeal, there was a spontaneous, fulsome response from the people, and they "offered willingly". "Every man according as he purposeth in his heart, so let him give; not grudgingly, or of necessity" (2 Cor 9.7). There is no suspicion of reluctance here.

God noted the extent of their giving, and the tonnage of precious metals is recorded here in v.7. Among other terms, an unusual Persian word is employed, "drams" (150) or "darics" (RV). Its usage would have been helpful for contemporary readers, many of whom had been familiar with the term during their days of exile. It should be an encouragement to us all that God does take note of sacrifice made in His interests as illustrated in the Lord observing proceedings as He sat "over against the treasury" (Mk 12.41).

Jehiel the Gershonite was responsible for managing the resources that were donated (v.8). Some suggest that his name means, "God lives", and who would doubt the meaning of his name in light of God's activity in the hearts of His people at this time? The Gershonites had been responsible for the curtains and coverings of the tabernacle, but that function was now a matter of history. However, there are no redundancies in the work of the Lord, and a new sphere of activity had opened up to this man. Sometimes it is evident that we have to move on in the Lord's service, that is, it may become apparent that our present activity is no longer viable and that new avenues of activity have to be explored. Change for the sake of change is reprehensible, but we do need to be sensitive as to when a particular ministry has served its purpose.

Verse 9 is a wonderful confirmation of the Lord's statement, "It is more blessed to give than to receive" (Acts 20.35). The hearts of these men were bursting with joy even although, in modern language, they had just emptied their bank accounts. It is a well-known fact that a man's happiness does not ebb and flow with the fluctuations of his savings, but that lesson is hard to learn. Here were people who had donated willingly, and with purity of motive, a "perfect heart", and for them the end result was sheer pleasure. What a contrast to those who harbour ambitions to be rich, and consequently pierce themselves through "with *many sorrows*" (1 Tim 6.10). Which would we rather be? Anyone whose compulsory reading included Silas Marner will never forget the miser's desolation at the loss of his hoard. It is fiction, but true to life. By contrast, the leaders here were thrilled to be benefactors.

As David witnessed this outpouring of generosity, and the subsequent ecstasy, his old leathery weather-beaten face was wreathed in smiles, for "David the king also rejoiced with great joy". The joy of the people was infectious, and there is surely a lesson in that for us. Sacrificial living brings joy, a joy that spreads to others. "I joy, and rejoice with you all. For the same cause also do ye joy, and rejoice with me" (Phil 2.17-18). May we be those who spread sunshine rather than gloom.

Verses 10-19: David's Worship

The "Wherefore" of v.10 relates to what has gone before. The reason for David blessing the Lord was his joy at seeing such a response to his appeal, such spontaneous open-handedness on the part of his subjects. David's poetic spirit had been stirred, and now he articulated his appreciation to God in the choicest of language, guided by the Spirit of course.

His prayer was public, "before all the congregation", in contrast to the private expression of worship on the day when he "sat before the Lord" (17.16). However, there are similar sentiments in both prayers, an indication that the way a man prays privately is often reflected in his public expressions of praise and supplication.

His first thought was to worship God on account of the greatness of His being. Addressing Him as Jehovah Elohim, he firstly acknowledged His eternal existence, the fact that He is "Blessed...for ever and ever". "Even from everlasting to everlasting, thou art God" (Ps 90.2).

God's "greatness" was mentioned for He is "the great God..." (Titus 2.13). Power, glory, victory and majesty are all ascribed to Him. The word "victory" (5331) also carries the thought of "for ever". These attributes are evidence of the fact that "all that is in the heaven and in the earth is thine". "The earth is the Lord's, and the fulness thereof" (Ps 24.1). The Creator God is unsurpassed in glorious majesty.

God is not only "head above all" (v.11), but "the kingdom" is His; "thou reignest over all" (v.12). So the Head of creation is the Head of the kingdom, whether you take that kingdom to mean God's rule in a general sense in

His universe, or, more particularly, the kingdom of Israel. The point is, God is absolutely sovereign.

At v.12 David pondered the practical issues of God's sovereignty. He is the One who bestows "riches and honour" and so, because of His beneficence the people had been in a position to give so bountifully. "Every good gift and every perfect gift is from above, and cometh down from the Father of lights" (James 1.17).

Any power the ruling classes wielded had been derived from Him. "Power and might" were in His hand, and it was His prerogative to "make great". They had derived their authority from Him. New Testament teaching confirms David's musings here. "There is no power but of God: the powers that be are ordained of God", and hence our responsibility to be subject to them (Rom 13.1).

David's prayer seems to switch between him speaking on behalf of the people using the plural pronoun "we" as at v.13, and then personal supplication as at v.17 - "I", and, "As for me". Brothers who participate publicly in a prayer meeting should keep in mind that it is wise to employ the plural pronouns, for they are speaking to God on behalf of the whole company.

Verse 14 seems to encapsulate the basic elements of Bible stewardship. David understood that neither he nor his people had any inherent power, or any ability to generate the resources required for building the temple. For that they had been dependent on God: "all things come of thee". Because all their resources had come from God, they really belonged to Him: "thine own". This meant that what they had given to God was really His own anyway! This is proper, legitimate spiritual recycling! The same principle is restated in the New Testament. We give to the Lord "as God hath prospered (us)" (1 Cor 16.2), so we too are responsible for what God has entrusted to us as stewards. The danger is that we see our financial resources as hard-earned cash to be hoarded for the sake of a feeling of security, or to be used selfishly in financing a lavish life-style. Whether what we possess is the result of diligent toil or prudent thriftiness, let us remember that it all belongs to Him, and He has the ability to "blow" on it should He see fit (Hag 1.9). David's subjects did not clasp God's resources with a tight fist, but, said the monarch, "of thine own we have given thee". The way in which they did it was so commendable, "so willingly". What an example! Let us remember that there will come a day when we will hear the summons, "give an account of thy stewardship" (Lk 16.2).

Frequently David had been described as "David the king", but here he asked, "Who am I?". As noted at 17.16, it was understandable for him to pose that question when he was just a boy in from the country (1 Sam 18.18), but this is "David the king"! His eminence had not inflated his ego; he felt his own nothingness and the humble circumstances of his people. Great men often felt insignificant in the presence of Deity. Abraham described himself as being "but dust and ashes" (Gen 18.27). It behoves us all to feel how unimportant we really are, for it is only then that we are usable in His hand.

In vv.15-16 David expressed the thought that because they were just strangers and sojourners like their forefathers, and because life was as fleeting as "a shadow", there would have been no expectation of them amassing the resources needed for God's house had He not supplied them. A lifetime of toil could never have done it. Thus, said David, it "cometh of thine hand, and is all thine own". Paul asked the self-important Corinthians, "what hast thou that thou didst not receive?" (1 Cor 4.7).

If life is as transient as is stated here, what point is there in frantically pursuing pleasures and riches? It would be far better to be wise in the use of the resources that God has directed towards us, like Moses, having "respect unto the recompense of the reward" (Heb 11.26).

In his prayer, David raised the thought of motives and integrity (v.17). There is no point in harbouring impure motives, for "thou triest the heart". There is no point in underhand dealing, for "thou…hast pleasure in uprightness". Ananias and Sapphira had evidently forgotten these basic facts about the character of God. It cost them their lives (Acts 5.1-10). Taking divine omniscience and divine pleasure into account will influence our thinking and behaviour significantly as with David here. "As for me, in the uprightness of mine heart I have willingly offered all these things." He was not making any boast about this to men. He was addressing God, the God whom he had just described as trying the heart. He was transparent before Him.

God had pleasure in David; now David expressed his personal pleasure in His people, having witnessed their bountiful giving: "now have I seen *with joy* thy people". It is so good when God's people afford their spiritual guides a good degree of pleasure. This is what Paul wanted from Philemon: "Yea, brother, let me have joy of thee in the Lord" (v.20). John had experienced it as he had heard of the consistency of Gaius. "I have no greater joy than to hear that my children walk in truth" (3 Jn v.4). May we all be a source of joy to those who watch for our souls.

In vv.18-19 David turns from praise to prayer: first of all prayer for the people, and then prayer for his son Solomon. There were two requests for his people. First, that their present attitude would be a permanent feature of their lives: "keep this for ever in the imagination of the thoughts of the heart of thy people". David was aware of the fact that there is a need for consistency and that embarking on the right road does not rule out deviation further down the track. Thus he prayed for their preservation.

Second, he prayed that God would "prepare" (3559), or establish their heart towards Him. There is always the need to focus the heart on God, to make Him the centre of our interests and affections. It requires divine help for this, and so David prayed.

David then prayed specifically for Solomon that he would have a "perfect heart". Verse 17 speaks of a tried heart and an upright heart. Verse 18 mentions a prepared heart. Now there is reference to a perfect heart, and David almost defines what he means by asking help for Solomon to keep God's commandments. A perfect heart is submissive to God's commands and obedient to His will: "*to do* all these things". David had made provision for "the palace". It was Solomon's responsibility to build it, but there was no point in embarking on the project if first of all he did not have the kind of heart that was submissive to God in the general round of life. "A temple without wholehearted devotion to the law was an empty gesture" (Thompson). Labour can never be in vain if it is "in the Lord", that is the labourer being subject to His authority as Lord of the life (1 Cor 15.58). Men ought to "serve as deacons, *if they be blameless*" (1 Tim 3.10, RV). Service and sanctity must go in tandem.

Professor Heading suggests the difference between commandments, testimonies and statutes to be as follows. "The 'testimonies' would be the tables of stone in the ark, while the 'commandments' would be the large amplification in the books of Moses; the 'statutes' suggest commandments in service, and for work in the land".

Verses 20-22a: Congregational Worship

Having worshipped and prayed, David now encouraged "all the congregation" to bless God, which they did to a man; note the repetition of the word "all". In fact that little word is sprinkled liberally throughout the whole chapter and is worthy of note.

David described God as "the Lord *your* God". They blessed "the Lord God *of their fathers*". It might be wrong to presume that the God of their fathers had not become their God, but it would be right to note that everyone must have a personal relationship with Him rather than relying on family history. God spoke to Jacob about being "the Lord God of Abraham thy father, and the God of Isaac" (Gen 28.13). Within a few verses, Jacob saw the need of making Him "my God" (v.21). Regeneration is "not of blood" (Jn 1.13), that is spiritual blessing is not hereditary.

As they expressed their worship, their posture is of note for they "bowed down their heads". In recent history a new expression has been coined - people speak of "body language", and body language is often a give-away as to a person's inner feelings. The bowed heads were an indication of reverence, a token of their sense of awe after hearing such a masterful description of the majesty of their God. It is significant that when the Lord Jesus spoke to His Father on the eve of His crucifixion, He "lifted up his eyes to heaven" (Jn 17.1). There was always a clear sky between Him and the Father, nothing that would ever have created any feeling of being uncomfortable. By contrast, a publican "would not lift up so much as his eyes unto heaven" (Lk 18.13).

"The king" also was acknowledged respectfully by the people. David's subjects stand as an illustration of Peter's command, "Fear God. Honour the king" (1 Pet 2.17).

Their appreciation was expressed in the multitude of offerings that were presented to the Lord the next day, and the occasion was savoured in that they "did eat and drink before the Lord". "Sacrifices in abundance" must have included many peace offerings, of which the offerers had their share. The vast number of offerings was surpassed on the day that the temple was dedicated (1 Kings 8.63), and yet written over it all are the words of the writer to the Hebrews, "it is not possible that the blood of bulls and of goats should take away sins" (10.4). Bless God for "the one sacrifice for sins" (v.12).

The fact that they were "before the Lord" explains the words "with great gladness". When God is given His place, and when His presence is sought, it will inevitably bring joy to His people. In the pristine days of Christian testimony, when the believers were continuing steadfastly, they "did eat their meat with gladness and singleness of heart" (Acts 2.42-47). We forfeit that joy when His position is usurped, and when His commands are ignored. "Before the Lord" is probably an indication that they were congregated in proximity to the tent where the ark was located temporarily.

Verses 22b-25: Solomon the King

There has been debate regarding the timing of the phrase, "they made Solomon the son of David the king the second time". Some see it as anticipating a proper coronation for Solomon after his hurried inauguration at the time of Adonijah's bid for power (1 Kings 1), and in that sense it is regarded as making him king "the second time". However, it does seem more in keeping with the context that right there and then, on the day of feasting, opportunity was taken to anoint him as king, giving due attention to the fact that David had just declared that such was the divine intention (28.5). It was "the second time" in that David had indicated it back at 23.1. His anointing in 1 Kings 1.39 would have been a further confirmation of his kingship.

At the time of Solomon's anointing, Zadok was anointed as high priest. Some have seen this as proof that the incident here was subsequent to the events of 1 Kings 1 and 2. However, that need not necessarily be the case. Abiathar and Zadok had operated jointly, and Zadok would emerge as the rightful high priest subsequent to Abiathar's defection to Adonijah (1 Kings 1.7). Possibly it was the anointing of Zadok here that prompted Abiathar to become an accomplice in the plot. Maybe he reckoned that if Adonijah secured the top political job, then he would have the top religious job restored to him, but we are back in the realm of conjecture. Whatever the circumstances, when eventually the dust settled Solomon was king and Zadok was priest.

Just as vv.26-27 give a summary of David's reign, so vv.23-24 give a summary of Solomon's accession and his early days as monarch. The phrase "the throne of the Lord" is interesting. It is an indication that Israel's king was acting in God's interests, he was administering as God's viceroy. David had described the kingdom as being "the kingdom of the Lord" (28.5). The Spirit now reinforces that concept by describing the throne as His. Even today, Christian leaders should keep in mind that they function by divine appointment and as responsible to "the chief Shepherd" (1 Pet 5.4).

As far as Solomon's literal throne was concerned, it was an exquisite structure that had no equal in the then known world, with its ivory, gold, and ornamental lions (1 Kings 10.18-20). We are told more about it than about the throne of God in Revelation 4.2! There, of course, the spotlight is upon the throne-sitter rather than on the throne itself.

Solomon "prospered" and no one could doubt it when reading the detailed account of his reign in 1 Kings. He prospered materially, with silver and gold becoming as commonplace as stones, and cedars as plentiful as sycomores (10.27; see also 2 Chr 1.15). He prospered intellectually for "God gave Solomon wisdom and understanding exceeding much, and largeness of heart, even as the sand that is on the sea shore" (4.29). He prospered culturally; he was a celebrated author and poet with a wide knowledge of flora and fauna on which to base his musings (4.32-34). He prospered politically, for during his reign "Judah and Israel dwelt safely, every man under his vine and under his fig tree" (4.25).

"All Israel obeyed him", and v.24 of this chapter expands that by telling us in effect that all the upper echelons of society "submitted themselves" to the one who was now described as "Solomon the king". "All Israel" had not obeyed David just so quickly when he came to the throne. Solomon enjoyed an immediate supremacy that his father had never experienced.

Apparently the word "submitted" (5414) has a literal meaning of giving or putting the hand under, a reference to them putting their hands under Solomon's and raising his hand to their lips as a token of allegiance (see Young's Literal Translation for example).

As far as submission was concerned, there was the brief initial scare when Adonijah attempted to seize the throne, but throughout the most of Solomon's reign there was complete submission to the king. It was only when he rebelled against God that some of his subjects began to rebel against him (1 Kings 11), and it did come out later that there had been undercurrents of discontent (12.3-4). The peace and prosperity of his reign point forward to the last millennium of human history when the Lord Jesus will reign over the world and impose His authority upon it. While the initial subjects of that kingdom will be the "righteous", the "sheep" of Matthew 25.32-34, as it runs its course there will be "a people that shall be born" (Ps 22.31). While each of them will acknowledge the authority of the King, it will be a grudging acknowledgement on the part of some, and thus the devil will find their hearts to be fertile soil in which to sow seeds of rebellion for the last great assault on the theocracy (Rev 20.7-10).

Verse 25 explains the reason for Solomon's greatness: "the Lord magnified Solomon exceedingly in the sight of all Israel", and as far as "royal majesty" was concerned he was quite unique. Other kings were unique in different ways. Hezekiah was unique as far as his trust in God was concerned (2 Kings 18.5). Josiah was unique in the way he committed himself wholeheartedly to God and His Word in order to effect revival (23.25), but the regal majesty of Solomon was unsurpassed. Never forget though, "a greater than Solomon is here" (Mt 12.42).

Verses 26-30: David...reigned...And he died

The book concludes with a summary of David's reign and a brief statement of his death. There is no lengthy obituary, but just a terse statement of fact. It has often been remarked that the Chronicler omitted much of the previous history if it had no bearing on his major theme of the building of a house for God. David's contribution to that had been cited, so there was now the brief record of his death; he exits the stage. There was no need to rehearse the details of the final illness that left him such a pathetic figure. There was no need to go into all the political intrigue that surrounded that last illness. It was all irrelevant to the Chronicler's purpose. He focuses on the house of God as an encouragement to his own generation to be busy in a similar project.

The Chronicler will commence the second book with a brief introduction to Solomon's reign and then get back to the point; "Solomon determined to build an house for the name of the Lord" (2.1).

At v.26 there is the reminder of David's humble origins, he was "the son of Jesse", and yet he "reigned over all Israel". The length of his reign receives mention, forty years, as do his respective seats of power, Hebron and Jerusalem.

"And he died". As with all others, it was inescapable. In his poem "The Spade", I. Y. Ewan penned these penetrating words:

Inevitable winner
Where sin has left its taint:
The master of the sinner,
The servant of the saint.

The fact that "he died in a good old age" is a testimony to the preserving hand of God upon him. Goliath had threatened to tear him apart. He escaped death by a hairsbreadth as more than once Saul's javelin missed its target. On an occasion his own men had threatened to stone him. His own son Absalom was intent on killing him. But with all that history he survived till old age and died of natural causes in his own bed. "But thou, O Lord, art a shield for me" (Ps 3.3).

The death of David stands in contrast to that of the Lord Jesus. David "died in a good old age, full of days". The Lord Jesus was "cut off out of the land of the living" (Is 53.8).

David was "full of...riches". He was a poor man who had become rich (1 Sam 18.23). The Lord Jesus, especially in His death, "became poor" (2 Cor 8.9). Messiah was "cut off" and had "nothing" (Dan 9.26, RV).

David was "full of…honour", whereas shame was connected with the death of the Lord Jesus Christ: Psalm 69.19 refers to reproach, shame, and dishonour.

After his death David left a son, for "Solomon his son reigned in his stead", but of the Lord Jesus it was said, "and who shall declare his generation?" (Is 53.8).

Samuel, Nathan and Gad were David's three biographers, encompassing the whole of his life, "first and last", that is from the time we are first introduced to him as the "ruddy" youth with the "beautiful countenance" (1 Sam 16.12), to the time we see him as a feeble old man shivering in his bed as he awaited death (1 Kings 1.1). Their stories are not necessarily part of the inspired record although doubtless there would be much duplication of material.

"The times that went over him" is an interesting phrase that encapsulates the shifting circumstances of David's life. He was a hero and then an outlaw. He was rejected and then enthroned. Sometimes his songs were exhilarating. On other occasions they were in the nature of a dirge. These diverse circumstances are illustrated in the Feast of Tabernacles when for the week of the feast the people lodged in makeshift booths. These comprised of, among other things, the interweaving of branches of weeping willows, and palm trees (Lev 23.40). Anne R. Cousin caught the atmosphere of it all in one of her hymns.

With mercy and with judgment
My web of time He wove,
And aye the dews of sorrow
Were lustred with His love.
I'll bless the hand that guided,
I'll bless the heart that planned,
When throned where glory dwelleth
In Immanuel's land.

The three narratives encompassed his whole reign, his power, his relationship with his own people Israel and with the nations around. Yet for all that, only three books were needed to tell the story. He was the greatest man of his generation, yet only three biographers were needed. By contrast, if everything that could have been recorded about the Lord Jesus had been recorded, "I suppose that even the world itself could not contain the books that should be written" (Jn 21.25). Great though David was, his greatness pales when he is placed side by side with the One who is David's Lord and David's Son (Mt 22.41-46). His brightness is eclipsed by Him who is "the root and the offspring of David, and the bright and morning star" (Rev 22.16).

And so the curtain falls on the man in whose heart a desire for a house for God was born, and whose single mindedness in latter years caused the dream to take root in the nation. Once more we salute his willingness to devote himself to the project although he would never see even the foundations dug, or the first stone laid. All of that would come within Solomon's remit, the record of which is contained in what we call 2 Chronicles. As stated at the start, as far as the Hebrew Scriptures are concerned, the two volumes are one, and so the narrative sweeps on relentlessly until eventually it comes to this: "the glory of the Lord filled the house of God" (2 Chr 5.14, RV). At last, David's aspirations had become concrete reality.

2 CHRONICLES

W. Gustafson

CONTENTS

BIBLIOGRAPHY

Ackroyd, Peter R. *The Dimension Bible Guides, 7: 1 & 2 Chronicles.* Dimension Books, 1969.

Not intended to be detailed exposition, but offers the non-professional reader guideposts and suggestions.

Allen, J. *What the Bible Teaches: Revelation.* John Ritchie, Ltd, 1997.

The author has been very thorough in his work on Revelation and has produced an outstanding book.

Allen, Leslie C. *The Communicator's Commentary: 1 & 2 Chronicles.* Word Books, Publisher, 1987.

Emphasizes God's ways with His people.

Archer, Gleason. *The NIV International Encyclopedia of Bible Difficulties.* Zondervan, 1982.

Defends the consistency and authority of the Bible.

Autrey, C. E. *Revivals of the Old Testament.* Zondervan, 1963.

Has some profitable observations about revivals.

Barber, Cyril. *The Books of Kings, Volume 1* (only for chapter 12). Wipf & Stock Publishers, 2004; and *Focus on the Bible: 2 Chronicles.* Christian Focus Publications, 2004.

These works have been greatly appreciated. However, one insight was found to be not in accord with the Word of God.

Barnes, William Emery. *The Cambridge Bible for Schools and Colleges: The Books of Chronicles.* Cambridge University Press, 1899.

This book has helpful comments on some of the kings.

Bennett, W. H. *The Expositor's Bible, Volume II (II Samuel to Job).* Baker Book House, 1903 and 1982.

Regrettably, critical aspects are allowed to penetrate his treatment of Biblical text.

Carroll, B. H. *An Interpretation of the English Bible: The Divided Kingdom and the Restoration Period.* Baker Book House, 1948.

A little profitable material was found in this work.

Constable, Thomas L. *The Bible Knowledge Commentary, Old Testament.* Victor Books, 1985.

A compilation of notes intended for the author's theology students, it is designed to lead to a better understanding of the Scriptures.

Coggins, R. I. *1 and 2 Chronicles.* Cambridge University Press, 1976.

Contains some profitable comments on the kings.

Courson, Jon. *The Application Commentary, Old Testament, Volume 1.* Thomas Nelson Publishers, 2005.

The author suggests some very good applications.

Criswell, W. A. *The Criswell Study Bible.* Thomas Nelson Publishers, 1979.

A premillenialist writer who has authored a number of outstanding books. His "Study Bible" has a good many profitable brief comments.

Curtis, Edward & Masden, Albert. *The International Critical Commentary: The Books of Chronicles*. T and T Clark, 1994.

This set may be complete by now. A different writer has written each commentary and they vary in quality and in theological presuppositions.

Dillard, Raymond B. *Word Biblical Commentary: 2 Chronicles*. Word Books, 1987.

A good commentary which is always worth consulting.

Edersheim, Alfred. *Bible History, Old Testament: Volumes V, VI, VII*. Wm. B. Eerdmans Publishing Company, 1954.

A clear simple review of the history of Israel from before the flood to the time of the Babylonian captivity. He was an outstanding Hebrew Christian scholar and is always worth diligent reading.

Ellicott, C. J. *Ellicott's Bible Commentary in One Volume*. Zondervan, 1971.

This work represents the careful analysis, critical selection and condensation of nearly 5,000 pages of the eight large volumes.

Erdman, Charles R. *Handbook to the Bible.* Wm. B. Eerdmans Publishing Company, 1973.

Erdman has written important paperback commentaries on most of the book of the Bible and they are all worth reading.

Farrar, F. W. *The Expositor's Bible, Volume 2: (II Samuel to Job)*. Baker Book House, 1903, 1982.

Thoughtful, but in places it manifests an unwise dependence on the Septuagint and follows some higher critical themes in vogue at the time of writing.

Fereday, W. W. *Solomon and His Temple;* and *Josiah and Revival.* John Ritchie, Ltd.

An assembly writer who has concise, helpful comments.

Flanigan, James. *What the Bible Teaches: Psalms*. John Ritchie, Ltd, 2001.

Flanigan has also written on Song of Solomon, three of the Minor Prophets, and Hebrews for "What the Bible Teaches". His material is always profitable and often Christ exalting.

Free, Joseph P. *Archeology and Bible History*. Van Kampen Press, 1950.

He writes from the position of a Bible believer and he often shows how archeology confirms the truth of Scripture.

Gaebelein, Arno C. *The Annotated Bible, Volume 1: Genesis to II Chronicles*; and *A Concise Commentary on the Whole Bible*. Moody Press; Loizeaux Brothers.

Among the best books for a Bible student's library. The Annotated Bible is especially helpful for lay people.

Habershon, Ada R. *Hidden Pictures in the Old Testament.* Kregel Publications, 1916, 1982.

A clear writer on Biblical subjects.

Haldeman, I. M. *Bible Expositions, Volume 1.* Dunham Publishing Company, 1964.

He has some good expositions in two volumes.

Heading, John. *Understanding 1 & 2 Chronicles.* Walterick Publishers, 1980.

An assembly writer who has also written two books for "What the Bible Teaches".

Henry, Matthew. *Commentary on the Whole Bible in One Volume.* Zondervan, 1961.

Dr. F. F. Bruce wrote that this work was, "One of the greatest theological classics of English literature…with his sure spiritual instinct for the sense of Scripture he presents its wholesome and abiding essence in a style of rare pithiness".

Hill, Andrew. *The NIV Application Commentary: 1 & 2 Chronicles.* Zondervan, 2003.

This commentary not only focuses on the meaning of the original text but also on present applications. The author explains what the Bible means and how it speaks to us today.

Jamieson, Fausset & Brown. *Commentary on the Whole Bible.* Zondervan, 1961, 1971.

C. H. Spurgeon wrote about this work: "It contains so great a variety of information that if a man had no other exposition he would find himself at no great loss if he possessed this and used it diligently".

Keil, C. F. & Delitzsch, F. *Commentary on the Old Testament: The Books of Kings,* and *The Books of Chronicles.* Wm. B. Eerdmans Publishing Company, 1875.

For many years this work has been a scholarly conservative reference work. He often quotes in Hebrew.

Kelly, William. *Lectures on the Books of Chronicles.* Bible Truth Publishers, 1963.

One of the early assembly writers who wrote prolifically and accurately.

Knapp, Christopher. *The Kings of Judah and Israel.* Triangle Press, 1908.

A very good commentary. Knapp is especially good in pointing out the moral lessons in 2 Chronicles.

Knapp, Christopher. *Life's Principles from Kings of the Old Testament.* AMG Publishers, 1998.

Some good applications.

Lockyer, Herbert. *All the Kings and Queens of the Bible.* Zondervan, 1961.

In this great book of royalty you have the rise and fall of mighty dynasties and kingdoms and all the subtle intrigues of court life.

Long, David Boyd. *Revival, A Study in Biblical Patterns.* John Ritchie, Ltd, 1993.

This assembly writer has written a profitable book on revival. He has an excellent applications in chs.29 and 34.

MacArthur, John. *The MacArthur Study Bible, New King James Version.* Word Bibles, 1997.

A well-known and often recommended writer.

MacDonald, William. *Believer's Bible Commentary.* Thomas Nelson Publishers, 1989.

The purpose of this commentary is to give the average Christian reader a basic knowledge of what the Bible is all about.

MacIntosh, C. H. *The MacIntosh Treasury.* Loiseaux Brothers, 1898, 1976, 1987.

Worth reading and especially evocative.

Maclaren, Alexander. *Expositions of Holy Scriptures, Volume 2: Second Kings, Chronicles, Ezra and Nehemiah.* Wm. B. Eerdmans Publishing Company, 1959.

Rich in spiritual insight and scholarship.

McConville, J. G. *The Daily Study Bible Series: I & II Chronicles.* The Westminster John Knox Press, 1984.

This book helps on technical points and has some excellent applications.

McShane, Albert. *I & II Kings.* John Ritchie, Ltd, 2002.

An assembly writer who has accurate and helpful applications.

Meyer, F. B. *Bible Commentary.* Tyndale House Publishers, 1979.

A popular devotional writer who is often helpful.

Moldenke, Harold N. & Alma L. *Plants of the Bible.* Chronica Botanica Company, 1952.

A very thorough work of 328 large pages and 36 pages of photos.

Murphy, James G. *The Books of the Chronicles.* T & T Clark.

A thoughtful work, but has only 154 pages.

Myers, Jacob M. *The Anchor Bible, II Chronicles.* Doubleday, 1965.

While attempting to validate the text of Scripture, the writer gives archeological data alongside the narrative.

Nelson Study Bible, NKJV. Thomas Nelson Publishers, 1997.

This study Bible combines a thorough exposition of Scripture with an accessible and spiritual style, and the annotations offer helpful explanations and theological insight.

Newberry, Thomas. *The Types of the Temple.* John Ritchie, Ltd.

A small book that exalts Christ and is helpful.

New Bible Commentary, Revised. Wm. B. Eerdmans Publishing Company, 1970.

New Bible Commentary, 21st Edition. Intervarsity Press, 1916, 1994.

New Layman's Bible Commentary in One Volume. Zondervan, 1979.

One of the editors writes: "We desire to place in the hands of Christians of all types and denominations a volume that takes its stand upon the historical and orthodox belief of the authority of Holy Scripture".

Dyer, Charles, & Merrill, Gene. *The Old Testament Explorer.* Word Publishing, 2001.

Page, John B. D. *Christ and Solomon's Temple.* Gospel Tract Publications, 1994.

Very helpful on the temple of Solomon. This book is the culmination of many years of study, research, writing and ministry by the author on the subject.

Parker, Joseph. *Preaching Through the Bible, Volume V.* Baker Book House, 1987.

C. H. Spurgeon said of Parker that "He condenses wonderfully, and throws a splendour of diction over all that he pours forth…one is struck with his singular ability and special originality".

Patterson, R. D. & Austel, Hermann J. *The Expositor's Bible Commentary, Volume 4: I Kings-Job.* Regency Reference Library, 1988.

In this book there are worthwhile comments on most chapters.

Payne, J. Barton. *The Expositor's Bible Commentary, Volume 4.* Regency Reference Library, 1988.

The author has also contributed to "The Wycliffe Commentary", and articles to "Bibliotheca Sacra".

Pierson, Arthur T. *The Bible and Spiritual Life.* Scripture Truth Book Company.

This book of fifteen splendid addresses emphasizes the fact that for all the cravings and crises of man's moral and spiritual life this Book of God is the exact provision, satisfaction and guide; that only He who, having made man and thus knows what is in man could have made a book which so anticipates and answers all the needs of his higher nature.

The Pulpit Commentary, Volume 6: 2 Chronicles.

Some comments worth considering.

Rawlinson, George. *The Bible Commentary, (F. C. Cook, Ed), Volume II and Volume III*. Baker Book House, 1971, 1981.

The Lives and Times of the Kings of Israel and Judah. James Family Christian Publishers, 1979.

This commentary has produced a good number of worthy additions.

Riddle, John. *Kings of Judah.* John Ritchie, Ltd, 2003.

This assembly writer has written three commentaries for "What the Bible Teaches" on Isaiah, Jeremiah, and Lamentations. He is worth considering.

Rodgers, William. *52 Bible Lessons, Series 3*. John Ritchie, Ltd; *52 Bible Lessons, Series 1*; and *Bible Notes and Expositions.* LM Press Limited, and John Ritchie, Ltd.

An assembly writer who has profitable and concise insights or comments not found anywhere else.

Rossier, Henri, L. *Meditations on 2 Chronicles;* and *Meditations on 2 Kings*. Believer's Bookshelf Inc. 1993, 1988.

This commentary has a good number of comments, insights and applications.

Ryrie, Charles Caldwell. *Ryrie Study Bible, Expanded Edition, KJV.* Moody Press, 1986, 1994.

A work that can be highly recommended.

Sailhammer, John. *First & Second Chronicles*. Moody Press, 1983.

This brief commentary, written by an evangelical, has profitable comments worth considering for most of the kings.

Scroggie, W. Graham. *The Psalms, Volume Five*; and *The Unfolding Drama of Redemption.* Fleming H. Revell Company, 1948, 1965.

Cyril Barber recommends the second book with these words: "A valuable set for the expositor…each book of the Bible is outlined and receives careful comment…numerous charts highlight God's redemptive program".

Selman, Martin J. *Tyndale Old Testament Commentaries: 2 Chronicles;* and *Tyndale Old Testament Commentaries: 1 Chronicles.* Intervarsity Press, 1994.

These commentaries are consistently accurate with good insights.

Shultz, S. J. *The International Standard Bible Encyclopedia, Fully Revised.* Wm. B. Eerdmans Publishing Company, 1986.

Slotki, I. W. *Books of the Bible: Chronicles.* The Soncino Press, 1952.

This commentary is designed primarily for the lay person and aims at giving direction for the understanding and appreciation of the Bible.

Smith, Wilbur, M. *The Glorious Revival under King Hezekiah.*

He has excellent material on the revival of Hezekiah's reign that is not found elsewhere.

Spurgeon, Charles H. *Men of the Old Testament.* Marshall, Morgan & Scott, 1960.

As with all his many books, worth considering.

Spurrell, Helen. *A Translation of the Old Testament Scriptures*. James Nisbet, 1985.

An interesting translation of the unpointed Hebrew Old Testament Scriptures.

Thiele, Edwin R. *The Mysterious Numbers of the Hebrew Kings, New Revised Edition.* Kregel Publications, 1983; and *A Chronology of the Hebrew Kings.* Academic Books, 1977.

Dr. Thiele has solved most of the problems related to the chronology of the Hebrew kings. By carefully studying the Biblical data, he determined the dating methods of the early Hebrew scribes; he has succeeded in producing a chronology that is consistent with most of the Scriptural records and the data of other material of the ancient world.

Thompson, J. A. *The New American Commentary: 1, 2 Chronicles.* Broadman and Holman Publishers, 1994.

His book on Chronicles is excellent with many useful comments.

Torrey, R. A. *Difficulties in the Bible.* Woodlawn, 1996.

His books are worth considering. He has some good answers to the difficulties in the Bible.

Traylor, John H. Jr. *The Layman's Bible Book Commentary: 1 & 2 Kings, 2 Chronicles*. Broadman Press, 1981.

Brief helpful comments on the kings.

Unger, Merrill F. *Unger's Commentary on the Old Testament, Volume 1.* Moody Press, 1981.

Written for lay people. Readily available rich thoughts.

Vine, W. E. *Expository Dictionary of New Testament Words.* Oliphants Ltd, 1940, 1956.

No student of the Scriptures can afford to be without this remarkable work.

Whitcomb, John C. Jr. *Solomon to the Exile, Studies in Kings and Chronicles.* Baker Book House, 1971.

Cyril Barber comments: "Recreates the Old Testament setting, graphically depicts the cause of the decline in Israel and Judah, and draws valid lessons from those incidents that are applied to the needs of the present".

Wiersbe, Warren, *The Bible Exposition Commentary, Old Testament History*. David C. Cooke, 2007.

This book is interesting and well worthwhile considering.

Wilcock, Michael. *The Bible Speaks Today: The Message of Chronicles.* Intervarsity Press, 1987.

This worthwhile commentary is very readable. He accurately makes the Chronicles come alive but also makes the message plain.

Williams, George. *The Student's Commentary on the Holy Scriptures*. Kregel Publications, 1956.

This commentary has material worth considering.

Williamson, H. G. M. *The New Century Bible Commentary: 1 and 2 Chronicles.* Wm. B. Eerdmans Publishing Company, 1982.

Making full use of a wide range of studies by Jewish and Christian scholars, this commentary offers a wealth of new insight and conclusions.

Wycliffe Bible Commentary. Moody Press, 1962.

Brief comments by evangelicals on each book of the Bible.

Zondervan King James Study Bible. Zondervan, 2002.

Has some comments that should be considered.

Zondervan Pictorial Bible Dictionary. Regency Reference Library, 1963, 1967.

Beautifully illustrated, and contains a wealth of material. However, it lacks cohesion and is not as good as some other Bible Dictionaries.

INTRODUCTION TO THE REIGN OF SOLOMON
(Chapters 1 to 9)

Originally 1 and 2 Chronicles were one book, but when the Septuagint (LXX) translation of the Old Testament into Greek was made, the translators divided it into two. The Chronicler is particularly concerned with the reigns of David and Solomon. There are 19 chapters about David and nine about Solomon. There are only two other kings given as many as four chapters: Jehoshaphat and Hezekiah. The accounts of David and Solomon are closely related. David did all that he could do to prepare for the building of the temple and Solomon actually built and dedicated it. "The reigns of the two kings are really a single unit, as Solomon's involvement in David's preparations has illustrated (1 Chr 22 and 28-29). The sense of partnership continues here, particularly in several passages unique to Chronicles where David is linked with Solomon (e.g. 2.3,7; 3.1; 6.42; 7.10; 8.14)" (Selman).

The beginning of the two reigns was very similar. 1 Chronicles 11.9 states, "So David waxed greater and greater: for the Lord of hosts was with him". 2 Chronicles 1.1 records about Solomon that "the Lord his God was with him, and magnified him exceedingly". It was, furthermore, central to David's desire for Solomon that the Lord would be with him, for the specific purpose of building the temple (1 Chr 22.11). "This…amounted to David's recognition that there was a total purpose for himself and Solomon together (see 1 Chr 17) which could only be achieved in Solomon's reign. It was Solomon who must build" (McConville).

"Of added significance is the fact that the Chronicler sought to show the relevance of the Word of the Lord (no matter how long ago it was given) to the needs of the remnant that had returned to Judah. This was done with a view to strengthening their faith. His intent was to develop an intrinsic spirituality as opposed to a formal adherence to the ritualistic observances of rites and ceremonies" (Barber).

God had already fulfilled the first part of the promise of His covenant with David (1 Chr 17.10-14), to "build an house" for him by ensuring that his son Solomon sat on the throne. The completion of the Davidic covenant was dependent on the fulfillment of two conditions imposed by the Lord and reiterated by David to Solomon: the building of the temple (1 Chr 28.6,10) and obedience to the commandments of the Lord (1 Chr 28.7-9).

The Chronicler omitted David's sin with Bathsheba, and only included two things derogatory to him. Guided by the Holy Spirit he had a purpose in doing so. In 1 Chronicles 13 David had a good motive when he wanted to bring the ark (which spoke of God's presence) to its rightful place in Jerusalem. But he did wrong to bring it up on a new cart. There was judgment instead of blessing in that Uzza was smitten. It was commendable that David realized his mistake three months later and wanted then to go by God's Word (1 Chr 15.2,13,15). None but the Levites should carry the ark. The writer of the Chronicles thus emphasized the importance of always moving according to the Word of God. Therein is a lesson even for today. All of God's people should have a good motive, for example in wanting to see souls saved. But it would be against the Word of God to pursue this good object by using unscriptural means or working with unscriptural organizations.

The other record of David's wrongdoing is in 1 Chronicles 21 where he numbered God's people in response to Satan's provocation. Because of this, God sent a pestilence in which 70,000 men fell (1 Chr 21.14). When David saw the angel of the Lord with a drawn sword in his hand, he had an excellent attitude in saying, "I it is that have sinned and done evil indeed; but as for these sheep, what have they done? Let thine hand, I pray thee, O Lord my God, be on me, and on my father's house; but not on thy people, that they should be plagued" (1 Chr 21.17). Right after this, the angel of the Lord commanded Gad to tell David to set up an altar in the threshing floor of Ornan the Jebusite (v.18). That is the exact place where Solomon built the temple (2 Chr 3.1). The writer of the Chronicles is especially interested in everything connected with the temple.

The Chronicler also gives a favourable account of Solomon by omitting any record of his 700 wives and 300 concubines who led him into idolatry when he was old (1 Kings 11.1-13). However, the writer hints at the wrong in having those pagan wives when he writes Solomon's words about the daughter of Pharaoh as recorded in 2 Chronicles 8.11: "My wife shall not dwell in the house of David king of Israel, because the places are holy, whereunto the ark of the Lord hath come". The Chronicler does not draw attention to the adversaries that God stirred up against Solomon because of his departure from the Lord. Neither does he record God's words to him that He was going to rend the kingdom in his son's days because of Solomon's sins. The writer of the Chronicles wants his readers to follow the good things about Solomon. He assumes that his readers also have the account of Solomon's reign in 1 Kings 1 to 11.

The historian largely followed the record of Solomon given in 1 Kings, although he not only omitted derogatory things about Solomon, but also some things that would enhance the reader's assessment of the king because they were not in keeping with his purpose. He did not record his very wise judgment between the two harlots (1 Kings 3.16-28) nor his wisdom shown in the administration of his kingdom (1 Kings 4).

Instead of recording all the blemishes found in 1 Kings in the lives of David and Solomon, "the Chronicler portrays glorious, obedient, all conquering figures who enjoy not only divine blessing, but the total support of the people as well; he presents to us not only the David and Solomon of history, but also the David and Solomon of his messianic expectation" (Dillard).

"Perhaps, therefore, we can say that Chronicles has simply taken the most positive view possible of Solomon's actual career. The Kings and Chronicles accounts, taken together, become another testimony - alongside the whole Biblical picture of David - to the way that God deigns to use great sinners in the work of his kingdom, so much so that the Old Testament's latest picture of Solomon does not even remember his sins" (McConville).

The writer, inspired by the Holy Spirit, wanted to present the reigns of David and Solomon as ideal. We read in 2 Chronicles 11.16-17 of the ones who gave up houses and lands to come from the northern tribes to sacrifice to the Lord God of their fathers, "So they strengthened the kingdom of Judah, and made Rehoboam the son of Solomon strong, three years: for three years they walked in the way of David and Solomon". The best three kings of Judah are each recorded as doing as David had done: Jehoshaphat (17.3), Hezekiah (29.2), and Josiah (34.2). Ahaz did not do as David had done (28.1), which is in direct contrast to the conduct of his son (29.2).

The first major theme of 2 Chronicles concerns Solomon's building the temple. God considered this so important that He guided the Chronicler to write extensively (six chapters) about its construction and dedication. The temple was Solomon's most important accomplishment. The writer omitted much that would not have contributed to his purpose, and he also added that which would further his design. Curtis & Masden have the most thorough comparison of the accounts of Solomon in 1 Kings 1-11 and 2 Chronicles 1-9. They found 39 differences, some major and some minor.

Selman shows that "Chronicles has produced a simplified but distinctive portrayal of this king. This is best demonstrated by setting out the total structure of Solomon's reign, which shows a basic chiastic formation.

1.1-17: Solomon's wisdom, wealth, and fame
    2.1-18: Solomon prepares for the temple
        3.1-5.1: Construction of the temple
        5.2-7.22: Dedication of the temple
    8.1-16: Solomon completes the temple and other building work
8.17-9.28: Solomon's wisdom, wealth, and fame".

Dillard has a much more elaborate chiastic scheme. He states, "The argument for viewing the Chronicler's Solomon narrative as a chiasm would be enhanced if it could be shown that the author in all probability also used the same device as the scaffolding for other narratives. H. G. M. Williamson has demonstrated that two passages which appeared to be in disjointed disarray are in fact examples of studied symmetry constructed in chiasms". (Dillard is referring here to Williamson's book on 1 Chronicles 2, and 1 Chronicles 11-12.)

"The repetition of the report of Solomon's wealth from 1 Kings 10.26-29 at the beginning and the end of the literary unit form an inclusio or envelope construction for the message (cp. 2 Chr 1.14-17; 9.25-28). The recognition of this literary feature has led to the discovery of a chiastic arrangement of the narrative of Solomon's reign" (Hill).

The actual construction of the temple and its dedication are manifestly the center of the chiasm. There is also a link between chapters 1-2 and 8-9. The theme of the temple is also included in these chapters.

The Chronicler uses the account of the building of the Tabernacle as a model for his description of the building of the temple. He presents Solomon as a new Bezaleel, and Huram as a new Aholiab. Of all the thousands who worked on the Tabernacle and the temple these are the only four named for what they did. It is significant that the only references to Bezaleel outside of the record of the building of the Tabernacle in Exodus are in Chronicles - 1 Chronicles 2.20; 2 Chronicles 1.5.

Solomon is a new Bezaleel. God chose Bezaleel and designated him by name for the construction of the Tabernacle (Ex 31.2; 35.30-36.2; 38.22-23). God also chose Solomon and designated him by name for the building of the temple (1 Chr 22.9-10; 28.6; 29.1). Bezaleel and Solomon are both of the tribe of Judah (Ex 31.2; 35.30; 38.22). They both received wisdom from God (Ex 31.3; 35.30-31; 2 Chr 1.7-12). For the writer of the Chronicles that wisdom was especially for construction of the temple. "Both build a brazen altar for the sanctuary (2 Chr 1.5; 4.1; 7.7) - significantly, the brazen altar is not mentioned in the summary list of Huram's work (2 Chr 4.11-16). Both make the sanctuary furnishings (Ex 31.1-10; 37.10-29; 2 Chr 4.19-22)" (Zondervan KJV Study Bible). "In Chronicles Hiram does not praise God for giving David, 'a wise son over this great people' (1 Kings 5.7), but for 'a wise son...that might build an house for the Lord' (2 Chr 2.12)" (Dillard).

Huram is a new Aholiab. Aholiab is given a role as helper in Exodus 31.6. In the Kings account the temple and the palace are both recorded as finished (6.38; 7.1) before the record of the work of Huram in 7.13-45, but in Chronicles Huram is involved with the building of the temple from the beginning just as Aholiab was in relation to the Tabernacle (Ex 31.6; 2 Chr 2.13). 1 Kings only speaks of Huram skilled in works of brass (7.14), but Chronicles records that Huram had the same skills as Bezaleel and Aholiab (Ex 31.1-6; 35.30-36.2; 38.22-23; 2 Chr 2.14). The writer of Kings records that Huram's mother was a widow of the tribe of Napthali (1 Kings 7.14), but Chronicles states that Huram's mother was of the daughters of Dan (2 Chr 2.14) in that way giving Huram the same tribal ancestry as Aholiab (Ex 31.6; 35.34; 38.23). McShane gives a good explanation of the discrepancy. "If 'Dan' there (2 Chr 2.14) refers to the town of that name, it was situated in the tribe of Napthali, and was originally called 'Laish', or 'Leshem' but when the Danites took it over they called it 'Dan' (Josh 19.47). Like Timothy in the New Testament, he was the son of a mixed marriage for his mother was an Israelite and his father a man of Tyre, yet grace triumphed over human failure and made their son a chosen vessel to furnish the courts of the Lord".

God gave the pattern for the Tabernacle to Moses (Ex 25.1-30.38;

especially 25.9,40; 27.8). He gave the pattern for the temple to David who gave it to Solomon (1 Chr 28.11-19; especially vv.11 and 19 which is not recorded earlier). God also has a pattern in the New Testament for local churches. It is an encouragement to follow that pattern to notice that in Exodus 39 we read ten times that the Lord "commanded" Moses, and the same expression eight times in ch.40. That is followed by the glory of God filling the Tabernacle in Exodus 40.34-35. The glory of God also filled the temple in 2 Chronicles 7.1-3.

The people contributed willingly and generously for both structures (Ex 25.1-7; 36.3-7). What is recorded about giving to the temple in 1 Chronicles 29.1-9,14,17 is not recorded earlier. God appreciates all giving from saints that is done willingly, for "God loveth a cheerful giver" (2 Cor 9.7).

"The spoils of war are used as building materials for both Tabernacle and temple (Ex 3.21-22; 12.35-36; see 1 Chr 18.6-11 - not mentioned in Samuel and Kings)" (Zondervan KJV Study Bible). In the two references in Exodus God's people "asked" (RV and JND) of the Egyptians. Both references tell of God giving them favour with the Egyptians and spoiling them. God told Abraham many years earlier in Genesis 15.14, "…afterward shall they come out with great substance". What was given to the Israelites could easily be looked upon as their wages for years of slavery.

Dillard gives profitable material on the succession of Moses and Joshua as a paradigm for that of David and Solomon.

Worship is very important to the Chronicler and he emphasizes it during Solomon's reign. Solomon begins by offering one thousand burnt offerings (1.6). The writer of Chronicles is concerned for the heart as well as the form of worship (1.11; 6.7-8,14,30; 7.10-11). "However, the real emphasis of Chronicles is to underline that God's forgiveness is constantly and unexpectedly available to anyone who comes to him in humble repentance. The prime motive for prayer in the temple is that there is always hope for sinners, as God affirms in his remarkable promises in 7.12-16" (Selman).

2 CHRONICLES 1

Solomon's Reign

Introductory

Verse 1 continues the thought of 1 Chronicles 29.25 and strikes the keynote of the first nine chapters - the greatness of Solomon. This is followed by three paragraphs describing three well-known characteristics of Solomon's reign: his worship (vv.2-6); his wisdom (vv.7-13); and his wealth (vv.14-17). Verses 2–13 follow 1 Kings 3.4-4.1 quite closely, but vv.14-17 are taken from 1 Kings 10.26-29. Since the Chronicler re-arranged the position for "his wealth" so radically, it shows that he deliberately wanted to link these things together because all three are related to the building of the temple (that follows in the next chapter). This chapter thus serves as a fitting introduction to the section that follows on Solomon's reign.

"The theme of 1 Chronicles (genealogy and history through David) lays the foundation for the great king (Solomon), who in turn foreshadows the Greater than Solomon, the Lord Jesus Christ, in His rule of peace and splendour in the millennial kingdom (cp. Ps 2.7-12; 72.1-20; Is 9.7; 11.1-10; 12.1-6; 35.1-10)" (Unger). The glory of that kingdom will far outshine the glory of Solomon's kingdom.

Solomon's name means peaceableness, peaceful, or great peace. His father gave his son that name realizing that he himself had been a man of war. David's victories in battle enabled his son to have a reign of peace. Wisdom, wealth, and peace will be manifested in a far greater degree in the millennial reign of David's Greater Son, our Lord Jesus.

God gave both wisdom and wealth to Solomon. The temple also brings the two together since it is the most significant example of Solomon's use of the wisdom that God gave him and the most important use of his wealth.

"All this arises from the picture of Solomon at worship. As one who offers sacrifice and especially as a man of prayer, Solomon shows himself to be suitably qualified to build a temple which will be a 'temple for sacrifices' (2 Chr 7.12; cp. 2.6) and 'a house of prayer' (Is 56.7; cp. 2 Chr 6.40; 7.14 etc.). In fact, the portrayal of the worshipping Solomon is the main focus of the chapter, since his wisdom and his wealth result from his praying" (Selman).

Outline of Chapter 1

Verse 1: Solomon's greatness.
Verses 2-6: Solomon's worship.
Verses 7-13: Solomon's wisdom.
Verses 14-17: Solomon's wealth.

Verse 1: Solomon's Greatness

The very first word, "And", indicates that the Chronicler is continuing the history of Israel given in 1 Chronicles which has a summary of David's reign as its conclusion (1 Chr 29.26-30). The last words of v.1, "magnified him exceedingly", are found also in 1 Chronicles 29.25. These words are a reminder that the same verb, "magnified", is used twice for Joshua (Josh 3.7; 4.14). Dillard writes, "suggesting that the Chronicler has used the succession of Moses and Joshua as a paradigm for the account of the succession of David and Solomon".

Selman has drawn attention to a convincing connection between God's blessing of David and the gracious favour He showed to David's son. "Every phrase in this verse illustrates that David's blessings continued under Solomon, as indicated by the addition of 'son of David' in this verse to the original text (1 Kings 2.46b). David had also been 'strengthened'... at the beginning of his reign (cp. 1 Chr 11.10), 'God was with him', had made him great (1 Chr 11.9) and 'made him exceedingly great' (also 1 Chr 29.25). This continuity...was God keeping His promises about establishing David's house (cp. vv.8-9; 2 Chr 6.3,10; 1 Chr 17.23-27)".

The word "strengthened" is used on a number of occasions in Chronicles. Since at least four of them refer to a king ascending the throne of David after overcoming difficulty (1 Chr 11.10; 2 Chr 12.13; 21.4 and also 25.3 where the same Hebrew word is translated "established"), it is possible that the writer of the Chronicles is making a summary allusion to the troubles described in 1 Kings 1 and 2 before "the kingdom was established in the hand of Solomon" (1 Kings 2.46b). On the other hand, Keil may be right when he writes, "But this view of the words is too narrow; the remark refers to the whole reign - to all that Solomon undertook in order to establish a firm dominion, not merely to his entry upon it. With this view of the words, the second clause, 'his God was with him, and made him very great,' coincides". Even if Keil is right, the first view above may obviously be included.

Solomon was God's choice and so we read, "the Lord his God was with him". David at least three times is recorded as expressing his desire for the Lord to be with Solomon (1 Chr 22.11,16; 28.20) and once notes that He was with the princes whom he calls to help Solomon (1 Chr 22.17,18).

Verses 2-6: Solomon's Worship

Kings has only one verse speaking of Solomon's worship (1 Kings 3.4), but the Chronicler has a much fuller account because worship is very important to him as is everything connected with the temple. The record of Solomon's worship adds to the qualifications of Solomon to build the temple. The expression "all Israel" (v.2) is a favourite of the writer of the Chronicles. Solomon's first act is similar to the first act of David after he was made king when he wanted to bring the ark up to its rightful place (1 Chr 13). "All Israel" is found in that chapter in vv.5-6, and 8. The phrase "sought unto it (the altar)" in v.5 is parallel to 1 Chronicles 13.3, RV: "for we sought not unto it (the ark) in the days of Saul". Most of the officials noted in v.2 are also listed in 1 Chronicles 28.1 at the last assembly of David. So Solomon's worship has continuity with his father David in his first and last assemblies.

"David had trained Solomon to be his successor...Of paramount importance was a strong, internal Godward relationship. The Chronicler was aware of this and began his treatment of the young king's reign with his worship of the Lord at Gibeon. And such was Solomon's desire to continue the godly leadership begun by his father that he included 'all Israel' in the event" (Barber).

The Chronicler is careful to record that Solomon offered his burnt offerings in the most appropriate place - at the Tabernacle of Moses (v.3) and at the brazen altar (v.5). Gibeon is seven miles north-west of Jerusalem.

Verse 4 is a parenthesis which repeats what has already been recorded in 1 Chronicles 13.14; 15.1; and 16.1. The words, 'he put' in v.5 of the AV are translated "was there" in the RV, JND and ESV. Barnes states, "In the Hebrew the position of a point makes the difference between these two translations". The phrase "was there" gives the best sense and is preferred by most critics. Solomon did not put the altar there.

Bezaleel is mentioned here in v.5 and in 1 Chronicles 2.20 but in no other book of the Bible except Exodus. The mention of his name is a reminder that as God used Bezaleel in making the Tabernacle and its furnishings so God was going to use Solomon's wisdom in building the temple and all that was to be in it. Solomon began his reign wonderfully by offering 1,000 burnt offerings to the Lord. (It must have been a very busy time for the priests!) His generous giving to the Lord was an inspiration to the exiles to whom the Chronicler was writing, and it should still inspire God's people today. The preceding verse in the record of 1 Kings states, "Solomon loved the Lord" (3.3). He magnificently expressed that love for the Lord.

Saints today have the privilege of Phillipians 3.3: "For we are the real circumcision, who worship by the Spirit of God and glory in Christ Jesus and put no confidence in the flesh" (ESV). The RV and JND translations are similar. A good number of saints who at one time met with assemblies of believers, but no longer do so, seem particularly to miss the way in which Lord's Supper offers an opportunity for collective worship.

Verses 7-13: Solomon's Wisdom

The writer of the Chronicles makes it clear that the Lord appeared to Solomon on the night following the 1,000 burnt offerings. God said to Solomon, "ask what I shall give thee" (v. 7). 1 Kings 3.5 states that God appeared to him in a dream. As God told Aaron and Miriam (in reference to Moses) in Numbers 12.6-8, that is not God's most intimate way of revealing Himself. "It seems certain that Solomon never knew God as his father knew Him. He lacked David's deep spiritual experience, never having suffered as he suffered. David's years of affliction gave him a knowledge of God from which we all benefit at this day as readers of his Psalms" (Fereday). It has been well said, "If David's heart had ne'er been wrung, David's songs had ne'er been sung". David is listed as one of the heroes of faith in Hebrew 11.32, but Solomon is not mentioned in that chapter. That night it was a dream, but the conversation was just as real to Solomon as a face-to-face conversation would have been. God's question was "intended to search the deeper feelings of his heart" (Edersheim). Verse 7 was a revelation of the grace of God and a test of the heart of Solomon.

God's invitation to Solomon to ask is a reminder that the Lord Jesus likewise invites His disciples to ask. "Ask, and it shall be given you; seek, and ye shall find; knock, and it shall be opened unto you. For everyone that asketh receiveth; and he that seeketh findeth; and to him that knocketh it shall be opened" (Mt 7.7-8). Also He said, "If ye abide in me, and my words abide in you, ye shall ask what ye will, and it shall be done unto you" (Jn 15.7).

Solomon having given to God that night God appeared to him and talked with him. Young King Solomon's answer delighted the heart of God (vv.8-12). He first of all acknowledged God's loving kindness to David in making him king in his father's stead (v.8). Then he asked God to establish His promise to David, probably referring to 1 Chronicles 22.9-10 (v.9). In the same verse he spoke of being king over a people "like the dust of the earth in multitude". That last part of the verse shows that God kept His promise to Abraham (Gen 13.16) and to Jacob (Gen 28.14).

"But he pleads with God that He has made him king, and implies therefore that God is bound to fit him for his office. That is the boldness permitted to faith - to remind God of His own past acts, which pledge Him to give what He has put us into circumstances to need. With beautiful humility, Solomon dwells on his youth and inexperience and on the vastness of the charge laid on him" (Maclaren).

David's words to Solomon, "Only the Lord give thee wisdom and understanding" (1 Chr 22.12) may have had much to do with Solomon's answer in v.10. Children perceive the value-system of their parents. Solomon deeply felt his own littleness and Israel's greatness. He was over-whelmed with his new responsibilities and his lack of experience to judge God's people. He wanted to "go out and come in before this people" (v.10). "Originally a military expression (cp. 1 Sam 18.13,16; 1 Chr 11.2), but here it means to govern the people adequately and with dignity befitting a king" (Myers). Solomon was wise to ask for wisdom so that he could lead God's people well.

All believers need wisdom from God, especially assembly leaders. James gives the promise of God, "If any of you lack wisdom, let him ask of God, that giveth to all liberally, and upbraideth not; and it shall be given him" (1.5). In the context James is especially referring to wisdom in trial, but surely the promise cannot be restricted to trials. The promise is very well illustrated in Solomon's request for wisdom.

James tells us later what God's wisdom is like: "But the wisdom that is from above is first pure, then peaceable, gentle and easy to be entreated, full of mercy and good fruits, without partiality, and without hypocrisy" (3.17). It should be noted that this wisdom is not first peaceable. That could be compromise or appeasement. It is first pure. But any person acting with wisdom from above will be as peaceable as possible consistent with the purity of the Word of God. Our Lord Jesus gives the same order in the Beatitudes. The only peace-making that is truly blessed in Matthew 5.9 is consistent with the purity of the previous Beatitude. True wisdom includes skill in personal relationships. Solomon asked for wisdom and knowledge. It is possible for a person to have a great deal of knowledge and only a very little wisdom. On the other hand, it is possible for a Spirit-made overseer not to have a great deal of theoretical knowledge but have a great deal of wisdom in dealing with assembly matters.

God was so pleased with Solomon having it in his heart to ask for wisdom and knowledge that He not only granted his request but also gave him what he did not ask for - riches, wealth, and honour (v.12). "It is small wonder that a prayer framed so thoughtfully, based so solidly, directed so rightly, and motivated with such concern for his fellows, brings Solomon the blessing he asks, and much more besides, from the God who is 'able to do far more abundantly than all we ask or think' (Eph 3.20)" (Wilcock). The record in Kings shows that Solomon excelled in wisdom: "Behold I have done according to thy words: lo, I have given thee a wise and understanding heart; so that there was none like thee before thee, neither after thee shall any arise like unto thee" (1 Kings 3.12). God was pleased that Solomon had the right priority. Surely this is a reminder that our Lord Jesus encourages all His own similarly to have the right priority. He said, "Seek ye first the kingdom of God, and His righteousness; and all these things shall be added unto you" (Mt 6.33).

The wisdom God gave Solomon enabled him to deal with the practical issues of life. This is clearly seen in the book of Proverbs.

The ESV gives an accurate and significant translation of v.13: "So Solomon came from the high place at Gibeon, from before the tent of meeting, to Jerusalem. And he reigned over Israel". JND and George Rawlinson have similar translations. The Chronicler omits any reference to Solomon sacrificing before the ark when he returned to Jerusalem. It is likely that he wanted to avoid anything that might detract from the picture of legitimate worship that he was so careful to develop in vv.3-6.

Verses 14-17: Solomon's Wealth

These verses have been taken almost word for word from 1 Kings 10.26-29 and they are repeated with changes in 2 Chronicles 9.25-28. The Chronicler gives them a new position very early in the record of Solomon. Their main purpose is to show that God kept His promise to give Solomon wealth (v.12). They also show that this wealth was useful for the building of the temple. Verses 14-17 "establishes the character of this reign as one of 'rest', in which hostilities have given place to trade, and war to peace" (New Bible Commentary, 21st Century Edition).

When David defeated the king of Zobah he took from him a thousand chariots and reserved from them a hundred chariots (2 Sam 8.4; 1 Chr 18.4). That seems to be the maximum number that David had. So, before Solomon chariots were used by Israel only to a small extent. Solomon made chariots a standard part of his army with 1,400 of them. Solomon's chariot cities have been confirmed by archeological discoveries at Megiddo. Some experts have claimed that they were store cities. More recently further research has confirmed that the structures were indeed stables. "Whether they were stables or storehouses, the fact is that Solomon built both 'cities of store' and 'cities for his chariots' (1 Kings 9.19)" (Thompson).

The only difference of any importance between these four verses and 1 Kings 10.26-29 is the addition of the word "gold" in v.15. That verse is a hyperbole. The writer of the Chronicles is bolder than the writer of the Kings in the use of this figure of speech. For Solomon to make silver and gold as plenteous as stones is especially significant at Jerusalem. "Jerusalem is one of the stoniest places in the world" (Barnes).

"There is no doubt at all as to the identity of the "sycomore tree" in 2 Chronicles 1.15. It is the well-known sycamore-fig...also sometimes called 'mulberry-fig' or 'fig-mulberry'. It should not be confused with the common 'sycamore' of eastern North America...The 'sycamore' of the Bible should not be confused with the English 'sycamore' which is a maple" (Moldenke). The fig-sycamore tree is still common in Palestine. The number of Solomon's chariots, the plentiful silver and gold, and luxury items like cedar are a measure of the wealth of Solomon.

The primary source of his wealth was trade. 1 Kings 10.22 records that the navy brought riches once every three years and 1 Kings 10.25 states that visitors brought riches including horses at a rate year by year. The kingdom of Solomon lies across the land bridge between the continents of Africa and Asia, which makes it easy to control the trade routes especially between Syria and Egypt. "The NIV follows a number of modern translations by referring to the land of Kue (...probably Cilicia to judge from ancient documents). The picture then suggests some sort of trade with horses and chariots as the commodities...There is, however, some uncertainty about the exact translation and meaning of these verses, and at present dogmatism should be avoided" (Thompson). Including the kings of the Hittites and the kings of Syria in the arrangement for trading enhances the picture.

2 CHRONICLES 2

Solomon's Reign

Introductory

This whole chapter is concerned with the preparations Solomon made for the building of the temple. Even though his father David had made extensive preparations, there were still more required. David anticipated this when he said, "and thou mayest add thereto" (1 Chr 22.14).

There are four touching verses in 1 Chronicles about David's preparations. "So David prepared abundantly before his death" (22.5). "Now, behold, in my trouble I have prepared for the house of the Lord" (22.14). David had an unusual amount of trouble and yet even in this he prepared for the house of the Lord. "Now I have prepared with all my might for the house of my God" (29.2). The next verse tells why he did it: "Moreover, because I have set my affection to the house of my God" (29.3). These verses are an encouragement to all in assembly fellowship to have affection for the assembly and to do all that can be done for it.

Verse 1 is a fitting introduction to the whole record of the building of the temple. When Solomon finished it similar words are found (7.11). The remainder of this chapter records the preparations of Solomon for the building of the temple, which is the first stage of the larger narrative.

Outline of Chapter 2

Verse 1:	Solomon's determination to build. For the remainder of the chapter, the Chronicler uses one of his favourite literary devices of structuring the chapter in a chiastic outline.
Verse 2:	Conscription of labourers.
Verses 3-10:	Solomon's letter.
Verses 11-16:	Huram's letter.
Verses 17-18:	Conscription of labourers.

"Repetition of vocabulary and themes is the hallmark of literature using chiastic structures; the Chronicler's fondness for the device should caution against labelling the repetition a product of a lapse of memory on the Chronicler's part" (Dillard).

Verse 1: Solomon's Determination to Build

The first portion of the verse is similar to the first phrase of 1 Kings 5.5. There it is part of Solomon's letter to Huram, but here, under the heading of Solomon's decision to build, the correspondence between Solomon and Huram forms an introduction to the narrative that follows.

"An house for his kingdom" denotes a palace for Solomon, which is referred to later in 2.12; 7.11; 8.1; 9.3 and 11. "However, unlike 1 Kings

7.1-12, the Chronicler includes no details of its building; perhaps he felt that to do so would detract attention from the more important temple theme. The fact that he includes a reference here is sufficient to show once again, however, that his purpose was not to deceive in any way, but that he expects of his readers good knowledge of the earlier account" (Williamson).

Solomon determined to build (v.1). He began to build (3.1) and he finished the work (5.1). His example is good to follow. Sometimes saints determine without then beginning, and sometimes saints begin without finishing.

"An house for the name of the Lord" calls to mind the book of Deuteronomy. In that book 21 times we read phrases similar to "the place which the Lord thy God shall choose" (beginning in ch.12). Nine times the words are added, "to place his name there". (These words are implied in the other places.) It is striking that we also find recorded 21 times the name of, "Jeroboam, the son of Nebat", the man "who made Israel to sin". He made Israel to sin by trying to keep them from going to Jerusalem where God had chosen to place His name. Jeroboam did so by putting a golden calf in Bethel for the Israelites to focus on instead of going to Jerusalem.

Verse 2: Conscription of Labourers

This verse is repeated in vv.17-18 with more details. It is given there to preserve the chiastic structure used by the writer. There are also further details about Solomon's servants in 8.7-9.

Verses 3-10: Solomon's Letter

Solomon sent to Huram the king of Tyre. Huram is the usual spelling for Hiram in Chronicles except in 1 Chronicles 14.1. Solomon still needed much cedar wood and fir for the temple. The most famous place for cedar trees was Lebanon. In the providence of God the king of that region was on friendly terms with David and Solomon. "As thou didst deal with David my father" (v.3) refers to 1 Chronicles 14.1 and 2 Samuel 5.11. They of Tyre had already sent "cedar trees in abundance" to David for the temple (1 Chr 22.4).

The Chronicler omits details that are given in 1 Kings 5.2-6 but he assumes that his readers know about them. Guided by the Holy Spirit he gives a much fuller account of Solomon's letter to Huram. Verses 4-6 have no parallel in Kings. Solomon gives a summary of what was to be done in the temple in the worship of the God of Israel (v.4). That is very important to the writer of the Chronicles.

Naturally, there are verses of instruction in the Pentateuch for each of the functions mentioned in v.4. Instructions are given in Exodus 25.6; 30.1-10; 37.25-29; 40.27 and Leviticus 16.13 for the burning of sweet incense, and in Exodus 25.23-30; 40.22-24; and Leviticus 24.5-9 for the continual shewbread. Burnt offerings are mentioned often in the Pentateuch, but the ones offered "morning and evening", "on the sabbaths", and "in the solemn feasts of the Lord our God" are all given in Numbers 28 and 29.

Verse 5 is reminiscent of the words of David: "the house that is to be builded for the Lord must be exceeding magnifical, of fame and of glory throughout all countries" (1 Chr 22.5), and of David's words in 1 Chronicles 29.1: "the work is great: for the palace is not for man, but for the Lord God". A great temple is befitting for a great God. Verse 5 explains why Solomon wanted the best craftsmen and the most precious materials for the temple. The words of the verse echo the words of Exodus 18.11; Psalm 95.3; 96.4; 97.9; and 135.5. When Solomon refers to "God above all gods", it does not imply that Solomon believed that any other gods actually existed. It was a way of expressing the greatness of the Lord God of Israel to Huram, a polytheistic pagan king.

The words of Solomon to Huram, "...seeing the heaven and heaven of heavens cannot contain him" (v.6), are a further testimony to Huram of the greatness of the Lord God of Israel. Solomon is testifying to him that, unlike all the false gods worshipped by the nations around, Jehovah far transcends His temple. Solomon used those words when dedicating the temple (1 Kings 8.27; 2 Chr 6.18). When Solomon says, "who am I?" (v.6), he is expressing that he does not consider himself worthy of the honour of building a temple for God. "Who am ?" is a common expression of humility used by Moses (Ex 3.11), and is also used by David three times (1 Sam 18.18; 2 Sam 7.18; 1 Chr 29.14). Solomon knows that even though the temple will not be able to contain such a transcendent God, yet it can be used "to burn sacrifice before him" (v.6).

The ESV has for the first words of v.7, "So now send me a man". Solomon has explained to Huram that he purposes to build a temple for his God and uses the words, "So now...", which is a transition marker between his introductory statement and the main part of his letter which is an entreaty. He requests a man skillful to work in metals and fabrics and who has the ability to engrave.

In 1 Kings, Solomon is not recorded as sending for Huram until after the temple and his own house are finished (1 Kings 6.38; 7.1,13-14), but the Chronicler records the request for Huram right away (before any work started). 1 Kings only states that Huram was skilled in brass (7.14), but the writer of the Chronicles records that Huram was skilled in all the skills of Bezaleel and Aholiab (Ex 31.1-6; 35.30-36.2; 38.22-23; 2 Chr 2.7,14). In both of these ways the Chronicler is strengthening his use of the account of the building of the Tabernacle as a model of his account of the building of the temple. (See also the Introduction to this commentary.)

The phrase, "Judah and...Jerusalem" (v.7), is only found here in the history of the united monarchy, but is found often during the history of the divided monarchy. David provided workers that were with Solomon. They would naturally be near the site of the building of the temple that is in Judah and Jerusalem. The last phrase of v.7, "whom David my father did provide", refers to 1 Chronicles 22.15; 28.21; 29.5. (All these details are found only in Chronicles.)

Solomon also requested trees from Lebanon: cedar, fir, and algum (v.8). The ESV has cypress instead of fir (as does the RV margin and JND). Since 1 Kings 10.11 and 12 record almug trees from Ophir and 2 Chronicles 9.10 and 11 records algum trees from Ophir; these are simply two different spellings for the same tree. Those verses indicate that Solomon got algum trees from Ophir and v.8 indicates that he also got algum trees from Lebanon. It is not likely that algum trees that were worth importing from Ophir also grew in Lebanon. The wood of algum trees seems to have been a precious wood useful for making furniture. "Solomon in the earlier part of his reign, before he engaged in commerce may easily have imagined that the algum wood, which the Jews were in the habit of importing from Phoenicia, grew in that country" (Rawlinson).

The phrase, "for I know thy servants can skill to cut timber" (v.8), shows that Solomon appreciated that skill. But Solomon's appreciation is even more emphatic in 1 Kings 5.6: "there is not among us any that can skill to hew timber like unto the Sidonians". Solomon offered, "my servants shall be with thy servants" (v.8). He probably made that offer because the task was so great. Solomon had 80,000 men as hewers in the mountain (vv.2,18). His unskilled workers would help under the supervision of the Sidonian skilled men. He gives the reason for the requests in these words: "for the house which I am about to build shall be wonderful great" (v.9). These words are in keeping with comments already made regarding v.5.

Solomon offered to pay Huram's servants, the hewers that cut timber, generously (v.10). The details of this verse supplement those of 1 Kings 5.11. The payment in 1 Kings was a yearly provision for the king's household as long as the building was going on and it is likely to have been in accord with the agreement of friendship that they made in 1 Kings 5.12. The payment here in v.10 is a one-time payment for the workers who cut timber. In 1 Kings there is no mention of barley and wine and the quantity of oil is much less, but the oil in 1 Kings is probably a much better quality of oil. Regarding the oil in 1 Kings Rawlinson writes, "The small amount of twenty cors of oil…was to be of superior quality ('pure oil' - literally 'beaten oil' - i.e. oil extracted from the olives by pounding, and not by means of the press)". In the view of the Chronicler, the important thing is that Solomon initiated the correspondence rather than Huram and Solomon set the terms of the payment.

"The great structure described in Ephesians 1-3 is here seen in type. That spiritual building which will be God's dwelling place throughout eternity is comprised of Jew and Gentile…Whether it be 'the holy temple' (Eph 2.21), or the peace which results from the breaking down of the middle wall (v.14), or the absence of 'enmity' (v.16), or being 'no more strangers and foreigners' (v.19), all of these are foreshadowed in this passage. In a future day when a greater than Solomon sits on his throne then, too, will

Jew and Gentile live together and God's house will be a house of prayer for all nations (Is 56.6-7; Micah 4.2)" (McShane).

Verses 11-16: Huram's Letter

"Then Huram…answered in writing" (v.11). These words are not in the account in 1 Kings. Regarding them, Rawlinson notes, "It seems to be implied that Solomon's communications had not been 'in writing'. Oriental monarchs, even at the present day, communicate mainly by accredited messengers. Autograph letters from king to king are rare".

Huram's reply here is considerably longer than that recorded in 1 Kings, partly because vv.13-14 are expanded from 1 Kings 7.13-14. The form of Huram's letter follows Solomon's letter closely. "(a) Theological and historical context (vv.11-12; cp. vv.3-6); (b) Huram-abi as chief craftsman (vv.13-14; cp. v.7); (c) Materials and payment (vv.15-16; cp. vv.8-10)…the temple, then, did not become a house of prayer for all nations by accident. The nations even played a part in its construction" (Selman).

The words of Huram (vv.11-12) have a parallel with the words of the Queen of Sheba. Solomon's wisdom (v.12) parallels 9.5-7; the love of the Lord in making Solomon king (v.11) parallels 9.8; and the blessing of the Lord (v.12) parallels 9.8. "It is one more characteristic of the Chronicler that he gives Huram's words in vv.11-12, like those of the Queen of Sheba in 9.8, that show the outside world recognizing that the presence and blessing of God are in Israel when it is ruled by God's chosen king" (New Bible Commentary).

Huram's letter indicates that he knew a great deal about Solomon and that Huram, David, and Solomon maintained close contact. The letter reveals a helpful, happy relationship. Both Huram and the Queen of Sheba use the word "Blessed" (v.12; 9.8). The word, used in this way, is found elsewhere in Chronicles only from the mouth of David (1 Chr 16.36; 29.10) and Solomon (2 Chr 6.4). The Hebrew phrase that is translated in v.12 as "prudence and understanding" is only seen elsewhere in 1 Chronicles 22.12 where it is translated, "wisdom and understanding". The RV has "discretion and understanding" in both places. Here in v.12 Huram praises Solomon for the qualities David desired for his son (1 Chr 22.12).

"A comparison with the parallel text vividly reinforces the Chronicler's view that Solomon's wisdom was particularly wisdom for building. In 1 Kings 5.7 Huram extols God's gift of a wise ruler, 'a wise son over this great people'; the Chronicler inserts instead, 'a wise son, endued with prudence and understanding, that might build an house for the Lord, and an house for his kingdom'" (Dillard).

The expression in v.12, "that made heaven and earth" and the expression in 1 Chronicles 16.26, "the Lord made the heavens" are the only two phrases in Chronicles that explicitly say that God is the Creator.

Huram's enthusiastic, clear comments about God in vv.11-12 are surprising. There are other declarations like this in the Old Testament - the

Queen of Sheba in 9.5-8; Cyrus in 36.22-23; Nebuchadnezzar in Daniel 4.34-37; Darius in Daniel 6.26-27 - but they do not necessarily imply conversion to God. If Huram was sincere in his statements in vv.11-12, his words come close to one who believed in the God of Israel. It is possible that Huram had come to know the God of the Hebrews as his own God through his long familiar dealings with David. On the other hand, it is possible that Huram used these words on the polytheistic principle of acknowledging Jehovah as the God of the Hebrews. His words could be carefully chosen by a practical businessman or may only be courteous words to a respected friend. Of the five Gentile rulers mentioned earlier, the Queen of Sheba is the one most likely to have come to a genuine faith in Jehovah (based on the words of the Lord Jesus in Matthew 12.42).

In regard to the phrase, "of Huram my father" (v.13), "it is generally agreed that this is a wrong translation, and the name, Huram, designates in this place the workman sent by the king of Tyre and not the king of Tyre's father...That Hiram (or Huram) was the name of the workman is certain from 1 Kings 7.13,40 and 2 Chronicles 4.11...With respect to the word ABI, which follows Huram, it is now commonly thought that it is either a proper name...or an epithet of honour attached to the word Huram, and grammatically in apposition with it. Translate...Huram, my master-workman" (Rawlinson).

Verse 14 states that Huram was "the son of a woman of the daughters of Dan". That indicates that she was a Danite. 1 Kings 7.14 records that, "he was a widow's son of the tribe of Naphtali", probably indicating that her first husband was of Naphtali. Her second husband was a man of Tyre. Since Huram's mother was an Israelite, that fact would help him in working with Israelites on the temple. However one accounts for the supposed discrepancy, it is clear that the writer of the Chronicles has recorded an ancestry from Dan to Huram-abi to enhance his presentation of him as a second Aholiab (Ex 31.6). The Chronicler also states that Huram's abilities were like those of Bezaleel and Aholiab rather than just a worker in brass as described in 1 Kings 7.14 (as noted already in the comments on v.7).

McShane's explanation of the discrepancy is helpful as explained previously in the Introduction to the Reign of Solomon.

"While Huram was a master workman, it was not left to him to design the things he made. Solomon remained the architect, and he, in turn, had received from his father David the God-given pattern of the house and its vessels" (McShane).

As a careful businessman, in v.15 the king of Tyre requested the payment first. Then he would have his men cut wood for Solomon. Since he used the words, "my lord", in reference to David in v.14 and Solomon in v.15, some commentators have taken this to indicate that Huram was a vassal of Solomon. "That may have been so, but it may also have been the language of a shrewd merchant to his client" (Thompson). It was extremely polite language.

Verse 16 is based on 1 Kings 5.8-9. "The present vocabulary of v.16 seems to reflect the post-exilic era. The mention of 'Joppa', not specified in 1 Kings 5.9, is almost certainly influenced by the transportation of timber for the second temple which arrived at the same port (Ezra 3.7)" (Selman). Jonah sailed from Joppa many years afterwards (Jonah 1.3). Centuries later, the Apostle Peter "tarried many days in Joppa with one Simon a tanner" (Acts 9.43).

Verse 16 tells of the journey of the logs from Lebanon to Jerusalem. "It was a long way…but Huram was no less skillful in their haulage than he was in their hewing" (McShane). The first part of the journey was the easiest, 20 miles from the forest to Sidon, mostly downhill. The second part was more difficult, 125-130 miles by sea from Sidon to Joppa. Joppa was the nearest seaport to Jerusalem. Logs could be attached together to make rafts and separated when they got to Joppa. The third part of the journey was the most difficult. Jerusalem was about 2,550 feet above sea level. From Joppa to Jerusalem was almost 35 miles as the crow flies. But since it was such a steep ascent with a rugged hilly terrain, they most likely had to travel up a winding route so that it would be nearer 50 miles. That made the journey about 200 miles in total.

Verses 17-18: Conscription of Labourers

Verse 17 makes clear what is not obvious in v.2. Those forced labourers were all "strangers". They were resident aliens, the descendants of the Canaanites whom the Israelites did not drive out, including the Gibeonites of Joshua 9.23. The phrase, "after the numbering wherewith David his father had numbered them", probably refers to 1 Chronicles 22.2. That verse records that David gathered the strangers. While it does not specifically mention numbering them, it is quite possible that he did. The total number that is given in v.17 is the exact total of the conscripted laborers mentioned in v.2 and v.18. "The total number employed…though large, cannot be considered excessive, when compared, for example with the 360,000 persons engaged for twenty years on the building of one pyramid" (Edersheim).

1 Kings 9.20-22 is reproduced quite closely in 2 Chronicles 8.7-9. Both of those passages indicate that none of the native Israelites were made bondmen. This seems to contradict 1 Kings 5.13-14 which is not recorded in Chronicles. There we read of a temporary levy of 30,000 from all Israel, but only 10,000 were actually at work in Lebanon at any one time. Two out of every three months were granted for home leave. It is not explained how they were selected, but it is possible that a good many of them may have volunteered since the work was for the house of God. These conscripted Israelites were much better off than the strangers who did not have time at home. Most likely their work was not as menial as the work of the resident aliens. Nevertheless, after Solomon died the people complained to Rehoboam in 2 Chronicles 10.4: "Thy father made our yoke

grievous". When Rehoboam sent Hadoram (who was over the tribute), the children of Israel stoned him with stones (2 Chr 10.18).

The only significant addition to the words of v.2 in v.18 is that the overseers were "to set the people a work". The overseers probably had whips or sticks to drive to work any that were sluggish.

Verse 18 states that there were 3,600 overseers, but 1 Kings 5.16 records that there were 3,300, who ruled over the people. 2 Chronicles 8.10 states that there were 250 Israelite chief overseers, which, added to the 3,600 makes 3,850. 1 Kings 9.23 records 550 chief officers (which, when added to the 3,300, makes 3,850). So the two accounts are in harmony. Of the chief overseers, 250 were Israelites and 300 were Canaanites.

2 CHRONICLES 3

Solomon's Reign

Introductory

Verse 1 tells how Solomon began to build the house of the Lord and 5.1 records that the work was finished. In between these two an account is given of Solomon building the temple including the Most Holy Place (chapter 3) and the furnishings (chapter 4). These two chapters are similar in structure and content. After recording details about the porch and the temple in 3.3-7, verse 8 of that chapter states that, "he made". These two words are recorded a total of eighteen times in these two chapters and verse 1 of chapter 5. This is another example of the desire of the writer of Chronicles to parallel the building of the Tabernacle in Exodus 36.8-39.42 where again the phrase "he made" is repeated over seventy times. The frequent use of this phrase indicates his overall leadership. Huram and those who were with him were the workmen.

Moses was careful to make everything as God had commanded him. Solomon likewise carefully followed the plans that God had given to his father David and that had been passed on to him (1 Chr 28.11-19).

God has a pattern for New Testament assemblies today. May the Lord encourage more and more believers to go by the pattern!

The temple of Solomon is especially linked with the Tabernacle of Moses in v.14 (writing about the vail). "Since none of these links occurs in 1 Kings 6-7, they are the Chronicler's way of underlining that the purpose of the tent, a travelling sanctuary, was fulfilled in the 'rest' signified by the temple" (Selman).

The writer of the Chronicles is so engrossed in the temple that he devotes the last thirteen chapters of 1 Chronicles to the preparations for it. A considerable part of that record is only found in Chronicles. In light of his interest, it is surprising that his account of the building of the temple and its furnishings is so brief. 1 Kings 6-7 (omitting the record of the buildings adjacent to the temple in 7.1-12) takes seventy-seven verses, where 2 Chronicles has only forty. The Chronicler knows that his readers have the fuller account in 1 Kings 6-7. "Since the Chronicles then goes on to devote more space to the opening ceremonies (chs.5-7) than to the building work, it is clear that his real concern is with the temple's meaning rather than its architectural details. In other words, the temple will be complete not when the last stone is in place but when God takes up residence" (Selman).

In the New Testament the word for the inner sanctuary of the temple (*naos*) is used "by Christ metaphorically of His own physical body (Jn 2.19,21). It is used in apostolic teaching, metaphorically, (1) of the Church, the mystical Body of Christ (Eph 2.21); (2) of a local church (1 Cor 3.16-17; 2 Cor 6.16); (3) of the present body of the individual believer (1 Cor 6.19);

(4) of the temple seen in visions in the Apocalypse; (5) of the Lord God Almighty and the Lamb, as the temple of the New and Heavenly Jerusalem (Rev 21.22)" (Vine).

These two chapters impress us with the magnificent beauty found inside the temple. But none of God's people ever saw that beauty other than the priests and the Levites. They were the only ones allowed inside. The only objects of beauty which the others were permitted to see were the two pillars and the doors in front of the temple. Only the high priest could enter into the Holy of Holies and that on one day of the year, the Day of Atonement. Even then he could only enter the Most Holy Place with blood that spoke of the blood of our Lord Jesus Christ.

Even the architecture of the building emphasized the great difficulty there was in approaching God. Hebrews 9.8 states that as long as the vail was standing in the temple "the Holy Ghost (was) this signifying, that the way into the holiest of all was not yet made manifest". God's people were thankful for the temple that spoke of the presence of God, the One who had drawn near to them, but the way to God had many restrictions.

If the unapproachable majesty of God is kept in mind, it leads to an increased appreciation of the greatness of the work of Christ on the cross. His acceptable sacrifice caused God Himself to rend in two the vail in the temple from the top to the bottom, thus making clear that the way into the Holiest was now open forever to human beings upon redemption of their souls (Mt 27.51). Not only so, but He has given His own people "boldness (or confidence) to enter into the holiest by the blood of Jesus" (Heb 10.19). No person could ever deserve such an unspeakable privilege. It is only by the grace of God and because of the infinite value of the sacrifice of Christ on Calvary.

Outline of Chapter 3

Verses 1-2:	The place and date for the start of the building of the temple.
Verses 3-7:	The dimensions of the temple including the porch and the Holy Place.
Verses 8-9:	The Most Holy House.
Verses 10-14:	The cherubims and the vail.
Verses 15-17:	The two pillars in the front of the temple.

Verses 1-2: The Place and Date for the Start of the Building of the Temple

Solomon started to build the temple (v.1). This is the task that more than any other will always be remembered as his service for God, and is especially true in the account of his life given in 2 Chronicles. Verse 1 is the only place where the temple site is designated and it is of special importance and interest. Jerusalem is identified first. It was the royal city and it was to become the holy city. Mount Moriah, where Abraham was willing to offer his son Isaac over 800 years before, is mentioned next (Gen 22.2,14 - the only other place where Moriah is mentioned in the Bible). Last of all, the location of the temple is identified with "the place that David had prepared in the threshing floor of Ornan the Jebusite".

"In Genesis 22.14 there is a wordplay linking God's provision of an alternative sacrifice with the establishment of a sanctuary. The Hebrew verb 'see' or 'reveal' also means 'see to' or 'provide'. So the statement of the future significance of this site in Genesis 22.14, playing on the two meanings of the one verb, according to the most likely rendering reads, 'in the mount of the Lord revelation shall be made'...It was David who received the promised revelation" (Leslie C. Allen).

In the same place where Abraham had a knife raised ready to plunge into his son's bosom, David "saw the angel of the Lord...having a sword in his hand stretched out over Jerusalem" (1 Chr 21.16). In the next verse David expressed genuine repentance (v.17). Then the angel of the Lord sent Gad to David to have him set up an altar in the threshing floor of Ornan the Jebusite (v.18). David offered burnt offerings and peace offerings on that altar and the Lord "answered him from heaven by fire upon the altar of burnt offering" (v.26). Evidently "this intervention of God in grace suggested to David that Jehovah had thus indicated His choice of site for the sanctuary" (Fereday). A little later David said, "This is the house of the Lord God" (1 Chr 22.1). So it was God Himself who chose the location of the temple. "What more appropriate place could be found for the temple of Jehovah?" (Habershon).

The date for the beginning of the building of the temple is given in v.2 as it is in 1 Kings 6.1 except that the name of the second month is omitted in Chronicles as is the reference to the exodus. The Chronicler is not as interested in the exodus as is the writer of 1 Kings. In relation to our calendar, the second month was from approximately the middle of April to the middle of May, an ideal time, the spring, to begin building. The following two months also were good for construction. It is interesting that building the second temple also began in the second month (Ezra 3.8).

Even though Solomon wholeheartedly wanted to carry out his God-given responsibility to build the temple, there was a delay in starting until the fourth year of his reign due to the time necessary to carry out all the preparations described in ch.2.

Verses 3-7: The Dimensions of the Temple Including the Porch and the Holy Place

Verse 3 refers to "cubits after the first measure". There were two different cubits. One of these was approximately 18 inches and the other approximately 21 inches. It is not easy to know which one was used. Using the smaller one, sixty cubits in length would be equal to ninety feet and twenty cubits for the breadth would be equal to thirty feet. The temple was not as big as might have been thought. But the main purpose of the temple was as a place in which God would dwell. It was not a building for a large congregation to gather. 1 Kings 6.2 gives the height as thirty cubits. Since the length and breadth are both twice as long as these dimensions were in the Tabernacle we might think that the height of the Tabernacle would have been fifteen cubits but the boards of that structure were only ten cubits high. That makes the temple three times as high as the Tabernacle. All the measurements given are interior measurements. (It is easy to see that the measurements were interior measurements since the wings of the cherubims together totalled twenty cubits, the measure given for the width of the temple.) The quality of the material and the workmanship made the temple glorious.

In v.4 the AV has the height of the porch as "an hundred and twenty" cubits. Rawlinson records that "the Arabic version and the Alexandrian Septuagint give 20 for 120…The true reading may be restored beyond any reasonable doubt; and the clause will then run thus - 'and the height was twenty cubits'…There is nothing surprising in the porch being ten cubits lower than the main building". Newberry is in agreement with this. He writes, "In 2 Chronicles 3.4 the porch is described as a hundred and twenty cubits high, but this is acknowledged to be a mistake arising from the transposition of letters; the Alexandrian copy of the Septuagint reads, 'twenty cubits'". Solomon overlaid the porch within with pure gold.

Verse 5 speaks of "the greater house" which is the Holy Place, the main chamber of the temple. The Holy Place was forty cubits long whereas the Holy of Holies was only twenty. The Holy Place was between the porch and the Holy of Holies. The word for "ceiled" is translated in the ESV as "lined". "The word translated 'fir' bears probably in this place, not the narrow meaning which it has in 2.8, where it is opposed to cedar, but a wider one in which cedar is included. From 1 Kings 6.15 it appears that the walls of the Holy Place were boarded with cedar while the floor was of fir" (Rawlinson).

"A distinctive feature of cedar wood is its virtual indestructibility. Apparently, a piece of worm-eaten cedar wood was never seen. The reason, says Newberry, is, 'The sap of the cedar is death to the worm; so that, instead of the worm destroying the cedar, the cedar destroys the worm'. This freedom from destruction of cedar wood by the worm, which is so unlike many other timbers is a remarkable picture of the incorruptible manhood of Christ…Thus, the cedar wood lining of the temple is symbolic of the risen Christ whose body is incorruptible" (Page).

The bodies of all other persons who have died see corruption, but the Apostle Peter said of our Lord Jesus in Acts 2.31, RV, "nor did his flesh see corruption". This was prophesied centuries before in Psalm 16.10. Peter quoted this verse in Acts 2.27 and Paul in Acts 13.35. Paul declared in Acts 13.36 that "David…saw corruption". Since His resurrection, the incorruptible body of the Lord Jesus is a body of glory (Phil 3.21, RV).

Both 1 Kings and 2 Chronicles speak of palm trees carved on the walls (1 Kings 6.29; v.5) and cherubims (1 Kings 6.29; v.7). Only Kings records knops (gourds) and open flowers (1 Kings 6.18), while only in Chronicles do we read of chains on the walls (v.5) and precious stones (v.6). There does not appear to be any reason why the walls could not have had all of the decoration that is recorded. Chain designs were also used on the two pillars (1 Kings 7.17 and v.16). Possibly the chains linked the palm trees together. Palm trees speak of victory and triumph (Jn 12.13; Rev 7.9). They could also speak of fruitfulness.

Page has another attractive application for the palm trees. "A missionary from the region told the author that if a palm tree were pulled over with a rope to an angle and released after a time, the tree would return to the vertical plane. This shows how a palm tree was known for its uprightness… The principle of this illustration may be applied to Christ. None is His equal in uprightness of character".

Verse 6 does not have any parallel in 1 Kings. It records that the gold was gold of Parvaim as if to suggest that it was the very best. "The reference to gold ornamentation is much greater throughout the Chronicler's account" (Coggins). The inside of Solomon's temple was a marvel of glory and majesty. Gold glittered everywhere in the interior. As if that was not enough, v.6 states that "he garnished the house with precious stones for beauty". 1 Chronicles 29.2 records that among the things that David prepared for the house of God were "onyx stones, and stones to be set, glistering stones, and of divers colours, and all manner of precious stones".

In Revelation 21.9 it is recorded, "I will shew thee the bride, the Lamb's wife". About the holy Jerusalem it is stated, "Having the glory of God: and her light was like unto a stone most precious, even like a jasper stone, clear as crystal" (v.11). Later it is recorded, "And the foundations of the wall of the city were garnished with all manner of precious stones" (v.19). "These precious stones aptly set forth those spiritual excellencies and perfections which will be conspicuous in the redeemed in glory, the workmanship of the ETERNAL SPIRIT, those GRACES of the Spirit of God which will be there in full bloom - 'open flowers', not simply graces in the bud and embryo, but in growth and perfection, which shall there appear in the clear radiance of the Divine presence, in all their spiritual beauty" (Newberry).

Of all the precious stones that Solomon used and David had prepared, only one is named and that is the onyx (1 Chr 29.2). This was one of the twelve precious stones for adorning the breastplate of the high priest (Ex 28.20). Even in the time of Job men understood the value of the onyx. Job 28.12 has this question, "But where shall wisdom be found?". Verse 16 gives one of the things said about wisdom, "It cannot be valued with the gold of Ophir, with the precious onyx, or the sapphire". The answer to the first question of v.12 is given in v.28: "the fear of the Lord, that is wisdom". There are also similar words in Psalm 111.10 and Proverbs 9.10: "The fear of the Lord is the beginning of wisdom". "Men of the ancient world viewed gold from Ophir and the precious onyx stone to be of immense value. But the value of wisdom could not be measured by such valuables - the worth of wisdom was, and is, immeasurable" (Page). Proverbs 8.22-31 and 1 Corinthians 1.30 both present our Lord Jesus as wisdom personified. Colossians 2.3 records about Him: "In whom are hid all the treasures of wisdom and knowledge".

Clearly Page believes that not only all that was inside the temple was overlaid with gold, but also all that was on the outside. He quotes the translation of JND for v.7: "He covered the house (i.e. the entire building), the beams (of the roof), the threshold (of the doors), and its walls, and its doors with fine gold". Later, he writes, "Outside the roof and walls were overlaid with gold". In his book *Christ and Solomon's Temple* the frontispiece shows the complete temple covered with gold. *Types of the Temple* by Newberry also has a frontispiece showing the outside covered with gold.

It is possible that Page and Newberry are right, but it is clear that McShane, for example, did not believe that the outside of the temple was overlaid with gold because he writes, "Apart from the pillars and the doors there was nothing particularly attractive about its appearance...Only on the outside were the stones seen".

Verse 7 also records that there were "graved cherubims on the walls". Fereday has precious thoughts about the first two times we read about cherubims. "(1) In Genesis 3.24 we see them placed forbiddingly at the gate of the garden after Adam's sin (living creatures doubtless). (2) In Exodus 25.18-20 we see golden cherubims upon the ark, beaten out of the same sheet of gold as the mercy seat. The contrast between these Scripture passages is instructive. The executors of God's judgment who are seen opposed to transgressors in Genesis 3 are seen in Exodus 25 looking down peacefully on the mercy seat from which the blood of the sacrifice was never lacking. Blessed be God, the atoning blood of Christ makes blessing sure for sinful men, and puts judgment far away".

Verses 8-9: The Most Holy House

The innermost sanctuary is called, "the most holy house" in v.8 and in v.10, and "the most holy place" in 1 Kings 6.16; 7.50; 8.6 and in 1 Chronicles 6.49; 2 Chronicles 4.22 and 5.7. Since it was the dwelling place of God who is thrice holy (Is 6.3), the names are very fitting.

The Most Holy House has an alternative name - "oracle" (eleven times in 1 Kings 6-8, and in 2 Chronicles 3.16; 4.20; 5.7,9). Oracle means "a source of wisdom" indicating that the Lord was heard there - "And there...I will commune with thee from above the mercy seat" (Ex 25.22). Of course, the mercy seat was in the Most Holy Place.

Verse 8 states that the length and breadth were each twenty cubits, 1 Kings 6.20 records that the height was twenty cubits, showing that it was a perfect cube. Since the Holy of Holies was a perfect cube it may signify the perfection of God's person. Only in this verse is the amount of gold specified that was used to overlay the Most Holy House - 600 talents of fine gold. This is only a small fraction of the gold that David had prepared (1 Chr 22.14), but it was still an enormous amount equal to twenty-three tons.

Only in v.9 do we read of the nails and the fifty shekels of gold (only about twenty ounces). Since gold is probably too soft to use as nails, a number of commentators take the fifty shekels to refer to the gold leaf used to cover the heads of the nails which were used to hold the sheets of gold in place on the walls. "This incredible detail tells us also of his thoroughness…the large and the small are equally his concern, extravagance and thoroughness admirably combined" (Wilcock).

"The upper chambers" are mentioned here (v.9) for the first time in 2 Chronicles but they are alluded to in 1 Chronicles 28.11.

Verses 10-14: The Cherubims and the Vail

Verses 10-13 describe the two large free-standing cherubims that were set up in the Most Holy Place. These two cherubims are one of the most unique features of Solomon's temple. "He made two cherubims of image work" (v.10). The NKJV has for the phrase "of image work", "fashioned by carving". There were no large cherubims in the Tabernacle, but there were two much smaller cherubims on the ark itself. The ark is the only piece of furniture that was both in the Tabernacle and the temple (5.7). These two large cherubims and other things used to decorate the inside of the temple may seem to go against the second of the ten commandments: "Thou shalt not make unto thee any graven image, or any likeness of anything that is in heaven above, or that is in the earth beneath, or that is in the water under the earth" (Ex 20.4). "Perhaps the commandment was understood to prohibit the making of likenesses only when there was a danger of their becoming objects of worship, and this danger was thought to be eliminated in a temple dedicated to the worship of Yahweh alone" (New Bible Commentary).

The Lord is recorded as dwelling between the cherubims (Num 7.89; 2 Kings 19.15; Ps 80.1; 99.1). Numbers 7.89 especially refers to the small cherubims above the ark. The other three references could include the large sculptured cherubims in the Most Holy House, and possibly also the cherubims carved on the walls.

The Chronicler omits three things about the cherubims that are recorded in 1 Kings. The large cherubims were made of olive wood and were ten cubits high (1 Kings 6.23). 1 Kings 6.25 (RV), records that the cherubims were of "one measure and one form".

"However, since the ark was only one eighth of the width of the Most Holy Place there was a lack of proportion. These two cherubims filled the room from wall to wall…They demonstrated the importance of the guardianship of God's glory...The fact that their wings touched each other, and also touched the side walls of the house, suggests the unity that befits the presence of God...This oily wood may have been chosen for its suitability for carving...The wood in the ark below them was shittim, so in the one compartment four woods met: cedar round the walls, fir on the ceiling, olive in the doors and the cherubims, and shittim in the ark. All of them were covered with gold" (McShane).

Verse 12, in describing the position of the other cherub as the same as the one described in v.11, shows that the position of the two cherubims side by side was identical. When the ark was in place (5.7) the cherubims stood on either side of it, like two sentinels guarding it. "Their wings reaching from one wall to another symbolized how completely they protected the ark" (Selman).

Verse 13 records two things not mentioned in Kings: "they stood upon their feet", and "their faces were inward". The AV margin and the RV both have for the last clause, "toward the house", and the ESV has similar words. In contrast to the two smaller cherubims that Moses made facing each other and looking down on the mercy seat, these two larger cherubims looked "toward the house". "This is in harmony with the reign of righteousness which is foreshadowed in Solomon and the temple. At that time, righteousness reigning and being established, these symbols of God's power can look outward in blessing, instead of having their eyes fixed on the covenant alone...When God has established his throne in righteousness, He can turn toward the world to bless it according to that righteousness" (Gaebelein).

Saints can look forward to the Millennium when righteousness will reign and can also look beyond that to the eternal state when righteousness will dwell, i.e. righteousness will be perfectly at home. There will be feigned obedience during the Millennium but no feigned obedience during the eternal state.

Verse 14 (RV) says, "he made the vail". Since the vail is not mentioned in Kings, this is an important addition to the parallel description given there. The temple also had wooden doors overlaid with gold, including the inner doors of the Most Holy Place (4.22; 1 Kings 6.31-32). The Tabernacle had a vail that separated the Holy Place from the Most Holy Place. "The Holy Ghost this signifying, that the way into the holiest of all was not yet made manifest" (Heb 9.8). The Chronicler records that the temple of Solomon had both doors and a vail separating the Holy Place from the Most Holy Place. This is like the description of Herod's refurbished temple according to Josephus (Holy Wars, 5.5). The writer of the Chronicles was especially interested in the vail because of its continuity with the Tabernacle of Moses. God's rending of the vail of the temple from the top to the bottom is especially important to all Christians. Now, believers can have "boldness (or confidence) to enter into the holiest by the blood of Jesus" (Heb 10.19).

The vail of the temple and the vail of the Tabernacle were very similar. Linen was the material for both vails. "Although not apparent in the English text, the two linens were different, which is evident from the Hebrew words used. 'Linen' (SHESH) for the Tabernacle vail is described as 'fine twined linen' which resulted from the high number of threads…and also denotes a remarkable whiteness in the linen. This exceptionally white and finely woven linen is figurative of the inherent righteousness and purity of Christ in His sinless Manhood, during the days of His humiliation on earth.

'Linen' (BUTS) for the vail of the temple is translated 'fine linen'… This linen was white but its striking feature was the effect of a glistening brilliance, resembling that of our Lord's raiment at His transfiguration. This sparkling bright linen for the vail of the temple portrays the same Christ in righteousness but now glorified, ascended and exalted" (Page).

Verses 15-17: The Two Pillars in Front of the Temple

"No feature of the temple architecture has generated as much interest as the pillars Jachin and Boaz" (Dillard). The Chronicler's account of the pillars is much shorter than the fuller account of 1 Kings 7.15-22. When v.15 states, "Also he made…two pillars", it refers to Solomon because he sent to Hiram, the king of Tyre, to send him Hiram, the metal worker, to do all the works of brass (1 Kings 7.13-14,40,45). Kings consistently names them both as Hiram. The Chronicler always names them Huram except in 1 Chronicles 14.1 where the name of the king is given as Hiram.

In v.15 the measurement is given as "thirty and five cubits high". 1 Kings 7.15, 2 Kings 25.17 and Jeremiah 52.21 each describe the pillars as eighteen cubits high. The word translated "high" in v.15 is translated "long" 21 times in the Old Testament. This may mean that the two pillars were made from a brass tube 35 cubits long. Therefore each pillar was 17½ cubits to which a base half cubit high was to be added, making a total of 18 cubits. Another, less likely, solution to the difference is that the Hebrew for 18 and the Hebrew for 35 are very similar.

The Chronicler gives the location of the pillars explicitly as being "before the house" in v.15, and "before the temple" in v.17. The ESV gives "In front of the house" (v.15), and "in front of the temple" (v.17). Jeremiah 52.21 is the only place where it is stated about the pillars that "the thickness thereof was four fingers: it was hollow". Newberry has a helpful comment: "The Hebrew word for 'pillar' signifies 'round pillar'…Those skilled in these questions say that the proportion of thickness and size here given are those whereby the greatest amount of strength is secured by the smallest quantity of metal. That is just like God in His perfect wisdom".

McShane, commenting on 1 Kings 7.15-22 regarding the chapiters on the top of the pillars and their decorations or ornamentation, appropriately writes, "Although there are five references to these pillars in 2 Kings 25.13-17; 2 Chronicles 3.15-17; 4.12-13 and Jeremiah 52.20-23, as well as here, it is almost impossible to determine their design or to be dogmatic as to their appearance". Significantly, Newberry also writes, "In the English translation there is constant confusion between the network or chequer work and the chain work or wreaths - seven chains suspended on each pillar. The confusion is not in the Hebrew Scriptures, which are perfectly clear and distinct - but in the translation. It is only from the Hebrew originals that it is possible to harmonize these various discrepancies".

The Chronicler only refers to the chapiters (v.15), the chains, and the pomegranates (v.16). 1 Kings also refers to "nets of checker work" and "wreaths of chain work" (7.17). "Lily work" is also referred to in 1 Kings 7.19. 1 Kings 7.18,20 and 2 Chronicles 4.13 indicate that the total number of pomegranates mentioned in v.16 was 200 for each pillar. The tops of the pillars were highly ornamented with awe-inspiring singular beauty. Those pillars formed an entrance in keeping with the beautiful interior of the temple.

When we read in v.17, "one on the right hand, and the other on the left", the writer of the Chronicles is referring to the entrance of the temple. Solomon called the names Jachin and Boaz. Jachin means, "He shall establish", and Boaz means, "In Him is strength". The "He" and "Him" in these meanings surely refer to God. "The two pillars called Jachin and Boaz are the symbols of the stability of the government of this earth in the glorious reign of Christ which is typified by the reign of Solomon and the house that he built" (Gaebelein). These two pillars are also a constant reminder of the presence and power of God.

"Their names, Jachin and Boaz, are something of a puzzle, but the most likely theory is that these were the opening words of two inscriptions. On the basis of the various expressions found in the Psalms it has been suggested that the inscription may have read roughly as follows: 'Yahweh will establish (jachin) thy throne forever', and 'In the strength (boaz) of Yahweh shall the king rejoice'. If this is correct, the pillars may have commemorated God's promise concerning the Davidic dynasty. There are hints later in Kings that in taking the throne a king stood by one of these pillars to pledge himself to keep God's covenant laws (2 Kings 11.14; 23.3)" (New Bible Commentary). In keeping with the references to Josiah in 2 Kings 23.3, 2 Chronicles 34.31 states that "the king stood in his place". Page and the New Layman's Bible Commentary also link the pillars with the promise of the Davidic dynasty.

These pillars have spiritual significance for us today. The Apostle Paul refers to three leading men, James the Lord's brother, and two apostles, Peter and John, as "pillars" (Gal 2.9). "The pillars can reasonably be considered pictures of the leaders of the church…the main stress in the description of them (the pillars) is on their heads. The heads of leaders should be like bowls filled with wisdom and understanding. The network echoes the girding of the loins of the mind (1 Pet 1.13); the pomegranates suggest fruitfulness of thought, and the chains restraint and submission as well as the linking together of that which is beautiful. The lilies speak of the pure mind (2 Pet 3.1). The many references Paul makes to the 'mind' in Philippians indicate its importance. The references to self-control, vigilance, sobriety, holiness, not being soon angry and not being violent in his qualifications of those aspiring to be overseers emphasize how vital are the virtues of the mind for those who are leading others (1 Tim 3.1-6; Titus 1.7-9)" (McShane).

"The Lord made Jeremiah 'an iron pillar'. This metaphor implies his strong spiritual stamina and his strength of character to withstand the ruthless onslaught from 'kings...princes...priests...and people'. They would 'fight' him but he would 'prevail' because the Lord promised, 'I am with thee' (Jer 1.18-19)...Jeremiah is an example for us to follow. Like 'an iron pillar' we should stand firm, knowing the Lord is with us (cp. 2 Tim 4.17)" (Page).

Believers collectively as a local church are also likened to a pillar. 1 Timothy 3.15 describes a New Testament assembly as "the house of God, which is the church of the living God, the pillar and ground of the truth". In the temple of Diana of the Ephesians there were 127 pillars, each bearing testimony to a man or an idol. The local assembly bears testimony to a risen Man who is truth personified. "The living God" is in contrast to all dead idols. The meaning of the names of the two pillars has precious application for a local church today. As already indicated, the meaning of Jachin is "He shall establish". God should establish each local assembly. The meaning of the other pillar is "In Him is strength". The spiritual strength of the local assembly is in God and not in itself. No wonder then that the Apostle Paul commended the overseers of the local assembly at Ephesus to God (Acts 20.32). Spiritual power is needed to carry out spiritual principles and that can come from God only.

The overcomer in Revelation 3.12 is promised that the Lord will make him, "a pillar in the temple of my God, and he shall go no more out". What an encouraging promise - a pillar eternally!

2 CHRONICLES 4

Solomon's Reign

Introductory

Chapter 4 is intimately connected with chapter 3. The use of short paragraphs that begin with the information that Solomon "made…" starts at 3.8 and continues in this chapter to v.19. The difference is that chapter 3 concentrates on the structure of the temple, whereas chapter 4 focuses on the furnishings of the temple.

This chapter follows 1 Kings 7.23-51 with some variations. "Since the Chronicler concentrates on the over-all impressions created by the gold and bronze as symbols of God's presence among His people, he omits detailed description of the stands (1 Kings 7.27-37), but adds features which speak both of God's presence and of a place for His people (vv.6b-9)…The pattern of Moses' obedience in constructing the Tent (cp. Ex 25-31 and 35-40) is therefore continued, in both cases culminating in God's house being filled with his glory (5.13-14; cp. Ex 40.34-38)" (Selman).

Outline of Chapter 4

Verse 1:	The brazen altar.
Verses 2-5:	The brazen sea or the large laver.
Verse 6:	The ten smaller lavers.
Verse 7:	The ten lampstands.
Verse 8:	The ten tables and the basons of gold.
Verses 9-10:	The courtyards, the doors, and the location of the brazen sea.
Verses 11-18:	The articles made of brass by Huram.
Verses 19-22:	The articles made of gold by Solomon.

Verse 1: The Brazen Altar

This verse does not have a parallel in Kings but the brazen altar is mentioned in 1 Kings 8.22,54,64; 9.25 and 2 Kings 16.14. The dimensions given of twenty cubits long and twenty cubits wide make it sixteen times as big as the brazen altar for the Tabernacle. The dimensions given in Exodus 27.1 and 38.1 are five cubits long and five cubits wide. Since the Tabernacle altar was only three cubits high, it could have been used without steps. But the altar for the temple was ten cubits high, which would require steps. Steps for an altar were forbidden in Exodus 20.26. That restriction no longer applied after the priests were clothed as directed in Exodus 28.42. 2 Kings 16.14 gives the location of the brazen altar as "the forefront of the house". 2 Chronicles 6.12-13 indicates more precisely that it was near the centre of the courts. The altar was the first thing one encountered coming inside the court. The brazen altar was a continual reminder that sinful man can only approach God through sacrifice, which looked forward to the perfect substitutionary sacrifice of Christ (Heb 9.12; 10.12).

It is striking that the measurements of the altar and the most holy house were exactly the same, twenty cubits square. Fereday writes, "... thus giving us the sweet assurance that the sacrifice of Christ is equal to all the demands of the holiness of God. What rest and peace this gives to conscience and heart".

"Although there was between the altar and the Most Holy Place this similarity in the sizes, there was a dissimilarity in the respective metals. All was gold in the Most Holy Place, but the altar was of brass, meaning it was overlaid with brass. Upon the altar the sin offering, amongst others, was offered, and so brass may symbolize the righteousness of God in judgment upon man's sin. The Most Holy Place was eventually filled with the glory of the Lord, which may signify that gold is a symbol of the glory of God. The fact that measurements of the altar and the Most Holy Place were equal suggests the equality between the various attributes of God. For instance, God is not more righteous than glorious. Neither is He more glorious than He is righteous. His righteousness equals His glory. This is true of all divine attributes. Whether it is the wrath of God or the love of God, both are equal" (Page).

However we should note that, "The Christian altar is not physical at all, and those who seek to perpetuate materialism in worship have no right to eat at this altar (Heb 13.10)" (Heading).

Verses 2-5: The Brazen Sea

The reason that it is called a sea is because of its great size. It could hold 3,000 baths (4.5), but it usually held only 2,000 baths (1 Kings 7.26). According to the "Tables of Measures" in the Newberry Bible 1 bath is equal to 7.5 gallons. That makes 3,000 baths equal to 22,500 gallons, an enormous amount of water. The location of the brazen sea is given in 1 Kings 7.39 and 2 Chronicles 4.10. The words in Kings are most easily understood: "and he set the sea on the right side of the house eastward, over against the south". The RV is even clearer, giving for the last three words, "toward the south".

The molten sea was cast like a huge circular bowl. The dimension from brim to brim was ten cubits. The thickness of the brim was "an handbreadth" (v.5). The handbreadth was equal to 3 or 4 inches. Subtracting two handbreadths from the diameter satisfies quite closely the formula for the relationship between diameter and circumference with the circumference of thirty cubits for the inside of the vessel.

1 Kings 7.24 records, "And under the brim of it round about there were knops compassing it, ten in a cubit". Verse 3 of this chapter says, "the similitude of oxen" and "two rows of oxen". Kings may be giving a generalized account while the Chronicler is being more specific.

The molten sea replaced the laver of the Tabernacle, but there are interesting points of difference between them. The laver was made from the women's brazen mirrors (Ex 38.8). The brazen sea was made from the spoils of David's conquests (1 Chr 18.8). In the case of the former, a woman's beauty is her distinction and she would naturally cherish that which shows it, but some women gladly gave up their mirrors to make a laver for the priests of God. Mirrors link cleansing with self-examination. In the latter, the spoils speak of victory in keeping with glories of the kingdom pictured in the reign of Solomon.

The dimensions and the capacity are not given for the laver of the Tabernacle, but they are both given for the molten sea. The laver and the brazen sea were both to be used for the priests. It is only the Chronicler who tells us the purpose of the brazen sea: "the sea was for the priests to wash in" (v.6). Because the brazen sea was five cubits high the priests could not dip their hands or their feet into it. It is probable that pipes were connected to the mouths of the oxen and they served as faucets to draw water. The priests were to wash their hands and their feet at the brazen sea before they went into the Holy Place. While serving in the temple the priests neither wore shoes nor gloves, so it was necessary for them to cleanse themselves lest they bring any defilement into the temple. How solemn that if a priest did not wash to clean himself when entering the Tabernacle or serving at the altar he would die (Ex 30.20-21). When the priests of Israel were consecrated, they had a complete bath (Ex 29.4). That complete ceremonial wash was never repeated.

This brazen sea has spiritual lessons for today. God expects holiness on the part of all who approach Him. The huge quantity of water in the brazen sea indicates that He has made ample provision for the cleansing of defilement. The brazen sea speaks of sanctification.

Two of the aspects of sanctification are illustrated here. First, there is positional sanctification, which takes place at the new birth, "the washing of regeneration" (Titus 3.5). This corresponds to the complete bathing of the priests at their consecration. Our Lord Jesus referred to this in John 13.10: "He that is washed needeth not save to wash his feet, but is clean every whit: and ye are clean, but not all". He knew Judas had never had the washing of regeneration.

Then there is the practical and progressive sanctification that is wrought by the application of the Word to the daily lives of saints in the power of the Holy Spirit. This corresponds to the priests washing their hands and feet. It also corresponds to our Lord Jesus washing the disciples' feet. He said to Peter, "If I wash thee not, thou hast no part with me" (Jn 13.8). It is important to notice that our Lord Jesus did not say, "no part in me". His actual words were, "no part with me". The words of Psalm 119.9 fit in with these thoughts: "Wherewithal shall a young man cleanse his way? by taking heed thereto according to thy word". Also, the psalmist David wrote, "Lord, I have loved the habitation of thy house, and the place where thy honour dwelleth" (Ps 26.8). In v.6 of the same psalm, he writes, "I will wash mine hands in innocency. so will I compass thine altar, O Lord".

In Revelation 4.6 there is an allusion to the molten sea. But what John saw in heaven was not a sea of water, but a "sea of glass like unto crystal". How fitting this is because the redeemed in glory no longer need any cleansing. They are already in an abiding, perfect state of holiness since they have seen our Lord Jesus as He is and they have been made like Him (1 Jn 3.2).

"The oxen speak of those who carry the burden and labour to bring the Word of God to the people of God that it may be applied to all who appreciate their need of holiness of life. The washed hands are a reminder of the works and the cleansed feet are a reminder of the walk of the people of God" (McShane).

Twelve oxen supported the molten sea, three of which faced each direction of the compass. All their hinder parts were inward. These oxen were probably life size. They were a reminder of how the twelve tribes encamped around the Tabernacle, three on a side, in their wilderness journeys to the Promised Land. "In the choice of oxen or bullocks as supporters of the basin, it is impossible to overlook the significance of this selection of the first and highest of the sacrificial animals to represent the priestly service, especially if we compare the position of the lions on Solomon's throne (1 Kings 10.20)" (Keil).

Verse 5 records, "…and the brim of it like the work of the brim of a cup, with flowers of lilies". The lilies are a reminder of the purity that God wants of all who draw near to Him. As lilies were sweet smelling (Song 5.13), so holy living is a sweet fragrance delightful to the Lord. Lives of holiness are also a testimony to others about our God.

Verse 6: The Ten Smaller Lavers

These portable lavers were something altogether new. There was nothing like them used in the Tabernacle. The first five words of v.6 correspond to 1 Kings 7.38, and the next twelve words correspond with 1 Kings 7.39. The Chronicler says nothing here about the wheeled bases for the lavers (recorded in 1 Kings 7.27-37), though he refers to them later (v.14). He does add what is omitted in Kings - information about the purpose of the lavers and the sea. The function of the lavers with regards to the burnt offerings (v.6) is to "wash in them", and the purpose of the sea is "for the priests to wash in" (v.6). The sea had the same purpose as the laver in the Tabernacle (Ex 30.17-21). This is another occasion where the writer of the Chronicles links the temple with the Tabernacle. The purpose of the ten movable bases regarding the burnt offerings is in keeping with the instructions in Leviticus 1.9,13, for washing parts of the burnt offerings. These portable lavers were large enough to handle oxen, the largest of the burnt offerings. The ten movable lavers were supplied with water from the great reservoir in the molten sea.

Verse 6 records that the burnt offerings were to be washed in the smaller lavers. After the burnt offering had been killed and cut in pieces,

God's Word directed that the priest "shall wash the inwards and the legs with water" (Lev 1.9,13). That makes the burnt offering a beautiful picture of the perfect sinlessness of Christ. 1 Peter 2.22 speaks of His legs, "Who did no sin, neither was guile found in His mouth". The sinlessness and guilelessness of Christ not only endured the test of scrutiny, but also the test of intimacy. Intimate John who leaned on His bosom wrote of Him that "in him is no sin" (1 Jn 3.5). That takes care of His pure inwards. Paul also wrote of Him that "he... knew no sin" (2 Cor 5.21).

Because the sinless Saviour died,
My sinful soul is counted free;
For God, the Just, is satisfied
To look on Him and pardon me.
(C. L. Bancroft)

Verse 7: The Ten Lampstands

Verses 7-9 have no parallel in Kings, although the summary in 1 Kings 7.48-50 mentions the candlesticks. In the temple there were ten golden lampstands with their seventy lamps. "The word is generally rendered, 'candlestick', but the word 'candle' never occurs in the sacred Scriptures, neither in the Hebrew nor in the Greek; it is always 'lamp' and 'lampstand'... The candle is self-sufficient and self-continuing; you have only to light it, and it burns from beginning to end. Not so the lamp, which is dependent on the OIL, typical of the HOLY SPIRIT" (Newberry).

The phrase, "according to their form" (v.7), is better translated, "according to the ordinance concerning them" (RV). Similarly in v.20 the phrase, "after the manner", is "according to the ordinance" in the RV.

In v.20 the context shows that the phrase there refers to the use of the lampstands, but the expression in v.7 may refer to the construction of the lampstands (Ex 25.31-39; 37.17-24). That would fit well with the desire of the Chronicler to parallel the work of the temple with the work of the Tabernacle. 1 Chronicles 28.14-18 also had a bearing on the construction of these ten golden lampstands.

"Unlike the brass used for the outside vessels which was not weighed, the gold for all these internal vessels was not only provided by David, but for each of them, he allocated a distinct weight (1 Chr 28.14-18). The pattern for all these was given to him and so he knew exactly the amount of precious metal needed. It has often been noted that no sizes were given for the golden candlestick of the Tabernacle, but its weight was one talent of pure gold. This settled, indirectly, its dimensions (Ex 25.39). Similarly the amount of gold set apart for these vessels decided their size" (McShane).

Verse 7 records that Solomon "set them in the temple". 1 Kings 7.49 and 2 Chronicles 4.20 are both more precise in recording that they were "before the oracle", i.e. before the Most Holy Place, five on the right side and five on the left side. Those ten lampstands made a lane of light in the Holy Place.

The number ten and its multiples have a prominent place in the arrangements for the temple. Besides all the measurements of the temple itself which were multiples of ten, there were ten brazen lavers set on ten bases, ten lampstands of gold, ten tables of gold, and a hundred basons of gold (vv.6-8).

"Numbers in Scripture have meaning. Ten is the number of responsibility, evidenced in the ten commandments of the Law. The prominence of ten in Solomon's temple is thus a reminder that everything was being set up on the ground of responsibility, and that the continuance of that marvellous system of glory and blessing depended upon the faithfulness of king and people" (Fereday).

The ten lampstands with their seventy lamps gave abundance of light in the temple. Light brings to mind two verses in Psalm 119 and one verse in Proverbs. Verse 105 of Psalm 119 says, "Thy word is a lamp unto my feet, and a light unto my path"; and in v.130 we read that "the entrance of thy words giveth light; it giveth understanding to the simple". Proverbs 4.18 says, "The path of the just is as the shining light, that shineth more and more unto the perfect day". All of God's people need the light of all the Word of God all the days of their life.

Paul is himself a good illustration of the light of Proverbs 4.18 in the three times his conversion is recorded in Acts. In Acts 9.3 there is "a light". When he tells of his conversion in Acts 22.6 he describes "a great light". Relating his conversion to King Agrippa in Acts 26.13 it "is a light from heaven, above the brightness of the sun" (and that was at noon). While the light was getting brighter, he was thinking less of himself. He calls himself first "the least of the apostles" (1 Cor 15.9). Later, in Ephesians 3.8, he says he is "less than the least of all saints". Still later he calls himself the chief of sinners (1 Tim 1.15).

In Revelation 2 and 3 seven local churches (assemblies) are represented by seven golden lampstands. As lamps are dependent on oil, which is a picture of the Holy Spirit, so each assembly is dependent on the Holy Spirit to be able to shine brightly in their testimony for their Lord Jesus Christ.

Verse 8: The Ten Tables and the Basons of Gold

The ten tables are only mentioned here and in v.19 but the plural, "tables", is also found in 1 Chronicles 28.16. "Table", singular, is found in 1 Kings 7.48, 2 Chronicles 13.11 and 29.18. It may be that even though there were ten tables only one was used at any given time. Another possible reconciliation is that the ten tables could have been considered as one unit.

The Tabernacle had only one laver, one lampstand, and one table. The temple had ten of each. Because 2 Chronicles 13.11 speaks of one lampstand and one table, that may have led to a "Jewish tradition that the temple contained both the new ten and the original one of each" (New Bible Commentary).

Because there were ten lampstands and ten tables and they were given the same location in the temple, five on the right side and five on the left, some commentators have thought that the lampstands were placed on the tables. Verse 19 indicates that the tables were for the shewbread and 1 Chronicles 28.16 seems quite conclusive that at the time of David and Solomon there were tables (plural) used for the shewbread. However one should note that 1 Kings 7.48 and 2 Chronicles 13.11 suggest that only one table was used for this purpose.

Since the tables were very close to the lampstands they were always in the light of the sanctuary. There is a connection between the light of the lampstands and the fellowship symbolized by the tables. This thought of light and fellowship is expressed in 1 John 1.7: "But if we walk in the light, as he is in the light, we have fellowship one with another, and the blood of Jesus Christ his Son cleanseth us from all sin". Surely such a walk is a blessed privilege for every child of God!

The size of the tables was limited by the amount of gold allocated for them in 1 Chronicles 28.16. Upon the table there was the shewbread, which spoke of Christ as the bread of life (Jn 6.35). "Christian fellowship is distinctive because, as the apostle of old says, 'our fellowship is with the Father, and with his Son Jesus Christ' (1 Jn 1.3). This glorious truth, which should thrill us, is foreshadowed in the tables of gold...Emphasis is on the gold - the glory of the temple. Our fellowship is with the Father who is 'the Father of glory', and with His Son who is 'the Lord of glory' (Eph 1.17; 1 Cor 2.8)" (Page).

The last part of v.8 states, "And he made an hundred basons of gold". "The word for 'basons' here is derived from the Hebrew verb meaning 'to sprinkle'" (The Nelson Study Bible). The priests used these basons for receiving and sprinkling the blood of sacrifice, or for liquid offerings, or for both.

Verses 9-10: The Courtyard, the Doors, and the Location of the Brazen Sea

The court of the priests (v.9) is the inner court of 1 Kings 6.36 and it was only for the priests. The great court was for all other worshippers. 1 Kings 7.9,12 tells of the great court.

This division into two courts emphasized the fact that in the Old Testament there was not the universal priesthood of all believers that would come about through the work of our Lord Jesus Christ on the cross. "For through him we both have access by one Spirit unto the Father" (Eph 2.18). Through Him, our Great High Priest, every believer has direct access to the throne of grace (Heb 4.14-16). In the Old Testament the priests were all descended from Aaron by physical birth. In the New Testament every believer is a priest by spiritual birth by being "born again" (1 Pet 2.5).

Martin Luther believed in the priesthood of all believers and probably most evangelicals also do today. In every New Testament local assembly every male believer in fellowship should be free to exercise his priesthood in public prayer, praise and worship in submission to the Word of God and under the control of the Holy Spirit (unless under discipline). Similarly, every female believer should also exercise her priesthood, but (according to 1 Corinthians 14.34) her participation should be inaudible in New Testament local church gatherings. This is in contrast to a humanly devised program for worship as is found in many places.

The doors for the court were overlaid with brass. "The doors speak of Jesus, our Door to the Father (Jn 10.9). Why were they made of brass? Because, throughout Scripture, brass is the metal of judgment and the only way we enter into the presence of God is by realizing that Jesus Christ our Door was judged for our sin" (Courson).

The writer of Kings records how the doors to the oracle were made of olive wood and the doors for the entrance of the temple were of fir, but all those doors were overlaid with gold (1 Kings 6.31-35). He also records that the hinges were of gold (1 Kings 7.50).

In v.10 the description of the location of the brazen sea is almost identical to that given in 1 Kings 7.39. The location of the brazen altar has already been discussed in the commentary on vv. 2-5 above.

Verses 11-18: The Articles Made of Brass by Huram

Verses 11-22 resemble closely 1 Kings 7.40-50. Verses 11-18 give a summary of the works of brass made by Huram. Verse 11 states that "Huram finished the work that he was to make for king Solomon for the house of God". How good it is for each believer to finish what God has for him or her to do! Even though he was a master workman in all metals, it seems he only made articles of brass. In his summary the Chronicler includes items that he has already written about such as the pillars (vv.12-13), the lavers (v.14), and "One sea and twelve oxen under it" (v.15). For the first time he mentions the bases (v.14) that are fully described only in 1 Kings 7.27-37. He also records for the first time smaller utensils like, "the pots, and the shovels, and the basons" (v.11), and "the fleshhooks, and all their instruments" (v.16). These smaller utensils were necessary for the ministry at the temple. Verse 16 says that the articles were made of "bright brass". That seems to indicate that the brass was polished after it was moulded.

It appears that the nearest place that had suitable clay ground for molding the vessels was in the Jordan valley near Succoth (v.17). "Excavations in this area have confirmed that Succoth was a center of metallurgy during the period of the monarchy" (Zondervan King James Study Bible).

The clay ground and the bright brass were both essential for making the things that God had planned for His house. "From the most humble conditions in earth have been produced the choicest of instruments God has used in His work. The brass was brought down to Jordan, a type of death and judgment, before it was brought up to adorn the temple courts.

Many would like to be chosen vessels for God's service but fail to realize the humbling experience essential to their making" (McShane).

It is clear that Huram made the articles of brass. In v.16, "Huram his father" should read "Huram-abi", or "Huram the master workman". Verse 18 records that "Solomon made all these vessels in great abundance". Solomon commissioned Huram to make them. This section closes with the words, "for the weight of the brass could not be found out", emphasizing the greatness of the achievement. Most of the brass, if not all of it, was taken from the two cities of Tibhath and Chun after David defeated Hadarezer (1 Chr 18.8).

"Again, brass speaks of judgment. Just as the weight of the brass used in the temple was too great to weigh, the judgment Jesus absorbed on our behalf cannot be measured" (Courson).

Verses 19-22: The Articles Made of Gold by Solomon

As in the previous eight verses there is a summary of the articles of brass that Huram made, so these verses give a summary of the work of Solomon in making the articles of gold. Verses 11-22 draw attention to the co-operation between Solomon and Huram. Huram and Solomon in a sense made all of the articles just as Moses and Bezaleel were equally responsible for making the Tabernacle (Ex 38.22). There is much more detail about the articles of brass (vv.11-18) than about the articles of gold (vv.19-22). Solomon had more direct control over the making of the articles of gold but, even so, Scripture does not tell if he constructed any of them personally.

"The differences in the metals are also significant. They illustrate the principle of gradation, whereby the costlier metals represent a greater degree of holiness. Thus, the bronze objects are all associated with the temple entrance, but the gold is reserved for the interior" (Selman).

Verses 19-22 closely parallel 1 Kings 7.48-50. The golden altar of v.19 is also called the golden altar in 1 Kings 7.48 (RV, ESV). The golden altar is called the "altar of incense" in 1 Chronicles 28.18, fittingly, because incense was burned daily on it (Lk 1.9). Before Solomon began building the temple, he said that he wanted to build "an house to the name of the Lord…to burn before him sweet incense… and for the burnt offerings morning and evening" (2 Chr 2.4). In the instructions for the temple the golden altar is only mentioned briefly and there is no detailed description of it given in the only three verses that relate to it (1 Kings 6.22; 7.48; 2 Chr 4.19). In contrast, fourteen verses are given over to the golden altar of the Tabernacle (Ex 30.1-10; 37.25-28).

Saints appreciate that our Lord Jesus Christ as our Great High Priest "ever liveth to make intercession" for us (Heb 7.25). "This grand truth is foreshadowed in the cedar wood used for making this altar, as it is not liable to pest attacks or rot. Therefore, the virtually indestructible cedar wood is a type of Christ in resurrection. The risen Christ 'ever liveth' and 'continueth ever' as our Great High Priest 'to make intercession' for us" (Page).

The psalmist David wanted his prayer to be as acceptable to God as the evening sacrifice with the accompanying sweet incense was to Him. Psalm 141.2 says, "Let my prayer be set forth before thee as incense; and the lifting up of my hands as the evening sacrifice". Incense is again linked with the prayers of saints in Revelation 5.8 and 8.3: "And another angel came and stood at the altar, having a golden censer; and there was given unto him much incense, that he should offer it with the prayers of all saints upon the golden altar which was before the throne". "The AV reading…shows that it is the incense that he is given that the angel adds to the prayers. The angel himself adds nothing; he adds to the prayers of saints that which has been given to him, the 'much incense' that speaks of Christ" (J. Allen). These verses show the importance of the prayers of saints to God.

Much incense is ascending
Before the eternal throne;
God graciously is bending
To hear each feeble groan.
To all our prayers and praises
Christ adds His sweet perfume,
And love the censer raises
Their odours to consume.
(Mary Peters)

The Chronicler mentions the tables in the last part of v.19 (already recorded in v.8). He does the same regarding the lampstands (v.20) that he has earlier described (v.7). The flowers of gold (v.21) refer to the ornamentation on the lampstands. The furnishings of the temple were designed to correspond to similar furnishings in the Tabernacle. Although there were ten tables and ten lampstands for the temple and only one of each for the Tabernacle, their functions remained the same.

The writer of the Chronicles records for the first time tongs (v.21), snuffers, spoons, and censers, as well as basons, all of gold (v.22). These articles were all necessary for ministry in the temple. In the last part of v.22 he mentions the doors of which he had already spoken (v.9). All the articles for the interior of the temple were made of gold that speaks of deity.

Edersheim, writing about the doors to the Most Holy Place, makes this significant comment: "These doors we suppose to have always stood open, the entrance being concealed by the great veil, which the high priest lifted, when on the Day of Atonement he went into the innermost sanctuary…This we conclude from the circumstance, that otherwise there would have been no use of a veil, and that we do not read of the high priest opening the doors on the Day of Atonement".

2 CHRONICLES 5

Solomon's Reign

Introduction

This chapter is the first of three dealing with the dedication of the temple. With the work for the temple finished (v.1), the remainder of the chapter tells of the climax, bringing the ark of God into the Most Holy Place. The ark was the most important vessel in the temple. It was the first Tabernacle vessel for which instructions were given for its construction (Ex 25.10-22). It was also the only piece of furniture used both in the Tabernacle and in the temple.

However, the great importance of the ark is that it signified the presence of God. This was demonstrated by the fact that the cloud of glory filled the temple after the ark was in its rightful place. The loss of the ark to the Philistines in the time of Samuel was lamented by Eli's daughter-in-law just before she died with these words, "The glory is departed from Israel: because the ark of God is taken" (1 Sam 4.21-22). The Psalmist records the same event by saying that God "delivered his strength into captivity, and his glory into the enemy's hand" (Ps 78.61). The ark was also the only vessel put into the temple with a special ceremony.

This account is a reminder of the occasion when David brought the ark from the house of Obed-edom to the tent he had pitched for it in the city of David (1 Chr 15.1-29). "But this time everything was on a grander scale; the ark's resting place was not to be a tent but the magnificent temple, and the sacrifices consisting of sheep and oxen beyond numbering (v.6)...the glory of the Lord, visibly manifested as a cloud filled the building (vv.13-14). This echoes the first setting up of the Tabernacle (containing the ark) by Moses (Ex 40.34-35). In both cases, the phenomenon indicated God's acceptance and approval of what was done" (New Bible Commentary).

God's glory in the Old Testament prepares the way for the full revelation of glory in the Son of God. "The Word became flesh and Tabernacled among us (and we beheld his glory, glory of the only begotten of the Father), full of grace and truth" (Jn 1.14, RV margin). Our Lord Jesus was the only perfectly balanced person who ever lived. He was the true meal offering (Lev 2.1), the fine flour with no unevenness in it. He had every desirable characteristic in perfect blend. Glory is associated with His birth (Lk 2.9) and with His transfiguration (Lk 9.31; 2 Pet 1.17). He was glorified as the Son of God when He raised Lazarus who had been dead for four days (Jn 11.4). He was glorified as the Son of Man at the cross for there we have the greatest display of moral excellence ever seen in a man, and there He fully glorified God (Jn 13.31). It is interesting that the brother of our Lord Jesus referred to Him as "our Lord Jesus Christ, the Lord of glory" (James 2.1, ESV).

David made a serious mistake when he tried to bring up the ark on a new cart and Uzza was smitten dead (1 Chr 13.1-14). It was understandable for the Philistines to put the ark on a new cart because they had neither the Word of God nor the Levites to carry out God's Word, but David should have known better. Thankfully, he realized his mistake three months later and resolved to do according to the Word of God when he said, "None ought to carry the ark of God but the Levites: for them hath the Lord chosen to carry the ark of God" (1 Chr 15.2). David said further to the Levites, "For because ye did it not at the first, the Lord our God made a breach upon us, for that we sought him not after the due order" (1 Chr 15.13). Solomon profited from his father's mistake and corrective action. May all saints see the importance of going by the Word of God, exemplified here by David.

"The Chronicler has made a number of brief but important additions to the comparable material in Kings (e.g. 5.11b-13a; 7.12b-15). This expansion contrasts with his treatment of the building work (chs.3-4) where the earlier account was reduced by almost 50%, confirming that the Chronicler's real interest is in what the temple signifies. Therefore these chapters are not so much about the temple of God as about the God to whom the temple belongs" (Selman).

There are a number of parallels in this chapter to David bringing the ark to the city of David (1 Chr 13 and 15). "Most important of all, a divine revelation is associated with each event (1 Chr 17.1-15; 2 Chr 7.12-22), in David's case followed by a prayer of thanksgiving (1 Chr 17.16-27), and in Solomon's preceded by a prayer of petition (2 Chr 6.12-22). Both of these messages from God are pivotal for the Chronicler's theology. The parallelism between the work of David and that of Solomon expresses its joint nature" (Leslie C. Allen).

"Solomon presides in the service as David did in bringing up the ark to Jerusalem…David, like a very good man, brings the ark to a convenient place, near him; Solomon like a very great man, brings it to a magnificent place" (Matthew Henry).

2 Chronicles 5.2-14 follows 1 Kings 8.1-11 closely. The special interests of the writer of the Chronicles are reflected in the addition of 5.11b-13a, and a slight change in v.4.

Outline of Chapter 5

Verse 1: All the work for the temple finished.
Verses 2-3: Solomon gathered all Israel.
Verses 4-6: The ark's last journey.
Verses 7-10: The ark's last resting place.
Verses 11-14: The glory of the Lord and the praise of Israel.

Verse 1: All the Work for the Temple Finished

This verse provides a transition between the building and the dedication of the temple. Solomon's finishing the work is a reminder of our Lord

Jesus: "My meat is to do the will of him that sent me, and to finish his work" (Jn 4.34). That was His satisfying portion and He did not rest content until He could shout victoriously on the cross, "It is finished" (Jn 19.30).

"The sense of fulfillment is brought out further in some of the language used. The word translated 'finished' (5.1) is *wattishlam*, which is linguistically akin to Solomon's name. Both words strongly suggest the idea of 'peace' (*shalom*). The 'finishing', therefore, is only an end in the sense of purpose. It opens on to something new, full of possibilities for good - for...*shalom* suggests all the richness and delight that are part of God's deepest purposes for humanity in creation" (McConville).

The account of the building of the temple begins and ends with a reference to David (3.1; 5.1). The writer of the Chronicles records Solomon paying tribute to David by putting all David's dedicated things into the treasuries of the house of God. Just as spoils of the Egyptians went into the building of the Tabernacle, so also the spoils of Israel's enemies went into the building of the temple. The Chronicler thus shows again that the work of the temple was a joint work of David and Solomon.

Several times the writer of the Chronicles refers to David dedicating things for the temple (1 Chr 18.8,11; 22.14; 26.26-27; 29.2-5). After using all that was necessary from these for the temple, Solomon faithfully put the rest in the treasuries which were most likely in the upper and side rooms of the temple (1 Kings 6.5-10).

Verses 2-3: Solomon Gathered all Israel

Solomon assembled all the leaders (v.2) and all the men of Israel (v.3) to bring up the ark as his father had done (1 Chr 13.1-3; 15.3). The ark is called "the ark of the covenant of the Lord" ten more times in 1 and 2 Chronicles, and once it is called "the ark of the covenant of God" (1 Chr 16.6). The ark had been in the tent that David had pitched for it in Zion (v.2; 1 Chr 16.1).

"Originally the name Zion was restricted to the southern portion of the hill rising on the east side of Jerusalem. Subsequently the name was extended to the northern portion on which the temple stood, and finally it connoted all Jerusalem. The verb 'to bring up' is exactly descriptive since the hill on which the temple stood was higher than the hill of Zion" (Slotki).

This dedication was, appropriately, held during the Feast of Tabernacles (the last feast of the year) in the seventh month (v.3). Part of that feast involved dwelling in booths (Lev 23.42-43). It was commemorative, reminding them of God's care for them as pilgrims through the wilderness. The ark had guided them all the way, and now it was going to have a permanent resting place. It is noteworthy that those who came back to Jerusalem from Babylon after their exile also dedicated the altar during the feast of Tabernacles (Ezra 3.4).

Since 1 Kings 6.38 states that the house was finished in the eleventh year and the eighth month, it is probable that Solomon waited eleven months to the next Feast of Tabernacles for the dedication, although commentators differ as to the exact time. It is possible that there were other matters that had to be arranged during those eleven months.

Verses 4-6: The Ark's Last Journey

1 Kings 8.3 records that the priests took up the ark, but here it is stated that the Levites did so (v.4). The writer of the Chronicles links up with David's words in 1 Chronicles 15.2: "None ought to carry the ark of God but the Levites". His words were based on the law of Moses (Num 3.31; Deut 10.8; 31.9), but the Chronicler is careful to record that the priests put the ark in the Most Holy Place because they were the only ones allowed to enter there (v.7). It has been suggested that the writer wanted to emphasize the difference between the priests and the Levites (1 Chr 23.24-32) and to put the latter in a favourable light.

The ark was brought up (v.5) from the tent that David pitched for it at Jerusalem (2 Sam 6.17; 1 Chr 15.1; 2 Chr 1.4). Because of the importance and solemnity of the occasion there were so many sheep and oxen sacrificed that they could not be numbered (v.6). "The Hebrew participial form, 'sacrificing' (v.6) would indicate that the sacrifices were being made as the ark progressed the short distance from the city of David to the temple. This view is strengthened by the precedent set by David when they brought the ark to Jerusalem (2 Sam 6.13). With each six steps taken by the priests carrying the ark, David sacrificed a bull and a fattened calf" (Patterson & Austel).

Regarding the sacrifices McShane writes, "These were almost certainly peace offerings that provided food for the crowds as well as giving God His due".

The Tabernacle of the congregation (or tent of meeting) and the holy vessels were also brought up (v.5). This was the original Tabernacle that had been in Gibeon (1.3). The term, "Tabernacle of the congregation", or "tent of meeting" is only used of the Tabernacle. The Tabernacle and the holy vessels were probably stored in the treasuries of the temple (1 Chr 26.20) as the "dedicated things" were (v.1).

Verses 7-10: The Ark's Last Resting Place

The ark of the covenant of the Lord (v.7) is called "the ark of the testimony" often in Exodus because God told Moses to "put into the ark the testimony which I shall give thee" (Ex 25.16) and Moses did so (Ex 40.20). The testimony consisted of the two tables of stone (Ex 31.18). The priests brought the ark into the Most Holy Place under the wings of the cherubim (vv.7-8). The ark is given great importance in Chronicles. It is mentioned there 49 times. It is interesting to note that there is an allusion to the ark in Asaph's Psalm (78.61) that has been referred to in the introduction. But Psalm 132 (whose author is unknown but whose subject is David) is the only Psalm that has a direct reference to the ark (vv.7-8). "With what eager anticipation they (the pilgrim bands) must have journeyed toward the very dwelling place of Jehovah, to kneel in worship at His footstool, His sanctuary. They call to Him, 'Arise, O Lord, into thy rest; thou and the ark of thy strength'. The Ark, symbol of His strength and power, had found a resting place, and to that place of Jehovah's rest in Zion pilgrims were now travelling" (Flanigan).

"Never before had it been in such a palatial setting. Even in the Most Holy Place of the Tabernacle, with its gold-covered wooden sides and its beautiful curtain ceiling, it had the earthen floor to rest on, but from this time until the Captivity it was completely surrounded by gold" (McShane).

According to the dates given by some, the Tabernacle was used from 1491 BC to 1012 BC (479 years) and this temple was used from 1012 BC to 610 BC (402 years). This would mean that the Tabernacle was in use 77 more years than the temple even though it was a portable structure. The ark had been separated from the Tabernacle from 1141 BC when the Philistines captured it until the time when it was put in its proper place in the temple in 1012 BC (129 years).

The RV and ESV for 1 Kings 8.8 and 2 Chronicles 5.9 do not refer to the staves being drawn out but rather to their length. Thus the ESV for 1 Kings 8.8 and 2 Chronicles 5.9 has, "the poles were so long that the ends of the poles were seen from the Holy Place before the inner sanctuary, but they could not be seen from outside". Of course, only the priests and Levites could go inside the Holy Place and could see this. The Word of God does not make this point concerning the staves clear, but there is a possibility that the poles were a help in guiding the high priest on the Day of Atonement. Exodus 25.15 states concerning the staves, "they shall not be taken from it". They were a reminder of God's faithfulness to them during forty years in the wilderness.

The last phrase of v.9 is, "And there it is unto this day". The ark may have been destroyed at the time when the temple was burnt (36.19). Verse 18 of that chapter tells of many vessels carried to Babylon. All the vessels that were brought back from Babylon are listed in Ezra 1.9-11 and the ark was not one of them. However, as the Chronicler wishes to emphasise the continuity between Tabernacle and this temple, he may be noting that so long as the temple lasted the ark was present. "It is a deliberate assertion of continuity between Solomon's temple and the temple of the Chronicler's day. The phrase, 'to this day', often seems to imply a sense of perpetuity" (Coggins).

The tables of stone (which Moses put in the ark 479 years previously in Exodus 40.20; Deuteronomy 10.5) were the only things in the ark (v.10). The Chronicler refers here to the covenant given at Sinai because the ten commandments as engraved on Moses' two tables of stone expressed the response that God expected from His covenant people that He had already redeemed from Egypt (Ex 20.2). Nehemiah acknowledged that the laws given at Sinai were "right judgments, and true laws, good statues and commandments" (Neh 9.13).

Verse 10, stating that there was nothing in the ark except the two tables of stone which Moses put there, seems to contradict Hebrews 9.4 which records, "wherein was the golden pot that had manna, and Aaron's rod that budded, and the tables of the covenant". "But not only according to the Talmud (Joma 52, b), but according to uniform Jewish tradition… what is mentioned in Hebrews 9.4 had really been placed in the Ark, although the emphatic notice in 1 Kings 8.9 (also in 2 Chronicles 5.10) indicates it was no longer there at the time of Solomon. It may have been removed previous to, or after the capture of the ark by the Philistines" (Edersheim).

"Again, we may observe that the items lost are restored to those whom the Lord calls 'overcomers' in Revelation 2-3. The 'hidden manna' is known only by revelation (Rev 2.17) and the 'tree of life' is also given (Rev 2.7)" (Heading).

"I believe the Holy Spirit includes this information to help us come to a very important understanding. That is, signs and wonders - budding rods and manna - as wonderful as they are, are not lasting. What lasts, what endures, what is absolutely essential is the Word of God.

According to Jesus, the greatest prophet who ever lived was neither Elijah, who called down fire from heaven, nor Moses, who parted the Red Sea. The greatest prophet who ever lived did no miracles whatsoever, John the Baptist" (Courson).

When our Lord Jesus went to the place where John at the first baptized we read, "And many resorted unto him, and said, John did no miracle: but all things that John spake of this man were true" (Jn 10.41). God's people are not performing signs wonders and miracles today, but can (like John the Baptist) give a true testimony by life and lip concerning our Lord Jesus Christ.

The ark is a beautiful picture of our Lord Jesus with the law inside illustrating how He kept the law perfectly. He was the only one who ever fully did so. In this context Hebrews 10 refers to Psalm 40.7-8 and tells of His words as he came into the world: "Then said I, Lo, I come: in the volume of the book it is written of me, I delight to do thy will, O my God: yea, thy law is within my heart". Psalm 2 is God's king and Psalm 1 is God's man. Psalm 1.2 states, "But his delight is in the law of the Lord; and in his law doth he meditate day and night". No one ever meditated as much on the Word of God as our Lord Jesus. He is the only perfectly sinless man who ever lived. For further material on the ark and its mercy seat see the volume in this series on *Exodus* by John Grant (pages 312-316).

Verses 11-14: The Glory of the Lord and the Praise of Israel

The parallel passage in 1 Kings 8.10 is very similar to the first half of v.11 and the last fifteen words of v.13. The Chronicler adds from v.11b to v.13a. The second half of v.11 shows that all the priests were there. The last part of v.12 shows that all the Levites were there and also gives the number of priests present as 120. Usually the priests served in turn in 24 courses (1 Chr 24.7-19), but on this important occasion all the priests were there without any reference to their turn or course. Similarly, in v.12 all the Levitical singers, who also ordinarily served by turn in 24 courses (1 Chr 25.9-31) took part in the dedication. "The singers, who had served since David's institution of them in two companies, some with the Tabernacle and some with the ark (1 Chr 16.37-42), were now united" (Fereday). Asaph, Heman, and Jeduthun represented the three Levitical groups of singers (1 Chr 25.1-4). Cymbals, psalteries, and harps, the instruments of the Levites (v.12), are also listed in 1 Chronicles 25.1.

The singers "stood at the east end of the altar" (v.12). In that way they could look at the altar and the temple beyond. What a sad contrast to this is found in Ezekiel 8.16 where the prophet saw in a vision "about five and twenty men, with their backs toward the temple of the Lord, and their faces toward the east; and they worshipped the sun toward the east". Thankfully, the Thessalonian believers did the opposite to these idolaters. They "turned to God from idols" (1 Thess 1.9).

"The 120 priests probably represented an *ad hoc* group of musicians, in keeping with the fact that the priests were not serving in their usual divisional rotations (5.12), though it is possible also that they consisted of five representatives from each of the twenty-four courses" (Dillard).

The 120 priests are a reminder of the 120 of Acts 1.15. On the day of Pentecost suddenly they were all filled with the Holy Spirit (Acts 2.2,4).

The "priests sounding with trumpets" (v.12) is a reminder that only the priests were to blow the silver trumpets in Numbers 10.8. The priests are also associated with trumpets in 1 Chronicles 15.24 and 16.6. The trumpets in a particular sense were the instruments of the priests.

The Chronicler is the first to refer to the Levites as "arrayed in white linen" (v.12) ("fine linen", RV). The ESV makes it clear (1 Chr 15.27) that not only was David clothed in "fine linen," but so also were the Levites. This seems to have been their special clothing since it is only mentioned in these two places, and in both it was in connection with bringing the ark to its rightful place. Fine linen was also the material for priestly clothing. This is another evidence of the high regard that the writer of the Chronicles had for the Levites.

The unity of the priests and the singers in their praise is emphasized by a two-fold reference, "as one, to make one sound" (v.13). What perfect harmony! How good when Romans 15.6 can be fulfilled in every assembly: "That ye may with one mind and one mouth glorify God, even the Father of our Lord Jesus Christ". The great Christological passage in Philippians 2.5-11 was not given because the Philippians needed correction on the person of Christ. It was rather given to encourage the Philippians saints to live harmoniously together. It also is an encouragement today to all saints in assembly fellowship to do the same.

They were praising the Lord with these words: "For he is good; for his mercy endureth forever" (v.13). God "inhabitest the praises of Israel" (Ps 22.3). There are identical or similar words in a number of passages - 1 Chronicles 16.34; 2 Chronicles 7.3,6; 20.21; Ezra 3.11; Psalm 106.1; 107.1; 118.1; 136.1; Jeremiah 33.11. In Psalm 136 the refrain is the phrase, "for his mercy endureth forever" in each of the 26 verses. This expression is centered on two attributes of God, His goodness and mercy. These are personified in Psalm 23.6: "Surely goodness and mercy shall follow me all the days of my life". Asaph, one of the leaders of song, wrote Psalm 73 that begins with the words, "Truly God is good to Israel", while in Psalm 103.17 David says that, "The mercy of the Lord is from everlasting to everlasting upon them that fear him".

"The Hebrew word for mercy is HESED (2617), 'loving-kindness; steadfast love; grace; mercy; faithfulness; goodness; devotion'. This word is used around 240 times in the Old Testament, and is especially frequent in the Psalter. The term is one of the most important in the vocabulary of the Old Testament theology and ethics…In general, one may identify three basic meanings of the word, which always interact: 'strength', 'steadfastness', and 'love'. Any understanding of the word that fails to suggest all three inevitably loses some of its richness…The association of HESED with 'covenant' keeps it from being misunderstood as mere providence or love for all creatures; it applies primarily to God's particular love for His chosen and covenanted people" (Vine's *Expository Dictionary of Bible Words*).

It was very appropriate for them to sing of God's mercy or steadfast love because in particular it refers to God's covenant commitment to David in 1 Chronicles 17.11-14, which had now resulted in this temple.

It was while they were praising the Lord that "then the house was filled with a cloud, even the house of the Lord" (v.13). This indicates that the Chronicler included vv.11b-13a to record an additional reason for the cloud filling the house of the Lord, namely, the praise of the priests and the Levites. This is a constant encouragement to God's people then and since to praise the Lord. Today every believer is a priest (1 Pet 2.5).

The cloud as a symbol of God's presence is also found in Exodus 13.21, Numbers 9.15-23 and Ezekiel 10.3-4. The next verse (v.14) makes it clear that it was a cloud of glory. The glory of the Lord filling the temple confirmed that God had accepted it as His dwelling place. Solomon was aware that heaven was God's dwelling place (6.21) and, "the heaven and heaven of heavens" would not be able to contain God (6.18). Later the rabbis referred to the cloud of glory as "Shekinah glory", Shekinah meaning "one who dwells".

"This marvelous manifestation of the cloud, which was the vehicle of the glory of God that filled the whole temple, occurred only at the placing of the ark. Afterwards the cloud of the divine glory was upon the mercy seat between the cherubim in the Most Holy Place, into which the high priest entered once a year on the Day of Atonement. But he was obliged to enter with a cloud of burning incense in his golden censer to cover the mercy seat. With the cloud of incense between himself and the mercy seat he was precluded from seeing the glory of the Lord (Lev 16.2,13)" (Page).

"In general the Chronicler has modeled his account of the building of the temple on the earlier manufacture of the Tabernacle; at completion both structures receive divine approval through the appearance of the cloud. The inability of the priests to perform their functions because of the presence of the cloud (5.14; 7.1-2) repeats the experience at the dedication of the Tabernacle (Ex 40.34-35)" (Dillard).

The cloud led Israel out of Egypt (Ex 13.21-22) and throughout their journey in the wilderness (Ex 40.38). The glory of God departed from the Tabernacle because of Israel's sin (1 Sam 4.21-22). But now the glory had returned. Later God's people would sin again especially with the abominable idolatries that Ezekiel saw in his vision in ch.8. In 9.3 he saw the glory of the God of Israel gone up to the threshold of the house. In 10.4 it was over the threshold of the house, and in 10.19 it was at the door of the east gate of the Lord's house. In 11.23 it was east of the city at the Mount of Olives. Ezekiel thus showed that God was reluctantly leaving His temple and His city. God allowed Ezekiel to see the glory of God returning from the east to the millennial temple (43.2) there speaking of a future day.

"There can be no doubt that this triumphant entrance of the ark into the temple is also a foreshadowing of the appearing of the Lord in His temple when He comes to set up His kingdom…The language of Psalm 24.7, 'Lift up your heads, O ye gates; and be ye lift up, ye everlasting doors; and the King of glory shall come in', will then be fulfilled.

If the temple is viewed as a type of a local church, for both are called 'the house of God', than the lesson it teaches us is that the presence of the Lord is the most important feature of it" (McShane).

2 CHRONICLES 6

Solomon's Reign

Introduction

Once the ark was present in the Most Holy Place and the cloud of glory had filled the temple (by which God had indicated His acceptance of it as His dwelling place), Solomon responded with praise and prayer. Chapter 6 gives the words of Solomon in three parts. Verses 1-2 - prayerful response to God for the cloud of glory; verses 3-11 - blessing the Lord before the whole congregation for His faithfulness to the house of David; and verses 12-42 - prayer of dedication for the temple. The parts increase in length from two verses to nine verses to thirty-one verses.

The first two parts look to the past, giving praise to God for His faithfulness in keeping His promises to dwell with His people (vv.1-2; cp. for example, Ex 25.8; 29.44-46), and ensuring that Solomon was placed on the throne of David (vv.3-11; cp. 1 Chr 17.10-15; 22.6-13; 28.2-10). The third part looks to the future, to the prayers that will be made in or towards the temple; examples of this are found in comparing vv.32-33 with 9.1-9, or vv.34-35 with 20.1-30, or vv.36-39 with 33.10-13. The dedicatory prayer has individual petitions, which form separate paragraphs.

There are several anthropomorphisms in this chapter. Verse 4 speaks of God's hands and God's mouth, v.20 about His eyes, and v.40 about His eyes and ears. "The word comes from two Greek words: *anthropos*, 'man'; from which we derive the discipline of anthropology (i.e. the study of human life), and *morphe*, 'form', as in morphology (the study of forms). When applied to God it means that we, because we cannot fully understand God, attribute to Him certain physical characteristics (e.g. hands, feet, eyes, and ears)" (Barber).

The prayer of Solomon is the second longest recorded prayer in the Word of God. It is a prayer about prayer. It marks the beginning of the function of the temple as the house of prayer. The only longer prayer recorded in the Bible is found in Nehemiah 9.

"The theme of the temple as a house of thanksgiving and of intercession clearly occupies a central place in Chronicles. This chapter forms a vital link between Chronicles' two major words from God. Its foundation is God's covenant promise to build David a house (1 Chr 17.10-14), and its development occurs in God's promise about the temple (2 Chr 7.12-22). It therefore shows how prayer plays a key role in the unfolding of God's will for mankind" (Selman).

This chapter follows 1 Kings 8.12-50 very closely. Nevertheless, there are a few changes worth noting, including two places where the Chronicler seems to have preserved a text that adds to Kings (vv.5b-6a,13). Two emphases may be discerned from what appear to be special contributions of the writer of the Chronicles. First, there are indications of an application to that day. For example, the Chronicler omits some of the details about the exodus (cp. v.11 with 1 Kings 8.21) and omits completely 1 Kings 8.50b,51,52b, and 53 which refer to it. Verse 16 has "walk in my law" instead of "walk before me" in 1 Kings 8.25. God's law had guiding principles for the daily life of His people. In the New Testament, God has foreordained that Christians today should walk in good works (Eph 2.10). Everything that pleases God is included in good works.

Second, the reduced emphasis on the exodus is replaced by a new prominence given to God's covenant with David. While on the one hand there are a number of references to the exodus showing that the deliverance from Egypt was important to the writer of the Chronicles (1 Chr 17.21; 2 Chr 5.10; 6.5; 7.22; 20.10), on the other hand, the reduction in detail and his use of a free citation from Psalm 132.8-10 (as a new ending in vv.41-42, in place of 1 Kings 8.50b,51,52b,53) shows that the covenant with David is even more important to the writer. The prominence given to the Davidic covenant is very evident!

Most probably the reason for these changes is because they have significance for post-exilic Israel. By preserving Solomon's request for God to continue keeping His promise to David (vv.16-17), the Chronicler is clearly indicating that even in his day there was still a future for the kingdom of David even though no longer was there a descendant of David reigning in Israel. The temple was a reminder to the post-exilic people that it was God's earthly dwelling place and invited them to confident prayer. They could pray for David's kingdom to come.

It is for this reason that we can say "the present passage is a beginning as well as an end, for it not only signals a fulfillment for God's plans for Israel, but also becomes a reference point for the stories of subsequent kings. The issue with each of them is whether they were able to secure the blessings of God through obedience. And the Chronicler's purpose is to present the people of his time with that challenge" (McConville).

Our Lord Jesus in John 14-17 gives different reasons for encouraging His people today to pray. "Jesus' teaching about prayer…has several emphases remarkably similar to this chapter. For example, there is a close connection between praying in Jesus name (e.g. Jn 14.13-14; 16.23-24) and praying towards the temple that bears God's name (e.g. vv.5,6,7, and 14 times in all in this chapter)…Another link is between the presence of the Holy Spirit with each Christian (e.g. Jn 14.16-18; Rom 8.26-27) and God's continual presence with Israel in the temple. The presence of God, by whatever means, is a real stimulus and encouragement to prayer" (Selman).

Outline of Chapter 6

Verses 1-2: Solomon's address to God in response to His glory.
Verses 3-11: Solomon's address to the people; a testimony to God's promise fulfilled.
Verses 12-13: Solomon's position in prayer.

Verses 14-17:	Solomon's request to God to fulfill His promise to David.
Verses 18-21:	Basic principles of intercession. Introduction to vv.22-42.
Verses 22-23:	Maintenance of justice.
Verses 24-25:	National defeat.
Verses 26-27:	Drought.
Verses 28-31:	Disasters and disease.
Verses 32-33:	Foreigners.
Verses 34-35:	Danger in war.
Verses 36-39:	Exile.
Verses 40-42:	The wonderful conclusion.

Verses 1-2: Solomon's Address to God in Response to His Glory

"Then said Solomon", are the first words of v.1 and they refer to the time when Solomon saw that the house that he had built was filled with a cloud and the glory of the Lord (5.13b,14), indicating God's acceptance of the temple as His dwelling place. Verses 1 and 2 are Solomon's response. In these verses Solomon addresses God, partly in prayer and partly in testimony. It filled Solomon with wonder to think that, though God is so great, He was willing to abide in the house that Solomon had built for His glory. Solomon was overwhelmed at the condescension of God, but even so he knew it was a fulfillment of God's desire to dwell among His own people. God still desires to be the centre of the lives of all His own people today. Even though the temple was so magnificent, he knew it was as nothing compared to the glory of heaven, God's holy dwelling place. Eight times in his prayer he states that God dwells in heaven (vv.21,23,25,27,30,33,35,39).

The rest of v.1 refers to what God had said as recorded in several verses of the Old Testament, especially the Pentateuch, about the gracious manifestations of His presence among His people. Solomon was reminded that God appeared to Moses in a similar way in Exodus 40.34-35. God told Moses in Leviticus 16.2, "I will appear in the cloud upon the mercy seat". God "dwelling in thick darkness" (v.1) indicates that God would veil His glory from human view, as He said to Moses at Mount Sinai in Exodus 19.9, "I come unto thee in a thick cloud". Even more so in Exodus 20.21: "and Moses drew near unto the thick darkness where God was". We read of the thick darkness at Sinai also in Deuteronomy 4.11 and 5.22. God cannot fully reveal Himself to man for we read His words in Exodus 33.20, "there shall no man see me, and live". The dark windowless Holy of Holies was a suitable place for God to dwell in thick darkness. There are a good number of other verses that speak of God's presence with His people - Exodus 13.21; 16.9-10; 19.16,18; 24.15-16; 25.22; 33.9-10; 34.5; Numbers 9.15-16; 12.5; Deuteronomy 4.7; 31.15; Psalm 18.11; 97.2.

Solomon is further amazed to think that he had the privilege of building a house in which God could dwell (v.2). In this verse he is especially contrasting the permanence of the temple to the Tabernacle, which was temporary and had to be moved from place to place. In 7.19-20, the requirement that men be faithful is given. God's people failed and the temple was twice destroyed (586 BC and AD 70). The Lord has promised that He will dwell in Zion forever (Ps 132.13-14). He has also promised His presence in companies gathered to His name alone in this church age (Mt 18.20) as long as those companies too remain faithful to Him (Rev 2.5).

Verses 3-11: Solomon's Address to the People; a Testimony to God's Promise Fulfilled

Solomon "turned his face, and blessed the whole congregation of Israel: and all the congregation of Israel stood" (v.3). This verse is almost identical to 1 Kings 8.14. The "congregation of Israel", mentioned twice in this verse, fits in well with the Chronicler's desire to emphasize (as he often does), "all Israel". Israel is mentioned a further seven times in 1 Kings 8.15-21 and eight in 2 Chronicles 6.4-11. The one that is missed in 1 Kings 8 is found here in v.11 referring to "the covenant of the Lord, that he made with the children of Israel". Solomon's address to the people is a further response of Solomon to the cloud of glory.

"Only three kings ever publicly blessed the people of God (so far as the records speak), and they were all outstanding types of Christ - Melchizedek (Gen 14.19); David (2 Sam 6.18); and Solomon. Then Solomon blessed Jehovah on the people's behalf" (Fereday). David blessed the people when he had put the ark in the tent of meeting at Zion and after he had offered burnt offerings and peace offerings.

Page enlarges on Fereday's words. "Each of these three kings portrays Christ. David prefigures Christ as the Warrior-King coming again with the saints to the earth. Solomon foreshadows Christ as the King of Peace during His millennial reign on the earth. Melchizedek typifies Christ as the King-Priest in the Millennium when as Priest He will sit upon His throne in the temple of that day."

After Solomon had blessed the people his first word in v.4 is "Blessed". Solomon is giving praise to the Lord God of Israel because of His faithfulness, fulfilling with His hands His promise to David that He made with His mouth. God used Nathan's mouth as "his mouth". Solomon is humbly acknowledging that all his labour and all the labour of the people in building the temple were "his hands". Human effort and divine sovereignty are subtly brought together here. All the rest of his address to the people expands on this, especially vv.10-11. Solomon was careful to give glory to God.

Paul similarly was careful in Acts 14.27 when he rehearsed before the assembly at Antioch, "all that God had done with them" (see also Acts 15.4). In 1 Corinthians 15.10 Paul records that he "laboured more abundantly than they all (i.e. all the apostles)". He was careful to give God the glory for his super-abundant labours by saying, "…yet not I, but the grace of God that was with me".

The Chronicler emphasizes God's sovereign choice in vv.5 and 6. God had not chosen a ruler until He chose David. It is true that God had chosen Samuel and others as leaders, but not one of them had superior authority as a king (v.5). God had selected Saul when the people of Israel demanded a king, but that was not a matter of God's initiative but the people's desire. God had indicated His displeasure at their actions: "the Lord sent thunder...And all the people said…we have added unto all our sins this evil, to ask us a king" (1 Sam 12.18-19). In contrast Samuel said, "The Lord hath sought him a man after his own heart" (1 Sam 13.14), referring to David the son of Jesse.

God had not chosen just any city where He wanted a house built so that His name might be there. "But I have chosen Jerusalem, that my name might be there." Those are the first words of v.6 and they are omitted in 1 Kings. This indicates a new concept for the temple. It was not only for the ark but it was also a place for His name. We have "name" in each of six consecutive verses (vv.5,6,7,8,9,10). "Name" is found in total 14 times in ch.6 and only 14 times connected with the Lord in all the other chapters. David is the first person recorded to think of building a house for the name of the Lord (v.7).

God commended David that it was in his heart to build a house for His name (v.8) even though God would not allow him to do so (v.9) because he had been a man of war and had shed blood (1 Chr 22.8-9; 28.3). These statements are not contradictory but rather complementary. God's appreciation of David's motive in wanting to build the temple is an encouragement for all saints to have a right attitude of heart before God which is essential for all godly living in His sight (vv.16,30; Prov 4.23). All our motives will be judged at the Judgment Seat of Christ (1 Cor 4.5). Our Lord Jesus considers our motives so important that a substantial part of the Sermon on the Mount deals with this (Mt 6.1-18). Here the next verse records that God assured David that his son would build the house (v.9).

"In 6.10 the NKJV endeavours to convey a Hebrew play on words that expresses this truth; Solomon filling his father's place was part of the fulfilling of God's promise. The New Testament is no stranger to this type of endorsement…Just as the note of fulfillment begins and ends Solomon's speech (6.4,10), so in Luke's Gospel the oral ministry of Jesus begins and ends on the note of Scripture fulfilled (Lk 4.21; 24.44)" (Leslie C. Allen).

"The moment that might have witnessed the utmost inflation of spiritual pride, the acme of ambition, the highest point of even a moral kind of grandeur, being touched, is saved from the peril. To the 'performing of the Lord' the glory is all given" (The Pulpit Commentary).

The Chronicler stresses God's fulfillment of His promise to David in setting Solomon upon the throne and enabling him to build the temple. But God did not do these things for the honour of David or Solomon, but rather for the glory of His name, "for the name of the Lord God of Israel" (v.10). Whenever God uses a believer in a special way that saint should be careful to give God the glory.

Solomon concludes his message to the people by referring to his placing the ark in the temple (v.11). He also identifies the covenant that God made with the children of Israel and the tablets of the Ten Commandments. Even in this verse that refers to the Mosaic covenant the Chronicler omits the reference to the exodus found in 1 Kings 8.21. The omission here again shows that he wanted to give prominence to the promise of God to David.

"The Ark and its precious contents, the tables of the covenant, was the most important of all the great treasures in the temple. This sacred chest was the symbol of the Lord's presence and the centre from which He communed with His people. No cloud nor outshining glory would have been seen in the temple had these things been absent. The stones were not made for the ark, but it was made for them, and they were secreted in it beneath the mercy seat, and could only be seen when this lid was removed. It was the only vessel in God's house which was used for permanent storage" (McShane).

Verses 12-13: Solomon's Position in Prayer

Solomon "stood before the altar of the Lord" (v.12). That would be the brazen altar, which stood in the court of the temple. The altar as the place for sacrifice had an important role in the dedication ceremony (vv.12,22; 7.7,9). Saints today have the privilege of offering sacrifices of praise to God (Heb 13.15) and also the sacrifices involved in obeying the injunction "to do good and to communicate" for, "with such sacrifices (plural) God is well pleased" (Heb 13.16; Phil 4.18).

The first word of v.13, "For", shows that v.13 explains v.12. The Kings account says nothing about the brazen scaffold and nothing about Solomon kneeling until the end of his prayer (1 Kings 8.54). Solomon is the first person recorded in the Bible kneeling to pray. It is worthy of note that the measurement of the scaffold is the same as that given for the brazen altar in the Tabernacle (Ex 27.1; 38.1).

Solomon humbly and dependently bowed his knees on the scaffold while he was praying to God. He knew that the kingdom over which he reigned was not his own. As David said, "He hath chosen Solomon my son to sit on the throne of the kingdom of the Lord over Israel" (1 Chr 28.5). The Hebrew word for "scaffold" is only this once so translated. Eighteen times out of 21 it is translated "bason". Unger helpfully writes, "a platform shaped like an inverted bason and attested archæologically both in Egypt and Syria".

Solomon "set the scaffold in the midst of the court" (v.13). That suggests that the scaffold or platform was set up temporarily for this special occasion. It may be assumed that it was near the altar (v.12). This word for "court" is a rare word and is used for the great court in 4.9 where it is distinguished from the court of the priests. Solomon prayed "in the presence of all the congregation of Israel" (v.12). A large crowd would be able to gather in the great court. Solomon being on that platform would be much more visible and more easily heard. Any brother that takes part in prayer or praise at a large meeting with hundreds of saints present should be able to do so with enough volume and clarity to enable the saints to hear him.

It is worth noting other Biblical expressions relating to prayer: we have *kneeling in prayer* in Psalm 95.6, Daniel 6.10, and Ephesians 3.14; *spreading/lifting hands towards heaven* is also found in other places (Ex 9.29,33; 1 Kings 8.54; Ezra 9.5; Job 11.13; Ps 28.2; 44.20; 141.2; 1 Tim 2.8).

"God has looked down upon three delightful spectacles of kings humbly praying before Him in Jerusalem:

1. Solomon at the dedication of the temple, when all was well (2 Chr 6.13).
2. Jehoshaphat in a day of peril from a great invasion (2 Chr 20).
3. Hezekiah when threatened by the blasphemous Rabshakeh, and the Assyrian hosts (Is 37.15).

Had those prayers practical value? Yes, a thousand times YES. It has been truly said, referring to Hezekiah, that 'a king in sackcloth was more to be dreaded than a king in a coat of mail'" (Fereday).

Verses 14-17: Solomon's Request to God to Fulfill His Promises to David

As in other prayers in Scripture, Solomon begins with praise (vv.14-15) and follows with petition (vv.16-17). The prayer has an impressive dignity and a gracious majesty with God being addressed three times with the words, "O Lord God of Israel". These words do not represent a composite title of God but rather two titles as shown in Darby's translation, "Jehovah, God of Israel", and the ESV, "O Lord, God of Israel". Verse 14 is similar to Deuteronomy 7.9. Throughout the rest of the prayer Solomon often refers to the Pentateuch especially Deuteronomy. The word for "mercy" in v.14 is HESED (2617) - loving kindness, steadfast love. (See three short paragraphs on Vine's comments on this word in ch.5 under v.13.) In v.14 Solomon praises God for His uniqueness. In the light of this verse, it is exceedingly sad that his wives "turned away his heart after other gods" when he was old (1 Kings 11.4). In v.15 Solomon praises God for His faithfulness in keeping His promise to David, even with similar words to those that he had used in his message to the people (vv.4,10). God's answer strengthened Solomon's confidence in prayer.

"'Now' (v.16), introduces Solomon's request, that God's promises to David's line should continue to 'be confirmed' (v.17)...David had made an identical petition (1 Chr 17.23-24), and both prayers indicate that God often looks for people to work with Him in prayer rather than Him fulfilling His purposes automatically (cp. 'Your will be done on earth as it is in heaven')" (Selman). A condition is given at the close of v.16 that the Davidic kings "walk in my law". The last words of David to his son Solomon (1 Kings 2.4) show that Solomon was repeating now the promise and the condition that he learned from his father. "'Keep' (v.16), for the future, contrasts with 'hast kept' (v.15), in the past" (Heading).

Because of serious unfaithfulness on the part of several of the Davidic kings, eventually God's people were without a king for many days (Hosea 3.4). Only David's Greater Son will fulfill the promise to David of an everlasting dynasty. The angel Gabriel in announcing to the virgin Mary the miraculous conception of our Lord Jesus told her, "the Lord God shall give unto him the throne of his father David: And he shall reign over the house of Jacob forever; and of his kingdom there shall be no end" (Lk 1.32-33). When Solomon prayed, "let thy word be verified" (v.17), he was holding God to His word and God's record of Solomon doing so is an encouragement for us to do the same.

"Another way to view the apparently double fulfillment is to note that the promise was conditional. When the promise was made, fulfillment was conditioned by obedience (1 Chr 28.9). When the conditions are not met, the promise remains to be fulfilled, but with a different person in view. The enumeration of the failure of the succeeding Davidic kings has the purpose in showing that the Person has not come who will fulfill the promise to David" (Sailhammer).

Verses 18-21: Basic Principles of Intercession

It overwhelmed Solomon to think that God who is so great would condescend to dwell with men on earth (v.18). "With men" is found only in the Chronicles account. Solomon's statement, "behold, heaven and the heaven of heavens cannot contain thee", is one of the most outstanding statements on the transcendence of God in all the Word of God. It is similar to what Solomon said to Huram in 2.6. God far transcends being contained by anything in all His creation. Solomon's temple was great for a great God, but it was not so very great. It was insignificant compared to God's greatness. While 2.6 emphasized the temple as a place of sacrifice, in this instance it is emphasized as a place of prayer. Those two things are combined in Isaiah 56.7.

Since Solomon had a clear understanding of the infinitude of God, it helped him to understand prayer. Solomon made it clear that God did not dwell in the temple as a man dwells in a house. The house confines the man, but the temple does not confine God. That is what Stephen said in Acts 7.48, "Howbeit the most High dwelleth not in temples made with hands", and Paul also said, "God...dwelleth not in temples made with hands" (Acts 17.24). Even so, Solomon knew that God had promised to dwell in a special way in the temple he had built (vv.1-2). It is because of the greatness of God that Solomon, eight times in the prayer to follow, refers to God hearing from heaven (vv.21,23,25,27,30,33,35,39). "For it is evident that Solomon did combine with his clear perception of the infinite exaltation of God a firm belief in His real presence in the temple" (Keil).

"Solomon's temple has gone, but a more wonderful thing has taken its place. The Church, composed of sinners drawn from amongst Jews and Gentiles, is now His temple (1 Cor 3.16); His house (1 Tim 3.15); His habitation (Eph 2.22)" (Fereday).

Selman has identified five basic essential principles of intercession in Solomon's prayer (vv. 19-21).

"a. The words for *prayer* are characterized by sincerity and urgency ('supplication' in vv.19,21,24,35, and 39, which is really a plea for mercy, as NIV in v.19; "cry" v.19; "call" v.33, RSV). [The ESV has "plea" or "plead" for each of the words translated 'supplication'.]

b. God is called upon to have His eyes open (vv.20,40), and especially to hear (vv.19, 20,21,23,25,27,30,33,35,39,40). [Knowing that God sees and hears enables praying in faith because He answers prayer.]

c. The prayers to be offered in or toward this house/place (vv.18,20,21, 22,24,26,29,32,33,34,38,40) come before God (v.19) in His heavenly dwelling. This is because God's name is on this temple…To pray in or towards this temple is to pray to or in the name of God to whom it belongs. [The first of 21 times in Deuteronomy where we read of the place, which the Lord your God shall choose (putting His name there), is linked with His habitation (12.5).]

d. God is accessible [in prayer] to anyone who acknowledges Jehovah as "my God" (vv.19,40), as "God of Israel" (v.14), or even as having "a great name" (v.32).

e. To forgive sins is the purpose of most of the prayers (vv.21,25,27,30,39). This is not to diminish the importance of other types of prayers, such as for guidance, meditation, or adoration, but to draw attention to humanity's basic need before God."

"Above all else, Solomon learned a lesson from his father, David, that was later crystallized by Isaiah the prophet. It is that 'the Lord's hand is not shortened, that it cannot save; neither his ear heavy, that it cannot hear: But your iniquities have separated between you and your God' (Is 59.1-2; cp. Ps 51.1-3). The temple as a 'house of prayer' serves to bridge the gap between God and His people caused by their sins because God is a 'forgiving' God" (Hill).

Five times in three verses Solomon pleads with God to "hearken" or to "hear" (vv.19-21). "Toward this place" is found in each of vv.20-21. Wherever the Jews were, they worshipped or prayed toward the temple (Ps 5.7; 28.2; 138.2; Jonah 2.4, and especially Daniel 6.10). Most of what follows in Solomon's prayer is an expansion of the simple words, "hear…and…forgive" (v.21). Verses 18-21 give the basic principles of intercessory prayer and most of the rest of his prayer gives the circumstances prompting intercession (vv.22-39).

Introduction to Verses 22-42

Solomon knew that stability had not yet come, so these verses are full of forebodings. "Solomon knew the terms of the covenant found in Deuteronomy 28-29, and the calamities he mentioned in his prayers are the very disciplines the Lord promised to send if Israel disobeyed His law. But Solomon also knew that Deuteronomy 30 promised forgiveness and restoration if God's people would repent and turn to the Lord" (Wiersbe).

In five of the seven paragraphs the calamities were the result of sin. The two that were not are described in vv.32-33 and vv.34-35. In each of those five paragraphs Solomon expected their repentance to lead to God's forgiveness and restoration. Verse 36 states, "there is no man which sinneth not". The word "forgive" is mentioned five times (vv.21,25,27,30,39), and once we have "maintain their cause" (v.39). The word "forgive" draws attention to the basic need of human beings before God. That word is a reminder of Psalm 130.3-4: "If thou Lord, shouldest mark iniquities, O Lord, who should stand? But there is forgiveness with thee, that thou mayest be feared". Saints of this dispensation can be thankful for the provision of 1 John 1.9 which is for all persons who have personally accepted the sacrifice of Christ: "If we confess our sins, he is faithful and just to forgive us our sins, and to cleanse us from all unrighteousness". God is not merciful and lenient to forgive our sins. Instead, He is faithful and just because He has provided a righteous basis for that forgiveness in the infinite value of the sacrifice of His beloved Son.

The structure of the remaining part of the prayer should be considered. There are seven paragraphs describing situations in which prayer might be offered, with a wonderful conclusion at the end (vv.40-42). The structure of those seven is "If…Then" as he makes his plea for the Lord to intervene. Each plea is an expression of Solomon's concern for his people. He not only wants God to answer his own prayers but also the prayers of his people (v.21).

The seven petitions deal almost exclusively with the affairs of the nation. The first one appears to be individual, but it is really a concern for maintaining justice. The petition for the stranger is to the end "that all people of the earth…may know that this house which I have built is called by thy name" (v.33).

Each time Solomon asks God to hear from "heaven". One of the times he pleads, "hear thou from heaven thy dwelling place" (v.30). Two of the times he has, "hear thou from the heavens, even from thy dwelling place" (vv.33,39). Solomon prays for the people of God in the double sense of representing them and interceding for them.

Verses 22-23: Maintainance of Justice

When a man is suspected of wronging his neighbour and there is no definite evidence against him, he is required to confirm his word by swearing with an oath solemnly taken before God's altar in the house of God. Solomon asks God to vindicate the one who is in the right according to the righteousness of his cause and condemn the guilty. Thus this plea is truly a plea for maintaining justice.

Similar action was to be taken for cases of suspected default (Ex 22.10-11), suspected theft (Lev 6.2-3), or suspected adultery (Num 5.19-22). God wanted righteous judgment to be carried out (Deut 25.1). 1 Timothy 5.21 emphasizes that there should be no partiality in assembly judgments. When Abraham was interceding for Sodom he pleaded, "Shall not the Judge of all the earth do right?" (Gen 18.25). He surely always will do right!

Verses 24-25: National Defeat

Though the main themes of the prayer were the Davidic dynasty, the temple, and prayer, two other themes are each mentioned a few times: war (vv.24-25, 34-37), and the land (vv.25, 27-28, 31,38).

God had warned His people that if they disobeyed His commandments then "ye shall be slain before your enemies" (Lev 26.17), and "the Lord shall cause thee to be smitten before thine enemies" (Deut 28.25). In Joshua's day Israel was smitten because of Achan's unjudged sin: "Therefore the children of Israel could not stand before their enemies" (Josh 7.12). Later, because of idolatry, the Lord had "delivered them into the hands of the spoilers that spoiled them, and he sold them into the hands of their enemies" (Judg 2.14). Unjudged sin in any assembly of God's people can hinder blessing in the gospel and result in judgment on some in the fellowship: "For this cause many are weak and sickly among you, and many sleep" (1 Cor 11.30).

If God's people were "put to the worse" before their enemies (v.24), the next verse (v.25) indicates that some might be taken captive. But since there were those who were expected to pray in "this house" (v.24), there would be far fewer captives than envisaged in the exile (vv.36-39). The parallel verse to v.24 in 1 Kings 8.33 adds the phrase "shall turn again to thee" which would indicate true repentance. If God's people also confessed God's name, prayed and made supplication before God in this house, then Solomon pleaded that God would forgive their sin and see that the captives were returned to their own land.

Verses 26-27: Drought

God had warned His people that if they sinned He would withhold rain from them (Lev 26.19; Deut 11.17; 28.23-24). Solomon pleads that this would change when "they pray toward this place, and confess thy name, and turn from their sin" (v.26). He gives two additional reasons why God should forgive their sin and send rain. First, the people are God's people by covenant - His servants and His people (v.27). Second, the land is God's: "thy land which thou hast given unto thy people for an inheritance" (v.27).

Rawlinson (in commenting on the parallel of v.27 in 1 Kings 8.36) writes, "Translate, 'when thou art teaching them (by Thy chastisement) the good way that they should walk in". God's chastening them by withholding the rain should lead to their repentance. Restoration is linked to God's people submitting to His chastening. If they did well in their submission, they may not need the same chastening in the future. God chastens those whom He loves (Prov 3.11; Heb 12.6). God never sends a trial to make any child of God bitter, but rather to make him better. However, a child of God can become bitter in a trial because of a wrong response to God's dealing. Our Lord Jesus also says, "As many as I love, I rebuke and chasten: be zealous therefore, and repent" (Rev 3.19). The words, "when thou hast taught them the good way, wherein they should walk" (v.27), parallels "make straight paths for your feet" (Heb 12.13). It is important today for each child of God to be exercised about any chastening that He sends. "Now no chastening for the present seemeth to be joyous, but grievous: nevertheless afterward it yieldeth the peaceable fruit of righteousness unto them which are exercised thereby" (Heb 12.11).

Verses 28-31: Disasters and Disease

"Israel's unique geographical location in the sole land bridge between the continents of Europe, Asia and Africa, and the large amount of commerce through the area, would have made the land subject to the easy spread of outbreaks and epidemics from the surrounding region" (Dillard). That God sent all those calamities as chastening is obvious since Solomon prays for forgiveness in v.30. Apart from the catastrophe of the caterpillar, all these disasters (v.28) are distinctly threatened in the Pentateuch. Each one is found either in Leviticus 26 or Deuteronomy 28, or in both. In the early part of each of those chapters God promised them blessing instead of disaster if they obeyed Him.

For the last part of v.28 and the first part of v.29 the ESV has "whatever plague, whatever sickness there is, whatever prayer, whatever plea is made by any man or by all your people Israel". That assumes that all is under God's control. "All your people Israel" includes each individual.

The most serious problem is disobedience due to the wickedness of the human heart. 1 Kings 8.38 (which is the parallel of v.29) has, "which shall know every man the plague of his own heart". "The heart is deceitful above all things, and desperately wicked: who can know it? I the Lord search the heart" (Jer 17.9-10). He knows it! Our Lord Jesus exposes the human heart as being full of all kinds of sin (Mk 7.21-23). God in His omniscience knows all the wickedness of the human heart, but thankfully He also knows when each individual is truly repentant and He thoroughly knows all the ways of each person. Therefore He is the only One who can justly recompense each one accordingly (v.30).

The outcome of the previous request was learning the good way wherein they should walk (v.27). Here the outcome is that they may have a reverential fear of God and so walk in His ways (v.31). The fear of God is linked with forgiveness in Psalm 130.4. Verses 30 and 31 emphasize God's intimate knowledge and concern for each one of His own people. In v.27 the land was given to God's people but here their fathers are said to have been given the land (v.31).

Verses 32-33: Foreigners

This is the most refreshing and fascinating of these paragraphs. Solomon envisages the wonderful possibility of a Gentile stranger coming from afar. He would come "for thy great name's sake, and thy mighty hand, and thy stretched out arm". The "great name" of God is quite a rare expression. "Great" is never linked with God's name in the Pentateuch even though we very often have the phrase, "thy mighty hand and thy stretched out arm". We have one or the other of the two parts of the phrase in five verses (Ex 3.19; 6.6; 13.9; Deut 9.26,29). We have both parts referred to in five verses (Deut 4.34; 5.15; 7.19; 11.2; 26.8), each time referring to God's deliverance of His people in the exodus. However, Deuteronomy 7.19 (after describing the exodus) shows that the expression should not be limited, by adding "so shall the Lord thy God do unto the people of whom thou art afraid". The "great name" of God is only once mentioned in the earlier historical books (Josh 7.9) and only twice in the Psalms (76.1 and 99.3). We find it here and in its parallel (1 Kings 8.42), in Jeremiah 10.6; 44.26; Ezekiel 36.23; and twice in Malachi 1.11.

When God called Abraham to leave Ur of the Chaldees and to go to Canaan, He declared that He wanted Abraham and his descendants to be a blessing to "all the families of the earth" (Gen 12.3). Isaiah 56.7 says, "mine house shall be called an house of prayer for all people" and "the sons of the stranger" are referred to in the previous verse (v.6). When God undertook for His people in a miraculous way it was a testimony to the nations (Ex 9.16; Josh 2.8-13; 4.23-24).

David predicted to the giant Goliath that his victory over him would have the result, "that all the earth may know that there is a God in Israel" (1 Sam 17.46). When Daniel was miraculously delivered from the den of lions King Darius said, "I make a decree, That in every dominion of my kingdom men tremble and fear before the God of Daniel: for he is the living God" (Dan 6.26). Jewish people prayed, "God be merciful unto us, and bless us; and cause his face to shine upon us; Selah. That thy way may be known upon earth, thy saving health among all nations" (Ps 67.1-2). The last verse of that Psalm has, "God shall bless us; and all the ends of the earth shall fear him" (v.7). God wants to bless every saint and make each one a blessing to others.

Solomon asks God to answer the stranger, "and do according to all that the stranger calleth to thee for", and then adds what he hopes will be the result: "that all people of the earth may know thy name, and fear thee, as doth thy people Israel, and may know that this house which I have built is called by thy name" (v.33). "What is especially notable is that foreigners could know and fear God 'as doth thy people Israel' (v.33). This hope of equality in worship was rarely expressed in the Old Testament (e.g. Gen 12.3; Is 19.24-25; Zech 8.20-22), and even Jesus' closest disciples found its fulfillment hard to take (Acts 10.1-11.18)" (Selman).

The visit of the Queen of Sheba described in 9.1-12 is one answer to this prayer, and so is the experience of the Ethiopian eunuch of Acts 8.5-39. Possibly he was from the same general area and with the same impulse to know Israel's God, even though a thousand years later. Fereday suggests: "with this difference: the Queen of Sheba got the blessing in Jerusalem, for all was in divine order in her day; the eunuch got the blessing going away from Jerusalem, the temple being then an empty shell, the Christ of God having been rejected".

Verses 34-35: Danger in War

The second request of vv.24-25 is like this one in that both are about war. There it was about defeat because of sin, but here it is victory following God's direction and their depending upon Him. When they pray towards God's house in Jerusalem, Solomon does not ask for forgiveness this time as he did in v.25, but he does ask that God would "maintain their cause" (v.35).

There are a number of records in 2 Chronicles of God answering this prayer. In 13.14-16 it was against the northern kingdom; in 14.9-12 it was against a million Ethiopians. In 18.31 we find that God saved the life of good King Jehoshaphat when he cried to God in the battle against Syria. In 20.5-17 they fought against the Ammonites and Moabites, and in 32.20-22 an angel of the Lord destroyed 185,000 Assyrians in one night (2 Kings 19.35).

God promised that if His people obeyed Him their enemies would be smitten before them (Deut 28.7). 1 Chronicles 5.20-26 provides great encouragement to trust God in the battle: "And they were helped against them, and the Hagarites were delivered into their hand; and all that were with them: for they cried to God in the battle, and he was entreated of them; because they put their trust in him". God knew that Israel were to be the first to go into captivity, yet when they trusted God He undertook for them.

"The New Testament battle is of a spiritual nature: 'Fight the good fight of faith' (1 Tim 6.12)…'I have fought a good fight' (2 Tim 4.7). Just as Solomon visualized the people being men of prayer in their warfare, so Paul was also a man of prayer; the great passage on Christian warfare terminates with the words, 'Praying always with all prayer and supplication in the Spirit'" (Eph 6.18) (Heading).

"The French writer, Voltaire, said, 'It is said that God is always on the side of the heaviest battalions', but the truth is that God is on the side of those who pray in His will" (Wiersbe).

Verses 36-39: Exile

This account of the seventh request about exile follows the record in 1 Kings 8.46-51 very closely except that almost all of the last two verses in that section of that chapter (vv.50-51) are omitted in 2 Chronicles, possibly because the first readers of 2 Chronicles had already experienced recovery from exile. The seventy years in Babylon is not the only captivity recorded in 2 Chronicles. 200,000 persons from Judah were temporarily taken captive by the northern ten tribes (28.8-15). Because of the great wickedness of Manasseh and the people, and their refusal to listen to God's reproofs, he was taken captive to Babylon where he humbled himself greatly before the Lord God of his fathers who brought him again to Jerusalem (33.11-13) - an example of an Old Testament prodigal saved late in life.

In v.36 Solomon's words, "for there is no man which sinneth not", recognizes the universality of sin very clearly. There are other verses that agree with that statement (like Romans 3.23), but two verses in Solomon's writings should especially be considered. Proverbs 20.9 records, "Who can say, I have made my heart clean, I am pure from my sin?". The implied correct answer is that no one can truthfully say that. Ecclesiastes 7.20 says, "For there is not a just man upon earth, that doeth good, and sinneth not".

God had warned His people that persistent rebellion would lead to their captivity in a foreign land (Lev 26.33; Deut 28.36). "Solomon knew that the worst would happen from his reading of the last words of Moses: 'when I shall have brought them into the land…then will they turn unto other gods…I know that after my death ye will utterly corrupt yourselves' (Deut 31.20,29). Solomon knew the consequences – the nation would be carried away captive" (Heading). That was the worst thing that could happen to the Jewish people. "The other disciplines took away from the Jews the blessings of the land, but captivity took them away from the land itself" (Wiersbe).

Just as Moses offered hope to Israel when they were repentant (Lev 26.40-42; Deut 30.10) so also Solomon offers hope to God's people when truly repentant. The words, "if they bethink themselves" (v.37), call to mind the words about the prodigal son in the far country: "when he came to himself" (Lk 15.17). Bethinking themselves was followed by confession (v.37).

"'Yet if they shall bethink themselves.' Literally, 'if they shall bring back to their heart' (margin). The promises of Moses, in Deuteronomy 30.1-3, are in Solomon's mind; and he here reproduces the exact phrase, which occurs in v.1. To 'bring back to the heart' is to 'reflect', 'to consider seriously'. 'We have sinned, we have done perversely (RV), and have dealt wickedly'. The words here used seem to have become the standard form of expressing contrition when the time of captivity arrived and the Israelites were forcibly removed to Babylon. We find the same three verbs occurring in exactly the same order both in the confession of Daniel (9.5), and in a Psalm (106.6) ascribed with much probability to the Babylonian period. The three expressions are thought to form a climax, rising from negative to positive guilt, and from mere wrongful acts to depravation of the moral character" (Rawlinson).

Again there would be forgiveness upon repentance but this time a deeper intensity can be seen. First there was bethinking themselves (v.37), then confession tripled (v.37). Returning to God in repentance was to be with all their heart and soul, then Solomon envisages the direction of their prayer to the things of God's choice - first the land, then the city as well as the temple (v.38). Their repentance with all their heart and soul calls to mind these words: "And ye shall seek me, and find me, when ye shall search for me with all your heart (Jer 29.13). Solomon prays that God would hear "their prayer and their supplications, and maintain their cause, and forgive thy people" (v.39).

"The spirit of Solomon's prayer takes on a new reality in the great intercessions of Nehemiah (1.4-11) and Daniel (9.3-19)" (Wilcock). Ezra's prayer (9.6-15) could be added to that list.

Verses 40-42: The Wonderful Conclusion

Verse 40 is very much like 1 Kings 8.52. Solomon's general conclusion (v.40) covers all his prayers and also the prayers of God's people to be made in the future: "let...thine eyes be open, and let thine ears be attent unto the prayer that is made in this place". Verses 20-21 and each of the seven requests had "in (or towards) this place (or house)". With God's omniscience He would know all the prayers thus uttered. In God's answer (7.15) He promises what Solomon prayed for, and in 7.16 He also promised that His heart would be there perpetually. Solomon's prayer here is similar to his prayer in v.20. Saints today have confidence that God answers prayer according to His will. "And this is the confidence that we have in him, that, if we ask anything according to his will, he heareth us: And if we know that he hear us, whatever we ask, we know that we have the petitions that we desired of him" (1 Jn 5.14-15).

Verses 41-42 are altogether different from 1 Kings 8.50b,51,53, suggesting that this part of the prayer is especially important to the Chronicler. The parallel in 1 Kings 8 bases the anticipation of a favourable response to the prayer on the special relationship between Jehovah and His people made in the Mosaic covenant at Sinai. In contrast, the Chronicler omits the reference to the exodus and Moses and bases the anticipation in the mercies of God to David (v.42). "Mercies" is translated from the plural of HESED (2617 - to which reference was made in the comments on v.14). Instead of referring to 1 Kings 8 (as the writer of the Chronicles did for the first 40 verses of this chapter), in vv.41-42 he refers to Psalm 132.8-10 written by either David or Solomon. Psalm 132 is unique in two ways. First, it is the longest of the fifteen Songs of Degrees (Psalms 120-134). Second, as noted previously, it is the only one of the 150 Psalms with a direct reference to the ark (v.8) although there is an allusion to the ark in Psalm 78.61.

Here in Chronicles Solomon calls, "Arise, O Lord God, into thy resting place, thou, and the ark of thy strength" (v.41). This is Solomon's summons to the Lord. David said, "I had in mine heart to build an house of rest for the ark" (1 Chr 28.2). The temple itself could not be built until there was rest from war (1 Chr 28.3). The pilgrims of Psalm 132 were travelling to the house of rest. The resting place is, of course, the Holy of Holies where the ark already was. This is not inconsistent with this summons. God would rest where the ark, the symbol of His strength, already sat. "Thy resting place", implies God's dwelling permanently in His house. The word "arise" calls to mind the words of Numbers 10.35: "And it came to pass, when the ark set forward, that Moses said, rise up, Lord, and let thine enemies be scattered". Solomon's summons to the Lord is very fitting at the dedication of the temple.

"Let thy priests, O Lord God, be clothed with salvation" (v.41). Psalm 132.9 has "clothed with righteousness". Salvation and righteousness are linked together in Isaiah 61.10: "I will greatly rejoice in the Lord, my soul shall be joyful in my God; for he hath clothed me with the garments of salvation, he hath covered me with the robe of righteousness". It has been well said, "God never gives righteousness as a covering, but what he looks for is righteousness as a character". Flanigan's words are fitting: "The priests would be clothed in their holy vestments, but more important was it that they should be suitably attired, morally, with righteousness".

"Let thy saints rejoice in goodness" (v.41). Psalm 132.9 has, "let thy saints shout for joy". This request and the earlier one about the priests in the same verse are both answered by the Lord in Psalm 132.16: "I will also clothe her priests with salvation: and her saints shall shout for joy". Solomon greatly desired God's people to rejoice in the goodness of God.

"O Lord God, turn not away the face of thine anointed" (v.42). "Though 'anointed one' occurs in both the Septuagint and Psalm 132.10, and is favoured by most commentators, the plural reading must be given serious consideration...Not only is it less easy to explain how an original singular might have been corrupted, but the plural is consistent with the priests and the saints as the two preceding objects of Solomon's prayer. In its favour, too, is the Chronicler's use of the only other instance of 'anointed ones' in the Old Testament (1 Chr 16.22; and parallel, Ps 105.15), and his interest in the Davidic dynasty and David and Solomon's joint kingship rather than in individual kings (cp. the preference for David and Solomon for an earlier singular form in 1 Chronicles 18.8 [cp. 2 Sam 8.8] and 2 Chronicles 7.10 [cp. 1 Kings 8.66]; cp. also 2 Chr 11.17; 30.26)" (Selman). Those commentators who prefer the singular "anointed" refer it to Solomon (1 Kings 1.39; 1 Chr 29.22).

To "turn away the face" from one who is asking is to disappoint him by refusing his request. It is clear from 1 Kings 2.16 that the phrase has this significance - "deny me not" has the AV marginal reading, "turn not away my face".

"Remember the mercies of David thy servant". "The repetition of God's 'great love' (HESED -2617) and the phrase 'David thy servant' in the final verse (v.42) has the effect of forming an *inclusio* or envelope construction with the opening petition of Solomon's prayer (vv.14-17). See especially 'covenant of love' (v.14) and 'your servant David' (vv.15-16)" (Hill).

Some commentators understand the phrase, "the mercies of David", to refer to the good deeds of David, but it seems best to take it as referring to God's mercies towards David. This is in keeping with the rest of the prayer, especially vv.14-17. It also agrees with what seems to be the meaning in the only other place in the Old Testament where we have the phrase (Is 55.3), and also harmonises with the meaning of mercy to David in Psalm 89.24,28. This is the meaning of Psalm 132.10-11. Solomon used the plural for the word "mercies" referring to the faithful loving kindness of God. Solomon was thus requesting God to fulfill His promise of a dynasty for David. The completion of the temple confirmed that hope. The Apostle Peter said in Acts 2.30 that Psalm 132.11 was fulfilled by our Lord Jesus. In a coming day when Israel is truly repentant our Lord will sit on the throne of David and there will be worldwide peace.

"It is interesting to compare this prayer with John 17, a passage popularly called 'the high priestly prayer of Jesus'. Both prayers are concerned with the glory of God, manifest in the cloud at the temple and in the presence of the Son of God (Jn 17.1,5,10,22,24); both prayers constitute somewhat of a 'charter' for the subsequent history of the people of God and are basically oriented to generations to follow (Jn 17.6,9,20). Both prayers occur at the completion of work undertaken by divine appointment (5.1; 6.10-11; Jn 17.4); both are concerned to solicit divine protection for those who follow (Jn 17.11-12,15). But for all their similarities, two prayers could hardly contrast more as the representatives of the old and new covenants" (Dillard). See also Selman's similar comparison between John 14-17 and 2 Chronicles 6 in the main Introduction above.

2 CHRONICLES 7

Solomon's Reign

Introductory

This chapter has two sections, both of which concern God's answer to Solomon's prayer (6.14-22). Verses 1-10 contain God's very public, dramatic, immediate, and emphatic confirmation of the prayer. This took place in the final acts of the dedication ceremony. Verses 11-22 give God's private answer to the prayer by His appearing to Solomon by night, thirteen years later.

"Chapter 7 is not only central to the message of Chronicles, but it is one of the most important chapters in the Old Testament. It offers hope to any who call on the name of the Lord, even if they have incurred God's wrath, because God's desire is for full reconciliation. The over-all theme is encapsulated in a passage most of which is unique to Chronicles (vv.12-16), and which contains one of the best-known verses in Chronicles (v.14)" (Selman).

"The double attestation of the temple, in 5.13-14 and 7.1-3a, reminds me of the twofold divine endorsement of Jesus, with a voice from heaven at His baptism and a voice from the cloud of glory at His transfiguration (Mk 1.11; 9.7)" (Leslie C. Allen).

This is a reminder of Aaron offering in connection with the Tabernacle "and the glory of the Lord appeared unto all the people" (Lev 9.23). "And there came a fire out from before the Lord, and consumed upon the altar the burnt offering and the fat" (Lev 9.24). It is also reminiscent of what we read about David in 1 Chronicles 21.26, which with 2 Chronicles 7.1-3 "testifies that the divine approbation was given as clearly at the completion of the temple as at the time of the original selection of the site" (Curtis & Masden).

Even though God's private answer to Solomon's prayer is so close to it in the text (6.14-42), 7.11 indicates that this appearance to Solomon did not occur until thirteen years later after Solomon had finished his own house as well as the temple. However, there was an immediate answer in vv.1-2. Both in Kings and in Chronicles God's words to Solomon in His appearance to him are looked upon as God's answer to his prayer.

God's response as recorded in Chronicles follows the parallel in 1 Kings 8.54a, 62-9.9 fairly closely with two exceptions. The Chronicler adds vv.1b-3 and vv.12b-16a, a very important addition. God's response to Solomon in vv.12-22 and especially v.14 is the basis for the remainder of the Chronicler's work. Because of the promise of v.14, God's people had three options: obedience, disobedience, or humble repentance. The last of these would lead to forgiveness, restoration, and healing through the grace of God.

"If disobedience had been rampant, all was not lost: there was an opportunity for obeying God's law of restoration. If every rule in the book had been broken, one more ruling is revealed, vibrant with grace and hope, here in 7.14" (Leslie C. Allen).

Humbling and repentance are more prominent from now on in Chronicles.

"Perhaps surprisingly, the New Testament makes no direct reference to this chapter, though it does develop several of its themes. The theme of answered prayer, for example, is central to the teaching of Jesus, and Christians are assured that God hears and answers prayers offered in Jesus' name (Jn 14.13-14)...Christians are invited, too, to pray toward God's heavenly temple, where the throne of grace promises mercy and grace in needed times (Heb 4.16). The availability of such a direct route to God's heavenly sanctuary offers even greater encouragement to draw near to God than Solomon had in his experience of God's glory (2 Chr 7.1-3, 15-16)" (Selman).

Outline of Chapter 7

Verses 1-10: God's immediate, public answer to Solomon's prayer.
  Verses 1-3: God's approval by fire and glory.
  Verses 4-7: The sacrifices of Solomon and the people.
  Verses 8-10: The Feast of Tabernacles and the dedication of the altar.
Verses 11-22: God's later, private answer to Solomon's prayer.
  Verse 11: God's house and Solomon's house all completed.
  Verses 12-18: God's response to Solomon's prayer.
  Verses 19-22: God's warning to Solomon and to the people.

Verses 1-10: God's Immediate, Public Answer to Solomon's Prayer

God's approval by fire and glory (vv.1-3)

The first nine words are the only part of this paragraph in common with 1 Kings (8.54a). The remainder is unique to Chronicles. On the other hand, the writer has omitted Solomon's blessing of the people recorded in 1 Kings 8.54b-61. There is no contradiction. Both records are true. "The Chronicler omits the account of Solomon blessing the people (1 Kings 8.54b-61)...because he was anxious to show (in a way that the Kings account does not) God's positive response to the prayer" (Williamson). The double manifestation of God's presence in the fire and the glory did show God's approval of the temple, the new altar (v.4.1), and the sacrifice, but especially of Solomon's prayer. The ESV for v.1 has, "As soon as Solomon finished his prayer", indicating that the fire and the glory came immediately after he had ceased praying. Thus the prayer, the fire, and the glory are linked together. God's approval is the most important part of the dedication. No one can sanctify apart from God Himself.

"And the priests could not enter into the house of the Lord, because the glory of the Lord had filled the Lord's house" (v.2). There was a very similar conjunction of events in 5.13-14.

"In consequence of the glory filling the temple, 'the priests could not enter' (v.2). This should not be confused with the previous occasion when the glory filled the temple. The priests then 'could not *stand*' there to minister but they were obliged to withdraw (5.14). This time, the priests 'could not *enter*' the temple owing to the glory, and so they had no alternative but to stay outside in the courts" (Page).

Moses himself could not enter the Tabernacle when the glory of the Lord had filled it (Ex 40.35). This fire (v.1) was in answer to Solomon's prayer. There was a similar fire in answer to the prayer of Elijah (1 Kings 18.38). When the people here saw the fire and the glory, they were so overwhelmed that "they bowed themselves with their faces to the ground…and worshipped, and praised the Lord" (v.3). This verse "is indeed a foreshadow of the age to come when a regenerate Israel will bow in worship before the glorified Messiah" (Page).

The fire in Leviticus 9.24 had a similar result: "when all the people saw, they shouted, and fell on their faces". The words that they used here in praising the Lord, "For he is good; for his mercy endureth forever", are an accustomed formula. They are found several times in Chronicles (1 Chr 16.34,41; 2 Chr 5.13; 7.3,6; 20.21) and in the Psalms (106.1; 107.1; 118.1,2,3,4; and in Psalm 136 at the close of each of the 26 verses). They were also used on the solemn occasion when the foundation of the temple was laid as described in Ezra 3.11.

The sacrifices of Solomon and the people (vv.4-7)

These verses are very similar to those in 1 Kings 8.62-64 except that v.6 is found only in Chronicles. "The king and all the people" in vv.4-5 is in keeping with the recurring theme in the book of Chronicles of national unity. "The king and all the people" offered sacrifices (v.4) and "dedicated the house of God" (v.5). The number of sacrifices in v.5 is exactly the same as the number given in 1 Kings 8.63. The total number seems incredible, and adding the sacrifices of the people would make it more so, but it is in keeping with the importance of the occasion. There were so many sacrifices that the brazen altar that Solomon had made (4.1) was not able to receive all the offerings, so Solomon hallowed the middle of the court for them (v.7). That would allow for a number to be offered at the same time.

The writer of Chronicles refers to the fat of the peace offerings, but only Kings records that the animals that Solomon offered were peace offerings (1 Kings 8.63). That indicates that even though Chronicles and Kings both tell of the offering of burnt offerings and meat offerings, most of the offerings were, in fact, peace offerings. That would provide food for all the people that were gathered together for the 14 days (vv. 7-10; 1 Kings 8.65) - 15 days if the day of dismissal is counted. The fat was burned before the people could eat any of the peace offerings (Lev 3.3). The priests may have made the offerings (even though it is not specifically recorded here but may be alluded to in v.6). The peace offerings must have been offered daily because the meat of that offering could only be eaten for two days and anything left over on the third day was to be burnt (Lev 7.16-17).

"In Roman times 256,500 paschal lambs are said to have been slaughtered in a few hours" (Curtis & Masden). "People cringe when we talk about sacrifices numbering this many. Why was there such a slaughter? Because God is painting a picture, showing us the seriousness of sin. The immensity of sacrifices offered point out that the price Jesus paid is immense, incomprehensible" (Courson).

Verse 6 records all who were present, priests, Levites, and all Israel, and reflect the Chronicler's interest in the Levites especially the musicians as is also found in 1 Chronicles 6.31-48; 15.16,27; 25.1-31 and 2 Chronicles 29.25-27. This verse also shows that the priests and the Levites took special care of the musical part of the worship and possibly also the sacrifices (vv.4,5,6,7). Trumpets are particularly linked with the priests (Num 10.8; 1 Chr 15.24; 16.6; 2 Chr 5.12; 7.6; 13.12,14). The instruments of the Levites were cymbals, psalteries, and harps (1 Chr 15.28; 16.5; 25.1,6), which King David had made (1 Chr 23.5; 25.1,6). The ESV and the RSV have, for the last part of v.6, "opposite them the priests sounded trumpets, and all Israel stood". "The expression 'opposite them' could just refer to an antiphonal arrangement with trumpets sounding alternately with the voices, but more likely refers to the respective positions of priests and Levitical musicians" (The New Layman's Bible Commentary).

Recording the hallowing of the middle court before the offering of sacrifices (v.7) reflects the concern of the writer of Chronicles that ritual procedures should be carried out correctly. "The middle of the court" (v.7) "was, in all probability, the rock upon which David offered the oxen purchased from Ornan" (Myers). "More likely Solomon used the bare rock for his sacrifice - the great rock es Sakhra now under the dome of the Mosque of Omar, which is believed to have stood in front of the temple and has every indication of having been an altar" (Curtis & Masden). See also 1 Chronicles 21.26.

The Feast of Tabernacles and the dedication of the altar (vv.8-10)

"All Israel" is a recurring theme in Chronicles as in v.8, which also notes a "very great congregation". The Chronicler adds "very" (which is not in 1 Kings) to emphasize the size of the gathering. The last words of v.8 show that God's people came from all over Israel, from the northern border to the southern. The last words of v.8, "unto the river of Egypt", refer to the southern border and are the same as is found in 1 Kings 8.65. They are both translated in the RV and ESV as "unto the brook of Egypt". So these words in 1 Kings 8.65 and 2 Chronicles 7.8 can hardly refer to the Lord's promise to Abraham in Genesis 15.18b where we read, "Unto thy seed have I given this land, from the river of Egypt to the great river, the river Euphrates". Robert Young's Analytical Concordance confirms that the Hebrew word for "river" in Genesis 15.18b is not the same as the Hebrew word for "river" in 1 Kings 8.65 and 2 Chronicles 7.8. It is most likely therefore, that the "river of Egypt" in Genesis 15.18b is the Nile itself rather than merely a brook.

These words "all Israel" are similar to those when David brought up the ark from Kirjath-jearim (1 Chr 13.5). Thus these three verses, 1 Chronicles 13.5, 1 Kings 8.65, and 2 Chronicles 7.8 indicate that David and Solomon came closest to possessing all the land promised to Abraham. God is always faithful in carrying out all of His promises, and so during the Millennium Israel will possess all of the land promised to Abraham.

"The words 'a very great congregation' in 2 Chronicles 7.8 are a reminder of Psalm 22.25. That precious Psalm, which describes Our Lord's experience as the Sin Offering in vv. 1-20, also speaks in the concluding verses of the far-reaching results of His sacrifice. Kingdom bliss is in view in v.25 - 'My praise shall be of thee in the great congregation'! Earth's long rejected Sovereign will return to Zion; and in the midst of Israel and many nations, all at last at rest and in peace, He will lead the song of praise to His God… Verse 22 of Psalm 22 is quoted by the Holy Spirit in Hebrews 2.12 and applied to the present time. 'I will declare thy name unto my brethren, in the midst of the church will I sing praise unto thee'. It is but a 'little flock' (Lk 12.32) when compared with the great congregation of the Kingdom age; but the church is all that He has during this period of His rejection, and it constitutes His present joy" (Fereday).

"Although he follows 1 Kings 8.65 in mentioning that the congregation had come from the maximum extent of the kingdom, at 1 Chronicles 13.5 he had already modified the parallel text (2 Samuel 6.1) to show David presiding over an assembly from the same extent ('from the Shihor of Egypt to Lebo-Hamath'), thereby further perfecting the parallel of David and Solomon" (Dillard).

The writer of the Chronicles gives the chronological details more clearly in vv.8-10 than those recorded in 1 Kings 8.65-66. The week-long dedication was from the eighth to the fourteenth day of the month, and was followed by the regular observance of the Feast of Tabernacles from the fifteenth to the twenty-second day of the seventh month. The final convocation of the Feast of Tabernacles (which is referred to as the eighth day and "a solemn assembly") was on the twenty-second day. It was to be a Sabbath day (Lev 23.39), and a solemn assembly (Lev 23.36). The twenty-third day of the month would be the day of dismissal. The days of dedication would include the Day of Atonement on the tenth, but the writer is silent about it. A similar two-week celebration occurred in the temple under good King Hezekiah (30.23).

The Feast of Tabernacles was one of the three feasts that every male was required to attend (Ex 23.14-17; 34.23; Deut 16.16). God promised His people that no one would even desire their land when they went up those three times a year (Ex 34.24). God knew that concern for their land would hinder their worship. We also learn from the mention of worship in Genesis 22.5 that we have to say to earthly cares as Abraham said to the two young men, "Abide ye here with the ass; and I and the lad will go yonder and worship". To make a modern day application, anxiety about earthly cares while at the Breaking of Bread will hinder worship.

Leviticus 23.42 is explicit about the Feast of Tabernacles: "Ye shall dwell in booths seven days". Solomon and his people did not do so. Nehemiah 8.17 records that the returned remnant "made booths, and sat under the booths: for since the days of Jeshua the son of Nun unto that day had not the children of Israel done so". It is no wonder that the last sentence of that verse reads, "And there was very great gladness". There is joy in obeying the Word of God (Jn 13.17; 15.9-11).

The last words of v.5 read, "all the people dedicated the house of God". The words, "they kept the dedication of the altar seven days" are found in v.9 but are not found in 1 Kings.

The eighth day of the Feast of Tabernacles (which was the last day of the feast) is reminiscent of the last day of the Feast described in John 7.37-38. "In that last day, that great day of the feast, Jesus stood and cried, saying, 'If any man thirst, let him come unto me, and drink. He that believeth on me, as the scripture hath said, out of his belly shall flow rivers of living water". Any person who wants God's salvation more than anything else is a thirsty sinner. This invitation is especially for them. This feast is the last of the seven and the one that had the most joy connected with it. They were to "rejoice before the Lord your God seven days" (Lev 23.40). Deuteronomy 16.15, RV, records, "thou shalt be altogether joyful".

"In John 4 He made a similar offer to a Samaritan woman who, having gone in for the pleasures of sin, was thirsting still. But here it was made to those who had just gone through a great religious feast, and indeed had completed a full year's round of religious observances. Was it possible that after all this there might be those still athirst for something better, those who were feeling that religion could no more satisfy their heart than could the pleasures of sin? If there were such, Christ's invitation was just what they needed" (Rodgers).

Verse 10 records that Solomon "sent the people away into their tents", i.e. "their homes". "The word 'tents' was used for 'houses' from an old habit of speech, which had come down from the time when the Israelites were a nomadic nation" (Rawlinson). The people were "glad and merry in heart for the goodness that the Lord had showed unto David, and to Solomon, and to Israel his people" (v.10). Instead of "David his servant" in 1 Kings 8.66, Chronicles has "David and Solomon", once more looking at the two together as one episode in the history of Israel. The Chronicler often brings together David and Solomon.

The response of the people was commendable. They were "glad and merry in heart". The Feast of Tabernacles itself was an occasion of rejoicing. The dedication of the temple that God had enabled Solomon to build, as

He had promised to David, made the occasion all the more memorable and joyful. They were obviously thankful for what God had done for David and Solomon and for what He had done for His people through them. It was truly a momentous and significant episode in the history of God's people.

The words in v.10, "glad and merry in heart", are translated as "joyful and glad of heart" in the RV and ESV. Verse 10 is a good summary of the first ten verses, showing that God's people were truly thankful for all the goodness of God to them. Since God has given far greater blessings to New Testament saints in the person of His Son, how thankful we should be! "Thanks be unto God for his unspeakable gift" (2 Cor 9.15).

It would have been wonderful if God's people had continued, united in joy before the Lord, as they were that day. It is important for believers today to be in fellowship with other believers so they can experience joy together. Saints need each other.

The Feast of Tabernacles commemorated their wilderness wanderings, and so it was fitting to have the dedication of the temple at the Feast of Tabernacles since with this permanent sanctuary there were to be no more wanderings.

Verses 11-22: God's Later, Private Answer to Solomon's Prayer

God's house and Solomon's house all completed (v.11)

Again one should note that the second answer to Solomon's prayer did not take place until 13 years later after Solomon had finished his own house (1 Kings 7.1). The writer of the Chronicles has only passing reference to the king's house (7.11; 8.11) while Kings devotes twelve verses to the buildings adjacent to the temple including the royal palace (1 Kings 7.1-12). "All of these were situated close by the temple and were viewed as a combined range of majestic buildings, so that the entire group is simply referred to as the king's house (1 Kings 9.1,10,15; 10.12)" (McShane).

God's response to Solomon's prayer (vv.12-18)

The Kings account links all that is recorded in v.11 to the occasion when the Lord appeared to Solomon the second time (1 Kings 9.1-2), but only the Chronicler has "by night" (v.12) which is a reminder of the first time that the Lord appeared to him (1.7). The first night was when God caused Solomon to excel in wisdom. His God-given wisdom helped in his prayer to which God is responding on this new night. The account in Kings has, "as he had appeared unto him at Gibeon" (1 Kings 9.2). "The omission of the Kings reference to Gibeon (v.12; cp. 1 Kings 9.2) is more likely to be deliberate; attention is now to be focused on Jerusalem" (Coggins).

Verse 12 is the only place where the temple is referred to as "an house of sacrifice". God clearly wanted His people to offer sacrifices only at the temple (Deut 12.13-14). The last part of v.12 is the beginning of God's response to Solomon's prayer.

It may seem strange that God did not give His second response to Solomon's prayer until 13 years later, but there may have been a more important reason why He appeared to Solomon at this time (rather than a more immediate response to his prayer). 1 Kings 6.38 records that the temple was completed in the eleventh year of Solomon's reign, and 1 Kings 7.1 states that Solomon spent 13 years building his own house which brings us to the 24th year of his reign when the Lord appeared to him. God's first appearance to him was early in his reign, possibly in the first year. That would make the second appearance 23 years later. 1 Kings 11.4 records, "For it came to pass, when Solomon was old, that his wives turned away his heart after other gods; and his heart was not perfect with the Lord his God, as was the heart of David his father". His departure in heart did not begin until after the 24th year of his reign, because God does not condemn him here. In God's response we have two verses encouraging him to walk as his father David did (vv.17-18) and four long verses (vv.19-22) warning him and the nation of the serious consequences of turning away. God's appearing to him twice made his departure all the more reprehensible (1 Kings 11.9).

The material between "have chosen" in v.12b to "have I chosen" in v.16a are only found in Chronicles. There are some parallels in God's response to Solomon's prayer. Verse 13 is representative of all the calamities spoken of in his prayer (6.22-39). The next verse begins with the words, "If my people". Solomon in his prayer referred to "thy people" ten times. "If my people, which are called by my name" indicates ownership. This wonderful promise was originally given to the nation of Israel. Today, God owns each believer, bought with the precious blood of Christ (cp. 1 Cor 6.19-20; 1 Pet 1.18-19). In 6.21-39 Solomon asks God to forgive five times (v.vv.21,25,27,30,39). Verse 14 is the best known and the best loved verse of all of Chronicles. It is a wonderful promise of forgiveness. The words of v.15 follow almost exactly word for word in answer to the request of Solomon in 6.40. Verse 16 answers the request of Solomon in 6.20.

Verse 14 is very important. It states the theology of the Chronicler. In chs.10-36 we see repeatedly his perspective: there is blessing for obedience and trouble for disobedience. But when God's people have sinned there is still the possibility of forgiveness and restoration after true repentance. The writer of the Chronicles often adds details to the account in Kings to emphasize his viewpoint.

There are four expressions, which give the right attitude for forgiveness and for restoration. They are best considered as four sides of the same attitude. These four are distinct from each other and in sequence. The first one is a key element: "shall humble themselves". It is humbling for any saint to acknowledge to God that he has been wrong. In so doing pride is subdued. Rehoboam (the first king of Judah after Solomon) is recorded three times as humbling himself with the princes of Judah (12.6,7,7) and once as humbling himself (12.12). There are 13 incidents (in the remainder of Chronicles) listed in the Introductory part of 2 Chronicles 12 where there was blessing as a result of humbling or lack of blessing because of refusal to humble themselves before God. Humbling is also involved in Leviticus 26.40-42 and Isaiah 66.1-2 but especially in Jeremiah 13.15: "Hear ye, and give ear; be not proud: for the Lord hath spoken". Jeremiah 13.17 says, "But if ye will not hear it, my soul shall weep in secret places for your pride". Jeremiah knew that pride would keep them from hearing as they should. This is illustrated in ch.42 of Jeremiah, when there were only a few of God's people left after all the others had been taken away captive. They begged Jeremiah to find out from God the way that they should go. They solemnly promised to obey (vv.5-6). God did not give direction to Jeremiah until ten days later because He wanted reality from them and He wants reality from His people today. Ten is the number of man's responsibility. After Jeremiah gave the direction (that God had given him), how sad to read the response (43.2): "Then spake Azariah…Johanan…and all the proud men, saying unto Jeremiah, Thou speakest falsely: the Lord our God hath not sent thee to say, Go not into Egypt to dwell there". But God had sent him to say just that! We should especially notice the word "proud". So they missed direction from God because of pride. This is a warning to God's people. Any believer can miss direction from God today because of pride.

There are three other expressions in v.14 about the right attitude. "Pray" here is a sincere acknowledgment of sin and a plea for mercy (like David in Psalm 51.1-3). "And seek my face": even in captivity God promised that they would find Him provided they "seek him with all thy heart and with all thy soul" (Deut 4.29). There are many encouragements later in 2 Chronicles for God's people to seek Him (11.16; 14.4; 15.2,4,12,13,15; 19.3; 20.3,4; 22.9; 26.5; 30.19; 31.21; 34.3).

"Turn" is one of the main synonyms for "repentance" in the Old Testament and in 2 Chronicles (15.4; 30.6,9; 36.13). To "turn" is to turn from every wicked way and to turn to God's way. "Pray" and "turn" are found often in Solomon's prayer and this verse is a direct answer to him. While God was graciously offering forgiveness, He was also protecting His own holiness by requesting genuine repentance.

God promised His people three things if they repented: He would hear, forgive, and heal. Right after the conditions of v.14 we read, "then will I hear from heaven". Newberry has the pronoun "I" as emphatic, showing how important it was for God to hear. God wants the prayers of saints to be real. "Forgive" is not found later in Chronicles. God's forgiveness is expressed in other ways such as God's wrath not being poured out (12.7; 30.8), God being found by His people (15.2,4,15), God answering an entreaty (33.13,19), and God pardoning (30.18-20).

"This last passage is particularly interesting; since it also contains the only other reference in Chronicles to God's healing (30.20). Both 7.14 and 30.18,20 indicate that forgiveness and healing are part of the same work of God" (Selman).

Pardoning mercy leads to healing mercy as in Psalm 103.3: "Who forgiveth all thine iniquities; who healeth all thy diseases". The three synoptic Gospels describe the case of the palsied man who experienced these mercies in the same order (Mt 9.2-8; Mk 2.3-12; Lk 5.18-26).

Verse 15 says, "The prayer that is made in this place". "Literally, as given in the AV margin, 'to the prayer of this place'. The unusual phrase seems chosen in order to include the two cases of prayers offered in (6.24) and towards (6.34,38) the sanctuary" (Rawlinson).

An outstanding statement about the presence of God in the temple (v.16) further strengthens the promise of restoration. God affirms that His name, His eyes, and even His heart would be there perpetually. After the words, "have I chosen" (v.16a), Chronicles follows 1 Kings 9.3b-9 quite closely to the end of the chapter.

"The idea of God having a heart is extremely rare in the Bible, and the only other explicit reference speaks of God suffering heart pains because of the evil of humanity (Gen 6.6; cp. also Gen 8.21; 1 Sam 13.14; Acts 13.22). Since the heart expresses the innermost parts of a person or thing, God here offers to humankind His deepest inner being, and reveals a wounded heart" (Selman).

God's response to Solomon's request about the dynasty of David (6.15-17, 42) is recorded in vv.17-18. Some of the words in God's response are quite close to those in Solomon's request. 6.16 reads, "There shall not fail thee a man...to sit upon the throne of Israel". 7.18 has, "There shall not fail thee a man to be a ruler in Israel". God Himself told Solomon that in order for the dynasty of David to be perpetuated he and his sons after him would have to be obedient like his father David (1 Kings 2.4; 8.25; 1 Chr 28.7,9).

Solomon himself turned away from God (1 Kings 11.4,9). God was so angry with him that He told him that He would rend the kingdom from him (1 Kings 11.11). 1 Kings 11.12-13 reads, "Notwithstanding in thy days I will not do it for David thy father's sake: but I will rend it out of the hand of thy son. Howbeit, I will not rend away all the kingdom; but will give one tribe to thy son for David my servant's sake, and for Jerusalem's sake which I have chosen". Twice in these two verses God told Solomon that His actions in judgment upon him were modified "for David's sake". God greatly appreciated David.

After the sins of Abijam (during his three year reign) we read an outstanding statement about David in 1 Kings 15.4-5: "Nevertheless for David's sake did the Lord his God give him a lamp in Jerusalem, to set up his son after him, and to establish Jerusalem. Because David did that which was right in the eyes of the Lord, and turned not aside from any thing that he commanded him all the days of his life, save only in the matter of Uriah the Hittite". Verse 5 is especially remarkable. After Jehoram's wicked reign of eight years in 21.7 God again acted according to His covenant with David.

McShane, in commenting on 1 Kings 9.4 (which is followed in 2 Chronicles 7.17), and most likely having 1 Kings 15.5 in mind, wrote, "Again the example of his father is set before him. Only by walking in his father's footsteps could he, and his posterity, retain the throne. The commendation given to David by the Lord may seem, in the light of his failure, to be more than warranted, but whatever the sins in his life, he had never turned to idolatry. Solomon was to imitate his father's virtues, but this did not imply that he was to look lightly on his father's failings".

McShane writes further about David: "Whatever David's failings he never engaged in idolatry…While it is wrong for us to try to grade sins as major and minor, it is evident that the one most detested by God is idolatry. He is a jealous God and will not tolerate any rival".

"There may have been some excuse for the kings of Israel to disregard the faithfulness of David, but the kings of Judah, who were reigning because of their relationship with him, were surely under an obligation to follow in his footsteps. Alas, most of them failed miserably to do so" (McShane).

Manasseh became an Old Testament prodigal saved later in life, but he was very wicked up until then. Ahaz also was wicked as were the last four kings. Zedekiah, the last son of David to reign on his throne, ceased to rule in 586 BC when the temple at Jerusalem was destroyed.

2 Chronicles 7.18 follows 1 Kings 9.5, but there are two changes in v.18 that are most likely deliberate and significant. These changes both emphasize God's commitment to the dynasty of David. Kings has, "as I promised to David", while Chronicles has, "as I covenanted with David". In this way, the Chronicler is magnifying the covenant. Kings has "a man upon the throne of Israel". Chronicles has "to be ruler in Israel". With this change the writer of Chronicles is thinking of the Messianic promise of the post-exilic prophet Micah since Micah 5.2 has the words, "to be ruler in Israel".

The second modification was a real encouragement to the readers of the Chronicles. "The author gives expression to his Messianic or royalist hopes: though the throne of David is vacant, the continuity of the Davidic dynasty remains. The dynastic promise has not lost its validity even with the loss of the throne…Though the temple had once been destroyed, God's choice of Jerusalem was still valid; though no descendent of David sat on a throne, the Davidic line had not failed (7.18). One would yet come, whose origins were of old, from ancient times, to be ruler over Israel (Micah 5.2)" (Dillard).

Our Lord Jesus, the greatest Son of David, was born in Bethlehem and he will yet come and reign over Israel and the world for a thousand years in His promised Kingdom!

God's warning to Solomon and to the people (vv.19-22)

This is the second response to Solomon's request about the dynasty of David in his prayer (6.15-17, 42). God had spoken to Solomon in the second person singular in v.17-18, "thee", "thou", about the necessity for obedience for the dynasty of David. Now in v.19 God shifts to the second person plural, "ye", to include all the people as well as Solomon, in warning about the fate of the nation if there were disobedience. The threatenings for disobedience in v.19-22 are similar to those in Deuteronomy 4.25-27; 28.15-68. The words of the last part of v.20, "will make it to be a proverb and a byword among all nations", are very similar to the words of Deuteronomy 28.37 and Jeremiah 24.9.

"Such judgment would actually reverse God's earlier promises - to be 'cast out of my sight' (v.20), is the opposite of the assurance that God's eyes are watching for one's prayers (vv.15-16). Interestingly, the situation in which such a disaster might arise is no different in kind from that described in v.13 which might result in restoration. The distinction between the salvation of v.14 and the judgment of v.20 is not that the people in the former case were any better, but that they repented. While judgment can be earned, restoration is an undeserved gift. Repentance and restoration, however, were God's expected norm" (Selman).

"Solomon's temple has long been destroyed; other structures have succeeded it; but Haggai 2.9, RV, teaches us that in God's sight the house has been one throughout. 'The latter glory of this house shall be greater than the former, saith the Lord of hosts'. Haggai 2.3 asks, 'Who is left among you that saw this house in her first glory?'...Even the temple that was built by Herod...was called by the Lord Jesus, 'my Father's house' (Jn 2.16). It is perhaps more remarkable that the temple in which the man of sin will sit is called 'the temple of God' in 2 Thessalonians 2.4 and Revelation 11.1" (Fereday).

"The destroyed temple will become an object lesson in disobedience. When the answer is given as to the reason for this destruction, namely, that it is because Israel had forsaken God and turned to idols, there is implied in that answer amazement at the fact that a people could be so foolish as to reject the God who had taken them out of bondage and made them into a great nation" (Patterson & Austel).

"And at this house, which was exalted, everyone passing by will be astonished" (v.21, ESV). Part of the astonishment is that a building so outstanding as the temple could be destroyed. It was destroyed in 586 BC. Here at the dedication of the temple in all its grandeur is a warning of what could and did in fact happen. The original readers of Chronicles have another temple in Jerusalem. Whether the same fate happens to that temple is dependent on whether God's people avail themselves of God's remarkable promise in 7.14.

Verse 22 refers to God's people and notes that they, "laid hold on other gods". In commenting on this McShane notes that "Israel taking hold upon (CHAZAQ - 2388) other gods is an interesting expression. It implies that they gripped them firmly, as did Adonijah and Joab the horns of the altar (1 Kings 1.50; 2.28)".

Saints today may think that they would never "lay hold on other gods", but in reality anything that takes our Lord Jesus' place in our affections is an idol. That is why John gives his exhortation in 1 John 5.21, "Little children, keep yourselves from idols".

"True praise is to be taken up with who God is, the Excellency of His Person, the evidence of His grace, the greatness of His works and His abiding love…The opportunity we have to praise the Lord and also bring before Him our troubles and our failures is a priceless privilege" (Barber).

"In this there is a weighty lesson. The most spiritual assembly, which according to the New Testament is a house of God, can be brought down to ruin as was the temple. Equally true is the fact that even though the founders of an assembly were careful to obey the Word of God this does not guarantee that their successors will be equally obedient. There can be various reasons for once prosperous assemblies to die out, but in not a few cases, the real cause can be traced to one factor, namely, departure from the Word of God" (McShane).

2 CHRONICLES 8

Solomon's Reign

Introductory

"The final section of Solomon's reign (chs.8-9) concentrates on the theme of praise for all that God has done for Solomon (see especially 9.8). This unit is clearly connected with the opening section about Solomon (2 Chr 1-2), which deals with Solomon's achievements and reputation. The chief difference is that whereas the earlier chapters describe Solomon's preparations in response to God's revelation at Gibeon, now that work is fulfilled. The real subject of chapters 8-9, therefore, is what God achieved through Solomon, rather than Solomon's own achievements" (Selman).

Barber writes similarly, "We are so prone to look at the effort we expend to accomplish a particular task that we seldom stop to thank the Lord for His enabling grace. A sub-theme, therefore, that runs through chapters 8 and 9 emphasizes the need for praise".

Since 5.1 and 7.11 record that the temple was finished, it may be surprising that the temple theme is again prominent in this chapter, but it is clearly quite deliberate. The Hebrew word translated "prepared" (KUN - 3559) in 8.16 - "Now all the work of Solomon was prepared" - is the same Hebrew word translated "set in order" in the last sentence of 29.35 - "so the service of the house of God was set in order". Verses 12-15 record how Solomon did this.

Another indication of this emphasis on the temple comes from the section between v.1 and v.12. Here we see repeatedly Solomon's success in building and fortifying cities. This accomplishment indicates God's blessings on Solomon and Israel for their faithfulness regarding the temple, and supports the principle that when worship is made a priority blessing from God will follow.

Selman offers another reason. "The subjects listed here occur in the same order as in the parallel passage dealing with the preparations for the temple (ch.2). Mention of the temple and royal palace (v.1 and 2.1) is followed by Solomon's relationship with Hiram king of Tyre (8.2 and 2.3-16), and by the contribution made by foreigners (8.7-10 and 2.17-18). Chapter 8 therefore shows that Solomon has obeyed the order to build the temple (2.1), and has completed the work (8.1; cp. v.16) with the aid of a Gentile king and Gentile conscripts. Comparison of ch.8 with 1.1-13 also demonstrates that these results are not ultimately attributable to Solomon's own efforts. It was God Himself who had begun the work by making unexpected promises to Solomon (1.7-12), who had seen it through to completion (cp. Phil 1.6)."

Similarly Thompson notes, "The true significance of this presentation of Solomon is that it is a model for the Kingdom of God. When God's domain has been fully established, there will be no want or ignorance. The powers of evil will be set in flight, but God will be truly worshipped. In this the greatness of Solomon's kingdom is a reminder that the Kingdom of God must finally triumph. When that happens, all his people will live under a reign that is far greater than anything Israel experienced under Solomon. Still, Solomon serves as a pointer to what the Kingdom of God will be".

Chapter 8 is parallel to 1 Kings 9.10-28. Although the Chronicler omits 1 Kings 9.11-17a and 24b, and adds 2 Chronicles 8.11b, 13-16a, the order of the material is practically the same in both histories and shows direct dependence on the account in 1 Kings even though there may also have been additional sources.

Outline of Chapter 8

Verses 1-10. Solomon's power.
 Verses 1-6: Solomon's building and fortifications.
 Verses 7-10: Solomon using foreign labour in his kingdom.
Verses 11-16: Solomon's worship.
 Verse 11: Solomon moves Pharaoh's daughter to the house he has built for her.
 Verses 12-16: Solomon's worship.
Verses 17-18: Solomon's wealth.

Verses 1-10: Solomon's Power

Solomon's building and fortifications (vv.1-6)

The twenty years in v.1 date from the beginning of the work on the temple in the fourth year of Solomon's reign - seven years for its construction to be completed, and thirteen years for the building of the royal palace.

Solomon's dominion is briefly described similarly to the description of David's achievements for his kingdom in 1 Chronicles 18. The emphasis here is on Solomon's building works: the verb "to build" occurs six times (vv.1,2,4,4,5,6) in this section and the whole land is included - "throughout all the land of his dominion" (v.6). His success in building the Lord's house and his palace in these twenty years encouraged him to build in other parts of Israel.

Verse 2 appears at first sight to contradict 1 Kings 9.12-13. Now the writer of the Chronicles must have been fully aware that his readers knew about the account in 1 Kings. Rather than a contradiction, v.2 is almost certainly a sequel to that account, declaring what happened to those twenty cities or villages. Huram returned them for one of two reasons, or possibly for both. 1 Kings 9.12 states that "they pleased him not", and the next verse records that he spoke disparagingly of them. That may be why he returned them. But it is also possible that those cities were collateral until Solomon could pay satisfactorily what he owed to Huram. The fact that Solomon had to build those cities before any of God's people could dwell there may indicate part of the reason why Huram was displeased with them.

The incident seems to have a happy ending in 1 Kings 9.14. "Clearly no offense was taken for Hiram gave Solomon a handsome gift of 120 talents of gold. If this came after all the building work was practically completed, it was a much needed bonus and helped to fill the coffers which by this time must have been drained to a low level" (McShane).

Even though the reign of Solomon is referred to as a reign of peace in Chronicles, the writer feels free to observe the only military victory of Solomon mentioned in Chronicles - that over Hamath-Zobah (v.3). 1 Chronicles 18.3-8 records that the people of Zobah were enemies of David and vv.9-10 notes that the people of Hamath were friendly to David. Solomon's referring to them as Hamath-Zobah indicates that they had come together.

Hamath was a city north of Damascus at Israel's most northern border (Num 34.8; Josh 13.5). It is recorded in 7.8 that there were some from Hamath at the dedication.

"His building of store cities in Hamath (v.4) shows that his authority was real, a factor underlined by the Chronicler's use of the word 'captured' (v.3, NIV)…It may be that these store cities played a significant role in Solomon's import of Anatolian horses, as well as being storage centres for grain" (Selman). (The fact that grain is the primary food for horses is probably also relevant.)

Because the AV has "Tadmor" in both 1 Kings 9.18 and 2 Chronicles 8.4 some think that they are the same city. But it seems more likely that there are two distinct cities. Tadmor (which is Palmyra) is 140 miles north-east of Damascus in the wilderness of Syria. In 1 Kings 9.18 the RV and ESV both have "Tamar". The ESV actually has, "Tamar, in the wilderness, in the land of Judah". Tamar is most often taken to be located 20 miles south-west of the southern end of the Dead Sea. Of all the cities mentioned in Kings, Hazor is the only one that we know to have been in the north. All the others were in the south (as Tamar was).

"By pairing Hamath and Tadmor the Chronicler shows Solomon's sovereignty over all the major arteries for trade with Mesopotamia: the main overland route (Hamath) and the desert shortcut (Tadmor) are in his control. Domination of these cities of the trade route to the north was fundamental to Solomon's endeavors and wealth" (Dillard).

Beth-horon the upper and Beth-horon the nether (v.5) are located on the ridge rising from the valley of Aijalon to the plateau just north of Jerusalem. 1 Chronicles 7.24 records that Sherah, the daughter or granddaughter of Ephraim, built those two cities. The district is memorable as the place where Joshua defeated the Amorites and where God smote many of them with hailstones from heaven (Josh 10.10-11). The road along this route was strategic and linked Jerusalem with the coastal highway. Both these fenced cities had walls, gates, and bars. This helped to protect Jerusalem from invaders from the north, for this route is the way by which they would come. Beth-horon the upper was 2,022 feet (620m) above sea level and eleven miles north-west of Jerusalem. Beth-horon the nether was 1,210 feet (370m) above sea level and about 1¼ miles further north-west from Jerusalem.

Baalath (v.6) is probably the city in Dan mentioned in Joshua 19.44. It was near the Philistines and could be used in defense against them. The chariot cities (v.6) refer to those cities mentioned in Kings such as Hazor, Megiddo, and Gezer where there is abundant archeological evidence of Solomon's building activity.

The RV adds to the words in v.6, "all that Solomon desired to build", the phrase, "for his pleasure" and Slotki also adds the same expression just before the words "in Jerusalem, and in Lebanon, and throughout all the land of his dominion".

Solomon was very wise to build defences to protect the land from its enemies. But this did not guarantee the safety of the land. It is safest for God's people to remember that, "except the Lord keep the city, the watchman waketh but in vain" (Ps 127.1), and, "The horse is prepared against the day of battle: but safety is of the Lord" (Prov 21.31). Saints should be careful not to forget their dependence upon God when there is a sense of natural security.

Solomon using foreign labour in his kingdom (vv.7-10)

This paragraph follows 1 Kings 9.20-23 fairly closely. The RV for the last part of v.8 is very similar to the AV of the last part of 1 Kings 9.21: "...raise a levy of bond service unto this day". Both passages make it clear that Solomon did not make slaves of any of the Israelites. The responsibilities of the Israelites were far less menial than those of the slaves. Israelites were men of war and chief of the captains of the chariots and the horsemen (vv.8-9). These Gentile slaves had much to do in helping build the temple and many other of Solomon's projects.

"It is surprising that such a variety of descendants of the Canaanite nations still existed in the days of Solomon. Though Joshua conquered them and captured their cities, he did not exterminate them, nor did their distinct identity disappear in the intervening years. Alas, quite a number of them were married into the families of Israel. They could not be treated as slaves. But some had no such connection to Israel, and these were the subjects of bondage" (McShane).

Deuteronomy 17.16-17 gives instruction for all the kings of Israel and Judah. The king was not to multiply horses (v.16) and not to multiply wives (v.17). Solomon multiplied both. Later, his wives were his spiritual downfall (1 Kings 11.4). There were 250 chief officers to rule over the people (v.10); however, 1 Kings 9.23 says 550. That difference is dealt with thoroughly in the comments on 2 Chronicles 2.17-18 (Conscription of Labourers).

Verses 11-16: Solomon's Worship

Solomon moves Pharaoh's daughter to the house he had built for her (v.11)

This is the first time that the Chronicler mentions Pharaoh's daughter. The fact of Solomon's marrying her is recorded in 1 Kings (3.1; 9.16; 11.1). But the record of the holiness of the ark as the reason for the move is found only in Chronicles (v.11b). 1 Kings 3.1 indicates that he married her early in his reign. The Chronicler emphasizes that all that is involved in the establishment of the temple and its worship was at Solomon's initiative by recording that he brought her up rather than that she came up as is suggested in 1 Kings 9.24.

There is no record that Pharaoh's daughter ever became a proselyte. So Solomon was concerned that there be a fitting distance between the temple and a devotee of a foreign religion. The daughter of Pharaoh's palace was close to the temple but far enough away so that she would not defile it.

It would also have been for the safety of Pharaoh's daughter to stay at a distance because of the holiness of the ark. 1 Chronicles 13.9-10 records how that Lord smote Uzza "because he put forth his hand to hold the ark".

"It is widely assumed that this has to do with her sex, but, since the context is about foreigners [the previous four verses have a lot to say about foreigners who were used as slaves], her paganism is the more likely reason (cp. Ezekiel 44.7-9). If the former were true, one would also expect separate accommodation for Solomon's Israelite wives, but mention is made only of new buildings in connection with his foreign wives (cp. 1 Kings 11.7-8)...The palace of David is assumed to be part of the temple complex...and is probably the one built by Solomon but linked with David because of the ark" (Selman).

"If, however, Pharaoh's daughter had become a believer in Yahweh... then it is possible that the real issue was her retinue (both male and female) who continued to serve her needs" (Barber). Whatever is the real explanation, the writer of the Chronicles records this incident (v.11) especially to demonstrate Solomon's concern for the holiness of the temple. This leads naturally to the worship by Solomon described in vv.12-16. "In fact, according to Jewish tradition, the daughter of Pharaoh actually became a Jewish proselyte" (Edersheim).

Solomon's worship (vv.12-16)

Verses 12-15 are an expansion of 1 Kings 9.25a. The last short sentence in 1 Kings 9.25 is the basis of the slightly fuller last sentence of v.16. Verses 13a and 14-16a are not found in Kings. The Chronicler omits the part of 1 Kings 9.25 that states, "and he burnt incense on the altar that was before the Lord". Some commentators on 2 Chronicles have wrongly thought that the writer of Chronicles omitted that because Solomon was wrong to do so.

McShane has written helpfully, "The statement that, 'he burnt incense upon the altar that was before the Lord' has been interpreted to suggest that he entered the Holy Place and burnt incense as though he were a priest. This is a misunderstanding of the passage. The idea is that, along with his sacrifices, incense was offered. He was not the bearer of it into the Holy Place any more than he was the one who put the burnt offering on the altar or that he built Millo with his own hands. By using the temple in this way he demonstrated to the people that it was the only center of worship and that it fulfilled all that was intended of it".

The first few words of v.13 are better translated, "as the duty of every day required" (RV and JND; ESV is very similar). Numbers 28.1-8 required a burnt offering with a meat offering, and a drink offering every morning and every evening. Interestingly, the very time at which our Lord Jesus was nailed to the cross (Mk 15.25), the third hour, 9am, was the time at which the morning lamb was offered. The ninth hour, 3pm, when the evening lamb was offered was the time at which our Lord Jesus cried with a loud voice (Mt 27.46). Then we read immediately after, "Jesus, when he had cried again with a loud voice, yielded up the ghost" (Mt 27.50). His cry now was John 19.30, "It is finished". God's first "Amen" to our Lord's triumphant cry, is recorded in Matthew 27.51, "And, behold, the veil of the temple was rent in twain from the top to the bottom". This must have startled the priest who was offering the evening sacrifice at that same time, and also the other priests when they heard about it! That event may well have had much to do with the statement in Acts 6.7, "a great company of the priests were obedient to the faith". God's second "Amen" was the resurrection (Rom 4.25).

Maclaren has written on "The Duty of Every Day" based on v.13 (RV). He notes, "There were then, these characteristics in the ritual of Solomon's Temple: precise compliance with the Divine commandments, unbroken continuity, and beautiful flexibility and variety of method".

After that he has a practical application, "'Even as the duty of every day required': the phrase may suggest three thoughts: that each day has its own work, its own worship, and its own supplies, 'even as the duty of every day required'...God's measure of supply is correct. If we were more faithful and humble, and if we understood better and felt more how deep is our need, and how little is our strength, we should more continually be able to rejoice that He has given, and we have received, 'even as the duty of every day required'".

There are other important particulars given in these verses. The burnt offering provided a means for an Israelite to be accepted by God. "It shall be accepted for him to make atonement for him" (Lev 1.4). It also symbolized the complete consecration of our Lord Jesus to the will of God, "all on the altar" (Lev 1.9). No wonder that John's Gospel is referred to as the burnt offering Gospel since John has a uniquely large number of references to the Lord Jesus' devotion to the will of God (Jn 4.34; 6.38; 10.17-18; 14.30-31;

18.4,11). The incense is symbolic of his prayers as in Psalm 141.2.

Solomon offered "according to the commandment of Moses, on the sabbaths, and on the new moons, and on the solemn feasts" (v.13, as in Num 28-29). The Chronicler uses the phrase in 1 Kings 9.25, "three times in a year", but adds the specific names of those feasts (v.13). All the males were required to attend all three (Ex 23.14-17; 34.23; Deut 16.1-17, especially v.16). Solomon's obedience to the commandments of Moses established the pattern of religious worship that would be continued for many years. He also established the temple and the altar of burnt offering as the only proper place for the worship of the Lord. He thus fulfilled one of the main purposes that he had for building the temple (2.4).

The writer of Chronicles focuses on Solomon. He offered the offerings. Solomon followed all the commandments of Moses. He appointed the services of the priests and the Levites as his father David had designated. Solomon gave commandments that were obeyed.

"The Chronicler does remind us that all was also 'according to the commandment of Moses', and 'according to the ordinances of David'. But this in no way detracts from Solomon's exalted position in the Chronicler's scheme of things; on the contrary, it shows us with what lofty company he is to be ranked" (Wilcock).

David gave commandments for the priests and the Levites in 1 Chronicles 23-26, "for so had David the man of God commanded" (v.14). This expression, "man of God", indicates that God guided him in these arrangements.

Concerning the phrase "man of God" Rawlinson writes, "This phrase, so common in 1 Kings...is rare in Chronicles, and is applied only to Moses (1 Chr 23.14), David, Shemaiah (2 Chr 11.2), and one other prophet (2 Chr 25.7,9)".

The example given in v.15 is an encouragement to all saints to obey all of God's commandments. Later the Chronicler tells us that the commandments of David and Solomon were committed to writing (35.4). The last words of v.15 are "concerning the treasures". Treasures are referred to in 1 Chronicles 26.20-28 and 2 Chronicles 5.1.

The translation of the first sentence of v.16 in the ESV seems smoother and clearer than the AV: "Thus was accomplished all the work of Solomon from the day the foundation of the house of the Lord was laid until it was finished". However the term "perfected" in the last sentence of the AV may be preferable to "completed" in the last sentence of the ESV. That also seems true for 1 Kings 9.25, which has in its conclusion the word, "finished", in the AV rather than "perfected". Solomon laid the foundation in ch.2. His work afterward is related in chs.3-8. There was no slacking of diligence until the temple was finished. The word "perfected" refers to more than the building of the temple. As suggested by Keil & Delitzsch the house of the Lord was only perfected when the prescribed sacrifices and worship were established. This verse with two occurrences of "the house of the Lord" makes it clear that the building is truly "the house of the Lord" and not the temple of Solomon.

Verses 17-18: Solomon's Wealth

These verses are parallel to 1 Kings 9.26-28. Ezion-geber is near the northern end of the Gulf of Aqaba, which opens into the Red Sea. 1 Kings 9.26 records that it is beside Eloth. It is difficult to account for the differences in the two accounts since no change is in keeping with the Chronicler's interest. Verse 17 indicates that Solomon took the initiative in the maritime venture with Huram, king of Tyre. Huram's people, the Tyrians were the best seamen of that day. They were renowned for their seamanship, as celebrated by the prophets (Is 23.1,14; Ezek 27).

Verse 18 records how Huram assisted Solomon: "And Huram sent him by the hands of his servants ships, and servants that had knowledge of the sea". Sending ships may possibly mean that Huram sent materials for the ships overland and the ships were built at Ezion-geber. The expert mariners whom he sent were a great help to the Jewish sailors who had less experience of the sea. They journeyed together to Ophir and returned with 450 talents of gold. This would have replenished Solomon's wealth after it had been reduced by so much being spent in building the temple, the palace, and other buildings.

The Kings account notes only 420 talents of gold. Scribal error is a possibility. One of the scribes could easily have made a mistake in copying the number since the Hebrew numerical letter for twenty is so similar to that for fifty. If this is the case then it is not known which account is correct. There is another possible solution. "Solomon may have given the thirty talents to Hiram for the service rendered by his men" (McShane).

The text does not reveal what they traded for the gold, but excavations have discovered at least two things that were dealt in. "The maritime venture of Solomon has been greatly illumined by the explorations and excavations of Nelson Glueck…Solomon had a seaport and a large copper and iron works at Ezion-geber, and to judge from the remains, there was also a naval yard there for the construction and repair of ships. Copper and iron were derived from the surrounding area…Finished products were apparently exported in barter trade" (Myers).

Rawlinson states, "The controversy concerning the locality of Ophir will probably never be settled. [He names nine different possible places!] Among the various opinions three predominate, all moderns except a very few being in favour either of Arabia, India or Eastern Africa…Arabia's claims are supported by the greatest number".

One of the lessons that Barber gives for saints today from the record of Solomon is, "Material possessions should not be the cause of arrogance or pride. Solomon's diligence in the worship of the Lord was not diminished as a result of the vast riches he amassed…He did not allow his riches to cause him to conclude that he no longer needed God. He reined in any temptation to pride and arrogance. Instead, he was diligent in every aspect of his worship. This truth is borne out by his conduct. He did not allow preoccupation with material possessions to push to the periphery of his life the daily, weekly, monthly and yearly requirement of the law. He took care to perform his duty as each day required (8.14)...In the building of ships, he did not succumb to pride that may have caused him to conclude that he had a monopoly on all wisdom. He gladly availed himself of the skills of the men of Tyre...In all things Solomon manifested a befitting humility".

2 CHRONICLES 9

Solomon's Reign

Introductory

This, the Chronicler's final chapter on Solomon, is reminiscent of his first. Both bring to our attention his wisdom and wealth. In addition to these God also promised Solomon outstanding honour (1.12). The Queen of Sheba's visit contributed to his international prestige, as we are reminded in vv.22,23,26. Chapter 9 follows the parallel in 1 Kings 10.1-28, and 11.41-43 quite closely.

"The chapter shows how far news of Solomon's wisdom had spread, stresses the superlative nature of that wisdom, and illustrates the wealth which flowed to Solomon in the form of gifts and tributes from foreign rulers" (New Bible Commentary, 21st Century Edition).

A number of unbiblical stories have accumulated around the visit. An example follows. "The Jewish romantic legend that the queen desired and received a son fathered by Solomon is unsubstantiated, as is the Ethiopic tradition that the royal Abyssinian line was founded by the offspring of Solomon and the Queen of Sheba" (Patterson & Austel).

Outline of Chapter 9

Verses 1-12:	The Visit of the Queen of Sheba.
Verses 13-21:	Solomon's wealth.
Verses 22-28:	Solomon's international supremacy.
Verses 29-31:	Conclusion of the reign of Solomon.

Verses 1-12: The Visit of the Queen of Sheba

Sheba probably refers to the south-western tip of Arabia (modern Yemen) 1,400 miles from Jerusalem. Sheba was known especially for its spice trade and caravans (cp. Is 60.6; Jer 6.20; Ezek 27.22-23). "To judge from the results of excavations so far published, Marib, the ancient capital of Sheba, was an imposing center of activity" (Myers).

The Queen of Sheba was a wealthy queen of a wealthy country and her caravan was in keeping with those riches. She came with "a very great company, and camels" (v.1). The "very great company" included servants (v.12). Her servants would do all they could to make her as comfortable as possible, but it still was a strenuous trip. It would take many weeks to complete the journey. The camels carried expensive gifts in keeping with the diplomatic protocol of that time (and still true today). Since she brought over four tons of gold besides spices and precious stones, she would require a good number of camels to carry it.

The fact that the account of the visit of the Queen of Sheba comes between passages (8.17-18 and 9.10-11 and 9.13ff) telling of Solomon's success in international trade, indicates that possibly her mission included trade agreements. But there is no reference to that in the record of her visit except perhaps in v.12. Verse 23 records that all the kings of the earth sought to hear Solomon's wisdom and the verse gives no hint of any business venture being involved.

"Several features of the passage comport well with its historical basis. Female rulers played important roles in pre-Islamic Arabia...and classical historians mention the fabulous wealth of the area" (Dillard).

William Rodgers has a number of valuable comments on this section that may be summarized as follows in the next two paragraphs.

The first verse of the Kings account has a very important clause that is omitted in Chronicles: "concerning the name of the Lord" (1 Kings 10.1). Since the fame of Solomon that she heard of included this, that would indicate that her interest in him was not merely in a wise man or even in a wise king. Her chief interest was in his relationship with his God. 1 Kings 10.2 and 2 Chronicles 9.1 state that "she communed with him of all that was in her heart". That is in keeping with her chief interest in Solomon. Probably most of her hard questions were religious difficulties. If they were only difficult questions to see how cleverly he would answer them they would come from her head instead of her heart. If this were correct, it would increase the point and force of our Lord's words about the Queen of Sheba that she came seeking the truth of God. Our Lord said, "She came from the uttermost parts of the earth to hear the wisdom of Solomon; and, behold, a greater than Solomon is here" (Mt 12.42).

The Queen of Sheba's visit was really an answer to Solomon's prayer in 2 Chronicles 6.32-33 concerning the stranger "that is come from a far country for thy great name's sake". Another answer to his prayer many years later is recorded in Acts 8 when the Ethiopian eunuch came from the same direction as she did and likely with the same impulse to know more about Israel's God.

Solomon was able to answer all her questions to her complete satisfaction (v.2). The first nine verses could be outlined as follows.

Verses 1-2: The Queen came and communed with Solomon.
Verses 3-4: What she saw.
Verses 5-8: What she said.
Verse 9: What she did.

The phrase, "the house that he had built" (v.3), could be his palace or the temple, but if there were a banquet it would be in his palace. Verse 4 implies a banquet - "the meat of his table...and the attendance of his ministers". Slotki comments regarding "the attendance of his ministers": "i.e. the excellent service of his well trained staff of waiters at the banquet". All that the Queen of Sheba saw (vv.3-4) was the result of Solomon applying his wisdom, and she was greatly impressed. The last thing that the Queen saw before "there was no more spirit in her" was "his ascent by which he went up into the house of the Lord" (v.4).

The comments of Rawlinson on "his ascent" are worth quoting. "All the old translators, and some modern commentators...understand this passage differently. They render, 'and the burnt offering which he offered in the house of the Lord'...But the authority of the best Hebraists is in favour of the rendering in our version (AV)...What the 'ascent' was is somewhat doubtful. Keil and others suppose it to be a private way by which the king passed from his palace on the western hill, across the ravine...and up the eastern hill, to the west side of the temple area. And this is a very probable explanation".

The Jamieson, Fausset & Brown Commentary writes about "his ascent": "This was the arched viaduct that crossed the valley from Mount Zion to the opposite hill...what for...magnificence was one of the greatest wonders in Jerusalem". While Solomon could "ascend", he was limited in his access to the temple. The Lord is "greater than Solomon", not least because He has access into "heaven itself", and by His death has opened up the way for believers so that we have better access than even Solomon had.

After the Queen had heard Solomon's wisdom (v.2), and seen the application of his wisdom and the splendour of his kingdom (vv.3-4), "there was no more spirit in her" (v.4). Twice we read in Joshua of persons who "had no more spirit" because of fear (Josh 2.11 [RV]; 5.1). In contrast, the Queen was overwhelmed in amazement.

Verses 5-8 state what the Queen said in her astonishment. She acknowledged that the report she heard in her own land about his acts and wisdom was true. It was so incredible to her that she did not believe it until she came. Now she exclaimed, "the one half of the greatness of thy wisdom was not told me: for thou exceedest the fame that I heard" (v.6). Her wonder calls to mind the experience of Thomas (Jn 20.24-28).

The Queen was favourably impressed with the happiness of Solomon's men and servants (v.7). Joy is a tremendous evangelistic force (Ps 40.2-3; 51.12-13; 126.1-3; Acts 2.46-47; Rom 14.17-18). It is recorded of the late Harold St John that after he was staying about three days in a hotel in Italy, a woman came to him with words like these, "Pardon me for speaking to you without a formal introduction, but since we are both British subjects in a foreign land I thought it would be all right. I have been watching you and I can tell that you have a peace and contentment that most people know nothing about. I would like to know the secret of it". So he told her of our Saviour the Lord Jesus Christ.

The Queen testified to the fact that the wisdom and wealth of Solomon were because of the Lord's blessing on the king and His love for the nation of Israel (v.8). Her testimony was no doubt based on what she heard from Solomon himself. The most significant change that the Chronicler has made to the Kings account of the visit of the Queen of Sheba is in this verse (v.8). In Kings, Solomon is set "on the throne of Israel" (1 Kings 10.9). But here he is set on the throne of God, "to be king for the Lord thy

God" (v.8). The writer of the Chronicles makes the same point in other passages that the throne and the kingdom belong to God (1 Chr 17.14; 28.5; 29.23; 2 Chr 13.8).

"The relevance for the post exilic community could not be lost. Israel may be under foreign domination (Persia), but the kingdom remains secure; God always was and remains the real King of Israel, even when no descendant of David sits on the throne, and He promises that the kingdom will endure forever (9.8)" (Dillard). The Chronicler has the word "establish" (v.8) which is omitted in Kings. That word would be a further encouragement to his readers.

"Solomon is only the temporary occupant. It is 'the Lord's throne', and today we rejoice to submit to the last and greatest of the rulers of God's choice. Where Christ by the Holy Spirit is enthroned in the hearts of His people, there the blessings are poured out" (Wilcock).

The Queen said that God's desire for the king was "to do judgment and justice" (v.8). That is why Solomon requested wisdom at the first (1 Kings 3.9; 2 Chr 1.10).

The Queen added to the wealth of Solomon with her expensive gifts - the 120 talents of gold, the precious stones, and the spices, which are noted as being in "great abundance…neither was there any such spice as the Queen of Sheba gave king Solomon" (v.9). Spices such as frankincense and myrrh ranked with gold as acceptable gifts to a king as in Matthew 2.11. All of those treasures were produced in her own land. Her country was one of the richest in the world, especially because of its trade in spices.

Unger writes about the parallel in 1 Kings 10.11-12, "the wealth brought to Solomon by his fleet (cp. 2 Chr 9.10-11) is not a break in the story of the Queen's visit; the parallel in Chronicles has the same thing. This note is introduced to accentuate Solomon's fabulous wealth and to show that he was able to give the Queen whatever she might desire". The Chronicler seems to be enhancing the role of Solomon. He does not write of the navy of Hiram alone (1 Kings 10.11), but of the joint effort of the servants of both kings (v.10). Verse 10 may have been suggested to the writer of the Chronicles by the mention of gold and precious stones in v.9. The mention of Huram's name in v.10 is a reminder that he had similar words of praise for the Lord God of Israel (2.12). Verse 11 tells of the things that Solomon made from the algum tree and adds, "there was none such seen before in the land of Judah". The Chronicler writes "the land of Judah" rather than "the land of Israel", because he is writing after the exile.

Verse 12 records what Solomon gave to the Queen. "Beside that which she had brought unto the king", "means that the king besides returning the Queen the value of her presents to him, also gave her additional gifts" (Barnes).

All too many today are not as noble as the Queen of Sheba. Many hear of One far "greater that Solomon". And like her, they do not believe the report. But unlike her they do not make any effort to test what they have heard. People today can assess the report with far less effort than the Queen of Sheba took to check what she heard. Any who do make a sincere effort find, like the Queen, that "the half was not told me" (1 Kings 10.7). Surely the statement of our Lord Jesus in Matthew 12.42 should be heeded by all, "The queen of the south shall rise up in the judgment with this generation and shall condemn it: for she came from the uttermost parts of the earth to hear the wisdom of Solomon; and behold, a greater than Solomon is here".

Verses 13-21: Solomon's Wealth

Verses 13-28 correspond quite closely to 1 Kings 10.14-29. Verses 29-31 correspond to 1 Kings 11.41-43. Solomon's wealth is expressed especially in gold. The weight of gold that he received in one year was 666 talents (v.13). Courson writes (around the year 2000) about those talents: "This would be equivalent to one billion dollars...Solomon was wealthier than any person who ever lived". It is not easy to imagine how great a sum of money that really is. It may help to consider that if Solomon spent $50,000 every day it would take him almost 55 years to spend $1,000,000,000 (according to the American system). "All, perhaps, that can be at present said with certainty is that Solomon's annual revenue exceeded that of Oriental empires very much greater in extent than his, and must have made him one of the richest, if not the very richest of the monarchs of his time" (Rawlinson).

The Amplified Bible and the Newberry margin both have "traders" instead of the word, "chapmen", of the AV (v.14). Wycliffe has "Chapmen (traders); literally, the men of the caravans". Verse 14 tells of more gold and silver coming to Solomon. The traders and merchants probably paid tribute for their caravans to pass into or through Israelite territory. The Queen of Sheba was not the only Arabian ruler to bring riches to Solomon, for we read here that "all the kings of Arabia and governors of the country brought gold and silver to Solomon". The income from the kings and governors was probably at least partly in the form of taxation from vassal states.

In v.15 the NKJV and the ESV both have "shields" instead of "targets" (AV). Solomon had much gold and he used it lavishly as in the case of these shields which were used for display rather than for battle. Gold is too expensive, too heavy, and too soft for use in warfare. (Later Shishak king of Egypt took away all the shields of gold that Solomon had made, 12.9.) Solomon put the shields in the house of the forest of Lebanon (v.16). The writer of Chronicles does not give a description of the house of the forest of Lebanon such as is given in 1 Kings 7.2-12. This building was so named because so much cedar was used in its construction. "It was in Jerusalem and seems to have existed as late as the time of Isaiah (Is 22.8) as an armoury" (Barnes).

Verses 17-19 describe the great throne that Solomon made. The throne may have been made of ivory (v.17) but as Rawlinson points out, "It is...

more probable that the substance was wood, and that the ivory, cut into thin slabs...was applied externally as a veneer. This is found to have been the practice in Assyria...The gold was probably not placed over the ivory, but covered other parts of the throne".

In v.18 the NKJV has "armrests" and the ESV has "arm rests", for "stays" in the AV. There were six steps with an armrest on each side of the step and with a lion on each side. The Chronicler does not mention that "the top of the throne was round behind" (1 Kings10.19), but he does record what is not mentioned in Kings - "a footstool of gold, which (was) fastened to the throne" (v.18). The lion is a natural symbol of sovereign power, since the lion is "the king of beasts". Twelve of them are a reminder of the twelve tribes of Israel. So Solomon's throne speaks of his sovereign power over the twelve tribes of Israel. "The dimensions of the throne...are not given. That they were well proportioned to the height, marked by six steps, may be taken for granted" (The Pulpit Commentary). The words at the end of v.19, "There was not the like made in any kingdom", emphasize the riches of Solomon.

Hill has an excellent comment on the "footstool" (v.18), (also found in 1 Chronicles 28.2). "The royal footstool is a symbol of a king's authority, a symbol of the peaceful rest enjoyed by his kingdom, and a sign of humble loyalty to the monarch on the part of his subjects. By means of this symbol the Chronicler recognizes that Israel's 'rest', whether in David's time or his own, is entwined with God's restful presence among His people...The temple will be built by 'a man of peace and rest' (1 Chr 22.9)". David was rejected as the builder of the temple because he was a man of war (1 Chr 22.8).

All the drinking vessels of King Solomon and all the vessels of the house of the forest of Lebanon were of gold (v.20). The ESV has for the last part of v.20, "Silver was not considered as anything in the days of Solomon". That was true because gold was so plentiful.

In v.21 we read, "the king's ships went to Tarshish". "Many suggestions have been made regarding the original site of Tarshish; most commonly identified with Tartessus in Spain...Scholars have often suggested that though the term Tarshish was originally a geographical name, it came to be applied to a type of ship used on long journeys...However, it is difficult to avoid the conclusion that the Chronicler considered these ships as travelling to Tarshish (9.21; 20.37). It is not necessary to conclude that the author was ignorant either of the type of vessel or of the geography, whatever the original meaning of the term; by the author's time it appears to have become a popular designation of a far distant place, roughly the equivalent of 'going to the ends of the earth'" (Dillard).

The Chronicler seems to be enhancing the role of Solomon in v.21 as he did in v.10. Here he only mentions "the servants of Huram", but in 1 Kings 10.11 "the navy of Hiram" is also noted. For "peacocks" (v.21) the ESV margin has "or baboons".

Verses 22-28: Solomon's International Supremacy

This paragraph has "all" in four of its verses. It begins with Solomon who "passed all the kings of the earth" (v.22) and "all the kings of the earth" seeking Solomon (v.23). It is centered in Solomon reigning over "all the kings" (v.26), and it concludes with "all lands" (v.28). Verses 27-28 are similar to 1.14-16, and vv.25-26 include statements from 1 Kings 4.21,26. Since we read of "a rate year by year" (v.24), that seems to indicate that the kings in vv.23-24 were tributaries to Solomon.

Matthew Henry writes:,

1. "Never any prince appeared in public with greater splendour than Solomon did.
2. Never any prince had greater plenty of gold and silver, though there were no gold or silver mines in his own kingdom.
3. Never any prince had such presents brought to him by all his neighbours as Solomon had.
4. Never any prince was so renowned for wisdom, so courted, so consulted, so admired (v.23)".

In v.25 we read of "four thousand stalls for horses", but in 1 Kings 4.26 we read of "forty thousand stalls of horses". Selman wisely writes, "Though certainty is impossible, a reasonable solution is to think of 1,400 chariots (1 Kings 10.26; 2 Chr 1.14) and twelve thousand horses (NIV, REB, NEB); rather than 'horsemen' (RSV and AV)...In this context, four thousand stalls is preferable to the 'forty thousand' in 1 Kings 4.26".

In relation to the extent of Solomon's kingdom it has been noted that "These limits of the kingdom of Solomon in Israel (v.26) correspond to those which God's counsels had assigned to His people in Joshua 1.4: they had never before been attained nor have they ever since. They will only be realized, and that in an even greater measure, in the future reign of Christ" (Rossier).

Regarding the description of the horses brought to Solomon (v.28), it is worth noting that in Deuteronomy 17.16-17 there are three things that the king was warned against multiplying to himself: horses, wives, and silver and gold. Putting trust in horses indicates a misplaced confidence (Ps 33.17; Is 30.16; Hosea 14.3). God wanted the king to trust in the Lord as we read in Psalm 20.7, "Some trust in chariots, and some in horses: but we will remember the name of the Lord our God". Also note Proverbs 21.31: "The horse is prepared against the day of battle: but safety is of the Lord".

God Himself promised Solomon riches. But Solomon did make a mistake in multiplying horses for himself. However, the most serious error he ever made was in multiplying to himself wives who, when he was old, "turned away his heart after other gods" (1 Kings 11.4) even as Deuteronomy 17.17 warns. (See the last paragraph of this chapter as to why the Chronicler does not record Solomon's turning away from God.)

Verses 29-31: Conclusion of the Reign of Solomon

Verse 29 begins, "Now the rest of the acts of Solomon, first and last...".

"The qualifying phrase ("first and last") is added frequently by the Chronicler, to the summaries taken from Kings (cp. 12.15; 16.11; 20.34; 25.26; 26.22; 28.26; 35.27)" (Curtis & Madsen).

The writer of the Chronicles describes other sources for information on the reign of Solomon (v.29). The RV and ESV both have "the history of Nathan" for the "the book of Nathan" as in the AV. This may indicate that his writings are wider in scope than the other two sources. Nathan told David of God's covenant with him (1 Chr 17). He rebuked David for his adultery and the resultant murder (2 Sam 12). He was a counsellor for both David and Solomon. He is linked with the first part of Solomon's reign (1 Kings 1.8, 10-11).

Ahijah the Shilonite played a very important part in the narrative of Kings. He was the one who told Jeroboam that the Lord God of Israel would give ten tribes to him as the first king of the northern tribes (1 Kings 11.29-39). He was also the one who told Jeroboam of God's judgment against him (1 Kings 14.2-18). Ahijah is probably the prophet who told Solomon that God would rend the kingdom from him (1 Kings 11.11-13). But he is only mentioned in 2 Chronicles here and in 10.15 because the Chronicler only writes about the kingdom of Judah and does not record Solomon turning away from the Lord in his last years. Ahijah is linked with the close of the reign of Solomon.

Iddo is mentioned three times in 2 Chronicles (9.29; 12.15; 13.22). He is never mentioned by name in Kings but, according to Josephus, he is the unnamed man of God from Judah in 1 Kings 13. He is called a seer in 12.15, and a prophet in 13.22. Naming these sources once again links Solomon with his father David who also received a similar epitaph (1 Chr 29.29).

2 Chronicles 9.29-31 corresponds to 1 Kings 11.41-43. Verse 29 is quite different from 1 Kings 11.41, but vv.30-31 are very close to 1 Kings 11.42-43. Verses 30-31 tell how long Solomon reigned over all Israel, how he slept with his fathers, and how he was buried in the city of David, and how Rehoboam reigned in his stead.

It is somewhat surprising that the record of Solomon concludes without any reference to his turning away after other gods as recorded in 1 Kings 11.1-40. There seem to be at least two reasons why the writer of the Chronicles omits that sad record. "First, he assumed the details were known by the readers from 1 Kings and felt no need to repeat them since they were not important to his overall purposes. Second, his interest in Solomon was primarily 'exemplary'. Solomon was an example of the promised descendant of David who, in the Chronicler's day, had not yet come. Insofar as the reign of Solomon represented the reign of the promised One, the Chronicler's interest was served...He was guided by his purpose, which was to build hope for the future rather than to lament the past" (Sailhammer).

INTRODUCTION TO THE DIVISION OF THE MONARCHY AND THE SUBSEQUENT HISTORY OF THE KINGS OF JUDAH (Chapters 10-36)

Introductory

Each of the first three kings of Israel reigned for 40 years. During that time the monarchy had ruled over a united nation except for the first seven years of David's reign, but now that unity was about to be broken. One of the most important events in the history of Israel was the secession of the ten northern tribes. During most of the two hundred years following the division there was hostility between the two kingdoms. There was a period of about 70 years of peace as a result of a fateful alliance. Jehoram, good King Jehoshaphat's son, married Athaliah, wicked King Ahab's daughter. Hostilities broke out again when the 100,000 Israelite soldiers that King Amaziah had hired were sent home in response to the message of a man of God. Those Israelite soldiers attacked cities of Judah (25.13).

"Historically, it marked the end of a major aspect of the great achievements of David, namely his uniting of different elements...This unity, together with the greatness it brought, would never be achieved again, the northern kingdom being destined to disappear for ever, more than a century before the Babylonian exile of southern Judah" (McConville).

The great schism that took place when the ten northern tribes separated from Judah has lessons for God's people today when we consider those responsible for the division: the ten northern tribes, Rehoboam, Jeroboam, and Solomon. Behind all is God, who was bringing to pass His judgment against Solomon for his idolatry.

The Ten Northern Tribes

The northern tribes are sometimes called collectively Ephraim since it was the most influential of the ten. The ten contributed to the division by acting proudly. The tribe of Ephraim on at least three previous occasions had done so.

In Joshua 17.14 the children of Joseph (which, of course, included Ephraim), said to Joshua, "Why hast thou given me but one lot and one portion to inherit, seeing I am a great people, forasmuch as the Lord hath blessed me hitherto?". Joshua, himself an Ephraimite, wisely challenged them to prove their greatness. In Judges 8.1 the men of Ephraim chided sharply with Gideon because he had not called them to the battle. The four tribes that Gideon had called were closer to the hill of Moreh (where the Midianites were) than Ephraim. Issachar was closer than any of the tribes but they did not complain at not being called. The men of Ephraim should have been thankful to be able to share in the glory of victory, but that was not enough for them. Gideon met their pride with a great deal of humility and he met their anger with a great deal of meekness. He answered their sharp chiding by saying, "What have I done now in comparison of you?

Is not the gleaning of the grapes of Ephraim better than the vintage of Abiezer? God hath delivered into your hands the princes of Midian, Oreb and Zeeb: and what was I able to do in comparison of you?" (Judg 8.2-3). It is no wonder that we read right after Gideon's words, "Then their anger was abated toward him, when he said that". It should be noted (as encouragement to take a humble place in difficulty) that Gideon did not lose anything by doing so. God gave him the honour of taking Zebah and Zalmunna, kings of Midian (v.12). Of course, kings are much more important than the princes that Ephraim took.

Our Lord Jesus never lost anything by humbling Himself, as Phillipians 2.5-11 shows. That great Christological passage was not given because the Philippians were wrong about the person of the Lord Jesus. It was given to encourage them in getting along with one another. Any person or group of persons acting like Ephraim should take warning. They will not always contend with someone as wise as Joshua or as meek and humble as Gideon. Sooner or later, they will meet someone like Jephthah as recorded in Judges 12.6 when 42,000 Ephraimites lost their lives. Proverbs 13.10 says, "Only by pride cometh contention". Other occasions which demonstrated division are found in in Judges 9.2 and 2 Samuel 2.8-10; 20.1. Now that kind of thinking was to split the nation until a day still future when they will be reunited (Ezek 37.15-23). "Another aspect of the matter manifested itself very quickly, which was that, in addition to rebellion against the house of David, there was apostasy from God and from His law. The ease with which Jeroboam won over the great majority of his people to his new religion of the calves showed that they were already away in heart from the Lord, as did also the fact that never afterwards was there any recovery on a national scale from this form of idolatry" (Rodgers).

Rehoboam

It is clear from the narrative that Rehoboam, by his childish and reprehensible arrogance, was largely responsible for the division. We read the expression, "my son", no less than 22 times in the book of Proverbs. All saints should take to heart what God says to each of His children. But it should not be lost sight of that Solomon no doubt hoped that these exhortations would have a good effect upon his own son Rehoboam. This view is supported by the expressions used in the fourth chapter where Solomon in giving his children the "instruction of a father" (v.1) clearly showed that he was passing on to them what his father David had taught him (vv.3-4).

"It is interesting to notice that the first lesson mentioned in this connection (v.5) is, 'Get wisdom, get understanding', which would suggest that when Solomon, at the beginning of his reign, responded to the Lord's offer in 2 Chronicles 1.7 to give him whatever he would request, by asking for wisdom and understanding, he was following the advice given him by David as recorded here in Proverbs 4. Similarly, that other great exhortation of this chapter, 'Keep thy heart with all diligence' (v.23), may be considered as a passing by Solomon to his children of the warning David had given him in 1 Chronicles 28.9, 'And thou, Solomon my son, know thou the God of thy father, and serve him with a perfect heart'" (Rodgers).

Solomon guided by the Holy Spirit gave exhortations in Proverbs that would have kept Rehoboam from his folly. One that was applicable to him and others involved in the sad division (and all since who have had to do with a similar difficulty) is Proverbs 17.14 (RV), "The beginning of strife is as when one letteth out water: therefore leave off contention, before there be quarrelling". "Its aptness was sadly evident, when that small trickle of a few rough words, spoken on either side, widened itself out into a mighty flood that carried all before it, just as has been the case on many another occasion since then" (Rodgers).

As far as Rehoboam himself is concerned Proverbs 15.1 is even more to the point, "A soft answer turneth away wrath: but grievous words stir up anger". When the king first turned to the old men for advice about the answer he should give to the demand of the people, the old men must have been greatly influenced in their counsel by this very verse. Their excellent advice was, "If thou be kind to this people...and speak good words to them, they will be thy servants forever" (2 Chr 10.7).

"But good advice, whether of his father's divinely inspired writings or of the men of experience whom he consulted, was lost on the headstrong young king. When the time appointed came, he answered them roughly (v.13) in 'grievous words' that stirred up their anger" (Rodgers).

Jeroboam

He had much to do with bringing about the division. The very day that Solomon promoted him to be "ruler over all the charge of the house of Joseph" (1 Kings 11.28), Ahijah could speak to him as one who already had a desire (v.37) to be king over Israel. And even though Ahijah told him that the Lord God of Israel would give ten tribes to him that did not justify his rebellion. It is noticeable that we read 21 times that Jeroboam the son of Nebat made Israel to sin.

Solomon

1 Kings 11.11-13 shows clearly that Solomon himself was the main cause of the trouble and that the division would be part of God's judgment on him for his idolatry. The division was the natural outcome of his sin. He would reap what he had sown (Gal 6.7). Solomon's love for "strange women" led to his building temples where they could worship their idols and that, in turn, led to Solomon placing a burden on his people by enlisting them for mandatory manual labour. At first, in the early part of his reign, he, to a large extent, avoided that. 1 Kings 9.20-22 makes it clear that he levied bond service only on the children of other nations that had been left in the land, and not on the children of Israel. Of those

strangers there were more than 150,000 (2 Chr2.17-18; 1 Kings 5.15). The part-time conscription of some Israelites, mentioned in 1 Kings 5.13-14, was to supervise the strangers (as hinted at in 1 Kings 9.22).

"It could scarcely be possible that the complaint had no foundation in fact. It would seem, therefore, that those who were at the first employed in official and honourable positions (while Solomon was in a good state of soul, and was engaged in building God's house) found themselves later bearing a heavy burden (when his wives had turned away his heart, and he was building idolatrous temples for them). His case is an example of what is at all times, almost universally true, that a saint who gets out with God will also get out with the people of God, and will have but small concern for their interests" (Rodgers).

"During the first 24 years of Solomon's reign it might appear that Pharaoh's daughter was his only wife (cp. 1 Kings 3.1; 6.37-7.1). This might be concluded from the statement in 11.1 that 'Solomon loved many strange women, together with the daughter of Pharaoh'...So it was during Solomon's declining years. Shrines to pagan gods with attending priests and guardian queens dotted the hills surrounding Jerusalem" (Whitcomb).

God

The Chronicler refers to the fulfillment of Ahijah's prophecy when he says that "the cause was of God" (10.15). The prophecy is given in 1 Kings 11.31-39. It is not recorded by the Chronicler in keeping with his policy of omitting most things critical of Solomon. He assumed his readers knew about it. The main point of it was that the northern tribes would be taken from Solomon's son because of Solomon's idolatry. On the one hand, the Chronicler does not give us the context of Ahijah's prophecy; yet, on the other hand, he has kept the sense that the division was caused by the over-ruling of God (2 Chr 10.15; 11.4). A consideration of God accomplishing His purposes through human mistakes and sins calls Psalm 76.10 to mind: "Surely the wrath of man shall praise thee: the remainder of wrath shalt thou restrain". Also, Genesis 50.20 records Joseph's words to his ten older brothers who had sold him into slavery: "But as for you, ye thought evil against me; but God meant it unto good, to bring to pass, as it is this day, to save much people alive". Acts 2.23, in Peter's words, gives the divine side and the human side of the cross in one verse: "Him, being delivered by the determinate counsel and foreknowledge of God, ye have taken, and by wicked hands have crucified and slain".

"The separation of the kingdom of Solomon into two weak and hostile states is, in one aspect, a wretched story of folly and selfishness wrecking a nation, and in another, a solemn instance of divine retribution working its designs by men's sins...One sentence draws back the curtain for a moment and shows us the true cause (10.15)...There is something very striking in that one flash, which reveals the enthroned God, working through the ignoble strife which makes up the rest of the story.

Again, the rending of the kingdom was the punishment of sin, especially Solomon's sin of idolatry which was closely connected with the extravagant expenditure that occasioned the separation. So the so-called natural consequences of transgression constitute its temporal punishment in part, and behind all these our eyes should be clear-sighted enough to behold the operative will of God" (Maclaren). 2 Chronicles 11.4 is also a reminder that "this thing is done of me".

After the Division

Following the separation the Chronicler focuses his attention on Judah, the southern kingdom, the place of the temple and David's throne. That does not mean that the concept of "all Israel" had ceased to be important to him. But God's purposes are to be worked out through the dynasty of David and the temple at Jerusalem. He does refer to the northern tribes whenever they are in contact with Judah. He is careful to record every time some from the northern tribes come to Judah. He considers them throughout their history as that part of Israel that has forsaken God and rebelled against the Davidic line, the only legitimate and God-given dynasty. (The northern tribes had nine different dynasties.) He writes about Judah at much greater length than the writer of the Kings. "The book of the Chronicles largely supplements all past history of the Jews by the introduction of very new matter...No other nation in the world ever had such a systematic preservation of contemporaneous literature as the Jews" (Carroll). The Chronicler gives many different sources for his additional material.

"The reign of David was the occasion for God's revelation of a theology linking palace and temple (1 Chr 17.12), while Solomon's reign saw the revelation of a theology of repentance and restoration (2 Chr 7.14). The coming chapters presuppose the first theology and find it necessary to invoke the second...Rehoboam's reign is used to portray contrasting scenarios: obedience spells divine blessing, while disobedience brings disaster. That is not to be the end of the story, however. God's ultimate will is positive rather than negative: He is just a prayer away, ever ready to answer a call from the contrite heart. The Chronicler is not interested in history for its own sake. His concern has to do with the perennial ways of God with His people. This makes his writings a good read for any Christian" (Leslie C. Allen).

All 19 kings of Israel, the northern tribes, were evil. The sin of Israel was much deeper and their departure from God was much sooner and more fully developed than in the south. It is no wonder that they went into captivity over 100 years before Judah. Edersheim enlarges upon Keil in the following words about Judah: "Idolatry never struck its roots deeply among the people, and this for three reasons. There was first, the continued influence for good of the temple at Jerusalem; and in this we see at least one providential reason for the existence of a central Sanctuary, and for the stringency of the

Law which confined all worship to its courts. Second, the idolatrous kings of Judah were always succeeded by monarchs distinguished for piety, who swept away the rites of their predecessors; while lastly and most remarkably, the reign of the idolatrous kings was uniformly brief as compared with that of the God-fearing rulers. Thus on a review of the whole period, we find that, of the 253 years between the accession of Rehoboam and the deportation of the ten tribes, 200 passed under the rule of monarchs who maintained the religion of Jehovah, while only during 53 years His worship was more or less discarded by the king of Judah. Years of public idolatry: under Rehoboam, 14; under Abijah, 3; under Joram, 6; under Ahaziah, 1; under Athaliah, 6; under Ahaz, 16; or in all 46 years, to which we add 7 for the later idolatrous reigns of Joash and Amaziah".

Rossier has written a profitable introduction to chapters 10-36. In this he states, "Solomon was not the true king according to God's counsels… The decree 'Thou art my Son: this day have I begotten thee' (Ps 2.7) did not relate to him, but directed hope to One greater and more perfect than he. But in order that this future Son might be 'the offspring of David', David's line must be maintained until His appearing; this is why God had promised David 'to give to him always a lamp, and to his sons' (2 Chr 21.7)…This entire second portion of Chronicles could thus be entitled, 'The history of grace to the kingdom of Judah'".

2 Chronicles 7.14 contributes largely to the last 27 chapters of 2 Chronicles, being a history of grace to the kingdom of Judah. The Chronicler records 13 instances where either there was humbling and God fulfilling His promise in 7.14 or a refusal to be humble. Only one of those 13 is recorded in Kings. (See the 13 listed in the introductory part of ch.12 in this Commentary.)

A remarkable and encouraging characteristic of Chronicles is that everything that could be the result of grace, even in the worst of kings, is carefully recorded. The Chronicler greatly appreciates each revival. But in spite of these revivals the evil of Judah became increasingly worse so that even good king Josiah could not avert the coming captivity. The writer only uses a few verses to deal with the four successors to Josiah because he wants to hasten to record their return from captivity, a glowing proof of the grace of God toward His people. It is seen in Chronicles that nothing was able to thwart the purpose of God, neither the malignant efforts of Satan nor the unfaithfulness of some of the kings.

There is also another way in which the last 27 chapters are a history of grace to the kingdom of Judah. God undertook to make known His ways of grace in a new manner while His people were still under the law. He did this by sending the prophets. There are 16 prophets named in 2 Chronicles and unnamed ones besides. These all had a combination of a ministry of grace and a ministry of judgment. There was a ministry of grace because God is a God of grace, and a ministry of judgment because the people were under the law and prophecy does not do away with the law.

"On the contrary, it rests on the law, while at the same time loudly proclaiming that at the least little returning to God, the sinner will find mercy...'When the prophets come on the scene', a brother has said, 'grace begins to shine anew'...Thus a special characteristic of God is expressed by the prophets...He is...a God who, while He shows His indignation against sin, takes no pleasure in judgment and whose true character of grace will always triumph in the end...The entire role of prophecy in Chronicles is expressed in Micah 7.18, 'Who is a God like unto thee, that pardoneth iniquity, and passeth by the transgression of the remnant of his heritage? he retaineth not his anger for ever, because he delighteth in mercy'" (Rossier).

Judah after the Division

2 Chronicles 10-12:	Obedience and blessing. Disobedience and disaster.
2 Chronicles 13-16:	Relying on God.
2 Chronicles 17-23:	An unholy alliance that led to compromise and far-reaching consequences.
2 Chronicles 24-26:	Three kings who began well and finished badly.
2 Chronicles 27-32:	Three kings who each were opposite to their fathers.
2 Chronicles 33-35:	Three kings and humbling before God.
2 Chronicles 36:	Four kings, exile, and return from captivity.

The Chronicler identifies the second section (chs.13-16) by the word for "rely" (SHA'AN - 8172) in these four chapters (13.18; 14.11 (as "rest"); 16.7,7,8), a word found nowhere else in the book. Reliance links these four chapters together. Linked with the main theme of reliance are two other words, "seek" (DARASH - 1875), found seven times (14.4,7,7; 15.2,12,13; 16.12) and "seek" (BAQASH - 1245) found twice (15.4,15). In summary, "seek" is used nine times in these four chapters but only 19 times in the remaining 32 chapters of 2 Chronicles. The opposite of "seek" is "forsake" (AZAB - 5800) which is in 13.10,11 and 15.2. It seems that these four chapters (13-16) are in direct contrast to the behaviour of Rehoboam as noted in 12.14: "...he prepared not his heart to seek the Lord".

In chs.33-35 the three kings (Manasseh, Amon, and Josiah) are a contrast in their attitudes toward repentance. Manasseh (in old age) and Josiah (in his youth) truly humbled themselves before God, while Amon never did.

"This kind of patterning supports the view that the Chronicler's aim was to draw out spiritual and theological principles rather than produce an alternative history to Samuel and Kings" (Selman).

Leslie C. Allen (earlier than Selman) also helpfully notices that the writer of the Chronicles emphasizes different sections. "The portrayal of three successive kings in 2 Chronicles 24-26 as running well at first and then dropping out of the spiritual race was intended as a serious admonition to maintain the faith".

2 CHRONICLES 10

Rehoboam's Reign

Introductory

Rehoboam was an important king who had the doubtful honour of being on the throne when the division of the nation took place. He was a weak, inexperienced character at the beginning of his reign. His own son Abijah said to Jeroboam and all Israel, "Rehoboam was young and faint-hearted, and did not show himself strong against them" (13.7, JND). Even though Solomon had so many wives Rehoboam is the only son mentioned in the Word of God (1 Chr 3.10). Solomon had 700 wives and 300 concubines. That large number would decrease conception rather than increase it. Solomon, in the first 9 chapters of Proverbs, twice refers to sons (8.4,31), but 15 times he gave counsel to his *son*. That adds weight to the argument that Solomon had only one son. Two daughters are mentioned briefly (1 Kings 4.11,15). Solomon seems to question the ability of his son to rule the kingdom (Eccl 2.18-19).

The Chronicler faithfully recorded the foolishness of Rehoboam and its consequences. This shows that he was not a narrow-minded Davidic nationalist who thought that Israel only needed a true son of David on the throne in order to prosper. Rehoboam was truly the legitimate Davidic king, but for most of his 17-year reign Judah did not prosper. "Pedigree is not enough. In fact, it is of no value without the wisdom that comes from the fear of the Lord" (Thompson).

"The Chronicler includes nearly all the material concerning Rehoboam from 1 Kings 12 and 14 but also adds to it in order to provide a pattern of failure (the division: 10.1-11.4) followed by a success through obedience (11.5-23) and of disaster brought about by pride followed by a measure of restoration consequent upon self-humbling (ch.12). This pattern sets the tone for much that is to follow" (Williamson). In this chapter the Chronicler follows 1 Kings 12.1-19 almost exactly.

Outline of Chapter 10

Verses 1-19: Israel's rebellion

Verses 1-5:	At Shechem Rehoboam hears conditions for reigning over all Israel.
Verses 6-11:	Advice for Rehoboam.
Verses 12-15:	Rehoboam's answer.
Verses 16-19:	Division of Israel from Judah, and Rehoboam's escape.

Verses 1-5: At Shechem Rehoboam Hears Conditions for Reigning over all Israel

If Rehoboam chose Shechem he was very wise. It is possible that this judicious decision was largely due to good counsel from the old men whose advice he later rejected. The honour of selecting the capital for the scene of the new king's coronation was the most likely thing to encourage the ten northern tribes to submit to the royal tribe of Judah a little longer. Shechem, at the base of Mount Ebal and of Mount Gerizim, was the place where Abraham built his first altar (Gen 12.6-7). It was Jacob's first home coming from Padan-aram (Gen 33.18-20). Joseph searched for his brothers there (Gen 37.12-14). Joshua gathered all Israel together there (Josh 24.1-25) and led them in renewing a covenant with the Lord (24.25-27) after the conquest of most of the land. Joseph's bones were buried there (Josh 24.32). Abimelech, Gideon's son, had reigned there (Judg 9.6-23). If Shechem was the northern tribes' choice, it was a wise concession on Rehoboam's part to go there to be made king. Shechem is more central than Jerusalem.

Israel had the privilege in popular assembly of approving the divinely appointed kings. They had already done so for Saul, David, and Solomon: for Saul at Mizpeh (1 Sam 10.17-24) and at Gilgal (1 Sam 11.14-15); for David at Hebron over Judah (2 Sam 2.1-4) and over all Israel, again in Hebron (2 Sam 5.3; 1 Chr 11.1-3); and for Solomon at Gihon in the Kidron valley on the outskirts of the city (1 Kings 1.38-40, 45) and in Jerusalem itself (1 Chr 29.27). The people thus ratified God's choices. God's name is mentioned in each of these coronations but His name is conspicuous by its absence on this occasion.

The Chronicler introduced Jeroboam without any explanation of who he was (v.2), showing that he assumed that his readers already knew from 1 Kings. Verse 15 is another instance where the writer of Chronicles assumed that his readers were acquainted with the prophecy of Ahijah in 1 Kings. The Chronicler has only a passing mention of Jeroboam and Ahijah in 9.29.

Jeroboam (v.3) was most likely the spokesman for the ten northern tribes. Probably no one else could have represented them better. He had been "ruler over all the charge of the house of Joseph" (1 Kings 11.28). Having been involved in the forced labour program, he knew the grievances at first hand. The writer of the Chronicles laid some of the blame for the division on Jeroboam. He especially blamed him for the continuation of the breach (13.5-12).

The northern tribes wanted a reduction in both heavy taxation and forced labour as conditions for them to recognize Rehoboam as king. They expected Rehoboam to relieve them and they said, "and we will serve thee" (v.4). Their request was compatible with a willingness to serve the new king loyally. "The tribes accusations against Solomon were serious. The phrases "harsh labour" (NIV; cp. Ex 5.9; 6.9) and "heavy yoke" (cp. Ex 6.6-7; Lev 26.13) charge him with oppressing Israel as Pharaoh had done… In no sense, therefore, can Chronicles be said to exonerate Solomon as blameless (*contra* Dillard), especially as a further analogy of Zedekiah and the Pharaoh of the Exodus is given as one of the reasons for the exile (cp. 2 Chr 36.13)" (Selman). "Although Solomon is glorified by the writer, he cannot and does not exclude the damaging reflection upon his role provided by this chapter, which is telling evidence to the effect that he does not completely distort history, painful though it might have been for him" (Myers). Rehoboam was prudent enough to ask for three days.

Verses 6-11: Advice for Rehoboam

Rehoboam wisely went first to the old men for counsel (vv.6-8). There is not much said about these men, but we do know from Solomon's Proverbs that he appreciated good advisers (Prov 11.14; 15.22; 20.18; 24.6). The counsel the old men gave is in tune with Proverbs 15.1: "A soft answer turneth away wrath". Matthew Henry has, "Good words cost nothing but a little self-denial, and yet they purchase great things".

Verse 8 begins to reveal the folly of Rehoboam. He wore his father's crown, but he did not have his father's wisdom. Neither wisdom nor grace runs in the blood. He forsook the counsel of the old men, the best advice he had. "He...took counsel with the young men that were brought up with him" (v.8).

To determine the age of Rehoboam at his accession is an interesting and difficult problem. 2 Chronicles 12.13 and 1 Kings 14.21 both say he had reached the age of 41. That age would be mature enough so that he could not plead the inexperience of youth as an excuse for his actions. But in the general narrative he seems to be a young man. Verse 8 talks of "the young men that were grown up with him" (RV). They are called "boys" in the Septuagint. Rehoboam's son Abijah referred to his father as "young" and "tenderhearted" (13.7) when he began to reign. These expressions can hardly be applied to a man of 41 at that time of Jewish history. Another difficulty is that his mother was an Ammonitess (1 Kings 14.31; 2 Chr 12.13). If Rehoboam was 41 at his accession, Solomon must have married an Ammonitess at least two years before his father David died. It is very unlikely that his father would have approved such a marriage. "We know that Solomon did marry many Ammonite women after he was established on the throne, and after the first fervour of his youthful piety had abated (see 1 Kings 11.1). Perhaps the best way of removing the whole difficulty would be to read in 1 Kings 14.21 and 2 Chronicles 12.13, '21' for '41'. The corruption is one which might easily take place, if letters were used for numerals" (Rawlinson). "There seems, therefore, considerable probability attaching to the suggestion that the notice of his age at his accession — 41 (1 Kings 14.21; 2 Chr 12.13) — is the mistake of a copyist, who in transcribing the figure misread the two letters — 21 — for — 41" (Edersheim).

Similarly, 2 Chronicles 22.2 says that Ahaziah was 42 when he began to reign. That is obviously the error of a copyist for 2 Kings 8.26 gives the right age as 22.

"The old men did not undertake to put words in Rehoboam's mouth, but the young men will furnish him with very quaint and pretty phrases... That is not always the best sense which is best worded" (Matthew Henry). In v.10 they advised him to say, "My little finger is thicker than my father's loins" (RV). This is paraphrased by the Targum, "my weakness is stronger than my father's might". "I will chastise you with scorpions" (v.11). Both expressions are hyperbole, one expresses greater power than his father and the other greater punishment.

"Various ancient authorities identify 'the scorpion' as a whip tipped with weights and barbs. There is no direct evidence as yet for the existence of such an instrument in ancient Israel or the contemporary ancient Near East...just as Rehoboam's little finger was thicker than his father's waist, so also the punishment he would inflict is similarly exaggerated. The yoke of Solomon had been burdensome, and in haughty arrogance Rehoboam would make it yet heavier; what a contrast to another son of David, one who was gentle and humble, and invited the weary and burdened to 'Take my yoke upon you and learn of me...For my yoke is easy, and my burden is light' (Mt 11.28-30)" (Dillard).

Verses 12-15: Rehoboam's Answer

Peer pressure and, in all likelihood, a puffed up sense of his own importance combined to do their worst for the king. His sense of his own insecurity led to an over-reaction that led to threats. He lacked the insight that his grandfather David had that the kingship was meant to further the interests of Israel (1 Chr 14.2, RV). Rehoboam wrongly thought that kingly power was a force to be used "roughly" (10.13). When he asked for counsel he only listened to advice that inflated his ego. "The incident is a warning to any who embark on new tasks involving authority over others" (Leslie C. Allen). Rehoboam answered like a tyrant. The Word of God exhorts submission to government but God's Word is against all tyranny.

The record of Rehoboam's rough answer is a warning to all who lead God's people. May the Lord encourage all such to be kind as the older men wisely counselled Rehoboam. 2 Timothy 2. 24-25 gives a New Testament view that would encourage such wisdom. "Influenced by a handful of callow novices and young court favourites, who, like himself, thought more of the rights of the king than of his responsibility to govern righteously, he replied with as rash and insolent a speech as was, perhaps, ever uttered from the throne of a civilized nation" (Knapp).

"The divine will takes on a special function in his overall history. At 1 Chronicles 10.14 and 12.23 mention was made of God turning Saul's kingdom over to David, in the second case with a reference to Samuel's two predictions to this effect. A noun related to the verb used there occurs here: 'the turn of events was from God' (v.15, NKJV)" (Leslie C. Allen). There is a specific reference to Ahijah's prophecy that he assumed his readers knew about (1 Kings 11.30-39). Rehoboam, Jeroboam, and the northern tribes were all responsible for their decisions and deeds but they worked out God's purposes. "Rehoboam's folly and arrogance worked out the ordained judgment of God, but they were folly and arrogance still" (Ellicott). Here in v.15, it is "of God" and in 11.4, "of me".

Verses 16-19: Division of Israel from Judah, and Rehoboam's Escape

The people answered the king in words similar to those used by Sheba, the son of Bichri in 2 Samuel 20.1 when leading a rebellion against David. In doing so they rejected their former hero and the founder of the God-given reigning dynasty. These words are a contrast to 1 Chronicles 12.18 when the Spirit of God clothed (AV margin) Amasai who declared loyalty to David: "Thine are we, David, and on thy side, thou son of Jesse: peace, peace be unto thee, and peace be to thine helpers; for thy God helpeth thee". (There are only two other times that the AV margin has "clothed": Judges 6.34 and 2 Chronicles 24.20.) 1 Chronicles 12.38 reads, "All these men of war...came with a perfect heart... and all the rest also of Israel were of one heart to make David king". No wonder v.40 reads, "there was joy in Israel". There is joy in any gathering of God's people when our Heavenly David gets His rightful place as Lord.

"To your tents" in v.16 is equivalent to saying, "Go to your homes", and it is a reminder of the days when they did dwell in tents. There were some from the northern tribes living in Judah and they were content to have Rehoboam reigning over them (v.17). Those same persons are referred to again in 11.3. In v.18 Rehoboam may have thought that Hadoram, who was over the tribute, was the best acquainted with their hardships and therefore could arrange some alleviation of the grievances. Rehoboam did not seem to perceive the seriousness of the situation. Hadoram would be the one man of Judah who would be the most vivid reminder of the reason for the rebellion. Hadoram was stoned with stones.

Stoning seems to have been the most usual way for mobs to take vengeance on those who had offended them. Moses expresses a fear (in Exodus 8.26) that the Egyptians would stone them if they sacrificed in Egypt. In Exodus 17.4, "Moses cried unto the Lord...they be almost ready to stone me". When David's own followers found Ziklag burned with fire and their wives and children taken captive, they also spoke of stoning David (1 Sam 30.6). The stoning opened Rehoboam's eyes to see the true gravity of the situation. "Rehoboam barely escaped with his own life. What should have been a glorious national celebration (v.1) turned into a humiliating rout for Judah's new king who fled his own coronation to escape assassination by his infuriated subjects" (Constable).

"Solomon forsakes God, and therefore his son after him is forsaken by the greatest part of his people...He that sins against God not only wrongs his soul, but perhaps wrongs his seed more than he thinks. When God is fulfilling His threatenings. He will take care that, at the same time, promises do not fall to the ground. When Solomon's iniquity is remembered, and for it his son loses ten tribes, David's piety is not forgotten, nor the promise made to him, but for the sake of that his grandson had two tribes preserved to him" (Matthew Henry). It was also appreciation for David that kept God from dividing the kingdom during Solomon's reign.

In v.19 the Chronicler has the same words as 1 Kings 12.19 about Israel in rebellion "against the house of David". But for the writer of Chronicles it pains him that 10 of the 12 tribes of the chosen nation are opposed to the chosen dynasty of God. The Chronicler never forgot that God's ideal was 12 tribes, not two. He refused to consider Judah and Benjamin as *all* the people of God. "If the southern kingdom is 'Israel' (12.6), so is the northern (10.16,19; 11.1)...From a southern perspective the Northerners were separated brethren, but they remained brethren (11.4). The Chronicler will not mince his words in criticizing the northern state, but his ecumenical spirit never allows him to disown estranged members of God's family" (Leslie C. Allen). From a northern perspective the Southerners were brethren (28.8,11). In Chronicles the context will indicate to whom "Israel" refers. The Chronicler focuses on the southern tribes with the Davidic dynasty. He only refers to the northern tribes when connected with Judah. The Northerners are brethren, but brethren in rebellion.

2 CHRONICLES 11

Rehoboam's Reign

Introductory

The first three years of Rehoboam's reign (described in this chapter) were his best. He seems to have matured and acted wisely in obeying Shemaiah the man of God (v.4), in fortifying cities (vv.5-12), and in acting wisely regarding his sons (v.23). Verses 1-4 follow very closely 1 Kings 12.21-24, but the rest of the chapter is almost entirely new material from sources of which the writer of the Kings either did not know or which he ignored. The Chronicler delights to record anything good produced in a bad king by the grace of God. The blessing of God for obedience is seen in the building recorded in vv.5-12, those coming from all the tribes of Israel (vv.13-17), and in children (vv.19-21).

Outline of Chapter 11

Verses 1-4: Rehoboam kept from war by Shemaiah's prophecy.
Verses 5-12: Rehoboam fortifying cities.
Verses 13-17: Priests, Levites, and others coming to Judah and Jerusalem.
Verses 18-23: Rehoboam's family.

Verses 1-4: Rehoboam Kept from War by Shemaiah's Prophecy

The 180,000 chosen men of v.1 is the same number as given in 1 Kings 12.21. This is plausible when we consider that the total for all Israel, in Numbers 1.46 and 26.51, is carefully detailed to be over 600,000. Of course, that was in Moses' day but the number would hardly be less in the days of Solomon. See also 1 Chronicles 21.5; 2 Chronicles 14.8; 25.5; 26.13. Shemaiah is the same prophet who confronted Rehoboam and the princes in 12.5. He also established one of the sources the writer of Chronicles used (12.15). The phrase in v.3, "all Israel in Judah and Benjamin" includes those who in 1 Kings 12.23 are called "the remnant of the people". They are those out of all the northern tribes who were with Judah and Benjamin by godly choice.

"The prophet exhorted Judah not to fight against their 'brethren'. The northern tribes were part of 'all Israel' (1 Chr 1-9) and therefore 'brethren' in the mind of the Chronicler and just as capable of repentance (28.6-15) as the south was of apostasy (28.1-5, 16-25). The phrase, 'to your tents, O Israel' (10.16), was a call to rebellion, but 'return every man to his house' was a call to abandon war" (Thompson). It took courage for the man of God to deliver such a message to a whole army getting ready for war. Shemaiah told them in "the words of the Lord" that "this thing is done of me". The southerners responded by obeying. Rehoboam foolishly did not take the advice of the old men (10.13) but now he, with all the others, obeyed the Word of God. The words "hearkened" (10.15), "hearken" (10.16), and "obeyed" (11.4) are all from the same Hebrew word (SHAMA - 8085).

"To proceed in this war would be not only to 'fight against (their) brethren' (v.4), whom they ought to love, but to fight against their God, to whom they ought to submit" (Matthew Henry). "Having earlier ignored the counsel of his elders, Rehoboam now heeded the counsel of the Lord and spared the lives of many Israelites. The Word of the Lord decreed the split, and the Word of the Lord ensured that the division was without bloodshed" (MacDonald).

This, the first of "two attempts to bring God's people together, which, though opposite in character, were alike in this, that God did not and could not bless either of them…The other was when Jehoshaphat, after a continuance of hostilities between the two kingdoms which had lasted through the reign of Rehoboam (1 Kings 14.30), Abijah (1 Kings 15.7), Asa (1 Kings 15.16), and part of his own (2 Chr 17.1), became friendly with Ahab king of Israel, and married his son Jehoram to Ahab's daughter Athaliah (18.1; 21.6); possibly hoping that the young pair might ultimately rule both kingdoms as a united nation. How wrong he was in his calculations we shall see later, but for the present it will suffice to point out that the Lord utterly condemned his course of action in the message sent to him in 19.2.

Now in the record of these movements there is much to be learned that is of present day value. The bringing together of God's people is a laudable and Scriptural aim, but there are wrong ways as well as right ways of setting about it. To fight with those who hold views differing from our own is certainly not a right way; but neither is it right that we should 'join affinity' (18.1) with such as are walking in disobedience to truth plainly taught in the Word of God, and which we ourselves profess to have learned therefrom. Union brought about in that way will prove costly in the end, even as it did for Jehoshaphat and his descendants" (Rodgers).

All believers should profit from Rehoboam's mistake. Instead of fighting, saints should act like gentlemen over every stand taken. Truth should be held in an upright manner. The truth never needs a lie to defend it or underhanded methods to sustain it. Paul writes in 2 Corinthians 4.2, "But (we) have renounced the hidden things of dishonesty, not walking in craftiness, nor handling the word of God deceitfully; but by manifestation of the truth commending ourselves to every man's conscience in the sight of God". Paul so acted that if every one of his adversaries could see every action that he took they would have every reason to believe he was doing it with a good conscience. He could say in Acts 24.16, "And herein do I exercise myself, to have always a conscience void of offence toward God, and toward men" (that does indeed take exercise). 2 Timothy 2.24-25 reads, "And the servant of the Lord must not strive; but be gentle unto all men, apt to teach, patient, In meekness instructing those that oppose themselves; if God peradventure will give them repentance to the acknowledging of the truth".

"Speaking the truth in love" (Eph 4.15) commends the truth. How praiseworthy it is to hold the truth with wisdom from above. "The wisdom that is from above is first pure, then peaceable, gentle, and easy to be entreated, full of mercy and good fruits, without partiality, and without hypocrisy" (James 3.17). Any person acting with wisdom from above will be as peaceable as practically possible consistent with the purity of the Word of God. This is the same order as our Lord Jesus gives in the beatitudes. Matthew 5.9 reads, "Blessed are the peacemakers: for they shall be called the children of God". The only peacemaking that is blessed is consistent with the purity of the previous beatitude, "Blessed are the pure in heart". Doing all this in love is far more likely to win others than by fighting with them. True unity is never achieved by force, but the respect of others and their submission is sometimes won by love.

Verses 5-12: Rehoboam Fortifying Cities

"The present verses bear upon…a period of piety and prosperity. This period is not recorded at all in Kings…But it is at the point of divergence from Kings, as so often, that he is most interesting. He has included the report of the period of Rehoboam's piety in pursuit of his careful policy of showing that, uniformly, piety is rewarded with blessing and apostasy with punishment…Having made the point, it must be admitted that he does not over-press the case for Rehoboam's piety. Much of the credit for the three-year period of stability which Judah enjoyed under him (v.17) evidently goes to the priests and Levites who came to Judah from all parts of Israel, even giving up their possessions to do so (vv.13ff), and indeed to other pious people also, who were determined to resist the path upon which Jeroboam was now embarked and who also came south…He also 'dealt wisely' in his government (v.23), which is more than our first encounter with him might have led us to expect. Perhaps his piety did not go much beyond this" (McConville).

It is probable that Rehoboam was humbled and subdued when he lost the greater part of the kingdom. For a while he walked in dependence upon God. The important lesson only lasted in its effect upon him for three years. Believers may expect to be tested again on truth previously obeyed. The fact that a believer has passed the test once does not mean that the test will never be repeated. Dependence upon God can never be dispensed with.

The word "built" in vv.5-6 is to be understood as meaning rebuilt or fortified. "All the places mentioned have now been identified. See the index in L. Grollenberg's 'Atlas of the Bible', 1956" (Myers). There are no cities fortified on the northern border. He may not have felt so threatened from the north and so he did not consider it as important to defend. It is also possible that Rehoboam did not fortify cities in the northern border because he hoped eventually to regain territory lost to the northern tribes. He was especially concerned about defence against Egypt. "No one of the

15 cities was really within the limits of the tribe of Benjamin. The writer uses the phrase 'Judah and Benjamin' merely as the common designation of the southern kingdom. (Compare vv.12 and 23)" (Rawlinson). "The line of fortresses…is…strategically well considered. Each fortress defends important roads into the heart of Judah" (Dillard).

Verses 13-17: Priests, Levites, and Others Coming to Judah and Jerusalem

After Moses found that Israel had worshipped a golden calf while he was on the mount with God he "stood in the gate of the camp, and said, Who is on the Lord's side? let him come unto me. And all the sons of Levi gathered themselves together unto him" (Ex 32.26). Now once again the Levites come to the side of God. The Chronicler is careful to record each time some come from the northern tribes to Judah. The priests and Levites had lost their jobs (v.14) and they were willing to sacrifice further by leaving "their suburbs and their possessions". Their good example had a positive effect on others. The writer of Chronicles emphasizes that these came from every tribe of Israel. They remained loyal to God in the midst of apostasy and rebellion. They separated from evil. "Wherefore come out from among them, and be ye separate, saith the Lord, and touch not the unclean thing; and I will receive you" (2 Cor 6.17).

"The Chronicler has enhanced the apostasy of Jeroboam in two ways. (1) He has added a reference to the goat idols, not known from Kings, and has thereby indicated a transgression of Leviticus 17.7. (2) He has also made explicit Jeroboam's rejection of the Levitical priests, rather than simply reporting his indiscriminate hiring practices as done in 1 Kings 12.32; 13.33" (Dillard).

In Deuteronomy we read 21 times of "the place" which the Lord their God would choose." To this is added 9 times that God would "place his name there". This addition is implied where it is not added. Significantly, 21 times we read of Jeroboam the son of Nebat having made Israel to sin. How did he make Israel to sin? He set up an altar in Bethel and one in Dan. With the altar in Bethel especially, he wanted to keep the people of the northern tribes from going to Jerusalem, "the place where the Lord had chosen to place his name there" (Deut 12.5). 2 Kings 17.21-23 reads "…and Jeroboam drave Israel from following the Lord, and made them sin a great sin. For the children of Israel walked in all the sins of Jeroboam which he did; they departed not from them; Until the Lord removed Israel out of his sight".

"Jeroboam and his sons" in v.14 could refer to his successors even though Nadab was the only son of Jeroboam to reign. All the kings of Israel followed in the sinful footsteps of Jeroboam. Alternatively, it is possible that Jeroboam's sons had positions of authority like Rehoboam's sons in vv.22-23.

"Now, we cannot over-emphasize the magnitude of a sin that destroys a nation. And I do not know of any sin but the sin of Adam more far-reaching in its consequences than the sin of Jeroboam" (Carroll). The "devils" (AV) (SAIYR - 8163) or "he-goats" (RV) of v.15 is "a term applied to demons… popularly believed to inhabit desert and waste places, not as pure spirits, but in corporeal form, ordinarily represented as hairy (hence goat-like)" (Curtis & Masden). 1 Corinthians 10.20 states, "the things which the Gentiles sacrifice, they sacrifice to devils ('demons', RV margin), and not to God".

Verse 16 speaks of "such as set their heart to seek the Lord God of Israel". The Chronicler uses the word "seek" which is his most important word to express spirituality. Seeking God here is linked with making up one's mind. They "set their heart". It is also linked with coming to the temple as the only God-ordained place of worship. "However much the Chronicler insists upon institutional correctness he never falls into the trap of equating it with reality in religion. That depends on the orientation of the heart of individuals…That seeking is the mark of reality. It is not the 'seeking' of those who have not found, and perhaps do not intend to find; but it is the seeking of those who have already found their God and who, because they have known Him, must come back to Him again and again. The Chronicler thus shares with the Psalmist the knowledge that true religion is characteristically a thirst (Ps 42.1ff). Perhaps it is this knowledge that leads him to imply that the position of the Northerners is not lost. Even those who now follow Jeroboam may yet return to the way of truth" (McConville).

The Chronicler does not always use the word "seek" for those who have already found their God. 2 Chronicles 34.3 records concerning Josiah, "For in the eighth year of his reign, while he was yet young, he began to seek after the God of David his father".

In v.17 we read that they "strengthened the kingdom of Judah, and made Rehoboam strong". They did this not only physically but spiritually as well. The last phrase of v.17 is the secret of Rehoboam's temporary piety: "for three years they walked in the way of David and Solomon". In 1 Kings 11.4-8 Solomon is contrasted most unfavourably with David. But the writer of the Chronicles idealizes Solomon here as he often does. David is an ideal role model. 1 Kings 15.5 is a remarkable testimony to him: "Because David did that which was right in the eyes of the Lord, and turned not aside from any thing that he commanded him all the days of his life, save only in the matter of Uriah, the Hittite". Both the Chronicler and the apostle appreciated the need of good role models. Paul wrote in 1 Corinthians 11.1, "Be ye followers of me, even as I also am of Christ". Men should be followed only in the measure that they follow Christ.

The personal exercise of the priests and the Levites to come to Jerusalem and that of others after them illustrates the first right step in bringing God's people together. It also illustrates that there is strength in convictions based on the Word of God (v.17). Whenever believers are willing to sacrifice for their convictions, they are truly a source of encouragement, a tower of strength, and a well of inspiration wherever they are found. They "Buy the truth, and sell it not" (Prov 23.23). Convictions should not be mere opinions. Sir Robert Anderson wrote well, "Opinions are our own and should not be too firmly held, but truth is divine and is worth living for and dying for. We are not called upon to die the martyr's death, but we are called upon to share the martyr's faith". Nature is said to abhor a vacuum. Nature also abhors a mental vacuum! When the mind is empty of truth it is easily filled with prejudices that may well call themselves convictions. But it is obvious that they are not based on God's Word. There surely is strength in convictions.

Verses 18-23: Rehoboam's Family

The Chronicler wants to show a third evidence of blessing in God's gift of children. Psalm 127.3 reads, "Lo, children are an heritage of the Lord: and the fruit of the womb is his reward". To the writer of the Chronicles a good number of children is a sign of blessing from God (1 Chr 3.1-9; 25.4-5; 26.4-8; 2 Chr 13.21; 21.1-3). While it is true that many children are an evidence of blessing, it is also true that many wives are an evidence of disobedience. Solomon had a bitter experience with his many wives (1 Kings 11.4). In spite of this bad example, Rehoboam took eighteen wives and sixty concubines. He thus followed his father in disobeying Deuteronomy 17.17 concerning the behaviour of Israel's kings: "Neither shall he multiply wives to himself, that his heart turn not away".

Of all his wives only two are named. The writer of the Chronicles may possibly be magnifying the dynasty of David when he tells (as the writer of Kings does not) that two of Rehoboam's wives were also descendants of David. The first one named is Mahalath. Both her father and mother are named. Since Jerimoth is not elsewhere named as a son of David, he must have been a son of one of David's concubines. Mahalath's mother is named as Abihail, the daughter of Eliab the son of Jesse. Eliab was David's oldest brother (1 Sam 17.13; 1 Chr 2.13). "Abihail cannot be held to be a second wife of Rehoboam, because v.19, 'Which bare him children', and v.20, 'And after her', show that in v.18 only one wife is named" (Keil). Jerimoth married his cousin. In v.20 the second wife is named - Maachah the daughter of Absalom. Maachah was really the granddaughter of Absalom. Daughter for granddaughter is a common Hebrew idiom. According to 2 Samuel 14.27 Absalom had only one daughter, Tamar by name. The same verse tells of three sons, but since Absalom himself in 2 Samuel 18.18 speaks of having no son, those three sons must have died in infancy or childhood. Maachah was named after her paternal great-grandmother (the mother of Absalom, 1 Chr 3.2). Since Absalom left no son, Maachah can only be the daughter of Tamar who, according to 2 Chronicles 13.2, was married to Uriel. There Maachah's name is given as Michaiah. Josephus confirms this by stating that Tamar was the mother of Maachah. The two wives named were Israelites of the royal family and not heathen. We have no record that any of Solomon's many wives were Israelites. Maachah was Rehoboam's favourite wife (v.21) and he wanted to make her son, Ahijah, king after him.

"In the Old Testament period polygamy was an accepted form of marriage, and concubines did not lack legal rights. Indeed in Judaism today, while monogamy is the prescribed form in Western and other countries which so legislate, polygamy is still permitted for Jews residing in Muslim states. In practice, at least from post-exilic times, economic factors probably made monogamy more expedient" (Leslie C. Allen). In the Old Testament polygamy was never commanded and never commended. Often sad results of polygamy are recorded as is the case here. Part of the sadness of polygamy is that favoritism is inevitable.

"It is not impossible that Rehoboam had eighteen wives and sixty concubines, twenty-eight sons and sixty daughters before the fifth year of his reign, i.e. by age 46 (12.13), though it does seem improbable that his harem could have been this large before his ascension. It is far more natural to see this as a total for his family through the duration of his reign of seventeen years. If the latter is the case, the Chronicler has chronologically relocated these genealogical notes to include them with the blessings of building programs (11.5-12) and a loyal populace (11.13-17), prior to narrating Rehoboam's disobedience and subsequent punishment...The genealogical section may also have the intent of explaining why the oldest son did not receive the kingdom" (Dillard). It is all the more probable if he began to reign at 21 years of age instead of 41 (see comments at 10.8 about Rehoboam's age at ascension).

"Our Authorized Version renders 2 Chronicles 11.23: 'he desired many wives' which seems to imply that Rehoboam sought them for himself. But this is not the case. The original has it, that he 'demanded (or sought)' these alliances for his sons, evidently to strengthen his connection with the noble families of the land" (Edersheim). The Revised Version has, "And he sought for them many wives". His wisdom in giving responsibilities to each of his sons helped to prepare each of them for a useful future.

"With regard to Rehoboam's family, it is obvious inbreeding is probably meant not as a fault but as a positive virtue, remembering the ancient traditions of Israel (Gen 24.3-4; 28.1-2) and the recent follies of Solomon (1 Kings 11.1-8). In this the son showed himself wiser than the father. The tone of this paragraph, like that of the previous two, is encouraging, and although it is possible to translate 11.23b in a way less complimentary to Rehoboam, it is more of a piece with the rest of the section if we take it as it stands in the RSV" (Wilcock). The RSV is similar to the RV in this part of the verse.

Rehoboam showed great wisdom in dispersing all his sons (v.23, RV). He most likely gave each of them positions of authority and gave them ample provision. He evidently wanted all of them to be content and not be jealous of their brothers. He sought a smooth transition to Abijah's reign when he died. Providing them with several wives each was another way to seek to make them contented. "To strengthen their position he married them to several wives apiece; and if these wives were drawn from the foremost families of each city, as most likely they were, that fact would make the worldly wisdom of Rehoboam yet more conspicuous. The 'many wives' of v.23 were sought for his sons, and not for himself as the RV shows" (Williams). The wisdom shown by Rehoboam had the desired result, for after he died Abijah took the throne without any recorded opposition from any of his many brethren.

2 CHRONICLES 12

Rehoboam's Reign

Introductory

Chronicles was written to encourage the returning exiles from Babylon and also to warn them. These important lessons for them are applicable to saints today. The promise of the key verse, 7.14, is critical to an understanding of 2 Chronicles: "If my people, which are called by my name, shall humble themselves, and pray, and seek my face, and turn from their wicked ways; then will I hear from heaven, and will forgive their sin, and will heal their land". This chapter is the first to record such a humbling before God. The grace of God was available for those who humbled themselves as it is also for saints today.

We should be thankful that the Chronicler, guided by the Holy Spirit, gives 13 occasions for our encouragement and warning in relation to 7.14, all but the 10th of which are completely omitted in Kings. Even in that case the record of Huldah's prophetic words has Josiah humbling himself once (2 Kings 22.19) whereas 2 Chronicles 34.27 has him humbling himself twice. The gracious promise of 7.14, which is only in 2 Chronicles, shows that God is far more anxious to bless His people than to carry out judgment. He looks for humbling and repentance and He is still the same today.

The 13 incidents are as follows.

1. The princes and the king humbled themselves before Shemaiah, and God reduced the punishment (12.6,7,12).
2. Asa refused to humble himself before Hanani the seer five years before he died (16.7-10). His remaining years on earth were away from God.
3. Jehoshaphat humbled himself before Jehu the son of Hanani (19.2-4). Most of the rest of ch.19 and 20.1-32 describe good things about Jehoshaphat and were at least partly a result of his humbling.
4. Joash refused to humble himself before Zechariah the son of Jehoida and had him stoned (24.20-22). The very next verse shows that he and the princes who turned him aside felt the governmental dealings of God (24.23-25).
5. Uzziah was "marvellously helped, till he was strong. But when he was strong, his heart was lifted up to his destruction" (26.15-16). He went into the temple to offer incense, which only the priests should do, and became a leper for the rest of his life.
6. Good King Hezekiah sent humbling invitations to the ten northern tribes to keep the Passover (30.1-9). In v.10 "they laughed them to scorn, and mocked them". How encouraging to read in v.11, "Nevertheless divers of Asher and Manasseh and of Zebulun humbled themselves, and came to Jerusalem". Because they willingly did so

they shared in the "great gladness" of v.21, the "gladness" of v.23, the rejoicing of v.25, and the "great joy" of v.26.

7. Hezekiah's heart was lifted up in 32.25 but, "Hezekiah humbled himself for the pride of his heart, both he and the inhabitants of Jerusalem" (v.26), so the wrath of God was postponed.
8. Manasseh was a very wicked king for about the first 50 years of his reign. When he was in affliction he humbled himself greatly before the God of his fathers and got to know "that the Lord, he was God" (33.12-13). For the last few years of his life he tried to undo his earlier wrongs.
9. Amon did wickedly and "humbled not himself before the Lord, as Manasseh his father had humbled himself" (33.23).
10. God greatly appreciated the way Josiah humbled himself before the Word of God (34.27). It is no wonder that he excelled, doing according to all of God's Word (2 Kings 23.25). This also explains why there was no Passover like the one he kept since the days of Samuel (35.18). The historian goes back farther in history to find one closer to the Word of God than the one kept by Hezekiah (30.26).
11. How sad it is that Josiah failed in his strong point in 35.22. He "hearkened not to the words of Necho from the mouth of God". He lost his life prematurely at the young age of 39.
12. The last king of Judah, Zedekiah, "humbled not himself before Jeremiah speaking from the mouth of God" (36.12). Because he refused to humble himself, how sadly touching it is that the last sight he got before the Babylonians put out his eyes was their murder of his sons.
13. 2 Chronicles 36.15-17 explains why Judah went into captivity. Those words are a warning and an encouragement. As long as saints are open to the Word of God and willing to humble themselves before Him there is a good possibility of recovery.

Outline of Chapter 12

Verse 1:	Rehoboam forsaking the law of the Lord.
Verses 2-4:	Shishak of Egypt attacking Judah.
Verses 5-12:	Judah's humble repentance.
Verses 13-16:	Rehoboam's reign concluded.

Verse 1: Rehoboam Forsaking the Law of the Lord

This tells precisely when Rehoboam forsook the law of the Lord. It was when God had established his kingdom and he had strengthened himself. The last statement is neutral by itself but, linked with the stress on humbling in v.6, appears to indicate that Rehoboam took wicked pride in what he had done. He seems to have made the mistake Moses warned God's people about in Deuteronomy 8.17-18: "And thou say in thine heart, My power and the might of mine hand hath gotten me this wealth. But thou shalt remember the Lord thy God: for it is he that giveth thee power to get wealth". He must have forgotten that it was especially the priests, Levites, and loyal believers from the northern kingdom that strengthened him; and also that it was while they walked in the way of David and Solomon that he was made strong. "Pride goeth before destruction, and a haughty spirit before a fall" (Prov 16.18). Pride led Rehoboam into a fall as it did later for Uzziah (26.15-16). "He forsook the law of the Lord and all Israel with him." As usual, the context helps us to know to whom the word "Israel" refers. Here evidently it denotes the southern kingdom. Possibly the word "Israel" is used to emphasize that their action is contrary to what it should have been. What a responsibility Rehoboam had. His bad example was followed by "all Israel". It is not clear why there are no details, because it is clearly implied in vv.1-2. 1 Kings 14.22-24 states that it was especially because of idolatry. Kings also states that it was Judah who sinned, but 2 Chronicles states that Rehoboam led them all into sin.

There is a significant change in the translation of v.1 in the RV and JND. The ESV and NASB are both similar: "when the kingdom of Rehoboam was established and he was strong". The verb "establish" (KUN – 3559) in Chronicles usually refers to God establishing a kingdom (1 Chr 14.2; 17.11; 28.7; 2 Chr 17.5). Even though God is not specifically mentioned here in so doing, it still seems probable that He established Rehoboam's kingdom. Young's Literal Translation of the Bible seems to confirm it: "And it cometh to pass, at the establishing of the kingdom of Rehoboam, and at his strengthening himself, he hath forsaken the law of Jehovah, and all Israel with him".

"As we assess the situation we note successive facts: 1) It was God who established Rehoboam; 2) only after that was Rehoboam able to strengthen himself; and 3) when he felt that he no longer needed the Lord (i.e. he was unfaithful to the Lord) he was taught that it is a very serious thing for anyone to turn his or her back to the Lord. To do so is to invite some form of chastisement. God often shows us our weakness in the very place where we thought we were the strongest" (Barber).

When the Chronicler writes in v.1, "he forsook the law of the Lord", he concentrates on the idea of personal disloyalty to God. Rehoboam gave up a personal commitment to God. God in turn had forsaken him (v.5). Sin is truly an offense toward God. David knew that he had sinned against Uriah and Bathsheba, but he also knew that, most seriously, it was sin against God (Ps 51.4). Joseph knew that to yield to Potiphar's wife would be sin against Potiphar, but would be, primarily, a sin against God (Gen 39.9). "It is because the modern world has largely rejected belief in the possibility of a personal relationship with God, and indeed of judgment, that it has difficulty in identifying anything as inherently wrong" (McConville).

Verses 2-4: Shishak of Egypt Attacking Judah

Most of v.2 is taken directly from 1 Kings 14.25. The last phrase of this verse, "because they had transgressed against the Lord", is where the Chronicler begins with new material, probably from the book of Shemaiah the prophet (v.15). He again draws from 1 Kings at v.9. So the writer of the Chronicles (writing from a divine standpoint) tells why Shishak attacked Judah (vv.2,5) and he gives a much fuller account of the invasion. Shishak was victorious over Judah not because of being superior militarily but because Judah had forsaken God. Three times we read of Judah forsaking the Lord (vv.1,5,5 (as "left")) and once that they transgressed against the Lord (v.2).

"Punishment for 'forsaking' God in this way is expressed in two ways. The one is specific, namely defeat at the hand of foreign enemies; cp. 7.19-22; 21.10; 24.23-24; 28.6; 29.6 with 8-9; and 34.25 with reference forward to the fall of Jerusalem. The other way in which 'forsaking' God is punished is by God 'forsaking' His people, usually with similar results, as v.5 of this chapter shows. This word-play occurs explicitly three times, at 12.5; 15.2; and 24.20, and it is implied at 1 Chronicles 28.9 and 20, though in rather different circumstances. Finally, it may be observed that a passage such as 15.2 suggests that to 'forsake' God is the exact opposite of 'seeking' Him" (Williamson).

"Solomon had joined affinity with Pharaoh by taking his daughter to wife; and whether this was merely to please himself, or that he expected to strengthen his kingdom by an alliance with so powerful a country, it all comes to naught, as do all such expedients where God's Word is disobeyed or ignored" (Knapp).

"The Chronicler's account (of Shishak's invasion), fuller than that of 1 Kings 14.25, had been thought untrustworthy historically until it was found that some of the extra details, especially in relation to the Sukkiim (v.3) had a plausible Egyptian background. This passage, then, is an important indicator that the Chronicler had access to at least some important historical sources in addition to earlier Biblical material" (McConville).

"Among the cities fortified by Rehoboam (11.6-10) which were taken by Shishak, we find in the Karnac inscription three only - viz. Shoco, Adorim, and Aijalon. Fourteen names, however, are lost in the commencement of the inscription, which is the place where the frontier towns towards the south would naturally have been mentioned" (Rawlinson). "Archæology throws some light on the invasion of Shishak. Not a great while ago, in uncovering the ruins of the temple of Karnak on the Nile, there was found the inscription of Shishak on his return from the invasion. It shows what cities he captured, and how he had taken away the treasures from Jerusalem…after thousands of years the spade keeps turning up proof of the truth of the Bible. When archæology first commenced the radical critics said that it would destroy the Bible" (Carroll). Nelson Gluech, the famous Jewish archæologist, said, "It can be stated categorically that no archeological discovery had ever controverted one Scriptural reference".

Verses 5-12: Judah's Humble Response

For the writer of the Chronicles the most important result of Shishak's attack was the humbling of the princes and the king. The Chronicler especially wants his readers to learn the theological significance of the attack (told so well in Shemaiah's pointed words in v.5): "Ye have forsaken me, and therefore I have also left you in the hand of Shishak". The princes of Israel in v.6 are the princes of Judah in v.5. The Lord told Moses, in Deuteronomy 31.16-17 that His people would forsake Him and He would forsake them.

"There is a striking double use of the word 'forsake' in the Hebrew of v.5, although the inflexibility of the English language does not permit its repetition: compare the RSV, 'You abandoned me, so I have abandoned you to the hand of Shishak'. There is spiritual logic at work here. The Chronicler's theology has a strongly moral tone: throughout his history he insists that God keeps short accounts and that to backslide is to forfeit His blessing in a life-shattering way…He seems to be writing as a pastoral theologian rather than as a purely systematic one, issuing incentives and sanctions as motives to keep his readers on the straight and narrow path of obedience to God" (Leslie C. Allen).

"In Jerusalem Rehoboam and the leaders of the people faced a serious dilemma. What were they to do? They met to discuss their most viable human options. Their combined wisdom, however, failed to produce a workable solution. Fortunately for them, the Lord did not leave them without knowledge of the cause of their misfortune" (Barber).

Suddenly Shemaiah approached them where they were meeting because of Shishak and came straight to the point: "Ye have forsaken me, and therefore have I left you in the hand of Shishak".

Verses 6-7 are the first illustration of the promise of 7.14. The promise is similar to the repeated record of the book of Judges: departure, defeat, desire, and deliverance. It was only after they cried to God that He sent a deliverer. See the introductory paragraphs for other illustrations of 7.14. Verse 6 records that, "the princes of Israel and the king humbled themselves". "Humbled" is found four times (vv.6,7,7,12). Since the princes are mentioned first, it would seem that they took the lead. The king should have done so but here he seems to be merely a follower. It appears that the princes were more spiritually sensitive to a message from the Lord than their sovereign. The king was slower, most probably because there was still pride unjudged within his heart. They said, "The Lord is righteous", which is similar to the words of Pharaoh, spoken insincerely, as given in Exodus 9.27 (after the plague of hail), and to those spoken by Daniel, sincerely, in his prayer recorded in Daniel 9.14. "The Lord is righteous", is a humble confession of sin, acknowledging that the Lord is right, they are wrong, and receiving just what they deserve. Even in the midst of punishment, it is not too late to repent.

"Here the character of repentance may be seen to correspond to that of sin. As sin is personal defection from the Lord with the absurd and heinous implication that God has not the right to be Lord over the individual's life - so repentance involves the affirmation that He does after all have that right. He is God and thus no theoretical proposition; He is God therefore entitled to be my Lord" (McConville).

Fulfilling the promise of 7.14 God said in v.7, "I will grant them some deliverance". The degree of deliverance is dependent on the degree of repentance. Because they would not willingly serve God, they would know the yoke of a different Lord. They were to be servants to Shishak that they might learn that it is far better to serve God than any other master (v.8). Maclaren has written on "Contrasted services" based on v.8. Here is one quote, "God's service brings solid good, the world's is vain and empty. God's service brings an approving conscience, a calm heart, strength and gladness. It is in full accord with our best selves. Tranquil joys attend to it. In keeping His commandments there is great reward; and that not merely bestowed after keeping, but realized and inherent in the very act".

Our Lord Jesus said in Matthew 6.24, "Ye cannot serve God and mammon". Mammon is earthly riches. Mammon can be used to serve, but every saint should be careful not to allow it to become his master. Our Lord said (Mt 11.29-30), "Take my yoke upon you and learn of me; for I am meek and lowly in heart: and ye shall find rest unto your souls. For my yoke is easy, and my burden is light". Just as God wanted Judah to learn from serving Shishak, so God wants each saint to learn when they depart (as stated in Jeremiah 2.19), "Thine own wickedness shall correct thee, and thy backslidings shall reprove thee: know therefore and see that it is an evil thing and bitter, that thou hast forsaken the Lord thy God, and that my fear is not in thee, saith the Lord God of hosts". Surely it is best for us saints to follow the well-known words, "Man's chief end is to glorify God and to enjoy Him for ever".

"Stripping the temple of all its golden vessels and ornaments symbolized the fact that the glory had already begun to depart. The continuance of the southern kingdom for another three hundred years is a marvelous tribute to the longsuffering of God!" (Whitcomb). Verses 9-11 are similar to 1 Kings 14.25-28. The first nine words of v.9 repeat part of v.2, showing that the Chronicler is returning to 1 Kings for his material.

Rehoboam's substitution of brass shields for Solomon's shields of gold vividly illustrates the fading glory of Judah, but this event also reveals the character of Rehoboam. Barber points out his feelings of inferiority: "Rehoboam suffered from lifelong feelings of inferiority created, not by the absence of a father, but by having a father who excelled in every area of his life. Success, it seemed, had been denied him. And so he resorts to strategies to make himself look good in the eyes of others".

When Shishak took away the shields of gold, Rehoboam would not enter the house of the Lord. So he had shields of brass made so that when he did eventually go in the shields of brass were a substitute for those of gold. Brass looks like gold and, when the sun is shining the shields would shine like gold. He was pretending that he still had the gold! Rehoboam's going up to the house of the Lord even though he had forsaken Him (v.1) is another evidence of his desire to keep up the right appearance at all costs. In just a few days all the wealth that David and Solomon had accumulated for many years (that was not already spent on the Temple and other buildings) was given to Shishak.

The AV margin for the last part of v.12 reads: "and yet in Judah there were good things". The first part of v.12 refers to vv.5-11 and the "good things" could refer to ch.11. It is also possible that there were a few good things in Judah as a result of the humbling of the leaders of Judah themselves. This is a reminder of Jehu's words to Jehoshaphat in 19.3: "Nevertheless there are good things found in thee". It is wonderful grace on God's part in a reign generally evil (v.14) that He acknowledged what was good.

Verses 13-16: Rehoboam's Reign Concluded

"There seems to be a contrast intended here between the earlier and later portions of Rehoboam's reign. In the earlier he strengthened himself throughout the whole of his dominion (11.5-12,17,23; 12.1); in the latter he was content to secure his capital" (Rawlinson). He reigned in the city of God's choice but he behaved very unbecomingly for one so privileged. In v.14 the negative assessment of Kings is increased. 1 Kings 14.22 states, "Judah did evil", while the Chronicler holds Rehoboam alone responsible and adds, "because he prepared not his heart to seek the Lord". His mother was Naamah an Ammonitess. She was an idolatrous woman who would give him a strong bias towards idolatry. Mothers can have a great influence for good or evil on their children. However, that is not the reason given in the next verse as to why he did evil. "He prepared not his heart to seek the Lord." If he had prepared or set his heart to seek God he could have overcome the bad influence of his mother. Both Hezekiah and Josiah had wicked fathers but by seeking God they were able to overcome that bad influence (31.21; 34.3). Rehoboam is also a contrast to Asa (14.4,7), Jehoshaphat (19.3; 20.3-4), Uzziah (26.5), Jotham (27.6), and also David who sought God's face (Ps 27.8). Verse 14 is not a contradiction of v.12, it is the summary of his whole reign, which was evil. The writer has enlarged it by adding the clause that explains why Rehoboam did evil.

Charles H. Spurgeon (in *Men of the Old Testament*) has only one chapter on any of the kings of Judah. That one chapter is on Rehoboam and Spurgeon comments on only one verse (12.14): "So I judge that this expression means first, that HE DID NOT BEGIN LIFE WITH SEEKING THE LORD…HE WAS NOT FIXED AND PERSEVERING IN HIS RELIGION. The original bears that sense." Regarding his first three years' reign he writes, "Thus he prospered; and you might have thought that, as his religion brought him prosperity, he would stick to it. Not he; there was no 'stick to it' in him…You see how readily Rehoboam went, first toward God, then toward idols, and then back again toward God. *He was always ready to shift and change*…There was not anything real and permanent in his religion; it did not hold him. He held it sometimes, but it never held him…But look you, sirs, *if there is no care about making the heart go right, it must go wrong*, because the natural tendency of our mind is toward evil…Then further, if we would be prepared to seek the Lord, there must be a *submission of ourselves to His guidance*".

The writer of the Chronicles in v.16 omits, "buried with his fathers" (1 Kings 14.31), possibly indicating a negative judgment.

"Based on scripture, I tried to imagine how King Solomon might have summed up his life in six words. As a young man he could have written: 'God has given me great wisdom'. But in his latter years, he might have said. 'Should have practised what I preached" (David McCasland, *Our Daily Bread*, 29th January, 2011).

2 CHRONICLES 13

Abijah's Reign

Introductory

The writer of Kings gave a negative report contained in eight verses of Abijah's brief reign of three years (1 Kings 15.1-8, where he is consistently called Abijam). The writer of Chronicles, guided by the Holy Spirit, takes 22 verses over one event in Abijah's reign. The Chronicler delights to record how Judah won a great victory because "they relied on the Lord God of their fathers" (v.18). This is an encouragement to the original readers. Imperfect people can have hope by relying upon the Lord God of their fathers. This is the first of four chapters that are linked together by the key word, "rely", found five times here (14.11 as "rest") and nowhere else in Chronicles. See the "Introduction to the Division of the Monarchy and the Subsequent History of the Kings of Judah" in this Commentary.

The writer of Kings gives this assessment of the life of Abijah in 1 Kings 15.3: "And he walked in all the sins of his father…and his heart was not perfect with the Lord his God, as the heart of David his father". Sadly, Abijah followed in the ways of his father, Rehoboam, rather than in the ways of his great grandfather David. In Kings it is recorded that it is only because of God's gracious covenant with David that his line is preserved. However, this chapter in Chronicles makes it clear that Abijah had more wisdom than his father. Abijah's speech indicates that he had a grasp of spiritual principles. It is never recorded that his father had.

So the Chronicler recorded one event in Abijah's reign that glorified God. Since this event is in the Word of God which also records the assessment of Abijah's reign in Kings, they are both true. No doubt the Chronicler agreed with the assessment of Kings but that does not hinder him from recording this positive event. He shows that Abijah rose to this one act of faith even though his life was characterized by displeasing God. He is thus able to put Abijah in a much better light because of his concern for the Davidic dynasty, the temple, priests, and Levites. Abijah expresses what the Chronicler surely believed about the position of Judah before God. The writer was encouraging all of Judah that had returned from Babylon to Jerusalem to be the ones to preserve the true worship of Jehovah. Similarly, the Apostle Paul exhorts Timothy and all the saints in 2 Timothy 1.14: "That good thing which was committed unto thee keep by the Holy Spirit which dwelleth in us". "That good thing" is the deposit of truth. Our Lord Jesus three times refers to the Holy Spirit as "the Spirit of truth" in His farewell ministry (Jn 14.17; 15.26; 16.13). The Spirit of truth that inspired every word of the Bible is well able to help each believer keep that good deposit.

The account in 2 Chronicles is very different from the account in 1 Kings. However, as noted above, both are true. Using Iddo's history ensured that the Chronicler's account was accurate and reliable. Carefully comparing the two suggests that the Chronicler used not only a source that is probably the story or commentary of the prophet Iddo (v.22), but also the Kings account. As suggested by Selman there are four things to be drawn from 1 Kings 15 in this chapter.

1. The war between Judah and Israel (1 Kings 15.6, 7; 2 Chr 13.2).
2. God was preserving Jerusalem and the dynasty of David as a lamp of testimony in the midst of darkness (1 Kings 15.4; 2 Chr 13.5-12).
3. The writer of the Kings records in 15.15 that Abijah commendably dedicated things for the house of the Lord, showing that he did not view Abijam altogether negatively. This is also indicated by the comment in the last part of v.3: "his heart was not perfect with the Lord his God, as the heart of David his father". The writer of the Kings is indicating that Abijah's heart was not perfect to the same degree as David's. He had already said this about Solomon in 11.4.
4. The writer of the Chronicles has structured his account from the opening and closing words of 1 Kings 15.1-8.

"Abijah's speech (vv.4-12) is parallel in style and content to one by Hezekiah (2 Chr 29.5-11; cp. 30.6-9)...Both speeches also have a stabilizing effect, Abijah following the catastrophe of the division, Hezekiah's after... the disastrous reign of Ahaz (ch.28)...Both speeches point to God-centred worship as the sole ground of future hope" (Selman).

Outline of Chapter 13

Verses 1-3: Unique introduction.
Verses 4-12: Abijah's challenging appeal to the northern tribes.
Verses 13-19: Judah's victory.
Verses 20-22: Contrast between the two rival kings, and conclusion.

Verses 1-3: Unique Introduction

The meaning of Abijah's name is "My Father is Jah", or "My Father is the Lord". It is possible that his name was changed to Abijam in the Kings account to distinguish him from a son of Jeroboam also named Abijah. Jamieson, Fausset & Brown give a more serious reason: "His name was at first Abijah (12.16); 'Jah', the name of God, according to an ancient fashion, being conjoined with it. But afterwards, when he was found 'walking in all the sins of his father', that honourable addition was withdrawn, and his name in sacred history changed into Abijam (Lightfoot)". It is noteworthy that the Chronicler does not give a spiritual evaluation of Abijah as we have in 1 Kings 15.3, possibly indicating that in spite of the good recorded here his reign as a whole did not have clear direction.

In vv.1 and 2 the Chronicler follows closely 1 Kings 15.1,2,6. Uniquely, this is the only time that he gives the chronological relation between a king of Judah and a king of the northern tribes, even though the writer of Kings notes this regularly. He does so here because the whole chapter speaks of the two kingdoms. This introduction is also unique because it relates to one of only three kings of Judah whose age at the beginning of his reign the Chronicler does not record. The initial division of the nation was from God. Humanly speaking, the foolishness of Rehoboam's answer was the reason that most of his subjects rejected him. The writer of the Chronicles knew that the continuation of the Jeroboam dynasty depended on his faithfulness to God (1 Kings 11.37-38). He failed grievously as his innovations proved (2 Chr 11.14-15; 13.8-9). "Accordingly the death of foolish Rehoboam and the accession of a new Judæan king afforded an opportunity to the Northerners to reject Jeroboam and revert to allegiance to the true, Davidic king" (Leslie C. Allen).

For Abijah's mother's name see the comments at 11.18-23. That shows that he was descended from David not only on his father's side but also on his mother's. Being doubly related to David may have aroused in Abijah a special interest in getting to know all that he could about his forefather as is displayed in vv.5-8a.

The figures given in v.3 for the size of the two armies are completely plausible upon considering the census figures Joab gave to David (2 Sam 24.9; 1 Chr 21.5). Abijah was courageous to face an enemy with an army twice as large as his own. This was probably because he relied on God as all Judah did (v.18).

Verses 4-12: Abijah's Challenging Appeal to the Northern Tribes

Abijah hoped that hostilities could be avoided and he also hoped that the Northerners would see that they could forsake Jeroboam and return to the Davidic rule. "Fair reasoning may do a great deal of good and prevent a great deal of mischief" (Matthew Henry). Mount Zemaraim is probably near Bethel (Josh 18.22). This speech of Abijah calls to mind Jotham's speech on Mount Gerizim to the men of Shechem (Judg 9.7-20). "For terseness, accusation, warning and appeal, the address is unsurpassed by anything in any literature of any time. Its merit was recognized even in his own day, for the prophet Iddo…did not neglect to record the eloquent king's 'sayings' (2 Chr 13.22)" (Knapp).

Abijah had great confidence in confronting Jeroboam and his army. His father Rehoboam gave all his sons responsible positions and made Abijah "chief" (11.22-23). That experience may have helped him in leadership.

In his magnificent speech Ahijah with amazing skill showed that God was with Judah. Firstly, he showed that the Davidic dynasty was the only God-given one (vv.5-8a). The Chronicler knew that God gave Jeroboam the right to rule over the ten northern tribes, but he also knew that Jeroboam had failed miserably to fulfill the conditions for his dynasty to be established by God. Secondly, Judah maintained the only true worship that God ordained in contrast to that of the Northerners (vv.8b-12). His speech is a masterpiece, which gave great weight to his final appeal in v.12. In v.4 he appealed to Jeroboam and all Israel but then he increasingly ignored Jeroboam. He referred to him in the third person in vv.6 and 8, and his final appeal left Jeroboam out altogether.

"There was no integrity in Jeroboam's dealings. His idolatrous practices, learned while in Egypt, gave him a foolish confidence in the gods he had created. So great was his confidence that he even carried them into battle" (Barber).

He reminded them that God gave the kingship over Israel to David forever, "by a covenant of salt" (vv.5-8a). Here Israel includes all twelve tribes. Abijah knew that they ought to have understood this (2 Sam 7.13,16; 1 Chr 17.14). Salt is well known as a preservative. Numbers 18.19 twice has "for ever" in connection with things given to Aaron and his family, "...by a statute for ever: it is a covenant of salt for ever before the Lord". The meaning is clearly an eternal covenant. Gabriel's words to Mary in Luke 1.32-33 show that the promise of the kingdom to David forever was to be fulfilled in Christ - "the Lord God shall give unto him the throne of his father David: And he shall reign over the house of Jacob for ever; and of his kingdom there shall be no end". Since God gave the kingdom to David and his descendants, it means that to reject that rule is equivalent to rejecting the rule of God.

Verse 7 speaks of "vain men, the children of Belial". In the New Testament Belial became a name of Satan (2 Cor 6.15). In the Old Testament it simply meant "worthlessness". The NIV has "some worthless scoundrels". Most commentators believe that these vain men were gathered around Jeroboam, thinking that "him" refers to Jeroboam. Williamson was probably the first modern commentator to point out that the antecedent of "him" is "his lord" in v.6, referring to Rehoboam. These vain men are therefore most likely the young men who "strengthened themselves against Rehoboam" and persuaded him to reject the wise, mature counsel of the old men. The Jewish historian Josephus was probably right so to interpret the verse since the phrase "vain men" or "some worthless scoundrels" (NIV) suggests a small group rather than "Jeroboam and all Israel" (10.3). Thus, Abijah is not criticizing the Northerners. Instead, he is apologizing for the mistake of his father. "This reflects both humility and tact on Abijah's part" (Thompson). "Now that he (Rehoboam) had died, there was no excuse for persisting in secession" (Leslie C. Allen). Eugene H. Merrill in the Bible Knowledge Commentary and Wilcock also see v.7 in a similar way.

In v.8 there is a clever and purposeful play on words. The word "withstand" (CHAZAQ - 2388) is used in the last part of v.7 in reference to Rehoboam not being able to "withstand" the "vain men". Here in v.8 it is used of the ten northern tribes withstanding the Lord's kingdom in the hands of the descendants of David. It made it look as though they preferred to trust in the idols that Jeroboam had made and had with him in the battle.

Abijah shows in vv.8b-12 that Judah was maintaining the true worship of God in contrast to the Northerners. They, with shameless boldness, had the golden calves with them in the battle even as God's people had the ark in the battle against the Philistines (1 Sam 4.3-17). Jeroboam said of those golden calves, "...behold thy gods, O Israel, which brought thee up out of the land of Egypt" (1 Kings 12.28). Ahijah the prophet said to Jeroboam (1 Kings 14.9) on behalf of the Lord God of Israel, "thou hast gone and made thee other gods, and molten images to provoke me to anger, and hast cast me behind thy back". Jeroboam had cast off the men that God had ordained to be priests (v.9) even as previously recorded in 11.14-15. The golden calves and Jeroboam's words about them are a reminder of the golden calf that Aaron made for God's people and the words of Aaron in Exodus 32.4, while they impatiently waited for Moses. God condemned that as idolatrous (32.8).

Abijah said (v.10), "But as for us, the Lord is our God", which is in strong contrast to the northern ten tribes. It calls to mind Joshua's words in Joshua 24.15, "...but as for me and my house, we will serve the Lord". Judah still served the Lord in contrast to the Northerners, although Abijah's loyalty to the Lord was only partial. There were sincere worshippers in Judah in spite of the king. In the beginning of v.10 Abijah said, "we have not forsaken him", and at the close of v.11 he said, "but ye have forsaken him". In between he tells of the continuation of God-given ceremonial in the temple by the priests and Levites.

In v.11 only one of the ten tables and only one of the ten candlesticks that Solomon had made is mentioned. "This passage suggests the view that, though Solomon made ten tables for the shewbread (4.8), it was only set upon one of them at a time. Solomon made ten candlesticks (4.7) but — as with the tables — one only was used at a time" (Rawlinson).

Abijah said (v.12), "God himself is with us for our captain". Deuteronomy 20.4 gives this promise: "For the Lord your God is he that goeth with you, to fight for you against your enemies, to save you". Joshua 5.14 records a pre-incarnate appearance of the Lord Jesus to Joshua, "...as captain of the hosts of the Lord am I now come. And Joshua fell on his face to the earth, and did worship, and said unto him, What saith my Lord unto his servant?". Abijah, in spite of his sin and shortcomings, appears to have an honest trust in the Lord whom he acknowledged as "captain", a divine leader taking control of the army. Abijah also refers to God's priests with trumpets sounding an alarm. God had promised "And if ye go to war in your land against the enemy...then ye shall blow an alarm with the trumpets; and ye shall be remembered before the Lord your God, and ye shall be saved from your enemies" (Num 10.9). Those trumpets spoke of divine power available for victory just as they did in Jericho many years before (Josh 6.16).

Abijah's final appeal at the end of v.12 is a concise and tactful climax. It is really an appeal to be re-united. He addresses them as, "O children of Israel", reminding them that they should all be together and he hoped that they would be once again united. He had said at the very beginning,

"Hear me, thou Jeroboam, and all Israel" (v.4). Now he leaves out Jeroboam altogether and goes on wisely to say, "Fight ye not against the Lord God of your fathers". They still have the same God. The words, "for ye shall not prosper", have a striking parallel in Gamaliel's advice to the Sanhedrin when they were thinking of killing the apostles in Acts 5.39: "But if it be of God, ye cannot overthrow it; lest haply ye be found even to fight against God". "Just as the apostles were bravely determined to 'obey God rather than men' (Acts 5.29), so Abijah, leading an out-numbered army (v.3), stands staunchly by his principles" (Leslie C. Allen).

The original division was of God, but there had been two changes since then and so there was no reason for it to continue. Rehoboam who had acted foolishly in rejecting the good advice of the old men had died. Secondly, Jeroboam had failed miserably to fulfill the conditions for God to establish his dynasty. The Chronicler regards each generation as individually responsible to God; therefore each generation should decide anew how they should act, even if it is different from the past. "You were subjects of Rehoboam, but God did not hold you to that when Rehoboam failed; you became subjects of Jeroboam, but God does not expect you to hold to that when there is a true king in the south again…Abijah…in this inspired moment grasped the truth. What matters is the kind of godly government seen in the Davidic king when they are what they should be, and the kind of godly worship seen in Solomon's temple when it operates as it ought" (Wilcock). The Northerners have forsaken God but Rehoboam also forsook God (12.1,5). The princes of Israel and the king had repented (12.6). Repentance was also open to the Northerners.

Verses 13-19: Judah's Victory

While Abijah pleaded with the northern tribes, Jeroboam took an unfair advantage and ambushed him (v.13). "He was so far from fair reasoning, that he is not for fair fighting" (Matthew Henry). It is obvious from the actions of Jeroboam that he is the one most responsible for the perpetuation of the division.

Even though Judah was out-numbered two to one and out-manœuvered, they won a great victory. Jeroboam's unfair ambush only enhanced the triumph. When the men of Judah saw the desperate plight they were in, with the battle both before and behind, "they cried unto the Lord, and the priests sounded with the trumpets. Then the men of Judah gave a shout…" (vv.14-15). David (who experimentally knew much about trusting God) said in Psalm 56.3, "What time I am afraid, I will trust in thee". It was while they were shouting that God smote Jeroboam and all Israel with him. In this divine supernatural intervention it is not known exactly what God did, but it is known that the victory was entirely from Him. Verse 15 records that "God smote Jeroboam"; and v.16 that "God delivered them into their hand".

Israel sustained the staggering loss of 500,000 chosen men (v.17). In hand-to-hand combat there can be a tremendous loss of life in a relatively short period of time. Verse 17 says, "There fell down slain…". "This word translated 'slain' (HALAL - 2491) strictly means 'pierced' and indicates both the killed and the wounded. This same word is translated 'wounded' in Lamentations 2.12" (Rawlinson). Overwhelming odds are no problem to the Lord. "It is a David and Goliath story which encourages a faithful minority to hold unto the truth…To rely is literally to lean; a related noun occurs in Psalm 18.18 where David attested that 'the Lord was my support' (ESV). Both contexts indicate that the term belongs to a situation of desperate crisis" (Leslie C. Allen). The key to victory is in v.18: "because they relied upon the Lord God of their fathers". In the Bible weakness can be a positive advantage when it leads to reliance on God as in 2 Corinthians 12.10, "when I am weak, then am I strong".

This is also a reminder of the victory of the 2½ tribes over the Hagarites on the east of Jordan as described in 1 Chronicles 5.20: "And they were helped against them, and the Hagarites were delivered into their hand, and all that were with them: for they cried to God in the battle, and he was entreated of them; because they put their trust in him". Even though later the 2½ tribes were the first ones to go into captivity because of idolatry (1 Chr 5.25-26), God honoured their trust in Him. Believers always need to have on the armour of Ephesians 6.10-18 for spiritual warfare. For example, when God's people engage in any special work of gospel testimony, it is like a battle for it involves a struggle against evil. It is very important to cry to God at such times. Abijah's victory and the victory of the 2½ tribes is an encouragement to do so.

Alexander Maclaren has a profitable message on 2 Chronicles 13.18, entitled "The Secret of Victory". In it he states, "The consciousness of weakness is the beginning of faith…Faith has an upper and an under side; the under side is self-distrust; the upper, trust in God…'What time I am afraid, I will trust in thee' (Ps 56.3)…Peril kills a feeble trust but vivifies it if strong. The recognition of danger is meant to drive us to God".

Because Judah relied upon the Lord God of their fathers they "prevailed" and found in God all that they needed. Because of Jeroboam's choice the northern tribes were not brought back to the house of God. Instead, they were brought under the children of Judah (v.18). The word for "brought under" is the same word translated "humbled" in 7.14 and 12.6. "This is an important final comment on Jeroboam's ill-fated attempt to resist God… The force of the use of the word here, however, is to show, with some irony, that he who will not humble himself before God will yet be humbled by God" (McConville).

One of the three cities captured was Bethel (v.19). It was the most important center for calf worship (1 Kings 12.28-29). Of course, the golden calves, ironically, could not even defend the shrine of one of them. Bethel later returned to the northern tribes (Amos 7.10-13). Since Baasha is recorded in 16.1 as fortifying Ramah, and Ramah is about five miles south of Bethel, most likely Bethel had returned to the North by then.

Verses 20-22: Contrast Between the Two Rival Kings and Conclusion

Jeroboam never recovered strength again from that humiliating defeat; "the Lord smote him, and he died" (v.20, RV). It is the same word as "smote" in v.15. The same language is used for Nabal's death in 1 Samuel 25.38. However, we know that Jeroboam did not die within ten days as Nabal did The Chronicler is not necessarily saying that he died suddenly or in any unusual manner. Instead he wants it known that Jeroboam's death was a judgment upon him for his sins. Comparing 1 Kings 14.20 and 15.9 shows that Jeroboam lived at least two years longer than Abijah, but the writer has no intention of referring to the history of Jeroboam again. So he writes of his death here.

In contrast to Jeroboam, Abijah waxed mighty (v.21). He had many children, which are a blessing from God (Ps 127.3). But sadly when he married so many wives it was in direct disobedience to the exhortation for future kings given in Deuteronomy 17.17: "Neither shall he multiply wives to himself". Abijah was the fourth successive king of Judah to multiply wives to himself. Thankfully, there was no king of Judah after him that so blatantly did so.

Verse 22 shows that the Chronicler had a source ("the story of the prophet Iddo") that the writer of the Kings did not have or did not choose to use. The AV margin and the RV as well as Helen Spurrell each have "commentary" instead of "story". JND has the word, "treatise".

"This chapter stands as the only assessment in 2 Chronicles of the 'sin of the North'. The Chronicler then…focuses the remainder of his attention on the Davidic kings of the southern kingdom" (Sailhammer).

2 CHRONICLES 14

Asa's Reign

Introductory

The writer of the Kings uses only 16 verses to write about Asa (1 Kings 15.9-24) whereas the Chronicler uses three times as many - 48 verses in three chapters. This is the third successive king to receive greater coverage in Chronicles than in the books of Kings. But, in contrast to Rehoboam and Abijah, the account in ch.16 is less complimentary than the account in Kings. (Chapters 14 and 15 are more complimentary.)

The first two kings of the divided monarchy, Rehoboam and Abijah, mostly displeased God, but occasionally did something that pleased Him. The next two kings, Asa and Jehoshaphat, mostly pleased God but occasionally displeased Him. The first two kings reigned a total of 20 years, the next two kings (who were both godly) thankfully reigned a total of 66 years.

As Payne has noted, the Chronicler, guided by the Holy Spirit, makes a series of contrasts between Asa's early godly years (which are recorded in chs.14 and 15) and the last few sad disappointing years (which are recorded in ch.16).

1. Asa faced an overwhelming opponent in Zerah with his million men, but later he faced a far weaker opponent in Baasha.

2. For the first enemy he relied on God but later, for the second enemy, he relied on the King of Syria.

3. Zerah and the Ethiopians were completely defeated by the Lord, and Judah had peace as the danger was gone. There was no such victory in his last years.

4. Asa responded to the Word of God in two opposite ways. He was encouraged and strengthened by Azariah's message from God. Later in life he was angry with Hanani the seer for his message from God and put him in a prison house. By giving these contrasts, the Chronicler is showing the blessings that come from seeking God and the foolishness of not continuing to seek Him in times of trouble.

In addition one might add:

5. Asa excelled in seeking God in his early years. The verb "to seek" is found eight times in chs.14 and 15. However, in his last two or three years he "was diseased in his feet, until his disease was exceeding great: yet in his disease he sought not to the Lord, but to the physicians" (16.12). He thus potentially exposed himself to the judgment of his own covenant (15.13).

6. Asa prospered in the first two chapters as a result of seeking God. Most likely the disease of Asa's feet was a discipline from God to encourage him to return to seeking Him. The Chronicler was amazed that Asa was so hardened that even in his serious sickness he still did not do so.

It is very interesting to notice (as Selman does) the remarkable parallels between Asa's reign and the reign of Hezekiah. Asa is not of the same stature as Hezekiah, but there are many similar characteristics in their reigns. Both prospered (14.7; 31.21) by doing that which was good and right in the sight of God (14.2; 31.20), by seeking God (14.4; 31.21), by serving Him from the heart (15.17; 29.10; 31.20), and by obeying His law and commandments (14.4; 31.21). They gathered the people together (15.9-10; 30.13) and made a covenant with them (15.12-15; 29.10). A very striking feature is that both kings welcomed the Northerners to worship at Jerusalem (15.9; 30.6-11). Both suffered a military invasion after it was obvious that the king and the people were in a good condition in relation to God, and both responded by declaring that relying on God was of first importance (14.9-11; 32.1,7-8). Neither responded well to the illness that they had (16.10; 32.25), though there is no record that Asa repented as Hezekiah did (32.26). Both were specially honoured at their funerals (16.14; 32.33). These parallels all point to a pattern of life that (in the main) the Chronicler commends to his readers.

One could also add that both had a miraculous victory over an invading army (14.12-15; 32.21-22).

Outline of Chapter 14

Verses 1-8: Asa's early reforms in his first ten years of peace.
Verses 9-15: Asa's victory over Zerah through his reliance on God.

Verses 1-8: Asa's Early Reforms in his First Ten Years of Peace

This account in Chronicles anticipates the revivals in the days of Hezekiah and Josiah. The ten-year period of peace noted in v.1 came about for two reasons: Abijah's victory (13.15-20), and as a reward for the faithfulness of Asa (as he himself said in v.7, "...we have sought the Lord our God...and he hath given us rest"). At this time Asa had the insight to see that peace was the Lord's doing, not his. The Chronicler adds the word "good" to the evaluation of Asa in 1 Kings 15.11 - "And Asa did that which was good and right in the eyes of the Lord his God" (v.2). The eyes of Asa himself were not important. The "eyes of the Lord" speak of the Lord's thorough discernment so that "all things are naked and opened unto the eyes of him with whom we have to do" (Heb 4.13). This is another parallel with Hezekiah since the phrase "good and right" only recurs in 31.20.

As a result of Asa's piety, five times we read of quiet or rest in the first seven verses, and we also read in v.6 of "no war". This is not really a contradiction to 1 Kings 15.16, "And there was war between Asa and Baasha king of Israel all their days". There were continuous hostilities but no special campaigns against each other. Scholars are not agreed on the exact nature of the idols mentioned in v.3 and v.5. The Chronicler omits all four references to the sodomites in Kings (1 Kings 14.24; 15.12; 22.46; 2 Kings 23.7), possibly because that was not practised much in post-exilic

Judah and so references to it would be somewhat irrelevant to his readers. We see Asa's faithfulness to the temple in vv.3 and 5. His faithfulness to the temple was a measure of his faithfulness to God. The importance of the temple was part of "the law and the commandment" of v.4. Verse 5 seems to contradict 1 Kings 15.14 about the high places. The high places that were removed here in v.5 have images linked with them. The high places in 1 Kings 15.14 that were not removed have no idols associated with them. So it appears that the high places where they worshipped the Lord only were spared (33.17). This same explanation can be given for 15.17: "But the high places were not taken away out of Israel". But for this verse the words "out of Israel" could refer to the fact that Asa did not have control of Israel. The verse in 14.5 is very specific - "he took away out of all the cities of Judah the high places and the images". This indicates that Asa's reform went beyond the principal cities to all the cities of Judah.

Verse 4 has the first mention in Asa's reign of his seeking God. In the three chapters we find this nine times (14.4,7,7; 15.2,4,12,13,15; 16.12). The Chronicler wants to encourage all his readers to seek God (see also 1 Chronicles 28.9; Jeremiah 29.13; Matthew 6.33). According to 1 Chronicles 28.9 seeking God is equivalent to knowing God and serving Him with a perfect heart and a willing mind.

Asa may have been in his early twenties when he began to reign. His father reigned for three years. Asa most likely saw the outstanding victory God gave to his father. That may have encouraged him to seek the Lord in his boyhood.

"There is a beautiful correlation between traditional faith and personal commitment in the phrase 'seek the Lord God of their fathers'. A new generation lays claim to a spiritual heritage and accepts the claims of the old faith in an ever-living God" (Leslie C. Allen). In most of Asa's years all that he did was rooted in knowing God and trusting Him. The Chronicler refers to "the Lord his God" in v.2. He himself speaks of "the Lord God of their fathers" in v.4, and "the Lord our God" in v.7. This is the second of four chapters that has the word "rely" five times, yet it occurs nowhere else in Chronicles. There is a relationship between seeking God and relying on God. Seeking God is more general, and relying on God is specific. Relying on God in times of crisis is most effective when it comes from those who are seeking Him.

At least in the first fifteen years of his reign (and possibly for thirty-five years), Asa acknowledged God in all his ways and was directed by Him in fulfillment of Proverbs 3.6: "In all thy ways acknowledge him, and he shall direct thy paths". He had the wisdom to build fortifications "while the land is yet before us" (v.7), i.e., while it was free from enemies. "He was no mere iconoclast. If he had the zeal to break down the images, he had also the wisdom to build fortified cities. To expose evil is very well, but to furnish the soul with truth is what protects it from the invasion of the enemy". (Knapp) The words in v.6, "in those years", refer to the ten years of v.1. This building program was a sign of God's blessing. Asa specifically strengthened the defences of Judah with walls, towers, gates, and bars. By slightly amending the Hebrew text some commentators translate v.7b as, "because we have sought the Lord our God…he has sought us".

The last sentence of v.7 states, "So they built and prospered". The people were inspired by Asa's words and by his example. There are significant instances of prospering or not prospering in the book of Chronicles. David encouraged Solomon to prosper (1 Chr 22.11,13). Solomon himself prospered in the beginning of his reign (1 Chr 29.23). Abijah warned the Northerners (2 Chr 13.12), "…for ye shall not prosper". Jehoshaphat encouraged his people in 2 Chronicles 20.20, "Believe in the Lord your God, so shall ye be established; believe his prophets, so shall ye prosper". Zechariah the son of Jehoida warned the people in 2 Chronicles 24.20, "Why transgress ye the commandments of the Lord, that ye cannot prosper?". 2 Chronicles 26.5 records concerning Uzziah that, "as long as he sought the Lord, God made him to prosper". 2 Chronicles 31.21 states about Hezekiah that "…he did it with all his heart, and prospered". 2 Chronicles 32.30 goes on to say that "Hezekiah prospered in all his works". 2 Chronicles 13.12 and 24.20 are warnings, but all the other verses encourage saints to prosper.

Interestingly, in v.8 the men of Judah were armed with spears as in 1 Chronicles 12.24 and the men of Benjamin were armed with bows as in 1 Chronicles 8.40; 12.2. They were all considered "mighty men of valour". Saints today can become mighty men and women for God spiritually by being "strengthened with might by his Spirit in the inner man" (Eph 3.16). The Holy Spirit especially strengthens us in prayer (Is 40.31; Ps 138.3) and the Word of God (1 Jn 2.14). We can be "strong in the Lord, and in the power of his might" (Eph 6.10), and we can "be strong in the grace that is in Christ Jesus" (2 Tim 2.1).

The mention of the total of his fighting men serves to show that when he was faced with Zerah the Ethiopian with a million men Asa was not depending on his army but on the Lord.

Verses 9-15: Asa's Victory over Zerah through his Reliance on God

The peace of the first eight verses is suddenly shattered. The Chronicler often writes of what commentators call "immediate retribution". But he does not always view enemies as agents of retribution from God. He has too realistic a view of life to do that. He observes reality too well to promise faithful believers that they will go through life "on flowery beds of ease".

Asa may have wondered why God had allowed this to happen. Many in Judah were trying to live godly lives and Asa himself had led an exemplary life. However, God did not intend this invasion as a punishment or a chastening. God allowed it to serve a totally different purpose, giving Asa an opportunity to express remarkable reliance on Him.

Crises come to most believers to a greater or lesser degree. God is well able to sustain when the difficulty comes. Every crisis is an opportunity to prove God's help in a fresh way.

The last seven verses of ch.14 tell of Asa relying on God. This is an encouragement to trust God in trouble, for He is able to meet any need, no matter how great the opposition. Believers are exhorted in Hebrews 4.16: "Let us therefore come boldly unto the throne of grace, that we may obtain mercy, and find grace to help in time of need".

Zerah comes with an intimidating army of a million men when Asa and Judah appear to be in a good spiritual condition. Mareshah (v.9) is 25 miles south-west of Jerusalem. It was one of the cities that Rehoboam fortified (11.8), "near the Via Maris, the coastal highway connecting Egypt and Canaan, making it strategically important" (The Nelson Study Bible, NKJV). In this crisis Asa went out against Zerah (v.10) and prayed a remarkable prayer (v.11). "He called upon the omnipotent God to help the powerless against the powerful" (Barber).

"He that sought God in the day of his prosperity could with holy boldness cry to God in the day of his trouble" (Matthew Henry). The Holy Spirit guided the Chronicler to write (v.11), "Asa cried unto the Lord his God". His words recall those of Jonathan to his armour-bearer in 1 Samuel 14.6: "...for there is no restraint to the Lord to save by many or by few". Those two won a great victory that day. The words of Asa's prayer, "in thy name we go against this multitude", bring to mind David's words to the giant Goliath in 1 Samuel 17.45, "I come to thee in the name of the Lord of hosts, the God of the armies of Israel, whom thou hast defied". What a marvelous triumph the boy David achieved that day! Asa's prayer expresses similar great confidence in God and great humility of mind. Instead of the word "rest" in "we rest on thee", the RV and ESV both have "rely". "'We rest on thee', he cries, and 'IN THY NAME we go...let not man prevail AGAINST THEE'. Is it any wonder that the deliverance granted is described in vv.12-15 in a similar strain: 'THE LORD SMOTE...they were destroyed BEFORE THE LORD, AND BEFORE HIS HOST'" (Rodgers)?

Rossier suggests that one of the two pillars before the temple named Boaz (which means "in him is strength") may have encouraged Asa to rely on the Lord who has strength available for those who trust Him, strength that is beyond the strength of any man. Asa's prayer is better known because of Edith G. Cherry's hymn, "We rest on Thee, our shield and our defender!". The hymn may have had much to do with the NKJV retaining the word "rest". In 6.34-35, Solomon prayed that the Lord would hear and answer His people's prayer in the time of battle. The Chronicler records several incidents that show God's response to His people's cries (13.14-18; 20.5-24; 1 Chr 5.20). 2 Chronicles 18.31 and 32.20-22 are the only ones also found in Kings but 18.31 gives more detail on Jehoshaphat's cry to the Lord when surrounded by enemies (1 Kings 22.32).

Alexander Maclaren notes concerning Asa's prayer: "The more humbly we think of our own capacity, the more wisely we shall think about God, and the more truly we shall estimate ourselves…So a profound self-distrust is our wisdom. But that should not paralyze us, but lead to something better, as it led Asa...Courageous advance should follow self-distrust and summoning God by faith…the all-powerful plea which God will answer… we may be quite sure of this, that if we have made God's cause ours, He will make our cause His, down to the minutest point in our daily lives".

Zerah's defeat was because of the faithfulness of Asa (14.2), and Shishak's victory over Judah was because of Rehoboam's sins (12.1-2).

"Secular history tells us nothing of this remarkable combat…The monuments, so they tell us, do not mention this extraordinary combat. For the believer, this silence is simple…And do you think that Zerah would proclaim his defeat? Have you ever found an inscription of Egypt, Syria, Moab, or Assyria where their kings recorded a defeat? On their part there is absolute silence. Later the king of Moab will proclaim his victories (on the Moabite stone), but not the defeat that preceded them. Such is the confidence that we can place in the authenticity of history written by man" (Rossier).

This is the second of four remarkable, miraculous deliverances that God gave to Judah which are recorded in 2 Chronicles (13.15-20; 20.22-24; 32.20-22). Only the last is also recorded in Kings. Here in v.12 we read, "So the Lord smote the Ethiopians". In v.13 "they were destroyed before the Lord, and before his host". We are not told how the Lord smote them and destroyed them, but this shows that the battle of God's people on this occasion was also the battle of the Lord Himself. The enemy fled to Gerar, 20 miles further south-west from Mareshah. Judah was able to smite all the cities round about Gerar "for the fear of the Lord came upon them" (v.14).

The spoils of Judah's victory were immense. Verse 13 says, "they carried away very much spoil". The RV has "booty". Verse 14 states that "there was exceeding much spoil in them". Verse 15 records that "They…carried away sheep and camels in abundance". Later, in 15.11 some of the spoil was offered in sacrifice to the Lord. In v.15, "the tents of cattle" refers to the living quarters of the cattle herders of that area. "The tents of cattle" and the "camels" in v.15 both indicate that nomadic herdsmen were associated with the Ethiopians. It is recorded in 16.8, NIV, that Libyans were included in Zerah's army. When the war was over they "returned to Jerusalem" (v.15). The Chronicler is interested in the facts of history, but he is much more interested (in these last seven verses) in giving encouragement to his readers to rely on the Lord in every crisis. God can give a similar victory in His will to helpless persons who rely on Him against any mighty enemy. No human or demonic forces can withstand God.

2 CHRONICLES 15

Asa's Reign

Introductory

Azariah the son of Oded met Asa and his army returning from the miraculous, God-given, victory over Zerah's host. He had a message of encouragement and of warning. It was timely and needed because God's people are in the greatest danger right after a victory. We should be most watchful even when the success is in response to relying on God. David is a sad example. The last three verses of 2 Samuel 10 tell of David's victory over Hadarezer and all the kings that were his servants. How sad to read of his moral fall in the next verses of ch.11. Asa's later history shows that he needed this warning; and all believers need the same encouragement and warning. No matter how well a Christian has gone on for God and no matter for how long, it is always necessary to heed the exhortation of 1 Corinthians 10.12, "Wherefore let him that thinketh he standeth take heed lest he fall". Saints are most vulnerable to a serious moral fall when they think they are invulnerable.

One should remember that this is the second of the two chapters that speak of Asa pleasing God. The events of the first 15 verses of this chapter are found only here in 2 Chronicles and not in Kings. The theme of seeking God is continued from ch.14. Seeking God is in the message (vv.2,4) and in the covenant (vv.12-13,15). It is stressed that the purpose of seeking God is to be found by Him (vv.2,14,15). Some commentators translate the verse as, "He will let himself be found of you".

Ever since the first parents of the human race sinned, God has been the prime seeker. God seeks individuals more than individuals seek Him. Romans 3.11 states, "There is none that seeketh after God". Persons only seek God after He has first been seeking them. The New Testament encourages people to seek God (Lk 13.24; Acts 17.27). Our Lord Jesus came to "seek and to save that which was lost" (Lk 19.10). He also states in John 4.23, "…the Father seeketh such to worship him". Of course we are then to seek Him. The Lord Jesus encourages us, in Matthew 6.33, "But seek ye first the kingdom of God, and his righteousness; and all these things shall be added unto you", and in 7.7, "seek, and ye shall find". Christians are thankful that God "is a rewarder of them that diligently seek him" (Heb 11.6). James encourages believers similarly in James 4.8: "Draw nigh to God and he will draw nigh to you". Saints should be careful to put away from their lives anything that hinders fellowship with God. Christians can say from experience like Asaph of old in Psalm 73.28, "But it is good for me to draw near to God". Thanks be to God that believers can have boldness (confidence) "to enter into the holiest by the blood of Jesus" (Heb 10.19). It is all because of the infinite value of the sacrifice of Christ on the cross.

Outline of Chapter 15

Verses 1-7: Azariah's message.
Verses 8-15: Asa's further reformation and covenant.
Verses 16-19: Asa's grandmother Maachah, the queen mother, removed.

Verses 1-7: Azariah's Message

This Azariah is mentioned only here. The Spirit of God came upon him to give a message, even as the Spirit of the Lord came upon Jahaziel in 20.14. Azariah deliberately went out to meet Asa and his army returning from the victory. He spoke with assurance, courage and authority, beginning with, "Hear ye me, Asa". The prophets of God are commanded in Jeremiah 23.28 to speak His Word faithfully. Azariah and Paul are good examples. Paul could tell the elders of Ephesus in Acts 20.27, "For I have not shunned to declare unto you all the counsel of God".

Azariah's message has three main points.

1. A statement that "if ye seek him, he will be found of you" (v.2b).

2. An exposition of illustrations from history, probably especially from Judges (vv.3-6).

3. An appeal by an exhortation and a promise (v.7).

The statement is based on Deuteronomy 4.29; 1 Chronicles 28.9; Isaiah 55.6; and Jeremiah 29.13-14. There is a warning that if they forsake Him He will forsake them. There is also a positive encouragement in the very first phrase of his message, "The Lord is with you, while ye be with him".

The exposition in vv.3-6 seems to draw illustrations from the book of Judges. Verse 3 appears to refer to the troubled periods when they did not regard, God or His law. The law existed just as God existed but the law was not taught - they had been "without a teaching priest". There were times when they had priests, but they did not have any priest that taught. Teaching was a responsibility of the priests (Lev 10.11; Deut 33.10; Mal 2.7). How important it is for God's people to be taught. Hosea 4.6 states, "My people are destroyed for lack of knowledge". Jeremiah makes a remarkable statement on behalf of God about the prophets who spoke without God sending them, "But if they had stood in my counsel, and had caused my people to hear my words, then they should have turned them from their evil way, and from the evil of their doings" (23.22).

It is important for every believer to be taught from the Word of God. Every teacher has a responsibility to obey the exhortation of 2 Timothy 4.2 - "Preach the word". All teaching should be based on God's Word. Every believer should be able to test all that they hear by the Word of God. If it agrees with God's Word we accept it, but if it does not, we should not accept it. "Prove all things; hold fast that which is good" (1 Thess 5.21).

We are reminded in v.4 that the book of Judges has a fourfold emphasis throughout - sinning, suffering or servitude, supplication, and salvation. This is similar to the Chronicler's emphasis of the promise of 7.14. The first part of v.5 calls to mind the words of Judges 5.6, "...the highways were unoccupied, and travellers walked through byways". Verses 5-6 tell of troubled times when they departed from God. When they did not turn to God things got worse and worse.

"Those difficult times were a consequence of having forsaken the Lord. God permitted those acts in order to compel His people to seek Him. When they did, He helped them" (Barber).

Here in Azariah's message he used past history as an incentive to living for God in the present. Paul was guided by the Holy Spirit to do the same in 1 Corinthians 10.1-11.

"Just as Azariah is exhorting pre-exilic Judah by referring to the past, so implicitly the Chronicler is challenging post-exilic Judah and preaching his own sermon via Azariah's. The proclaimed word spans the centuries, living and powerful (Heb 4.12)" (Leslie C. Allen). "One of the most encouraging aspects of the Chronicler's theology is his insistence upon the openness of God to receive back his wayward children, even after great apostasy. And he is no less willing if any should return to him only because they have exhausted all other possibilities" (McConville). The word "departure" would be better than the word "apostasy" in the above quote because no true child of God can ever apostatise.

Verse 7 gives the appeal with an exhortation and a promise. The exhortation to be strong is often found in the Word of God (Deut 31.6-7,23; Josh 1.6-7,9; 1 Chr 22.13; 28.10,20; 2 Chr 32.7; Hag 2.4; Zech 8.9,13; Eph 6.10 and 2 Tim 2.1). Often it is linked with being of good courage. In Joshua 1.6, Joshua was to be of good courage to dispossess seven great nations and divide the land. God knew that he would need even greater courage to observe to do according to all the law (in v.7) so God told him there to be "very courageous". After a lifetime of experience Joshua knew that God's people would need to be "very courageous to keep and to do all that is written in the book of the law of Moses" (Josh 23.6).

For v.7 JND has, "But as for you, be firm and let not your hands be weak". That translation helps to emphasize that Azariah wanted Asa and all of God's people to profit from the mistakes of history.

The appeal finishes with a promise: "for your work shall be rewarded". This is almost identical to Jeremiah 31.16: "...for thy work shall be rewarded". The exhortation and the promise call to mind the exhortation and the promise of 1 Corinthians 15.58: "Therefore, my beloved brethren, be ye steadfast, unmovable, always abounding in the work of the Lord, forasmuch as ye know that your labour is not in vain in the Lord".

Verses 8-15: Asa's Further Reformation and Covenant

In v.8 for "Oded the prophet", the margin of the NKJV has, "Following Masoretic Text and Septuagint, Syriac and Vulgate read, 'Azariah, the son of Oded' (compare v.1)". The ESV has "Azariah the son of Oded". Asa responded enthusiastically to the prophecy, took courage and continued more fully the work of reformation, which he had already begun. This time he not only removed idols out of Judah and Benjamin but also out of the cities he had taken from Mount Ephraim. The Hebrew word for "be ye strong" in the exhortation of v.7 is (CHAZAQ – 2388). It is the same Hebrew word used in Asa's response in v.8, "he took courage".

It is probable that Azariah's message gave Asa the necessary spiritual strength and courage to remove his grandmother from her position as queen mother and destroy her idol (v.16).

He also "renewed the altar of the Lord". This is the same altar upon which Solomon offered burnt offerings to the Lord in 8.12, but does not necessarily imply that there was an earlier desecration. After over 50 years of use the altar needed some maintenance that may have been deferred. This calls to mind Elijah who, in 1 Kings 18.30, "repaired the altar of the Lord".

"Asa 'renewed the altar of the Lord (v.8)'. I have no doubt that here is a matter, as in many other passages, of renewing the sacrifices regularly offered on the altar according to the law...Wherever we find true and energetic separation from the defilement of the world, it does not take long for the worship of God's children to resume its honoured place" (Rossier).

It is delightful to read in v.9 that "they fell to him out of Israel in abundance, when they saw the Lord his God was with him". "Their coming was a great encouragement to him, for the reason of their coming was because 'they saw that the Lord his God was with him'...the invitation he gave them to the general assembly (was) a great encouragement to them" (Matthew Henry).

This is the second correct way described in Chronicles to bring God's people together. The first was individual exercise (11.13-14) on the part of priests and Levites who willingly sacrificed further by leaving their suburbs and their possessions because of conviction based on the Word of God. Those priests and Levites were living out the truth of Proverbs 23.23: "Buy the truth, and sell it not". The cost of truth never exceeds its value. Their good example had a good effect on others. "And after them out of all the tribes of Israel such as set their hearts to seek the Lord God of Israel came to Jerusalem to sacrifice unto the Lord God of their fathers" (11.16). The third and last right way is described in 30.1-11 where Hezekiah sent wise letters to invite all the twelve tribes to the Passover. Some were too proud to accept the invitation but a number "humbled themselves, and came to Jerusalem" (30.10-11).

"The Lord his God was with him" brings to mind Genesis 39, which is very encouraging. There it is stated of Joseph four times that the Lord was with him. Acts 7.9 reads, "And the patriarchs, moved with envy, sold Joseph into Egypt: but God was with him". The fact that God was with him made a very great difference in Joseph's life. We read in Genesis 39.2 that in Potiphar's house "the Lord was with Joseph". Verse 3 tells us that "his master saw that the Lord was with him, and that the Lord made all that he did to prosper in his hand". How good it is when saints have God with them to such an extent that even their unsaved employers can see it. Joseph was unjustly put in prison but the Lord was still with him (v.21). Verse 23 reads, "The keeper of the prison looked not to anything that was under his hand; because the Lord was with him, and that which he did, the Lord made it to prosper".

"The Lord his God was with him" is also a feature of David in 1 Samuel 18. We read there in v.12, "And Saul was afraid of David, because the Lord was with him, and was departed from Saul". The previous verse records that Saul twice tried to kill David with a javelin. Verse 14 records, "And David behaved himself wisely in all his ways; and the Lord was with him". The Lord being with David enabled him to behave himself very wisely (vv.14-15). The last part of that verse states that when Saul saw that, he was afraid of David. Later on in the same chapter, vv.28-29 record: "And Saul saw and knew that the Lord was with David, and that Michal Saul's daughter loved him. And Saul was yet the more afraid of David". In summary, three times in 1 Samuel 18 the Lord was with David and three times (as a result) Saul was afraid of him. That record is also an encouragement to us to seek the Lord so that we can have His presence with us.

The name of Simeon here in v.9 is a little puzzling. Simeon seems to have been included as one of the northern tribes in 1 Kings 11.31. Their territory at the first was to the south of Judah (Josh 19.1-9; 1 Chr 4.24-43). Some of the Simeonites may have been assimilated with Judah, but some of them must have migrated north because in 34.6 they seem to be in the north and here in v.9 these Simeonites seem to have come from the north. Certainty is not possible at present.

In v.10 they gathered together in Jerusalem in the third month of Asa's fifteenth year for a covenant ceremony. The third month seems to show that this assembly was probably part of the Feast of Weeks or Pentecost, which was one of the three in the year which all the males were to attend (Ex 23.14-17; 34.22-24; Lev 23.15-21; Deut 16.9-10,16). "The Chronicler possibly intended to make a connection with the Feast of Weeks because of the verbal similarity in Hebrew between 'weeks' (shabuot) and the verb 'swear' (shaba) which is prominent in vv.14-15" (Thompson).

This assembly is typical of those of other kings in Chronicles, including David (1 Chr 13.2-5; 15.3; 28.8; 29.1ff), Solomon (2 Chr 1.3; 5.6), Jehoshaphat (2 Chr 20.4-5,18), Hezekiah (2 Chr 29.28; 30.2,25), and Josiah (2 Chr 34.30,32; 35.18). "This no doubt reflects the importance of the assembly in the period from Ezra and Nehemiah onwards (e.g. Ezra 3.1; 10.12; Neh 8.1ff; 13.1), and witness to the significant role played by the people as in this covenant ceremony (cp. v.13)" (Selman).

They offered to the Lord generously out of the spoil that they had taken 700 oxen and 7,000 sheep (v.11). God by His grace had given His people the victory. It was only fitting that out of the spoils they should glorify God with this generous offering.

Verses.12-15 record the covenant that they all made "with all their heart and with all their soul" (v.12). Those same words are almost identically repeated in v.15. Since v.12 in the RV refers to the covenant (because the Hebrew does have the article), this covenant may refer to the Sinai covenant of Exodus 19.5-8. If so, the tradition of the Sinai covenant was being applied to new circumstances. Commentators are not all agreed on this. Some consider it as a binding agreement to follow the king in seeking God. The king's command in 14.4 is now honoured enthusiastically. Here, seeking God is equal to a total commitment to God individually and collectively. There was not only an individual responsibility to a total commitment but also a corporate responsibility to keep the covenant intact by exacting the maximum penalty on the covenant breakers. It is possible that (in their zeal) Asa and the people of Judah went too far in their reform, even to an extreme, when they decreed that anyone who would not seek the Lord God of Israel should be put to death.

The penalty of death (v.13) seems harsh to us but it is as stated in Deuteronomy 13.6-10 and 17.2-7. We have no evidence that this was ever carried out. In spiritual terms, "It signifies that they would henceforth put the judgment of God's Word upon everything that did not honour and glorify him" (Haldeman).

The New Testament also states that some should be excluded from a local assembly (1 Cor 5). Anyone guilty of any of the sins listed in v.11 of that chapter should be put away with a view to their restoration to God and the assembly. This is vastly different from putting to death! Yet both Testaments agree that a commitment to God is very solemn.

They confirmed the covenant with an oath, as we have it in Deuteronomy 29.12,14 and Nehemiah 10.29. The loud voice, the shouting, the trumpets, and the cornets in v.14 seem to be normal at such an important religious celebration. There were three more musical instruments in 1 Chronicles 15.28 to make noise when they brought the ark up to Jerusalem to its rightful place. "The importance of the occasion probably also explains the reminder of the time of David and Solomon. The acclamation and rejoicing (vv.14-15) are linked with David (1 Chr 15.25,28), and rest on every side with Solomon (1 Chr 22.9,18)" (Selman). "And all Judah rejoiced at the oath". We also read of joy or rejoicing in 1 Chronicles 15.25; 16.10; 2 Chronicles 23.13,18,21; 30.25, and "great joy" in 1 Chronicles 29.9 and 2 Chronicles 30.26. The writer of the Chronicles takes notice that the Lord matched the wholehearted response of the king and the people with His own favourable response.

Alexander Maclaren writes on 2 Chronicles 15.15 in a piece entitled, "The Search that Always Finds": "The words express in simplest form what should be the chief desire of our heart and occupation of our lives...But our text lays emphasis on the wholeheartedness of the people's seeking God... We are not required to seek nothing else in order to seek God wholly... but He does ask that the dominant desire after Him should be powerful enough to express itself through all our actions, and that we should seek for God in them, and for them in God...the one token of it which the text specifies is, casting out our idols. There must be detachment if there is to be attachment...To seek him with the whole heart is to engage the whole of self in the quest, and that is the only kind of seeking which has the certainty of success...Whilst to seek is to find him, in a very deep and blessed sense, even in this life; in another aspect all our earthly life may be regarded as seeking after Him, and the future as the true finding of Him".

Verses 16-19: Asa's Grandmother Maachah, the Queen Mother, Removed

Since Maachah was Abijah's mother (11.20-22), she was really Asa's grandmother. The same Hebrew word for mother is also used for grandmother. The importance sometimes attained by a queen mother is seen in other women - for example, Bathsheba, Jezebel, and Athaliah. Since Asa's mother may have died at a young age, that would increase his grandmother's influence. The Hebrew word for "idol" (used only for her idol - here and at 1 Kings 15.13) suggests the possibility of it being something horribly obscene, something shockingly repulsive. The writer of the Chronicles approvingly records that Asa's loyalty to God was greater than his loyalty to his grandmother. He took from his grandmother the honour and dignity that she had as queen mother and burnt her idol at the brook Kidron. Asa is the first king recorded as destroying idols. After Asa, other idols were so dealt with (2 Kings 23.4-6,12; 2 Chr 29.16; 30.14). Since Maachah had an idol, she certainly was not seeking the Lord God of their fathers as they had covenanted to do (vv.12-15). After her idol was destroyed, she may have agreed to seek the Lord and thus avoided being put to death; but the Chronicler does not say so.

Asa is to be commended for removing his grandmother from being queen mother and destroying her idol. William Rodgers wrote, "Maachah had got doing pretty much as she liked in the reign of her husband Rehoboam (11.21-22), and in that of her own son Abijah (13.2), so it must have required more than ordinary firmness on the part of her grandson Asa to oust her from her long held position as head of the royal household, and to smash her favourite idol". This is the most outstanding evidence of Asa's reformation. He made no allowances for natural ties when God's honour was involved. He had already displayed that good trait by destroying all the idols his fathers had made (1 Kings 15.12). His action is in keeping with the later teaching of our Lord Jesus in Luke 14.26: "If any man come to me, and hate not his father, and mother, and wife, and children, and brethren, and sisters, yea, and his own life also, he cannot be my disciple". Since He also taught elsewhere love for our enemies (Mt 5.44), "hate" has to be taken in comparison to love for the Lord Jesus. Matthew 10.37 makes this clear: "He that loveth father or mother more than me is not worthy of me: and he that loveth son or daughter more than me is not worthy of me".

The sons of Levi answered Moses' call in Exodus 32.26 after the camp was defiled by idolatry: "Who is on the Lord's side?". About 3,000 men (including relatives) were slain that day by the sons of Levi (v.28-29). God's appreciation is shown in the blessing of the tribe of Levi in Deuteronomy 33.8-11.

Before the Lord used Gideon to deliver his people from the Midianites, He wanted him to begin by destroying his father's altar of Baal and the grove that was by it and by using the wood to offer his father's bullock on an altar to the Lord his God. He was afraid to do it by day so he did it at night (Judg 6.25-27).

It is very important that all assembly decisions should be made without preferential treatment of relatives. In 1 Timothy 5.21 Paul wrote, "I charge thee before God, and the Lord Jesus Christ, and the elect angels, that thou observe these things without preferring one before another, doing nothing by partiality". This makes clear that not only do God the Father and the Lord Jesus Christ know, but even the elect angels know if anything is done with partiality.

Verse 17 may seem to contradict 14.3 in relation to Asa destroying the high places. Verse 14.3 tells of the idols connected with the high places, whereas v.17 has no mention of them. This indicates that those high places were places where they worshipped the Lord their God only (33.17). It is also possible that the Chronicler inserted in v.17 the words, "out of Israel", to indicate that Asa did not remove the high places from the cities of the northern kingdom over which he had no control. That is clearly the meaning of "out of Israel" in 15.9. In contrast 14.5 says explicitly, "out of all the cities of Judah".

When v.17 says that "the heart of Asa was perfect all his days", it does not mean that Asa was morally perfect. For the Chronicler soon afterwards (16.1-10,12) records some serious transgressions by this king. The expression only means that Asa was free from idolatry (1 Kings 15.14). 1 Kings 11.4 states that Solomon's "heart was not perfect with the Lord his God, as was the heart of David his father", when his heart turned away after other gods. So David was perfect in the same way that Asa was perfect.

Asa enriched the house of God (v.18) by bringing into it the things his father had dedicated. This was probably the booty taken when Abijah defeated Jeroboam as described in 13.16-20. The things that Asa himself dedicated probably came from the booty taken when he defeated Zerah and his allies (14.13-15). This was very becoming since it was God Himself who enabled Abijah and Asa to be victorious.

Verse 19 is reconcilable with 1 Kings 15.16, "And there was war between Asa and Baasha king of Israel all their days". Kings refers to what we would call today a "cold war" existing constantly between them. 2 Chronicles refers to no open conflict, in keeping with the last phrase of 15.15: "the Lord gave them rest round about". It is more difficult to reconcile the 35th year of Asa in v.19 and the 36th year of Asa in 16.1, since Baasha died in Asa's 26th year (1 Kings 15.33; 16.8). A possible solution will be discussed in the comments on 16.1.

2 CHRONICLES 16

Asa's Reign

Introductory

This chapter is in stark contrast to the previous two. Chapters 14 and 15 show the great spiritual height to which Asa attained, but chapter 16 shows how far he fell. In the first two chapters describing the early part of his reign we see him strong in relying on God but in this chapter we see him weak in relying on human aid. Jeremiah wrote years later, "Thus saith the Lord; Cursed be the man that trusteth in man, and maketh flesh his arm, and whose heart departeth from the Lord" (Jer 17.5). It seems difficult to understand such a change in Asa. Surely the Chronicler meant this chapter as a warning just as chapters 14 and 15 were an encouragement to trust God. Asa began so well and ended so poorly. Knapp writes, "His end was as humiliating as his beginning had been brilliant". Surely all need to take heed to 1 Corinthians 10.12: "Wherefore let him that thinketh he standeth take heed lest he fall". George Muller is said often to have prayed, "Lord; let me not die a wicked old man".

There is a serious chronological difficulty in the first verse. It says that Baasha came up against Judah in the thirty-sixth year of the reign of Asa. 1 Kings 16.8 shows that Elah the son of Baasha began to reign in the twenty-sixth year of the reign of Asa (right after his father had died), indicating that Baasha had died about ten years before the thirty-sixth year of Asa's reign! Kiel writes, "The older commentators, for the most part, accepted the conjecture that the thirty-fifth year (in 15.19) is to be reckoned from the commencement of the kingdom of Judah; and consequently, since Asa became king in the twentieth year of the kingdom of Judah, Baasha's invasion occurred in the sixteenth year of his reign, and the land had enjoyed peace till his fifteenth year". In support of this theory, the Hebrew word MALKUT (4438) is often translated "kingdom" as in 2 Chronicles 1.1; 2.1; 7.18; 11.17; 12.1; 33.13; Ezra 1.1; and Nehemiah 9.35. It is translated "realm" in 2 Chronicles 20.30 and Daniel 1.20.

Thiele has popularized this view so that some modern commentators refer to his book, *The Mysterious Numbers of the Hebrew Kings*. It is not always realized that Keil knew about this theory years before Thiele wrote. This is one possible solution and it does avoid the necessity of amending the text. But Dillard's first objection to this idea is formidable: "Of the hundreds of bits of data for the chronology of the divided monarchy, this would be the only occasion of dating from the schism. It would be unique to this passage and therefore, a case of 'special pleading' to appeal to it".

Another possible solution, first given by Keil, prefers to regard the number "thirty-five" in 2 Chronicles 15.19 and the number "thirty-six" in 16.1 as a copyist's error for "fifteen" and "sixteen" respectively. Archer (who is the most thorough and the most satisfying in dealing with this problem) also prefers this solution. He points out that, "if the number was written in numerical notation of the Hebrew alphabetic type (rather than the Egyptian multiple-stroke type used in the Elephantine Papyri), then 'sixteen' could quite easily be confused with 'thirty-six'. The reason for this is that up through the seventh century BC the letter *yod* (=10) greatly resembled the letter *lamed* (=30), except for two tiny strokes attached to the left of the main vertical stroke".

If this is the true solution for the discrepancy it would be similar to 2 Chronicles 36.9, which gives the age of Jehoiachin as eight at the time he began to reign, whereas the parallel passage in 2 Kings 24.8 gives the true age as "eighteen". Another similar instance is in 2 Chronicles 22.2, which gives the age of Ahaziah, the son of Jehoram, as "forty-two" when he began to reign, whereas 2 Kings 8.26 gives the correct age as "twenty-two".

Edersheim also considers this the only satisfactory solution. He writes, "There is manifestly here a copyist's mistake, and the numeral which we would substitute for 35 is not 15 (as by most German commentators) but 25 - and this for reasons too long to explain".

Edersheim's suggestion of substituting 25 for 35 in 15.19 seems to be the best solution. That would also mean that 26 would be substituted for 36 in 16.1.

Asa's very poor response to the rebuke of Hanani indicates that in the last years of his life he was away from God. Asa had done so well in seeking God as shown by chapters 14 and 15, but of the last three years of his life, when the disease of his feet became very severe, v.12 states, "yet in his disease he sought not to the Lord, but to the physicians".

Since he died in his 41st year, it is far easier to believe that godly Asa was away from God for 15 years rather than 25 years (which it would be if 15 is a substitute for 35). Asa is the only godly king who had a godly son, Jehoshaphat, who began to reign when he was 35 (20.31).

Since Asa was only away from God for 15 years, then 20 years of godly reign could have been a good influence on Jehoshaphat. The "very great burning for him" in 16.14 was an honour given to him most likely in appreciation for the first 26 years of his life, rather than just 16. Having said this, while God knew the exact state of his heart, the people of Judah were certainly not as discerning of his departure from God.

Outline of Chapter 16

Verses 1-6: War with Baasha.
Verses 7-10: Hanani's message.
Verses 11-14: Conclusion of Asa's reign.

Verses 1-6: War with Baasha

These verses parallel 1 Kings 15.17-22. Baasha had been continuously hostile and now he is especially stirred up against Asa, probably because so many of his people defected to him (15.9). Rossier helpfully comments,

"This principle occurs again and again: those who, like Baasha, still maintain a profession of true religion, though mixed with deadly error, cannot tolerate near them a testimony which attracts souls". Baasha built Ramah (v.1) which is five or six miles north of Jerusalem. By doing this he effectively stopped all movement into Judah from the north and all movement toward the north out of Jerusalem. Asa was right in wanting to take action, but the action he took was shocking.

"Jeremiah 41.9 refers to a pit (or cistern) made by Asa 'for fear of Baasha king of Israel'. God would thus, in this incidental way, remind us by this late and last historical notice of King Asa what was the beginning of his decline - 'The fear of man (which) bringeth a snare' (Prov 29.25)" (Knapp). In v.2 Asa took silver and gold out of the treasures of the house of the Lord and out of the king's house. The Kings account significantly says that he took all the gold and the silver that was left (1 Kings 15.18). Asa gave up the results of his own piety described in 2 Chronicles 15.18, and the blessing of God of 14.13-14. These things all belonged to God but Asa gave them to a heathen king to try to get him to break his league with Baasha. Believers should be careful that they do not give time, treasures, and talents that belong to God to someone else. Ben-hadad was wrong to break his league with Baasha and Asa was wrong to try to get him to do it. The most serious downfall of Asa was in giving up his trust in the Lord and putting his trust in a mere man.

The RV margin and the NIV have for the opening words of v.3: "Let there be...". This is the first time the Word of God tells us of any king calling on a heathen power against his brethren. This is also the first time we learn of a league between Abijah and Ben-hadad's father. Evidently Baasha had first succeeded in getting the king of Syria to break his league with Abijah, Asa's father. Now Asa wanted the king of Syria to break his league with Baasha. Ben-hadad was agreeable to the plan and the price and so he attacked Israel from the north and caused Baasha to stop building Ramah (vv.4-5). Ben-hadad showed by his reaction that he was fickle and ready to accept the bid most favourable to him.

The first phrase in v.6 is more concise than the parallel in Kings. Here we have, "Then Asa the king took all Judah". 1 Kings 15.22 has more detail: "Then king Asa made a proclamation throughout all Judah; none was exempted". This indicates that Asa made a thorough conscription to dismantle the fortification of Ramah and used the material for two fortifications of his choice, one at Geba and one at Mizpah.

Verses 7-10: Hanani's Message

These verses are altogether omitted in Kings. This is one of the most important additions to Asa's history given by the writer of the Chronicles. Hanani courageously faced King Asa, the most influential person in Judah, to rebuke him for relying on the king of Syria instead of relying on the Lord his God. There are other records of prophets rebuking kings. Samuel spoke against Saul in 1 Samuel 13.13-14 and 15.14-29. Nathan spoke against David in 2 Samuel 12.1-14, and Gad also spoke against him (24.11-14). Shemaiah spoke against Rehoboam (2 Chr 11.2-4; 12.5). In later years Isaiah spoke against Hezekiah (Is 39.3-7), and Jeremiah spoke against Jehoiakim (Jer 36.27-32), Coniah (Jer 22.24-30), and Zedekiah (Jer 21.3-7; 2 Chr 36.12). The most famous instance of a prophet warning a king not to trust in political alliances is found in Isaiah 7 when the prophet warned Ahaz to trust the Lord rather than trust the king of Assyria. That chapter contains the well-known "Immanuel" passage.

Asa may have congratulated himself that his expedient had worked so well. We should understand that just because a course of action is successful, it does not necessarily mean that it is right in the eyes of God. He had succeeded in getting a good result but at what a cost materially and spiritually. He missed the much better result that God intended, i.e. a defeat of Syria as well as Israel - "therefore is the host of the king of Syria escaped out of thine hand" (v.7). Asa had missed a wonderful opportunity. Hanani's rebuke was intensified by a contrast with Asa's earlier victory over two enemies (v.8). "Since the Libyans are not mentioned in the earlier account (14.9-15), the mention of both here suggests understanding Hanani's speech as implying victory over two foes as well" (Dillard).

Verse 9 explains why he was victorious before, and why he could have been victorious again by trusting the Lord. To enable his readers to understand, Hanani vividly likens God to a human being with eyes. He describes the eyes of the Lord as searching throughout the whole world to help those who rely upon Him. Hanani's sharpest rebuke follows immediately: "Herein thou hast done foolishly". Samuel said the same to Saul in 1 Samuel 13.13. How sad to read Asa's response (v.10) - he was "wroth with the seer", and "in a rage with him". Saddest of all, Asa had him put in a prison house. This considerable blot tarnished his character.

From the time of Saul, the first king of Israel, prophets had given to kings messages, some of which were rebukes, but never before had a king punished a prophet. Later Micaiah was put in prison (18.26) as was Jeremiah (Jer 20.2). Even worse, Zechariah the son of Jehoiada the priest was stoned to death (24.20-22) and Urijah (who prophesied in the name of the Lord) was killed by king Jehoiakim (Jer 26.20-23). How solemn it is that such a good king as Asa did this to Hanani and oppressed some of the people at the same time. Even today it is possible for a teacher of Scripture to be put into a figurative prison and made to feel it in one way or another for the "crime" of giving a message from God that is resented.

While Barber's book on 2 Chronicles is of great value, it seems in error here in doubting that God sent Hanani to rebuke king Asa (in vv.7-9). He writes, "Was he truly delivering the word of the Lord or did he presume that inasmuch as he still held prophetic office God would still use him?". Again, it seems wrongly, he writes, "Was Hanani's rebuke really the word of the Lord to Asa or was Hanani claiming that his own sentiments were an expression of God's will?". Similarly, it seems wrong to suggest that "he ignored all the good Asa had done". Verse 8, coming from Hanani's lips, is all complimentary concerning Asa's wonderful reliance on God when there were a million Ethiopians against Judah. Verse 9 is one of the best loved verses of 2 Chronicles: "For the eyes of the Lord run to and fro throughout the whole earth, to shew himself strong in the behalf of those whose heart is perfect toward him". Surely these are the words of the Lord rather than simply those of Hanani himself.

There is a good likelihood that Baker is also wrong about Hanani's predicted wars. "But what of the predicted wars? They never came. Did the prophet speak on his own authority? It would appear as if he did, leaving us to wonder if the Lord really sent him". There are three verses that speak about wars between Rehoboam and Jeroboam continually (1 Kings 14.30; 15.6; 2 Chr 12.15). There was war between Abijah and Jeroboam (2 Chr 13.2). There are also two verses that write about war between Asa and Baasha all their days (1 Kings 15.16,32). While we do not have any later record of war between Judah and Israel, yet most students believe that there was trouble between the two countries until Jehoshaphat "joined affinity with Ahab" (18.1). Even in the first part of the reign of Jehoshaphat, he felt it necessary to strengthen himself against Israel (17.1). Barber over-emphasizes how discouraging Hanani's message was to Asa, but in reality v.8 was an encouragement for Asa to rely again on the Lord as he had marvelously done before (14.11). Verse 9 is a real encouragement for saints of all ages to trust God.

Corrective ministry should be given in the same way that the speaker would like to receive it. That would be carrying out the golden rule our Lord Jesus gave in Matthew 7.12: "Therefore all things whatsoever ye would that men should do to you, do ye even so to them". Otherwise the ministry will be counter-productive. 2 Corinthians 2 and 7 especially show how much love the Apostle Paul had for the Corinthians when he wrote his first epistle to them, so full of correction. He was so concerned for them that he sent Titus to find out how they had responded. When Paul got to Troas and a door was opened to him of the Lord, he had no rest in his spirit because he could not find Titus. So he went on to Macedonia (2.12-13). That unfinished story has its sequel in 7.5-11. Paul had been cast down, but God comforted him with the news that Titus brought about the Corinthians. They had made things right.

That justifies two balancing statements. On the one hand, it would be a good thing if all corrective ministry (all need correction sometimes) was given out with some of the love which the Apostle Paul showed for the Corinthians. On the other hand, it would be wonderful if all corrective ministry was received as the Corinthians received it, for they made things right. These two things are not always true.

Verses 11-14: Conclusion of Asa's Reign

Although these verses are based on, and remain in substantial agreement with, 1 Kings 15.23-24, the Chronicler has rewritten this paragraph. Verse 11 is the first time in 2 Chronicles that the Chronicler gives his most important literary source - "the book of the kings of Judah and Israel". It is mentioned also in 1 Chronicles 9.1. This source cannot be our present 1 and 2 Kings (that has only a small part of the material on Asa found in Chronicles), and is now lost. In the following chapters this title or similar titles occur several times (20.34; 24.27; 25.26; 27.7; 28.26; 32.32; 33.18; 35.27; 36.8). In the parallel portion in 1 Kings 15.23 we read of, "the book of the chronicles of the kings of Judah". But never once in any of these other nine references does the writer of the Chronicles refer to the kings of Judah alone. Whenever we read of the kings of Judah we also read of Israel. In this way the historian wanted to show that Judah was part of the inclusive Israel, which he considered an ideal.

Verse 12 tells us that in his 39th year Asa "was diseased in his feet, until his disease was exceeding great". The Chronicler does not make it clear what the disease was, but he does stress that Asa should have taken it as a warning from God. All illness is not a warning from God, but it should exercise the hearts of saints as to its cause. Conventional medicine and skill can bring recovery but all healing ultimately has God as its source (Ps 103.3). Paul referred to Luke as "the beloved physician" in Colossians 4.14, making it obvious that he availed himself of Luke's God-given medical abilities.

Asa failed to seek God in his military crisis but not only then. He also failed to seek God in his personal crisis. In both cases he relied on human aid instead of relying on God. He had done so well in seeking the Lord in his earlier years. Now he is not condemned for going to physicians, but he is condemned for going to physicians without seeking God at all in the matter. The writer of the Chronicles is amazed that Asa did not turn to the Lord when he was so seriously ill. Hezekiah, who excelled in trusting the Lord (2 Kings 18.5), is a good example of how one who trusts should react in serious sickness (2 Kings 20.1-3). Even in the miraculous cure of Hezekiah means were used (2 Kings 20.7), showing that it is not wrong to use such methods so long as one seeks God first. Every saint should be exercised by any chastening that God sends into their lives (Heb 12.11).

Asa displayed in this instance the same mind he had already manifested when Baasha came against him, "a state of mind which Bengal rightly characterizes as theoretical orthodoxy combined with practical atheism" (Edersheim).

Verse 13 states that Asa died in his 41st year. When he began to reign, Jeroboam was reigning over Israel. During Asa's reign he saw six other kings of Israel in power: Nadab, Baasha, Elah, Zimri, Omri, and Ahab. These represented four rival dynasties.

The Chronicler has much more information (v.14) about Asa's burial than does the writer of Kings. "The use of the plural - 'sepulchres' - will not seem strange, if we remember that a tomb in Judæa was ordinarily an excavation in the solid rock containing a number of cells each capable of holding a body" (Rawlinson). The "very great burning" was not cremation but rather was a bonfire of some kind in honour of King Asa. Cremation was only used in extraordinary circumstances (1 Sam 31.12). Both 2 Chronicles 21.19 and Jeremiah 34.5 indicate that it was usual to have a burning at the burial service of a king. Even though Asa finished so badly, he was one of Judah's best kings and the people honoured him at his burial. Jehoshaphat, another of Judah's good kings, followed Asa. Asa's best years (when relying on God) had a good influence on his son. No other Judæan king did as well in following his father in virtue as Jehoshaphat.

2 CHRONICLES 17

Jehoshaphat's reign

Introductory

Chronicles devotes four chapters to Jehoshaphat and almost as many verses as in the four chapters given over to Hezekiah. The section on Hezekiah is longer than that for any other Judæan king. Jehoshaphat therefore must be one of the most important characters to the Chronicler.

Jehoshaphat illustrates the folly of an unequal yoke. The exhortation of 2 Corinthians 6.14, "Be ye not unequally yoked together with unbelievers", is followed by five questions that all expect a negative answer and all enforce the leading exhortation. William Rodgers suggests that those five questions hint successively at business life, social life, political life, matrimonial life, and religious life. Jehoshaphat entered into each of these unequal yokes to some degree. The Chronicler records four of them. There was a marriage involving an unequal yoke when Jehoshaphat's son, Jehoram, married Athaliah, the daughter of two wicked parents, Ahab and Jezebel (18.1). This led to a social unequal yoke, in 18.2, when sheep and oxen were killed by Ahab for him in abundance and for those who were with him. That led to a third unequal yoke in the religious realm, in going with Ahab against the Syrians for Ramoth-gilead because that city was a Levitical city and a city of refuge (18.3). After Ahab died, Jehoshaphat made a business unequal yoke with Ahab's son, Ahaziah (20.35-37). The last unequal yoke (which is not recorded in 2 Chronicles) is a political unequal yoke. In 2 Kings 3.6-12 he went with Jehoram, another son of Ahab, and the king of Edom with their men to try to break the growing power of Moab.

A believer should not deceive himself or herself into thinking that they will win an unsaved spouse to Christ. It may happen, it sometimes does happen, but there is no guarantee that it ever will happen, and it hardly ever happens until after years of misery for the disobedient child of God. One sister told me, "I am thankful that God has saved my husband, but before He did, I went through ten years of misery. If ever you know of a young sister contemplating marrying an unsaved man, tell her from me not to do it".

I heard of a sister (who was thinking about marrying an unsaved man) telling Charles Spurgeon, "I intend to win him for Christ". After Spurgeon brought the Word of God to bear on the subject, she kept repeating her intention. Finally, Spurgeon asked her to get up on a table, which she did. Then he asked her to lift him up onto the table. She replied, "I could never do that". Then he easily pulled her down and said, "That is what will happen if you marry him. You will not be able to lift him to your level but he will easily bring you down to his level"!

Wilcock sees many valuable lessons for overseers in the shepherd work of Jehoshaphat. He writes, "The New Testament clearly envisages plural and corporate leadership in the church, rather than a 'one man band'. Indeed even the Israelite kings knew something about shared ministry, consulting with advisors, and prophets, and their own sons as co-regents, and we shall learn from them some thoroughly New Testament lessons on the subject...First Jehoshaphat cultivates his own relationship with God... This personal devotion is the prime requirement for a basis of pastoral care". The Apostle Paul addresses the overseers from the assembly of Ephesus, "Take heed therefore to yourselves, and to all the flock, over the which the Holy Ghost hath made you overseers" (Acts 20.28). Paul writing to Timothy (who was to do some teaching at Ephesus) says in 1 Timothy 4.16, "Take heed unto thyself, and unto the doctrine (thy teaching, RV)". Overseers and teachers should both be concerned first about their own personal devotion and submission to the Word of God.

In the much larger picture of Jehoshaphat that the Chronicler gives, we can see a shepherd of the people of God in his weakness. (Interestingly, Wilcock points out that Jehoshaphat's weakness is actually related to his excellence as a shepherd. He cares for his people with a soft heart. His troubles begin when he is not sufficiently hard-hearted. He genuinely cares for his people but he lacks discernment. He does not have the ability to say "No". "It is the other side of his splendid qualities that makes him a good shepherd: so kind, so large-hearted, so concerned for everyone, so willing to help".)

The record of Jehoshaphat has five parts.

1. Jehoshaphat's character and organization (17.1-19);
2. Jehoshaphat's sinful alliance with Ahab (18.1-34);
3. Jehoshaphat's favourable response to God's rebuke and his reformation (19.1-11);
4. God's reward for Jehoshaphat's trusting God (20.1-34);
5. Jehoshaphat's commercial alliance and God's rebuke (20.35-37).

As usual, the Chronicler, guided by the Holy Spirit, shows that faithfulness and obedience are rewarded. The presence of the Lord in blessing and help is mentioned four times (17.3; 19.6,11; 20.17). The Chronicler also warns that wrong alliances are met with a definite rebuke (19.1-3; 20.37) and punishment (20.37). The most important lesson to be seen here is that one must not only be devoted to the Lord, but one must also avoid entanglement with any ungodly person or group.

Outline of Chapter 17

Verses 1-6:	Character and rule of Jehoshaphat.
Verses 7-9:	Teaching throughout the land.
Verses 10-13a:	Blessing and tribute to Jehoshaphat.
Verses 13b-19:	Details of Jehoshaphat's army.

Verses 1-6: Character and Rule of Jehoshaphat

This wonderful chapter has no parallel in 1 Kings except for the first eight words (15.24). It well illustrates the valuable supplementary character of Chronicles. This chapter has one of the best scenes for the kingdom of Judah. "The main theme occurs in vv.1-6, where God's activity on behalf of Judah is balanced by Jehoshaphat's practical faith. God is mentioned four times, twice describing what He has done for Jehoshaphat in vv.3,5 and twice concerning Jehoshaphat's attitude to Him in vv.4,6" (Selman).

The very first verse states that he "strengthened himself against Israel". He does that especially in "the cities of Ephraim, which Asa his father had taken" (v.2). "This is worthy of notice. Israel and Israel's king were ever a snare to the heart of Jehoshaphat. But in the opening of his course, in the season of his early freshness, he was able to fortify his kingdom against the power of Israel. Now, one frequently observes this in the history of Christians; the evils which in after life prove their greatest snares are those against which there is the greatest watchfulness at first. Most happy it is when the spirit of watchfulness increases with our increasing knowledge of the tendencies and capabilities of our hearts" (Mackintosh).

Most of the good kings of Judah did not finish as well as they began. "But perhaps the most remarkable of all the references made to it is one made incidentally and by implication in v.3 where we read that Jehoshaphat 'walked in the first ways of his father David'. Here it is clearly suggested that even in David's case his first ways were his best…His sin with Uriah's wife occurred after he had settled down in his kingdom, and his pride which led him to number his people developed in an even later stage of his life" (Rodgers).

Verse 3 states that "he sought not unto Baalim" (the first mention of Baal in 2 Chronicles) as Ahab and Jezebel led Israel to do. Verse 4 adds that he "walked…not after the doings of Israel". There was pressure to condone the idolatry of the ten northern tribes. It was strong pressure because of relationship. Pressure to depart from God's Word can be strongest from relatives, especially when they have the same background of faith and there is some acknowledgement of God. How sad that Jehoshaphat began so well and yet, ironically, he changed his thinking about Israel in 18.1.

In v.3 we read that the Lord was with him, as He was with Solomon (1.1), Abijah and Judah (13.12), and Asa (15.9). The Lord's presence in blessing and in help is mentioned three other times (19.6,11; 20.17). Verse 3 goes on to state: "because he walked in the first ways of his father David". "Seeking", in v.4, is a favourite expression of the Chronicler for evaluating spirituality: "But (he) sought to the Lord God of his father". Jehu praised him with the words of 19.3: "thou…hast prepared thine heart to seek God". Verse 20.3 says that "Jehoshaphat feared, and set himself to seek the Lord". The last mention of the king is in 22.9, as one "who sought the Lord with all his heart".

Dillard draws attention to a number of ways in which we see in Asa and

Jehoshaphat, "like father, like son".

1. Both took away the high places where idols were worshipped (14.3; 17.6). Both spared the high places where they worshipped the Lord their God (15.8; 20.33). See the Appendix to Chapter 30 regarding the high places.
2. Each enjoyed the rewards of their piety in building (14.7; 17.2,12), peace (14.1; 17.10), and large armies (14.8; 17.12-19). The Lord was with both (15.9; 17.3), and the fear of the Lord was on the surrounding nations (14.14; 17.10; 20.29).
3. Prophets rebuke each for foreign alliances (16.7-9; 19.1-3; 20.37).
4. Two prophets prophesied during the reign of each. Azariah and Hanani for Asa, Jehu and Eliezer for Jehoshaphat. Like Asa and Jehoshaphat, the relationship between two of the prophets was that of father and son - Hanani (16.7) was the father of Jehu (19.2; 20.34).
5. Twice the Chronicler compares Jehoshaphat to his father Asa (17.4; 20.32). Elijah pairs Asa and Jehoshaphat together as a standard of comparison against Jehoram (21.12).

Payne has three more likenesses.

1. As Asa accomplished his first reform (14.1-8) so Jehoshaphat removed idolatry, taught the Law of the Lord throughout Judah, and strengthened his kingdom (ch.17).
2. Azariah encouraged Asa, which led to further reform (15.1-7). So also the rebuke of Jehu (19.2-3) led to further reform in Jehoshaphat's reign.
3. Each had a miraculous deliverance from a large army by trusting God (14.9-13 and 20.1-30).

One could add two more likenesses: each sought God (Asa in 14.4,7; Jehoshaphat in 17.4; 19.3; 20.3; 22.9), and no other father and son among the kings of Judah did so well in pleasing God as these two.

The writer of the Chronicles gives the same message in chs.17-20 about Jehoshaphat as he did in chs.14-16 about Asa. That message emphasizes the supreme importance of depending on God, the blessing of loyalty and the danger of disobedience.

"Therefore the Lord established the kingdom in his hand" (v.5). Wealth, honour, and fame are usual rewards bestowed on a faithful king as recorded by the Chronicler. They were enjoyed by David (1 Chr 29.14-16), Solomon (2 Chr 9.13-27), at this time by Jehoshaphat (17.5; 18.1), later by Uzziah (26.5,8,15), and Hezekiah (32.27).

"And his heart was lifted up in the ways of the Lord" (v.6). Here the Chronicler shows "the exceptional nature of the king's spirituality" (Leslie C. Allen). This is the only place in Chronicles where the phrase "his heart was lifted up" is used in a positive sense. Its usual use in Chronicles and in the rest of the Old Testament is negative, as in being haughty or proud. Verse 26.16 records that Uzziah's "heart was lifted up to his destruction", and Hezekiah's lifting up of his heart brought wrath upon him (32.25), although the next verse states that he "humbled himself for the pride of his heart". The verb "lifted up" means to be high, and, when used with "heart" elsewhere, means to have a high, haughty, and proud attitude; but here it refers to his high ideals or high spiritual ambition to follow the Lord. "Ambition is a virtue when practised within the guidelines of 'the ways of the Lord'" (Leslie C. Allen). Jehoshaphat's high aims are seen in destroying the idols and in his wanting all of God's people to be instructed in the law of the Lord (vv.7-9). Verses 1-6 can be summed up in these words: Jehoshaphat sought God and found God in His goodness in his life and reign.

Verses 7-9: Teaching Throughout the Land

"Also in the third year" (v.7) is probably the first year of his effective rule. He had ruled as co-regent with his father Asa during his father's last three years because Asa was diseased in his feet. Jehoshaphat had a true shepherd's heart. What he knew of God's ways and commandments (vv.3-4), he wanted all of God's people to know. Jehoshaphat was an ideal shepherd king who was subject to the law himself and wanted all of God's people to be subject to it also. He initiated an itinerant Bible teaching team. This is the first time in Chronicles that such a ministry is explicitly mentioned. Jehoshaphat's name means "the Lord will judge or rule". As his name implies, he wanted the will of God to rule among his people. He knew that the people would have to know the will of God before they could obey it. He appointed five princes, nine Levites, and two priests. Various parts of the Old Testament describe priests teaching, but this is the first time that we read of Levites doing so. This probably encouraged Levites to teach in Nehemiah 8.7-9. It seems that all 16 of them were "apt to teach" (1 Tim 3.2). David Boyd Long writes, "This would give balance and variety to all the teaching, something best done through different types of teachers rather than a stereotyped one-man-ministry type of arrangement". "The role of the princes…appointed by Jehoshaphat, himself, shows that the king was prepared to organize his whole kingdom for the purpose of propagating the law" (McConville). These teachers went throughout the cities of Judah and taught the people (v.9). Teaching is emphasized in these three verses by being mentioned three times. They taught from the book of the law that they had with them. The Lord's people need teaching from God's Word today by men fitted of God to teach. Everyone in every assembly, in a greater or less degree, should be able to test all they hear by the Word of God. 1 Thessalonians 5.21 states, "Prove all things; hold fast that which is good".

Verses 10–13a: Blessing and Tribute to Jehoshaphat

Verses 1-9 tell of his concern for the things of God. Now the following verses tell of the resultant blessing. "And the fear of the Lord fell upon all the kingdoms of the lands that were round about Judah" (v.10). They had a healthy respect for Jehoshaphat. We also read of this for David (1 Chr 14.17), Asa (2 Chr 14.14), and again for Jehoshaphat (20.29). God promised in Deuteronomy 11.22-25: "For if ye shall diligently keep all these commandments...the Lord your God shall lay the fear of you and the dread of you upon all the land". Immediately after Jacob commanded his family to put away the strange gods that were among them, we read in Genesis 35.5 that "the terror of God was upon the cities that were round about them, and they did not pursue after the sons of Jacob". In Joshua's day God did similarly (Josh 2.9,11; 5.1). Proverbs 16.7 states, "When a man's ways please the Lord, he maketh even his enemies to be at peace with him". In Acts 2 (right after we learn of the believers' steadfastness) we read in v.43, "And fear came upon every soul". After Ananias and Sapphira died in judgment, Acts 5.11 states, "And great fear came upon all the church, and upon as many as heard these things". Because of the fear in Jehoshaphat's day, "they made no war against Jehoshaphat".

Verse 11 tells of the tribute brought to the king, especially by the Arabians. The animals that they gave were very suitable for extensive sacrificial uses as well as for food and clothing. Even some of the Philistines brought presents. In v.5, "all Judah brought to Jehoshaphat presents". The assurance is given in the New Testament to the Corinthians that if they prophesied in an orderly way, unbelievers or unlearned would fall on their faces and acknowledge that God was truly in the midst of the assembly (1 Cor 14.24-25).

Verses 12 and 13a state that the prosperity of Jehoshaphat enabled him to build castles and cities of store and to have much business in the cities of Judah. Barber does well in summarizing the blessing of the Lord upon Jehoshaphat. "(1) God protected His people by filling their enemies with fear; (2) former enemies began to bring him tribute; (3) and Jehoshaphat increased in material and numerical strength".

Verses 13b-19: Details of Jehoshaphat's Army

This listing of Jehoshaphat's army is one of four found in 2 Chronicles (14.8; 17.13b-19; 25.5; 26.11-15). Five captains of his army (and the men with each of them) are mentioned in vv.14-18. The first three are of Judah and the last two are of Benjamin. Verse 16 records, "Amasiah the son of Zichri, who willingly offered himself unto the Lord". He is the only one of Jehoshaphat's men of whom this is said. The first two captains had more men than Amaziah did, "but no service could be done with a higher motive than his. We are told of him that he 'willingly offered himself as a freewill offering', not merely to Jehoshaphat, but unto the Lord" (Rodgers). This is similar to the Macedonians in 2 Corinthians 8.1-5. They gave more than Paul expected, and they gave beyond their power. Paul gives us the secret of their giving in v.5: "they...first gave their own selves to the Lord, and unto us by the will of God". If one first gives himself to the Lord, the Lord has everything: one's time, one's treasure, and one's talents. This is the same order as characterized Amaziah - it was "unto the Lord" first. Other captains may have done their "military duties as Amaziah did, because of loyalty to Jehoshaphat's person, or from a sense of duty, or even because of a warlike disposition. But he did it because he believed it to be the work the Lord had for him to do; it was for the Lord's land, and for the Lord's people" (Rodgers). Rossier suggests that Amaziah's willing service is one of the fruits of the teaching of the law of the Lord in vv.7-9.

The total of the men in vv.14-18 comes to 1,160,000, which is exactly twice as many as the total for Asa's army in 14.8 (580,000). It must have included all the men that could be enrolled in the army. This large number seems to be a militia reserve since they are distinguished from the regular army in the fenced cities of Judah (v.19). Payne has written two articles in *Bibliotheca Sacra* entitled, "The Validity of the Numbers in Chronicles". He points out that the Hebrew word for "thousand" (ELEP - 505) has other possible translations. The actual number may therefore have been less than those given above. He writes, "The claims so often repeated about impossible numbers in Chronicles simply are not true".

Jehoshaphat's large army probably included a good number from the northern tribes who fell to his father Asa "in abundance, when they saw that the Lord his God was with him" (15.9). In 2 Samuel 24.9 there were 800,000 valiant men of Israel who drew the sword, and 500,000 of Judah. The total number in 1 Chronicles 21.5 is even higher for David's men who drew the sword. Considering the men who fell to Asa and the number of David's men who drew the sword, the Chronicler's figure of 1,160,000 is quite reasonable. The only difficulty with this solution is that the numbers given in 2 Chronicles 17 are only given for Judah and Benjamin. However, it is possible that, once the men left the northern tribes, they were considered as belonging to the tribe in whose territory they dwelt.

It should be noted that it was not Jehoshaphat's large army that made the surrounding countries have a healthy respect for Jehoshaphat and Judah. It was the Lord Himself who rewarded Jehoshaphat's seeking God (v.10).

2 CHRONICLES 18

Jehoshaphat's Reign

Introductory

The Word of God is very clear in chapter 17 that Jehoshaphat was a good king. Chapter 18 is just as clear that the good king did wrong, for which he receives a definite rebuke from the prophet Jehu in 19.2. Ahab excelled in wickedness (1 Kings 16.30-33). 1 Kings 21.25 especially states this: "But there was none like unto Ahab, which did sell himself to work wickedness in the sight of the Lord, whom Jezebel his wife stirred up". Darby translates the last part of 2 Chronicles 18.1 as, "allied himself with Ahab by marriage". The ESV has, "he made a marriage alliance with Ahab". His son Jehoram married wicked Athaliah (the daughter of Ahab and Jezebel who was even more evil than her husband). It is possible that Jehoshaphat had a good motive in the marriage, thinking that the twelve tribes could be reunited. But if so, he was very wrong! The twelve tribes were not unified as he may have hoped, but there was one good aftermath of the alliance. The war between Israel and Judah ceased, but the sad consequences far outweighed that one good outcome. That one decision had very far-reaching sad results, for Jehoshaphat personally and for Judah nationally.

The marriage must have taken place early in the reign of Jehoshaphat and Jehoram must have married when he was 15 or 16, or possibly even younger. When Jehoram died at 40 (2 Kings 8.17; 2 Chr 21.5) his youngest son Ahaziah was 22 (2 Kings 8.26). Accordingly, Jehoram must have married in the eighth or ninth year of Jehoshaphat's reign. Most of the rest of ch.18 is set in the seventeenth year of his reign. We know that because 1 Kings 22.51 declares that Ahaziah the son of Ahab began to reign in the seventeenth year of Jehoshaphat. Of course, he began to reign right after his father Ahab died.

There were sad personal consequences. That matrimonial unequal yoke led to four other unequal yokes (as pointed out in the introductory notes to ch.17). Jehoshaphat almost lost his life. He was rebuked by Jehu the son of Hanani in 19.2 and by Eliezer in 20.37. Even though he was doing wrong, the Lord responded to his cry in 18.31 and saved his life. However, the Lord chastened him in 20.37 by breaking his ships. Also his son Jehoram slew all his own brethren (21.4). It is likely that Jehoshaphat did not live to see the murder of all the rest of his sons by Jehoram.

There were sad national consequences. While Jehoshaphat reigned for 25 years God blessed Judah nationally, but the next 15 years were evil because of this one wicked woman Athaliah. For eight years Jehoram "walked in the way of the kings of Israel, like as did the house of Ahab: for he had the daughter of Ahab to wife" (21.6). Jehoram's son, Ahaziah, reigned for one year, and 22.3 records that "He also walked in the ways of the house of Ahab: for his mother was his counselor to do wickedly". When he died, his mother Athaliah destroyed all the seed royal of the house of Judah (or so she thought) and usurped the throne for six years. Except for a one-year-old boy, Joash, she exterminated the line of the Messiah. As someone has said, "All the purposes of God for all eternity hung on the slender thread of a one year old baby boy but they were secure."

Since there were such serious consequences to Jehoshaphat's decision, it is a warning to all to be vigilant in all decisions. Young persons especially should be careful in the choice of a life partner. In Deuteronomy 7.4 God tells why He did not want His people to make marriages with the nations around them, "For they will turn away thy son from following me". God greatly appreciates it when His people follow Him. He does not want anything to turn them aside. An unsaved life partner can turn anyone away. It happened to King Solomon in 1 Kings 11.4, "For it came to pass, when Solomon was old, that his wives turned away his heart after other gods: and his heart was not perfect with the Lord his God, as was the heart of David his father." See also the third and fourth paragraphs of the commentary on ch.17.

Outline of Chapter 18

Verses 1-3:	Alliance with wicked Ahab.
Verses 4-14:	Misleading prophecies.
Verses 15-22:	Micaiah's prophecy.
Verses 22-27:	Micaiah's prophecy rejected.
Verses 28-34:	Micaiah's prophecy fulfilled.

Verses 1-3: Alliance with Wicked Ahab

How sad that Jehoshaphat, who was one of the godliest kings ever to sit upon the throne of Judah, was linked with Ahab who excelled in wickedness (1 Kings 21.25)! "Now Jehoshaphat had riches and honour in abundance" (v.1). This phrase may be repeated here from 17.5 to indicate that Jehoshaphat had no need to make alliance with the ten northern tribes. (These first two verses are different from the first three verses of 1 Kings 22.) This focuses attention on Jehoshaphat (the one with whom the Chronicler concerns himself) rather than on Ahab. Verses 3-34 follow 1 Kings 22.4-35 except for 18.31b.

This is the largest body of material by far from Kings used by the Chronicler. He had at least three good reasons for including this amount. "1) The story concerned a true prophet of the Lord, Micaiah. 2) The Chronicler desired to contrast strongly the insistence upon the orthodox faith by the king of Judah with the lawless religion of the north. 3) The story was recounted here to highlight Ahab's wickedness and prepares the way for the timely rebuke administered to Jehoshaphat by the prophet Jehu, the son of Hanani, in the next chapter (19.2-3)" (Unger).

"And after certain years…" (v.2). This was the 17th year of Jehoshaphat's reign, at least eight years after Jehoram married Athaliah (see above). "And

Ahab killed sheep and oxen for him in abundance, and for the people that he had with him". "The enemy does not attack his kingdom, he attacks his heart. He comes not as a lion, but as the serpent. Ahab's 'sheep and oxen' are found more suitable and effectual than Ahab's men of war... Jehoshaphat's kingdom is fortified against Ahab's hostilities, but his heart lies open to Ahab's allurements. This is truly solemn...The devil has always found religious and benevolent objects most effectual in their influence upon the people of God. He does not come at first with something openly ungodly" (Mackintosh). Jehoshaphat's role is enhanced by the deference shown to him and those with him. This is not recorded in Kings; Ahab probably wanted to flatter Jehoshaphat before making his proposal.

It seems like another weakness of Jehoshaphat to allow himself to be so impressed with Ahab's lavish banquet that he was off his guard when Ahab "persuaded him to go up with him to Ramoth-gilead". Once Jehoshaphat accepted Ahab's sumptuous meal it was difficult for him to say no to Ahab's request to go against Ramoth-gilead. It is safer for God's people to be careful never to allow themselves to become a debtor to the world. "The Hebrew word rendered 'persuaded' is a strong one: it is used in Deuteronomy 13.6 of enticement to apostasy, and so it connotes leading someone spiritually astray...The whole story is made to revolve around the concept of manipulation, human and divine" (Leslie C. Allen). "Persuaded" is in Hebrew (SUT - 5496). "Jehoshaphat did not realize that the cunning and wily Ahab was drawing him into a trap. And this...shows Jehoshaphat's gullibility. He was honest in his dealings with others, and he expected them to be honest in their dealings with him. He did not expect Ahab to be devious and deceitful" (Barber).

The Chronicler leaves out 1 Kings 22.3, thus reducing the importance of Ahab in the narrative. Jehoshaphat responded to Ahab's question about going to war with him by saying, "I am as thou art, and my people as thy people" (v.3). That is altogether opposite to the statement of Jehu in 19.2, "Shouldest thou help the ungodly, and love them that hate the Lord?". How sad for such a godly king as Jehoshaphat to put himself on the same level as wicked Ahab! It was sadder still to put his own people equal to the ten northern tribes when, at that time, there were only 7,000 that had not bowed the knee to Baal (1 Kings 19.18). Jehoshaphat repeated the response to Jehoram the son of Ahab in 2 Kings 3.7 but it was opposite to the thoughts of Elisha the man of God. Elisha made a big difference between Jehoshaphat and Jehoram in 2 Kings 3.13-14. Ramoth-gilead belonged to Israel, but now it was in the hands of the enemy. It was a Levitical city and a city of refuge. To recover it for God was truly a good work, but it was wrong for Jehoshaphat to try to do so in association with wicked Ahab.

Verses 4-14: Misleading Prophecies

Even though Jehoshaphat was making a serious mistake, he very properly felt his need of enquiring of the Lord that day (v.4). It would have been far better for him to have done this before he committed himself in v.3. He also felt his need of enquiring of the Lord in 2 Kings 3.11. Jehoshaphat wanted the enquiry to be made "to day" because it was very important to him.

Edersheim states, "At any rate, it was - as the event proved - too late now to withdraw, whatever the word of Jehovah might be. In truth it was only what may always be expected when those who serve and love the Lord allow themselves to be entangled in alliances with ungodly men, where one step leads to another, and one inconsistency involves the next, till at last we recoil when it is too late to withdraw, and the only thing consistent is to be inconsistent in owning God where His will can no longer be obeyed. But even then it is good for it is the first step to repentance".

Ahab gathered 400 prophets who all said, "Go up; for God will deliver it into the king's hand" (v.5). These 400 were prophets of Ahab (vv.21-22) as Elisha confirms (2 Kings 3.13). Although Jehoshaphat lacked discernment (as to how serious was Ahab's departure), he had discernment enough to know that these were not true prophets of the Lord. So he asked for a prophet of the Lord in v.6. "But Jehoshaphat's conscience bothered him. He felt uneasy. It was his practice to seek God's will, and he sensed inwardly that he had too hastily consented to something without consulting the Lord. To allay his misgivings he suggested that they inquire of the Lord in order to ascertain His will" (Barber). It would be enough for Jehoshaphat to have even one true prophet of the Lord to counterbalance the other four hundred. Ahab answered in v.7 about Micaiah, "There is yet one man, by whom we may inquire of the Lord: but I hate him, for he never prophesied good unto me, but always evil". Ahab's confession is interesting. It indicates that Micaiah had spoken to him in the past, and that each time Micaiah had reproved him Ahab refused to accept it.

Ahab is like the rebellious Israelites of Isaiah 30.10: "Which say to the seers, See not; and to the prophets, Prophesy not unto us right things, speak unto us smooth things, prophesy deceits". Jehoshaphat is opposite to Ahab in his attitude to the Word of God. He is in the habit of receiving every word that comes from God. He bowed to God's rebuke later from Jehu (19.2-3). May the Lord help every child of God to be like Jehoshaphat in submission to God's Word.

Jehoshaphat genuinely feared the Lord and rebuked Ahab, "Let not the king say so". Ahab also hated Elijah (1 Kings 18.17; 21.20). Ahab may not have mentioned Elijah because his whereabouts were unknown to him. Even Micaiah had to be brought from prison. The "officer" that Ahab called to fetch Micaiah in v.8 is really a "eunuch", according to the margins of RV and JND.

Zedekiah had made himself horns of iron. Now, while Micaiah is being summoned, he uses them dramatically when he says in v.10, "Thus saith the Lord, With these thou shalt push Syria until they be consumed". He was possibly referring to God's promise by Moses in regard to Joseph in Deuteronomy 33.17: "his horns are like the horns of unicorns: with them he shall push the people". Jehoshaphat wanted to enquire of the Lord (Jehovah) in v.4. All the 400 prophets used another name for God (Elohim) in v.5. Again in v.6 Jehoshaphat wanted a prophet of Jehovah (v.10). After Zedekiah's dramatic prophecy using Jehovah, all the other prophets were encouraged to repeat their earlier prophecy in the next verse, but this time, instead of Elohim, they used Jehovah as Zedekiah had done.

Micaiah's answer in v.13 is a good resolve for all who speak for God: "As the Lord liveth, even what my God saith, that will I speak". When asked in v.14 (if they should go up to Ramoth-gilead), Micaiah must have answered mockingly when he said, "Go ye up, and prosper, and they shall be delivered into your hand".

Verses 15-22: Micaiah's Prophecy

Ahab could likely tell by the tone of his voice that he was mocking. Verse 15 indicates that most likely Ahab and Micaiah had gone through one or more similar procedures before. Once Ahab challenged him, Micaiah must declare the truth, and he was ready to do so. In v.16 he predicted that only Ahab, who should have been a shepherd to Israel, would fall. In v.17 Ahab spoke to Jehoshaphat words that show that he thought Micaiah had personal hostility towards Ahab. Micaiah in v.18 twice referred to the Lord, the true source of his message, rather than any personal enmity to Ahab. None of God's people should ever act like Ahab. We should never blame a messenger of God for the message that he brings from the Lord, even if it is solemn. In the vision that Micaiah described he showed that it was the Lord's purpose that Ahab fall at Ramoth-gilead. God was going to use a lying spirit in the mouth of all Ahab's prophets. Elijah faced 450 prophets of Baal in 1 Kings 18.22 and now Micaiah faced 400 prophets of Ahab.

In v.19 the Lord's question, "Who shall entice Ahab…that he may…fall", illustrates the truth that God, in His sovereignty, can use evil spirits, or even Satan himself, to accomplish His purposes (Job 1.12; 2.5-6; Lk 22.31-32; 2 Cor 12.7). Satan and his agents can only go as far as God allows them. Genesis 50.20 and Psalm 76.10 show that God can even use wrongdoing to fulfill His plans. The words of v.22, "these thy prophets", emphasize the difference between Ahab's prophets and the true prophet of God. William Cowper said, "He who hates truth will be the dupe of lies". Ahab did not want the truth as the context shows.

The vision of Micaiah in vv.19-21 does trouble some saints. Torrey gives a good explanation. "At first glance it appears here as if the Lord sanctioned and took part in lying and deception. What is the explanation? It is found clearly given in the context. Micaiah, speaking by the Holy Spirit, is seeking to dissuade Ahab and Jehoshaphat from going to Ramoth-gilead…But that Jehovah was not really a party to the deception appears clearly in the narrative if we take it as a whole. So, far from being a party to the deception,

He sends His own prophet to warn them that the spirit that spoke by the false prophets was a lying spirit, and to tell them the exact facts in the case as to what the issue of the battle would be. If they would choose to listen to God and His prophet, they would be saved from calamity; but if they would not listen to God and His prophet, then God would give them over to the working of error, that they should believe a lie".

In *Bibliotheca Sacra* (published by Dallas Theological Seminary), Volume 155, Number 617, January-March, 1998, there is a thorough article regarding this subject by Robert B. Chisholm Jnr, entitled, "Does God Deceive?".

Verses 23-27: Micaiah's Prophecy Rejected

Zedekiah had dramatically demonstrated with horns to encourage going up to Ramoth-gilead in v.10. Of all the 400 prophets of Ahab, Zedekiah's pride was probably hurt the most by Micaiah's prophecy. Apparently he greatly desired to diminish the effect of Micaiah's exposure of a "lying spirit". Insultingly, he "smote Micaiah upon the cheek", although Micaiah had the last word with Zedekiah in v.24. How sad that Jehoshaphat saw Micaiah treated so shamefully and never said a word on his behalf. Jehoshaphat's silence itself was shameful. This suggests that when we entangle ourselves with the ungodly, we are likely to get into circumstances that will lead us to behave disgracefully (like the ungodly). Zedekiah was told that he would be so frightened on that day that he would try to escape for his life. That fear would be a contrast to the bravado he displayed in striking Micaiah.

Ahab would not believe Micaiah's message because he did not want to believe it. He so deeply resented Micaiah's answer that he sent him back to prison with his last words, "until I return in peace". Micaiah responded nobly with the final word in v.27. His answer defended the honour of the Lord. He was appealing to one test of a true prophet in Deuteronomy 18.21-22. In his last words he called upon all who heard him to be witnesses, "Hearken, all ye people". The outcome of the battle would show that he was right. "Jehoshaphat…sat beside Ahab, and beheld the Lord's prophet first struck, and then committed to prison, simply because he would not tell a lie to please a wicked king, and harmonize with four hundred wicked prophets. What must have been the feelings of Jehoshaphat when he beheld his brother smitten and imprisoned for his faithfulness in testifying against an expedition in which he himself was engaged" (Mackintosh).

Verses 28-34: Micaiah's Prophecy Fulfilled

Jehoshaphat led some of Judah to Ramoth-gilead with Ahab and his army. It is not stated anywhere how many from Judah went with Jehoshaphat to battle. Besides, 19.1 tells only of Jehoshaphat returning to his house in peace. It may have been just a guard of soldiers that he had with him to make this visit (v.3). Ahab rejected Micaiah's message, but he feared that it might be true. In a cowardly way he suggested (v.29) that Jehoshaphat go into battle with his robes while he disguised himself. He thus willingly exposed Jehoshaphat to extreme danger. Jehoshaphat did not discern the wickedness of Ahab's cowardly suggestion. God knew, but neither one of the two kings knew that the king of Syria would command, "Fight ye not with small or great, save only with the king of Israel (v.30). He was hoping to thwart God's purpose. The very orders of the King of Syria in v.30 were arranged by God to bring about the death of Ahab. His orders, when carried out, also allowed all the others to return in peace as Micaiah had predicted.

"The words about Jehoshaphat with which v.31 concludes - 'and the Lord helped him; and God moved them to depart from him' - are an addition by Ezra, not found in the parallel passage of 1 Kings 22.32. They are significant, moreover, in at least three ways. (1) showing the seriousness of Jehoshaphat's deviation, how he would forthwith have reaped a fatal blow from his sinful alliance with Ahab, had not God intervened; (2) suggesting the reality of his faith, that when 'Jehoshaphat cried out', this was not just an expression of fear on his part but was apparently a prayer for Divine help; and (3) demonstrating the greatness of the grace of God, rescuing men without a need for manmade alliances, or even, as in this case, in spite of them" (Payne).

Jehoshaphat cried out in the battle in v.31 as Judah under Abijah had done before him (13.14-15), and also the sons of Reuben, and the Gadites, and the half tribe of Manasseh (1 Chr 5.18-20). There was an immediate answer to his ejaculatory prayer. These three references are among the many encouragements in God's Word for all of God's people to avail themselves of the power of prayer. It is also significant that the Lord (Jehovah, the Covenant-keeping One) helped Jehoshaphat, and that God (the Creator God) moved the men to depart from him. The omnipotent God can turn man as He wills. God delivering Jehoshaphat is a good illustration of Peter's words in 2 Peter 2.9: "The Lord knoweth how to deliver the godly out of temptations". Jehoshaphat would have perished if God had not intervened for him.

Verse 33 shows that even though Ahab disguised himself and encouraged Jehoshaphat to go into battle with his robes on, he did not succeed in thwarting the purpose of God. Ahab's actions only served to show the more clearly that God purposed and accomplished Ahab's death. The arrow was guided by God and found the disguised Ahab in his most vulnerable spot. "Rarely has history so visibly and in every detail taught its Divine lessons" (Edersheim). In spite of Ahab's wickedness he died like a brave hero propped up in his chariot facing his enemies until sunset, and then died.

"The incidents recorded in this chapter were of the utmost importance to the people for whom the Chronicler wrote. The voice of the prophets had been neglected and few were prepared to acknowledge their authority in Israel. The fulfillment of Micaiah's predictions would reinforce the role of those who were truly God's representatives" (Barber).

2 CHRONICLES 19

Jehoshaphat's Reign
Outline of Chapter 19

Verses 1-3: Jehu's rebuke of Jehoshaphat's alliance with Ahab.
Verse 4: Jehoshaphat leading Judah in restoration.
Verses 5-11: Jehoshaphat's appointment of judges.

Verses 1-3: Jehu's Rebuke of Jehoshaphat's Alliance with Ahab

The Chronicler, guided by the Holy Spirit, has in chapter 19 and 20.1-34 material omitted in Kings. He has phrased v.1 as a fulfillment of Micaiah's prophecy in 18.16. A contrast is clearly seen in Ahab who did not return in peace. Jehoshaphat may have been very grateful that God made a difference between Ahab and himself even though he had mistakenly said in 18.3, "I am as thou art".

Jehu the son of Hanani knew (v.2) that he was risking being put in prison like his father (16.10) when he courageously rebuked Jehoshaphat. He was the brave prophet who in 1 Kings 16.1-7 rebuked Baasha the king of Israel 31 years earlier in the 26th year of the reign of Asa. So Jehu was mature and he knew accurately the sad condition of the northern tribes. Jehu gives God's estimate of Ahab in v.2: "…the ungodly…them that hate the Lord". Believers ought only to love what God loves. They should love the world evangelistically as God does (Jn 3.16), and should also hate everything that God hates. Psalm 97.10 says, "Ye that love the Lord, hate evil". They should hate every system that God hates and yet, at the same time, should love the individuals in the system. The phrase, "love them that hate the Lord", in v.2 does not imply so much emotional attachment as deliberate choice. Elsewhere in God's Word "loving" and "hating" are used to convey preference as in Luke 14.26 and Luke 16.13. Rossier notes, "The second phrase is even more serious than the first. Loving the world involves associating one's self with it, becoming jointly liable with it in its enmity against God. 'Ye adulterers and adulteresses', says James, 'know ye not that the friendship of the world is enmity with God?' (James 4.4). 'No man can serve two masters', says the Lord Jesus, 'for either he will hate the one and love the other, or else he will hold to the one, and despise the other' (Lk 16.13)". Surely Christians should have compassionate love for the lost, even enemies (Mt 5.44) as the Lord Jesus perfectly lived out (Lk 23.34), but should never become unequally yoked with unbelievers (2 Cor 6.14).

"Therefore is wrath upon thee from before the Lord" (v.2). Leslie C. Allen says, "The reference to God's wrath is not easy to explain, since it has no verb with it in the Hebrew. The RSV may be correct in interpreting 'wrath has gone out' (as the ESV also has), in which case the reference is to Jehoshaphat's humiliating defeat (see 18.16 and cp. 20.37)". Many commentators think the invasion of ch.20 is the expression of God's wrath. This may be so, but there is no confession in Jehoshaphat's prayer in 20.6-12 as we might have expected.

Jehu softened the condemnation with a word of commendation (v.3). Jehoshaphat had removed idolatry: "thou…has prepared thine heart to seek God". That was opposite to Rehoboam in 12.14: "And he did evil, because he prepared not his heart to seek the Lord". Jehu seems to have anticipated Jehoshaphat's favourable response by his acknowledgement of "good things found in thee".

Jehoshaphat responded to Jehu's rebuke much better than did his father Asa when Jehu's father Hanani rebuked him (16.7-10). Jehoshaphat took this reproof to his heart and conscience. He did not answer, but his actions showed that he was repentant. All the good of the rest of this chapter and 20.1-34 is a result of his humbling himself at Jehu's rebuke. Asa would not humble himself at Hanani's censure and as a result he was away from God for the last five years of his life. When Jehoshaphat saw Ahab wrongfully put Micaiah in prison it helped him to see how wrong his own father had been to incarcerate Hanani.

Verse 4: Jehoshaphat Leading Judah in Restoration

Jehoshaphat went personally from the southern extremity to the northern extremity of his realm. He went where the people were. "Many of his subjects had never seen their king in person, and to have him visit their small city or village must have had an impact on them" (Barber). In v.4, "again" is a reference to 17.7-9, even though there he acted indirectly, through those he sent to teach. "And brought them back unto the Lord God of their fathers." It is easy to believe that his alliance with idolatrous Ahab had a bad effect on his kingdom. Whether that was so or not, he was an instrument in God's hand in a genuine turning to the Lord on the part of the people. It is encouraging that God used Jehoshaphat in this way immediately after he took to heart Jehu's rebuke. Jehoshaphat acted like his ancestor David when the joy of God's salvation was restored to him in Psalm 51.13: "Then will I teach transgressors thy ways; and sinners shall be converted unto thee".

Verses 5-11: Jehoshaphat's Appointment of Judges

Jehoshaphat initiated judicial reform throughout the land of Judah. Here again he showed a pastoral care for his people even as he did in 17.7-9 when he sent travelling teachers to them. He set judges in all the fenced cities of Judah (vv.5-7). The Nelson Study Bible points out that "the role of Jehoshaphat's judges differed from that of the heroic leaders who led Israel before David's time (Judg 2.16). The judges that Jehoshaphat appointed served as local officials in the fortified cities". Jehoshaphat also set judges in Jerusalem (vv.8-11). Interestingly, "Lord" is found nine times in the eight verses (vv.4-11). Besides that, Jehoshaphat had made two speeches emphasizing the presence of the Lord. In the beginning of his first speech he speaks of His being with them "in the judgment" (v.6). At the end of the second speech he says, "the Lord shall be with the good" (v.11).

Leslie C. Allen draws attention to God's presence. Thus he links 19.4-11 and 20.1-30 in a memorable way. He labels the first section, "God's Presence in Social Reform" and he labels the second section, "God's Presence in Deliverance". Jehoshaphat not only appointed judges, but in his speeches he gave spiritual principles which were to help them in judgment. These same principles are essential today for all who lead God's people. Some of these principles are from Deuteronomy 1.16-17 and 16.18-20.

Verse 6 is an encouragement to overseers who sometimes have difficult decisions to make. The more that they realize that they are not merely judging for man but for the Lord, the more they can count on God to help them. The words of v.6, "...who is with you in the judgment", recall the words of Moses in Deuteronomy 1.17, "...the judgment is God's". In v.7 Darby rightly translates, "let the terror of Jehovah be upon you", for it is a different Hebrew word from that in v.9 which indicates a reverential fear of the Lord. They were to dread the just anger of the Lord if they were unrighteous, took bribes, or respected persons in judgment. The deaths of Nadab and Abihu, the sons of Aaron (Lev 10.1-2), and the two sons of Eli, Hophni and Phinehas (1 Sam 4.11), are examples of the terror of the Lord. Jehoshaphat insisted that the judges should be like the Lord in their judgment. The more that saints imitate God the more they please God. The RV of Ephesians 5.1 states, "Be ye therefore imitators of God, as beloved children". Because Christian masters in Ephesians 6.9 know that their own Master in heaven is completely impartial, it should affect their treatment of their slaves. It should also affect the way Christian employers treat their employees.

May the Lord help every assembly to act with the wisdom "from above" which does not have any partiality (James 3.17). Jehoshaphat's judges were not only to judge for the Lord and with the Lord, but also to judge like the Lord. "Shall not the Judge of all the earth do right?" (Gen 18.25). Jehoshaphat states in v.7 that the Lord our God does not take gifts. Jehoshaphat himself had allowed his judgment to be affected by being overly impressed with the gift of a sumptuous meal from wicked Ahab (18.2), but v.7 seems to indicate that he had learned that he should not have done so.

In v.8 Jehoshaphat set judges in Jerusalem. It is interesting that "the chief of the fathers" were now to share in the judgment. In David's day judgment seemed to be confined to 6,000 Levites (1 Chr 23.4). This court in Jerusalem was to be like a supreme court as well as a local court. It was to handle major cases including homicide and appeals. Jehoshaphat charged them in v.9: "Thus shall ye do in the fear of the Lord, faithfully, and with a perfect heart". The reverential fear of the Lord makes one faithful. Nehemiah 7.2 states, "That I gave my brother Hanani, and Hananiah the ruler of the palace charge over Jerusalem: for he was a faithful man, and feared God above many". This is the only verse in the Bible about this Hananiah and he is the only one recorded who "feared God above many". That made him faithful. The fear of the Lord also gives the wisdom, which is so necessary for proper judgment. We have almost identical words in three successive books of God's Word - Job 28.28; Psalm 111.10; and Proverbs 9.10: "The fear of the Lord is the beginning of wisdom". The fear of the Lord should, for example, keep all from cheating when submitting their income tax returns, even if any of them have reason to believe that they could get away with it!

Verse 10 records the words, "between blood and blood". The judges were to determine the degree of blood guiltiness. They were not only to make judicial decisions, but they were to "warn them". Jehoshaphat was told in v.2 that "wrath has gone out" (RSV and ESV) referring to his humiliating defeat (18.16). Now, he is concerned that no wrath should come upon them because of trespassing against the Lord.

In v.11 there is a distinction explicitly made between "all matters of the Lord" and "all the king's matters". Amariah the chief priest was to be over the former. Zebadiah was to be over the latter. There were therefore two divisions. One handled religious affairs and interpretations of the law. The other handled criminal and civil cases. Levites who were not judges "shall be officers before you". They were to help in different ways. As a result of Jehoshaphat's actions there was "greater spiritual order than at any time since Solomon" (MacArthur). There should be order in every assembly: "Let all things be done decently and in order" (1 Cor 14.40). Jehoshaphat's closing words encourage decisive action - "Deal courageously, and the Lord shall be with the good". Psalm 11.7 declares, "For the righteous Lord loveth righteousness".

2 CHRONICLES 20

Jehoshaphat's Reign

Introductory

This is a thrilling chapter to read, and the first 30 verses are especially so. Jehoshaphat's deeply moving prayer in vv.5-13 is one of the most remarkable ever recorded. This is the third king's prayer in 2 Chronicles. Solomon's is recorded in 6.14-42 and Asa's in 14.11.

"Chapter 20 contains one of the outstanding stories not only in Chronicles but in the whole Bible. It describes first of all a unique Israelite victory. Though on other occasions God enables Israelite forces to be victorious, here the credit is due entirely to God while the army is reduced to the level of spectators. Secondly, it is the showpiece of Chronicles' account of the Divided Monarchy (chs.10-36). Israel's faith and trust and God's actions on Israel's behalf are presented in particularly glowing terms. Even the triumphs of other kings (e.g. 13.3-19; 14.9-15; 26.6-15) pale into insignificance in comparison with what is achieved here" (Selman).

None of the events of the first 30 verses of this chapter are found in Kings. 1 Kings 22.45 states, "Now the rest of the acts of Jehoshaphat, and his might that he shewed, and how he warred, are they not written in the book of the chronicles of the kings of Judah?". The Chronicler has provided this additional information and omits this reference from his own reign summary (20.34).

"The account is significantly structured. Apart from the outer frame, which highlights the reversal of circumstances (vv.1-4, 28-30), it falls into three divisions. (1) Jehoshaphat's prayer (vv.5-13); (2) the Lord's response (vv.14-19); (3) the great victory (vv.20-27). At the center of each is the crucial statement, and these are all linked by a key word: v.9, 'we stand before this house, and in thy presence'; v.17, 'stand ye still, and see the salvation of the Lord with you'; v.23, 'the children of Ammon and Moab stood up against the inhabitants of mount Seir, utterly to slay and destroy them'" (Zondervan KJV Study Bible).

The Chronicler delights to encourage his readers with the record here of humbling, repentance, and complete dependence on God when the nation is threatened with a grave and serious danger. Most of this chapter is an encouragement for all saints undergoing trial to keep depending on God.

The last three verses of the chapter are a record of Jehoshaphat's alliance with Ahaziah the son of Ahab in a commercial venture that God rebuked. The positive result of the first 30 verses is balanced by this serious failure in Jehoshaphat's life - his willingness to yoke himself with the house of Ahab, and his people with idolatrous Israel. Jehoshaphat entered into one more unequal yoke: with Jehoram, another son of Ahab. This is recorded in 2 Kings 3. On that occasion, were it not for the miracle wrought by Elisha, all of the army could have perished from lack of water. That incident has similarities to the incident here, but the differences are too great for this account to be based on 2 Kings 3.

Outline of Chapter 20

Verses 1-4: Judah invaded by a great multitude; fear and fasting.
Verses 5-13: Jehoshaphat's remarkable prayer.
Verses 14-21: God's answer through Jahaziel and the response.
Verses 22-30: The astounding victory.
Verses 31-34: Concluding comments on Jehoshaphat's reign.
Verses 35-37: Jehoshaphat's alliance with wicked Ahaziah.

Verses 1-4: Judah Invaded by a Great Multitude; Fear and Fasting

The Moabites and the Ammonites came against Jehoshaphat. We learn from v.10 and vv.22-23 that men from Mount Seir were with them. Reports came to Jehoshaphat of a great multitude that was already at En-gedi about midway on the western shore of the Dead Sea, only about 25 miles south of Jerusalem. No figures are given for the invading army but the Judæans clearly believed that it had overwhelming numbers.

"We are in far less apprehension for Jehoshaphat when we behold him the object of the enemies' hostilities than when we beheld him the subject of Ahab's kindness and hospitality. And very justly so, for in the one case he is about to be cast simply on the God of Israel, whereas in the other he was about to fall into the snare of Satan...When the world smiles, we are in danger of being attracted; but when it frowns, we are driven away from it into our stronghold; and this is both happy and healthful" (Mackintosh).

Jehoshaphat feared, and quickly decided that his only hope was in the Lord. He was acting like David in Psalm 56.3: "What time I am afraid, I will trust in thee". Christians are not exempt from fear, but thankfully they have a God to whom they can take their fears. In his fear Jehoshaphat turned to prayer and to fasting (v.3) rather than to despair (vv.6-12). Jehoshaphat led his people in seeking the Lord (vv.3-4).

"Seek" is a key word in his reign (17.3,4; 18.4; 19.3; 22.9). Jehoshaphat had a greater trust in God than in his military forces. He proclaimed a fast throughout all Judah. There was a good response to his proclamation. "All Judah" is repeated (vv.3,13,15,18,27) and the reference to "all the cities of Judah"(v.4) and all the women and children (v.13) speak of a wonderful response. His going throughout the land (19.4) as well as setting judges throughout all the fenced cities of Judah (19.5) probably built up good will towards Jehoshaphat so they readily responded to his call for a fast. Special fasts were sometimes held to seek God's help in particular circumstances (Judg 20.26; 1 Sam 7.6; Ezra 8.21-23).

"The news caused Jehoshaphat to summon all Judah to prayer. In this respect his action set a precedent that was followed in World War II. Hitler's army was only a week or two from crossing the British Channel and invading England when King George called the nation to prayer. Churches were left open twenty-four hours a day so that people could enter them and pray. God, however, heard their prayers...He turned the tide of war and miraculously delivered His people" (Barber).

Verses 5-13: Jehoshaphat's Remarkable Prayer

Jehoshaphat stood "...praying for the nation, appealing to the promises, the glory and the reputation of God which were at stake since he was identified with Judah". Then the same writer sums up his prayer well, "In his prayer he acknowledges God's sovereignty (v.6), God's covenant (v.7), God's presence (vv.8-9), God's goodness (v.10), God's possession (v.11), and their utter dependence on Him (v.12)" (The MacArthur Bible Commentary).

Jehoshaphat stood "in the house of the Lord" because he knew that was the right place to seek God's face (vv.5,9). It was "before the new court". This probably designated the "great" court or outer court of the Temple (4.9), called "new", possibly because it had been repaired or enlarged.

Some commentators believe that the invasion was the expression of God's wrath of which Jehu spoke to Jehoshaphat in 19.2: "...therefore is wrath upon thee from before the Lord". If that is so, then "this is a fine instance of a guilty servant seeking refuge in the bosom of the very God who is justly smiting him" (Williams). The rhetorical questions of vv.6-7 reinforce the certainty of what is said. Jehoshaphat appealed to facts from God's Word, including reference to Abraham 1,000 years before. This appeal to the Word of God in his prayer recalls our Lord's words in John 15.7: "If ye abide in me, and my words abide in you, ye shall ask what ye will, and it shall be done unto you". May the Lord help every Christian to love the Word of God and to trust God as Jehoshaphat clearly did.

"Jehoshaphat made a threefold appeal: (1) 'Art thou not the true God who is omnipotent and able to help us in our helplessness?'; (2) 'Art thou not our God who hast given us this land forever and so art bound to help us against enemy invaders?'; (3) 'Art thou not the God especially of this temple and promised Solomon that thou wouldest answer prayer from this place?' (Rawlinson). Jehoshaphat's prayer is in four sections.

Praise for God's sovereign power (v.6)

This is especially appropriate since the most crucial need for Judah was due to their powerlessness (v.12). His words in v.6, "...rulest not thou over all the kingdoms of the heathen? and in thine hand is there not power and might?", are similar to David's words in 1 Chronicles 29.12. Chronicles emphasizes that God is in heaven because that is where He hears prayer. This is seen especially in Solomon's prayer (6.21,23,25,27,30,33,35,39; cp. Ps 11.4; 103.19; 115.3).

Praise for the gift of the land and the temple (vv.7-9)

Jehoshaphat is especially thankful for the gifts of the land and the temple promised to Abraham, Moses, David, and Solomon. "Abraham thy friend" recalls Genesis 18.17: "shall I hide from Abraham that thing which I do?". This is the first time in the Bible that he is called the "friend of God". He is never called this in the book of Genesis, but he is seen on friendly terms with God in three ways.

1. The climax of his obedience was when he was willing to offer Isaac (James 2.21-23, "and he was called the Friend of God"). Our Lord Jesus said in John 15.14, "Ye are my friends, if ye do whatsoever I command you".

2. God told Abraham about His plan to destroy Sodom and Gomorrah. Our Lord Jesus said in John 15.15, "Henceforth I call you not servants; for the servant knoweth not what his lord doeth: but I have called you friends; for all things that I have heard of my Father I have made known unto you".

3. In Abraham's intercession for Sodom, he spoke with God as a man with his friend (cp. Exodus 33.11, "And the Lord spake unto Moses face to face, as a man speaketh unto his friend"). 200 years after this prayer God Himself refers to Abraham as "my friend" (Is 41.8).

Verse 9 is an excellent summary of Solomon's prayer in 6.14-42. Immediately after Solomon finished praying, "fire came down from heaven, and consumed the burnt offering and the sacrifices; and the glory of the Lord filled the house" (7.1). Again, in 7.12, "the Lord appeared to Solomon by night, and said unto him, I have heard thy prayer". Now Jehoshaphat is appealing to God in accordance with God's response to Solomon's prayer. Recalling earlier promises of God is also a feature of other prayers in Chronicles (1 Chr 17.21-22; 29.15,18; 2 Chr 6.5-17). Using promises of God from His Word in intercessory prayer is a principle of effective prayer. Thankfulness for the past gives fresh assurance for the future, especially in times of stress.

Complaint against invaders (vv.10-11)

Jehoshaphat reminded God that He did not allow Israel to attack these nations when they were travelling towards Canaan (Deut 2.4,9,19). He implied that it would not be consistent for God to allow these same nations (who were ungrateful invaders) to cast Judah out of the possession God Himself had given them. The Edomites were descendants of Esau. Ammon and Moab were descendants of Lot. All of them were distant relatives. Jehoshaphat called on God to honour Israel's former obedience and to keep His promise (v.11).

"The prayer is most precious and instructive - full of divine intelligence. They come, says he, 'to cast us out of thy possession, which thou has given us to inherit'. How simple! They would take what God has given! This was putting it, as it were, upon God to maintain His own covenant" (Mackintosh).

Plea for help (v.12)

Jehoshaphat made a specific request only at the end of his prayer. They had no power, no plan, and because their eyes were upon the Lord they had no panic. "The final phrase, 'We do not know what to do, but our eyes are upon You', is one of the most touching expressions of trust in God to be found anywhere in the Bible. To recognize one's weakness is a position of much strength (compare John 15.5; 2 Corinthians 12.9)" (Selman). "It is at Wits' End Corner that you meet the miracles, says the Psalmist (107.27-28)" (Wilcock). In v.12 Jehoshaphat is like his father Asa in 14.11. The final appeal in v.12, "our eyes are upon thee", is a beautiful expression and reminiscent of Psalm 123.2: "Behold, as the eyes of servants look unto the hand of their masters, and as the eyes of a maiden unto the hand of her mistress; so our eyes wait upon the Lord our God, until that he have mercy upon us". Christians should never be without hope. The saints' response in the darkest hour should be: "our eyes are upon thee". Jehoshaphat's prayer revealed great confidence in God and thankfulness for past deliverances. Philippians 4.6-7 is a precious promise, but it is important that the two words in v.6 there, "with thanksgiving", are not forgotten. Thanking God for help in the past helps Christians to enjoy the peace of God in the present. Their little ones and children were all with Judah and so were encouraged to learn the necessity of waiting on God (v.13).

Maclaren has some excellent things to say on the last phrase of v.12: "...we have no might against this great company that cometh against us; neither know we what to do: but our eyes are upon thee". Some choice quotations are: "Our text is the close and climax of Jehoshaphat's prayer, and as the event proved, it was the most powerful weapon that could have been employed, for the rest of the chapter tells the strangest story of a campaign that was ever written...We see here the confidence of despair... the very depth of despair sets them to climb to the height of trust...firm is the trust which leaps from despair!...Wise and happy shall we be if the sense of helplessness begets in us the energy of a desperate faith. For these two, distrust of self and glad confidence in God, are not opposites, as naked distrust and trust are, but are complementary...We see here the peaceful assurance of victory that attends on faith". Jahaziel told them in v.15, 'the battle is not yours, but God's', and in v.17, 'stand ye still and see the salvation of the Lord with you'. No wonder that the message was hailed as from heaven, and put new heart into the host, or that, when the messenger's voice ceased, his brother Levites broke into shrill praise as for a victory already won...For if we begin our warfare with an appeal to God, and with prayerful acknowledgment of our own impotence, we shall end it with thankful acknowledgment that we are 'more than conquerors through him that loved us'" (Rom 8.37) (Maclaren).

Verses 14-21: God's Answer Through Jahaziel and the Response

God gave a very encouraging answer through the Spirit of the Lord coming upon Jahaziel. His unusually long genealogy traces his pedigree back five generations to Asaph the chief Levitical musician when David organized the Temple personnel (1 Chr 16.5). David's day is a reminder of a new era of grace in the provision of the Temple. Asaph is listed as the composer of 12 of the Psalms (50, 73-83). "Jahaziel's words in v.15, 'the battle is not yours but God's', reflect the spirit of David against Goliath in 1 Samuel 17.47" (Payne). "Twice the prophet exhorts the king and the people in the very words that Jehovah used to encourage Joshua when the death of Moses had thrown upon him all the heavy responsibility of leadership: 'fear not, nor be dismayed' (vv.15,17; Josh 1.9)" (Bennett). Twice he encourages them with these words, "go ye down (go down) against them" (vv.16-17). Twice he tells them in v.17, "The Lord will be with you". Twice he said, "the battle is not yours, but God's" (v.15, cp. v.17). Persons with anxious hearts and minds appreciate the repetition of assuring words.

The words of v.17a, "stand ye still, and see the salvation of the Lord", recall Exodus 14.13 which gave a wonderful promise of a great miracle. "Exodus 14.13-14 offers a particularly close analogy, which suggests that the Chronicler saw this incident as a unique parallel to the exodus itself. Only in these two passages are the following phrases combined: 'do not be afraid', 'take your stand', 'see the Lord's deliverance', while the two statements in vv.15 and 17 that Judah does not have to fight are but a negative version of 'the Lord shall fight for you' (Ex 14.14)" (Selman). Verse 17 makes it clear that Jehoshaphat and his army would only be joyful spectators. The God who defeated Goliath and Pharaoh and his host is still Israel's God and ours as well. Jahaziel told them (v.16) exactly where to find the enemy on the morrow. The climax of his message was the promise of God's protective presence, "the Lord will be with you" (v.17).

Verse 18 describes the positive response of Jehoshaphat and his people with praise and worship. That response was as important as any military preparation. The prayer meeting was turned into a praise meeting. Their humble attitude expressed reverence for God and His Word, confidence in His promise, and thankfulness for such an unusual deliverance. It is the praise of faith that dares to give God credit for telling the truth. Dependence on God was more important than merely winning the battle. Some Levites stood up to praise the Lord God of Israel with a loud voice (v.19). They all regarded the victory as already obtained.

"Early the next morning they prepared to obey the Divine direction (v.20). It was to be a battle such as had never been witnessed since Jericho had fallen at the blast of the trumpet of the Lord when His ark compassed its walls. And they prepared for it in such manner as host going to battle had never done...If never before an army had so marched to battle, never, even in the marvelous history of Israel, had such results been experienced" (Edersheim). Rising early the next morning indicates their confidence based on Jahaziel's word the day before. In v.20 Jehoshaphat has come all the way from "fear" in v.3 to a new confidence in God. His exhortation to all Judah, "Believe in the Lord your God, so shall ye be established", was similar to Isaiah's appeal to Ahaz (Is 7.9). The words of Isaiah 7.9 confirm the words of Jehoshaphat in v.20 in a negative way, "If ye will not believe, surely ye shall not be established". "The thought may be paraphrased. **Trust** in the Lord your God and you will find Him **trustworthy**. There is in the exhortation a call to commitment. The trustworthiness of the Lord cannot be known until one begins to make decisions on the basis of His promises, staking wealth and welfare on the outcome" (McConville). The Hebrew wordplay could also be rendered, "Have firm faith and you will stand firm".

In v.21 they appointed singers to praise, singing what appears to be the Chronicler's favourite Psalm 136 (cp. 1 Chr 16.34, 41; 2 Chr 5.13; 7.3,6). The phrase "the beauty of holiness" is repeated often in the Old Testament. Most commentators prefer to refer to the singers in "holy array" or "holy attire". Their battle cry was replaced by singing.

The Hebrew word translated "mercy" is a precious word, sometimes translated "loving kindness". "The Hebrew word is HESED (2617), used about 250 times in the Old Testament. It means loyal, steadfast or faithful love and it stresses the idea of the belonging together of those involved in the love relationship. Here it connotes God's faithful love for His unfaithful people" (Ryrie's note on Hosea 2.19).

So great was their trust that the singing choir went in front of the army. All of Judah went out to be passive spectators of the power of the Lord shown in a marvelous way. Their action recalls Psalm 20.7: "Some trust in chariots, and some in horses: but we will remember the name of the Lord our God".

Maclaren writing on "Believe in the Lord your God, so shall ye be established" notes: "The exhortation in our text, which is Jehoshaphat's final word to his army, has in the original, a beauty and emphasis that are incapable of being preserved in translation. There is a play of words, which cannot be reproduced in another language, though the sentiment of it may be explained. The two expressions for 'believe' and 'be established' are varying forms of the same root-word; and although we can only imitate the original clumsily in our language, we might translate in some such way as this: 'Hold fast by the Lord your God, and you will be held fast', or 'Stay yourselves on Him and you will be stable'...Put out your hand and clasp Him, and He puts out His hand and steadies you".

Maclaren goes on to state three things: to whom we are to cling, how we are to cling, and what the consequences of clinging are. We are to cling to "'the Lord your God', and not even the Bible that tells you about Him...it is He that is the Object to which our faith clings...'Believe in His prophets, so shall ye prosper'. The immediate reference, of course, was to the man who the day before had assured them of victory. But the wider truth suggested is that the only way to get to God is through His Word that speaks of Him...The object of faith proposed to Judah is not only 'the Lord', but 'the Lord your God'". His promise must be appropriated personally.

"How we cling...and I mean that we should try to commit our way unto the Lord, 'to rest in the Lord and wait patiently for him'. The submissive will which cleaves to God's commandments, the waiting heart that clings to His love, the regulated thoughts that embrace His truth, and the childlike confidence that commits its path to Him — these are the elements of that steadfast adherence to the Lord which shall not be in vain" (Ps 37.5,7).

"The blessed effects of this clinging to God 'so shall ye be established'. That follows as a matter of course...'The law of the Lord is in his heart', says one of the Psalms, 'none of his steps shall slide'. The man who walks holding God's hand can put down a firm foot, even when he is walking in slippery places (Ps 37.31)" (Maclaren).

Verses 22-30: The Astounding Victory

"When they did but begin the work of praise, God perfected the work of their deliverance" (Matthew Henry). Verses 22-23 record how the invaders were defeated. The men of Mount Seir were smitten first by the others, possibly suspected of some treachery. Then the rest destroyed one another (v.23) (cp. Judges 7.22 which tells of Gideon's victory). When Judah looked upon the multitude in v.24 they were all dead. In v.25 "dead bodies" seems unlikely as an item in a list of plunder. Some ancient authorities have "garments", a common item of plunder. The ESV has "clothing" instead of "dead bodies". There was so much plunder in v.25 that it took three days of gathering. The enemies all lying dead and the enormous amount of booty reflect the greatness of the victory that God gave them. Such an astounding victory prompted praise and joy among the Lord's own people (vv.26-28) but great fear among their enemies (v.29).

On the fourth day they blessed the Lord in the valley of Berachah, which means "Blessing". They did not even wait until they got to the house of the Lord in Jerusalem. "The assemblage of v.4 was to ask help of the Lord. The assemblage of v.26 was to bless the Lord. The 'fear' that Moab inspired preceded the prayer meeting of v.4; the 'joy' that God inspired (v.27) followed the praise meeting of v.26" (Williams). They all returned to Jerusalem with joy, Jehoshaphat leading them, "for the Lord had made them to rejoice over their enemies" (v.27). They came with musical instruments to the house of the Lord (v.28). They most likely returned to the Temple to give thanks together to the Lord in the very place they had prayed together (vv.5-12). This is like the Samaritan leper in Luke 17.15-16 who returned to give thanks to the Lord once he saw that he was cleansed. Psalm 50.23 states, "Whoso offereth praise glorifieth me". The leper, with a loud voice, glorified God (Lk 17.15). The next verse tells us how he glorified God, by "giving him thanks". Even though nine others were cleansed, our Lord Jesus said in Luke 17.18, "There are not found that returned to give glory to God, save this stranger". It glorifies God whenever a stranger gets saved. It glorifies God to a greater degree when that person allows himself to be led by the Word of God to be baptised, to meet in fellowship with God's people, and so be a partaker at the Breaking of Bread where God can be honoured in thanksgiving.

Verses 31-34: Concluding Comments on Jehoshaphat's Reign

It might have been expected that vv.35-37 would come before vv.31-34. But it is easily explained because the Chronicler follows the same order as in 1 Kings 22.41-50. Verse 32 is a general positive assessment of the reign. He "departed not" from "that which was right in the sight of the Lord" as, sadly, his father had done for the last five years of his life. So he did better than his father. "Yet for all his virtues, he was not immune from a besetting sin, to which he was to surrender again (vv.35-37)…The tenor of the king's life was good, despite temporary lapses…A similar lapse is recorded in the case of the people in v.33" (Leslie C. Allen).

The high places in v.33 were most likely places where they worshipped the Lord their God only (as in 33.17) since there is no mention of idols. Nevertheless, such high places were forbidden in Deuteronomy 12.13-14. The last part of the verse explains why they did so, "for as yet the people had not prepared their hearts unto the God of their fathers". Jehu told Jehoshaphat, "thou…hast prepared thine heart to seek God" (19.3). Even though Jehoshaphat was such a godly leader, he was unable to get them to follow him in this. "A good example and good teaching are not enough when those who see and hear do not commit themselves in turn" (Leslie C. Allen). The Chronicler wanted his readers to see the necessity of continuing faithfulness and watchfulness. In v.34 he gives a prophetic source, Jehu the son of Hanani, as his most important authority for the record of Jehoshaphat.

Verses 35-37: Jehoshaphat's Alliance with Wicked Ahaziah

These three verses are somewhat of an anti-climax to the first 30 verses of this chapter. The passage in 1 Kings 22.48-49, and this one, are not contradictory but supplementary. Kings does not say anything about Eliezer or why the ships were broken. Kings tells us that they were Tarshish ships — a class of ships built for long journeys and able to go all the way to Tarshish — and that their destination was Ophir. The ships were built at Ezion-geber, the same place where Solomon built a navy (1 Kings 9.26). This alliance with Ahaziah must have taken place shortly after the death of Ahab. Ahaziah only lived for a little more than a year after him (see 1 Kings 22.51; 2 Kings 3.1).

Verse 37 tells of Eliezer's rebuke of Jehoshaphat, another instance of the Chronicler's use of prophetic warnings. All that we know of Eliezer is in this verse. "Jehoshaphat's devout life did not sanctify this venture; rather Ahaziah's corrupt life defiled it" (Thompson). The ships were broken because a holy God will not tolerate unholy alliances. "With this the Chronicler's account of this enterprise concludes; while in 1 Kings 22.49 it is further stated that, after the destruction of the ships first built, Ahaziah called on Jehoshaphat still to undertake the Ophir voyage in common with him, and so to build new ships for the purpose, but Jehoshaphat would not. The ground of his refusal may easily be gathered from v.37 of the Chronicle" (Keil). Alliance with the wicked for commercial reasons is not less displeasing to the Lord than alliance with the wicked for war. Both A. R. Fausset's Bible Dictionary and Cyril A. Potts in his Dictionary of Bible Proper Names give the meaning of Ezion-geber as "the giant's backbone". Knapp gives "the devil's backbone" and states that "there is always something of the wiles or power of Satan in these unequal yokes". Someone has well said, "If you marry a child of the devil you can expect to have trouble with your father-in-law". Jehoshaphat made one more unequal yoke not reported in Chronicles (2 Kings 3.7-14). This was with Jehoram another wicked son of Ahab. Jehoshaphat again said, "I am as thou art". But, significantly, Elisha made a big difference between Jehoram and Jehoshaphat. He rebuked Jehoram (v.13) and then he said, "As the Lord of hosts liveth, before whom I stand, surely, were it not that I regard the presence of Jehoshaphat the king of Judah, I would not look toward thee, nor see thee" (v.14). How sad that the reign of Jehoshaphat (which was wonderful in so many ways) ended on the sad note of his unholy alliance.

2 CHRONICLES 21

Jehoram's Reign

Introductory

Chapters 21 and 22 show the serious and far reaching consequences of good king Jehoshaphat's mistake in having his son Jehoram marry Athaliah, the wicked daughter of Ahab. Ahab married Jezebel, a woman more wicked than himself (1 Kings 16.31 and 21.25). Athaliah is called a wicked woman (2 Chr 24.7). Jezebel was Athaliah's mother and she raised her daughter to be like herself. Ahab was greatly influenced for wickedness by his strong-willed wife, Jezebel. Ahab's son-in-law, Jehoram, was also greatly influenced for wickedness by *his* strong-willed wife, Athaliah.

God blessed Judah during Jehoshaphat's reign of 25 years, but the next 15 years were disastrous. Jehoram reigned for eight years and "he walked in the way of the kings of Israel, like as did the house of Ahab for he had the daughter of Ahab to wife" (v.6), and then Ahaziah reigned for one year and "his mother was his counseller to do wickedly" (22.3). Athaliah herself usurped the throne for six years. Jehoram was the son of one of the best kings of Judah, but he himself was one of the worst. He and his son, Ahaziah, were the first kings of Judah about whom the Chronicler had nothing commendable to say. Jehoram undid all the good of Jehoshaphat and Asa. The writer of the Chronicles records the words of Elijah the prophet contrasting the reigns of Jehoshaphat and Asa, which were so different from the reign of Jehoram (vv.12-13). Judah was brought almost to the brink of ruin in 15 years through the evil influence of one wicked woman, Athaliah (21.6; 22.3; 22.10-12). Other counsellors of the house of Ahab helped her (22.4). Because of the evil influence of Athaliah and the house of Ahab, there was actually a house of Baal that was destroyed along with Mattan the priest of Baal (23.17). Surely the record of these two chapters is a forceful illustration of the solemn consequences for any saint of disobeying 2 Corinthians 6.14-18.

"Chapters 21-22 belong together, as evidenced by a number of common expressions. In addition to 'the house of Ahab' (21.6; 22.3) these include the death of the royal 'princes' (21.17; 22.8; cp. 21.4), the 'youngest son's' preservation (21.17; 22.1; cp. 22.11-12), invasion by Arabian raiders (21.16-17; 22.1), and the fact that both kings 'did evil in the eyes of the Lord' (21.6; 22.4)" (Selman). The good of Jehoshaphat was still remembered (21.12; 22.9). Ahaziah, Jehoshaphat's grandson, was slain by Jehu, who was raised up by God to execute judgment against the house of Ahab. Yet they buried him out of respect for Jehoshaphat, "who sought the Lord with all his heart" (22.9). Neither Jehoram not his son Ahaziah followed Jehoshaphat's example of seeking God (17.4; 19.3; 20.3; 22.9), yet it is because of the good king's mistake in having his son marry Athaliah that they were so closely linked to the house of Ahab.

The writer of the Kings writes only nine verses about Jehoram (2 Kings 8.16-24) while the Chronicler has 20. The writer of the Chronicles omits only a little of 2 Kings but adds the account of Jehoram killing his brothers (21.4), the erection of the high places and leading Judah astray (21.11), the letter from Elijah (21.12-15), the loss of land and family to the Philistines and Arabians (21.16-17), and the manner of his death as prophesied by Elijah (21.18-20).

Verses 1-4 have no parallel in 2 Kings, vv.5-7 are parallel with 2 Kings 8.17-19, vv.8-10 are parallel with 2 Kings 8.20-22, and v.20 is parallel with 2 Kings 8.24. Jehoram is also called Joram in 2 Kings 8.21,29; 9.14-23; and 1 Chronicles 3.11

Outline of Chapter 21

Verse 1: Jehoshaphat's death and Jehoram reigning in his stead.
Verses 2-4: Jehoram's murder of his six brothers and some of the princes.
Verses 5-11: The character of Jehoram's reign.
Verses 12-15: The writing of judgment from Elijah the prophet.
Verses 16-20: The fulfillment of the judgment.

Verse 1: Jehoshaphat's Death and Jehoram Reigning in his Stead

"It seems like a relief of spirit to read the words, 'Jehoshaphat slept with his fathers' (21.1), as we feel assured that he has at last got beyond the reach of the enemies snares and devices; and further, that he comes under the Spirit's benediction, 'Blessed are the dead which die in the Lord; for they rest from their labours', - yes, a rest from their conflicts, snares and temptations also" (Mackintosh).

Verses 2-4: Jehoram's Murder of his Six Brothers and Some of the Princes

Six brothers are named in v.2. The second Azariah is given as Azaryahu in the NKJV. These two may possibly have had different mothers. Jehoshaphat is referred to as "the king of Israel". The Chronicler seems to regard Judah as the rightful successor of the united Israel. He uses the term "Israel" for the southern kingdom a number of times including, in v.4, "princes of Israel". See also 12.1,6; 15.17; 28.19,27. In v.3 Jehoshaphat followed the example of his great grandfather, Rehoboam, who had also chosen which of his sons he wanted to reign (11.22). We read of Rehoboam in 11.23: "And he dealt wisely, and dispersed of all his children...unto every fenced city: and he gave them victual in abundance". So Jehoshaphat gave his other sons "great gifts of silver, and of gold, and of precious things, with fenced cities in Judah" (v.3).

Jehoram murdered all of his brothers because they were potential rivals to the throne (v.4). In view of the fact that Athaliah murdered her own grandchildren (22.10) and that Athaliah's mother was a murderess, there is a good likelihood that she suggested to Jehoram that he should kill his brothers. Elijah said that his brethren were better than him (21.13). This may well have been because none of them had such a wicked wife as he had. The fact that his brethren were better than he was may be an added reason why he killed them. It is possible that his brothers had expressed disapproval of Jehoram's policies. The princes of Israel, slain at the same time, may also have disapproved.

Two other persons are recorded who sought to eliminate all potential rivals. Abimelech in Judges 9.5,56 and Jehu in 2 Kings 10.6-11. "Ironically, Jehoram's efforts to safeguard his royal position put at risk the very continuance of the dynasty, the massacre being the first in a sequence of events which will result in its near extinction" (McConville). Four times violence is recorded against the royal family (21.4,17; 22.8-9; 22.10-11) so that the Davidic line was completely exterminated except for a one-year-old baby boy. Satan did his utmost these four times to thwart God's purpose in having the Messiah born of the line of David. So the purposes of God for His blessed Son and the blessing of mankind hung on the brittle thread of the life of this baby, but God's purposes were secure nevertheless.

Verses 5-11: The Character of Jehoram's Reign

2 Kings 1.17 and 3.1 indicate that Jehoram had a co-regency with his father. In v.6 Athaliah so wickedly influenced Jehoram that he abolished the worship of the Lord and did what he could to introduce all the corruptions of the northern kingdom including the worship of Baal. Jehoram brought Judah down to the level of the northern kingdom. The ten northern tribes were passing through the darkest days of their history. There were only 7,000 who had not bowed the knee to Baal (1 Kings 19.18 and Rom 11.4). It is possible that the house of Baal that had to be destroyed in 23.17 was built during his reign with his approval and direction. Jehoram was so wicked that God would have completely destroyed him and his house had it not been for His promise to David (v.7). The promises to David of 2 Samuel 7.12-16 and 1 Chronicles 17.11-14 are here called a covenant. God was faithful to His promise.

The changes in v.7 from 2 Kings 8.19 seem to be significant. "The house of David" in v.7 (instead of Judah in Kings) is directly opposed to "the house of Ahab" in v.6. "David his servant's sake" in Kings has become "the covenant that he made with David". The only other time that the Davidic covenant is mentioned in Chronicles is in 2 Chronicles 13.5. Both passages refer back to 1 Chronicles 17.11-14. It was because of the same covenant that God had preserved the southern kingdom to Rehoboam after Solomon's sins of idolatry in his closing years (1 Kings 11.4,36). God promised "to give a light to him (David) and to his sons forever" (v.7). Unger writes, "Evil men and their dark deeds could not extinguish that light. It would eventually be realized in David's greater son, 'the light of the world' (Jn 8.12)". Rossier states, "The royal house was spared only in view of the future heir who was to descend from it". The promise of a "light" to David and his sons forever seems to be a figurative way of saying that David would always have a descendant for the throne. The same expression in 1 Kings 15.4 and 2 Kings 8.19 supports this interpretation.

The metaphor of the lamp for the lasting dynasty of David is to be fulfilled ultimately in David's greatest son, our Lord Jesus Christ (Lk 1.32-33). The Chronicler has a greater interest in the lampstand shining in the temple than the writer of Kings. The phrase, "according to the ordinance", for the lampstand in 4.7,20, RV, is found in 2 Chronicles 13.11 but has no parallel in Kings. Leslie C. Allen writes, "In 13.11 he mentioned 'the lampstand of gold' being in the temple as an ingredient of legitimate worship... The Chronicler seems to have consciously related the metaphor and the religious ritual of the ever-burning lamp: instead of referring to lampstands in the plural as elsewhere, he mentioned only one. It is probable that he viewed the perpetually burning light of the lampstand(s) as a symbol of the perpetuity of the Davidic line".

All the rest of this chapter could be considered as God punishing Jehoram. While the Davidic covenant promised the preservation of the Davidic dynasty it also warned that individual kings would be punished for departure from God (cp. 1 Chr 28.9; 2 Chr 7.19-22). The first punishment recorded is a rebellion by Edom (vv.8-10a) and a revolt by Libnah, a city of Judah (v.10b). Edom and Libnah had been in subjection before. God allowed them both to succeed in their revolt because of Jehoram's apostasy.

During Jehoshaphat's reign, 1 Kings 22.47 states that "There was then no king in Edom: a deputy was king". In light of this verse, where 2 Kings 3.9 tells of the king of Edom with King Jehoshaphat, it is best to understand that the king of Edom was merely assuming the status of king. Verse 8 of our chapter records that when the Edomites revolted they made themselves a king. Jehoram tried to subdue the rebellion but the attempt ended in defeat. Edomite forces surrounded his armies. By night, he managed to break through and escape. 2 Kings 8.21 states that "the people fled into their tents". It seems that the others escaped as best they could. This implies a battle ending in defeat. Jehoram could not subdue Edom.

Even though the writer of Kings tells us of these two revolts, it is only the Chronicler who specifically tells us why (that is characteristic of him): "because he had forsaken the Lord God of his fathers" (v.10b). To forsake God is the opposite of seeking Him. "If Jehoshaphat's virtue was to seek God (17.4; 19.3; 22.9), his son's vice was to forsake Him. The Chronicler's view of moral providence was a high one: he delights to demonstrate how God keeps short accounts in the payment of moral debts. So if the reward of his father's seeking God was the consolidation of his kingdom (17.5), Jehoram's own recompense for forsaking Him was its depletion. Evil does not go unpunished" (Leslie C. Allen).

Jehoram encouraged worship in the high places in contrast to his grandfather Asa (14.3) and his father Jehoshaphat (17.6). He was the first king to make them. He also compelled Judah to commit spiritual fornication (v.11).

Verses 12-15: The Letter of Judgment from Elijah the Prophet

The only part of the remainder of the chapter that is found in Kings is the notice of the death of Jehoram. The next incident noted by the Chronicler describes a writing to Jehoram from Elijah the prophet. Kings has recorded much about Elijah referring to him by name 66 times. Elijah was especially raised up of God to confront Ahab and his Baal worship. This is the only occasion the Chronicler mentions Elijah. Since Jehoram behaved like the house of Ahab (because he had the daughter of Ahab to wife), it is very fitting for Jehoram to be rebuked by Elijah. Similarly, Jehu was especially raised up of God to execute judgment against the house of Ahab (2 Kings 9.7-9). Jehu also slew some of the royal family of Judah, including Jehoshaphat's grandchildren (2 Chr 22.7-9), because of their connection with Ahab. They buried Ahaziah because "he is the son of Jehoshaphat, who sought the Lord with all his heart" (2 Chr 22.9). Even when Jehu killed relatives of Jehoshaphat, there was still respect shown for his memory. How striking that is since it is only because of the good king's mistake (in having his oldest son, Jehoram, marry Athaliah) that the judgment had to be executed.

The time of Elijah's translation cannot be exactly fixed with certainty. In 2 Kings 3.11 it says, "Here is Elisha the son of Shaphat, which poured water on the hands of Elijah". That in itself does not prove that Elijah had already ascended. It only shows that Elisha had served Elijah. Some students point out that Elijah could not have written a letter to Jehoram since he had already gone home to heaven. Strictly speaking, v.12 does not speak of a "letter" but of a "writing". According to Strong's Concordance, in the many times that the AV has "letter", not once does it have the Hebrew word for "writing" that is in v.12. Elijah could have written this after Jehoram murdered his brothers and before he was translated. Elisha could have delivered it on behalf of Elijah after his ascension. This is the only known writing of Elijah.

But even if we assume that Elijah had already ascended before Jehoshaphat died, there is still a satisfactory explanation. God could easily have revealed to Elijah all the wickedness that Jehoram would do after his father's death and the resulting judgment. The writer of the Chronicles sometimes wrote of prophets predicting disaster to kings before the event. He wrote of Shemaiah and Rehoboam (12.5-8); Hanani and Asa (16.7-9); Jehu and Jehoshaphat (19.2-3); Zechariah and Joash (24.20); and Elijah and Jehoram in this chapter. Predicting the future accurately is supernatural.

Archer deals well with the problems about this writing. He gives the reign of Jehoram (852-841) and concludes, "In all probability the letter of

Elijah to Jeroboam was composed in 847 and delivered to him that same year, shortly before Elijah was taken up into heaven by a celestial chariot of fire (2 Kings 2.1)".

It is pleasant to notice that though Asa's last five years were not as good as his earlier years, and even though Jehoshaphat made the same mistake a number of times (attempting to make an unequal yoke with the house of Ahab), yet their "ways" on the whole were such that Elisha could hold them up as a positive example.

Verses 12 and 13 state why there was judgment on Jehoram and on the people. In v.13 Jehoram had made them go "a whoring", i.e. to go after false gods. Today saints commit spiritual adultery by being on intimate terms with the world. "Ye adulteresses, know ye not that the friendship with the world is enmity with God?" (James 4.4, RV). Because the people went a whoring, they would suffer as v.14 states: "Behold, with a great plague will the Lord smite thy people". Plague (as in the case of some of the plagues of Egypt) has the meaning of general calamity rather than the narrow meaning of pestilence. In due time enemies invaded the land (vv.16-17).

Verses 16-20: The Fulfillment of the Judgment.

Because Jehoram had slain his brethren, then in judgment against him, his children, his wives, and all his goods would also feel the great plague (v.13); and in v.14 he himself would have great sickness and die a painful death (fulfilled in vv.18-19). In due time all his sons were slain except the youngest (v.17). The justice of the governmental dealing of God is seen in that the man who murdered all of another man's sons except one now has all his sons murdered except one. His punishment fits the crime. He also lost some of his wives at the same time. His kingdom was so weak that Jehoram is not recorded as trying to recover his wives.

In vv.8-10 the Edomites and Libnah revolted because "he had forsaken the Lord God of his fathers" (v.10). In v.16, "the Lord stirred up against Jehoram…"; and in v.18, "And after all this the Lord smote him in his bowels". In v.17, "the king's house" was probably a royal residence outside Jerusalem. Surely Jehoram found out experimentally that "the way of transgressors is hard" (Prov 13.15). Jehoram's youngest son is called Jehohaz in v.17 and once Azariah in 22.6; but in ch.22, he is called Ahaziah eleven times.

The reaction of the people when he died (vv.19-20) gives three more evidences of the judgment of God on Jehoram. The people made no burning for him (v.19); he "departed without being desired" (v.20); he was not buried in the sepulchres of the kings (v.20). In these three ways he was buried without honour. Herbert Lockyer wrote, "One day Robert Murray McCheyne, the Scottish saint, wrote in his diary, 'O God, for grace to live, so that when dead, I shall be missed'".

2 CHRONICLES 22

Ahaziah's and Athaliah's Reigns

Introductory

This chapter emphasizes the influence of the house of Ahab (vv.3,4,7,8) during the reigns of Ahaziah (vv.1-9) and Athaliah (vv.10-12). Athaliah, the daughter of Ahab and mother of Ahaziah, continued to be dominant. She named her son after her wicked brother in the north. That was bad enough but, more seriously, she was also "his counseller to do wickedly" (v.3). Athaliah (as the queen mother) and other advisers of the house of Ahab made their influence felt during Ahaziah's brief reign. After he died, Athaliah usurped the throne for six years. So, for both reigns and also for the reign of Jehoram (21.6), the house of Ahab effectively influenced Judah, especially through Athaliah. She succeeded in practically obliterating any distinction between the religious life of the northern kingdom and that of the southern.

The names of their kings show that Judah and Israel were very close at that time. No other kings are named Jehoram or Ahaziah, yet both names are used of successive kings in Judah and Israel. Ahab (the king of Israel) had two sons who reigned successively, Ahaziah and Jehoram. Jehoshaphat (the king of Judah) had a son Jehoram who reigned after him; Ahaziah reigned after Jehoram in Judah. In summary, Ahaziah and Jehoram ruled in Israel while Jehoram and Ahaziah ruled in Judah.

The Chronicler's account of Ahaziah is much shorter than that of Kings (2 Kings 8.24-10.14). The account in Kings has many details of the coup of Jehu and the fulfillment of prophecy against the house of Ahab. The writer of the Chronicles omits much of that material and concentrates on that which is connected with the southern kingdom. The verses in Chronicles parallel to the record in Kings show that the Chronicler had the Kings account before him (compare 2 Kings 8.26-29 with 2 Chronicles 22.2-6). He also seems to depend on his reader's knowledge of that account (22.7-8). See also the introductory section for 2 Chronicles 21.

Outline of Chapter 22

Verses 1-9: Ahaziah's reign.
Verses 10-12: Athaliah's reign.

Verses 1-9: Ahaziah's Reign

"The inhabitants of Jerusalem" (v.1) made Ahaziah the youngest son of Jehoram king in place of his father. This is only recorded in Chronicles. "The inhabitants of Jerusalem" may be the same as "the people of the land" who had a part in deciding who was to reign in times of crisis (26.1; 33.25; 36.1). This seems to indicate that there was some difficulty as to who should reign. It is also possible that "the inhabitants of Jerusalem" were some in Jerusalem who acted without considering others outside the capital. "The band of men" referred to in v.1 were probably Philistines (21.16).

Since Jehoram was only 40 years old when he died, Ahaziah could not be 42 years old when he began to reign (v.2). 2 Kings 8.26 gives his age as 22, which is very likely correct. The age of 42 is most probably the result of a copyist's error. It is remarkable that there are so few such errors! The doctrine of inspiration is not affected since that refers to the original Hebrew and Greek Scriptures. Verse 2 refers to Athaliah as "the daughter of Omri". The Hebrew word for "daughter" can also be translated "granddaughter"; for Athaliah was the daughter of Ahab and the granddaughter of Omri (21.6). Omri was the first king of his dynasty to reign. Athaliah apparently was not taken captive with other wives of Jehoram as described in 21.17. Since Ahaziah was 22 when his father died at the age of 40, that means that his father was only 18 when he (Ahaziah) was born and he was the youngest of Jehoram's sons. This is possible when we realize that early marriages were often entered into in that area and at that time; and also when we remember that Jehoram had several wives (21.17).

The words, "He also" in v.3 were added by the Chronicler to indicate that in his mind the reigns of Jehoram and Ahaziah are linked together. The writer of the Chronicles also introduced and emphasized wicked counsel. Counselling is mentioned in each of three successive verses (vv.3,4,5). The dependence of Ahaziah on counsellors from the house of Ahab is a chief characteristic of his reign. It seems that Ahaziah more thoroughly submitted to the evil influence of the house of Ahab than did his father. Athaliah used her position as queen mother to the full and we read in v.3 that "his mother was his counseller to do wickedly". The other counsellors of the house of Ahab were probably of her choosing (to give all the greater weight to her advice). Verse 4 states, "they were his counsellers after the death of his father to his destruction".

Almost every ruler depends on advisers. But each is responsible as to how he acts on the advice given to him. The United States President Harry Truman had on his desk the saying, "The buck stops here". He was accepting responsibility for his actions, as all should do. Ahaziah could have been pleasing to God in his reign if only he been like the man of Psalm 1.1: "Blessed is the man that walketh not in the counsel of the ungodly". Bad counsel has ruined the lives of many young persons going to college or beginning their working life.

Jehoram and Joram in v.5 and v.7 are the same, with simply longer or shorter variants of the name. Ramah in v.6 is an abbreviated form of Ramoth-gilead in v.5. Azariah in v.6 refers to Ahaziah. The ESV has Ahaziah. JND and RV both refer to Ahaziah in the margin.

As a result of the counsel, Ahaziah "went with Jehoram…to war against Hazael king of Syria…and the Syrians smote Joram" (v.5). Jehoram returned to be healed in Jezreel. Ahaziah went down to see his uncle Jehoram (v.6). Since there is so little detail about the war against the Syrians, we do not know whether Ahaziah went down from Ramoth-gilead or from Jerusalem.

Jehoram, like his father Ahab, went to war against Syria at Ramoth-gilead (1 Kings 22.4) and, like his father, had the help of a king of Judah. Ahab had the help of good king Jehoshaphat (1 Kings 22.4,29). Jehoram had the help of Ahaziah. Jehoram of Israel, like his father, lost his life as a result (1 Kings 22.34,37). Jehoram was wounded by the Syrians in battle and later killed by Jehu (2 Kings 8.29; 9.24; 2 Chr 22.5).

The paragraph in vv.7-9 seems to be based on the much longer account given in 2 Kings 9.1-28 and 10.12-14. It is likely that the Chronicler expected his readers to be familiar with this and so did not think it necessary to explain the identity of Jehu. He wanted to tell briefly what happened to Ahaziah and his family. He added a sentence at the beginning (v.7) to show that what happened was the judgment of God on Ahaziah's unfaithfulness: "And the destruction of Ahaziah was of God by coming to Joram". He also added the last half of v.9: "And the house of Ahaziah had no power to hold the kingdom" (RV). When Ahaziah died at the young age of 23, he had no adult son who could be his successor. That verse is a transition to the following account of Athaliah, usurping the throne, for it sets the stage for the event recorded in v.10.

There are some differences between the details of 2 Kings and here. In 2 Kings 9.27, Ahaziah is killed first and "the brethren of Ahaziah" afterwards as described in 2 Kings 10.12-14. The writer of the Chronicles records Ahaziah being slain afterwards (vv.8-9). He may have wanted to finish with the judgment upon Ahaziah in his death. 2 Kings 9.28 records Ahaziah being buried "in his sepulchre with his fathers in the city of David". Since v.9 does not record the place of his burial, it can be taken as an indication by the Chronicler that Ahaziah did not please God. He himself was not worthy to have his burial recorded in Chronicles, but since he was the grandson of Jehoshaphat (who sought the Lord with all his heart, v.9), it was only fitting that he should have a decent burial, out of respect for his grandfather. It was in keeping with that respect for Ahaziah to be buried in Jerusalem as 2 Kings 9.28 records. Verse 9 gives the final evaluation of Jehoshaphat by the writer of the Chronicles. The godly reign of that king is a great contrast to the wicked reigns of Jehoram and Ahaziah. How sad that the mistake of good King Jehoshaphat in having his son Jehoram marry Athaliah (the daughter of Ahab and Jezebel) had so much to do with the evils of the reigns of Jehoram and Ahaziah. Those related to Ahaziah who were killed in v.8 are best considered as "kinsmen" or "relatives".

It is more difficult to reconcile the movements of Ahaziah shortly before he died, as recorded in 2 Kings 9.27 and 2 Chronicles 22.9. The Chronicler was no doubt chiefly concerned to bring out the theological implications of what had happened. Ahaziah met his death as a result of visiting his uncle Jehoram in Jezreel where he was recovering from being wounded by the Syrians. God had anointed Jehu to cut off the house of Ahab. Just as Ahaziah had followed the house of Ahab in wickedness, and he himself was a grandson of Ahab, so he died with them under the judgment of God. The writer of the Chronicles is the only one to refer to Ahaziah hiding in Samaria (v.9). "There is ironic justice in the death of Ahaziah: he who lived by the counsel of the Omrides shared their fate; he who had taken advice from Samaria found no refuge there at the time of his death" (Dillard). He died the same day as his uncle. So the king of the northern kingdom and the king of the southern kingdom were both killed the same day. Ahaziah was the sixth king from Solomon and the first king of Judah to die violently. The Chronicler has given another illustration of God's justice in bringing retribution for wickedness.

Verses 10-12: Athaliah's Reign

Barber offers a good summary of the three reigns connected to Athaliah. "So far we have considered the life of the king nobody wanted, and the short lived reign of the king nobody knew, and now we read about Athaliah, the queen whom everybody hated."

It is especially noticeable that the writer of the Chronicles does not give the age of Athaliah when she began to reign; nor did the writer of Kings. Neither regarded her as a legitimate ruler, so the usual introductory and concluding notices about her reign are omitted. She truly was an illegitimate usurper. The Chronicler followed the Kings account (2 Kings 11.1-3) closely but with the significant addition (v.10) of the phrase "of the house of Judah". Athaliah wanted to destroy all the descendants of David, who was of the tribe of Judah. God would not permit this.

The writer of the Chronicles alone states that Jehoshabeath was the wife of Jehoiada the priest. This is the only recorded marriage of one from the royal line with one from the priestly line. Jehoiada was considerably older than Jehoshabeath (24.15). She was the sister of Ahaziah, born to Jehoram by another wife (other than Athaliah), according to the Jewish historian Josephus. As the sister of Ahaziah, Jehoshabeath had access to the baby.

Athaliah had a grandfather, a father, and two brothers who reigned in succession in the northern kingdom. She also had a father-in-law, a husband, and a son who reigned in succession in the southern kingdom. But that entire honour was not enough for her. She desperately wanted to reign herself. She was also anxious for the worship of Baal to continue in Judah. Once she saw that her son was dead, she cruelly destroyed the entire seed royal, including her own grandchildren. She probably concentrated on the males who could be potential successors to Ahaziah. The fact that Jehoshabeath was spared supports that. But since she was the wife of the high priest, it is possible that that also was a factor in her escape from the wholesale slaughter.

Even though Jehu so thoroughly massacred the house of Ahab, he did not succeed in killing Athaliah. Her massacre of the seed royal was the fourth killing of the royal family in less than ten years. It brought the house of David to the verge of extinction. The fact that the line of David survived demonstrates God's faithfulness to His promise. Behind Athaliah's action was Satan who wanted the line of Messiah cut off to oppose the purposes of God for His Son. It is thrilling to see how God over-ruled. Satan used other attempts to cut off the line. "These attempts to eliminate the royal line did not take God by surprise. He foreknew what would happen and sovereignly orchestrated events so that there would always be a descendent of David to sit on David's throne" (Barber).

Verse 11 tells of this woman Jehoshabeath who is a contrast to Athaliah. Courageously, she risked her life to save the baby boy by putting him and his nurse in a bedchamber, a convenient hiding place. The bedchamber was a room where mattresses and bedding were stored. Later, she and her husband removed him to a safer hiding place. Verse 12 states that "he was with them hid in the house of God six years". Joash was probably raised in the home of the high priest in one of the buildings of the court of the temple.

This is a reminder of Moses in the ark of bulrushes at the brink of the river (Ex 2.3) and the young child Jesus taken to Egypt to escape the desire of Herod to kill Him (Mt 2.13,16). Pharaoh, Athaliah, and Herod were all over-ruled by the thrilling providential working of God. "The fact that royal infants may regularly have been put into the care of wet nurses or foster mothers becomes the key to Jehoshabeath's frustration of Athaliah's plans; the sucking child was overlooked and could have escaped detection as he grew by mingling with the priests children" (Dillard).

Another contrast is given here. The Chronicler gave the boy Joash his royal title as king even before he was crowned (23.3), regarding him as the legitimate king even while Athaliah reigned as a usurper. Just as Herod the king was opposed to the One who was "born King of the Jews" (Mt 2.2), so there was opposition here. Athaliah and the baby boy were rivals. Surely "God hath chosen the weak things of the world to confound the things which are mighty" (1 Cor 1.27).

After the death of Ahaziah, there are three unique things worthy of note.

1. This is the only time that there was a break in 400 years in the reigning of successive Davidic kings in Judah.
2. This is the first and only time either in Judah or Israel that a queen ruled. "Even the wife of the reigning king is never directly spoken of as queen. Jezebel and Maacah are called queens, but in each case it is as queen mother (the mother of the reigning king), and not as wife or ruler (2 Kings 10.13; 1 Kings 15.13)" (Lockyer).
3. This was the only time that a priest (Jehoiada) had such a leading role in the affairs of Judah.

2 CHRONICLES 23

The Overthrow of Athaliah and the Crowning of Joash

Introductory

This chapter tells of Jehoiada the high priest leading the overthrow of Athaliah, the crowning of Joash, and the subsequent reformation. 2 Kings 11.4-20 gives a briefer account of these events. The very first verse of this chapter suggests that the Chronicler had another source (besides the Kings account) since he gives the names of five captains of hundreds, who are completely absent from the account in Kings. There the writer emphasizes the part the military played in the coup in protecting the king and the palace, while the writer of Chronicles emphasizes the part that the Levites played in protecting the temple. The two accounts supplement each other, but do not contradict each other. Keil very thoroughly demonstrates that the accounts harmonize. "But if...the two accounts be recognized to be extracts confining themselves to the main points, excerpted from a more detailed narrative of the events from a different point of view, the discrepancies may at once be reconciled".

There are additions in this account that show the singular interests of the Chronicler. He is especially concerned for the sanctity and the personnel of the temple. Its holiness and cleanliness are to be preserved (vv.6,19). He has explicit instructions for the duties of the Levites, including the porters and musicians (vv.4,7-8,13,18-19). This was a special encouragement to the priests and Levites in the days of the Chronicler. He is the only writer who records that "Jehoiada and his sons anointed him" (v.11b). It is very sad to think that Zechariah was probably one of the sons who anointed Joash as king. In 24.21-22 we learn that Joash had him stoned for giving a message from God.

The Chronicler is also concerned to show that God's promise concerning the house of David was fulfilled. Both Kings and Chronicles refer to Joash as "the king" and "the king's son", but the writer of the Chronicles goes further. He writes, "Behold, the king's son shall reign, as the Lord hath said of the sons of David" (v.3b). This is an important addition. He also writes of the restoration of temple worship as established by David (v.18). This was an incentive to his post-exilic readers. Since God preserved the Davidic line when it was so close to being exterminated, God could do it again. Another descendant of David could rule again! Eventually He came, the Lord Jesus, the One who is still destined to rule universally.

The people are prominent in the Kings account, but the Chronicler particularly emphasizes their part in the coup. References to the chief of the fathers (v.2), all the congregation (v.3), and all Judah (v.8), "give them additional prominence as a covenant people (cp. vv.1,3,16)" (Selman). The writer calls attention to the coronation of Joash as being similar to the coronation of David, especially in his emphasis on "all the people" (vv.5,6,10,13,16,17,20,21). Those eight references are double the number found in 2 Kings 11 (vv.14,18,19,20). "The Chronicler indicated by its frequent usage that it was not merely the priests and Levites who were involved in the coup but the whole nation" (Thompson). This was similar to the occasion when David was given his rightful place as king, "…and all the rest also of Israel were of one heart to make David king" (1 Chr 12.38). Another similarity is, "there was joy in Israel" (v.40d). Here in this chapter all the people willingly and joyfully took part in the coronation, but this is almost equally so in 2 Kings 11. It is recorded twice there (vv.14,20) and thrice here (vv.13,18,21). What a day of rejoicing for the godly. For six years they did not know that God's promise of a descendant of David for the throne had not failed. Now they see it fulfilled in the seven-year-old king!

Jehoiada and his wife Jehoshabeath acted nobly in faith as his words in v.3 indicate: "Behold, the king's son shall reign, as the Lord hath said of the sons of David". What the Lord had said enabled them to act in faith in spite of the danger, difficulty, and work. God gave Jehoiada the needed wisdom so that all his careful plans succeeded, "all proving that whatever be the cunning and craft of the devil in Athaliah, it must succumb to the wisdom of God and of faith" (Knapp). This is an encouragement to act in faith and dependence on the Word of God. They also had patience along with their faith, waiting for God's time. Faith and patience go together - Isaiah 28.16d: "…he that believeth shall not make haste", and Hebrews 6.12: "…them who through faith and patience inherit the promises". "A woman's ruthlessness (Athaliah's) is outwitted by a woman's cunning (Jehoshabeath's)" (Farrar).

Jehoiada and Jehoshabeath are commendable in different ways. Jehoiada courageously led others in what he was convinced was right in the sight of God. Jehoshabeath was heroic in a quieter but very necessary way in aiming for the goal they both wanted. "The complementary roles of Jehoiada and his wife well illustrate the mutual dependence of those with different gifts and tasks within the church" (McConville). This couple working together call to mind another outstanding couple in the New Testament, Aquila and Priscilla, who are always mentioned together and are an inspiration to every Christian couple, as are Jehoiada and Jehoshabeath.

Outline of Chapter 23

Verses 1-11: Joash anointed king.
Verses 12-15: Athaliah's reaction.
Verses 16-21: Reformation.

Verses: 1-11: Joash Anointed King

Jehoiada and his wife Jehoshabeath carefully kept the secret of Joash for six years. Jehoiada was biding his time until the child was old enough to be presented to the people. The disgust of the people with Athaliah's reign had also probably reached a peak. The military commanders (v.1) were willing and the Levites longed for a return to the regular services for the worship of the Lord. Jehoiada is often spoken of as high priest; for example 2 Kings 12.10 and 2 Chronicles 24.11 both refer to him in this office. Verse 1 of this chapter says that he "strengthened himself", that is he took courage or "showed himself courageous". "The high priest, whose normal duties lay in the realm of sacrifices and offering incense, became on this occasion more like the commander-in-chief of an army" (McShane).

Even though all the names of v.1 with the exception of "Elishaphat" can be found elsewhere in priestly or Levitical lists (Williamson), it does not necessarily mean that the writer of the Chronicles intends his readers to consider the names as Levites. It is certain that he has emphasized the part of the priests and the Levites in the coup, but it is at least possible that he is giving the names of the military officers mentioned in Kings. In v.1 the men are identified as "captains of hundreds". In the parallel account in 2 Kings 11.4, this phrase seems to refer to military officers. "Unless 23.7,9 are the exception, there is no passage where the Levites are themselves described as organized in units of 'hundreds'; in one passage, the officers of hundreds are distinguished from the Levites (1 Chr 26.26; cp. Num 31.51-54)" (Dillard).

There are three covenants mentioned in this chapter. In v.1 Jehoiada made a covenant with the captains. In v.3 the whole congregation made a covenant with the king. Finally Jehoiada, all the people, and the king made a covenant (v.16). "Here, the restoration of a son of David to the throne is accompanied by these three covenants, as a sign that the covenant, the original one between God and David, cannot be broken" (Wilcock).

Verses 2-3 are not found in Kings. In v.2 the captains gathered the Levites from all the cities of Judah and the chief of the fathers of Israel to Jerusalem. The captains of v.1 are the military leaders, the Levites of v.2 are the religious leaders, and the chief of the fathers in v.2 are the civil leaders. Jehoiada wanted them all to help to enthrone Joash as king. In v.3 the writer of the Chronicles refers to Joash as the king even while Athaliah is still reigning. He looked forward, even in post-exilic days, in the fond hope that one day the Davidic dynasty would be established again in Israel. Jehoiada appealed to God's promise (v.3), "the king's son shall reign, as the Lord hath said of the sons of David". By this appeal he was making clear why they should all do what they could so that a son of David could reign again. The Chronicler (in referring to God's promise) was also stating the reason for the coup.

It was regarded as commendable for leaders to respect the congregation. Here in v.3 is found the term "all the congregation", the first mention of the congregation since Jehoshaphat's reign (20.5,14). The covenant in this verse probably had the terms of the kingship of Joash and the regency of Jehoiada.

Jehoiada gave explicit instructions (vv.4-5). He wanted as many military men and Levites as possible present without any suspicions being aroused. The Sabbath was shrewdly chosen as the day when the "courses" of the Levites were relieved and probably also the military officers. Verse 8 specifically says, "Jehoiada the priest dismissed not the courses". Jehoiada also wanted men to be in the most strategic positions.

Jehoiada was concerned for the sanctity of the temple (v.6). He wanted only the priests and they that ministered among the Levites to go into the house of the Lord; for they were the only ones who were holy and the only ones allowed to enter. All the rest of the people were forbidden to go in. The Levites were to be with the king at all times (v.7). Special precautions were taken throughout to protect his life. In v.8 the Levites and all Judah did everything that Jehoiada had commanded. Those going off duty were detained in the temple area. So there were twice as many men as usual. Jehoiada gave spears and bucklers and shields (that had belonged to King David) to the captains of hundreds (v.9). If the captains had carried their own weapons into the area it might have aroused suspicions. How fitting that these could be used to help make a son of David king. Since they were not of gold or silver, Shishak king of Egypt did not take them when he took away the treasures of the house of God (12.9). Jehoiada saw to it that Joash was fully protected with armed men near the altar and the temple from the right side to the left (v.10).

The ceremony in v.11 was a coronation and an anointing. This is the fullest account in Chronicles of such an occasion, and two of the three main characteristics are found only here. One of these is the crown, which was borne by high priests as well as by kings. In Exodus 29.6 and Leviticus 8.9 it is called a "holy crown". The other characteristic is the "testimony", which most probably refers to a copy of the Law that the king was to write for himself (Deut 17.18-20). He was to read it all the days of his life. It was called "the testimony" because it continually testified to his obligation to fear God and do according to God's Word. It also testified to the blessing to him and his people for obedience and curses for disobedience. His anointing speaks of Joash being chosen by God to rule as king.

There are a few implications that foreshadow things to come. The hidden king is a reminder of the One who is in the presence of God at His right hand (the true Heir to the throne of Israel and the universe) but who is not yet manifested. Just as the wicked rule of Athaliah was just before the rule of the king who rightfully belonged on the throne, so the Antichrist will rule in Jerusalem just before our Lord Jesus Christ comes to reign. The many around Joash when he is made king is a reminder of the "ten thousands of the saints" that will come with the Lord Jesus Christ.

Verses 12-15: Athaliah's Reaction

The palace where Athaliah lived was close to the temple. It was easy for her to hear the noise made by the people acclaiming Joash as king (v.12). When she went to investigate and saw the boy with a crown on his head (v.13), she was completely taken by surprise. She thought that she had killed all possible rivals (to the throne). After reigning for six years as queen she must have had only a very few supporters among the common people since so many knew of the proposed coup (v.3), yet Athaliah had not learned of it. On the other hand, those listed in v.3 had bound themselves with an oath and it is also likely that there was only a short time between this covenant and the successful implementation of the agreed plan. What a shockingly abrupt awakening it was for the queen! Athaliah was even more alarmed to realize that her guards were in open revolt against her, and all the people were rejoicing to have the boy as king. The word "princes" in v.13 is translated as "captains" in the RV and ESV.

Athaliah hearing the noise is reminiscent of Adonijah and his supporters with him when they heard the noise of the people at Solomon's anointing as king over Israel (1 Kings 1.39-41, 45-46).

The king stood at his pillar (v.13), which is probably one of the two great pillars, Jachin and Boaz, at the entrance to the temple. The rejoicing of all the people in v.13 is the first rejoicing recorded since 20.27. The words found in v.13, "also the singers with instruments of musick, and such as taught to sing praise", are found only in Chronicles in keeping with the interest of the writer. "Treason" being repeated in v.13 suggests intensity. Athaliah's words, "Treason, Treason", are extremely ironic when the violent circumstances by which she seized the throne are called to mind. She was the real traitor. Joash had a legal right to the throne. Her cry was a frantic cry of desperation, knowing that she could not escape death. Her words have a special irony in that they do not condemn Jehoiada, her guard, or the people but only herself. "So much are the enemies of the truth hardened in their perceptions...By Athaliah's own standards there can be no treason, since, for her, power is rightly held by those who can hold it" (McConville).

Jehoiada's words in v.14, "have her forth of the ranges", are given as "Have her forth between the ranks" in the RV. Jehoiada wanted the captains of hundreds to be careful about two things. Anyone who wanted to rescue Athaliah was to be slain with the sword; no one is recorded as coming to her aid. Also he said to the captains, "Slay her not in the house of the Lord". Ironically Jehoiada's own son was slain in the house of the Lord (24.21). The RV reads for v.15, "So they made a way for her; and she went to the entry of the horse gate", suggesting that they allowed her to walk out of the temple, not only unharmed but untouched. As she was leaving the temple she knew from Jehoiada's words that they would not execute her there. It appears that she walked proudly to her death. When it is seen as defiance of the judgment of God, it is in keeping with her entire wickedly willful life. She was slain at the entry of the horse gate which was a fitting end to her life since her wicked mother Jezebel was trampled to death by horses (2 Kings 9.33). Athaliah like her husband Jehoram departed without being desired (21.20). Since there are none of the usual statements about her (either here or in Kings), it shows once again that neither historian considered her a legitimate ruler.

Verses 16-21: Reformation

Immediately after the coronation of Joash, Jehoiada began reforms that were very important. He made a covenant between himself, all the people, and the king (v.16). This corresponds to 2 Kings 11.17, except that there we have the Lord instead of "him" (Jehoiada). This difference is easily reconciled. Since Jehoiada was God's high priest, he acted as God's representative. He used the opportunity of the great gathering in the temple and the rejoicing to bind the people afresh to God with a solemn covenant, "so that the joyous festival of homage to the young king became on this occasion identical with that of renewed allegiance to Jehovah" (Rawlinson, quoting from Ewald). The nation had first made a covenant at Sinai (Ex 34.3-8). They renewed the covenant in the fifteenth year of Asa (2 Chr 15.9-15) after the partial departure of Rehoboam and Abijah. Now Jehoiada led the people in renewing the covenant for the third time after 15 years of evil reign. Later Hezekiah (29.10) and Josiah (34.31-32) did the same after Judah had again fallen away from God.

The people then destroyed the house of Baal and his altars and his images. Jehu also did similarly (2 Kings 10.26-28). If one truly loves God one should hate everything that God hates. Psalm 97.10 says, "Ye that love the Lord, hate evil". The people also slew Mattan the priest of Baal, as God's word declared should be done (Deut 13.5-10). Mattan and Athaliah are the only ones recorded as slain in this coup. An execution like this was also carried out by Elijah in 1 Kings 18.40 and by Jehu in 2 Kings 10.25.

The events of vv.18-19 are not found in the parallel account except for the simple notice in 2 Kings 11.18, "And the priest appointed officers over the house of the Lord". This shows that it was important for the priests and Levites to follow the instructions of David and Moses and to protect the sanctity of the temple. The priests and the Levites had the oversight of the temple in their hands. Each of them had tasks assigned to them by David (1 Chr chs.15-16 and 23-27). As usual, the Chronicler traces the general arrangement of the house of the Lord and the singing back to David, but he traces the burnt offering back to Moses. The reinstatement of the Davidic monarchy had a fitting accompaniment in the re-institution of Davidic practice.

"Ever since the death of Jehoshaphat the temple and its worship had been neglected. As high priest he (Jehoiada) took prompt action to restore its services…And so a day that had started out with careful planning but without anyone knowing what might happen, ended with the Lord once again at the centre of His people's lives" (Barber).

The porters were stationed at the gate of the temple (v.19) as designated in 1 Chronicles 26, so that no ritually unclean person could enter. (This gives a Scriptural illustration of the presence and the duties of an assembly.)

This continues the concern expressed in vv.6 and 14. No unclean person should be allowed into assembly fellowship today. Local assemblies should be composed only of saints (1 Cor 14.33) sound in life and doctrine.

The second stage of the coronation is given in v.20. Jehoiada organized a procession to bring down the king from the house of the Lord to the king's house, so that he could sit upon the throne of the kingdom. This thrilling scene was a fitting climax to that day. Verse 21 states that all the people of the land rejoiced, which was a response often found in Chronicles when the Lord's will was being obeyed. This joy was added to the joy of the temple worship of v.18 and also the joy of v.13 at the presence of the boy king. It is recorded that "The city was quiet" (v.21). The Chronicler several times uses the word "quiet" to indicate the blessing of God when the will of God is being carried out (14.1,4-5; 20.30). In v.21 the writer of the Chronicles adds a note about the mode of Athaliah's death not given in v.15.

"The entire country was thrilled with what had transpired...The corrupt queen killed, and the rightful heir on the throne, marked a turning point in the nation, and in this case, a turning in the right direction. One fact made plain in these verses, and one which at times is overlooked is that if there be a desire to establish what pleases God, it must include the destruction of what is contrary to Him. To allow the evil worship of Baal to continue would have left a strong temptation for some in the nation to go back to it. True love of the Lord, means to truly hate what He hates" (McShane).

2 CHRONICLES 24

Joash's Reign

Introductory

The record of Joash is probably the saddest in the book of Chronicles. He owed his life to Jehoiada and his wife, Jehoshabeath. Joash, as a result of Jehoiada's skillful planning, began reigning at the age of seven. He pleased God while Jehoiada was alive. He initiated repairing the temple. How sad and tragic that after the death of Jehoiada, he deliberately turned his back on God. With atrocious ingratitude he even commanded that Jehoiada's son, Zechariah, be stoned for giving a message from God.

This is the first of three chapters that belong together. Each tells of early success contrasted with later failure. Each tells of blessing for obedience and trouble for departure. It is possible that the Chronicler had in mind the righteous man who turns from his righteousness and dies while set on that course (Ezek 18.24-26). This pattern has already been seen in Rehoboam (chs.11-12) and Asa (chs.14-16), "But it plumbs new depths in chs.24-26. Positive balancing factors at the end of these reigns are no longer found (cp. 12.12; 16.14), and each concludes in disaster" (Selman). The greatest change for the worst was in the reign of Joash. The only balancing factor is recorded in v.27, "the repairing of the house of God" and that is referring to his early years. The writer of the Chronicles uses these three historical records as a triple warning against getting away from God.

Each of these three kings forsook the Lord. In the reign of Joash "they left the house of the Lord God of their fathers, and served groves and idols" (24.18). At 25.27 we read that "Amaziah did turn away from following the Lord", and in 26.16, concerning Uzziah, that "he transgressed against the Lord his God". Each of these three spurned good advice to their own hurt (24.19-21; 25.15-16; 26.18-19). Kings has no parallel to the three clauses about departure, neither any parallel to the verses about good advice. While the writer of Kings does record the departure of Solomon, he does not record the failures of these three. Proverbs 12.15 records, "The way of a fool is right in his own eyes: but he that hearkeneth unto counsel is wise". Proverbs 12.5 states that "the counsels of the wicked are deceit". Either by rejecting wise counsel or accepting bad counsel, each of these kings was led astray with sad results.

Joash may have had a relationship with God with the help of Jehoiada but he may never have felt his need of having direct communion with God. Faith in the living God must be personal. "Thousands of godly souls remain in a condition of childhood, depending first of all on their parents, then later upon their spiritual leaders, instead of depending upon God and the Word" (Rossier). The record of Joash shows that he lacked spiritual maturity. Psalm 118.8 (the central verse of the Bible) says, "It is better to trust in the Lord than to put confidence in man". The next verse is even more striking. "It is better to trust in the Lord than to put confidence in princes". Even though princes may be the best of men, no one can be trusted so completely and thoroughly as the Lord. All must put confidence in the Lord Himself.

Once again Maclaren has some significant and helpful comments, this time on Joash. "There is no telling the amount of mischief that pure weakness of character may lead into...we see in Joash what a strange, awful strength of obstinate resistance, a character weak as regards its resistance to man, can put forth against God. He never attempted to say 'No' to the princes of Judah, but he could say it again and again to his Father in heaven...the murder of Zechariah was beyond the common count of crimes; for it was a foul desecration of the Temple, and an act of the blackest ingratitude to the man who had saved his infant life, and put him on the throne, an outrage on the claims of family connections, for Joash and Zechariah were probably blood relations".

This chapter is parallel to 2 Kings 12. It has the same general order of events but has some very important matters which are not mentioned in Kings (especially vv.3,7,9, 15-22). The most important addition is in vv.15-22, in relation to Joash forsaking God after Jehoiada died. 2 Chronicles treats the matters common to both narratives in quite a different way from Kings. Key words set the tone for each of the two main sections of ch.24. First, Joash "repairs" the temple. Appropriately, the word "repair" is in the introduction (v.4) and conclusion (v.12) of the main part dealing with the temple. The king's attitude toward the temple is very significant since God's Word teaches that the worship of God is the most important priority for any person. The second section is in total contrast. Its central theme is "forsake" (vv.18,20,24).

Outline of Chapter 24

Verses 1-16:	Faithfulness while Jehoiada lived.
Verses 17-27:	Departure after Jehoiada died.

1-16: Faithfulness while Jehoiada Lived

There is a good commendation of Joash in v.2, but it is ominous, preparing us for a change when Jehoiada dies. He had the influence of godly Jehoiada in contrast to his father and his grandfather who were influenced by a wicked woman, Athaliah. Joash may have leaned too much on Jehoiada so that when that prop was gone he fell.

Verse 2 "provides the outline for the Chronicler's treatment of Joash - the good years while Jehoiada was alive (vv.1-16), and the turn to evil after his death (vv.17-22) (Zondervan Study Bible). (See also the note from the same source for 25.1.)

Verse 3 is found only in Chronicles. Many of David's seed had been murdered in recent years. by Jehoram (21.4); by Jehu (2 Kings 10.12-14); by a band of men that came with the Arabians (22.1); and by Athaliah (22.10). Since the line of David had almost been completely destroyed, it was important to rebuild the family. Jehoiada fixed the number of wives he took for Joash at "two". That indicates a concern for succession in the Davidic line and also a discouragement of excessive polygamy. Jehoaddan of Jerusalem, the mother of Amaziah, was one of these wives (25.1). Since Amaziah was 25 when he began to reign and Joash died at 47 years of age (24.1), Joash was 22 when Amaziah was born. That means that Joash had married Jehoaddan at least by the time he was 21.

Verse 4 begins the record of the repair of the temple. Jehoiada and Joash may have discussed the need for this, but for some reason Jehoiada was not enthusiastic enough to get started. His old age might have been a factor. Joash may have been grateful for the temple being his refuge in infancy or he may have been grateful that he was crowned king there or indeed he may have been grateful for both of these reasons. Whatever his motive was, he is to be commended for taking the initiative and following through until the repair was completed. Joash is a contrast to the sons of Athaliah (v.7). The fixed purpose of Joash to repair the house of the Lord is the opposite of its destruction by them.

Joash sent the priests and the Levites to collect money for the repair of the temple (v.5). He may have suspected that they would be dilatory so he said, "See that ye hasten the matter". The next sentence of the same verse says, "Howbeit the Levites hastened it not". Possibly this was because the funds collected were barely sufficient for the service of the house of God so that there was very little left over for the repair. It is very unusual for the Chronicler to write anything negative about the Levites. The Word of God does not tell how long before the 23rd year Joash gave the instructions for the collection. 2 Kings 12.4 mentions three sources of revenue but Chronicles emphasizes only one - the half shekel taken of every man when there was a census (Ex 30.12-16).

"The tabernacle of witness", or "the tent of testimony" is only found here in v.6 and four times in Numbers (9.15; 17.7,8; 18.2). The Chronicler uses several terms for the Tabernacle but most often "the Tabernacle of the Lord" (1 Chr 16.39; 21.29; 2 Chr 1.5) and "the Tabernacle of the congregation" (1 Chr 6.32; 9.21; 23.32; 2 Chr 1.3,6,13; 5.5. Verse 7 again has information found only in Chronicles. The sons of Athaliah had broken into the temple and ransacked it for the worship of Baal. Most likely they caused extensive damage. They must have done it before the band of men that came with the Arabians in 22.1 murdered them.

The priests were hesitant in carrying out the king's plans. "Their hesitation is understandable if as some suggest, the king was imposing on the priesthood a burden formerly carried by the royal treasury" (The Baker Commentary on the Bible). Joash rebuked Jehoiada and indirectly the Levites (v.6), even though Jehoiada had encouraged the priests to take the money to repair the breaches (2 Kings 12.4-5). 2 Kings 12.7 states that he also rebuked the other priests.

The first plan did not work so Joash made another arrangement. At the king's commandment they made a chest (v.8), but it was Jehoiada who carried out the king's commandment, bored a hole in the lid of the chest, and set it beside the altar (2 Kings 12.9). "The arrangement for collecting the contributions 'saved the faces' of the priests to some extent, for the gifts were handed to them, and by them put into the chest. But, of course, that was done at once, in the donor's presence. If changes involving loss of position are to work smoothly, it is wise to let the deposed officials down as easily as may be" (Maclaren). Verse 8 records that the chest was "set...without at the gate of the house of the Lord". The chest may have been beside the altar at first as above. Later, it may have been set outside the gate for easier access.

"Not all the money brought to the temple was used for repairs, for the priests had a portion that was not taken from them. When any trespassed, he had to repay for the loss sustained, and add a fifth part. When the trespass was against the Lord, then the recompense could go to the priests who were His representatives. This money was still to be retained by them, and not put into the chest. In the case of anyone offering a sin offering and giving the priest a gift for his services, then this money also was to be retained, and not used for the repairs" (McShane).

The proclamation made throughout Judah and Jerusalem is only recorded in v.9. Joash hoped that with the chest and the proclamation the people would be more liberal, knowing that the contributions were to be used specifically for the repair of the temple. The phrase "Moses the servant of God" (v.9) is found only four times in the Old Testament (1 Chr 6.49; 2 Chr 24.9; Neh 10.29; Dan 9.11) in contrast to "Moses the servant of the Lord" (v.6) (18 times in the Old Testament: Deut 34.5; Josh 1.1,13,15; 8.31,33; 11.12; 12.6,6; 13.8; 14.7; 18.7; 22.2,4,5; 2 Kings 18.12; 2 Chr 1.3; 24.6). Verses 10-11 imply that there were free will offerings as well as tax. The response was overwhelming, so the second plan was truly successful after the first had failed. The giving was so generous that the chest was filled and emptied over and over again. Verse 11 ends, "they...gathered money in abundance". This generous giving is a reminder of the giving for the Tabernacle, which was "much more than enough" (Ex 36.5). The rejoicing in giving calls to mind the people and David rejoicing when they gave willingly for the original temple as recorded in 1 Chronicles 29.9.

In v.11 the Chronicler draws attention to the Levites who brought the chest to the king's office. As often as he could the writer put the Levites in a good light. They are not mentioned in the parallel portion in 2 Kings. In fact, the Levites are only mentioned once in Kings (1 Kings 8.4). Verse 11 states that the king's scribe and the high priest's officer came when the chest was full and emptied it. Those two were responsible for the contribution. 2 Kings 12.10-11 makes it clear that they put the contributions in bags and ascertained how much had been given. Those two checked each other and prevented suspicion of either.

The king and Jehoiada "gave it to such as did the work" (v.12). 2 Kings 12.15 states, "Moreover they reckoned not with the men, into whose hand they delivered the money to be bestowed on workmen: for they dealt faithfully". We read similar words in 2 Kings 22.7 about the workmen who did the repairs in the reign of Josiah. That does not mean that this example should be followed today. "The times of Joash and Josiah were exceptional. In each reign a great spiritual revival was in progress. After many years of grave transgressions the people (or at least a remnant of them) were turning back to their God. Hearts and consciences were in exercise concerning His Holy will. This being so, precautionary measures against fraud were scarcely necessary" (Fereday).

We should notice that even in days of spiritual revival the king's scribe and the high priest's officer were a check on each other. Romans 12.17 states, "Provide things honest in the sight of all men". In the New Translation by Darby, there is a footnote for the word "provide": "Taking care by forethought that there should be what is comely and seemly". There were large sums of money contributed by various Gentile assemblies for the relief of needy brethren in Jerusalem. They wanted Paul to carry the gifts to Jerusalem. But he insisted on having companions, men chosen by the assemblies for that purpose. He wrote, "Providing for honest things, not only in the sight of the Lord, but also in the sight of men" (2 Cor 8.21).

Judas was most likely chosen by his companions to have charge of the bag. He certainly was not chosen for his spiritual grace, but perhaps for his business ability. Many years after Judas had gone "to his own place" (Acts 1.25), John wrote what he did not know while Judas was living: "This he said, not that he cared for the poor; but because he was a thief, and had the bag, and bare what was put therein" (Jn 12.6). It is possible that the apostles had the sad case of Judas before their minds when they said in Acts 6.3, "Wherefore, brethren, look ye out among you seven men of honest report, full of the Holy Ghost and wisdom, whom we may appoint over this business". Those were the men to care for the widows. Even that work was to be done by spiritual men. Thank God for every Spirit-made overseer who has been successful in the business world or a profession. But it should be remembered that mere success in these spheres does not of itself qualify a man for overseership.

The workmen in the days of Joash and Josiah "dealt faithfully". 1 Corinthians 4.2 says, "It is required in stewards, that a man be found faithful". The NIV for part of v.13 reads, "They rebuilt the temple of God according to its original design". God gave the pattern to David who also gave it to his son Solomon (1 Chr 28.11-12). God also had a pattern for the Tabernacle. Ten times we read in Exodus 39, "as the Lord commanded Moses", and eight times in Exodus 40. After the work on the Tabernacle was finished, it is no wonder that we read in Exodus 40.34 that "the glory of the Lord filled the Tabernacle". God also has a pattern for New Testament assemblies today. May the Lord encourage all to go by that pattern for the glory of our Lord Jesus Christ.

The giving was so bountiful that there was money left over after the temple had been repaired (v.14). They made articles for use in the temple with the surplus. 2 Kings 12.13 seems at first to contradict this but it does not. The writer of the Kings wanted to impress on his readers that the repairs to the building were not delayed by spending money for vessels for the house of God. He does not state that the vessels were made after the temple was repaired, but the Chronicler does. The last sentence of v.14 shows that offerings were faithfully given by the people as long as Jehoiada lived. Verse 15 records that Jehoiada was "full of days" when he died. This expression is used for only four others: Abraham (Gen 25.8, JND), Isaac (Gen 35.29), Job (Job 42.17), and David (1 Chr 29.28).

Jehoiada was given the honour of being buried among the kings (v.16). No other person who was not a king has been recorded as having this privilege. It was given to him largely because "he had done good in Israel, both toward God, and toward his house" (v.16). It may also in part be attributed to his marriage to Jehoshabeath, the daughter of King Jehoram, and also the fact that for all practical purposes he essentially held the kingly office for a number of years until Joash was old enough to reign. The writer of the Chronicles says that Jehoiada had done good in Israel. He is thus speaking of Judah as the true Israel. What a deplorable contrast (to the honour given to Jehoiada at his death) to read in v.25 concerning Joash that "they buried him not in the sepulchres of the kings". The Chronicler sometimes uses contrast as a literary device, as he does here. "It is to his (Jehoiada's) eternal credit he held fast to his integrity during the evil reigns of Jehoram, Ahaziah, and Athaliah" (Barber).

Verses 17-27: Departure after Jehoiada Died

The death of Jehoiada was likely to have been a traumatic experience for Joash, but how sad that he so quickly went against all that had been taught him, thus displaying a serious weakness of character. What a dramatic contrast there is between v.2 and vv.17-18. Verses 15-22 are not found in 2 Kings but are important for understanding the last days of Joash. The princes had taken part in putting him on the throne (23.2,13,20) but probably not for the best reasons. Athaliah of the house of Ahab had corrupted the father and grandfather of Joash. We could not expect anything better of her. But it is very regrettable that the princes should be the seducers of their king. They enticed him with flattery. Joash had been receptive to the good advice of Jehoiada, but then yielded himself to their bad advice.

Four kings of Judah before him got into serious trouble by heeding bad advice. Rehoboam (10.8-11), Jehoshaphat (18.2), Jehoram (21.6), and Ahaziah (22.3-4). Verse 18 states, "And they left (or forsook) the house of the Lord God of their fathers". Joash had earlier begun the repairs of the house of the Lord. "House of the Lord" or its equivalent is found 15 times in this chapter but v.18 gives it its fullest title. The Chronicler thus emphasized the seriousness of the departure. Because of this trespass, "wrath came upon Judah and Jerusalem" (v.18). The verse does not explicitly say that the wrath was from the Lord but this word for wrath (QASEP - 7110) is used in Chronicles only for the wrath of God (1 Chr 27.24; 2 Chr 19.2,10; 29.8; 32.25,26). Forsaking the house of the Lord (v.18) is equivalent to forsaking the Lord Himself (v.20).

God's righteousness (v.18) judged their evil doings, and God's mercy (v.19) sent prophets to bring them back. The words, "bring them back" (NIV), are from the same Hebrew word as "turn" in the encouraging promise of 7.14. This means that there was a message of hope right after the terrible departure recorded in vv.17-18. The people listened to the princes when they departed from God, but they would not listen to the prophets trying to bring them back. So God in His grace sent the one person to whom they would be most likely to listen (v.20). If they would respond to anyone, it would be Zechariah the son of Jehoiada. All the people should have been grateful to Jehoiada. Joash himself owed more to him than anyone else. Zechariah was one of only three recorded with whom the Spirit of God clothed Himself - Gideon in Judges 6.34 to deliver Israel from their enemies and Amasai in 1 Chronicles 12.18 to declare loyalty to David.

Zechariah "stood above the people" (v.20) so that he could be easily heard like Ezra later who "stood upon a pulpit of wood" (Neh 8.4). It is also like Baruch the son of Neriah who read the words of Jeremiah in "the upper court" (RV) to the people assembled below (Jer 36.10). The climax of Zechariah's short message is recorded in v.20: "because ye have forsaken the Lord, he hath also forsaken you". The theology of retribution is simple. Those who seek God prosper and those who forsake Him cannot prosper. The writer of the Chronicles uses the verb translated "prosper" (TSALEACH - 6743) often as in 1 Chronicles 22.11,13; 29.23; 2 Chronicles 7.11; 13.12; 14.7; 18.11,14; 20.20; 24.20; 26.5; 31.21; 32.30).

There are a number of ironies in v.21. The people, who would not obey the commandments of the Lord (v.20), readily obeyed the king's wicked commandment to stone Zechariah (v.21). Zechariah, the son of Jehoiada, who had saved the life of Joash and saved the throne for him, was murdered by the order of Joash in the very place where "Jehoiada and his sons" had anointed him king and protected him (23.11). Jehoiada, who did not want blood to be shed in the temple because he was concerned for its sanctity, installed the king who would one day murder his son in that very place!

The people conspired against Zechariah and stoned him (v.21). Years before, wicked Jezebel conspired against Naboth and had him stoned (1 Kings 21.8-14). Verse 22 emphasizes touchingly the base ingratitude of Joash. He "remembered not the kindness which Jehoiada his father had done to him". The man who could so easily forget God (vv.17-18) could also easily forget the kindness of Jehoiada. The Hebrew word for "kindness" is CHESED (2617). It is used about 250 times (in the Old Testament) of God, sometimes translated "lovingkindness", but much more often translated "mercy". The word means faithful, loyal, or steadfast love.

The heinous nature of this act is magnified by the kindness of Jehoiada to Joash. His actions illustrate the depths to which a man may be plunged by sin. There lies within every person, whether a believer or an unbeliever, the germ of every kind of sin. It only takes the right combination of circumstances to bring it out. For a believer, one of those circumstances would have to be that he or she is away from God. Surely all have to pay heed to the exhortation of 1 Corinthians 10.12: "Wherefore let him that thinketh that he standeth take heed lest he fall". Thankfully, our Lord Jesus is "able to keep you from falling" (or "stumbling", RV) (Jude v.24). A child of God can still stumble and fall but if so it is because of failure to look to Him who can keep His own from stumbling.

When Zechariah died he said, "The Lord look upon it, and require it" (v.22). In Genesis 9.5 God Himself used the same word: "And surely your blood of your lives will I require". When Joseph's ten older brothers heard the governor speaking roughly to them, they said to one another "We are verily guilty concerning our brother, in that we saw the anguish of his soul, when he besought us, and we would not hear: therefore is this distress come upon us" (Gen 42.21). They remembered vividly the anguish of their brother, even though it was 22 years earlier! Significantly, Reuben commented in the last part of the next verse, "therefore, behold, also his blood is required".

Zechariah's dying words may not be from a spirit of revenge. "This prayer should not be considered unfavourably with those of Jesus and Stephen (Lk 23.34; Acts 7.60). For one thing, Jesus actually quotes this incident in pronouncing the same judgment on his contemporaries (cp. Mt 23.33-36; Lk 11.47-51). For another, Zechariah is not looking for personal revenge but asking God to act in keeping with His declared principles of justice" (Selman).

The punishment was not long in coming - "at the end of the year" (v.23). The words in v.23, "destroyed all the princes of the people from among the people" are very significant. The princes were the leaders in departure (v.17) and these words indicate that all of the princes and only the princes were selectively destroyed!

On the other hand it should be pointed out that it is a mistake to think that there is no grace in the Old Testament. Since our Lord Jesus is grace personified (Titus 2.11) and "grace and truth came by Jesus Christ" (Jn 1.17), it is no wonder that there is more grace in the New Testament. Nonetheless God acts in grace a number of times in 2 Chronicles. There is grace here. "The Chronicler mentions the kindness (CHESED) shown Joash by Jehoiada, and CHESED is the Old Testament counterpart of the New Testament *charis* 'grace' (v.22)...The word DARASH (1875) - "require" in v.22 - has in some Old Testament contexts been translated either 'enquire' or 'require'. Its root is to 'ask' or 'seek' and it does not necessarily look at revenge. In reality, Zechariah may have been asking God to seek out the evildoers with a view to bringing them to repentance" (Barber). That is at least a possibility.

The majority of commentators believe that this is the incident to which the Lord Jesus referred in Matthew 23.35 and Luke 11.51. The Jewish Bible has the books of the Old Testament in a different order and 2 Chronicles is the final book. So our Lord referred to the first murder (of Abel in Genesis) and to the last recorded murder (of Zechariah in 2 Chronicles). One difficulty is that in Matthew we have, "the son of Barachias", and Zechariah in 2 Chronicles is the son of Jehoiada. There are three possible solutions.

1. Barachias could be another name for Jehoiada.
2. Barachias could be a title for the priest.
3. Barachias could be the father of Zechariah and Jehoiada could be the grandfather of Zechariah. Since Jehoiada was 130 when he died, he could easily be Zechariah's grandfather. This is the most likely solution.

Since the man whom the Spirit of God used to write the book of Zechariah was the son of Berechiah (Zech 1.1), a few believe that he is the one referred to in Matthew, but there is no record that he was martyred. He lived over 300 years later than Zechariah the son of Jehoiada. Archer gives the most thorough account of those believing that the Lord Jesus referred to the one who lived over three centuries later.

Verse 23 records that "all the spoil was sent to the king of Damascus". Criswell has an excellent explanation for this designation rather than "the king of Syria". "It is not unusual for Biblical writers to refer to kings of various nations and empires as the king of their respective capital cities. Here for instance, Ben-hadad, known to the Chronicler as the king of Syria (Aram), is identified as the king of Damascus, which is the capital city of Syria. Ahab is known as the king of the Northern Kingdom (Israel), but on occasion he is referred to as the king of Samaria (1 Kings 21.1). Hiram (Huram) is called the king of Tyre (Phoenicia) on several occasions. In keeping with this precedent, Jonah spoke of the king of Assyria as the king of Nineveh, which is its capital city (Jonah 3.6)".

In v.24 we read that a small company of Syrians was able to defeat a very great host of God's people. In contrast to this defeat, God used only 300 with Gideon to defeat 135,000 Midianites (Judg 7), 1,000,000 Ethiopians were overcome in answer to Asa's reliance on the Lord (14.9-12), and also a great multitude of Moab, Ammon, and Mount Seir were defeated in answer to godly Jehoshaphat's prayer in ch.20.

The Lord Himself delivered them to defeat "because they had forsaken the Lord God of their fathers" (v.24). Moses warned that this would happen (Lev 26.17). The Chronicler makes plain the exact correspondence between the offence and the punishment because he often gives an evaluation from God's point of view (that is missing in 2 Kings).

The last words of Zechariah's message clearly show that, in God's governmental dealings, the punishment fits the crime. They forsook the house of the Lord (v.18, RV), which was the same as forsaking the Lord (v.20). Because of that God forsook them (v.20). The writer of the Chronicles uses this word "forsake" precisely to show the justice of God. He states that this is why they were defeated (v.24). He uses the same Hebrew word in v.25 when he records that Joash was "left' or "forsaken" "severely wounded" (ESV) and to disloyal servants.

The Chronicler used two other words to emphasize the appropriate justice of God's dealings: "conspire" and "slew". In v.21, they "conspired" against Zechariah. Later in v.25, "his own servants conspired against him for the blood of the sons of Jehoiada". "This disloyalty is really part of a greater loyalty to God by Joash's servants" (Coggins). "The outrage of his murdering the son of Jehoiada, the priest, was too much for them" (Thompson). Joash "slew" Zechariah in v.22 and therefore his own servants "slew" him in v.25. The RV margin states that for "sons" in v.25, the Septuagint and the Vulgate read "son". The ESV reads similarly.

The Chronicler often tells us that righteous kings are buried with honour among the kings, and unrighteous kings in ignominy are not buried there (21.19-20; 28.27). Here the refusal to bury unrighteous Joash among the kings (v.25) is in sharp contrast to the righteous priest Jehoiada being so honoured (v.16).

The writer of the Chronicles is the only one who tells us that the conspirators who slew Joash had foreign mothers, one an Ammonitess and one a Moabitess. "It is as if the Chronicler seeks to emphasize the irony of the situation since these 'mixed blood' Israelites have a greater sense of justice than the king and citizens of Judah" (Hill). Even though they were rightly concerned for justice, they were wrong to take matters into their own hands and commit murder.

In v.27 we have "his sons" mentioned. The only son of Joash that we know of is Amaziah. Since Joash was the only son of David left, it was important that he have male children. The Hebrew word for "story" in v.27 is MIDRASH (4097). The only other place that we have that Hebrew word is 13.22. The exact meaning is not known. It may simply mean "annotations", "theological commentary", or "treatise". "The intriguing comment that it contained many prophecies 'about' (REB, NEB, NIV) or 'against' (GNB, NRSV, RSV) Joash presumably refers to v.19 and reflects Chronicles, continuing emphasis on prophetic interpretation of history" (Selman). The ESV has "the many oracles against him". The RV margin has, "the greatness of the burdens uttered against him".

2 CHRONICLES 25

Amaziah's Reign

Introductory

Amaziah is the second of three successive kings, the first part of whose reign was good and the last part poor. In Amaziah's case there is not as great a contrast between the first and last parts of his reign as in the case of the other two. This is mainly because the first portions of the reign of Joash and Uzziah were both much better than the first part of the reign of Amaziah and much longer. He is to be commended in that he did not slay the children of the assassins of his father (v.4), as the Word of God instructs (Deut 24.16). On the other hand there is no record that he asked God about going against Edom. It was a mistake to rely more on numbers than on God. It was an even greater mistake to hire soldiers from Israel. To Amaziah's credit, in response to a message from a man of God, he sent the soldiers from the northern kingdom home and he trusted God.

The critical point of his life is recorded in v.14 when he turned to the idols of the Edomites. In v.16 he threatened to kill a prophet unless he forbore to give God's message. Because God had given him a victory over Edom his heart was lifted up with pride to his own destruction. He challenged the northern kingdom that was much stronger than Edom. His humiliating defeat led to a conspiracy that simmered for many years before he was assassinated.

The comments of Selman on the value of reading yet another depressing story of a wayward king deserve consideration. "Firstly, repeated stories about sinful rulers testify to God's patience. Secondly, people who turn away from God after receiving His grace are also found in the Christian church (e.g. 1 Cor 5.1-13; 2 Tim 2.16-18; Rev 2.4-6, 20-25). Thirdly, such incidents are exemplary warnings to others not to fall into the same temptation (1 Cor 10.11-13; cp. Rom 15.4). Fourthly…No-one is immune from pride and complacency (1 Cor 10.12; 1 Jn 1.8,10), but God's forgiveness to anyone who falls is always close at hand (cp. Ps 51.7-15; 2 Chr 7.13-16; 1 Jn 1.9; 2.1-2)".

The Chronicler's account of Amaziah's reign follows closely 2 Kings 14.1-20, although 25.5-16 has much more detail about his victory over the Edomites than the one verse of 2 Kings 14.7. Verses 5-16 and also v.20 must have come from a source available to the Chronicler but not identified for his readers.

Outline of Chapter 25

Verses 1-4:	Amaziah's accession.
Verses 5-13:	Amaziah's victory over the Edomites.
Verses 14-16:	Amaziah's apostasy.
Verses 17-24:	Amaziah's war with Joash of Israel.
Verses 25-28:	Amaziah's end.

Verses 1-4: Amaziah's Accession

In v.1 the Chronicler provides a simple introduction to the record by noting Amaziah's age at accession, the length of his reign, and his mother's name.

He then gives an overall assessment of the man: "he did that which was right in the sight of the Lord but not with a perfect heart" (v.2). That assessment indicates that Amaziah was half-hearted. "The writer appears to be motivated by his outline, which covered the good years first and then the reversion to evil. Negative comments about these kings are held to the second half of the account of their reigns, whereas in Kings the summary judgment about their reigns…is given immediately" (Zondervan Study Bible). "Not with a perfect heart", is in contrast to the charge of good king Jehoshaphat to the men who were to judge in Jerusalem (19.9): "Thus shall ye do in the fear of the Lord, faithfully, and with a perfect heart". That is good advice for all who serve God today. Verse 16.9 holds out a wonderful promise: "The eyes of the Lord run to and fro throughout the whole earth, to show himself strong in the behalf of them whose heart is perfect toward him". May the Lord help all to have the right attitude toward God in order to be strengthened by Him.

2 Kings 14.3 has another phrase qualifying Amaziah's obedience, "yet not like David his father". David set a high standard of wholehearted devotion to the Lord for the kings who were to follow him. 2 Kings 14.3 adds, "he did according to all things as Joash his father did", and that included the rejection of a prophet sent to him by God.

The men who murdered his father were right to be grieved and to consider that Joash was very unjust to have Zechariah the son of Jehoiada stoned (v.3). But, as noted above, they were wrong to take the matter into their own hands. That should not have been condoned. Verse 4 records that Amaziah did not slay the children. The Wycliffe Bible Commentary gives this note: "The citation from the law of Moses is evidence that Deuteronomy is not a late composition as the higher critics hold".

"Amaziah was knowledgeable of the Mosaic Law and did not follow the precedent set in other Near Eastern countries whereby one's entire family would be exterminated for the sins of one member (Deut 24.16; cp. Jer 31.29-30; Ezek 18.1-20)" (Barber). Amaziah's respect for the Word of God indicates that he must have read it as all kings were expected to do (Deut 17.18-19). If only he had continued with this attitude how different his life and reign would have been! Verse 4 is a necessary explanation for such unusual behaviour. Following the Word of God makes persons distinctive. "The note of moderation is one that correspondingly speaks to all in a position of authority. Many a mother or father knows the temptation to crack the nut of a child's offence with the sledgehammer of fury" (Leslie C. Allen).

"There is no need to see a tension between this law and the principle enunciated in Exodus 20.5f…The difference between Exodus 20.4ff and

Deuteronomy 24.16 is that the former speaks of God's own application of His justice and love in history, according to His mysterious ways, while the latter legislates for human judicial processes" (McConville).

Verses 5-13: Amaziah's Victory over the Edomites

The military enrollment by Amaziah in v.5 was similar to that of Asa (14.8) and Jehoshaphat (17.14-19). He mustered from Judah and Benjamin those who were 20 years old and upward. The following verses show that he wanted to fight against Edom. The Edomites had been lost to Judah during the reign of Jehoram (21.10). He now wanted to regain the territory for Judah. He had 300,000 men, which was far less than Asa or Jehoshaphat had because of losses such as those incurred by Joash (24.23-24). Instead of relying on the Lord with these 300,000 men, he hired a further 100,000 mighty men from Israel. He trusted in numbers rather than trusting in the Lord. Psalm 20.7 states, "Some trust in chariots, and some in horses: but we will remember the name of the Lord our God". But his error was even more serious in that these soldiers came from Israel that had departed from the Lord.

God in mercy sent an unnamed man of God to Amaziah (v.7). Moses is the first person in the Bible to be called a "man of God" (Deut 33.1). "Man of God" is used of 13 different individuals including three unnamed men and an angel of the Lord. The man of God told Amaziah why soldiers from Israel should not go to fight with his soldiers. Firstly, the Lord was not with Israel (that is, the northern kingdom) as the explanatory note, "with all the children of Ephraim", makes clear. Since Ephraim was the prominent tribe, the term "Ephraim" refers to all the northern kingdom. The man of God emphasized that God's presence was only assured for the southern kingdom, and that to make an alliance with the north was to reject God's presence and would mean sure defeat for Judah no matter how valiantly and courageously they fought (v.8). A second reason (by implication) for not using soldiers from Israel was that they were not necessary. God is not dependent on numbers to achieve victory.

Becoming intimately linked with the ungodly invites disaster. "It should not have been necessary to remind Amaziah of this, he must have known how disastrous Jehoshaphat's alliances with Israel had been" (Riddle). Amaziah expressed his concern to the man of God about the 100 talents of silver he had already given to the army of Israel (v.9). The man of God answered beautifully, "The Lord is able to give thee much more than this". In effect the man of God told Amaziah, "Lose your silver or lose the battle". "Amaziah lost the 100 talents of silver by his obedience; and we find just that sum given to his grandson Jotham as a present (27.5); thus the principal was repaid, and, for interest, 10,000 measures of wheat and as many of barley" (Matthew Henry).

To Amaziah's credit he dismissed the mercenaries from Ephraim (v.10) and sent them home, even though probably reluctantly. They left in great anger, mostly because they felt cheated out of the plunder that they would have received in the battle. Amaziah put his trust in the Lord as his fathers had done (14.11; 20.12). The events in vv.11-12 are parallel to 2 Kings 14.7 which tells of the victory of Amaziah over Edom in the Valley of Salt, which was probably a marshy plain at the south end of the Dead Sea. It was the scene of one of David's victories (1 Chr 18.12). 2 Kings 14.7 records that "He…took Selah by war, and called the name of it Joktheel unto this day". Joktheel may mean, "subdued by God" (McShane) or "God destroyed". Verse 12 has no parallel in Kings. The taking of 10,000 Edomites to the top of the rock and casting them down from there so that they all were broken to pieces seems very brutal (v.12). "To us this sounds like a barbaric way of dealing with prisoners taken in war. In the ancient Near East, however, it was looked upon as a way of ensuring that a defeated enemy could not mount a counter-attack for at least a generation" (Barber). This method of execution was common among pagan nations. Amos 1.11 states about Edom that "he did pursue his brother with the sword, and did cast off all pity, and his anger did tear perpetually, and he kept his wrath for ever". The soldiers of Ephraim that had been dismissed retaliated (v.13) (likely when Amaziah went south to fight Edom) by raiding towns of Judah on the unprotected northern border. They probably began at Samaria and went as far as Beth-horon. They took much spoil and killed 3,000 civilians. They thus manifested their character and showed another reason why God was not with them. "This was a cruel and unnecessary act of aggression against the members of their own extended family" (Barber).

It is worthy of notice that Judah did not entirely escape the consequences of Amaziah's hiring soldiers from the northern kingdom (vv.10,13). He surely did the right thing to respond to the man of God and send them home, but it would have been much better if he had never hired them in the first place. God forgives our sins and our mistakes when we confess them to Him (1 Jn 1.9), but sometimes there are consequences even from forgiven sins.

"Adept as the Chronicler is at selecting the facts which best teach the lessons, he will not manipulate them. He is quite prepared, for example, to record how the immediate result of Amaziah's obedience to the first prophet was not success but trouble (25.7-10, 13). But the story as a whole shows clearly that he who obeys is blessed and he who rebels is punished" (Wilcock). McConville says something similar: "These details, which show that retribution was not immediate, together with the description of the Israelite rampage (v.13), which does not follow neatly from Amaziah's positive response to the first prophecy, show that the Chronicler had respected his historical material, and not tailored it to his theological ends".

Verses 14-16: Amaziah's Apostasy

Amaziah brought with him the gods of the children of Seir when he came from the slaughter (v.14). The Edomites were called "children of Seir" because Mount Seir was part of their territory (Deut 2.5). Since God gave Amaziah a remarkable victory, it would have been becoming for him to have a grateful heart. There can be danger in success. Amaziah's victory was followed quickly by his becoming a slave to their idols. He became guilty of terrible ingratitude. Instead of a grateful heart he committed blatant idolatry. He "bowed down himself before them, and burned incense unto them" (v.14). Wicked Ahaz did similarly (28.23), sacrificing to the gods of Damascus.

Amaziah's idolatry was the height of absurdity. It was sheer, senseless madness. God had given His people an exceptional deliverance from Egypt, and the gods of Edom were absolutely impotent and unable to deliver the Edomites from Amaziah. It is almost incredible that he did so foolishly. "Amaziah went to battle having rid his army of idolatrous mercenaries from Israel, and returned with the idols of his vanquished enemies. How quickly he turned from God to idols" (Riddle). How much better it was when the Thessalonians "turned to God from idols" (1 Thess 1.9).

God's anger was kindled against Amaziah for this folly, but in mercy He sent an unnamed prophet to him (v.15) to help him see his error. The prophet rebuked him for his idolatry and for his stupidity. Amaziah had responded well to the earlier man of God (vv.7-10); but in contrast here (v.15) he probably would have carried out his threat and killed the prophet as his father had done if the man had continued.

Before the prophet forbore altogether, he courageously gave even more solemn, alarming words to Amaziah from God. Amaziah wanted to stop God's voice, but it continued. The prophet knew that God had determined to destroy Amaziah, not so much for his idolatry as for his refusal to hear His messenger, which was equivalent to rejecting God Himself. He had a second opportunity but he spurned it and sealed his own fate.

The Chronicler uses a clever play on words (as he sometimes does) showing how serious it was for Amaziah to refuse to listen. "I know that God hath determined to destroy thee." The word "determined" is related to the words "counsel" used twice in v.16 and "took advice" in v.17. Amaziah implied that the prophet should not speak since he was not in the king's council, but the prophet shows that he had God's counsel, which is far greater than the king's. He threatened the prophet with death but, like a boomerang, he met a violent end determined by God as eventually took place (v.27). He rejected the word of the prophet (v.16) and preferred his own advisers (v.17), but the following course of events shows that he could not avoid God's will however much he wanted to.

Verses 17-24: Amaziah's War with Joash of Israel

These verses follow 2 Kings 14.8-20 quite closely with only minor deviations. Here, in v.17, Amaziah challenged Joash (a variant of Jehoash), "Come, let us see one another in the face". It can sometimes mean simply, "meet one another". But it can carry the meaning of meeting in battle as it does here and in v.21. Amaziah's victory over Edom had inflated his ego and emboldened his vanity and pride so that he foolishly challenged a far stronger foe than Edom. He was puffed up with a sense of self-importance, so with a streak of foolhardiness he made the ill-advised challenge. Though at first (when he renamed the rock "Joktheel") he seemed to realize that God had a part in the victory over Edom, he soon forgot God's part and took the glory for the victory to himself. He no longer needed God. Pride, which implies a lack of dependence on God, was a particularly heinous sin in His sight and in the view of the writer of the Chronicles. Proverbs 29.23 says, "A man's pride shall bring him low". Proverbs 16.18 is probably the best-known verse in in the book about pride and it records, "Pride goeth before destruction, and a haughty spirit before a fall". Amaziah was not the only person ruined by pride. His son Uzziah made the same mistake (26.16). Pride is in every human heart and can easily spring up, especially if nurtured by success. May the Lord help all to "walk humbly with thy God" (Micah 6.8). That is the safest place to be. "God resisteth the proud, and giveth grace to the humble" (1 Pet 5.5; James 4.6). The fall of Satan was due to pride (1 Tim 3.6). In Proverbs 6.16-17, "A proud look" is the first thing listed (of seven) that God hates and that are an abomination to Him.

Joash's fable (about the arrogant thistle in vv.18-19) is a reminder of Jotham's allegory about the bramble in Judges 9.7-15. "The contrast between the northern and southern kingdoms in point of military strength and resources, and the disdainful tolerance with which the former regarded the latter, could hardly have found more forcible expression" (Ellicott's Bible Commentary in One Volume). The parable itself (v.18) was very insulting. It was like waving a red flag before a bull. But the moral of the fable (v.19) and the advice Joash gave was very good. He correctly understood the motive of Amaziah. He could discern that behind the threatened attack was pride generated by his victory over Edom. In effect Joash told Amaziah two things: "You are only a thistle and you are filled with pride".

Joash gave Amaziah good advice when he said, "why shouldest thou meddle to thine hurt?" (v.19). It is like king Solomon's wise counsel in Proverbs 20.3, "…every fool will be meddling", and in Proverbs 26.17, "He that passeth by, and meddleth with strife belonging not to him, is like one that taketh a dog by the ears". Peter gives similar advice in 1 Peter 4.15: "But let none of you suffer as…a busybody in other men's matters". It is not the business of pilgrims and strangers to meddle in the affairs of the world around us. Good King Josiah lost his life by doing so (35.20-24).

"But Amaziah would not hear" (v.20). "The word 'listen' ('hear', AV) has connotations which make the phrase suggest not only rejection of Joash's advice but disobedience to God. The consequences are predictable: humiliating defeat and loss of national wealth (vv.21-24)" (McConville). Amaziah had a serious failing in that he was so reluctant to recognize and follow sound advice. This was manifest both when the prophet spoke to him and in his response to the advice of Joash, and calls to mind the words of Solomon in Proverbs 15.32: "he that refuseth instruction despiseth his own soul: but he that regardeth reproof getteth understanding".

All but the first five words of v.20 are unique to Chronicles and provide a characteristic touch. The words serve to link this event specifically with what has gone before. God was working behind the scenes of human history, moving events to judge Amaziah and Judah for their idolatry. It is only here that the plurals "them" and "they" are found, showing that the people shared the guilt of idolatry. God used this pride to bring about the mortifying defeat of Amaziah and Judah.

Joash was so confident of his superiority, when he saw that war was inevitable, that he went on the offensive and launched an attack in Amaziah's own territory at Beth-shemesh, 15 miles west of Jerusalem (v.21). Beth-shemesh is the first place in Israel where the ark came from the Philistines (1 Sam 6.12-14). "Judah was put to the worse before Israel" (v.22) which was a humiliating defeat. Joash took Amaziah prisoner (v.23) and brought him to Jerusalem. Joash further humiliated Amaziah and Judah by breaking down 400 cubits of the wall (600 feet/185 metres) (v.23) and taking treasures from the house of God and the king's palace (v.24). The part of the wall that he broke down was the most vulnerable part facing north.

Joash also took hostages but most likely many fewer than the captives of Judah (28.8-15). Those captives were returned to Judah in response to Oded the prophet of the Lord. The mention of this Obed-edom (v.24) is found only in Chronicles, which is again a characteristic touch. "The fact that Jehoash was not afraid to do so in Jerusalem shows how far the sons of Jeroboam had moved the north from reverence for the ancient national shrine. But neither Jehoash nor Jehu before him pressed their advantage to overthrow the Davidic dynasty" (The New Layman's Bible Commentary).

The writer of the Chronicles does not tell us when Amaziah was released but the notice that he gives in v.25 that he (Amaziah) outlived his captor by 15 years has often been taken as an indication that he was released when Joash died. Thiele has argued that it was when Amaziah was taken prisoner that the people made Uzziah his son king. It was a crisis that made the people intervene. So Amaziah only reigned on his own for five years and Uzziah had co-regency with him for twenty-four years. It seems likely therefore that nine years after his captivity (when his captor died) he was released and for the last fifteen years of his life he was co-regent with Uzziah.

"For many years Old Testament scholars have noticed that a total of 128 regnal years for the rulers of Judah from the accession of Athaliah to the end of Azariah (Athaliah 7 years, Joash 40 years, Amaziah 29 years, and Azariah 52 years) was about a quarter of a century in excess of the years of contemporary Assyria, but they had no idea as to what was responsible for this excess. Azariah's overlap of 24 years with Amaziah provides the answer" (Thiele).

Amaziah wanted to avenge the looting and murder by Israel. He may also have hoped to be reimbursed for the loss of the hundred talents of silver (v.9). Behind that, the real reason for his wanting to go against them was the pride generated by his earlier victory over Edom. But behind even that, was God Himself. Amaziah had worshipped the Edomite gods, "… the result was that he himself was defeated, not simply by a sequence of military events or by an over-confident character, but by the God he had turned away from (25.14-16, 20)" (Wilcock).

Verses 25-28: Amaziah's End

These verses are almost the same as those of 2 Kings 14.17-20. The only real exception is the opening words of v.27, which is a negative review explaining why there was a conspiracy. It is noteworthy that the conspiracy that led to his death is recorded to have arisen "from the time that Amaziah did turn away from following the Lord" (v.27, RV). That time is recorded in vv.14 and 20 which indicates that his death as a result of a conspiracy occurred many years afterwards. "However, divine judgment in Chronicles can often take place at a later date (cp. chs.21-23)" (Selman). In 2 Kings, only the fact of the conspiracy is mentioned. The words in v.27, "they made a conspiracy", indicate that no individual conspirators are named. That in turn seems to show that there was a general disaffection against Amaziah.

His foolish decision to fight Israel and the thoroughly inglorious defeat may have turned a good number of his subjects against him. That disaster may have precipitated the conspiracy against him as a further punishment from God. "He fled to Lachish", which was 30 miles south-west of Jerusalem. It was one of the cities that Rehoboam fortified (11.9). Palace guards and dungeon walls could not keep out the judgment of God in Exodus. Only the blood of the lamb could do so (Ex 12). Even the best-fortified city could not prevent God's wrath from reaching Amaziah. The assassins followed him to Lachish and slew him there. The assassins were honourable enough to see that he had a kingly burial: "And they brought him upon horses" (v.28). The Hebrew text, "upon the horses" suggests it was likely the very same horses by which he had fled to Lachish.

Most of the record of Amaziah is negative with the exception of his going by God's Word in not killing the children of his father's assassins and in his victory over Edom. "Instead of royal building programs, the walls of Jerusalem are destroyed; instead of wealth from the people and surrounding nations, the king is plundered; instead of a large family, there are hostages; instead of peace, war; instead of victory, defeat; instead of loyalty from the populace and long life, there is conspiracy and regicide" (Dillard). Amaziah was the second king to die by a conspiracy, but in contrast to the northern kingdom (which had nine different dynasties), Judah always installed a son of the slain king thus maintaining the Davidic dynasty. God providentially overruled.

2 CHRONICLES 26

Uzziah's Reign

Introductory

Uzziah is the third of successive kings the first part of whose reign was good and the last part poor. There is a much greater contrast between the two parts of Uzziah's reign than those of his father Amaziah. It is delightful to read the first fifteen verses for they are a real encouragement to seek God. But the last eight verses are a solemn warning against pride. Every saint is faced with the challenge of finishing well.

There were other kings of Judah who began well and did not finish well besides these three. How much better it is to be able to say like the Apostle Paul in 2 Timothy 4.7, "I have finished my course". There is only one other person specifically recorded in the New Testament as having finished his course and that is John the Baptist who is so commended in Acts 13.25. In effect Paul was saying that John the Baptist fulfilled the purpose that God had for him, which is a very high commendation. May the Lord give grace to all to finish as well as they began, or to do even better.

"In Amaziah, son of Joash, king of Judah, and in Uzziah, his son and successor, we have two men of similar type, both the good and bad features in the career of the father being reproduced and emphasized in that of the son. Amaziah had peace and a measure of prosperity in the early part of his reign, and so had Uzziah to even greater degree. The former made use of the opportunity this afforded him to enroll and equip a large army (25.5), and the latter on a still greater scale did the same (26.11-15). Amaziah met with success in his war with the Edomites (25.11-12), while Uzziah conquered the Philistines and Arabians and extended his fame to the borders of Egypt (26.6-8). The father, owing to his success, became 'lifted up' with pride to his own ruin (25.19,23); so did the son in a yet more daring way, and with a still more dreadful outcome (26.16,19)" (Rodgers).

Uzziah did better than his father in two ways. Amaziah did what was right but not with a perfect heart, while Uzziah seems to have sought God with a perfect heart (26.5). Again Uzziah did better than his father in that he never worshipped idols (25.14).

There was no king in Israel or Judah who seems to have had such a variety of interests and accomplishments, with the exception of Solomon. He was a king (v.1), a warrior (v.6), a builder (vv.6,9,10), a husbandman (v.10), and an engineer (v.15) for the greater part of his reign. But Uzziah was not content with all of that so he sought also to be a priest (v.16). The sad result was that he finished his days as a leper (v.21).

He was the first king of real stature since Jehoshaphat who died about 84 years earlier. Uzziah's reign was the most prosperous (excepting that of Jehoshaphat) since the days of Solomon. His fall is one of the greatest recorded in Old Testament history. There is a striking similarity to the fall of Satan, recorded in Isaiah 14.13-14 and Ezekiel 28.17 and referred to in 1 Timothy 3.6. Uzziah and Satan were both lifted up with pride. One can hardly imagine a more sorrowful end to an otherwise successful reign.

Uzziah's father Amaziah was also lifted up with pride (25.19) and so also was Hezekiah (32.25-26). Pride was not only a problem then, but still is today. The very first words of the Sermon on the Mount are, "Blessed are the poor in spirit" (Mt 5.3). Our Lord Jesus wants all His own to be truly humble (as He was). He also said (Lk 22.27), "For whether is greater, he that sitteth at meat, or he that serveth? is not he that sitteth at meat? but I am among you as he that serveth". One has well written, "Wouldst thou be chief, then lowly serve. Wouldst thou go up, then go down, but go as low as ere you will, the Master has been lower still".

There are a number of kinds of pride. There is pride of face; some are proud of their appearance. There is pride of lace; some are proud of the clothes they wear. There is pride of place; some are proud of the position they have. There is pride of race; some are proud that they are white and some are proud that they are black. The subtlest one of all is pride of grace. One brother said to another, "I always thought that you were humble, until you told me you were humble"! There is also pride of wealth and pride of ability. Even God-given success can lead to pride just as it did with Uzziah (v.16). A person proud in heart tends to forget God (Deut 8.14) (cp. Deut 8.2; Prov 15.33; Is 57.15; Jer 9.23-24; 13.15,17; 43.2; Mt 5.3; 18.4; 1 Cor 8.1; 10.12; 13.4; Phil 2.5-8; 1 Tim 3.6; 1 Pet 5.5-6). All these verses are an encouragement to humility and a warning against pride.

The vision Isaiah had (Is 6) took place "In the year that king Uzziah died", and in the temple which was the scene of Uzziah's trespass (v.1). The leper king's death and the remembrance of his presumptuous sin and its punishment had a profound effect upon Isaiah so that he took up the language of a leper, "Woe is me! for I am undone; because I am a man of unclean lips, and I dwell in the midst of a people of unclean lips" (v.5). Isaiah knew that a leper was to cry, "Unclean, unclean" (Lev 13.45). Isaiah was not a physical leper, but he knew that he was unfit for God's holy presence, especially after he heard one seraphim cry to another and say, "Holy, holy, holy, is the Lord of hosts: the whole earth is full of his glory" (v.3).

The prophet's iniquity was taken away and his sin purged by a sacrifice. "It seems that in the history of Uzziah this great truth is particularly brought to light: Grace based on sacrifice is the only resource of the best of kings and of the greatest of prophets" (Rossier).

The experience that Isaiah had and the resulting judgment on the king seem to be reflected in some parts of his prophecy. He often refers to that which is "unclean"; as in 52.11, "touch no unclean thing…be ye clean that bear the vessels of the Lord", and 64.6, "But we are all as an unclean thing, and all our righteousnesses are as filthy rags". The vivid description of the nation given in 1.5-6 appears to be that of a person covered from head to foot in leprous sores in various stages of disease. "On the other hand, when we find that Isaiah, no less that twenty-five times, speaks of the Lord as, 'the Holy One of Israel', a title found not more than seven times in all the other Scriptures, we cannot but feel that Uzziah's fate and his own vision had left a powerful impress upon his spirit" (Rodgers).

The writer can never forget when he heard Isaiah 64.6 quoted for the first time in his life Even though I was a Sunday school teacher, I did not know that that verse was in the Bible. I could not adequately express in words how terrible I felt after three years of self-improvement, three years of church attendance, three years of Sunday School work, and two years of preaching to men at work (on our lunch hour) about not drinking, not smoking, and not carrying on with women, to find out from God's Word that the very best that I had done was only filthy rags in the sight of God. I am thankful that both preachers quoted that verse. I got saved at the close of the meeting the following Sunday night. No one gets truly saved who does not at least see that, in their natural condition, they are unfit for God's presence.

Outline of Chapter 26

Verses 1-5:	Introduction.
Verses 6-8:	Uzziah's foreign wars.
Verses 9-10:	Uzziah's building and agriculture.
Verses 11-15:	Uzziah's army.
Verses 16-23:	Uzziah's pride and downfall.

Verses 1-5: Introduction

Verses 1-2 correspond to 2 Kings 14.21-22 and vv.3-4 to 2 Kings 15.2-3. There is usually some difficulty implied when the people have a part in putting a king on the throne (cp. 22.1; 33.25; 36.1). As previously suggested, this probably took place at the time Uzziah's father Amaziah was taken captive (25.23). Eloth (v.2) was very close to Ezion-Geber where Solomon and Jehoshaphat had ships. Both of those places were very important seaports for commerce and economic growth. The control of Eloth was lost during the reign of Jehoram (21.8-10). The Chronicler carefully notes that Uzziah built and restored Eloth after his father died. Thus he completed the war against Edom that his father began. Restoring Eloth enabled the beginning of prosperity unequalled in Judah since the days of Jehoshaphat. This may have been one of Uzziah's most significant accomplishments. The words, "after that the king slept", confirm that he ascended the throne prior to the death of his father.

Uzziah is introduced twice because vv.1-2 form the conclusion to Amaziah's reign as given in 2 Kings 14.21-22. This may be for emphasis. The account of Uzziah begins with vv.3-4 (as in 2 Kings 15.1-2) to which the Chronicler has added his own material (v.5). "Though Uzziah reigned for fifty-two years (v.3), his reign included co-regencies with his father Amaziah (probably for twenty-four years) and his son Jotham (for ten years)" (Selman). Even though it was such a long reign, 2 Kings covers it in only nine verses. Here vv.5-20 deal with material found only in 2 Chronicles.

Nevertheless, the fact that the age of sixteen is mentioned for the second time in v.3 (the first is in v.1) is a reminder that youth is often very important to God (as with Samuel, David, Joash, Josiah, Daniel and his three companions, and Timothy). Verse 4 states that Uzziah did "according to all that his father Amaziah did". The writer of the Chronicles was comparing the first part of the reign of Amaziah with the first part of the reign of Uzziah.

It is possible for strong leaders today to allow their God-given strength to be their downfall as Uzziah so forcefully illustrates.

Uzziah had Zechariah who helped him spiritually (v.5), even as Uzziah's grandfather had Jehoiada (24.2). Verse 5 states, "And he sought God in the days of Zechariah". These words and the remainder of the verse lead the reader to expect a change, as did the words of 24.2. They also imply that Zechariah may have died before Uzziah. This is the only time in Scripture that this Zechariah is mentioned. Seeking God became the predominant characteristic of the greater part of Uzziah's reign. Doing "that which was right in the sight of the Lord" (v.4), and seeking God (v.5), thus bringing blessing, are a favourite emphasis of the Chronicler.

Verse 5 records that Zechariah "had understanding in the visions (Hebrew 'seeing') of God" (AV margin, and RV margin). He had a good influence on Uzziah and his "influence was based on his experience of the 'seeing' of God. Such a man would unquestionably be humble-minded, and anyone influenced by him would be humble-minded too. But when that influence was removed by Zechariah's death, the king, like so many others, was found unfit to stand alone, and the pride of his heart manifested itself" (Rodgers). For "the visions of God" the RV margin states, "Many ancient authorities have, 'the fear'". The ESV has "Zechariah, who instructed him in the fear of God".

Verses 6-8: Uzziah's Foreign Wars

The practical side of v.5, "God made him to prosper", is given in detail in vv.6-15. Uzziah had prosperity and the blessing of God in three areas: war (vv.6-8), building and agriculture (vv.9-10), and the army (vv.11-15). He fought against three enemies to the west and south. He may have wanted to have control of trade routes in keeping with the building of Eloth (v.2). First, he defeated two major cities of the Philistines, Ashdod and Gath, as well as Jabneh (v.6). He consolidated his victories by building cities in the region of Ashdod (margin) and among the Philistines. He most likely fortified these cities in the conquered territory. Second, he defeated the Arabians of in Gur-baal (v.7). Third, he was victorious over the Mehunims (v.7). God helped Uzziah against each of these three enemies. It is no wonder that he was successful. After his victory over these adversaries, the Ammonites probably did not want to go to war against him. Instead they gave him gifts (v.8) and possibly agreed to be his vassals. We read in the same verse, "his name spread abroad even to the entering in of Egypt". The Chronicler favourably compared Uzziah's reign with the reigns of David and Solomon. In 1 Chronicles 14.17 we have a similar statement, which serves likewise as a summary expression of the blessing of God on David. Both David and Uzziah won the respect of all the neighbouring nations. Solomon and Uzziah both used Eloth profitably (8.17).

Verses 9-10: Uzziah's Building and Agriculture

Uzziah was rightly concerned with both foreign and domestic affairs. All the activities in vv.6-15 are worthy of praise for the larger part of his reign and were more varied than any other king of Judah since Jehoshaphat who died about 84 years before Uzziah began to reign. Verse 8 states that "he strengthened himself exceedingly", and v.15 records that "he was marvelously helped, till he was strong". In vv.9-10 Uzziah was occupied with building and agriculture. "Abundant evidence for these activities of Uzziah abounds in numerous excavated sites in the Negev around Beersheba, where cisterns, farms and artifacts have been located" (Unger).

The building work in Jerusalem (v.9) was necessary because of the damage done while his father reigned. Specific notice should be taken of "the corner gate" in 25.23 and "the corner gate" in v.9. "But by far the most important undertaking of the reign of Uzziah was the restoration and fortification of the northern wall of Jerusalem, which had been broken down in the time of Amaziah (25.23)" (Edersheim).

There may also have been damage from an earthquake (Amos 1.1; Zech 14.5). Carmel in v.10 may actually be the city with that name that is eight miles south of Hebron. Large flocks could graze there (1 Sam 25.2,4,7). On the other hand it is possible that instead of Carmel, it should read "fruitful fields" as in the AV margin and the RV. "Husbandmen and vine dressers" (v.10) may have worked on royal estates (cp. 1 Chr 27.25-31). "Evidence for some of the officials in charge of such workers has come from seals bearing the name of Uzziah/Azariah, one of which was actually found in a cistern at Tell Beit Mirsim. The rather touching description 'he loved the soil' is unique in the Bible" (Selman). "Towers in the desert" (v.10) may have had a threefold purpose of observation, defence, and shelter for his cattle. The many wells that he dug provided an ample supply of water for all his animals and all his servants (v.10).

Verses 11-15: Uzziah's Army

Verse 12 states that there were 2,600 heads of fathers' houses (RV) who had men under them. Verse 11 seems to indicate that Hananiah, one of the king's captains, had most to do with organizing the army in "bands".

Jeiel and Maaseiah under him helped in this. Verse 13 records, "And under their hand was the power of an army" (AV margin and RV margin), or "and under their hand was a trained army" (RV). The words, "to help the king" (v.13) link with v.7, "and God helped him", and v.15 "marvellously helped". We have similar help recorded for the 2½ tribes in 1 Chronicles 5.20, for David (1 Chr 12.1,18, 21-22), for Solomon (1 Chr 22.17), and for Hezekiah (2 Chr 32.3). It is worth noticing (v.14) that no longer were the soldiers required to provide their own arms, but now the king supplied them, setting a new precedent. Verse 15 seems to suggest that some kind of catapult was used, but since they were not known until the fifth century BC, it is more likely that the inventions may refer to protective devices so that men on the tops of walls could shoot or hurl stones safely.

"The Israeli general and scholar Yigael Yadin had plausibly identified the 'devices' (v.15) with special structures added to towers and battlements… They were wooden frames into which round shields were inserted to form a protective barrier behind which archers and stone throwers could safely stand instead of crouching awkwardly" (Leslie C. Allen).

"Further evidence of God's blessing is to be found in Uzziah's well-trained and well-equipped army that was of sufficient significance to be mentioned in the annals of Tilgath-Pilneser II of Assyria. He records a campaign against a coalition of kings one of whom was 'Azriau' from 'Juda' (viz. Uzziah from Judah). That the other kings were not mentioned in the Assyrian king's annals is important for it shows Uzziah's unquestioned prominence as the leader of the western alliance" (Barber).

"Verse 15 forms an inclusion with verses 7-8 by repeating the three key terms, fame, helped and powerful/strong (v.15), which characterize the section. The adverb 'marvellously' (NRSV, RSV) or 'wonderfully' (REB, NEB) always implies that God is the subject, cp. GNB, 'the help he received from God' (cp. Is 28.29; 29.14; Joel 2.26; Ps 31.21)" (Selman).

Verses 16-23: Uzziah's Pride and Downfall

The prosperity of vv.1-15 led to pride in v.16 and that led to presumption. Verse 16 records, "But when he was strong, his heart was lifted up to his destruction". Those words illustrate well the truth of Proverbs 16.18, "Pride goeth before destruction, and a haughty spirit before a fall". The material in vv.5-20 is found only in Chronicles except for the last five words of v.20. Those words and vv.21-23 correspond to 2 Kings 15.5-7. He "transgressed against the Lord his God" (v.16). God had decreed that only the priests the sons of Aaron should enter the temple and they only should offer incense (Ex 30.7-8; Num 3.10,38; 16.40; 18.7). It is true that Solomon offered sacrifices at the temple, but he did so on altars outside in the courtyard (6.13; 7.7). According to the law no man was allowed to be king and priest. David was a king and a prophet (Acts 2.30), but he never tried to be a priest. Our Lord Jesus has a perfect right to be "a priest upon his throne" in a coming day (Zech 6.13).

"Let us note that it was 'when he became powerful' that he succumbed to the kind of temptation that faces strong leaders. He became headstrong and thought himself incapable of failure. His opinion of himself blinded him to any consequences of his action. He did not pause to think of what God's Word might teach" (Barber).

Azariah the priest went in after Uzziah, and with him 80 priests of the Lord, who were valiant men (v.17). They truly were intrepid because it took moral courage to confront the king. Withstanding the king was very risky. They could no doubt remember Joash who slew Zechariah the priest in the temple (24.21-22). The Chronicler always refers to the king by the name, Uzziah, except in the genealogy of 1 Chronicles 3.12, the only place where he uses his other name Azariah. The writer of the Chronicles may have wanted to call the king Uzziah consistently to distinguish him from the priest Azariah who led 80 of his colleagues to withstand him.

"His name signifies 'Strength of the Lord', and this seems to underline the references to 'strengthened' and 'strong' in 2 Chronicles 26.8,15,16. The other name Azariah by which he is usually called in the record of 2 Kings, means 'Help of the Lord', and is even more clearly hinted at in the references to 'help' in 2 Chronicles 26.7,13,15, for it is in each case the Hebrew word 'azar', from which the name Azar-iah is compounded. This is the more remarkable because of the fact that Chronicles never uses the name Azariah as his (apart from the occurrence in the genealogy of 1 Chronicles 3.12), but mentions it in v.17 as that of the priest who withstood him. The 'Strength of the Lord' was for Uzziah's 'help' as long as he sought Him and kept humble; but when 'his heart was lifted up' in self-will, it was put forth against him. And the leper king is not the only person who has found this to be true" (Rodgers). The Hebrew word for "help" is AZAR (5826).

"Uzziah's earlier faithfulness is unable to prevent Judah's gradual destruction, though the full consequences are not felt till Ahaz's reign (ch.28). The seriousness of the problem is indicated by two phrases. Firstly, pride here and in 25.19 is a matter of the 'heart' being 'lifted up'... Secondly, Uzziah is unfaithful (vv.16,18, NIV; transgressed/trespassed, AV). This is the most important expression for sin in Chronicles...The term has not appeared since Rehoboam's time (12.2), but will now become a regular theme to the end of the book (28.19,22; 29.6,19; 30.7; 33.19; 36.14). Though Uzziah's pride did not cause the exile...From now on, Judah's end is definitely in sight" (Selman).

The priests had the Word of God for what they said to the king (v.18). He wanted to burn incense at the altar of incense and he became incensed against the priests (v.19). Verse 19 speaks twice about Uzziah being wroth against the priests. Even though what Uzziah did was very serious, he was not smitten with leprosy until after he was enraged against the priests and would not repent despite hearing their rebuke based on God's Word. He became leprous rather than any other disease because it was considered a sign of special divine judgment. This might not have happened if only he had repented when he heard the rebuke of the priest. "He who wanted too much ends up with less than he previously had. Yet the Chronicler desires his readers to appreciate that, great as his sin was, his fate was not irreversible until he sealed it by willful refusal to climb down from his high and mighty attitude" (Leslie C. Allen). Uzziah, smitten suddenly with leprosy, demonstrates forcefully that no person is so great that he does not have to answer to God.

In the first 15 verses Uzziah had enjoyed signs of divine blessing: God's help, victory in war, building projects, wealth, fame, and a large army. Now he had a sign of divine judgment. There is a parallel to an earlier such case recorded in Numbers 12.10: "And Aaron looked upon Miriam, and, behold, she was leprous". Those words are similar to v.20 here, "and Azariah... looked upon him, and, behold, he was leprous in his forehead". Another case of leprosy as a divine judgment is found in 2 Kings 5.27 in relation to Gehazi for his covetousness.

Numbers 3.10,38 and 18.7 all prescribe death as the penalty for what Uzziah did and Numbers 16.40 implies death as the penalty. Leprosy was like a living death. Aaron said of his sister Miriam (after she was struck with leprosy in Numbers 12.12), "Let her not be as one dead, of whom the flesh is half consumed". Leprosy is mentioned no less than five times in vv.19-23. Disease is noted at least twice before by the Chronicler as a consequence of departure from the Lord - Asa in 16.12 and Jehoram in 21.18.

"It was a punishment that answered the sin as face does face in a glass. (1) Pride was at the bottom of his transgression, and thus God humbled him and put dishonour upon him. (2) He invaded the office of the priests in contempt of them, and God stuck him with a disease which in a particular manner made him subject to the inspection and sentence of the priests; for to them pertained the judgment of the leprosy (Deut 24.8). (3) He thrust himself into the temple of God, whither the priests only had admission, and for that he was thrust out of the very courts of the temple, into which the meanest of his subjects that was ceremonially clean had free access" (Matthew Henry).

"Though Uzziah had many noble qualities and greatly blessed his nation, his pride led to his downfall. The root form of the word translated 'pride' means 'to be high'. Its usage is often linked to parts of the body (Is 2.11,17), as, for example, the eyes (Ps 101.5; Is 5.15), the heart (Ezek 28.2,5,17), the spirit (Prov 16.18; Eccl 7.8), and one's speech (1 Sam 2.3) (cp. Jer 48.29)" (Barber).

"The problem of pride lies in the variety of ways it can appear. Some can be quite humble in many ways, yet as proud as peacocks in some other way" (McShane).

In v.20 the priests could see that "he was leprous in his forehead". His thoughts had been puffed up with pride. On the forehead of the high priest was "HOLINESS TO THE LORD" (Ex 28.36-38). The priests thrust the king out of the temple because they knew it was a holy place. What Uzziah did was truly rebellion against the Lord and His holiness. Even though he defiantly resisted the persuasions of the priests based on God's Word, he "himself hasted to go out, because the Lord had smitten him" (v.20).

Uzziah's submission in hasting to go out may suggest that his pride was gone and that once more he truly feared the Lord. He learned by experience what Nebuchadnezzar learned similarly years later (Dan 4.37) - "those that walk in pride he is able to abase". The judgment on Uzziah reflects three earlier Old Testament incidents involving two of Aaron's sons in Leviticus 10.1-3, Korah and 250 men in Numbers 16.33,35, and Jeroboam in 1 Kings 12.33; 13.1-5. The two sons of Aaron offered incense in an unholy manner and Korah, the 250 men with him, and Jeroboam were all laymen who tried to act as priests in offering incense. "The link with Numbers 16 is especially close, however, and shows not only that Uzziah should have known better, but also that God does not stand idly by when His holiness is tampered with" (Selman). "Holiness becometh thine house, O Lord, forever" (Ps 93.5), and note the use of "thy holy temple" in Psalm 79.1.

Uzziah was not only barred from the courts of the temple but he was also barred from the palace. He was a leper until the day of his death (v.21). Once he was smitten with leprosy his son Jotham began his ten-year co-regency. The law required Uzziah's isolation (Lev 13.46; Num 5.1-3). Since other kings that were afflicted with serious disease still had something to do in the government of the nation, it is possible that Uzziah had some part to play (but not publicly, in contrast to others like Asa in 16.11-13, and Jehoram in 21.18-19). "Jotham his son was over the king's house, judging the people of the land" (v.21). He acted as the executor.

Verse 22 is the first reference to any canonical prophet, but the writing of Isaiah referred to is not the prophecy of that name in our Bibles but rather a writing that we no longer have. Isaiah also wrote about Hezekiah (Is 36-39) and had visions during the reign of Uzziah but it was not until the year of Uzziah's death that he received God's call to service (Is 6.1-8).

The pride of Uzziah and the sin of presumption to which it led followed him to his grave. He was not interred in the royal sepulchres but in the field that belonged to the kings. They must have thought that the corpse of a leper would have polluted the royal tombs. He was buried in isolation even as he had been alone most of the time for the last few years that he lived. The last words of v.23, "Jotham his son reigned in his stead", simply mean that he no longer was reigning as co-regent but had begun to reign as king by himself.

2 CHRONICLES 27

Jotham's Reign

Introductory

The previous three kings each had a period in their reign when they did well followed by a time when they did poorly. Now we have a change in three alternating kings. It is remarkable how closely these parallel the three generations (two kings who were righteous with a king that was wicked between them) of Ezekiel 18. In vv.5-9 of Ezekiel 18 we have a righteous man described who corresponds with Uzziah's son Jotham (2 Chr 27.2,6). In Ezekiel 18.10-13 the righteous man's son turns out to be exceedingly wicked as did Ahaz, the son of Jotham (2 Chr 28.1,2,19). Ezekiel 18.14-17 tells of the son (of that wicked man) who seeing the evil that his father had done, turns from the evil and does righteously. This is the case of Hezekiah, the son of Ahaz (2 Chr 29.2; 31.20,21).

"Finally, in vv.21-22 there is seen another evil generation, but in this instance the wicked person ultimately repents and is forgiven. And that this was the experience of Manasseh, the son of Hezekiah, we learn from 2 Chronicles 33.12-13. Thus the Israelites who first heard Ezekiel's message had concrete examples in the history of their own recent kings of what he was endeavouring to set before them" (Rodgers). It is truly remarkable that such an excellent king as Hezekiah, by the grace of God, came between the two wickedest kings of Judah, Ahaz and Manasseh.

"This three generation sequence of a faithful man followed by a wicked son and a faithful grandson corresponds exactly to the situation described in Ezekiel 18.1-20…the basic principle is that each person is responsible to God for their own behaviour, with its corollary that no-one is bound by their upbringing or their environment. This was potentially of great significance for the Chronicler's generation…Jotham's example shows they had every opportunity to obey God faithfully and every hope of seeing signs of his blessing" (Selman).

Jotham is the only king with nothing recorded against him personally in Kings or Chronicles. Abijah has nothing written against him in Chronicles, but the writer of the Kings gives a negative record of him. It is surprising that the Chronicler has so little recorded about good King Jotham. It may possibly be because so much of his 16 year reign was for 10 years as co-regent with his father, and it could be that he had his son Ahaz reigning with him for a couple of years.

However, it is also possible that the 10 years during which he was co-regent with his father are excluded from the fifteen years. That is the likely explanation for the reading in 2 Kings 15.30, "the twentieth year of Jotham the son of Uzziah".

This short chapter on Jotham is similar to the account in 2 Kings 15.32-38. It contains all the facts of the Kings account except the notice of war with Syria and Israel (v.37). The writer of the Chronicles provides a much fuller note of Jotham's building work (vv.3b-4) and the whole account of the war with the Ammonites (v.5). The Chronicler, as his custom was, gave theological reflections on his history. He states that he followed his father in doing that which was right in the sight of the Lord, but he did not follow his father's wrong of entering the temple to burn incense (v.2). He also records that he "became mighty, because he prepared his ways before the Lord his God" (v.6).

"The chapter is structured in a symmetrical fashion. At its heart lie two evidences of God's favour in vv.3-4 and 5. This twinned element is surrounded by the secret of Jotham's success in vv.2 and 6. Encircling that are the two initial and closing formulas of his reign in vv.1 and 7-9, each including a statement of his sixteen years' reign, a repetition which finds a parallel in the case of Jehoram at 21.5,20. We shall find that ch.28, similar in form but diverse in content, functions as the negative counterpart of ch.27" (Leslie C. Allen).

Outline of Chapter 27

Verses 1-2: Jotham's accession.
Verses 3-5: Jotham's activities.
Verse 6: The secret of Jotham's success.
Verses 7-9: Jotham's obituary.

Verses 1-2: Jotham's Accession

In v.1 the writer of the Chronicles as usual gives the king's age at accession (25 years) and his length of reign (16 years). The Chronicler gives the mother's name for 9 of the 19 kings of Judah including Jotham. Interestingly, the writer of the Kings gives the mother's name for 16 of the 19, but only one of the 19 kings of Israel (Jeroboam in 1 Kings 11.26). Perhaps this is because all the kings of Israel were evil (including Jeroboam). But we do not know why the writer included the mother's names of five kings of Judah that were evil (Amon and the last four kings) when other kings of Judah were also evil. He gives the mother's name of Manasseh who was very wicked until very near the end of his long reign. It is well known that mothers can have a profound influence for good or evil on the lives of her children.

The behaviour of Jotham was pleasing to God as was the behaviour of his father before his fall (v.2). Jotham felt keenly the consequences of Uzziah's sin in wanting to offer incense in the temple. He profited from his father's mistake and he carefully avoided doing the same. The phrase in v.2, "howbeit he entered not into the temple of the Lord", can be taken grammatically as something negative against Jotham. A few commentators take it that way, but the context is against doing so. This verse also teaches that the one act of wrongdoing on the part of Uzziah did not nullify the good character of his reign.

"The one lesson which can be learned from him is that while it is good to imitate those leaders, who have lived their lives for the advancement of God's kingdom, yet their failings must not be imitated nor should their errors be adopted. He learned from his father the costliness of acting wrongly, and was preserved from repeating the same mistake. Those kings in Judah who walked in the ways of David, and were praised for doing so, were never guilty of copying his behaviour with Bath-sheba" (McShane).

The last sentence of v.2 is significant: "And the people did yet corruptly". In spite of Jotham's good behaviour, the people behaved badly. The writer of the Chronicles does not condemn Jotham for this. The rulers were very important in leading the people in their attitude towards God, but the people were ultimately responsible for their own attitudes and actions. "The people can contradict the attitudes of their rulers, whether the ruler be the wicked Athaliah or the good Jotham" (Thompson).

"Up to this point, the general perspective of Chronicles has been that the character of the king determines the moral judgment of the people. Here we see a divergence between the king's godliness and the popular apostasy of the people, a distinction that, later, could permit anticipating judgment despite the good qualities of a good king (cp. 34.27,28)" (Baker Commentary on the Bible).

Verses 3-5: Jotham's Activities

Jotham profited from 10 years of co-regency with Uzziah. He vigorously continued his father's activities that increased the material prosperity of his subjects. The first part of v.3 is taken from 2 Kings 15.35 which refers to Jotham building the high gate of the house of the Lord which was on the north side of the temple. "The 'high gate' led from the king's house to the temple (see 2 Chr 23.20), and Jotham's building it (rebuilding or repairing) is very significant. He wished free access from his own house to that of the Lord…This is one of the secrets of his prosperity and power" (Knapp). Ophel (v.3) is the southern slope of the temple hill. Verse 4 gives more of Jotham's building activities. The word "built" is found four times in vv.3-4. The seal of Jotham was found at Ezion-Geber indicating that there was activity at that seaport.

Verse 5 records Jotham's victory over the Ammonites. Since they gave gifts to Uzziah (26.8), it is likely that they stopped doing so when he became a leper. After Jotham defeated them they paid tribute of a hundred talents of silver and more besides. In 25.6 Amaziah had hired 100,000 mighty men out of Israel for 100 talents of silver. In v.7 a man of God told him, "O king, let not the army of Israel go with thee; for the Lord is not with Israel". Amaziah said to the man of God (v.9), "But what shall we do for the hundred talents which I have given to the army of Israel?". And the man of God answered, 'The Lord is able to give thee much more than this". Here in 27.5 is a fulfillment of 25.9.

Verse 6: The Secret of Jotham's Success

"So Jotham became mighty" (like his father) because the Lord helped him. But, unlike his father, Jotham evidently never forgot that the Lord was his true source of strength. This evaluation given by the Chronicler guided by the Holy Spirit again shows that blessing from the Lord follows obedience. Surely v.6 is an encouragement for all today to seek spiritual strength from the Lord by doing as did Jotham who "prepared his ways before the Lord his God", or, as the RV has, "ordered his ways". An alternative to "prepared" or "ordered" is in the margin of the AV - "established his ways". An ordered life will be an established life. It is very personal: "before the Lord his God".

Only three are recorded in God's Word who "walked with God". Enoch (Gen 5.24), Noah (Gen 6.9), and Levi (Mal 2.6). Four are recorded as having walked "before" God: Abraham and Isaac (Gen 48.15), David (1 Kings 3.6), and Hezekiah (2 Kings 20.3). Those four are a link with Jotham who "prepared his ways before the Lord his God".

Maclaren comments: "The rest that we hear of him in Chronicles is a mere sketch of campaigns, buildings, and victories, and then he and his reign are summed up in the words of our text, which is the analysis of the man and the disclosure of the secret of his prosperity: 'he became mighty, because he prepared his ways' — and more than that, 'He prepared them before the Lord his God'...The secret of true strength lies in the continued recognition that life is lived 'Before the Lord our God'".

Verses 7-9: Jotham's Obituary

The writer of the Chronicles omits what we read in 2 Kings 15.37: "In those days the Lord began to send against Judah Rezin the king of Syria, and Pekah the son of Remaliah". But the initial stages of that war may be indicated in what is stated here in v.7, "all his wars". "The Syro-Israelite league had been formed at the close of the reign of Jotham (2 Kings 15.37), although its full effects only appeared when Ahaz acceded to the throne" (Edersheim). "Hostilities apparently broke out before the death of Jotham; but nothing of importance was effected until the first year of his successor" (Rawlinson). It is likely that the Chronicler omitted any direct reference because he considered that it was not a judgment against Jotham but against Judah, just as the writer of the Kings recorded it, and more especially against Ahaz (2 Kings 16.5; 2 Chr 28.5).

All that is stated in v.8 had already been recorded in v.1. It is possible that the writer repeated the information because Jotham was faithful to God right to the end and made significant accomplishments in a relatively brief period of time. But it is difficult to assign any similar reason for 21.5 being repeated in v.20 for Jehoram, a wicked king. Jotham was honourably buried in the city of David and most likely greatly lamented by his people.

2 CHRONICLES 28

Ahaz' Reign

Introductory

It is striking how often, especially among the kings of Judah, godly fathers had wicked sons: Jehoshaphat had Jehoram 21.1; Jotham had Ahaz 27.9; Hezekiah had Manasseh 32.33; and Josiah had three wicked sons, Jehoahaz, Eliakim, and Zedekiah 36.1,4,10. Ahaz (being a wicked king) was the second of three alternating kings that parallel the three generations of Ezekiel 18, as noted in the first paragraph of the introduction to Jotham's reign in Chapter 27 of this commentary.

Ahaz was a thoroughly wicked king who completely forsook the Lord and gave himself utterly to idolatry. The more God smote him for his wickedness, the more he sinned against Him. Ahaz was the exact opposite of his father in almost every way.

Ahaz was the third king of Judah for whom the Chronicler did not have one good thing to say. The other two were Jehoram in ch.21 and Ahaziah in ch.22 (omitting Athaliah who usurped the throne and reigned illegally).

Jotham and Ahaz both reigned for 16 years but what a difference there was; 16 godly years followed by 16 wicked years. Verse 27.2 states that Jotham "did that which was right in the sight of the Lord'. In contrast, 28.1 records that Ahaz "did not that which was right in the sight of the Lord". The writer of the Chronicles does not record one bad thing about Jotham and he does not record one good thing about Ahaz.

Another similarity in these two chapters is the Hebrew verb for "be strong" or "strengthen" (which is found three times in these two accounts). The same verb is found twice in ch.27 in a positive sense - "prevailed" in v.5 and "became mighty" in v.6. This verb is found once in 28.20 in a negative sense - "strengthened him not". "The Chronicler would have his readers view the reigns side by side as a challenge for them - and so for us - to decide which king is to be the role model to follow" (Leslie C. Allen).

Ahaz came to the throne in difficult circumstances. Even though his father was a godly king, v.27.2 states that "the people did yet corruptly". Two deadly enemies, Pekah the king of Israel and Rezin the king of Syria (who had begun the war with Judah before Jotham died, 2 Kings 15.37) were probably encouraged to go aggressively against Jerusalem since Ahaz was only a youth of 20 years. Isaiah records (7.2) that when it was told the house of David that "Syria is confederate with Ephraim", "his heart was moved, and the heart of his people, as the trees of the wood are moved with the wind". Isaiah then encouraged Ahaz: "Take heed, and be quiet; fear not, neither be fainthearted for the two tails of these smoking firebrands" (Is 7.4).

He told Ahaz (Is 7.6) that Rezin and Pekah were planning to dethrone him and set up a man of their choosing on Judah's throne, "the son of Tabeal". Isaiah assured Ahaz (v.7), "Thus saith the Lord God, It shall not stand, neither shall it come to pass". Of course, Ahaz neither deserved, nor ever is said to have showed any gratitude for, God's intervention. This incident was another attempt by the devil to cut off the Davidic line of the Messiah. Isaiah warned Ahaz (v.9), "If ye will not believe, surely ye shall not be established". Isaiah also gave him a sign when he prophesied the virgin birth of the Messiah (vv.14-16). Thinking of the attempt to cut off the Messianic line helps us to understand why Isaiah speaks of the house of David (vv.2 and 13) rather than the personal name of Ahaz. It also explains Isaiah's prophecies concerning the Messiah not only in ch.7, but also in 9.6,7 and 11.1-5,10. God's purposes for the throne of David and the Messianic line could not be frustrated.

"In vain did Isaiah warn him, rebuke him, offer him signs, threaten him, urge him to rely on Jehovah (Is 7.4-17; 8.1-4; etc); he…ever trespassed more and more (2 Chr 28.22), till, at the age of thirty-six (2 Kings 16.2), when he was in the very prime of life, God cut him off…and so stopped the further degradation of His people" (Rawlinson). God's Word says that "deceitful men shall not live out half their days" (Ps 55.23).

Ahaz reigned at a very critical time in Judah's history. It was during his reign and the ninth and last year of the reign of Hoshea (the last king of Israel) that the king and many of the northern tribes were taken captive by Assyria. That ended the divided monarchy. It would have been wonderful if Ahaz had repented personally and had then led the southern kingdom in repentance when he saw that the northern kingdom had been defeated and for the most part taken into captivity. But instead he increased in his wickedness.

Thiele believes that the fall of the ten northern tribes occurred in the 13th year of Ahaz. He writes in his preface to *A Chronology of the Hebrew Kings*, "It is my hope that those who carefully study these findings will discover doubts and perplexities beginning to vanish and will find new confidence in the veracity of the Word of God".

By the end of the reign of Ahaz there was only one king over the covenant people because there was no longer a king reigning over the ten northern tribes. The writer of the Chronicles (near the end of the chapter) seems to be making a statement of this new circumstance in a threefold way. In v.19 he refers to Ahaz as "king of Israel", and in v.23 he speaks of his subjects as "all Israel". In v.27 he even refers to the span of Judæan monarchs as "kings of Israel".

"His full name as appears in the Assyrian state records was Jehoahaz (i.e. 'the possession of Jehovah'), but the Spirit of God strikes the Jehovah syllable out of his name, and invariably calls him 'Ahaz', i.e. 'possession'. Such was his life, he was led and influenced and possessed by anyone or anything except God" (Williams).

This account in Chronicles is akin to the account in 2 Kings 16. In addition to the introduction and conclusions being similar, both accounts have Ahaz' apostasy and war with Syria and Ephraim (vv.1-15; 2 Kings 16.1-6). Both have an appeal to the king of Assyria (vv.16-21; 2 Kings 16.7-9). Both have the further apostasy of Ahaz (vv.22-25; 2 Kings 16.10-18). The Chronicler gives details about the defeat of Judah, as well as describing how the prophet Oded delivered the captives of Judah that Ephraim had taken (vv.9-15) which is not recorded in 2 Kings. The writer of the Chronicles omits things recorded in 2 Kings and seems to assume that the record of 2 Kings is known. He is especially concerned to add material omitted in 2 Kings, making his account supplemental to that record.

The Chronicler refers often in this chapter to the taking of Judæan captives (vv.5,8,11,13,14,15,17). "This theme anticipates the exile itself, indicating that Ahaz' actions jeopardized the very existence of God's covenant people. The reasons for this are developed in the second section (vv.16-21), where the key word is 'help' (vv.16,21, also v.23)…The occurrences in vv.16 and 21 are especially significant, since they mark the beginning and end of the paragraph, in both cases as part of phrases that are additional to Kings…Judah went into captivity because Ahaz sought false help from the king of Assyria and also from the gods of Damascus (v.23)" (Selman). Verse 3 also anticipates the exile with these words, "he… burnt his children in the fire, after the abominations of the heathen whom the Lord had cast out before the children of Israel".

The writer of the Chronicles compares Ahaz with its first king Rehoboam. Rehoboam "forsook the law of the Lord" (12.1) and "transgressed against the Lord" (v.2). As a consequence, Shishak king of Egypt "took away the treasures of the house of the Lord, and the treasures of the king's house; he took all" (v.9). Ahaz caused Judah to be defeated "because they had forsaken the Lord God of their fathers" (v.6), and "he…transgressed sore against the Lord" (v.19), and "in the time of his distress did he trespass yet more against the Lord" (v.22). Ahaz also took treasure out of the house of the Lord and out of the house of the king to pay Assyria for help that he never really received. In Rehoboam's case the humbling of themselves by the princes and the king diminished the divine "wrath" (12.6,7,12). In the case of Ahaz there was no humbling and divine "anger" brought disaster and was still not satisfied at the close of his reign (vv.9,25).

The Chronicler probably had other sources available to him that the writer of Kings did not have or did not use. He, guided by the Holy Spirit, has made it clear that there was an almost complete reversal of what is recorded in ch.13.

1. Ahaz made molten images for Baalim for worship (v.2) even as Jeroboam had golden calves to worship and, "them that are no gods" as Abijah charged the Northerners (13.8-9).

2. Ahaz shut the doors of the temple (v.24), put out the lamps, and stopped the burning of incense and the burnt offerings (29.7) These

additions by the writer of the Chronicles show that the boast of Abijah of 13.11, "we keep the charge of the Lord our God", was no longer true.

3. At the time of the division righteous individuals left the North to strengthen Judah (11.13-17) but during Ahaz' reign righteousness was found in the North (28.9-15). At the time of the schism Judah was obedient to the words of Shemaiah the man of God: "Ye shall not go up, nor fight against your brethren" (11.2-4). Now it was Israel that was obedient to the words of Oded the prophet of the Lord regarding their brethren (28.9-15).

4. The military results are also reversed. In 13.11 it is stated that the Northerners had forsaken the Lord God and therefore "God delivered them into their hand. And Abijah and his people slew them with a great slaughter" (13.16-17). Verse 28.5 states about Ahaz: "And he was also delivered into the hand of the king of Israel, who smote him with a great slaughter". The next verse tells us why: "because they had forsaken the Lord God of their fathers" (v.6). In Abijah's reign Israel was "brought under" (13.18) whereas in Ahaz' reign, "the Lord brought Judah low because of Ahaz" (28.19).

"In the plainest possible way, by using identical words and reversing their references, the Chronicler shows that divine favour does not belong automatically to any place, community, or form of religion as such, but only to those whose hearts are right with God" (Wilcock). The bad behaviour of Ahaz and the people of Judah put the good behaviour of the Northerners in a more favourable light. "These changes show that apostasy in the South had reached the same depths as that in the North at the time of the schism" (Dillard).

Outline of Chapter 28

Verses 1-4:	The character of Ahaz.
Verses 5-8:	The Syro-Ephraimite war.
Verses 9-15:	The message of Oded and its results.
Verses 16-21:	The appeal to the king of Assyria.
Verses 22-27:	The apostasy and death of Ahaz.

Verses 1-4: The Character of Ahaz

Verse 1 seems to indicate that Ahaz was thirty-six years of age when he died. Hezekiah was twenty-five when he began to reign (29.1). That would indicate that Ahaz was only eleven years of age when Hezekiah was born. While this is not probable, yet it is possible since some boys begin to mature physically much more rapidly than others.

There are two additional possible solutions. The Septuagint for this verse has twenty-five years. Those five extra years added to the life of Ahaz when he died would mean that Ahaz was sixteen when Hezekiah was born (which is a much more probable age for the fathering of children). The only problem with this solution is that the Septuagint in the parallel text in 2 Kings 16.2 has twenty years instead of twenty-five years as it has for 2 Chronicles 28.1.

Another possible solution is that the Chronicler is only referring to the years that Hezekiah reigned alone when he writes that he reigned for sixteen years. He did have the co-regency with his father for two or three years. If we added those years to eleven, we would have Ahaz at thirteen or fourteen years when Hezekiah was born. The only problem with that solution is that the writer of the Chronicles states (26.3) that Uzziah reigned fifty-two years and we know that includes two co-regencies, one of twenty-four years and the other of ten years. We cannot explain why he would not include the co-regency with his father in 28.1.

These verses give a similar account to that of 2 Kings 16.2-4 except that the Chronicler has an addition (vv.2b and 3a). The writer of the Chronicles is emphasizing with those additions the unbridled wickedness of Ahaz. The very first verse shows that Ahaz was the opposite of his father. Verse 27.2 says about Jotham, "And he did that which was right in the sight of the Lord". This verse says about Ahaz, "but he did not that which was right in the sight of the Lord". There are many kings for whom it is recorded, "he did evil in the sight of the Lord" or similar words (20 times in 2 Kings and nine times in 2 Chronicles: 12.14; 21.6; 22.4; 33.2,6,22; 36.5,9,12). But Ahaz is the only king with the assessment: "he did not that which was right in the sight of the Lord". The writer of the Chronicles possibly recorded it in this way to emphasize the contrast to his father. "Ahaz grew to adulthood without a strong God-consciousness. Does this seem far-fetched? It is not. It takes place daily in the public schools where our children are taught things that deliberately contradict what is taught in the home. And such teaching has a corrosive effect on the child as well as society" (Barber).

Verse 1 is also unique in that there are only four other verses (besides this and the parallel verse in 2 Kings 16.2) where criticism is expressed for not following the example of David: 1 Kings 11.4 for Solomon; 1 Kings 14.8 for Jeroboam; 1 Kings 15.3 for Abijah; and 2 Kings 14.3 for Amaziah. Four kings are commended for following David's example: Asa (1 Kings 15.11); Jehoshaphat (2 Chr 17.3); Hezekiah (2 Kings 18.3; 2 Chr 29.2); Josiah (2 Kings 22.2; 2 Chr 34.2).

Ahaz walked in the ways of the kings of Israel (v.2) like wicked Jehoram (21.6) and like wicked Ahaziah (22.4). Ahaz of Judah should not be confused with Ahab of Israel who reigned over one hundred years earlier. All the kings of Israel were evil. The Chronicler adds what is not recorded in Kings: "he…made also molten images for Baalim" (v.2). Ahaz is the only king recorded besides Jeroboam (in the North) who made molten images. Even though Ahaz walked in the ways of the kings of Israel, yet Pekah the king of Israel was one of his chief enemies.

Ahaz was the first king of Judah who burnt his children in the fire (v.3). His grandson Manasseh followed him in this (33.6). Amon may also have done so, but it is never explicitly stated in the Word of God. 2 Chronicles 33.22 states that, "he did that which was evil…as did Manasseh his father", which may imply that he did. Kings has even a stronger implication in the words of 2 Kings 21.21: "And he walked in all the way that his father walked in". 2 Kings 16.3 records "son" but Chronicles has "children" and makes it explicit that he "burned" them. That made his sin even worse. Ezekiel 16.20-21 seems to indicate that the victims were first slain and then burnt (Edersheim). This was one of the abominations committed by the heathen whom the Lord had cast out before the children of Israel, and was also one of the reasons why the ten northern tribes were taken into captivity (2 Kings 17.17-18). The law prohibited this (Lev 18.21; 20.2-5; Deut 18.10). Leviticus 20.2-5 is especially strong in condemnation. It is also referred to in Psalm 106.37-38 and Ezekiel 23.37-38. Good King Josiah stopped the practice in 2 Kings 23.10.

How horrible that any king of Judah would so cruelly treat any of his children in this gruesome way. He burned at least two of his own children and possibly one of them was heir to the throne of David. Following the wicked ways of the northern kings was bad enough, but it was even worse to imitate the Canaanites who were so wicked that God ordered their expulsion from the land. Jeremiah refers to the valley of the son of Hinnom as Tophet and the valley of slaughter (Jer 7.31-32; 19.2-6). Good King Josiah defiled the place (2 Kings 23.10). Afterwards, rubbish was continually burnt there south of Jerusalem so it became a fit emblem for Gehenna, the place of eternal conscious punishment. Gehenna is the Greek equivalent of two Hebrew words meaning "Valley of Hinnom" and was used (as "hell", AV) by the compassionate Lord Jesus.

"In grace the Lord sent the prophet Isaiah to meet with King Ahaz. God promised Judah deliverance from her enemies, and to prove the sincerity of His words Ahaz was told that he could ask for any sign he chose (Is 7.11) — the more difficult the better. With hypocrisy that makes our flesh crawl, the faithless king replied: 'I will not ask, nor will I test Yahweh'. He lacked the honesty to put God to the test even when invited to do so. Isaiah then gave the virginal conception of the Messiah (Is 7.14). Still Ahaz would not believe" (Barber).

Other kings of Judah allowed their subjects to sacrifice and burn incense in high places but Ahaz was the first king of Judah recorded who actually did so himself (v.4). This verse makes the idolatry and apostasy of Ahaz more explicit.

Verses 5-8: The Syro-Ephraimite War

"Never surely had a man greater opportunity of doing well than Ahaz had...and yet here we have him in these few verses.

Wretchedly corrupted and debauched. He had had a good education given him...(but) he did not that which was right in the sight of the Lord' (v.1), nay, he did a great deal that was wrong, wrong to God, to his own soul, and to his own people; he walked in the way of the revolted Israelites and the devoted Canaanites, made molten images and worshipped them...

He forsook the temple of the Lord and sacrificed and burnt incense on the hills, as if they would place him nearer heaven, and under every green tree…To complete his wickedness, as one perfectly divested of all natural affection as well as religion…he 'burnt his children in the fire to Molech' (v.3).

Wretchedly spoiled…The Syrians insulted him and triumphed over him…and carried away a great many of his people into captivity. The king of Israel, though an idolater too, was made a scourge to him and 'smote him with a great slaughter'" (Matthew Henry's Commentary).

The war was so named because an alliance of Syria and Ephraim was pitted against Judah. Ephraim refers to the northern kingdom of Israel. This war is also referred to in 2 Kings 15.37, 16.5, and Isaiah 7.1-6. Some commentators add Hosea 5.8-6.6. Instead of presenting Syria and Ephraim as a coalition (as in 2 Kings 16.5 and Isaiah 7.2), the writer of the Chronicles records two separate attacks. He disapproves of foreign alliances because they indicate a failure to trust in the Lord (16.2-9; 19.2; 25.6-10). Dillard suggests that the Chronicler wanted to present the Northerners in a good light as in vv.9-15 so he may have avoided making it obvious that they had made an alliance with a pagan country. Treating Ephraim as an entity instead of a member of a coalition also emphasized more directly the reversal of roles recorded in Abijah's defeat of Jeroboam in 13.13-18.

Although both 2 Kings 16.5 and Isaiah 7.1 tell of the alliance being unable to prevail against Ahaz and Jerusalem, the writer of the Chronicles chose to focus on the defeat of Ahaz in keeping with his theology that evil kings are defeated in war. He emphasizes that the defeat of Ahaz and Judah was from God because of their departure from the Lord God. "Wherefore the Lord his God delivered him into the hand of the king of Syria…And he was also delivered into the hand of the king of Israel" (v.5). The defeat by Syria was great, but the defeat by Israel was even greater. All the men that Pekah slew in v.6 were valiant men. But being valiant did not avail because "they had forsaken the Lord God of their fathers" (v.6). The phrase "delivered… into the hand of" does not mean that Ahaz himself was delivered into the hand of these two enemies, but rather that his army was defeated. Never in all the history of Judah were so many recorded as slain - "an hundred and twenty thousand in one day" (v.6).

The losses given in v.6 are large but Rawlinson records some other great losses recorded in history. "Darius Codomannus lost 100,000, or 110,000, at Issus, out of probably 131,200. Out of 300,000, 100,000 are said to have fallen at Platæa. At the battle of Tigranocerta the Armenians lost 150,000 out of 260,000".

Verse 7 adds the losses in Ahaz' court and the loss of one of his relatives to the disastrous total of v.6. The specific names given suggest that the Chronicler had a source that was not available to the writer of 2 Kings. Since Ahaz was only 20 years of age when he began to reign, his sons would have been too young to be in the battle. Maaseiah must have been a younger son of the late king Jotham. The title "second to the king" (AV margin, RV margin, and JND) is only found elsewhere in Esther 10.3 (JND). His loss, the death of the governor of the house, and the one who was second to the king would likely have had a devastating effect on Ahaz' court officials.

The writer of the Chronicles deliberately uses the word "brethren" (vv.8,11,15). He wants to remind his readers that there is a unity between the northern tribes and the southern tribes in spite of the division that took place in the early part of Rehoboam's reign. The Chronicler's quotations of the words of Oded, "the Lord God of you fathers" (v.9), and "the Lord your God" (v.10) point the reader in the same direction.

Verses 9-15: The Message of Oded and its Results

"The Chronicler gives the reason for these misfortunes. The king and his people 'had forsaken the Lord God of their fathers' (28.6b). God, however, was more gracious than the Judahites deserved. As the men of Israel returned to their homes, Oded, a prophet of the Lord, met the army and questioned them about the propriety of what they were doing. The people of Judah were their relatives. They came from the same family. Oded then challenged them to let the captives go, reminding them that they had sinned in their attitude toward those in Judah and had incurred God's wrath. The men of Israel listened to him and in a magnanimous way did as he had instructed" (Barber).

These seven verses are delightful reading in the midst of twenty sad verses about the wickedness of Ahaz. "Then follows one of the beautiful scenes in Chronicles. This dark chapter is relieved by this mercy that was shown" (Gaebelein). "This episode is one of the most unexpected (and attractive) in the whole of Chronicler's work" (Coggins). "We come now to one of the most fascinating paragraphs in the whole of Chronicles" (Wilcock).

This is the only place where we read of this Oded the prophet (v.9). It is the fourteenth of fifteen times recorded that a prophet or a man of God, or a seer, or a priest, gave a message from God, but this is the only time a message is given to someone other than a king (1 Chr 17.1-15; 21.9-12; 2 Chr 11.2-4; 12.5-8; 15.1-8; 16.7-9; 18.18-27; 19.2-3; 20.37; 21.12-15; 24.20; 25.7-9, 15-16; 28.9-11; 36.12). 2 Chronicles 15.1 and 8 tell of an earlier Oded who may have been an ancestor of this man. This Oded courageously went to meet the victorious army, not with words of flattery but with words of warning even as Azariah did (15.2). Similarly, when Jehoshaphat returned from a battle in which he almost lost his life and Ahab was killed, Jehu the son of Hanani bravely rebuked him.

God sovereignly controlled events in bringing judgment on Judah and also in alleviating the terrible consequences of the judgment. Thus God blended mercy with judgment. The kindness shown to the captives is reminiscent of the kindness of Elisha to the men who had come to take him captive after they themselves had been taken captive (2 Kings 6.21-23).

The prophet Oded met the returning victorious army and told them that the real reason for their victory was that they were the instruments of God's judgment on Judah (v.9b). He sternly rebuked them for going too far and venting their own wrath upon their brethren. They went beyond what was allowable: "a rage that reacheth up unto heaven" describes the magnitude of their fury. "Not merely with a rage beyond all measure, but a rage which calls to God for vengeance. Cp. Ezra 9.6" (Keil).

Oded rebuked them for wanting to make slaves of all their brethren that they had taken captive (v.10). Leviticus 25.39-43,46 forbade making any one of their brethren a bondman. The fact that these captives were not the men who fought against them but women and their children added to the guilt of the northern kingdom. Oded aimed at their conscience when he said, "but are there not with you, even with you, sins against the Lord your God?" (v.10). This question is reminiscent of our Lord's teaching against censorious judgment (Mt 7.1-5). That question and the statement in v.11, "the fierce wrath of the Lord is upon you", was really an invitation to repentance, something never heard of before in the northern kingdom.

"Oded's words, 'the fierce wrath of the Lord is upon you' (v.11) produce such an impression on the consciences of these four faithful men that they repeat: 'There is fierce wrath against Israel' (v.13). God speaks through their mouth, because the word has first of all exerted its authority on their consciences, and it possesses a power of conviction that brings souls into subjection" (Rossier). Oded finally demanded, "send back the captives" (v.11, RV), and warned them of "the fierce wrath of the Lord" if they did not obey. "The speech, which was a model in respect of compact brevity, lofty eloquence, clear statement, pathetic appeal, resistless logic, and which must have been delivered with combined boldness and persuasiveness, made a deep impression" (The Pulpit Commentary).

The response of four of the leaders of Ephraim (vv.12-13), the armed men, the princes, and the entire congregation (v.14) shows the effectiveness of prophecy. Surprisingly, the Northerners responded to God's word whereas Judah under Ahaz did not. Since the Chronicler gives the names of these four men it is another of the indications that he had a source that the writer of the Kings did not have or did not use (v.12). These four leaders "stood up against them that came from the war". They opposed any suggestion of making the captives all slaves. It is possible that the record of these four "heads of the children of Ephraim" assuming the lead on behalf of the captives is an indication that the king of the Northerners was already fallen. It is remarkable that soldiers gave up the prisoners they had captured from Judah and the plunder. "Such magnanimous behaviour is unusual in the ancient world, since plunder was the payment for service soldiers expected" (Thompson).

These four men took the lead in caring for the captives in a number of ways including anointing them (v.15). They applied balms and oils to the wounded. All the feeble ones were carried on asses to Jericho, the city of palm trees. This was an occasion of being "Good Samaritans" nationally. The conduct of these four men especially "was morally beautiful…And the righteous Lord who loveth righteousness has seen to it that these men of tender heart and upright conscience should be 'expressed by name'… the God of Israel has placed it on eternal record…that men might know that He never forgets a kindness done to His people, even when they suffer, under His government, the just punishment of their sins". (Knapp). Hebrews 6.10 comes to mind, "For God is not unrighteous to forget your work and labour of love, which ye have shewed toward his name, in that ye have ministered to the saints, and do minister".

Verse 14 indicates that these four men acted with the general approval of the army, the princes and the whole congregation. These four, and all the Northerners who helped, were fulfilling the Old Testament standard of showing love even to the enemy. Exodus 23.4 states, "If thou meet thine enemy's ox or his ass going astray, thou shalt surely bring it back to him again". It is recorded in Proverbs 25.21: "If thine enemy be hungry, give him bread to eat; and if he be thirsty, give him water to drink". They had been fighting against the Southerners as enemies, but the Southerners and Northerners were really brethren. Believers today have a closer relationship with one another since the Holy Spirit indwells each one. It is written in Leviticus 19.18, "Thou shalt not avenge, nor bear any grudge against the children of thy people, but thou shalt love the neighbour as thyself: I am the Lord". Compare Matthew 5.44 with Luke 23.34: our Lord Jesus lived out in perfection what He taught, "Father, forgive them; for they know not what they do".

"That fact at the beginning of the history of the two separated kingdoms, and this at the end of it, finely correspond to each other. In the one place it is a Judæan prophet who exhorts the men of Judah, in the other an Ephraimite prophet who exhorts the Ephraimites, to show a conciliatory spirit to the related people; and in both cases they are successful" (Keil).

"This is a beautiful incident, and full of interest, as showing that even in the period of national decline, there were not a few who steadfastly adhered to the Law of God" (Jamieson, Fausset & Brown).

A good number of commentators link this incident (vv.9-15) with the parable of the Good Samaritan in Luke 10.30-35. Edersheim is the most commendably reverent: "Without presuming to affirm that this episode was in the mind of the Lord when He spoke the parable of 'the Good Samaritan', there is that in the bearing of these men who are expressed by name which reminds us of the example and the lessons in that teaching of Christ". He goes on to point out that there were in all likelihood others who participated in this good deed.

Verses 16-21: The Appeal to the King of Assyria

Verse 16 states that Ahaz appealed to the kings of Assyria. The RV margin has, "Many ancient authorities read king." The one king is named in v.20, Tilgath-pilneser, and he is also referred to in v.21. Seven times the Chronicler unexpectedly uses the plural "kings" when the singular "king" would be expected (1.17,17; 9.14; 28.16,23; 30.6; 32.4). Three of them are "kings of Assyria" (28.16; 30.6; 32.4). Selman writes, "which may if taken together refer generally to the Assyrian empire".

Ahaz was in desperate straits. The Syrians and Ephraimites were in the north and the Edomites and the Philistines were in the south.-

"The historical substance of this paragraph (vv.16-21) comprises an appeal by Ahaz to Tilgath-pilneser III of Assyria...This situation is not described in any other Biblical text, though 2 Kings 16.6 points in the same direction. However, increased knowledge of Assyrian movements from texts discovered at Nimrud has convinced most scholars that this represents an accurate portrayal of the situation" (Williamson).

Earlier kings of Judah who had been faithful to the Lord and trusted Him had seen God defeat enemies many times. The writer of the Chronicles delights to record how God helped them and others when they trusted Him (1 Chr 5.20; 12.18; 15.26; 2 Chr 14.11; 18.31; 20.4,9; 25.8; 26.7,15; 32.8).

But sadly, Ahaz did not trust in the Lord because he consistently acted like a politician. As a matter of expediency, he appealed to Assyria to help him in defiance of the pleadings of Isaiah to trust the Lord for deliverance (Is 7.7-9) and in spite of the warnings that an appeal to Assyria would result in suffering at their hand (Is 7.17-20). The words of Ahaz recorded in 2 Kings 16.7 in his appeal to Tilgath-pilneser, "I am thy servant and thy son", show that Ahaz was putting complete trust in the king of Assyria and was willingly reducing the status of Judah to a vassal of Assyria.

"For" in v.17 introduces the explanation for the appeal by Ahaz to Assyria. The prophets rebuked Edom's ever-present readiness to take advantage of Judah in distressful calamity and their lack of pity (Ezek 35.5; Amos 1.11; Obadiah vv.10-14). Verse 18 continues the explanation. The Philistines took revenge for Uzziah's victory over them (26.6).

"For", in v.19 introduces the real reason for the troubles of Ahaz, "For the Lord brought Judah low because of Ahaz". Judah had recently been very high in wealth and power. Ahaz' troubles (which increased at every turn) were all due to his sin. "For he made Judah naked", or "he cast away restraint" (RV margin).

That variation in translating the original Hebrew clause in the RV margin is remarkable. There are hardly any three words that could more accurately describe the day in which we live. There are persons who want increasingly to "cast away restraint". One writer for television has recently stated, "My goal is to get men and women and boys and girls to laugh at incest, adultery, and homosexuality. If I can get them to laugh at those things, I will take away their inhibitions against them". That surely is a wicked goal, and the saddest thing is that today there are many persons with similar wicked aims. Phillips translation of Romans 12.2a is particularly valuable: "Don't let the world around you squeeze you into its own mould". It seems that the world around us is desperately trying to squeeze us into their way of thinking. No Christian should allow this to happen.

Ahaz allowed lawlessness to spread rampantly and "transgressed sore against the Lord". It seems strange that he should be called "king of Israel", but it should be noted that all Judah is referred to as all Israel (v.23) and that the kings of Judah (v.27) are referred to as "kings of Israel". The Chronicler sometimes uses "Israel" as equivalent to "Judah" (12.1,6; 15.17; 20.34; 21.2,4). "King of Israel" (v.19) is equivalent to "king of Judah" (21.2). Ahaz was wicked but he was still king.

Verse 20 shows that the appeal of Ahaz to Tilgath-pilneser was disastrous, for he "distressed him, but strengthened him not". The words added to the last words of v.21, "but he helped him not", do not really contradict what is recorded in 2 Kings 16.9, "And the king of Assyria hearkened unto him: for the king of Assyria went up against Damascus, and took it, and carried the people of it captive to Kir, and slew Rezin". The Chronicler assumes that his readers know what is in the Kings account and he supplements it. What the king of Assyria did for Ahaz (2 Kings 16.9) was a help; even though it was only a little in contrast to the distress he caused him.

Judah became a vassal state of Assyria. The tribute was very costly (v.21) and it led him on to further idolatry. The tribute the king of Assyria demanded was extremely upsetting. The first cost to Judah (the first word in v.21 is "For") was the plundering of the temple, the palace, and the possessions of the princes to pay the tribute. JND uses the word "stripped". Thompson and Keil use the word "plundering". Matthew Henry writes about Ahaz that "he enslaved himself", and "he impoverished himself", referring to 2 Kings 16.7-8. 2 Kings 16.8 is parallel to 2 Chronicles 28.21. But there were other consequences to follow. Judah's treasures were depleted in vain. "As we summarize Ahaz' reign we find that throughout his years on the throne he constantly made the wrong decisions and relied on the wrong people for assistance. Like someone caught in a whirlpool, his waywardness constantly sucked him downward…and he drew Judah down with him" (Barber).

Verses 22-27: The Apostasy and Death of Ahaz

"Ahaz was now the vassal of Assyria and compelled along with his people to pay a heavy tribute every year. Isaiah continued to minister in Judah, but we do not read of the king humbling himself and pleading with the Lord for His mercy. Instead, he intensified his idolatrous practices out of the misguided belief that if all the gods that he worshipped combined their strength, he would have success. Unfortunately for him he ignored the truth contained in the history and writings of his own people…And Ahaz is not alone. People today ignore the teaching of God's Word…The only sure guide is a thorough knowledge of the Scriptures" (Barber).

"In the time of his distress" (v.22) was an opportunity for him to seek the Lord. 2 Chronicles 6.28-30 could have been an encouragement for

Ahaz to do so. How wonderful it would have been if he had done as his wicked grandson did: "when he was in affliction, he besought the Lord his God, and humbled himself greatly before the God of his fathers" (33.12). The two words used, "distress" in v.22 and "affliction" in 33.12, are from the same Hebrew word TSARAR (6887). Instead of humbling himself, Ahaz hardened himself in idolatry. "The more he multiplied his gods the more he multiplied his sorrows and the more he multiplied his sorrows the more he multiplied his gods" (Maclaren). The RV has for the last words of v.22, "this same king Ahaz", which "puts Ahaz in the class of Athaliah who was called 'that wicked woman' (24.7)" (Traylor). These words also are reminiscent of 32.30: "this same Hezekiah" in a good sense, and 33.23 (RV) in a bad sense: "but this same Amon trespassed more and more".

Verse 23 is even more pitiful than earlier verses: "For he sacrificed unto the gods of Damascus, which smote him". Of course, those gods did not really smite Ahaz but he thought that they did. The Chronicler is giving the motive for the action of Ahaz. "The words which follow - 'And he said, Because…help me' – are exegetical, setting forth the king's motive more plainly, and in a greater number of words" (Rawlinson). Ahaz could not or would not see that it was the Lord who smote him because of his sins (vv.5,6,9,19). Kings records Ahaz seeing an altar that he liked in Damascus and sending to Urijah the priest the fashion of it and the pattern for him to make an altar like it (2 Kings 16.10-16). Ahaz disgracefully used that pagan altar to take the place of the brazen altar of God.

Since Damascus was by this time Assyrian (2 Kings 16.10a), "Interpreters until recently had assumed that the price of a nation's submission to the empire of Assyria included their compulsory worship of its deities…Recent studies, however, have indicated that such was not necessarily the case" (Payne). Instead of recounting the story of the altar, the writer of the Chronicles chose rather to give greater evidence of the increasing apostasy of Ahaz.

The word play on the word "help" brings out the sad irony of Ahaz seeking "help" from any other source except the Lord, the only One who could truly "help" him. He first sought "help" from Assyria (v.16). Later, he turned for "help" to the gods of the king of Syria, after they had defeated Judah (v.23). Ahaz rejected the one source from which he could have received the "help" he so desperately needed and wanted. Those gods to which he turned "were the ruin of him, and of all Israel" (v.23). Of course, those gods that are helpless did not bring about the ruin; it was rather Ahaz' worship of those gods that brought that about.

In v.24 it is recorded that Ahaz "cut in pieces the vessels of the house of God"; this probably refers to 2 Kings 16.17. 2 Chronicles 29.18-19 indicates clearly that Ahaz did not destroy all the vessels. "The divinely–appointed sphere of men and women in the assembly is as a sacred vessel of the house of God, the privilege (yes, privilege) of exhibiting the headship of Christ in the assembly is another. Both, alas, are cut in pieces in many places today" (Riddle).

Verse 24 states that "Ahaz shut up the doors of the house of the Lord". This implies that the services in the Holy Place were discontinued altogether. The only sacrificial services left were at the new pagan altar that was outside the Holy Place. Thankfully, "in the first year of his reign, in the first month", Hezekiah the son of Ahaz, "opened the doors of the house of the Lord" (29.3). It was also on the first day of the month (29.17). Ahaz "made him altars in every corner of Jerusalem" (v.24). "And in every single city of Judah he made high places to burn incense to other gods" (v.25, NKJV). No wonder that the last words of v.25 are, "and (he) provoked to anger the Lord God of his fathers". Ahaz was so strongly in favour of the spread of idolatry that even good King Hezekiah did not succeed in eliminating it. There was still some idolatry connected with Ahaz that Josiah rooted out (2 Kings 23.12).

"This infatuated king surrendered himself to the influence of idolatry and exerted his royal authority to extend it, with the intensity of a passion-with the ignorance and servile fear of a heathen (v.23) and a ruthless defiance of God" (Jamieson, Fausset & Brown).

This record of Ahaz shows that Judah had sunk to the same low level of apostasy as the northern kingdom at the time of the schism. In 13.8-9 it is recorded that "there are with you golden calves, which Jeroboam made you for gods…that are no gods". There never was such idolatry in Judah until the reign of Ahaz. In 13.11 it is stated, "ye have forsaken him". The defeat in v.6 of this chapter was "because they had forsaken the Lord God of their fathers".

There are also likenesses between Ahaz and Ahab. Both established idolatry as an institution. They both provoked the Lord God to anger (1 Kings 16.33; 2 Chr 28.9,25).

Ahaz is the fourth king of Judah who was not buried in the sepulchres of the kings (v.27). Jehoram was the first (21.20), Joash was next (24.25), and Uzziah was third (26.23). Of the four Uzziah was closest to being buried there; he was buried in a field that belonged to the sepulchres because he was a leper. All four of these kings were buried with their fathers in the city of David (in the account in 2 Kings). That may look like a contradiction but is not. The Chronicler acknowledges that they were buried in the city of David, but not in the sepulchres of the kings. The people seemed to have in their power to decide whether a king should be buried in these sepulchres. They seemed to be quite accurate in their judgment because it was only good kings who were buried there. Since Ahaz had not walked in the ways of David his father during his lifetime, he was not buried in the same place as David.

This sad chapter explains why the exile eventually had to take place. When Ahaz died Judah had reached its lowest level yet, religiously and politically. "Ahaz died and was buried in dishonour. And such would have been the fate of the kingdom too were it not for Hezekiah his son whose faith in Jehovah in an hour of ultimate crisis was God's reason for extending the nation's existence yet another hundred years" (Whitcomb).

The record of Ahaz in 2 Kings 16 and 2 Chronicles 28 is a solemn warning. God gave the pattern of the temple to David who gave it to Solomon (1 Chr 28.11-13). Ahaz grievously departed from that pattern. He was zealous religiously but only to promote idolatry. Over and over again the writer of the Chronicles states that the troubles of Ahaz were because of his sin (vv.4-5,6,9,19,25a). It is no wonder that he finished up by closing the doors of the house of the Lord and that he died in the prime of life. May all be warned to keep close to the Word of God.

2 CHRONICLES 29

Hezekiah's reign

Introductory

Hezekiah illustrates an important lesson to any who may despair because of a poor spiritual lineage, or to any who may presume spirituality merely because of a good one. This is especially important in this day when so many want to evade accepting responsibility for their own actions. Hezekiah reigned between the two worst kings of Judah, his father Ahaz and his son Manasseh. One cannot help wondering how Hezekiah could be so good with a father so bad and how a father so good could have a son so bad. This clearly shows that heredity and environment do not necessarily determine and excuse a person's character. Each one is responsible for the development of his own character before God whether there is a good background or a poor one. God is able to work in the life of anyone who wants to please Him. In his book of Bible Lists, Willmington notes only four godly sons of godless fathers: Jonathan, Asa, Hezekiah, and Josiah. (Saul, the father of Jonathan, and Abijah, the father of Asa, were not as wicked as the other two.)

Hezekiah and Josiah were the two godliest descendants of David to sit upon his throne. They wonderfully responded to God's grace. The sovereign grace of God is seen in raising up Hezekiah, the son of wicked king Ahaz, and, 57 years afterward Josiah, the son of wicked king Amon. While Hezekiah and Josiah were reigning God blessed Judah thus showing the importance of good leadership.

Hezekiah is a very remarkable king whom God raised up to lead His people through one of the most crucial periods of the nation's history. He led them successfully and he knew that the glory belonged to God (29.36). Hezekiah was truly an emergency man of God, for Judah was at the point of dissolution. God used him for a recovery that gave a fresh lease on life and enabled Judah to stay in the land almost a century and a half longer than the ten northern tribes.

"Hezekiah...came to the throne of Judah at one of the lowest points in his nation's history. His father had closed the doors of the temple and encouraged the worship of all the gods of the heathen" (Barber).

There are eleven chapters about Hezekiah, more than for any other of the kings except David and Solomon (2 Kings 18-20; 2 Chr 29-32; Is 36-39). Most of 2 Chronicles 29-31 is not found elsewhere. The reign of Hezekiah especially illustrates the difference between the character of the book of Kings and the character of the book of Chronicles. 2 Chronicles has three whole chapters on religious reforms (chs.29-31) and only one chapter on civil, political, and domestic affairs (ch.32). 2 Kings 18-20 are (apart from the first seven verses of 2 Kings 18 on the religious reforms) entirely about civil, political, and (to a lesser extent) domestic matters.

Hezekiah's name means "Strength of Jehovah". He truly lived up to the meaning of his name. He excelled in trusting the living God (2 Kings 18.5) and he inspired his people to have confidence in God. In chs.29, 30 and 31, the revival that took place in the first year of Hezekiah's reign is recorded. Hezekiah's father, Ahaz, was a wicked king as stated in 2 Chronicles 28.1: "...he did not that which was right in the sight of the Lord, like David his father". In striking contrast, v.2 of this chapter reads about Hezekiah that "he did that which was right in the sight of the Lord, according to all that his father David had done". The next verse says that he "opened the doors of the house of the Lord" which is another stark contrast to his father of whom we read in 2 Chronicles 28.24 that he "shut up the doors of the house of the Lord".

In the revival that took place in Hezekiah's reign there were at least five important returns.

1. A return to God and to His house.
2. A return to blood sacrifice.
3. A return to the Word of God.
4. A return to the place where the Lord had chosen to place His name.
5. A return of singing and rejoicing.

Worshipping God is very important to the Chronicler so he records (in ch.29) how the temple was cleansed and rededicated so that both the Passover and regular worship could be reinstated.

Outline of Chapter 29

Verses 1-3: Introduction to Hezekiah's good reign.
Verses 4-11: His invitation and exhortation to the priests and Levites.
Verses 12-19: Cleansing the temple.
Verses 20-24: Atoning sacrifices.
Verses 25-30: Burnt offerings and worship with musical accompaniment.
Verses 31-36: Offerings of the congregation.

Verses 1-3: Introduction to Hezekiah's Good Reign

Hezekiah's mother may well have been a godly woman who had a good influence in moulding her son for God, although the writer of the Chronicles does not say so. Her name is only partially given in 2 Kings 18.2 - "Abi"; here her name is given in full - "Abijah". Her father Zechariah could be the faithful witness of Isaiah 8.2. There are three other possibilities for this Zechariah: (1) the one who was a real help to Uzziah as long as he lived (26.5); (2) the Levite who helped to cleanse the temple (v.13); (3) viewing "daughter" as possibly a descendent of Zechariah, the prophet-priest (24.20). Any one of the four homes would be likely to be a godly home. At this time three or perhaps four prophets were at the peak of their ministry: Isaiah, Hosea, Micah, and possibly Nahum. It is likely, directly or indirectly, that they had something to do with the revival. Isaiah was especially close to Hezekiah as described in Isaiah 37, 2 Kings 19, and 2 Chronicles 32.20 when they are both recorded as praying. In summary, Hezekiah seems to have had a godly mother, a grandfather who was godly in the last few years of his life, and he also came under the godly influence of three or four prophets, especially Isaiah.

"Too little is said in praise of mothers. The late Sydney J. Harris pointed out that 'the commonest fallacy among women is (the belief) that simply having children makes one a mother — which is as absurd as believing that having a piano makes one a musician'. Billy Graham's admonition comes closer to hitting the mark. He said, 'Let your home be your parish, your little brood your congregation, your living room a sanctuary, and your knee a sacred altar'" (Barber).

The Chronicler shows in v.2 that there was a return to the era of David and Solomon. When Ahaz died Hezekiah became the first king of the surviving kingdom. In the remaining years of its history only Hezekiah and Josiah were good kings. The other six were all evil except for the last few years of Manasseh. Three good kings are likened to David in 2 Chronicles: Jehoshaphat in 17.3, Hezekiah in this verse, and Josiah in 34.2. Asa is also likened to David in 1 Kings 15.11. David's love for God's house is seen repeatedly in his history and in his psalms. Hezekiah's love for God's house is seen in these three chapters.

The first recorded step that Hezekiah took to turn Judah back to God was to open and repair the doors of the house of God, which had been shut by his father Ahaz in 28.24. "Repaired them" included overlaying them with gold (2 Kings 18.16). This is the beginning of the longest account of any revival in Biblical history. The revival that took place in Hezekiah's day began at the right time and the right place. It began right away, "in the first year of his reign, in the first month" (v.3), and v.17 adds "the first day of the first month". When Hezekiah ascended the throne he knew exactly what he wanted to do. He could see that his father unsuccessfully had tried one thing after another instead of looking to God, the only One who could help. That was a lesson for Hezekiah. It is easier to take the right stand at the beginning than to shift to it afterwards. To give up bad habits by degrees is not promising. When conscience has no doubts and the Word of God is clear there should be no hesitation. The psalmist in Psalm 119.60 says, "I made haste and delayed not to keep thy commandments". Any Christian troubled with a sinful habit does not get the victory by giving it up gradually.

Verses 4-11: His Invitation and Exhortation to the Priests and Levites

As a wise king, Hezekiah assembled the priests and the Levites for the work of cleansing the temple, work that only they could do. "The east street" was the open space opposite the temple entrance (which was on the east side).

The priests and the Levites had to sanctify themselves to be useful in their office (v.5). Hezekiah was talking about ceremonial cleanliness but it has more than ceremonial significance. Even today, if one wants to be used of the Lord to cleanse anything, one has to be clean oneself. One has to be right before God to be used of God to make anything right. One must pay heed to oneself before trying to correct others (Ezra 7.10; Mt 7.1-5; Acts 20.28; 1 Tim 4.16; Titus 2.3-5). After the Levites and the priests first sanctified themselves they were to sanctify the house of the Lord, and "carry forth the filthiness out of the holy place" so that both they and the temple would be fit for His presence.

2 Corinthians 7.1 is an exhortation for all: "Having therefore these promises, dearly beloved, let us cleanse ourselves from all filthiness of the flesh and spirit, perfecting holiness in the fear of God". There is nothing like the fear of God to regulate one's thinking. No one knows what a person is thinking unless the thoughts are spoken, but God knows. "The fear of the Lord is to hate evil" (Prov 8.13).

Hezekiah not only began his revival at the right time (which was right away) but at the right place. Judah was paying tribute to the Assyrians. Before dealing with the Assyrians, Hezekiah knew that the most important thing was a right relationship with God. Only then could they count on God's help against their enemies. God and worship in His temple must come first before they could expect Him to turn from His wrath and bless them. Hezekiah was following the priority that our Lord Jesus enunciated years later in Matthew 6.33: "But seek ye first the kingdom of God, and his righteousness; and all these things shall be added unto you". This same principle is taught in the first two of the Ten Commandments in Exodus 20.2-6. Revival, like God's judgment, must begin at the house of God (1 Pet 4.17 and Ezek 9.6: "begin at my sanctuary"). Civil, political, and domestic matters could all come afterwards. May God help each one to put God and His things first in one's life. "The importance of Hezekiah's reign can only be adequately explained in the light of his Godward relationship, for nothing is more central to the Chronicler's message than the proper worship of the Lord" (Barber).

In vv.6-7, all that Hezekiah said about "our fathers" was especially true of his own father Ahaz - "they...have not burned incense nor offered burnt offerings". This may seem to contradict 2 Kings 16.15. However, the burning of incense and the burnt offering there were upon the altar that wicked king Ahaz had copied from an altar that he had seen in Damascus. Hezekiah rightly did not consider those sacrifices as truly offered to the Lord.

The word "Wherefore" is used in v.8 because of all the sins of God's people as shown in the previous two verses. Hezekiah was reminding the priests and Levites of the reason for the wrath of God being upon them. He thoroughly explained to the priests and the Levites why they should cleanse the temple. The godly king had the discernment and the humility to say that all the calamities that had befallen them were due to their departure from God. Hezekiah knew that when the king and the people followed God there was prosperity; and when the king and the people forsook God there was adversity. In the Old Testament in the dealings of God with Judah and Israel, blessing followed obedience and suffering followed disobedience more surely and directly than is now the case, in either national or individual life. However, it still remains true at least in measure (Gal 6.7-8; Hebrews 12.5-11). The primary reference of "captivity" in v.9 seems to be to ch.28 where the idea of captivity is repeated eight times (vv.5,8,11,11,13,14,15,17). Though Ephraim had returned her captives (v.15), Judah's other enemies had not done so (vv.5,17) and thus some of the people of Judah were still in captivity.

This revival began in Hezekiah's heart - "Now it is in mine heart" (v.10). God's interests so gripped the heart of Hezekiah that he was able, by God's using him, to affect the hearts of all the people of Judah. "Also in Judah the hand of God was to give them one heart to do the commandment of the king and of the princes, by the word of the Lord" (30.12). Verse 31.21 states, "And in every work that he began...he did it with all his heart, and prospered". This is another way in which Hezekiah was like David who spoke to God of "the uprightness of mine heart" (1 Chr 29.17). In the next two verses David prayed for the hearts of the people and for the heart of Solomon. In 1 Chronicles 29.3, he said, "I have set my affection to the house of my God". Solomon could say, in 2 Chronicles 6.8, "But the Lord said to David my father, Forasmuch as it was in thine heart to build a house for my name, thou didst well in that it was in thine heart". God especially wants the hearts of His people. Proverbs 4.23 says, "Keep thine heart with all diligence; for out of it are the issues of life", and Proverbs 23.26 exhorts, "My son, give me thine heart". Maclaren puts it well: "That strong young heart showed itself kingly in its resolve as it had shown itself sensitive to evil and tender in contemplating the widespread sorrow".

Hezekiah called them Levites in v.5 to remind them of their relationship to God and now he calls them "my sons" (v.11) to remind them of their relationship to himself; but he quickly goes on to reiterate the fact that "the Lord hath chosen you". He concludes his exhortation to the priests and Levites by saying, "My sons, be not now negligent". He addresses them in a kind and fatherly way, as all leaders should. Surely Hezekiah is displaying a shepherd heart in so speaking to them as "My sons". Hezekiah's saying, "the Lord hath chosen you", is another link with David; for David also refers to them as "chosen" in 1 Chronicles 15.2 (the only other time in Kings or Chronicles that they are referred to in this way). There are four mentions of David later in the chapter: vv.25,26,27,30. Hezekiah used the word "now" to the priests and Levites (v.5), and in v.11 uses the same word again. He is thus encouraging them to take action in cleansing the temple.

Verses 12-19: Cleansing the Temple

The response of the Levites is seen in vv.12-15. In v.12 there are two from each of the divisions of the Levites: Kohathites, Merarites, and Gershonites. In vv.13-14 there are two sons of Elizaphan, and two sons from each of the three families of the singers: Asaph, Heman, and Jeduthun. Special mention is given to the family of Elizaphan who had been a chief of the Kohathites in the days of Moses (Num 3.30). Naming the three families of singers is another link with David (1 Chr 25.1-7). These 14 chiefs named in vv.12-14 took the responsibility of gathering their brethren together for the important work of cleansing the temple. The record of the 14 names of these Levites is in keeping with what is known about the reign of Hezekiah in that there was literary activity (this included five chapters of Proverbs - chs.25-29, and possibly also chs.1-9, as well as Psalms 120-134).

In the revival that took place in Hezekiah's day there was a return to the Word of God, as v.15 indicates. Everything in the cleansing of the temple was done "according to the commandment of the king, by the words of the Lord". In the three chapters (29, 30, 31) God's word is referred to at least 10 times (29.15,25; 30.5,12,16,18; 31.3,4,21,21). Examples are "the words of the Lord", "the word of the Lord", "the commandment of the Lord", "the law of Moses", "the law of the Lord", and "as it was written". While Hezekiah's wicked father was on the throne Isaiah said, "To the law and to the testimony: if they speak not according to this word, it is because there is no light in them" (Is 8.20). Ahaz did not respond well, but Hezekiah responded wonderfully. May the Lord help every one of His own to respond well to the Word of God throughout life.

The priests alone cleansed the inner part of the house of the Lord from which the Levites were excluded (v.16). This is another indication of their care to do everything according to the word of the Lord. The Levites could not go into the Holy of Holies but they could take the "uncleanness" ("filthiness" in v.5) that the priests brought out and take it to "the brook Kidron". "Uncleanness" would include not only dirt that had accumulated by neglect but also objects of pagan worship and the things that go with them (which Ahaz had put in the temple). In 15.16 (RV) the record is given of good King Asa who, over 200 years before, regarding his grandmother's idol, had "cut down her image, and made dust of it, and burnt it at the brook Kidron". Years later good King Josiah cast the dust of the false altars into the same brook (2 Kings 23.12). Casting into the brook Kidron was a decisive finish with all that was thrown into it, as also in 2 Chronicles 30.14. The first thing that is said of the actual cleansing is that "the priests went into the inner part of the house" (v.16). God works from the inside out, unlike man. 1 Samuel 16.7 states "man looketh on the outward appearance, but the Lord looketh on the heart". Our Lord Jesus said, in Matthew 23.25-26, "Woe unto you, scribes and Pharisees, hypocrites! for ye make clean the outside of the cup and of the platter, but within they are full of extortion and excess. Thou blind Pharisee, cleanse first that which is within the cup and platter, that the outside of them may be clean also". When the heart is right, the outside will be right according to all that the person knows from the Word of God.

It took sixteen days to cleanse the temple (v.17).

Verses 18-19 stress the proper recovery and cleansing of the temple implements. All the "filthiness" and "uncleanness" had to be put out before the temple of the Lord would be fit for the presence of God. Psalm 93.5 states, "holiness becometh thine house, O Lord, for ever". The local assembly is a temple of God (1 Cor 3.16; 2 Cor 6.16). Any unjudged sin of the nature of those sins given in 1 Corinthians 5 should be dealt with as with leaven, to use the illustration employed by the Apostle.

1 Corinthians 3.17 (RV) gives a solemn warning: "If any man destroyeth the temple of God, him shall God destroy; for the temple of God is holy, which temple ye are". The word "destroy" can also be translated "corrupt, defile or mar". The RV correctly translates that word "destroy" twice in the same verse. This emphasizes that the punishment fits the crime. The more seriously any person corrupts, defiles or mars an assembly the more seriously God will corrupt, defile or mar him. There is another word for "corrupt" It is the intensive form of the word used here. God can be thanked for every time that He has intervened before an assembly has become "utterly corrupted".

The Word of God teaches that believers should not jump to the wrong conclusion that a child of God who has experienced personal calamity has been guilty of serious sin. Saints should profit from the mistake of Job's three friends; they thought that Job was surely guilty of gross sin.

But, having said that, there are times when God acts in such a way that it appears that the calamity was God's direct governmental dealing. The author is aware of incidents of this kind. One man vowed that he was going to drive hundreds of miles to split an assembly. On the way he was killed in an automobile accident. Known cases of this kind could be multiplied.

Verses 20-24: Atoning Sacrifices

Then (after receiving the good news from the priests and Levites as related in vv.18-19), Hezekiah rose early. This indicates how important the restoration of temple worship was to him. John Heading says well, "Many times in Jeremiah, God is depicted as rising early to speak urgently through His prophets". In fact, ten times in Jeremiah God is pictured as rising early to speak through His prophets with an important message for His people (Jer 7.13,25; 11.7; 25.4; 26.5; 29.19; 32.33; 35.14,15; 44.4). Once Jeremiah referred to himself as rising early (Jer 25.3). Hezekiah's rising early is in keeping with his putting God first. He gathered together the rulers of the city (the civil leaders). It is instructive that Hezekiah began with the priests and Levites (v.4), then with the civil leaders (v.20), then on to all the people (v.31, including some from the ten northern tribes).

Hezekiah brought the rulers of the city to the temple and they offered

28 animal sacrifices for a sin offering with a threefold purpose: "for the kingdom, and for the sanctuary, and for Judah" (v.21). The kingdom seems to refer to the political, royal aspect of the nation while Judah more clearly refers to the people themselves (in v.24 the phrase "for all Israel" is used twice). They had all corrupted themselves. Of course, the sanctuary refers to the temple but it could include the temple personnel, the priests and the Levites. The seven bullocks, the seven rams, and the seven lambs comprised the burnt offering while the seven he goats comprised the sin offering. Seven in the Bible speaks of that which is complete. These four sevens speak of the completeness of their repentance. The larger number of sacrifices than on the Day of Atonement also contributed to the sense of completeness. They were deeply conscious of the seriousness of their sin. The last sentence of v.21, which refers to "the priests the sons of Aaron", is another emphasis on the return to the Word of God. Only the persons whom the Bible designates to offer the sacrifices are commanded to do so by the king.

Some good writers believe that only the he goats were atoning sacrifices. However, in the light of burnt offerings being used for atonement in Leviticus 1.4; 16.24, and Job 1.5, it is at least possible that all these 28 animal sacrifices were for atonement (see Leslie C. Allen and Selman). The emphasis in v.22, for all the 21 burnt offerings, is on the shedding of blood. We read in Leviticus 17.11: "for it is the blood that maketh an atonement for the soul". The focus on the blood speaks of the precious blood of Christ (1 Pet 1.18-19).

The blood is emphasized in vv.22-24 by being mentioned four times. Blood is also sprinkled by the priests in 30.16. There was a return to blood sacrifice. In a survey of 45 writers only Wilbur M. Smith draws attention to a record of "blood" as part of a sacrifice offered by the Israelites since the time of the exodus, a period of 765 years! The only mention is when wicked king Ahaz made an offering on the altar that he had copied from one in Damascus (2 Kings 16.13). Of course, blood was actually shed during that time in connection with sacrifice. For example, when Solomon was dedicating the temple many animals were slain, offered, and their blood shed but there is no specific mention in Scripture of the word "blood". There is mention of "the blood of war", "the blood of the slain", the shedding of "innocent blood", and "the blood of Naboth", but no mention of "blood" in connection with a sacrifice acceptable to God. However, "blood" is often referred to at this point.

Here is the first mention of a sacrifice for atonement since Israel came into the land of Canaan. Here is the only mention of reconciliation in all the Old Testament historical books. Here is recorded the first Passover in 725 years, since Joshua 5.10-11. It seems certain that they did keep other Passovers but they are not recorded in any detail. (35.18 implies that there were other Passovers.) Any true revival amongst God's people will result in a real appreciation of the atoning death of the Lord Jesus Christ and

His cleansing blood (1 Jn 1.7). That appreciation will be reflected in the content of gospel preaching. The blood in the New Testament is always closely associated with the Person of Christ. How fitting that is, for the infinite value of Christ gives infinite value to His sacrifice.

Preaching that tries to add to or subtract from the sacrifice of Christ should not be tolerated.

Leslie C. Allen notes regarding v.23 that (as in Leviticus 1.4 & 4.24) "In each of these instances 'laid' (their hands) is a little weak; 'pressed' would convey the meaning better; for the Hebrew word has the sense of leaning one's weight upon". Looking at the 21 offerings as atoning, in v.22, they could be considered as atoning for sins in general and the seven he goats in v.23 as atoning for specific sins. In Leviticus 16.21 the laying on of hands is explicitly linked with confession of sins. This verse states that the he goats were brought "before the king and the congregation; and they laid their hands upon them". Very likely it was the king and the leaders who laid their hands on the he goats as representing the people. The next verse explicitly says that it was for "all Israel". By laying their hands on the he goats they were identifying themselves with the offering. Thus the sins of the people were transferred to the animals, so those seven he goats died as substitutes for the people. 2 Corinthians 5.21 brings before us the truth that "he (God) hath made him (Christ) to be sin for us, who knew no sin; that we might be made the righteousness of God in him". The laying on of hands illustrates the necessity of a sinner personally acknowledging his sinnership before God and personally accepting the sacrifice of Christ for himself.

The shepherd heart of the king led him to command that the burnt offering and the sin offering should be made for "all Israel" (v.24). "All Israel" is emphasized by its repetition in this verse. This prepared the way for Hezekiah to invite all Israel, including the ten northern tribes, to the Passover in ch.30. Ultimately, what gave these sacrifices value was that they all pointed forward to the perfect sacrifice of Christ (1 Pet 3.18).

Verses 25-30: Burnt Offerings and Worship with Musical Accompaniment

Some commentators suggest that these offerings were simultaneous with the offerings of vv.21-24. However, those offerings were for atonement whereas these offerings are for consecration (v.31). After atonement was made (in vv.21-24), they could praise God and worship as is described in vv.25-30. The word "worshipped" is found three times in these verses. David is mentioned four times, thus giving another illustration that Hezekiah was pleasing God as he did. There is also an emphasis in vv.25-30 on everything being done according to the Word of God.

Hezekiah ordered the Levites to praise God with musical instruments (vv.25-26). The musical instruments were not originally used in the Tabernacle but they were commanded later through the prophets David,

Gad, and Nathan, inspired by God. The Chronicler here considers David among the prophets. Thus the use of musical instruments was "according to the commandment of the Lord", as Chronicles emphasizes. Peter calls David a prophet in Acts 2.29-30. The fact that Gad and Nathan spoke in this way is nowhere else recorded in the Bible. Solomon also used musical instruments at the dedication of the temple, as his father David had ordered (7.6).

The burnt offerings here in v.27 (and also in v.32) were used in a different way from those in vv.21-24. Burnt offerings are linked with a variety of attitudes in worship. In vv.21-24 they are linked with atonement. Here they are associated with the worshipers consecrating themselves wholly to the Lord; so Hezekiah could say in v.31, "Now ye have consecrated yourselves unto the Lord". Later, in vv.31-35, burnt offerings are linked with thank offerings.

We should notice especially in v.27 that "when the burnt offering began, the song of the Lord began also", and it "continued until the burnt offering was finished" (v.28). Meyer writes helpful words: "Self sacrifice and the surrender of the heart and life to God always leads to joy". Long's words are also worth quoting: "It was the sense of giving to God the worship His heart desired that stirred such spontaneous singing".

In v.29 the king is specifically mentioned as bowing and worshiping with everyone else. In v.30 we see that they sang inspired words - "the words of David, and of Asaph the seer", both authors of many psalms. They sang old words with a new holy joy and gladness. "Worshipped" is in three consecutive verses: vv.28,29,30. Christians have more joy when they realize that it is a side effect of worshipping God. We should also notice in v.30 that "they sang praises with gladness". The nearest New Testament counterpart to vv.25-30 is Ephesians 5.19 (RV): "speaking one to another in psalms and hymns and spiritual songs, singing and making melody with your heart to the Lord". That is one of the results of being filled with the Spirit or controlled by Him. Hezekiah and those with him also sang with their hearts.

The Greek word for "making melody" is *psallo*. Robert Young in his Concordance gives the meaning of *psallo* under 1 Corinthians 14.15 as, "to sing praise with a musical instrument". This has been thought by some to give Scriptural proof of the use of instrumental music in the meetings of the saints in apostolic days. But this is refuted in a booklet entitled *Instrumental Music in the Assembly - Is it Scriptural?* by W. E. Vine and William Rodgers. Vine agrees with Young's meaning "in the use of the verb, mentioned in the Septuagint version of the Old Testament, but as I point out in my *Dictionary of New Testament Words* under the word MELODY, it was used in New Testament times simply of singing a praise or singing a hymn, as is clear from various passages. See for instance, James 5.13, 'let him sing praise' (RV), which simply means that a cheerful believer is to praise the Lord; it clearly does not mean that he must have an instrument to do it with". William Rodgers wrote about "Ephesians 5.19, where the same word *psallo* is translated 'making melody', and this is to be done, not 'on a harp' but 'in your heart'. If we make good use of this instrument, we shall have little need of any other".

Verses 31-36: Offerings of the Congregation

The third group of offerings was different from the previous two (vv.20-30). The other offerings were public but these were individual offerings made by "as many as were of a free heart" ("willing heart" in RV, JND, ESV).

David used the same word "consecrated" as is used in v.31 in 1 Chronicles 29.5: "And who then is willing to consecrate his service this day unto the Lord?". (The margins of the AV and the RV both have "Hebrew, to fill his hand".) This is yet another link with David, in keeping with v.2. Since they were consecrated on the ground of the sacrifice (which spoke of the sacrifice of Christ), now Hezekiah invited them to "come near". This is similar to Hebrews 10.19,22: "Having therefore, brethren, boldness to enter into the holiest by the blood of Jesus...Let us draw near". The king further invited them to bring "sacrifices and thank offerings". The congregation did so in response to the king's invitation and brought burnt offerings. The burnt offerings especially were linked with a willing heart. In a burnt offering the whole animal went up to God and none was left for the one who offered it. This is a reminder of the secret of the liberal sacrificial giving of the Macedonians in 2 Corinthians 8.5 - they "first gave their own selves to the Lord". If this is done, then the Lord has everything: our time, our treasure, and our talents. The word "willing" (RV) is from the same root as "willingly" (occurring seven times in 1 Chronicles 29) linked with giving for the building of the temple during David's reign. A "willing heart" is also linked with giving for the Tabernacle (Ex 25.2; 35.5,22).

In vv.32-33 the large number of animals sacrificed shows the overwhelming response of the people. God takes note of what is given to Him for these animals were counted! They spoke to Him of His blessed Son.

Ordinarily the killing and the flaying of the burnt offering was the duty of the individual offerer. Here the priests and the Levites did it, probably because there were so many individuals offering at the same time (v.34). It is striking to notice that the Levites "were more upright in heart to sanctify themselves than the priests". The priests did not respond as well as the Levites to the revival of Hezekiah. However, this is not surprising since Urijah the priest followed wicked King Ahaz in departing from the Lord (2 Kings 16.10-16) by making an altar like the one he had seen in Damascus. It is likely that other priests helped him and still other priests knew what Urijah was doing and did not try to stop him. Knowing human nature a little, it is easy to believe that it takes more grace for leaders in departure to humble themselves than those who have merely followed. The small number of the priests who were sanctified necessitated that the Levites helped them.

The peace offerings of v.35 symbolized fellowship and communion. They were only partially offered to God, "the fat of the peace offerings"; the rest was returned, part to the officiating priest, and part to the offerer and his family. Drink offerings symbolized the joy of giving. The last sentence of v.35 is a summary of the whole chapter: "So the service of the house of the Lord was set in order". The temple was cleansed; the people were restored, and now offered worship to the Lord.

The last sentence of v.35 has two consequences in v.36. First, Hezekiah and all the people were joyful; a second consequence was that they fittingly acknowledged God in the revival. On the one hand it was a matter of grace, and on the other hand it was a response of obedience to God's written word. The fact that it was done suddenly was a special evidence of God's working. Their humility was very becoming; it is always becoming to walk humbly with God (Micah 6.8).

2 CHRONICLES 30

Hezekiah's Reign

Introductory

Chapters 29 and 30 really belong together. They both have a similar structure. First is an invitation to worship: 29.4-11; 30.6-12. This is followed by an act of purification: 29.20-36; 30.15-27. Praising, rejoicing, singing, and gladness are in both chapters (29.27,28,30,36; 30.21,23,25-26), emphasizing that there was a return of joy and singing in Hezekiah's revival. There was much praising, singing, and rejoicing in David's day but little for the 300 years afterwards. There appear to be only twelve verses indicating joy, gladness, or God's people praising, singing, or rejoicing throughout this period of their history (1 Kings 8.66; 2 Kings 11.20; 2 Chr 5.13; 7.10; 15.15; 20.19,22,27; 23.13,18,21; 24.10). Here in these two chapters there are eight verses for just the first year of Hezekiah's reign! There truly was a return of joy and gladness!

Chapter 30 does have two emphases of its own. The first is that all Israel is invited to this Passover. The second emphasis is on the Passover itself. The actions of King Hezekiah in this chapter are a reminder of the period of David and Solomon as was also true in chapter 29. Both are mentioned in 30.26. Since they were the last to reign over all Israel, they are closely linked with the theme of "all Israel" (vv.1,5; 31.5). David is associated with the phrase "Beersheba to Dan" in v.5; the only other place the Chronicler has the same phrase is in 1 Chronicles 21.2, during David's reign. David is also linked with the musical instruments of v.21. Solomon is associated with God hearing prayer (vv.18-20,27; see also 6.14-42). Many of the words of the promise to Solomon in 7.14 are repeated in this chapter: "humble" (v.11), "pray" (vv.18,27), "seek" (v.19), "turn" (vv.6,9), "hear" (vv.20,27), and "heal" (v.20). What a precious promise is found in 7.14: "If my people, which are called by my name, shall humble themselves, and pray, and seek my face, and turn from their wicked ways; then will I hear from heaven, and will forgive their sin, and will heal their land". The God of Abraham, Isaac, Jacob, David, and Solomon is a living God always ready to hear and answer the prayers of those who fulfill the conditions of this verse.

Outline of Chapter 30

Verses 1-5:	The decision of the king and the congregation.
Verses 6-12:	The letters of invitation.
Verses 13-22:	Celebrating the Passover.
Verses 23-31.1:	Continuing the blessing.

Verses 1-5: The Decision of the King and the Congregation

In v.1 there is a summary of the first nine verses. The next eight verses give more details. Within the first three years of Hezekiah's father's reign

(2 Kings 15.27; 16.1) King Pekah, the son of Remaliah, led the ten northern tribes in slaying 120,000 valiant men of Judah (2 Chr 28.6). Hezekiah was so concerned for the unity of all Israel that in spite of what Pekah had done these 14 years before he still invited all Israel to come to Jerusalem. The verses clearly show that there was no wish for revenge in the heart of Hezekiah. The unity of all Israel seems to have been forgotten for about 250 years (since Solomon died) except by Elijah (1 Kings 18), about 180 years earlier, when he took twelve stones to build an altar, one stone for each of the twelve tribes. Another evidence of Hezekiah's concern for all Israel is that he named his son Manasseh after one of the important tribes of the northern kingdom.

"The Passover may have been appropriate at the inauguration of a new reign because it commemorated Israel's beginning as a nation (cp. Ex 12.27; Deut 16.1; the second month is that of Hezekiah's first full year, cp. 29.3)" (Selman).

In v.2 there is described a commendable harmony between the king and the people. Everyone acted willingly. This is in contrast to King Asa who "commanded Judah to seek the Lord God of their fathers, and to do the law and the commandment" (14.4). King Hezekiah consulted with the people instead of commanding them. The first two words of v.5 beautifully say, "So they", not the king only! The assembly or the congregation was very important to the Chronicler and to Hezekiah for it occurs nine times in this chapter: vv.2,4,13,17,23,24 (twice), 25 (twice). This indicates the unity among God's people. The phrase "all the congregation" in Chronicles is linked only with David (1 Chr 13.2,4; 29.1,10,20), Solomon (2 Chr 1.3; 5.6; 6.3,12-13), Joash's coronation (23.3) and Hezekiah (29.28; 30.2,4,23,25 twice). This feature is another link with David and Solomon as well as other links pointed out at verses 29.2,10,11,14,21-31, and in the second paragraph of the introduction for this chapter.

Two reasons are given in v.3 as to why they could not keep the Passover in the first month. Another reason is given in 29.17 where we read that the temple was not cleansed in time because it took 16 days to carry out that work. Hezekiah and the congregation had the Word of God for keeping the Passover in the second month (Num 9.10-11). There we read, "If any man...be unclean...or be in a journey afar off, yet he shall keep the Passover unto the Lord. The fourteenth day of the second month they shall keep it". Wilcock puts it well; "Defilement and distance are the permitted grounds for postponing the festivals". It was mostly defilement here in 2 Chronicles 30 that hindered them from keeping the feast in the first month. Hezekiah was rightly very concerned to remove the defilement. In keeping the Passover in the second month according to Numbers 9.10-11, Hezekiah had God's instruction for so doing; thus he was not like Jeroboam, the first king of the northern tribes who "ordained a feast in the eighth month, on the fifteenth day of the month...even in the month which he had devised of his own heart" (1 Kings 12.32-33).

Beersheba is the southernmost extremity and Dan the northernmost extremity of all Israel. The phrase "as it was written" (v.5) refers to Deuteronomy 16.1-8 where the Passover was to be kept in the place where the Lord had chosen to place His name rather than, as in Exodus, by the family at home.

Verses 6-9: The Letters of Invitation

Since v.1 is a summary, the letters mentioned in vv.6-9 are the same as are mentioned there. It is a surprise that they do not mention the Passover, even though it is specifically mentioned in v.5; and there is an invitation in the letters to "enter into his sanctuary" (v.8). It is a loving invitation, but a humbling invitation with hope of recovery. Hezekiah is not being Pharisaical since he used similar words when addressing the priests and Levites (29.6-9). He pleads movingly and effectively. He puts the response he wants in five different ways: "turn again unto the Lord…be ye not stiff-necked…yield yourselves unto the Lord, and enter into his sanctuary… and serve the Lord your God". He refers delicately to their calamities.

The very first words of the invitation, "Ye children of Israel", are an acknowledgment that the ten northern tribes are part of Israel; which is not meant to be divided. He goes on to say, "turn again unto the Lord God of Abraham, Isaac, and Israel". Repeating Israel as the name of Jacob adds force to his first use of the name for all his descendants.

"Stiff-necked" is stubborn disobedience; "enter into his sanctuary" is the call to come to the God-ordained centre. The Passover was one of the three yearly feasts that every male should attend (Ex 23.14-17; 34.23-24; Deut 16.16). To obey this exhortation would be decisive proof of truly yielding themselves to the Lord. That yielding to the Lord is the heart of his invitation.

"The Lord your God is gracious and merciful" is taken from Exodus 34.6. The call for Israel to return, significantly, is found at both the beginning and the end of the invitation (vv.6,9). This shows that God would much rather that His people return than that He should turn His back on them. Hezekiah is showing the fulfillment of God's gracious promise. The key words, "turn" and "return" (vv.6,9), is the same Hebrew verb translated "turn" in 7.14. The words in v.11, "humbled themselves", also are a reminder of that precious promise.

In the invitation, "frequent quotations from other Scriptures are evident, especially in relation to God's character. God's turning to those who repent, for example, is found in Solomon's dedicatory prayer (e.g. 1 Kings 8.33-34; 2 Chr 6.24-25; 7.14) and in Jeremiah (3.22; 15.19; 31.18-19) and Zechariah (1.2-6). That He is *gracious and compassionate* (v.9, NIV, REB, NEB) is one of the most frequent confessions of faith (e.g. Ex 34.6; Ps 103.8; Neh 9.17,31), and that He is the *God of Abraham, Isaac and Israel* (v.6) recalls His answer to Elijah's prayers (1 Kings 18.36)" (Selman).

The posts would be runners or couriers. Hezekiah's wisely written invitation was met with a mixed response from the northern tribes. This is similar to the response to the gospel in Acts 17.32,34 and Acts 28.24. Some of the Israelites who mocked may have thought that Hezekiah was very presumptuous. They could have thought it very unbecoming for him to invite Israelites to Jerusalem, but Hezekiah was thinking of God. He knew that the Lord God had put His name in Jerusalem for all Israel. One can be bold when one sees that God's worship, God's way, and God's will have a claim on all of God's people. Hezekiah knew that the rending of the ten tribes from the house of David was of God; so he did not seek the ten northern tribes for himself, but he sought them for God. William Kelly puts it well: "The more you draw near to God, the more you love the people of God. It is because God was so great in Hezekiah's eyes that the people of God were so dear to Hezekiah; and so he claimed them for God, and called them to come out from their abominations". Some were too proud to accept the humbling invitation so they expressed their pride in scornful laughter and mocking.

Verse 18 shows that some from Ephraim and Issachar accepted the invitation, and speaks of a multitude. Thank God they "humbled themselves"; they would have had to humble themselves to accept.

Thiele, an expert on the chronology of the kings, places the fall of the northern ten tribes at 723 BC during the reign of Ahaz. Hezekiah was hoping that some who remained still in the north would realize the seriousness of their predicament and would respond favourably to the invitation.

The Chronicler was thankful for every member of the northern tribes who humbled himself to come to Jerusalem and so is careful to restrain any temptation to pride on the part of the people of Judah by acknowledging that the overwhelming response was due to the grace of God, as was the case in 29.36.

Verses 13-22: Celebrating the Passover

The "feast of unleavened bread" (also in v.21) took place immediately after the Passover, symbolizing the life of practical holiness that should follow redemption. Since the two festivals were so closely linked together, either designation is acceptable. The Passover is referred to six times in this chapter (vv.1,2,5,15,17,18). The "very great congregation" was made up of an overwhelming number from Judah (v.12) and those who humbled themselves from the northern tribes (vv.11,18).

The priests had cleansed the temple and the people cleansed the city of Jerusalem from religious defilement. Just before the Passover, a very great congregation took away all the altars that were in Jerusalem and cast them into the brook Kidron (see comments on the brook Kidron under 29.16 in this commentary). Many of these would be altars that king Ahaz had made in every corner of Jerusalem (28.24). Many would be altars for idolatry, but also included were altars where they worshipped the Lord (33.17). After the Passover, all Israel that were present "threw down the high places and the altars out of all Judah and Benjamin, in Ephraim also and Manasseh, until they had utterly destroyed them all" (31.1). This was so contrary to human thinking that Sennacherib, king of Assyria, actually thought that was a reason why Judah could not expect God to help them (32.12): "Hath not the same Hezekiah taken away his high places and his altars, and commanded Judah and Jerusalem, saying, Ye shall worship before one altar, and burn incense upon it?". So there was a return to the place which the Lord their God had chosen to place His name. (See appendix on "The return to the place where the Lord had chosen to place His name".)

The Passover lamb was a type of the future redeeming substitutionary death of Christ, the true Lamb of God who would truly take away the sin of the world (Jn 1.29; 1 Cor 5.7). The priests and the Levites had to be sanctified before they could offer the sacrifices. "It is clear then, that it was one thing to be a priest or Levite, but quite another to be fit at any given time to *act* as such" (McConville). This shows that God is concerned about the condition of those who handle holy things. There were priests, and even some Levites, who were not whole-heartedly behind Hezekiah's reforms until the remaining hardness of their hearts was melted by the zealous devotion of the congregation.

Ordinarily the fathers would sacrifice their own Passover lambs for their families (Deut 16.5-6). The next verse gives the reason why the Levites did it "according to the law of Moses" instead - because many of the people were not sanctified. Their obedience in following the Word of God to carry out the service of God honoured Him and His Word. The Chronicler delights to see God's written revelation being carried out.

In Exodus 12.7,22-23 the sacrificial blood was applied to the lintel and the two side posts. But now the priests received the sacrificial blood from the Levites and sprinkled it on the altar.

The importance to the writer of the Chronicles of the Levites' exercise is seen in the prominence given to them in v.17 and also in v.22.

When Hezekiah saw that a multitude from the northern tribes were not cleansed according to the purification of the sanctuary (vv.18-19), he did not think to himself, "It will serve them right if God strikes them down dead". Instead, his compassion for them is seen in his prayer for them (which is a reminder of Solomon's prayers). Hezekiah may have been encouraged to pray as he did by God's Word to Solomon as recorded in 7.14: "If my people, which are called by my name, shall humble themselves, and pray, and seek my face, and turn from their wicked ways; then will I hear from heaven, and will forgive their sin, and will heal their land". In effect, he is pleading for the promise of that verse to be honoured. For those from the northern tribes had humbled themselves, turned back to God, and were seeking His face: therefore, they fulfilled the conditions of the promise. Hezekiah had confidence in the goodness of God. He was also persuaded that, although they were not ceremonially clean at this time, it was more important to God that they were seeking Him from the heart.

Hezekiah's intercession is deeply touching and so is God's answer (v.20). The phrase "healed the people" could refer to physical healing. It seems more likely that it is spiritual healing that is in mind since Hezekiah prayed for forgiveness. So here we have a moral, spiritual healing as in Psalm 41.4: "I said, Lord, be merciful unto me: heal my soul; for I have sinned against thee". A similar thought is found in Hosea 14.4: "I will heal their backsliding". God was true to His promise, as He always is. "The Lord hearkened", means the Lord heard and answered. The Chronicler uses the same Hebrew word "healed" as in the promise of 7.14. This prayer and its answer is another indication that Hezekiah excelled in trusting God (2 Kings 18.5). Here is an encouragement to his first readers and to us.

"Prayer was effective in overriding purely ritual considerations according to the Chronicler...The Chronicler was not content with a religion of mere external correctness but delighted in the one who 'sets his heart on seeking God'" (Thompson). The Holy Spirit inspired the writer of the Chronicles in all that he wrote.

Hezekiah displays a wonderful balance. He had a heart for all of God's Word and also for all of God's people. He had a genuine desire that all of God's people should obey the Word of God. All believers should have the same desire. Hezekiah wisely insists that they "turn again unto the Lord", which implies turning from unscriptural practices of many years duration. By wanting all God's people to come to Jerusalem, the place where God had chosen to place His name, and (at the same time) to come with a spirit of humble submission, he illustrates the principle of exercising care in reception.

"Great gladness" was experienced by all from the northern tribes who had humbled themselves: they shared in the "gladness" of v.23, the "rejoicing" of v.25, and the "great joy" of v.26. Being consciously in God's will always brings joy and gladness, even as our Lord Jesus confirmed in John 13.17; 15.9-11. As the hymn writer puts it:

> When we walk with the Lord,
> In the light of His Word,
> What a glory He sheds on our way!
> While we do His good will
> He abides with us still,
> And with all who will trust and obey.
>
> Trust and obey;
> For there's no other way
> To be happy in Jesus,
> But to trust and obey.
> (John H. Sammis)

There is no record of gladness, rejoicing and great joy during Josiah's

Passover even though it was closer to the Word of God (35.18). Perhaps there was more joy at Hezekiah's Passover because at Josiah's most of the people only turned to the Lord feignedly (Jer 3.10).

"Spake comfortably", is literally "spake to the heart". Simply put, one can say that he spoke encouragingly to all the Levites.

Verses 30.23-31.1: Continuing the Blessing

See the comments on 30.2 for "the whole assembly". The whole congregation of God's people found such great gladness in keeping the Feast of Unleavened Bread that they decided to keep it a further seven days, something that we never read of happening again in the Word of God. This would remind the readers that Solomon celebrated for two weeks when dedicating the temple (7.9-10 but, more clearly, in 1 Kings 8.65-66). Here one can see the joy that goes with obedience to the recovery of lost truth.

The large number of animals given by Hezekiah and the princes may have contributed to the decision to keep the Feast seven more days. In the phrase, "a great number of the priests sanctified themselves", we see many of them experiencing a revival of consecration.

There is an emphasis in v.24 on the large number of animal sacrifices rather than the number of people. The great amount of offerings that Hezekiah gave to the congregation shows that he was not only a good leader but generous. The princes followed his good example.

Verse 25 gives the make-up of the "very great congregation" of v.13. It included "strangers that came out of the land of Israel, and that dwelt in Judah". There was a return to the Law of Moses in the mention of the stranger keeping the Passover (Num 9.14). The word "all" (which is found twice in this verse) is stressed.

In v.26 there is another indication that there was a return to the Word of God in this revival. It would be necessary to go back in history all the way to Solomon's day to find a Passover like this one. However, in Josiah's day, there was none like the Passover in the eighteenth year of his reign since the days of Samuel, which would be further back (35.18). Josiah's Passover was closer to the Word of God. We read about the Feast of Tabernacles in Nehemiah 8.17: "for since the days of Jeshua the son of Nun unto that day had not the children of Israel done so. And there was very great gladness". God's people had actually kept the Feast of Tabernacles before, but they had omitted dwelling in booths until Nehemiah's day.

May the Lord encourage all to go as close as they can to the Word of God. It is possible for anyone to become extreme by going very close to one part of the God's Word and neglecting another part that should regulate how the first part is taken. But that is not going too close to the Word of God; it is not going close enough. God's Word is a balanced book; the closer one is to the Bible, the more balanced one will be.

As one example of the balance in the Word of God one can note 1 Kings

12 and 13. In 1 Kings 12 Rehoboam made a fatal mistake in forsaking the advice of the old men. But, in the very next chapter, not 20 chapters later, the man of God from Judah lost his life because he took seriously the words of the old prophet of Bethel. Proverbs 16.31 says: "The hoary head is a crown of glory, if it be found in the way of righteousness". See also the comments on a return to the Word of God as in 29.15. "Great joy" always abounds when God's people go by His Word and separate themselves from sin as symbolized in the Feast of Unleavened Bread. Joy is a tremendous force in evangelism too!

"The priests the Levites arose and blessed the people" (v.27) with the priestly blessing of Numbers 6.22-27, as Moses directed. "Their prayer came up to his holy dwelling place, even unto heaven." These words are a reminder of Solomon's prayer in ch.6, when he used similar words four times (vv.21,30,33,39). It is only by inspiration of the Holy Spirit that the Chronicler can give information here that only God would know. God's people departed with the prospect of God's blessing on their subsequent lives. The joy of worship issued in a challenge for them as they left Jerusalem. Lives that had been so blessed needed to be changed; so, in the next verse, they banish from their midst all that was not of God.

The first part of 31.1 is similar to the first part of 2 Kings 18.4 with one significant difference. There Hezekiah is the subject, but here it is "all Israel". "All Israel that were present" does not refer to the people of the northern kingdom especially, but rather to the whole congregation, all who had been present at the Passover. "All Israel" is to be understood as in 30.21. God's people had displayed a unity in keeping the feasts of the Passover and Unleavened Bread. Since the house of the Lord was completely cleansed (ch.29), and Jerusalem itself (ch.30.14), so now the land should be completely cleansed as well. "They realized that purity and singleness of heart were the keys to God's continued blessing" (Barber).

John Heading makes a valuable application of this by writing: "They were now so satisfied with the house and service in Jerusalem, that the rest of the land had to be consistent with it. In other words, religious activity outside a local church must be consistent with the holy service in actual gatherings of the Lord's people...The early Christians in Ephesus burned their 'curious arts' so that their outside life should be as holy as the new life found in the newly-formed church at Ephesus (Acts 19.19)". Refer to the comments on the high places in 30.14 and the Appendix below on "The return to the place where the Lord had chosen to place His name".

APPENDIX

The Return to the Place where the Lord had Chosen to Place His Name

In 14.3 and 17.6 we read that Asa (and Jehoshaphat after him) "took away the high places", but, in 1 Kings 15.14; 22.43 and 2 Chronicles 15.17; 20.33, it says that King Asa and King Jehoshaphat did not remove the high places. On the surface this looks like a contradiction, but in reality it is not. There are only four writers (of 45 writers consulted) who recognize that some of the altars destroyed in 31.1 were altars for worshipping God (Edersheim, Payne, Rawlinson, and Rodgers). The best writer for clarity, simplicity, and profitable application on the high places is Rodgers. His solution is simple and convincing.

There were two kinds of high places: high places where they worshipped idols, and high places where they only worshipped the Lord their God (33.17). In the first two references above, where it says that they "took away the high places", there is also reference to the idols. In the other four places where they did not take away the high places, nothing is said about idols. This makes clear that those two good kings destroyed the high places where they worshipped idols, but they spared the high places where they worshipped the Lord. Hezekiah was the first king to destroy them all (30.14; 31.1).

This was so contrary to human thinking that Sennacherib actually thought the fact that Hezekiah had done so was a reason why they could not expect God to help them (32.12): "Hath not the same Hezekiah taken away his high places and his altars, and commanded Judah and Jerusalem, saying, Ye shall worship before one altar, and burn incense upon it?". Some of God's people in Hezekiah's day may have thought that Hezekiah was bigoted and narrow-minded, but it should never be forgotten that he had the Word of God for doing it. Deuteronomy 12.13-14 says, "Take heed to thyself that thou offer not thy burnt offerings in every place that thou seest: But in the place which the Lord thy God shall choose in one of thy tribes, there thou shalt offer thy burnt offerings". Whatever anybody thought of Hezekiah, what God thought about him is noted in 31.20: "Hezekiah… wrought that which was good and right and truth before the Lord his God". God's commendation is the most important of all. Whatever God's people thought of Hezekiah while he lived, what they thought about him when he died is stated in 32.33: "And Hezekiah slept with his fathers, and they buried him in the chiefest of the sepulchres of the sons of David: and all Judah and the inhabitants of Jerusalem did him honour at his death". Hezekiah was the only king of whom it is recorded that "they buried him in the chiefest of the sepulchres of the sons of David". Here is another illustration of 1 Samuel 2.30: "them that honour me I will honour".

Of course, high places where they worshipped idols were much more dishonouring to God than the high places where they worshipped the Lord. But both were alike in this - they had no Scriptural authority for their existence. By application, today, there are still two kinds of high places. There are places in Christendom that are honey-combed with so much that is contrary to God's Word that any of God's people who know His Word (at least in measure) would not have anything to do with them.

However, there are also high places that have so much good about them that good brethren, like Asa and Jehoshaphat, would spare them and even attend them. May the Lord help each one to abide by the Word of God. God does get delight from individual believers, wherever and under whatever banner they gather, and some of them would put many of us to shame. But, the only corporate gathering that has Scriptural support for its existence is composed of God's people gathered simply to the precious name of our Lord Jesus Christ (Mt 18.20).

2 CHRONICLES 31

Hezekiah's reign

Introductory

The breaking down of the altars and high places in Judah, Benjamin, Ephraim, and Manasseh (v.1) was a direct consequence of the Passover kept in chapter 30. Verse 1 is parallel to 2 Kings 18.4, and vv.20-21 are parallel to 2 Kings 18.5-7a. The rest of this chapter is unique to Chronicles.

This is the third chapter in which Hezekiah leads so that God gets His rightful place among His own people. Chapter 29 presents the cleansing of the temple. Chapter 30 describes the celebration of the Passover. This chapter presents the orderly arrangement for the continuation of worship in the temple. Hezekiah re-established the priestly and Levitical services and restored the giving of tithes for their support. In his leadership he provided the necessary stimulus, but a hearty response from the people was crucial. The Chronicler emphasizes this in speaking of their response (v.5), as "abundance", "the tithe of all things", and "abundantly". Four times in vv.6-9 we have "heaps" and in v.10 "that which is left is this great store".

"Service cannot continue otherwise, and this is illustrated in Nehemiah 10.39 where, in Nehemiah's restoration of the temple service, the people declared, 'We will not forsake the house of our God', that is, they would bring all the gifts necessary for its service. But a short time later when such gifts were not being brought, Nehemiah had to exclaim, 'Why is the house of God forsaken?' (13.10-11)" (Heading).

The writer of the Chronicles in his portrayal of Hezekiah shows that his reign is like the reigns of David and Solomon. Hezekiah appointed the courses of the priests and Levites as Solomon had done (8.14) and as David did (1 Chr 23-26). David and Solomon both gave of their own wealth for the temple (1 Chr 29.1-5; 2 Chr 8.12-13). Hezekiah also gave of his own property (v.3), and manifested a real desire to follow the "law of the Lord" (v.3) as David and Solomon did before him (1 Kings 2.3; 1 Chr 16.40; 22.12; 2 Chr 6.16). "The Chronicler is fond of showing that faithful and generous kings prompt similar generosity in the population (31.5-10; 24.8-14; 1 Chr 29.6-9)" (Dillard). 1 Chronicles 29.9 records, "Then the people rejoiced, for that they offered willingly, because with perfect heart they offered willingly to the Lord: and David the king also rejoiced with great joy". Hezekiah blessed the people (v.8) as did David (1 Chr 16.2) and Solomon (2 Chr 6.3). "The Chronicler presents Hezekiah as the ideal successor of David" (Coggins).

God's people and Hezekiah himself were blessed as a result of their response to God (vv.8,10,21; 32.29: "God had given him substance very much").

Outline of Chapter 31

Verse 2: Organizing the work.
Verse 3: Providing the materials.
Verses 4-10: Contributing the tithes and the offerings.
Verses 11-19: Distributing the tithes and the offerings fairly.
Verses 20-21: Commendation of Hezekiah.

Verse 2: Organizing the Work

"Hezekiah appointed the courses of the priests and the Levites." The priests would be responsible for the burnt offerings and peace offerings. However, "The 'burnt offerings' and the 'peace offerings' which they were to offer to the Lord (v.2) did not mean that these were the only sacrifices they were to offer. It was the Chronicler's way of referring to the entire sacrificial system (e.g., as we might say, 'from A to Z'; cp. Numbers 28-29)" (Barber). The Levites would be responsible for singing, praising, gate keeping, and other duties. The king was acting according to the directions of David given in 1 Chronicles 23-26. The twenty-four courses enabled the priests and the Levites to share in the service. This principle of serving by courses is illustrated by Zacharias the priest and father of John the Baptist: "And it came to pass, that while he executed the priest's office before God in the order of his course...And it came to pass, that, as soon as the days of his ministration were accomplished, he departed to his own house" (Lk 1.8,23). It was necessary for Hezekiah to re-establish the twenty-four courses of the priests and the Levites because they fell into disuse during the reign of wicked King Ahaz. The arrangement provided for the continuance of temple worship. These arrangements are a reminder of the exhortation to New Testament assemblies, "Let all things be done decently and in order" (1 Cor 14.40).

"Hezekiah's organizational acumen was one fine way in which he endeavored to 'seek his God' (v.21). The Chronicler's use of his characteristic language of spirituality shows how he was able to invest the most mundane of religious tasks with an aura of devotion...One senses his thrill as he thought back to the glory of the achievements of David and Solomon and back further to the Mosaic Tabernacle evoked by the archaic term 'camp' (v.2)...This hive of religious industry called the temple was for him the focus of work done for God and in line with His will. Such is the lofty perspective that animated the Chronicler's thinking, and he commended it to every priest and Levite involved in their everyday, repetitive tasks" (Leslie C. Allen).

Verse 3: Providing the Materials

"The contribution of the king from his own possessions" (ESV) is noted. His possessions are listed in 32.27-29. From these Hezekiah gave for the offerings commanded in Numbers 28 and 29. "There were needed for these purposes in the course of a year nearly 1,100 lambs, 113 bullocks, 37 rams, and 30 goats, besides vast quantities of flour, oil and wine for the accompanying meat and drink offerings" (Rawlinson). Hezekiah followed the example of David (1 Chr 29.1-5) and Solomon (2 Chr 8.12-13).

Verses 4-10: Contributing the Tithes and the Offerings

Because Hezekiah set a good example (v.3) he had a moral right to command "the people that dwelt in Jerusalem to give the portion of the priests and the Levites, that they might be encouraged in the law of the Lord" (v.4). "The portion" due included tithes, first fruits, and some of the sacrifices. Hezekiah wanted them to be supported so that they could give themselves to the services of the temple and to teaching without having to work to provide for themselves. In Nehemiah it is recorded that he "perceived that the portions of the Levites had not been given them: for the Levites...were fled everyone to his field" (13.10). The New Testament never teaches tithing, but it does teach systematic, proportionate giving to the Lord: "Upon the first day of the week let every one of you lay by him in store, as God hath prospered him" (1 Cor 16.2). Giving to the Lord should not be "grudgingly, or of necessity: for God loveth a cheerful giver" (2 Cor 9.7).

Supporting priests and Levites is similar in principle to supporting the Lord's servants today. While the work of priests and Levites was obvious to all in Jerusalem, the needs of workers, especially pioneer workers, and those labouring among small and financially poor assemblies, today may be less obvious. More support is needed for such than for those moving among saints who are in more comfortable circumstances. The Lord has "ordained that they which preach the gospel should live of the gospel" (1 Cor 9.14).

Andrew E. Hill in *The New Application Commentary* has much profitable material on Hezekiah the Encourager (pages 601-605). Hill refers to 30.22 and 32.6-8. Chapter 30.22 states, "And Hezekiah spake comfortably unto all the Levites". The AV margin has, "to the heart of all". In 32.6, "and spake comfortably to them", the AV margin has again, "spake to their heart". Verse 32.8 tells of the good result of Hezekiah speaking to their hearts: "And the people rested themselves upon the words of Hezekiah king of Judah". One might add 31.4 to the theme of Hezekiah the Encourager, for Hezekiah wanted the Levites to be encouraged in the law of the Lord. How helpful it is in every assembly for there to be some who encourage like Hezekiah or like Barnabas in the New Testament (Acts 11.23-24).

The greatest emphasis in vv.4-19 is the overwhelming response of the people. "There is good evidence that this was a recurring problem in the post-exilic period (cp. Neh 10.35-39; 12.47; 13.10-13; Mal 3.8-10), so that the Chronicler may well have hoped to challenge his readers by his description of the people's enthusiastic response" (Williamson). The last two references especially support what Williamson has written. "As soon as the commandment came abroad" (v.5). The meaning is probably that, contrary to Hezekiah's intention, his command to the residents of Jerusalem became unexpectedly well known.

Verse 5 shows that the response was immediate and wholehearted:

"brought in abundance" and "the tithe of all things brought they in abundantly". The "children of Israel" (v.5) included people from all the cities of Judah besides "the people that dwelt in Jerusalem", who were especially invited (v.4). "A worshipping people will always be a generous people, especially when their leaders set the example, and Judah was no exception" (Wiersbe). The first fruits were for the priests (Num 18.8,12). The tithes were for the Levites (Num 18.21), but the Levites were to give "a tithe of the tithes" to Aaron the priest (Num 18.26-28).

Verse 6 includes people from the northern ten tribes that had moved to cities in Judah. It speaks of "the tithe of holy things" which Slotki says, "were legally exempt from the tithe" but were nonetheless brought. The heaps began to be established in the third month with the grain harvest (the Feast of Pentecost) and finished in the seventh month with the fruit and vine harvest (the Feast of Tabernacles) (v.7). According to the record, chapters 29, 30, and 31 were all within the first year of Hezekiah. The temple was cleansed in the 1st month (ch.29), the Passover was celebrated in the 2nd month (ch.30), and the offerings were collected in the next five months (ch.31).

The people gave so generously that there was abundance left over that they put into heaps. Those heaps, laid up in a response beyond their expectation, surprised Hezekiah and the princes (v.8). It calls to mind three other occasions when there was similar giving. The Macedonians gave far more than Paul ever expected (2 Cor 8.1-5). Their giving was "beyond their power" (v.3). In v.5 Paul gives the secret of their giving: "And this they did, not as we hoped, but first gave their own selves to the Lord, and unto us by the will of God". So their giving was even beyond the level that Paul hoped for. If we give ourselves first to the Lord He has everything - our time, our treasure, and our talents. Exodus 36.5 records, concerning the offering for the Tabernacle: "The people bring much more than enough for the service of the work, which the Lord commanded to make". David could say about the offering for the temple in 1 Chr 29.2, "I have prepared with all my might for the house of my God", and in v.3 he states why he gave so much: "because I have set my affection to the house of my God". David rejoiced to see his good example of giving followed by his people: "Now have I seen with joy thy people, which are present here, to offer willingly unto thee" (1 Chr 29.17). The people gave willingly and joyfully. Surely our Heavenly David rejoices to see His good example of giving being followed by all His own people (2 Cor 8.9).

Thy life was given for me!
Thy blood, O Lord, was shed
That I might ransomed be,
And quickened from the dead;
Thy life was given for me;
What have I given for Thee?

(Frances Ridley Havergal)

Verse 8 gives a becoming response by Hezekiah and the princes when they saw what the people had brought. The Lord had given them plentiful harvests and the Lord had put it into their hearts to give. The Lord's people readily responded to God's working and their actual giving led Hezekiah and the princes to bless the Lord and His people. As David said in 1 Chronicles 29.14, "of thine own have we given thee".

Hezekiah questioned the priests and the Levites as to how there were such heaps (v.9). Azariah the chief priest answered, "we have had enough to eat, and have left plenty: for the Lord hath blessed his people; and that which is left is this great store" (v.10). This Azariah is not likely to be the Azariah who led 80 priests against king Uzziah (26.17) since that was some 45 years earlier.

The fact that "a great amount was left over (v.10) is an interesting anticipation of Jesus feeding of the five and four thousand (Mt 14.20; 15.37; etc.)" (Selman).

Verses 11-19: Distributing the Tithes and the Offerings Fairly

The bountiful heaps received were faithfully stored, maintained and distributed equally among the families of the priests and Levites. The writer of the Chronicles emphasizes that the work was thoroughly and faithfully carried out. The ESV makes "faithfulness" clear in the following three verses. Verse 12 says, "And they faithfully brought in the contributions;" and v.15 says of the six men named under Kore that they "were faithfully assisting him" The last part of v.18 reads, "for they were faithful in keeping themselves holy".

At the king's commandment they prepared chambers in the house of the Lord (v.11). The tithes and first fruits could be piled in heaps in the open because of the rainless Palestinian summers, but it was necessary to store them before the rains came. Cononiah the Levite was in charge of the storing, and his brother Shimei was next to him. There were ten men named to be assistants in the work. Scripture records their names, possibly indicating that God takes notice of all who work for Him. The king and Azariah, the ruler of the house of God, appointed all these capable men (vv.12-13). Kore the Levite was in charge of the distribution. Kore has the same name as the grandson of Korah of 1 Chronicles 9.19. Kore had six assistants, named here, who lived in the priestly cities (vv.14-15). The cities of the priests are noted in Joshua 21.13-19. The "most holy things" of v.14 included the shewbread, the meal offerings, and other offerings that were eaten by the priests while on duty in the temple. Kore and his assistants were to give equitably to their brethren "as well to the great as to the small" (v.15).

A very careful and thorough distribution was made to all who were entitled to a share of the things given. No one was forgotten or overlooked (vv.16-19). Verse 16 refers to the priests and Levites while on duty. The phrase, "from three years old and upward" (v.16), possibly refers to the fact that at that time children were weaned when three years of age. Verse 17 records, "the Levites from twenty years old and upward". At first, the age for Levites to begin their service was thirty (Num 4.3). Later, God Himself told Moses that the age was to be "twenty-five" (Num 8.24). David, toward the close of his reign, reduced the age further to twenty (1 Chr 23.24). Verse 17 includes both priests and Levites. The next verse shows that the children, the wives, their sons, and their daughters were also counted in (v.18). The priests off-duty were included (v.19). The administration was done efficiently. A New Testament application is given in 2 Corinthians 8.21 - "Providing for honest things, not only in the sight of God, but also in the sight of men".

Verses 20-21: Commendation of Hezekiah

This is an extension of the favourable assessment given in 29.2. It has a parallel in 2 Kings 18.5-7a. "Even parallel passages such as this, however, reveal the Chronicler's distinctive style and vocabulary. One characteristic emphasis is that at various stages a note is made that work on the temple was properly completed and its services restored (cp. 7.11; 8.16; 24.13-14; 29.35). No doubt the author had in mind the almost fatal delay in the construction of the second temple (Ezra 3.1-6.22)" (Selman).

"This review also links Hezekiah with David in his wholehearted devotion to God and with Solomon in his concern for the Lord's Temple" (Hill). These two verses are a fitting conclusion to the three chapters describing Hezekiah's reign, for all that he did as recorded, he did it with all his heart, and prospered (v.21). The whole revival in his reign began in his own heart as he himself said in 29.10, "Now it is in mine heart...".

Part of 2 Kings 18.7a has the closest phraseology to the parallel verses of Chronicles 31.20-21: "he prospered whithersoever he went forth". For the last five words of v.20, "before the Lord his God", Unger has this insightful parenthesis: "(the expression hinting at his firm faith in God)". 2 Kings 18.5 states that he excelled in trusting God: "He trusted in the Lord God of Israel; so that after him was none like him among all the kings of Judah, nor any that were before him".

The expression in v.21, "he did it with all his heart", is a reminder of other verses that encourage all to be wholehearted. Deuteronomy 6.5 exhorts, "And thou shalt love the Lord thy God with all thine heart". Solomon in his prayer to God in 2 Chronicles 6.14 spoke of the "Lord God of Israel...which keepest covenant, and shewest mercy unto thy servants, that walk before thee with all their hearts". During good King Asa's reign, 15.15 states, "And all Judah rejoiced at the oath: for they had sworn with all their heart".

There are other verses that promote wholeheartedness when they use the term a "perfect heart". 1 Chronicles 12.38 speaks of "those who came with a perfect heart to Hebron, to make David king". No wonder that v.40 states that "there was joy in Israel". Today there is joy in any assembly in the measure that they all with a perfect heart want our Lord Jesus to have His rightful place among them. In 1 Chronicles 28.9 David encouraged his son Solomon to serve God "with a perfect heart". David rejoiced in 1 Chronicles 29.9 that his people "with perfect heart…offered willingly", and the people themselves rejoiced. 1 Kings 11.4 records that "when Solomon was old…his wives turned away his heart after other gods: and his heart was not perfect with the Lord his God, as was the heart of David his father". Hanani's words to King Asa in 16.9 are a great encouragement to have a perfect heart: "For the eyes of the Lord run to and fro throughout the whole earth, to shew himself strong in the behalf of them whose heart is perfect toward him". King Jehoshaphat charged those who were going to judge in Jerusalem (19.9), "Thus shall ye do in the fear of the Lord, faithfully, and with a perfect heart". There is a warning about Amaziah in 25.2: "And he did that which was right in the sight of the Lord, but not with a perfect heart". Immediately after Isaiah told Hezekiah that he was going to die, Hezekiah prayed unto the Lord about his having a perfect heart (2 Kings 20.3; Is 38.3).

The last word of v.21, "prospered", calls to mind God's promise to Joshua (Josh 1.8): "…then thou shalt make thy way prosperous, and then thou shalt have good success". It is also a reminder of the blessed man of Psalm 1, "…whatsoever he doeth shall prosper" (v.3). Jehoshaphat exhorted his people in 20.20, "believe his prophets, so shall ye prosper", and 26.5 states about Uzziah that, "as long as he sought the Lord, God made him to prosper". Isaiah prophesied about the Lord Jesus that "the pleasure of the Lord shall prosper in his hand" (Is 53.10). All God's future purposes will come to fruition in His hand, which is one of the results of His infinite sufferings on the cross. Other places the Chronicler uses the word, "prosper" are 1 Chronicles 22.11,13; 29.23; 2 Chronicles 7.11; 13.12; 14.7; 18.11,14; 24.20; 32.30.

Williamson suggests that this two-verse evaluation of Hezekiah serves as a literary marker. It ends the three chapters that have been mostly unique to the Chronicles, and it marks a return to being more largely dependent on Kings. The last word of v.21 is another reminder that Hezekiah is like Solomon (7.11; 32.30).

2 CHRONICLES 32

Hezekiah's reign

Introductory

Hezekiah is the third king of Judah to be faced by an enemy (32.1-23) after pleasing God. (Hezekiah had pleased God early in his reign: see chapters 29,30,31.) Asa in 14.9-13 faced an enemy after pleasing God, and Jehoshaphat similarly in 20.1-30. In all three cases it was a test allowed by God to refine these kings and to bring out the best in them. Satan tries to bring out the worst in the saints. In each of these times God was glorified by a miraculous deliverance that He gave in answer to each of these kings trusting Him.

The Chronicler reverses the balance of the writer of Kings. The writer of the Chronicles has much more about the reforms than the account in Kings. Kings has only a few verses about the reforms, but the Chronicler has three chapters! For the record of Sennacherib coming against Jerusalem, the Chronicler, with only 23 verses, has considerably less than Kings which has 62 verses (2 Kings 18.13-37; 19.1-37)! The writer of the Chronicles assumes that his readers are familiar with the account in Kings. The fuller account in Kings and in Isaiah is needed to best understand some of the things recorded in this chapter. Even though the Chronicler's record is much shorter, he has a section of his own about Hezekiah's preparations (vv.2-8) including vv.6-8 that tells of Hezekiah speaking comfortably to the captains and the people encouraging them to trust God.

"The author of the Chronicles has arranged his narrative rhetorically so as to make the various events form a climax: first, the speeches of the servants of Sennacherib; then the letter to Hezekiah to induce him and his counsellors to submit; and finally, the attempt to terrify the people in language intelligible to them" (Keil).

Verses 9-19 record the threatening speeches in which pride, disdain, and persuasion were skillfully blended in an attempt to impress the hearers with the irresistible power of Assyria and the complete hopelessness of their case. The Assyrian propaganda cleverly tried to turn an act of obedience to God (destroying all other altars) into a reason why they could not expect God to help them. Those speeches were insulting blasphemies delivered with insolent irreverent defiance. Sennacherib did not count on the loyalty of the people of Judah to their king and the power of Jehovah.

The book *Life's Principles from the Kings of the Old Testament* (Knapp) has an excellent outline for the reign of Hezekiah. "Following God in the Crises of Life…Succeeding in the Crisis of Choice (2 Chr 29.2). Perhaps the most important choice of Hezekiah's life was his decision not to follow the example of his father Ahaz…Succeeding in the Crisis of Invasion (32.1-23)…Succeeding in the Crisis of Sickness (2 Kings 20.1-11; 2 Chr 32.24; Is 38.1-22)…Stumbling in the Crisis of Prosperity (32.25-31)…Perhaps the single most important application from the life of Hezekiah is that no matter how godly we become, we are never beyond stumbling, and we never outgrow our need for God's grace and help".

"All who have accepted Christ as their Saviour face adversity (Jn 16.33; Acts 14.22)...Because trials are part of everyone's life, this chapter about good King Hezekiah contains some important truths that we do well to learn... The fact that a good man like Hezekiah had to face adversity was designed to reassure the returned exiles (and us) that their present hardships were not necessarily an indication of God's displeasure" (Barber).

Outline of Chapter 32

Verses 1-8:	Hezekiah's preparation for invasion.
Verses 9-19:	Sennacherib's taunting verbal attacks.
Verses 20-23:	The Lord's miraculous deliverance for Hezekiah and Judah.
Verse 24:	Hezekiah's sickness and prayer.
Verses 25-26:	Hezekiah's pride.
Verses 27-31:	Hezekiah's riches and honour.
Verses 32-33:	Conclusion.

Verses 1-8: Hezekiah's Preparation for Invasion

"After these things and this faithfulness..." (v.1; RV, JND, Berkeley). "These things" refers to all the reformation recorded in chs.29, 30, and 31. "This faithfulness" refers to a time a little earlier (31.20): "And thus did Hezekiah throughout all Judah, and wrought that which was good and right and truth before the Lord his God". The RV margin for "truth" has "Heb. faithfulness". "After these things and this faithfulness" came not blessing but Sennacherib. Maclaren has a substantial and profitable section on v.1 entitled, "A Strange Reward for Faithfulness": "His invasion increased dependence on God...Ah! dear brethren, anything that drives us to His breast is a blessing". God's miraculous deliverance was a fitting reward for Hezekiah's faithfulness and trust.

2 Kings 18.13 states that Sennacherib came in the fourteenth year of Hezekiah. "Under this dynasty Assyria reached the zenith of its power" (Slotki). Verse 1 here tells of Sennacherib encamped against the fenced cities, but it does not even imply that they were captured. The Chronicler only says that Sennacherib "thought to win them for himself". According to the Taylor Prism, Sennacherib captured 46 cities of Judah and a huge number of prisoners. 2 Kings 18.13 harmonizes with the claim on the Taylor Prism. "Sennacherib's invasion of Judah was perhaps the greatest threat to the kingdom's existence before its fall at the hands of Babylon" (McConville).

"The phrase (lit.) 'set his face for war against Jerusalem' (v.2) marks the climax of his campaign, though it also forms a fascinating contrast with Jesus' determination to 'set his face to go to Jerusalem' (Lk 9.51, NRSV,

RSV) for a totally different purpose" (Selman). Luke 9.51 also calls to mind Isaiah's prophecy concerning the Lord Jesus in Isaiah 50.7: "For the Lord God will help me; therefore shall I not be confounded: therefore have I set my face like a flint, and I know that I shall not be ashamed". Nothing could turn the Lord Jesus aside from going to the cross. As in the hymn by James G. Deck,

> Unmoved by Satan's subtle wiles,
> By suffering, shame, and loss;
> Thy path, uncheered by earthly smiles,
> Led only to the cross.

It was very important to Sennacherib for Judah to remain as a loyal vassal. He most likely thought that the best way to keep control of Judah was to neutralize the good influence of Hezekiah, which is what he actually tried to do.

The first thing Hezekiah did in his preparations was that he took counsel (v.3) with his princes as he had done before (30.2); this time it was to stop the waters of the fountains. This was a defensive measure as v.4 explains: "Why should the kings of Assyria come, and find much water". Sennacherib had taunted in 2 Kings 19.24 that he had drunk strange waters. Hezekiah saw to it that Sennacherib would have no water to drink near Jerusalem. No water to drink would be a real distress to invaders because the land around Jerusalem was destitute of water. The "kings of Assyria" may refer to kings of lesser kingdoms who were obligated by oath to support Assyria in battle.

Hezekiah also made sure that the people in Jerusalem would have plenty of water to drink. Even though 2 Kings does not record this, 2 Kings 20.20 confirms vv.3-4. Sennacherib threatened that they were in danger of dying by famine and by thirst. Hezekiah showed great foresight in providing plenty of water to drink. Hezekiah's tunnel (in v.30) was probably already built.

The second preparation that Hezekiah made is described in v.5 - "he strengthened himself", or "he took courage" (RV) as 1 Chronicles 11.10; 2 Chronicles 12.1; 15.8; 23.1; 25.11; 26.8, and "he built up the wall that was broken, and raised it up to the towers". The phrase, "another wall without" (v.5) indicates an outside wall as an additional means of defense. "This last statement has been thought to be confirmed by the discovery of the remains of an outer wall 'which may date as far back as Hezekiah'" (Curtis & Masden). He "repaired Millo in the city of David, and made darts and shields in abundance" (v.5). With the darts he armed the people offensively and with the shields he armed them defensively. Referring to Millo is a deliberate comparison between David in 1 Chronicles 11.8 and Hezekiah. "Confirmation that Hezekiah devoted much attention to the city walls in his defensive measures comes from Isaiah 22.8-11. Moreover, recent archeological evidences point in the same direction" (Williamson). "A part of the western wall of Jerusalem which could have been erected under Hezekiah's supervision is over 20 feet thick. It could easily have withstood Sennacherib's powerful battering rams" (Barber).

The third preparation that he made is given in v.6: "And he set captains of war over the people". All assemblies need overseers who will lead and guide according to the Word of God in all their difficulties.

The fourth and last preparation that Hezekiah made was also the most important: "he...spake comfortably to them saying..." (v.6). The AV margin has, "spake to their heart". His heart-encouraging message is given in vv.7-8. Hezekiah had encouraged the Levites (30.22) by speaking to their heart. Other places where we have this thought include Genesis 34.3; 50.21; Judges 19.3; Ruth 2.13; 2 Samuel 19.7; Isaiah 40.2; and Hosea 2.14. Besides the two times Hezekiah is recorded as "speaking to the heart", he also encouraged the Levites in 31.4 when "he commanded the people that dwelt in Jerusalem to give the portion of the priests and the Levites, that they might be encouraged in the law of the Lord". How helpful for assemblies when the saints encourage one another as Hezekiah did. Saints sometimes need correction, but often need something for their hearts!

Verse 7 begins with these words, "Be strong and courageous". Hezekiah had already strengthened himself (v.5) and he excelled in trusting God (2 Kings 18.5). He strengthened them and encouraged them to trust in the living God. Hezekiah's first four words are almost identical to those of Deuteronomy 31.6-7; Joshua 1.6,9; 10.25; 1 Chronicles 22.13; and 28.20. He encouraged them not to be afraid or dismayed even though there was a multitude against them, "for there be more with us than with him". These words are similar to those of Elisha to his servant when the servant was alarmed at so many Syrians encamped against them (2 Kings 6.16). However, Hezekiah referred to God Himself instead of the angelic host of God, as was the case with Elisha. The New Testament supports the same truth as in Romans 8.31 and 1 John 4.4.

Verse 8 commences: "With him is an arm of flesh". Those words are reminiscent of Jeremiah 17.5: "Thus saith the Lord; Cursed be the man that trusteth in man, and maketh flesh his arm, whose heart departeth from the Lord". An arm of flesh is a contrast to the arm of the Lord. Hezekiah goes on to say, "but with us is the Lord our God to help us, and to fight our battles". There are many verses in Scripture that no doubt encouraged Hezekiah to speak of the Lord our God fighting our battles - for example Exodus 14.14,25; Deuteronomy 1.30; 3.22; 20.4; Joshua 10.14,42; 23.3; 2 Chronicles 20.29. "For the Hebrews, that epithet, 'the Lord our God' (32.8) is a reminder of God's election of the nation of Israel and his mighty deliverance of his people from Egyptian oppression at the Exodus (cp. Ex 8.10)" (Hill). This calls to mind the words of Abijah to Jeroboam just before he won a victory over him: "And, behold, God himself is with us for our captain" (13.12). The repeated "with us" in vv.7-8 can be compared with the "Immanuel" of Isaiah 7.14. The RV margin has, "That is, God is with us"; see also Isaiah 8.10. What a good result there was because of Hezekiah speaking to their heart; "And the people rested themselves upon the words of Hezekiah, king of Judah". The AV margin for "rested" has "leaned". Hezekiah's words to the heart not only encouraged his own people but they are recorded to encourage all saints ever since.

"When from this account we turn to the prophetic narrative in Isaiah 22, we feel that it had not been always so (v.11), but that through the admonitions of the prophet, what had been at first confidence in the strength of their defenses, became transformed into trust in the living God" (Edersheim). Edersheim may be right. There is no doubt that Isaiah and Hezekiah were a good influence on each other, and we can be sure that Hezekiah himself was truly trusting God when he was encouraging God's people to do so.

Verses 9-19: Sennacherib's Taunting Verbal Attacks

In these provocative oral assaults we have an example of ancient propaganda using psychological warfare. In these eleven verses, the Chronicler has condensed the 30 verses of 2 Kings 18.13-37 and 19.9-13. In six verses (vv.10-15) he has in a masterly way combined several messages recorded in twenty-four verses in Kings (2 Kings 18.17-25, 26-35; 19.9-13). Verse 9 says, "After this did Sennacherib...send his servants to Jerusalem". His servants are given in 2 Kings 18.17 by their titles as Tartan, Rabsaris, and Rabshakeh. Rabshakeh means "chief officer", or "chief cupbearer". He is the spokesman. Sennacherib himself was at Lachish.

In v.10 Sennacherib asked, "Wherein do ye trust?". This is the most important matter to the Chronicler who has already given the answer in vv.7-8. He omits, therefore, anything that would take away from his account of Hezekiah trusting God. He omits the record in 2 Kings 18.14-16 of Hezekiah's submission at first to Sennacherib and paying him silver and gold. He also omits the possibility that Hezekiah may have trusted Egypt (2 Kings 18.21,24). In a masterly way the writer of the Chronicles greatly abbreviates the account of the attack by taunts and threats. He describes a speech (vv.9-16), letters (v.17), and loud shouts to intimidate (v.18). Rabshakeh, on behalf of Sennacherib, wanted to break the morale of the people, shake their confidence in God, and incite them to rebel against Hezekiah.

In the very accusation that Hezekiah is misleading the people (vv.11-12), he gives away the fact that he does not truly understand the situation. What Hezekiah did as described in v.12 was in response to God's Word. But Rabshakeh thought that what Hezekiah did would be a reason why they could not expect God to help them since Hezekiah had destroyed God's altars and high places. The Assyrians had completely misunderstood the situation, and unsaved people sometimes misunderstand saints today.

They did not understand how much "one altar" meant to God and how different God was from the idols of the nations.

Regarding v.13, "'My fathers' i.e. 'my predecessors upon the throne of Assyria'. It is the usual practice of Assyrian monarchs to call all their predecessors their 'ancestors'. Sennacherib really belonged to a dynasty that had only furnished one king before himself" (Rawlinson).

In vv.13-15, Sennacherib appealed to history. His boast in these verses, that no god of any of the lands he had defeated was able to deliver them from his hand, only confirmed the fact that they were not real gods in the first place! Five times in these three verses he referred to "mine hand". He referred twice more to "mine hand" in v.17. In 2 Kings 18.34 some lands are specified that were defeated by Assyria and Samaria is included. Sennacherib finished v.15 with these words, "how much less shall your God deliver you out of mine hand?". He was insolently insulting God by implying that God was inferior to all the other gods.

"Sennacherib's pride causes him to esteem his own power much higher than that of the God of Israel…Sennacherib despises and blasphemes the Lord, and likens Him to idols (see vv.14,15,16,17,19) and this stands out in our account whose brevity contrasts with those of Kings and Isaiah" (Rossier).

Verses 16-18 (especially the words in v.16, "against the Lord God, and against his servant") recall Psalm 2.2: "The kings of the earth set themselves, and the rulers take counsel together, against the Lord, and against his anointed". The whole thought of that verse is similar to the thought of the Chronicler. The writer of the Chronicles has given his own summary addition in v.16. He appears to know that his readers are familiar with the fuller account in 2 Kings. He is freely admitting that he has abbreviated his account. Sennacherib in his hatred links Hezekiah with the sovereign God. What a privilege this was for godly King Hezekiah!

Verse 17 begins with, "He wrote also letters". "Or 'a letter' as in 2 Kings 19.14. The plural form of the word seems to be used sometimes of a single document" (Rawlinson). 2 Kings records that when Hezekiah received the letter, he went up into the house of the Lord and spread it before the Lord. His trustful prayer is recorded in 2 Kings 19.15-19. This calls to mind our Lord Jesus spending all night in prayer to God in Luke 6.12. The previous verse states part of the reason for His all-night prayer: "They were filled with madness; and communed one with another what they might do to Jesus". There was a rise of opposition at that critical time of His public ministry, but there was another reason for that long time in prayer. He was about to choose His twelve apostles. The two reasons for His all night prayer were the schemings of evil on the part of men and the purposes of grace on the part of God. All saints should follow His example when there is opposition or when choices have to be made.

Verse 18 refers to the speech of Rabshakeh who is not mentioned by title in Chronicles. (In keeping with the supremacy of God in relation to the foolishness of men, Isaiah 2.11,17 records: "The Lord alone shall be exalted in that day".) The expression "Jews' speech", or "Jews' language" is found only here and in 2 Kings 18.26,28; Nehemiah 13.24; and Isaiah 36.11,13. We do read of "the language of Canaan" in Isaiah 19.18. Rabshakeh wanted to make sure that the people on the wall would understand his speech so he spoke in the Jews' language and wanted to make sure that they heard him, so he spoke with a loud voice. The Chronicler, in the last three clauses of v.18, writes of a motive for this action. A motive is not given in 2 Kings, but it is in harmony with that account. Rabshakeh hoped to turn the people against Hezekiah and gain the city that way, but the people showed their loyalty to Hezekiah by not answering a word just as the king had commanded (2 Kings 18.36).

"Hezekiah did the right thing in commanding his delegation: 'Answer him not' (2 Kings 18.36); for the only answer the Assyrian could possibly understand would be the language of action in the form of supernatural judgment" (Whitcomb).

In v.19 we read of "the God of Jerusalem". We also read in Psalm 135.21, "Blessed be the Lord out of Zion, which dwelleth at Jerusalem". God made special choice of Jerusalem. This verse is a significant summary of the boastfulness of the Assyrians. They equated God with false gods, which was the serious fallacy in their arguments. The Lord is not merely one god among many. He is the only true and living God. The very insolence of the message of vv.9-19 provided justification for the stirring trust that Hezekiah expressed in vv.7-8.

Verses 20–23: The Lord's Miraculous Deliverance for Hezekiah and Judah

The only effect of all the Assyrian speeches was that it drove Hezekiah and Isaiah to prayer. Both of those men felt keenly the dishonour done to the Lord and they were stirred to the heart to pray (v.20). "The juxtaposition of Hezekiah's address (vv.7-8) with the Assyrian taunts has elevated the confrontation from a simple issue of military superiority into a direct challenge to God's sovereignty and power. Thus, in the concluding paragraph (vv.20-23), Hezekiah acts in the only appropriate manner — prayer — and the outcome is decided entirely by divine intervention as a vindication of faith" (Williamson). Verse 20 states that Hezekiah and Isaiah "cried to heaven", which means that their prayers reached the throne of God. In v.20 "heaven" is used reverently for God as in Daniel 4.26; Matthew 21.25; Luke 15.18,21.

The Chronicler concentrates on the answer to the prayers of v.20 by recording the response in the very next verse. The Lord answered these prayers by sending an angel (v.21) that destroyed 185,000 Assyrians in one night (2 Kings 19.35). Here in v.21 additional information is given that the losses were especially "all the mighty men of valour" and "the leaders and captains". Our Lord Jesus asked Peter (after Peter had smitten off the ear of a servant of the high priest in Matthew 26.53), "Thinkest thou that I cannot now pray to my Father, and he shall presently give me more than twelve legions of angels?". A legion in the Roman army consisted of 3,000 to 6,000 men. Since one angel in one night could do what is recorded about the Assyrians, it is difficult to imagine what at least 36,000 angels could have done! Our Lord Jesus went on to say, "But how then shall the scriptures be fulfilled, that thus it must be?". The Chronicler heightens the direct intervention of God by adding (what is omitted in Kings), "So he returned with shame of face to his own land". 2 Kings 19.37 and Isaiah 37.38 both give the names of his two sons who smote him with the sword, but the Chronicler's account in the last part of v.21 is more affecting: "they that came forth of his own bowels slew him". That happened twenty years later!

Verse 22 summarizes the Lord's deliverance. This is one of the great historical examples of God's intervention on behalf of His people, ranking with Israel's crossing of the Red Sea. "From the hand of Sennacherib" is a direct contrast to Sennacherib's word, "mine hand", used 7 times in vv.13-17. God's power and Hezekiah's leading God's people to trust the living God is completely vindicated. The Assyrian monuments record Sennacherib's boast that he had shut up Hezekiah at Jerusalem "like a bird in a cage", but those monuments do not record Sennacherib's humiliating defeat. So, in reality, his boast was really a cover up for his serious defeat as a result of the prayers of Hezekiah and Isaiah. For the last phrase of v.22, "guided them on every side", the Septuagint has, "gave them rest on every side". The NASB has in the margin, "Another reading is 'gave them rest'". This rest is seen as a blessing that can be enjoyed as a reward for faithfulness as was the case for Asa (14.1,5-7; 15.15), Jehoshaphat (20.30), but most particularly for Solomon (1 Chr 22.9).

Verses 22-23 record the honour that came to Hezekiah as a result of the great victory that God gave to him - "Many brought gifts unto the Lord to Jerusalem". "Many" most likely refers to neighbouring peoples who by the defeat of the Assyrian army were also freed from that dreaded enemy. They too may have felt impelled to show by their gifts their gratitude to the God of Israel who had wonderfully worked for the defeat of Assyria. It is a reminder of the principle stated in 1 Samuel 2.30: "...them that honour me, I will honour". Others were rewarded for their faithfulness: David (1 Chr 14.17), Asa (2 Chr 14.5-7; 15.15), Jehoshaphat (17.10-11; 20.29), Uzziah (26.5), and especially Solomon (1 Chr 22.9; 2 Chr 1.1; 9.23-24). Verses 22-23 underline the spiritual message that the writer of the Chronicles wants his readers to see.

Scroggie writes this note for Psalm 75: "A comparison of this Psalm with the 76th, 46th, 47th, 48th; Isaiah 10.32-33; other passages, leads to the view that the occasion of it is the miraculous deliverance of Jerusalem from Sennacherib's army. But whether this was the occasion or another, the teaching of the psalm is plain, namely, that God is sovereign in His own world, a truth which is demonstrated by the fact that He delivers the righteous and punishes the wicked".

Both Clarke and John Phillips in their commentaries on the Psalms believe that the miraculous deliverance for Hezekiah and Judah (vv.20-23) is the background for Psalm 46.

Verse 24: Hezekiah's Sickness and Prayer

The phrase, "in those days", is intended to link Hezekiah's sickness with the Assyrian invasion chronologically. 2 Kings 20.7 states that his sickness was a boil. The Chronicler very briefly describes Hezekiah's sickness, but he assumes that his readers are familiar with the much longer account in 2 Kings 20.1-11 which gives details of Hezekiah's prayer and the miraculous sign. The RV margin has "wonder" for "sign". God responded to Hezekiah's prayer by giving him a promise of fifteen more years and confirming the promise with a sign. "Hezekiah quite properly asks for a sign to assure himself of his recovery. His hypocritical father, in mock modesty, refused to ask for a sign. He used a pious phrase in his refusal, saying, 'I will not tempt the Lord'. But he was not asked to 'tempt God'. God Himself had told him to ask for a sign" (Knapp).

In reference to 32.24, "God also gave Hezekiah a sign. Contrary to all established laws, and to confirm His Word, the Lord caused the shadow of the sun to go back ten degrees...How He arranged this is not known. Critics, of course, claim that this is scientifically impossible and that for such an event to take place the earth would have had to suddenly reverse its rotation with catastrophic results. That it happened is attested by the embassy from Babylon" (Barber).

Today saints usually look for assurance from the Word of God instead of looking for a sign. But there are times when the Lord does give special guidance, always in harmony with His own Word. For example, some missionaries and other workers in their call to public service were given confirmation that could easily be described as a sign.

Hezekiah was so precious to God that He took notice of his tears and answered his prayer for recovery. (Believers in every age are similarly precious to God though He has taught us the wisdom to ask if it be "according to his will" and for His glory, 1 Jn 5.14-15.) When Hezekiah prayed in his serious sickness he did much better than Asa (16.12) of whom it is recorded that "in his disease he sought not to the Lord, but to the physicians". Hezekiah already had a prayer answered for healing very early in his reign (30.18-20).

"Though it is not at first apparent, the moment we turn to the next chapter we are confronted with a problem, for Hezekiah's son Manasseh is said to have been enthroned at the age of twelve. This implies that if Hezekiah had died from his illness he would have left no heir to sit on David's throne (contrary to 2 Samuel 7.13b,16). God's promise would have become null and void...Another view is to look upon Manasseh sharing the throne as co-regent with his father...this latter view...allows the commonly accepted practice of a co-regency" (Barber & Thiele).

Verses 25-26: Hezekiah's Pride

How sad it is to read of King Hezekiah in v.25 that he "rendered not again according to the benefit done unto him". Hezekiah did not follow the psalmist David's exhortation in Psalm 103.2: "Bless the Lord, O my soul, and forget not all his benefits". Hezekiah was not as concerned as the writer of Psalm 116.12 to render to God for all His benefits: "What shall I render unto the Lord for all his benefits toward me?". The next phrase of v.25 records why he failed: "for his heart was lifted up". It calls to mind the failure of Uzziah (26.16) - "But when he was strong, his heart was lifted up to his destruction". Hezekiah said after his prayer for healing was answered, "I shall go softly all my years" (Is 38.15). Whatever else the phrase, "go softly", may signify, it surely implies humility. How wonderful if he had kept that resolve! But how sad that he did not. His pride is seen especially after receiving the Babylonian ambassadors (v.31). Even for a "second Solomon", pride brings wrath from God. The first thing of seven things that God hates and that are an abomination to Him is "a proud look" (Prov 6.16-19).

Verse 26 states that "Hezekiah humbled himself for the pride of his heart, both he and the inhabitants of Jerusalem". Because of that humbling the wrath of God was postponed until more than a century later. This was another fulfillment of God's promise in 7.14. This verse also points forward to a greater judgment, probably referring to the Babylonian exile but not as explicitly as 2 Kings 20.16-18 and Isaiah 39.5-7.

"There seems to be an allusion here (v.26) to something not related in Kings - perhaps to the self-humiliation of Hezekiah, whereof Jeremiah speaks as following on a certain prophecy uttered by Micah (Jer 26.19). The prophecy of Micah (3.12) is by some referred to the earlier part of the reign of Hezekiah; but there is nothing to show that it was not delivered about this time" (Rawlinson).

Hezekiah was right to be thankful that God's wrath would not come in his days (2 Kings 20.19), but he does not seem to have risen to having the same care for God's people as did David: "And David spake unto the Lord when he saw the angel that smote the people, and said, Lo, I have sinned, and I have done wickedly: but these sheep, what have they done? let thine hand, I pray thee, be against me, and my father's house" (2 Sam 24.17).

Verses 27-31: Hezekiah's Riches and Honour

In the times of the Old Testament "riches and honour" were evidence of the favour and blessing of the Lord: God gave Israel temporal blessings. In the New Testament we read, "Blessed be the God and Father of our Lord Jesus Christ, who has blessed us with all spiritual blessings in heavenly places in Christ" (Eph 1.3). Two statements are especially significant: "God had given him substance very much" (v.29), and "Hezekiah prospered in all his works" (v.30).

There are some good spiritual lessons that can be gleaned from Hezekiah's wealth. There were "treasuries for silver, and for gold, and for precious stones". Saints can be spiritually rich. Silver speaks of redemption, gold of deity, and precious stones speak of Christ-like character formed in the saints. These three things are what should be built on the foundation (1 Cor 3.12). How good it is when all assembly saints are contributing to the spiritual treasures of the assembly. The spices speak of the fragrance of Christ. "The shields speak of the protection of the doctrines concerning Christ, while the jewels speak of the value Christ sees in His people (Mal 3.17; Mt 13.46; Ex 28.21). The storehouses of Hezekiah (v.28) would refer typically to a local church filled with the Scriptures (corn), spiritual joy (wine), and the Spirit for worship and service (oil)" (Heading).

There were certain "cities, and possessions of flocks and herds in abundance" (v.29). "Ellicott's commentary suggests that the word rendered 'cities' here appears to mean watch towers or forts for the protection of flocks and herds" (Riddle). There is some archaeological evidence to suggest a prosperous reign. Verses 27-29 provide another likeness to Solomon (9.23-28) as is given in v.23.

The Chronicler sees the successful building of "Hezekiah's tunnel" as another evidence of divine favour (v.30). Since his tunnel is not mentioned in v.3, it was probably built earlier. It is very unlikely that such a huge undertaking could have been completed in time after the threat from the Assyrians first became known. Hezekiah's tunnel was a remarkable feat of engineering. The tunnel links the Gihon Spring with the pool of Siloam. "The Siloam Inscription", inscribed by the very engineers who constructed the tunnel, was found near the Siloam end of the tunnel. The tunnel is 1,777 feet (almost 550 metres) long through solid rock, often 60 feet (18.5 metres) below the ground and large enough to walk through, averaging two feet (0.6 metres) in width. The distance in a straight line is only 1,104 feet (340 metres). The inscription tells of the excitement of the workers on the project as they drew near to each other. (They worked from opposite ends toward the middle.) They met almost exactly in the middle!

Again in v.31 the writer of the Chronicles assumes that his readers are familiar with the fuller accounts in 2 Kings 20.12-19 and Isaiah 39.1-8. But in this one verse the Chronicler records two things not recorded in the fuller accounts. Isaiah 39.1 states one reason for the visit of the ambassadors: "At that time Merodach-baladan, the son of Baladan, king of Babylon, sent letters and a present to king Hezekiah: for he heard that he had been sick, and was recovered". 2 Kings is similar. That was kind of the king of Babylon. Here in v.31 is the only place where we read of another reason: they "sent unto him to inquire of the wonder that was done in the land" (which was the going back of the shadow by ten degrees). The Babylonians were greatly interested in astronomy.

The writer of the Chronicles is also the only one who states that "God left him, to try him, that he might know all that was in his heart" (v.31). Really, Hezekiah himself left God out because there is no record that he thought it was necessary to ask God about the matter at all. Of course, this does not mean that God was ignorant, for 1 Chronicles 28.9 states, "the Lord searcheth all hearts, and understandeth all the imaginations of the thoughts". Also 2 Chronicles 6.30 records: "whose heart thou knowest; (for thou only knowest the hearts of the children of men)". But God did this for Hezekiah's sake. Just as God's leadings in the wilderness 40 years was for the sake of the Israelites (Deut 8.2), "…to humble thee, and to prove thee, to know what was in thine heart", this test revealed to Hezekiah his pride and led him in humility to God.

God's tests are "to provide an opportunity for people to show heartfelt repentance. God tests in order to refine, to stimulate repentance and to deepen faith (cp. Gen 22.1; Ex 20.20; Deut 8.16)" (Selman). Hezekiah failed in this test but he was better off spiritually to judge the pride of his heart. Verses 27-31 give the riches and honour of Hezekiah, but v.31 is one exception to the overall prosperity of Hezekiah.

"It is interesting to note that two ostensible reasons are given for this embassy, yet behind them lay a third - the real cause of it - which is only hinted at…But what is meant by the words in 2 Kings 20.13: 'And Hezekiah hearkened unto them'? Although they are followed by a statement that he showed them all his treasures, they are not preceded by any request on their part to view these, and it is most unlikely that they mean no more than this. It is now well known from Assyrian and other records that Merodach-baladan had all his days been struggling against the power of Assyria, and had been endeavouring to stir up rebellion against that empire wherever he could. There can, therefore, be little doubt that the real object of his embassy to Hezekiah was to obtain his aid and alliance; and if so, the display of the treasures follows naturally upon the statement that he hearkened to them, as an endeavour on his part to show them how valuable his alliance would be" (Rodgers). At this time Babylon was gradually gaining power as Assyria was gradually declining in power. Sennacherib and his insulting representatives drove Hezekiah to his knees. But Merodach-baladan succeeded against Hezekiah with his favour and flattery. Saints have more to fear from favour and friendship from the world than from their fury and their frown.

Noticing the real aim of the ambassadors from Babylon helps to understand the severity of the words of Isaiah to Hezekiah after they left. Otherwise, what Hezekiah did might seem trivial. It would have been good if Hezekiah had done with the ambassadors what Solomon did with the Queen of Sheba in 9.4 - he showed her "his ascent by which he went into the house of the Lord". Solomon was thus showing the Queen of Sheba about his relationship with his God.

"The test of a true believer is not that one never falls but that, when it happens, he or she repents sincerely and, drawing on God's grace, continues along the Christian path, chastened but not devastated by his experience" (Leslie C. Allen).

Verses 32-33: Conclusion

In v.32, "his goodness" is translated in the RV "good deeds", as the same Hebrew word is translated in the AV of Nehemiah 13.14. Chapter 35.26 refers to Josiah's "goodness" and, again, is translated in the RV by "good deeds". The Chronicler wanted Hezekiah to be remembered for his "good deeds" rather than his failings. The "vision of Isaiah" was the same title given by Isaiah to his prophecy in Isaiah 1.1.

Although in v.33 the RV has "ascent" for "chiefest", it is still possible that a special place of honour for the burial place of Hezekiah is indicated. In spite of his failure in v.31, v.33 records that, "all Judah and the inhabitants of Jerusalem did him honour at his death". He was an outstanding king who pleased God most of his reign and who was genuinely concerned for his people. He surely deserved all the honour that they gave him at his death. 2 Kings 18.5 states that he excelled in trusting God. This chapter records three answers to Hezekiah's prayers: against the Assyrians (v.21); regarding his sickness (v.24); for forgiveness (v.26). His prayers are part of his "good deeds" (v.32) and that is likely the most encouraging fact about him - that God hears and answers prayers of those who trust Him. Proverbs 25.1 records that "men of Hezekiah king of Judah copied out" some of the proverbs of Solomon. Almost all of chs.29-32 of 2 Chronicles show beyond question that Hezekiah deserved the entire honour that he was given.

2 CHRONICLES 33

Manasseh's Reign

Introductory

Manasseh in his wickedness is a stark contrast to Hezekiah in his godliness. Thiele, in his careful study, *A Chronology of the Hebrew Kings*, suggests that Manasseh began reigning when he was twelve as a co-regent with his father Hezekiah for ten years. If Thiele is right, Manasseh's departure from God is all the more reprehensible for it would mean that he had his godly father with him until he was 22 years of age. Instead of following the good example of his father, he followed the wicked example of his grandfather Ahaz. Manasseh was the wickedest of all the kings of Judah and the one most responsible for Judah's going into captivity (2 Kings 21.10-16; 23.26-27; 24.3-4; Jer 15.4).

The first ten verses of this chapter follow closely 2 Kings 21.1-10 but the rest of the account in Kings is very different from the Chronicler's record. The writer of 2 Kings, guided by the Holy Spirit, focused on the depth of Manasseh's sins, which made the exile certain. He did not include the account of Manasseh's repentance. The Chronicler, likewise guided by the Spirit, did record his repentance, in keeping with his purpose to encourage the returning exiles. It is possible that the writer of the Chronicles had sources that the writer of 2 Kings did not have. All historians, then and now, are discriminating in their reliance on the records available to them. The Chronicler and the writer of Kings were both extremely selective in their use of material. The writer of Kings emphasized that God was righteous in bringing about the captivity because of Manasseh's wickedness. There is no contradiction. The Chronicler supplements the record of the Kings.

What an encouragement for those who had come back from the Babylonian exile (to whom the Chronicler is writing). Just as they had been captive for their sins in Babylon, so Manasseh was captive for his sins in Babylon. Just as he was restored to the land, so they had been restored to the land. Manasseh's repentance is overwhelmingly remarkable - even more so than his wickedness. Gaebelein writes, "Jewish tradition often refers to Manasseh's conversion as the greatest encouragement to repentant sinners".

In the New Testament, there are records of how, when, and where thousands were saved. However, there are not many saints of the Old Testament about whom we know how, when, and where they were made right with God. Manasseh is one of them, an Old Testament prodigal forgiven. Josiah, in the next chapter, is another (v.3).

Outline of Manasseh's reign

Verse 1: Manasseh's long reign.
Verses 2-8: Manasseh's sins.

Verses 9-10: Manasseh's sins summarized.
Verses 11-13: Manasseh's captivity, repentance, and restoration.
Verses 14-17: Manasseh's reforms.
Verses 18-20: Summary and conclusion.

Verse 1: Manasseh's Long Reign

Manasseh was given the same name as Joseph gave to his oldest son in Genesis 41.51. Manasseh means "made to forget", "one who forgets", or "forgetting". "This man was well named…and although he was young when he began to reign, he quickly forgot all that he should have remembered" (Scroggie). The writer of the Chronicles does not give the name of his mother (as he had done for all the previous kings except Jehoram and Ahaz), and does not give any mother's name again in his book. Manasseh reigned for 55 years, longer than any other king of Judah or Israel.

Verses 2-8: Manasseh's Sins

The first characteristic of the Chronicles in this paragraph "is that at several points Manasseh followed the direct example of Ahaz (cp. vv.2-6 with 28.2-4,25). The latter has replaced Ahab as Manasseh's model (cp. 2 Kings 21.3), which is quite appropriate since Ahaz figures directly in Chronicles (ch.28) but Ahab only indirectly (e.g. 18.1-34; 21.6)" (Selman). These verses emphasize the religious aspects of his wickedness, including idolatry (vv.3-7) and almost all forms of the occult (v.6). He did evil (v.2) like his wicked grandfather Ahaz in doing "the abominations of the heathen whom the Lord had cast out before the children of Israel" (28.3).

"Abomination" is the strongest word for God's disapproval. The Hebrew word is TOEBA (8441). It shows that they deserved to go into captivity. There is a progression of evil: in v.2, "evil"; in v.6, "much evil"; and in v.9, "They did evil more than did the nations, whom the Lord destroyed" (RV). The Chronicler in v.3 has two plurals: "Baalim" ("Baals", JND), and "groves" ("Asherahs", JND), whereas 2 Kings 21.3 has two singulars, "Baal", and "grove" ("Asherah", JND). Again in v.6, the writer has the plural, "children", whereas 2 Kings 21.6 has the singular, "son". How sad that Manasseh made his own children pass through the fire. Paganism is not only offensive to God but degrading to humanity. The Chronicler's use of the plurals may be intended to emphasize Manasseh's wickedness.

In these verses "God's promise about the temple (vv.4,7-8) and the extent of Manasseh's evil (vv.6,9) are both mentioned twice" (Selman). Manasseh probably did not feel the slightest shame as he sinned publicly and conspicuously. In v.6 he did most of the things forbidden in Deuteronomy 18.10-12, all abominations to the Lord. Almost the whole field of occult activity is covered. Manasseh did so many things unworthy of the Lord's name (vv.4,7). In v.7, Williams considers "a graven image of the idol" (RV) to be the most debased of all forms of idolatry. He gives details as to why this was so particularly offensive. Manasseh set it right in the house of God as if that was where it belonged. It seems as if the Holy Spirit guided the Chronicler to place this at the end of Manasseh's sins as a tremendously tragic climax. In all that he did he was provoking the Lord to anger.

"What Manasseh began to practise was a form of religious pluralism, not unlike the pluralism of our own day...This fallacy is possible even today because relativism has been widely taught in our schools, and people no longer believe that there are any criteria by which truth can be determined...One of the problems of pluralism is that when people are in a crowd and 'everyone is doing it' they feel safe. What they fail to realize is that death is a personal experience that each of us must face alone...Our society has cut itself off from the truth...Truth, we are told, 'is relative and there is no such thing as absolute truth'" (Barber).

Verses 9-10: Manasseh's Sins Summarized

What a summary! In v.2, he had done "like unto the abominations of the heathen, whom the Lord had cast out (YARASH – 3423) before the children of Israel". But even more, he not only did that himself but he "made Judah and the inhabitants of Jerusalem to err, and to do worse than the heathen". The writer of Kings does not state whom he seduced, but the writer of Chronicles says specifically, "Judah and the inhabitants of Jerusalem" (v.9).

"The verb 'destroyed' (SHAMAD – 8045) in v.9 is an intensification of 'cast out' in v.2. It is a hint that not merely loss of land, but loss of life would be a fitting reprisal for the way that the king and the people spurned their religious heritage" (Leslie C. Allen). In v.10, the Lord spoke to them all, but they would not hearken. 2 Kings 21.11-15 states what the Lord said. The Lord's message was not heeded. They were more stubborn and perverse than the people of Nineveh (Mt 12.41). Refusing to hearken to God speaking is the ultimate sin in provoking Him as Asa and Joash found (16.7-10; 24.20-22), and as is narrated in the summary of 36.15-16 where the reasons for their being taken into captivity are given.

The writer of 2 Kings records that much innocent blood was shed (21.16), immediately after he states what the Lord said to them. "The tradition may be true which says, Isaiah 'was sawn asunder'...with a wooden saw. Josephus does not mention this, though he does say that Manasseh 'barbarously slew all the righteous men that were among the Hebrews. Nor would he spare the prophets'" (Knapp). As wicked as Manasseh's grandfather Ahaz was, there is no record that he shed innocent blood except for that of his own children in the fire (28.3). Manasseh's shedding innocent blood has much to do with why they eventually had to go into captivity as 2 Kings 24.4 records: "And also for the innocent blood that he shed: for he filled Jerusalem with innocent blood; which the Lord would not pardon". When Manasseh repented God forgave him for all his personal sins but there were still national consequences to some of his forgiven sins.

Verses 11–13: Manasseh's Captivity, Repentance, and Restoration

Some commentators have questioned whether the Chronicler's account in vv.11-20 is truly historical. "There is valuable circumstantial evidence which has persuaded a good number of scholars that historical events underlie the Chronicler's narrative. The Assyrian records mention Manasseh. He is listed among twenty-two kings…who were summoned to Nineveh…to bring building materials for a new palace" (Thompson). "In the Assyrian records is a report of Necho, an Egyptian king who was carried captive to Nineveh and sent back to his throne…This incident, which all critics accept, is almost a parallel case to Manasseh's experience" (The Zondervan Pictorial Bible Dictionary).

"Wherefore", because of the wickedness of Manasseh and his people and their refusal to hearken to God's Word, the Lord sent the Assyrians, who took Manasseh "among the thorns" (v.11), or "with hooks" (RV margin). Where other historians see political movements, the Chronicler often sees the hand of God behind the secondary causes of events. "Assyrian kings sometimes thrust a hook into the nostrils of their captives and so led them about, a practice illustrated in many Assyrian reliefs in the British museum" (Curtis & Masden). A nose ring completely humiliated Manasseh before his captors as he was treated as a wild animal and taken to Babylon. "Recent discoveries reveal Babylon, and not Nineveh, was at this time the residence of the Assyrian Monarch" (Williams). This verse is a warning to all. If one will not humble oneself before God's Word, God may choose to speak more drastically even as he did with Manasseh.

"It is interesting to note that Manasseh's fate was not in the hands of the Assyrians. God was sovereignly orchestrating events to achieve his purpose…he was bound with bronze shackles (possibly reserved for royal persons) and taken to Babylon" (Barber). It was the Lord who also brought the Assyrians against them (v.11) and it was the Lord his God who brought him again to Jerusalem (v.13).

Manasseh's grandfather Ahaz was delivered into the hand of the king of Assyria and into the hand of the king of Israel because of his sins. He was not as responsive to God's dealings as was Manasseh (28.22). In contrast to Ahaz, Manasseh humbled himself greatly before the God of his father (v.12). That was fitting since he was guilty of great wickedness. His captivity brought him to his senses. God never sends trouble to make a person bitter but rather to make them better. Some do get bitter because they react like Ahaz. Manasseh took God's dealings wisely. His thinking was like that of the Psalmist in Psalm 119.75: "I know, O Lord, that thy judgments are right, and that thou in faithfulness hast afflicted me". Just as Joseph's ten older brothers in the adversity of being imprisoned paid attention to their consciences, so Manasseh's conscience must have been activated to remember his godly father's teaching and the warnings of the prophets. Joseph's ten older brothers said, "We are verily guilty concerning our brother, in that we saw the anguish of his soul, when he besought us, and we would not hear; therefore is this distress come upon us" (Gen 42.21).

2 Chronicles 7.14 illustrates a theme of the Chronicler. This is the most outstanding example of the many instances of humbling in the book. Verses like Luke 14.11; 18.14; James 4.6, and 1 Peter 5.5 are an added encouragement for believers to humble themselves before God. When Manasseh humbled himself the Lord God of his fathers truly became his God.

After his prayer was answered he knew that the Lord was God (v.13). The Hebrew word for "know" (YADA - 3045) is the same as in 2 Kings 5.15 when Naaman said after being miraculously cleansed of leprosy, "now I know that there is no God in all the earth, but in Israel". Such knowledge is not gained by understanding alone, but it is acquaintance with the living Person, like the knowledge which loving persons have of each other. This word "know" carries the idea of experience. Thank God that He responds graciously and wondrously to genuine repentance. This is one of the greatest miracles of grace on record. What an illustration of the exceeding riches of His grace to the most ungodly (Eph 2.7). Manasseh forgiven calls to mind Micah 7.18: "Who is a God like unto thee, that pardoneth iniquity, and passeth by the transgression of the remnant of his heritage? he retaineth not his anger forever, because he delighteth in mercy".

Verses 14-17: Manasseh's Reforms

The first words of v.14, "Now after this", indicate that Manasseh did these reforms after returning from Babylon. These verses show how their land was healed in response to Manasseh humbling himself greatly before the God of his fathers. Manasseh by his wickedness undid the good his father had done and now, after his repentance, he tried to undo the wrongs that he had done. Of course, any of the innocent persons he had killed could not be brought to life again. Since it is very likely that he humbled himself late in life there was a limit to what he could do.

The Chronicler's record of Manasseh's repentance is a partial answer to a problem in 2 Kings 21. Since Manasseh was so bad why did Judah not go into captivity sooner? If the writer of the Kings knew of his repentance he may not have included it since there was so little that could be accomplished in reform. The following all believe Manasseh's captivity, humbling and restoration were late in his life: Barber, Bennett, Edersheim, Eerdman, Rawlinson, and Shultz. The following four writers specifically say it took place five or six years before the end of Manasseh's life: Ellison, Payne, Selman, and Unger.

The healing of the land promised in 7.14 is seen in three ways: building and extending Jerusalem's city walls, organizing the army outside Jerusalem (both in v.14), and restoring true worship (vv.15-16). Building and repairing are mentioned often in 2 Chronicles in association with spiritual prosperity (11.5-10; 14.6-7; 17.12; 26.9; 27.3-4). "Reorganizing the army (v.14b) is another common feature of faithful kings in Chronicles (cp. 11.5-12; 14.6; 17.12-19)" (Selman).

Manasseh removed the idols (v.15) in keeping with turning "to God from idols to serve the living and true God" (1 Thess 1.9). He repaired the altar and offered thank offerings (v.16). This shows that Manasseh was grateful to God for His grace to him. Similarly, the Apostle Paul was thankful to God for His grace to one who was before "a blasphemer" against the Son of God, "a persecutor" of the people of God, and "injurious" to the work of God. Paul writes that he "obtained mercy, because I did it ignorantly in unbelief" (1 Tim 1.13). He considers himself the chief of sinners (v.15). John Newton expressed his gratitude in his famous hymn:

> Amazing grace, how sweet the sound,
> That saved a wretch like me!
> I once was lost but now am found,
> Was blind but now I see.

Every believer can thank God for His grace and say like the psalmist David, "He hath not dealt with us after our sins; nor rewarded us according to our iniquities" (Ps 103.10). How wonderful to read that God is going to take delight forever in the "exceeding riches of his grace in his kindness toward us through Christ Jesus" (Eph 2.7). What a contrast to 2 Chronicles 33.16, where Manasseh commanded Judah to serve the Lord God of Israel, is found in v.9 when he made them all to err. In v.17 they were sacrificing in the high places which was forbidden in Deuteronomy 12.13-14. Now it is "unto the Lord their God only" which is much less serious than sacrificing to idols. See the Appendix at the close of chapter 30.

Verses 18-20: Summary and Conclusion

This is an expansion of the summary given in 2 Kings 21.17-18. The most important difference is that the Chronicler emphasizes the importance of the change in Manasseh in order to rightly understand his reign, especially his prayer (vv.19,12-13) and his humbling of himself (v.19, RV, and v.12). The writer reminds us of the sins of Manasseh, but he wants his readers to understand that God's grace triumphed over Manasseh's sins. The Lord's desire then was, as now, "not willing that any should perish, but that all should come to repentance" (2 Pet 3.9). The Lord wanted to bring him back by the ministry of seers (vv.10,18). When he and his people would not respond the Lord sent him to Babylon, where he humbled himself, prayed, and was entreated of God. "Josephus says that all the rest of his time he was so changed for the better that he was looked upon as a very happy man" (Matthew Henry).

The Chronicler's final recording of his sin is a reminder that no person is so bad that they cannot be welcomed back to God. The first part of Manasseh's reign is a warning and the last part is an encouragement.

Rossier has an interesting suggestion for v.20: "Only Manasseh after his repentance seems to me to have personally chosen the place of his burial, feeling himself unworthy of the royal sepulchres. If this is so, it adds a touching feature of his humiliation".

Amon's reign

Introductory

This takes into account the material in 2 Kings 21.18-26. In 2 Kings it seems to be more a sequel to the account of Manasseh but in 2 Chronicles the account of Amon is significant because of two expressions that do not occur in 2 Kings. Both expressions are found in v.23: "he humbled not himself before the Lord, as Manasseh his father had humbled himself", and "Amon trespassed more and more". Selman links the three kings in chs.33-35 together regarding repentance. Manasseh repented, Amon did not, and Josiah did (34.27).

Amon's father reigned longer than any other king of Israel or Judah, but Amon only reigned two years. His reign was "short and sinful". He did wickedly like his father, but the Spirit of God guided the Chronicler to record in v.23, "And (he) humbled not himself before the Lord, as Manasseh his father had humbled himself". That indicates that God holds persons responsible for knowing of His dealings with their relatives, especially parents and grandparents. Manasseh did not humble himself until about 60 years of age. Amon may have thought that he could have his fling and repent late in life like his father, but such an opportunity never came. He died at 24 years of age. Something similar is seen in the fifth chapter of Daniel. Daniel reminded King Belshazzar of God's dealing with his grandfather Nebuchadnezzar in humbling him in vv.18-21. Then Daniel drove it home to Belshazzar's conscience in v.22: "And thou his son, O Belshazzar, hast not humbled thine heart, though thou knewest all this".

Outline of Amon's reign

Verse 21: Amon's name.
Verse 22: Amon undoing the good of his father's reform.
Verse 23: Amon's wickedness.
Verse 24: Amon's assassination.
Verse 25: Amon's successor.

Verse 21: Amon's Name

Amon's name is identical to that of an Egyptian deity, the chief object of worship at Thebes. His father gave him that name when he was doing wickedly. He is the only Jewish king who bears the name of a foreign deity (Bennett). Just as Manasseh could not undo all the evil he had done in Judah, even so he could not go back and change the son he had raised to be a pagan. There are sometimes serious consequences even to forgiven sin as in Manasseh's case.

Verse 22: Amon Undoing the Good of his Father's Reform

Amon did wickedly as his father did before his repentance. There is no record that he shed innocent blood like his father. When his father tried to undo some of the evil that he had done, "he took away the strange gods, and the idol out of the house of the Lord, and all the altars" casting them out of the city (v.15). Since Manasseh did not burn them with fire (as Deuteronomy 7.5 says should have been done), it was easy for Amon to bring them back into use. So Amon undid most of the good his father had done in the closing years of his reign, showing the great necessity for Josiah to purge the land of idolatry.

Verse 23: Amon's Wickedness

He literally "multiplied trespass" (AV margin). It seems that "he tried to show how much evil could be compressed into a little time...He made no secret of his departure...He revelled in trespass" (Parker).

Verse 24: Amon's Assassination

Amon was assassinated as a result of an insurrection in the palace but not among the people. Amon rebelled against God and his own servants rebelled against him. He met the same fate as Joash (24.25) and Amaziah (25.27). In both of these cases the conspiracy was associated with the judgment of God and the assassination of Amon seems to be of the same nature.

Verse 25: Amon's Successor

The unexpected death of Amon led to a crisis. The people of the land slew all the assassins. They acted decisively in making Josiah king in his stead. They thus perpetuated the Davidic dynasty as in 22.1 and 26.1. They did so again in 36.1.

2 CHRONICLES 34

Josiah's Reign

Introductory

Josiah was the last good king of Judah. His name means "given of Jehovah". "This is suggestive. Such a pious and conscientious king was a priceless gift to the people of Judah at a critical juncture" (Fereday). He was the fulfillment of a prophecy given over 300 years before by the man of God of Judah in 1 Kings 13.2. Cyrus, king of Persia, was also named about 150 years before his birth (Is 44.28; 45.1). Josiah was the last king to be buried in Jerusalem. He was the only king who had more than one son to reign after him. He had three sons to follow him after his reign.

Since Josiah was so tender and humbled himself when the Word of God was read to him (34.27), it is easy to understand how he excelled in going according to all the Word of God (2 Kings 23.25). Hezekiah excelled in trusting God (2 Kings 18.5). There was no Passover like the one Hezekiah kept since the days of Solomon (30.26). But for the Passover Josiah kept there was none like it since the days of Samuel the prophet (35.18). It was necessary to go further back in history to find a Passover as close to God's Word as the one Josiah kept.

Josiah's reforms in 2 Kings are distinguished from any taken by earlier kings of Judah. But in Chronicles the distinctiveness of his reform is diminished somewhat, partly because the Chronicler records a larger number of earlier reforms and partly because the writer emphasizes the importance of Hezekiah's reform. Josiah's reformation is like his great grandfather Hezekiah's, but Rodgers draws attention to the fact that Josiah deserves a higher place in esteem than merely as an imitator of Hezekiah. His purging of the land was more thorough and more extensive than Hezekiah's reform. Whitcomb gives an amazing list of twelve things accomplished during Josiah's reform movement. All the idolatrous influences that had been allowed to accumulate in Israel, in Jerusalem, and in the Temple courts are astounding. Most striking perhaps is Josiah's destruction of the high places of idolatry (2 Kings 23.13) which Solomon had made for his heathen wives in 1 Kings 11.5-8. They must have been spared by even the best of the kings before Josiah!

Both Kings and Chronicles focus almost exclusively on the great religious reformation of Josiah. Both agree that the climax was in the eighteenth year of Josiah, and the Chronicler makes it clear that he actually began the reformation six years earlier. The reformation began in the 12th year of Josiah's reign and Jeremiah was called by God in the next year (Jer 1.2). Jeremiah may have been an encouragement to the comprehensive and extensive nature of the reform. Although the reformation was very thorough, it was almost entirely external and never effected any real change in the hearts of most of the people. This is clear from Jeremiah

3.10: "Judah hath not turned unto me with her whole heart, but feignedly, saith the Lord", and also their very quick return to idolatry after Josiah's death.

Josiah's humbling himself before God, seeking God and honouring the temple as the means of proper worship, and the Word of God as the rule book of life were all ideals important to the Chronicler and so he commends these things to his readers.

"Despite the inevitability of the disaster (vv.24-25,28), God's covenant can still be renewed by people who take His Word seriously" (Selman).

Outline of Chapter 34

Verses 1-2:	Introduction.
Verses 3-7:	The removal of idolatry from Jerusalem, Judah, and Israel.
Verses 8-13:	The Temple repairs.
Verses 14-15:	The discovery of the book of the law.
Verses 16-18:	Shaphan brings the book and reads it to the king.
Verses 19-21:	Josiah's response.
Verses 22-28:	Huldah the prophetess.
Verses 29-33:	Covenant renewal.

Verse 1- 2: Introduction

He "walked in the ways of David his father". This introduces a link between Josiah and David. In the next verse (v.3) Josiah follows David in seeking David's God (and also in vv.21 and 26) where the same word for "seek" is translated "inquire". Those three verses are unparalleled in Kings. They indicate that the kingdom was his first priority (Mt 6.33). The Hebrew word for "seek" and "inquire" is (DARASH - 1875). Josiah follows David also in taking responsibility for the temple (v.8) and obeying God (v.31).

Manasseh may have tried to help his grandson spiritually during the last five years of his life. Josiah was six when Manasseh died. A few kindred spirits who lived at Jerusalem at the time when he was sixteen may have encouraged him: Hilkiah the high priest, Shaphan the scribe, Huldah the prophetess, and possibly Zephaniah the prophet. Zephaniah was Josiah's own cousin, the descendant of Hezekiah (Zeph 1.1). It is not likely that Jeremiah had any influence on Josiah at this time since Jeremiah lived in Anathoth in Benjamin and did not receive his call till five years afterwards, in the thirteenth year of the reign of Josiah (Jer 1.2; 25.3).

Josiah's reign has several parallels to the reign of Joash. Both began to reign as boys. Both collected funds for temple repairs and both were involved in the actual repairs. Both stood in the king's place in the temple precincts (34.31; 23.13). There was a covenant made in the temple during the reigns of each (34.29-33; 23.16). A very important contrast between the two is that Joash was true to the Lord only as long as Jehoiada lived

(24.2,17-18). It is recorded in (34.33) about Josiah: "And all his days they departed not from following the Lord, the God of their fathers".

Besides Josiah, the only other kings compared favourably to David are Asa (1 Kings 15.11), Jehoshaphat (2 Chr 17.3), and Hezekiah (29.2). We also read in 2 Chronicles 11.17 that during the reign of Rehoboam, "three years they walked in the way of David and Solomon". Josiah is the only king of whom we read such a high commendation: "and (he) declined neither to the right hand nor to the left" (v.2). That expression, "to the right hand or to the left", is found at least eight times in God's Word (Deut 5.32; 17.20; 28.14; Josh 1.7; 23.6; Prov 4.27; 2 Kings 22.2). The Deuteronomy 17.20 reference is in the context of instruction for the future kings of Israel. These passages emphasize the importance of complete undeviating obedience to God's Word. Going beyond the Word of God and falling short of the Scriptures are both deviations and equally problematic. Enthusiastic newly saved people may have a tendency towards going beyond the Word of God. Older believers may have a tendency towards falling short of what God's Word says. May the Lord help each one to be like Josiah, and, better yet, to be more like the only perfectly balanced person who ever lived, our Lord Jesus who was "full of grace and truth" (Jn 1.14). He was the true meal offering of the fine flour with no unevenness in it. He had every desirable characteristic in perfect blend.

Verses 3-7: The Removal of Idolatry from Jerusalem, Judah, and Israel

The author of Chronicles lovingly gives the chronology of the spiritual progress of Josiah's reformation. In the eighth year of his reign, when he was sixteen, he began to seek after the God of David his father. That sounds like a New Testament conversion with the time given. Other kings who sought God include David (1 Chr 28.8-9), Solomon (2 Chr 1.5), Asa (14.4,7), Jehoshaphat (22.9), Uzziah (26.5), and Hezekiah (31.21). Josiah began seeking God personally and privately which led to his public purging of the land. "While he was yet young" may be intended to explain why Josiah did not take public action at that time. He was most likely still ruling under the constraint of a regent.

Josiah began his great reform movement when he was 20; this seems to be when he reached the age of majority. In 31.17 it is given as the age when the Levites began their life work. Now Josiah could rule by himself. This brought to a fruitful climax his aspirations that began when he was sixteen. Many Christians look back to their teenage years when they first were saved and decisions were made that determined the way they would live in their later lives.

The reform of his grandfather Manasseh may have had a part in motivating Josiah. The horror of the two years of wicked reign by his father and Amon's subsequent assassination may have made him resolve to do differently. Here is a young man of 20 who set out to accomplish great things for God. There is great encouragement in the Word of God for young men. All of the following were young men when God began to use them: Joseph, Samuel, Jonathan, David, Elihu, Daniel and his three companions, Timothy, and Titus, as well as Hezekiah and Josiah. Jeremiah and Zechariah (among the prophets) were both young when first spoken to by God.

It took real courage for Josiah to destroy all the idols of the land. In Judges 6.25-27, when the Lord wanted Gideon to break down his father's altar of Baal, Gideon was afraid to do it in the daytime so he did it at night instead. Josiah was very much alone in his purging the land. In these five verses "he" is mentioned seven times. In v.4 we read, "And they brake down the altars of Baalim in his presence". The wording suggests that they might not have done it had he not been present to see that they did. Wilcock especially emphasizes how alone Josiah was in his reform. In contrast, in Jehoshaphat's day at a time of crisis we read, "out of all the cities of Judah they came to seek the Lord…all Judah stood before the Lord…all Judah… fell before the Lord, worshiping the Lord" (20.4,13,18). In Hezekiah's day, there are at least seven verses in ch.29-31.1 that show that God's people were supporting Hezekiah's action. Jeremiah 3.10, quoted earlier, shows that only a small number were with Josiah in heart.

In vv.3-5 Josiah began with Judah and Jerusalem. All servants should begin near home. One is reminded of Moses and the golden calf (Ex 32.20) in v.4, where Josiah broke the idols in pieces and made dust of them. In his zeal for God (v.6) he extended his purging as far as Napthali on the northern border of the land. Since the decline of Assyria, Josiah was caretaker for Israel at least at first, possibly as a vassal of Assyria. He wanted all of Israel for the Lord. Hezekiah was concerned for the spiritual welfare of the northern kingdom and Josiah followed his example but in much more favourable circumstances. Verse 7 says, "throughout all the land of Israel". The expression "land of Israel" is found only five times in Chronicles, once each during the reign of Solomon (2.17), Hezekiah (30.25), Josiah (34.7), and twice during that of David (1 Chr 13.2; 22.2).

God's people are not called upon to be iconoclasts (as Josiah was), yet there are lessons for today from these verses. Demetrius the silversmith complained to his fellow craftsmen in Acts 19.26, "this Paul hath persuaded and turned away much people, saying that they be no gods, which are made with hands". After the uproar in the theatre the town clerk dismissed them saying, "these men…are neither robbers of churches, nor yet blasphemers of your goddess" (Acts 19.37). That shows clearly that Paul often spoke against idols but he never once spoke against Diana of the Ephesians. This is a valuable lesson. It should be made clear in preaching the gospel that no one is saved by religion, but one should not pick out one particular religious group to ridicule from the platform. Paul wrote in 1 Corinthians 10.14, "flee from idolatry", and in Colossians 3.5, "Mortify…covetousness, which is idolatry". One may not be in danger of having idol statues but could have idols in the heart. The Apostle John wrote in 1 John 5.21, "Little children, keep yourselves from idols". Anything today that takes the place in the affections of that which belongs to our Lord Jesus is an idol.

Notice the order of Josiah's action. First he purged the land and the temple. Then he repaired the house of the Lord his God. Only after those two things did he want to call the people to keep the Passover. As in Josiah's day, purging is necessary if God is to be glorified. One should not be concerned about purging defilement in religious places outside but should be concerned about purging defilement within. 1 Corinthians 5.7 states, "Purge out therefore the old leaven". The Corinthians put away the wicked person, so Paul could write in 2 Corinthians 7.11, "In all things ye have approved yourselves to be clear in this matter". There should also be a cleansing in our individual lives continually. 2 Corinthians 7.1 says, "Having therefore these promises, dearly beloved, let us cleanse ourselves from all filthiness of the flesh and spirit, perfecting holiness in the fear of God". (See comments on this verse at 29.5.) This is especially necessary in assembling together with other believers at the Lord's Supper. There should be self-examination beforehand (1 Cor 11.28).

Verses 8-13: The Temple Repairs

"Unfortunately, the sense of continuing action is obscured...by the translation 'when he had purged', but the Hebrew clearly means 'to purge'" (Selman). Most translations miss the true meaning. The NIV translation for v.8 is good: "In the eighteenth year of Josiah's reign, to purify the land and the temple, he sent...to repair the temple of the Lord his God". Young's Literal Translation of the Bible comes closest to that of all the translations reviewed. Josiah takes the initiative for the repairs in the eighteenth year of his reign. Similarly in time past other kings - David, Solomon, Joash, Hezekiah - took the initiative for construction and repairs.

The other two officials with Shaphan in v.8 are not mentioned in the parallel account in Kings that notes that the keepers of the door gathered the money of the people. The Chronicler, as he delights to do, is more specific in naming the Levites as the ones who collected the money. In his concern for all Israel, he tells us that the money was from "Manasseh and Ephraim and of all the remnant of Israel". "All the remnant of Israel" (v.9) has no equivalent term in 2 Kings 22. A sense of common feeling, with the Chronicler's own readers, is implied. The Levites may have gone with Josiah as he purged the northern part of Israel and collected money from them as well as collecting some at the temple. Israel united is seen in principle during Hezekiah's reign and is repeated here. In v.21, when Josiah sent to enquire of the Lord, he said, "...for them that are left in Israel and in Judah". Here in v.9, Myers suggests that the Chronicler may be "stressing his favourite theme of all Israel having a share in the temple as the true centre of worship".

Here in v.12 we read that "the men did the work faithfully". "We gather from vv.8-13, that the relations between the carpenters and the masons and their overseers were cordial and harmonious. These verses make delightful reading, and they remind us of how agreeably Boaz and his harvestmen wrought together (Ruth 2.4)" (Fereday). It is also a reminder of the days when Nehemiah built the wall when "the people had a mind to work" (Neh 4.6). The words written to slaves in Colossians 3.23, "And whatsoever ye do, do it heartily, as to the Lord, and not unto men", have an application to every believer.

There were two good reasons why the repair was successful. First, as noted above, the workmen did their work faithfully. The other reason for the success was the effective leadership of the Levites (vv.12-13). This is something that the Chronicler emphasizes but not the writer of Kings. It is not necessary to think that the Levites used their musical skill in construction work. The reference to their expertise in music could be looked upon as a passing comment similar to the reference to the occupation of the Levites in the next verse. The emphasis is on the supervising role of the Levites that is important to the writer of the Chronicles. The Levites gave ample leadership to all the work that was being done.

Verses 14-15: The Discovery of the Book of the Law

The Chronicler follows 2 Kings 22.8-20 very closely but he adds the first verse of this section (v.14) to show why he is including all these verses. In Kings the account of the reform is after the discovery of the book of the law. But the Chronicler shows us that the reform began six years before the discovery of the book of the law. "Verse 14 emphasizes that it is only because of the repairs of the temple that the book was found in the first place. So the Chronicler regards the finding of the book of the law as a reward for Josiah's faithfulness and an incentive for greater acts of obedience" (Williamson). He delights to show repeatedly that righteousness is rewarded. The finding of the scroll is the result of the reform rather than its primary cause.

Hilkiah the high priest found the book in the house of the Lord. The discovery is introduced twice: first, by an objective report in v.14 and then, by a personal testimony in v.15. Sailhammer makes the interesting and noteworthy observation: "As the temple once protected the house of David (22.10-12), so now it protected the Law of Moses. The temple had preserved from destruction the two foundational pillars of Israel's faith, the law and king". Hilkiah delivered the book to Shaphan who did wisely in reading it (2 Kings 22.8). How important it is for every child of God to read the Word of God. The Word of God can save from wrong doctrine and wrong deeds. Psalm 119.11 states, "Thy word have I hid in my heart, that I may not sin against thee". Our Lord Jesus said to the Sadducees in Matthew 22.29, "Ye do err; not knowing the scriptures".

"The English translation of the title as Book of the Law is somewhat misleading. For example, it was almost certainly a written scroll (cp. Jer 36.2;

Ezek 2.9- 10). Also 'law' (TORA) is better understood as 'teaching, instruction', so that a better alternative might be 'Scroll of the Teaching' or even 'Scroll of (God's) Instruction'" (Selman). Spurrell has "scroll" instead of "book".

Many commentators believe the book found was Deuteronomy or at least a part of Deuteronomy. Dillard gives seven features that favour the identification with Deuteronomy. Anyone interested might appreciate Thompson's comments on "The Date and Authorship of Deuteronomy" (he has 22 pages) in The Tyndale Old Testament Commentaries.

Finding the book was a crucial turning point for Josiah and his kingdom. It shows the importance of the Word of God for any revival and even for daily living. Long gives good applications as to how the effect of the authority of the Scriptures can be lost today. While there are plenty of Bibles in our day and good commentaries on them, the Bible can be lost in more ways than by misplacing it. He quotes H. W. Soltau (one of the men in the movement recovering assembly truth in the early 19th century) from his booklet, *They Found it Written*: "...men who searched the Scriptures with great diligence and were so driven that, as they found something that had been lost to them, they immediately started following it". Long finishes by saying, "True revival will always spring from obedience to God's Word, and will produce more obedience to that Word". Fereday makes a good observation when he says, "One of the happiest results of the Protestant Reformation was that the Scriptures became available to the people in many lands. Once more men were allowed to listen to the voice of their God apart from human interpolations".

Verses 16-18: Shaphan Brings the Book and Reads it to the King

It seems as if Hilkiah the high priest esteemed the book of the law more than Shaphan the scribe, at least at first. Hilkiah referred to it in v.15 as, "*the* book". Shaphan only referred to it in v.18 as, "*a* book". Shaphan first told the king of the obedience of the servants, overseers, and workmen. "He says nothing of the newfound treasure as yet. It may not have been a treasure in his eyes. Like many at the present time, he was more occupied with 'workmen' and 'money' than with God's book, which He has 'magnified', not merely above all Christian work or missionary enterprise (though these have their place), but above all His name (Ps 138.2). Shaphan did not despise the book, but he had not yet, like many a modern scribe, realized the importance of that blessed volume" (Knapp).

Verses 19-21: Josiah's Response

In v.19, the Word of God worked effectually on Josiah as it did years later on the Thessalonians (1 Thess 2.13). When Josiah heard God's description of their apostasy and the terrible consequences of God's wrath, he was utterly overwhelmed with holy horror and so he rent his clothes. The rending or tearing of garments was a sign of great distress (e.g. Gen 37.34; 2 Kings 19.1; Job 1.20). It is difficult to imagine how a king of David's line did not know about this book of the law, especially since God had commanded each king in Deuteronomy 17.18-19 to "write him a copy of this law in a book…And it shall be with him, and he shall read therein all the days of his life". But it is easy to believe that in the first 50 years of wicked apostasy in the reign of Manasseh it was hidden in the Temple. It may also have been hidden during Hezekiah's reign when the kingdom was in danger of invasion. During later persecutions, scrolls were hidden in caves like those near the Dead Sea where so many priceless manuscripts have been found (Whitcomb).

"Josiah was so filled with awe at what he heard (cp. Deut 30.15-20) that he burst into tears and tore his clothes as a sign of his deep grief. When he regained his composure his first thought was how to avert the disaster that threatened his people. He was aware of the history of the kings and knew of other times when the nation had entered into a solemn covenant with the Lord (cp. 29.10; 30.8; 32.26; 33.13). The repentance of the people had been accompanied by a postponement of the judgment, and Josiah hoped that God would do the same again" (Barber).

Josiah quickly realized that what he was hearing was the Word of God even though Shaphan only referred to it as a book and did not repeat the words that Hilkiah had said about it - "I have found the book of the law". He also responded by sending "to enquire of the Lord". "Though 'enquire' translates the same word as 'seek' in v.3, here (and in v.26) it has the sense of asking for specific guidance rather than describing Josiah's basic orientation towards God" (Selman). Other kings received messages from God; but Josiah actually and urgently sought for a message from God. He immediately felt his need to consult God.

"One of the strongest links with Deuteronomy is its repeated references to a Book of the Law (Deut 28.61; 29.21; 30.10; 31.26; cp. Josh 1.8; 8.31,34; 23.6; 24.26). Another is the phrase 'all the curses written in' (v.24; in place of 'everything written in', 2 Kings 22.16), referring to the contents of the Book of the Law in Deuteronomy 29.20,21,27; Joshua 8.34. Further connections with Deuteronomy include the centralizing of worship (vv.3-7,33; cp. Deut 12), the centralized Passover (35.1-19; cp. Deut 16.1-8), and above all the covenant ceremony (vv.29-32; cp. Deut 31.10-13)" (Selman).

One of the persons Josiah sent to enquire of the Lord in v.20 was Ahikam who saved Jeremiah's life in Jeremiah 26.24. He was also the father of Gedaliah, the governor of Judah, after the fall of Jerusalem (Jer 40.7).

Verse 21 notes that the enquiry was also, "for them that are left in Israel and in Judah". In contrast, 2 Kings 22.13 only has "for the people, and for all Judah". The Chronicler wished to include all Israel even as he had in v.9; because he saw that the sins revealed in the book referred to all of God's people.

Verses 22-28: Huldah the Prophetess

Hilkiah the high priest and the other four officials (sent by Josiah to enquire of the Lord) went to Huldah the prophetess, the wife of Shallum the keeper of the wardrobe. Deborah (Judg 4.4), Anna (Lk 2.36), and the four daughters of Phillip (Acts 21.9) were other prophetesses of God. There are two prophetesses who opposed the things of God: Noadiah (Neh 6.14) and Jezebel (Rev 2.20). Shallum had a trusted position, probably that of making and maintaining priestly and Levitical garments. Those garments would need to be washed because the blood of the sacrifice would have been splattered on them. He may well have been the uncle of Jeremiah (Jer 32.7). Huldah lived in Jerusalem "in the second quarter" (RV). One might ask why Hilkiah and the four others with him did not go to Jeremiah or to Zephaniah? Jeremiah lived in Anathoth in Benjamin just three miles from Jerusalem. He was called to be a prophet just four years previously (Jer 1.2) and he was very young at the time (Jer 1.6). Zephaniah was also preaching, but he too was young. Neither of them was in Jerusalem at the time.

In vv.23-28 we have Huldah's authoritative message. Four times she says, "Thus saith the Lord" (vv.23,24,26,27). She was the mouthpiece of God at a critical time in the history of Judah and Israel. In v.23 she says, "Tell ye the man that sent you to me". Verses 23-25 are to "the man", and vv.26-28 are to "the king". "It is interesting that Huldah did not refer to Josiah as 'the king' in her first reference to him, but simply as 'the man'. This was not disrespectful, but apparently was God's way of emphasizing the frailty of one who, though king, needed His help desperately" (Whitcomb). Keil's comment is worth repeating: Huldah indicates "that the word announced to him applied not merely to the king, but to everyone who would heed the word, whereas the second portion of her reply showed reference to the king alone".

The first part of Huldah's message to Josiah, in vv.23-25, was very solemn. In 2 Kings 22.16 we read, "...all the words of the book", but the Chronicler has instead, "...all the curses that are written in the book" (v.24), referring especially to Deuteronomy 27-29 (and if the whole of the Pentateuch is the book found, also passages like Leviticus 26). This part of her message declares that the exile is certain. God Himself will bring the terrible evil upon His people (vv.24,28) because they have forsaken Him (v.25). God's wrath could be turned away in Hezekiah's day (29.10; 30.8) but now it can no longer be quenched.

But the second part of Huldah's prophecy shows that hope is not altogether gone. In v.27 God greatly appreciated Josiah's tender response to His word. Humbling oneself is a key theological theme of the Chronicles. There are a number of cases: 12.6; 30.11; 32.25-26; 33.12. There are also cases where some did not humble themselves: 16.7-10; 24.20-22; 26.15-16; 33.23; 36.12. (See the extensive notes on "humbling oneself" in the introductory part of chapter 12 herein.) None of these are recorded in Kings. The only case of humbling oneself recorded in Kings is Josiah. 2 Kings 22.19 has one reference in Huldah's message to Josiah's humbling himself, but here in v.27 we have Josiah humbling himself twice recorded.

This suggests that the Chronicler is encouraging his readers to follow Josiah's example; all of which correlates with a theme of the Chronicles noted in 7.14. In keeping with 7.14 is Josiah's enquiry, asking God's will in vv.21 and 26 which develops the same verb used of his seeking God as a boy of sixteen in v.3.

Walter Kaiser, quoted by Thompson, looks on "2 Chronicles 34.1-33 in three steps centered on the theme of human humbleness:

1. humbling oneself before God (vv.1-13).
2. humbling ourselves before God's Word (vv.14-28).
3. humbling ourselves before God's people (vv.29-33)".

It is essential for each believer today to humble oneself if one wishes to live in the will of God.

Huldah, speaking for God, promised Josiah that he would be gathered to his grave in peace and would not see the evil that God was going to bring on the people. Since he died violently as a result of an arrow in battle, some suggest that part of the prophecy was not fulfilled. It is much more preferable to see that it was fulfilled in one of two ways. "For the Israelite to 'die in peace' meant to die in a state of fellowship with God as a true believer, whether in the front line of battle or at home in bed. In contrast to this, 'there is no peace, saith my God, to the wicked' in Isaiah 57.21" (Whitcomb).

Dillard gives an alternative way of seeing that Huldah's prophecy was fulfilled. "A more natural understanding does not require literary critical effort. The compilers of Kings and Chronicles apparently understood the first half of Huldah's prophecy (going to his grave in peace) as defined by the second half (not seeing the destruction of Jerusalem)".

Verses 29-33: Covenant Renewal

Josiah, like Hezekiah before him (2 Kings 20.19), was comforted that the evil would not come in his day. Both humbled themselves. But in contrast to Hezekiah, Josiah was not content that he himself would escape the coming judgment by the grace of God. He wanted others of his people also to escape. First of all, Josiah saw to it that the book of the law would be made known to as many as possible. He gathered all the people together "great and small: and he read in their ears all the words of the book of the covenant" (v.30). All people, whether young or old, whether great or small, need the Word of God all the time but especially in a time of crisis. The reading was for everyone, not just the religious leaders. The reading of the law once in every seven years (commanded in Deuteronomy 31.10-13) most likely had not been observed since Manasseh began to reign.

While vv.29-32 follow 2 Kings 23.1-3 fairly closely, the three most important changes should be noted. First, in v.30 the reading is "Levites" instead of "prophets" as in 2 Kings 23.2. Levites prophesy in 1 Chronicles 25.1-3 and 2 Chronicles 20.14. The writer of the Chronicles is noticeably favourable to the Levites. Second, in v.32, the Chronicler emphasizes that it was the king's initiative to get the people to make this commitment (contrast 2 Kings 23.3). The third change is also in v.32: "In contrast to his source (2 Kings) the Chronicler wanted to single out that 'the inhabitants of Jerusalem' were participants in the covenant ceremony (v.32). He was sensitive to the fact that they were the human targets of God's prophetic judgment against Jerusalem (vv.24,27-28)...and now divine wrath loomed over them. In their desire to avert it they penitently participated both in the pledge of commitment and in the Passover celebration (35.18)" (Leslie C. Allen).

Reading the book of the covenant was not enough for Josiah. He led all his people into a renewal of the covenant. Josiah knew that it was important for God's people to hear the Word of God because it showed why a renewal of the covenant was necessary. Other good leaders of Judah in earlier days held a special service when they and God's people pledged themselves to God: Asa (15.12-15); Jehoiada (23.3,16); and Hezekiah (29.10). Josiah accomplished this without the threat of death as in Asa's day (see 15.13).

"Josiah was a man thoroughly in earnest. He felt the power of truth in his own soul, and he could not rest satisfied until he gathered the people around him, in order that the light which had shone upon him might shine upon them likewise. He did not, he could not, rest in the fact that he was to be gathered to his grave in peace" (Mackintosh).

Heading writes, "The last three verses present the effects of the Word, on the king (v.31), on Jerusalem (v.32), and on Israel (v.33)...But there is a difference: for Josiah it was 'with all his heart'. This is not recorded of the others; for them it was mostly outward, instead of inward as in Josiah's case. It derived from the testimony of Josiah and lasted only as long as he lived (v.33; Jer 3.10) where their 'whole heart' was not set on the things of God". Heading also draws attention to the fact that the word "all" is found eleven times in vv.29-33. "It implies the necessity for moral completeness in revival and in the maintenance of its lasting effects".

"Jeremiah the prophet, who lived in Anathoth north of Jerusalem and prophesied during the reign of Josiah, sensed the people's apathy and indicted them for their failure to seek the Lord with all their heart (cp. Jer 3.6-10; 4.22; 5.2,7b-8,31; 6.10,13-14; 8.5-6,9b,12a; 9.3,13,23-24; etc.)" (Barber).

"The king's initiative in getting them to make the commitment is also emphasized (v.32; contrast 2 Kings 23.3). It is echoed too in v.33, along with his continuing influences for good. The result was that, just as the 'God of his father David' became 'his God' (vv.3,8); so the 'God of their fathers' became 'their God' (vv.32,33). The process of making the traditional faith one's own is beautifully repeated. Josiah taught others the lesson of a living faith he had learned earlier" (Leslie C. Allen).

The Chronicler himself has added v.33 as a summary and a conclusion to ch.34. It is noteworthy that he refers to "all the abominations out of all the countries that pertained to the children of Israel" for the Chronicler looks on all Israel as one and that all in Israel would serve the Lord their God as long as Josiah lived.

Fereday's summary is excellent. "Never was the written word more respected than by Josiah, and never was Jehovah's land and sanctuary more thoroughly purified of everything that was contrary to His will. How pleasant to God!"

Josiah demanded that all in Israel should obey the renewal covenant. The first nineteen verses of the next chapter show that they owed their obedience to God. The Passover is the great reminder of what God first did for them. Jeremiah, who prophesied during most of Josiah's reign, looked forward to a new covenant in which a revolutionary change of heart would enable them to truly respond to it. The abiding lesson of Josiah's reformation is that the heart must be changed before there is genuine service to God. Our Lord Jesus tells us that the human heart is full of all kinds of sin (Mk 7.20-23). Josiah, in contrast to the people, turned to the Lord with "all his heart" (v.31, cp. 2 Kings 23.25).

2 CHRONICLES 35

Josiah's Reign

Introductory

This chapter is in two main parts: vv.1-19 - Josiah's Passover; and vv.20-27 - Josiah's death. Kings allows only three verses for the Passover, but Chronicles nineteen. The Chronicler is dependent on Kings for vv.1a, 18a, and 19. Since the account in Chronicles follows right after the renewal of the covenant (34.29-33), it seems to form part of it. This Passover account gives a much more positive image of the reform than Kings which has so much about removing every trace of idolatry. "The Chronicler's concern is rather to encourage the right use of the *temple* (vv.2,3,8,20), its *service* (vv.2,10,15,16), and its *offerings* (vv.7,8,9,12-14,16)" (Selman).

There are five points of special interest in this Passover account:

1. The necessity of returning the ark to its rightful place (v.3).

2. The diligence of Josiah to have everything done according to the Word of God in the writings of David and Solomon (vv.4,15) and Moses (vv.6,12-13). "Just as Josiah acted on what he found written in God's Word, so the Biblical record of Jesus' Passover sacrifice at Calvary still offers a fresh dynamic for life and worship" (Selman).

The Levites fervently served all the people first (vv.11-13). Afterwards, they prepared for themselves and the priests (v.14) and then for the singers and the porters (v.15). Their prominence is of special interest to the Chronicler.

3. Everyone was in his place. The king stood in his place (34.31). The priests and the Levites were in their place (v.10). The singers and the porters were in their place (v.15). How good it is when everyone in assembly fellowship is in the place that God wants him or her to be. No one is seeking a place for which God has not fitted him or her. No one is shirking a place of responsibility for which God has fitted him or her and where he or she is needed.

4. No wonder then that there was no Passover like this one since the days of Samuel, about 500 years earlier (v.18). As noted previously there was no Passover like the one kept by Hezekiah since the days of Solomon (30.26), but it was necessary to go further back in history to find one like Josiah's because his was closer to the Word of God.

5. God wanted His people of old to keep the Passover in order to remind them of what He had done for them in delivering them. He had delivered them by the blood of the lamb from bondage and from the judgment that fell on the Egyptians. The Passover lamb is typical of Christ as 1 Corinthians 5.7 makes clear, "For even Christ our passover is sacrificed for us". "The Lord's Supper differs somewhat from the Passover in that it is not a mere memorial of a great deliverance, but a remembrance of the *Person* who wrought the deliverance for us. 'This do in remembrance of me', are our

Lord's words in Luke 22.19" (Fereday). In Luke 22.15 the Lord expressed intense desire, "With desire I have desired to eat this passover with you before I suffer". He knew with perfect divine knowledge the intensity of the suffering He would endure (Jn 18.4). We can thank God that this did not override the intensity of His desire to do His Father's will.

Outline of Chapter 35

Verses 1-6: Passover preparations.
Verses 7-9: Passover provisions.
Verses 10-15: Passover celebration.
Verses 16-19: Passover concluding summary.
Verses 20-27: Josiah's death.

Verses 1-6: Passover Preparations

The first part of v.1 is a summary of vv.1-19. This is a Passover to the Lord. John 6.4 notes, "And the passover, a feast of the Jews, was nigh". John 7.2 reads, "Now the Jews' feast of Tabernacles was at hand". Both Passover and Tabernacles were "feasts of the Jews" in contrast to Leviticus 23.2,4 - "feasts of the Lord". The question should be asked, "Are our hearts going out towards Christ and God as heartily as Josiah's heart went out to the Lord so long ago?".

"The Passover began the year for God's ancient people. It had been instituted on the night the Lord delivered them from the might of Pharaoh of Egypt, and it concluded on the day the Lord Jesus was crucified. His blood took the place of the lamb that had been slaughtered, and it is His blood that to this day covers and protects those who trust in Him" (Barber).

The Chronicler is careful to state in v.1 (omitted in Kings) that this Passover was kept on the fourteenth day of the first month. As in the days of Hezekiah, officials were appointed and encouraged before the actual Passover (29.4,5,11). Verse 2 implies that the priests required special encouragement in contrast to the eager willingness of the Levites to serve (29.34). In vv.3-6 Josiah instructs the Levites with seven imperatives. He dignifies the Levites by saying they are "holy unto the Lord" (v.3).

The instructions about "the holy ark" in v.3 are puzzling because there is no record of the ark ever being removed from its place. Faithful priests could have removed the ark at the time when Manasseh was so vehemently opposed to God. It is also possible that the ark was hidden when Judah was threatened by Assyria. Some commentators would translate the word for "Put" as "Leave". McConville suggests another possible solution: "The likeliest interpretation, therefore, is that Josiah deliberately re-enacted the placing of the ark in the temple as a symbolic gesture…as a declaration that Judah was ready to start again". This is the last historical reference to the ark in Scripture.

It was very important that the ark be restored to its rightful place before the Passover could rightly be held in Jerusalem. "But the ark spoke to God of Christ, and Josiah very properly spoke of it as 'the holy ark'. It was the most expressive of all the types of the Levitical economy: our Lord's incorruptible humanity is set forth in the shittim wood; His deity in the gold which covered it, and His accomplished sacrifice is suggested in the blood on the Mercy Seat (or propitiatory) upon which the golden cherubim looked down...Christ is God's true centre, and this must be made clear (at least in type) before the Passover could be acceptable to Jehovah" (Fereday). The ark was the very first part of the Tabernacle to be made (Ex 25.10-22). There is only one Saviour for sinners and there is only one gathering centre for saints: the same Person in both cases - our Lord Jesus Christ. We have His own words in Matthew 18.20: "For where two or three are gathered together in my name, there am I in the midst of them". The name to which we are gathered is His full name: Lord Jesus Christ. Lord speaks of His Lordship, Jesus speaks of His Person, and Christ speaks of His work. The word "gathered" is in the passive, which simply means that these two or three do not gather themselves together. Someone else is the Gatherer - the Holy Spirit. *He* would not sanction any group that is indifferent to any one of these!

In v.3 the Chronicler must have used "Levites" in the general sense, including priests, because only priests were allowed to enter the Holy Place (cp. 29.5). Josiah wanted their service to be "according to the writing of David...and according to the writing of Solomon" (v.4). He also wanted it to be "according to the word of the Lord by the hand of Moses" (v.6). Significantly, he wrote that the Levites taught "all Israel".

In vv.5-6 the Levites were given a very prominent role in the Passover. Each family grouping was to be served by a part of a Levitical family. Their service was to kill the Passover lamb and prepare it for the people while the priests took care of the blood. Although the heads of family households ordinarily killed the Passover animals (Ex 12.3–6,21), yet the practice of killing by the Levites begun at Hezekiah's Passover is now continued. In 30.17 the Levites killed the Passover lambs because some of the people were ritually unclean. The practice seems to have been normalized by the time of Josiah. When the Chronicler wrote in v.6, "according to the word of the Lord by the hand of Moses", he evidently referred to the principle of killing the Passover lamb rather than to the one who does it. He also referred forward to v.13.

Verses 7-9: Passover Provisions

Verse 7 notes that Josiah gave liberally to the people for the Passover as David did for the temple (1 Chr 29.2-5). Josiah's officials followed his generosity as in David's day when David's giving was followed by the giving of others (1 Chr 29.6-9), and so also with Hezekiah (30.24). They not only gave generously, but also willingly (v.8). In v.8 we find reference to "rulers of the house of God". That phrase is found (with "ruler" in the singular) three times (1 Chr 9.11; 2 Chr 31.13; Neh 11.11). The total number of the small cattle was 37,600 and of bulls or oxen 3,800. These totals are just about double the offerings at Hezekiah's Passover (30.24) but are much less than at the dedication of the temple (7.5).

This Passover was truly an outstanding event. The fact that bulls and oxen are mentioned indicates that provision was made not only for the Passover, but also for burnt offerings, thank offerings, and the Feast of Unleavened Bread (v.17). The writer of the Chronicles often tells of freewill, joyful giving by king and people (1 Chr 29.2-14; 2 Chr 1.6; 7.5; 17.16; 24.8-14; 29.31-36; 30.24; 31.13-14). He wanted all his readers to know the joy of giving to the Lord willingly.

Verses 10-15: Passover Celebration

"'The service was arranged' is a rare but significant phrase occurring additionally in the Old Testament only at 2 Chronicles 8.16; 29.35, meaning that everything had been done as God required. Since it appears elsewhere only in concluding summaries, its appearance in v.10 underlines the importance of preparing properly for worship, including the contribution of the king and lay leaders (vv.2,7-8)" (Selman). The NIV has "the service was arranged" in v.10 in place of the AV translation, "the service was prepared".

The priests and the Levites were in their place (v.10). The singers and the porters were in their place (v.15). See the comments in the Introductory remarks about everyone being "in his place", under the 4th point of special interest. Verse 10 reads, "according to the king's commandment". To emphasize that this Passover is celebrated according to the written Word of God, v.12 notes, "according...as it is written in the book of Moses"; in v.13, it is "according to the ordinance", and in v.15, it is "according to the commandment of David, of Asaph, and Heman, and Jeduthun the king's seer".

"Preparation for worship is especially important in Chronicles, and may be compared with the extensive preparation for the temple (1 Chr 22) and with Hezekiah's concern for self-purification at the Passover (29.15,17)" (Selman).

The Levites both killed the Passover lambs (vv.6,11) and skinned them while the priests took the blood to the altar. Having the Levites and the priests do that was an adaptation from Exodus 12 relating to the first Passover in Egypt when each household put the blood of the lamb on the two side posts and the lintel. In v.13, "they roasted the passover with fire", following the instructions given in Exodus 12.8-9. That constituted the Passover meal, which was the second part of the Passover celebrations. The first part was offering the sacrifice (vv.11-12). The distribution is given in vv.13b-15. The other holy offerings were boiled. In v.13, the Levites "divided them speedily among all the people". That emphasized their willing service. The original Passover was to be eaten in haste (Ex 12.11).

Note the element of haste in the service of the Levites. The priests had such an enormous task in offering the burnt offerings and the fat that they were busy until night. The Levites prepared for all the people first. Afterwards, they prepared for themselves and the priests and for the singers and the porters. The Chronicler emphasizes that the Levites had a significant role in every part of the celebration. The unselfish care of the Levites for others at the Passover was much more commendable than the attitude of the carnal Corinthians at the Lord's Supper (1 Cor 11.17-22, 27-34)!

"For a time the streaming of celebrants to receive the animals for the ceremony, the process of slaying and skinning the animals, and the removal of the portion used as burnt offerings turned the temple into a vast hive of activity. All these actions were largely dictated by the centralized nature of the celebration. The prescription of Exodus 12 would have been inappropriate in the temple setting…The offerings probably included fellowship offerings, the fat portions of which were burnt on the altar (Lev 3.6-16). The burnt offerings and the fat offerings (v.14) may refer to the more regular sacrifices" (Thompson).

Verses 16-19: Passover Concluding Summary

All was done "according to the commandment of king Josiah" (v.16). This summary confirms the faithfulness of Josiah. Here was a leader who wanted to get as close to God's Word as he could. He excelled in that (2 Kings 23.25). It is good for all to have that same desire. Some saints may think this would be extreme but surely all believers should want to be like our Lord Jesus who never deviated in the slightest degree from God's Word. He said to the scribes and Pharisees, "these ought ye to have done, and not to leave the other undone" (Mt 23.23). He commended them for their care in tithing, but condemned them for omitting the weightier matters of the law, judgment, mercy, and faith. He lived out in perfection all that He taught. The parameters of the Word of God guided His every thought, word, and deed to perfection.

In v.17 the Passover is combined with the Feast of Unleavened Bread as is also found elsewhere. Israelites from north and south, "the children of Israel", kept this Passover (v.17). The Chronicler records that, "there was no passover like to that…from the days of Samuel". 2 Kings 23.22 has, "from the days of the judges". Since Samuel was the last of the judges, the change of terminology is readily understandable.

"But the pinpointing of Samuel seems to have had a deeper significance. Earlier in Chronicles Samuel was represented as adopted into the Levitical clan (1 Chr 6.26-28, 33-38; cp. 1 Sam 1.1; 8.2). A Levite led the nation's worship! This provided an old precedent for Levites taking a more prominent role and having a high status in religious worship" (Leslie C. Allen) "In verse 18, 'the kings of Israel': the Chronicler omits 'and Judah'; the unity of the people of God is again his concern. This is underlined by his own addition of the closing part of the verse, the purpose of whose detail is to make the same point in a different way" (Williamson). The last verse reminds us of 34.8 and its eighteenth year, and it is almost the same as 2 Kings 23.23. That eighteenth year of Josiah's reign was an eventful year, for him and for the nation.

Hezekiah's Passover took place just after the captivity of the northern kingdom. Josiah's Passover was shortly before the captivity of the southern kingdom. "The sands of time were running out for guilty Israel, and soon their 'place and nation', would be extinguished by the righteous judgment of God, not to be restored until the appearing of Christ; yet, before the stroke fell, the remnant left in the land experienced one of the brightest moments that Israel had ever known. This was due instrumentally to the faith of the king, whose mind and heart had been reached by the Word of God, and who desired that both himself and the people might be wholly obedient thereto. All this is encouraging to us today. We are living in the late evening of the Church dispensation; but God is as willing as ever to grant blessing and joy to those whose hearts are true to Him" (Fereday). "During Josiah's Pascal week the rich helped the poor to provide all that was necessary for the great feast; the singers led the praises of the congregation; and the porters guarded the door against all intruders (vv.7,8,15). When the hearts of the people are right with God, they are generous, praiseful, and watchful. May the Holy Spirit make all these things true of us at this time also" (Fereday). In all that Josiah did that day for the Passover he manifested that he was a good leader. We have the brightest Passover kept shortly before the darkest hour!

"Thus we find three inseparable things in this chapter. They make up the greatness of this ceremony...the year of the restoration of the temple and of setting the ark in its place — the year of the discovery of the book of the law — that year the Passover was celebrated and worship was recovered. So it is in our days too. When the Assembly of the Living God, the dwelling place of God through the Spirit, is known; when the Word of God, the whole Word and nothing but the Word, is discovered and brought to light as the one and only rule for the Christian; then worship can take place in an intelligent manner around the memorial of the death and to the glory of our Lord Jesus Christ" (Rossier).

Verses 20-27: Josiah's Death

The Chronicler gives a summary of Josiah's work in the 18th year of his reign (34.8-35.19) when he writes, "After all this, when Josiah had prepared the temple..." (v.20). The renewal of temple worship and of the Passover was the climax of Josiah's reform and repairs, which the writer of the Chronicles greatly appreciated. A great contrast to this is Necho's invasion thirteen years later and Josiah's actions then.

God's people enjoyed peace and prosperity for the next thirteen years but they are passed over in silence because the people had only feignedly turned to the Lord as Jeremiah records in 3.10.

After years of pleasing God in obedience to His Word, Josiah deliberately and heedlessly went into conflict. Surely this is a warning to all. So many of the good kings of Judah did not finish as well as they began: Asa, Jehoshaphat, Joash, Uzziah, Hezekiah, and Josiah. One must be dependent on God if one wants to finish well. No matter how close one is to God and no matter for how long, the exhortation of 1 Corinthians 10.12 must be heeded: "Wherefore let him that thinketh he standeth take heed lest he fall". If any one does fall it will be because of a lack of dependence on the One who can keep from falling (Jude v.24) and even stumbling (RV).

2 Kings 23 uses only two verses to deal with Josiah's death - vv.29-30. The Chronicler has additional material to explain why he died so tragically. Necho warns Josiah, "Forbear thee from meddling with God, who is with me, that he destroy thee not" (v.21). Proverbs 26.17 has a warning: "He that passeth by, and meddleth with strife belonging not to him, is like one that taketh a dog by the ears". He did not have any business entering into this conflict when it did not concern God's people though he may have thought it did. God's people today should not be involved in the politics of the world. The believer's business is not to change the culture of the world. Instead, it is to do all one can to see others won for the Lord Jesus and their lives changed for His glory. Our Lord said to Pilate, "My kingdom is not of this world: if my kingdom were of this world, then would my servants fight, that I should not be delivered to the Jews: but now is my kingdom not from hence" (Jn 18.36). Saints can accomplish more by praying than by voting.

Verse 22 states that Josiah "hearkened not unto the words of Necho from the mouth of God". A message from God is sometimes given through a man or woman who is not a true servant of God as in Numbers 22.20,35; 23.5,16; 2 Chronicles 2.11-12; 9.8; 36.22-23 and John 11.49-51. Necho's words came true. Josiah died as a result of going to battle against him. Josiah's death was tragic, but the manner of it added to the tragedy. He had excelled in tenderly hearkening to God's Word. Now he failed in his strong point as other Old Testament saints did. There is no record at all of Josiah's spreading the matter before God. He had the good example of Hezekiah who received a disturbing letter on behalf of a mighty king and took it before the Lord (2 Kings 19.14).

It was not only tragic that he lost his life by not hearkening to God, but it is also ironic that he died like the wicked king Ahab. Ahab excelled in wickedness (1 Kings 16.30,31,33,and especially 21.25). Josiah excelled in going according to all the Word of God. Now he died like one who was so wicked. Josiah disguised himself (v.22) as Ahab had done in 18.29. This shows that in all probability he did not have a good conscience about the matter. It is not surprising that Ahab disguised himself when he heard that God had purposed that only the king of Israel should fall in battle. He wanted to avert that calamity. At the same time he encouraged Jehoshaphat to wear his royal robes and expose himself to the death Ahab wanted to avoid. But Josiah should have known better. God never needs deceit or underhand methods to sustain His truth. Josiah used subterfuge when he disguised himself. No matter how much guile characterized us in our unsaved days, we should be through with it now. "All guile" is one of five things that Peter states that we should be "laying aside" (1 Pet 2.1). We should all try to be like our blessed Lord Jesus of whom Peter writes, "Who did no sin, neither was guile found in his mouth" (1 Pet 2.22). Even though guile was sought for it could not be found in His blessed Person. The sinlessness and guilelessness of Christ not only endured the test of scrutiny, but also the test of intimacy. John who leaned on His bosom wrote of Him, "in him is no sin" (1 Jn 3.5).

Besides disguising himself as Ahab had done, there are other explicit links between them. Archers hit each of them (18.33; 35.23). Each king said, "I am sore wounded" (18.33, RV, and 35.23), and was propped up in his chariot before he died (18.34; 35.24). The climactic irony is that Josiah died like Ahab who hated the Lord (19.2). Josiah's death was out of keeping with his life, but the Chronicler manages to give a warning that for anyone to disregard a message from God is sheer folly.

Josiah knew from Huldah's prophecy that the righteous judgment of God upon Judah would not be executed while he lived. So his life was exceedingly important for Judah. Huldah's "communication should have made him act with less precipitation, and with a more exercised heart than he manifested when he went up against the King of Egypt. The knowledge that their well-deserved judgment was soon to overwhelm Israel, and that there was no remedy for their sins…ought to have prevented him going up against Pharaoh, when the latter did not attack him, and even warned him to forbear; but he would not hearken, and was lost through a hardihood which was not of God" (J. N. Darby as quoted by Fereday).

Josiah was fatally wounded at Megiddo. "Megiddo was the scene of a great victory when Barak and Deborah moved in faith against the Canaanites, for God was with them (Judg 5.19); Megiddo was now the scene of a disastrous defeat, for God was not with Josiah in his foolish enterprise" (Fereday).

"They might well mourn, for the disaster in the valley of Megiddo was the end of the Kingdom of Judah. The crash must needs come, for Jehovah had spoken of it years before; but it is sorrowful that the folly of one of the brightest saints that ever lived should have hastened it! This reflection should serve to take out of us all every vestige of self-confidence" (Fereday).

Huldah had prophesied (34.28) that Josiah would be gathered to the grave in peace. Since he died as a result of a fatal wound in battle, it may seem that this prophecy was not fulfilled. In this context see the relevant comments under 34.22-28. "This much can be said for the manner of his death: his body did not lie on the battlefield to run the risk of desecration but was buried in peace in Jerusalem (cp. the fate of Saul in 1 Chronicles 10.8-12)" (Thompson).

His servants showed their love and devotion to Josiah on the battlefield by the way they cared for him after he was wounded. They took him out of one chariot that probably was damaged and put him in another and brought him to Jerusalem. All the people loved him and mourned for him extensively (v.24). Three times mourning or lamenting are mentioned in keeping with the shocked emotions of the nation. It also shows the high esteem and respect of the people for King Josiah. This surely was a very sad day in the history of Judah.

"God was real to Josiah. The Lord never appeared to him as he had done to others in the past, but from the time Josiah set out to seek the Lord, the Lord became increasingly personal to him" (Barber).

The most notable lament was Jeremiah's. He thought highly of Josiah and appreciated the justice of his administration (Jer 22.11,15-16). The last part of v.25 reads, "they are written in the lamentations". This is often taken as a reference to the book of The Lamentations of Jeremiah. But since that book deals with the fall of Jerusalem rather than the death of Josiah, this may refer to some other book long since lost. Josiah's renewed covenant (34.29-33) was quickly given up after he died. Jeremiah could look forward to a day when a new covenant would be written on the hearts of individuals, a new covenant that would produce a genuine change (Jer 33). Josiah's reforms could delay the coming captivity but could not avert it. Jeremiah was called of God in the thirteenth year of Josiah's reign. He outlived Josiah to the time of the captivity more than 20 years later.

"Someday, wrote the prophet Zechariah a century later, Israel will mourn for the Messiah they crucified, even 'as the mourning of Hadadrimmon in the valley of Megiddon' (12.11), a remarkable evidence of the intensity and universality of Judah's mourning for Josiah" (Whitcomb).

Josiah's failure makes all who read of it look forward to another, greater, Son of David who will rule in righteousness without any lapse whatsoever. In the meantime, as Ezekiel proclaims, "I will overturn, overturn, overturn… until he comes whose right it is; and I will give it him" (21.27).

The Chronicler does not dwell on Josiah's unfortunate death, but on his "goodness". The "goodness" of Hezekiah is noted in 32.22 and of the high priest Jehoiada in 24.16: "he had done good in Israel, both toward God, and toward his house". The last phrase of v.26, "according to that which was written in the law of the Lord", is a reminder of the manner in which Josiah excelled all other kings (2 Kings 23.25).

2 CHRONICLES 36

The Reigns of the Last Four Kings, the Exile, and the Hope of a Return

Introductory

Chapter 36 records very briefly the reigns of the last four kings of Judah, an explanation for the exile, the fall of Jerusalem and the temple, and the hope of a return. Josiah is the only king to be succeeded by more than one son. He was followed by three - Jehoahaz, Jehoiakim, and Zedekiah. Keil's words are worth quoting: "As the kingdom of Judah after Josiah's death advanced with swift steps to its destruction by the Chaldeans, so the author of the Chronicles goes quickly over the reigns of the last kings of Judah, who by their godless conduct hastened the ruin of the kingdom".

For most of the kings of Judah the Chronicler provides more extensive records than are found in Kings. Before this chapter, there are only two reigns where the writer has less material. Kings has 11 verses for Ahaziah - 2 Kings 8.25-29; 9.16,21,23,27-29, whereas Chronicles has only nine - 2 Chronicles 22.1-9. For Amon, Kings has eight verses - 2 Kings 21.19-26, and Chronicles only five - 2 Chronicles 33.21-25.

Ahaziah, Amon, and all four kings in this chapter were wicked.

For the first, Jehoahaz, both Kings and Chronicles have four verses. But for each of the last three kings, Chronicles has much less than Kings and increasingly so. Chronicles has only 10 verses for Zedekiah and the fall of the temple while Kings has 20.

The Chronicler for the first time omits any notice of the deaths of these kings. "The reigns of four kings have been presented almost as if they were one, and the increasing brevity of their description most effectively underlines the increasingly unstoppable threat of exile" (Selman).

Another effect of the very brief treatment of the last four kings is that it contributes greatly to the contrast to the two chapters describing good King Josiah's reign. Josiah's tender response to the Word of God (34.27) is in stark contrast to that of each of these four who rejected it, especially Jehoiakim who cut up the Word of God and burned it (Jer 36.23) and Zedekiah who "humbled not himself before Jeremiah the prophet speaking from the mouth of the Lord" (2 Chr 36.12). The reason for the captivity is given in vv.12-16. The importance of the Word of God in all this is a lesson for saints at all times.

Each of the four has at least two names. It is likely that there are only two kings of Judah (before these four) to have had at least two names in the Old Testament. Uzziah is referred to as Azariah eight times in 2 Kings and four times as Uzziah. The Chronicler always referred to him as Uzziah, except in 1 Chronicles 3.11 where he is referred to as Azariah. Jehoram's son is called Jehoahaz in 2 Chronicles 21.17, Azariah in 22.6, and Ahaziah 11 times in ch.22. Jehoahaz is also named Shallum in Jeremiah 22.11

and 1 Chronicles 3.15. The king of Egypt changed the name of Eliakim to Jehoiakim (v.4). The king of Babylon changed the name of Mattaniah to Zedekiah (2 Kings 24.17). Probably both wanted to remind the kings of Judah that they owed allegiance to another, greater, king. Both names given had the name of Jehovah so these changed names were not like those of Daniel and his three companions. They had idolatry linked with them. Jehoiachin had also the name of Jeconiah (1 Chr 3.16) and Coniah (Jer 22.28).

The author of the Chronicles seems to give the birth order of four of Josiah's sons (1 Chr 3.15). His firstborn son Johanan may have died before his father or with his father at Megiddo. 2 Kings 23.30 and 2 Kings 24.18 which were 11 years apart, make it clear that when Jehoahaz was 23, Zedekiah, the youngest sibling, was only ten years of age. Jehoiakim, the second oldest, was 25. But in 1 Chronicles 3.15 Shallum is given as the youngest son. Zedekiah and Shallum had the same mother (2 Kings 23.31; 24.18), which may explain why they are listed next to each other. One possible solution is that Shallum is put last because his reign was so much shorter than the reigns of Zedekiah and Jehoiakim.

Each of the last four kings was exiled to another country, the first one was exiled to Egypt and the last three to Babylon. "The final collapse under Zedekiah is therefore merely the final stage in a process that has long been inevitable. This arrangement had its own momentum, since the race to the exilic tape began as far back as Ahaz (28.5,8,11,13), Hezekiah (29.9; 30.9), and Manasseh (33.11)...Individual actions and even deaths are less important than that the kings experienced exile together because of the attitudes described in verses 12-16" (Selman).

Josiah was the last king of Judah to have political autonomy. Jehoahaz was dethroned by Necho the king of Egypt and exiled to Egypt. Necho put Eliakim (Jehoiakim) the half-brother of Jehoahaz on the throne and Judah became a vassal state. During the reign of Jehoiakim, Babylon defeated Egypt and Judah then became a vassal state of Babylon until they were carried away captive to Babylon itself.

Even though the writer of the Chronicles records these four reigns so briefly, he is careful to describe in each reign what happened to the temple. Some commentators believe that when Necho took tribute from the land in such a large amount (v.3), part of the payment may have come from spoiling the temple. While that is possible, it seems unlikely due to the fact that Jehoiakim taxed the people to pay the tribute (2 Kings 23.35). Some of the information about the temple in vv.7,10 and 18 is found only in Chronicles. "He has traced from its muted beginnings (v.3) a crescendo in terms of the temple's deprivation (vv.7,10,18), and this reaches its climax in its eventual destruction (v.19). Thus, there is a sense in which the Chronicler had drawn a deliberate parallel between the fate of the temple and that of the Davidic dynasty" (Williamson). The destruction of the temple is also recorded in 2 Kings 25.9 and Jeremiah 52.13.

The writer of the Kings places the responsibility for the exile on Manasseh (2 Kings 24.3-4) on account of the innocent blood that he shed. Even though Manasseh had a conversion experience very late in his reign, there are consequences even for forgiven sins. For the last few years of his reign he tried to undo the wickedness he had done previously. But he could never bring back to life the innocent persons he had slain. The writer of the Chronicles extends the blame to the whole nation rather than one individual or one generation. He explicitly shows in vv.12-16 that the king, the priests, and the people were all equally responsible for the exile.

Outline of Chapter 36

Verses 1-4: The reign of Jehoahaz.
Verses 5-8: The reign of Eliakim (Jehoiakim).
Verses 9-10: The reign of Jehoiachin.
Verses 11-19: The reign of Zedekiah, his fall, and the fall of the temple.
Verses 20-24: The hope of rebuilding the temple.

Verses 1-4: The Reign of Jehoahaz

Jehoahaz was the last king to be put on the throne by the people. They also chose Ahaziah for the throne (22.1), Uzziah (26.1), and Josiah (33.25). The king of Egypt chose Jehoiakim to reign (v.4), and the king of Babylon chose Zedekiah to reign (2 Kings 24.17). Possibly because of a reign of only three months, his is the least fully documented. It is surprising that the Chronicler did not record that Jehoahaz did evil as recorded in 2 Kings 23.32. Possibly, the people chose Jehoahaz to reign because he had anti-Egyptian sympathies like his father. But that is probably the reason that Necho put him down at Jerusalem and carried him to Egypt where he died (2 Kings 23.34).

"Jeremiah, who had his finger on the pulse of the people, instructed them not to mourn for Josiah (now dead only three months), but to mourn for Joahaz (Jehoahaz), for he would never again see his homeland" (Barber).

Necho took Jehoahaz's brother Eliakim and changed his name to Jehoiakim. Eliakim means, "God will establish", and Jehoiakim means, "Jehovah will establish". This "indicates a deference to the feelings of the sovereign, or rather to the people over whom he was appointed, which is in keeping with the politic character of Necho" (Murphy). Since Necho changed his name, even though only slightly, it was a reminder to Jehoiakim that Judah was now a vassal state. Because of that fact, Necho could put down Jehoahaz and demand tribute. The tribute he demanded (v.3) was much less than that which the king of Assyria imposed on Hezekiah (2 Kings 18.14).

"It is interesting, yet sad, to see the contrast between the story of Exodus and the one here. There, the Passover was observed at the time when Israel was freed from Egypt, and this same deliverance was celebrated by this king's father. Most likely he was alive at the time, and helped to share in the celebration, but now he is taken prisoner to the very land from which his people were freed. When Israel left Egypt they brought with them treasures of silver and gold, but now the descendants of the people then enriched, are sending their wealth back to the very place from which their forefathers had obtained it" (McShane).

Since the Passover was celebrated in the 18th year of Josiah's reign (35.19) and Josiah reigned for 31 years (34.1), Jehoahaz would be 13 years younger than the 23 years of age he was when he began to reign. So Jehoahaz would have been 10 years old when Josiah kept that Passover.

Verses 5-8: The Reign of Jehoiakim

Verse 5 records that the reign of Jehoiakim "was evil in the sight of the Lord his God". Jeremiah portrays his wickedness with a masterly hand (Jer 22.13-19). Jehoiakim taxed the people to pay the tribute while he himself was living in luxury (Jer 22.13-14). He withheld the wages of those that worked on his luxurious home. No king of Judah is recorded as having such disrespect for the Word of God as Jehoiakim. In Jeremiah 36 it is recorded that he cut up the Word of God and then burned it.

Verses 6-7 are the only verses of the first ten of this chapter that have any information not found in 2 Kings. Verse 6 says that Nebuchadnezzar "bound him in fetters to carry him to Babylon". But we do not know from that whether Jehoiakim was actually carried to Babylon or only threatened with deportation. However, since the phrase, "bound him with fetters to carry him to Babylon", is only found elsewhere of the exile of Manasseh in 33.11 and of Zedekiah in 2 Kings 25.7, Jeremiah 39.7 (RV), and 52.11 with almost identical words, it seems probable that he was actually carried to Babylon, albeit temporarily. "Further, the background for vv. 6-7 is greatly enhanced if the Babylonians' theft of the temple vessels is the same as that described in Daniel 1.1-2...Jehoiakim could have been taken to Babylon on either occasion, though he obviously found it no easier to accept Babylonian sovereignty than he did God's authority" (Selman). (He is referring to two occasions recorded in a Babylonian chronicle.)

Verse 7 is not in 2 Kings but is confirmed by Daniel 1.1-2. The word "also" in v.7 supports what has been said about Jehoiakim actually being carried to Babylon: "The Chronicler twice uses the doom-laden words 'to Babylon', in v.6 about the king and in v.7 about the temple treasure. Exile, and the end of the temple and throne, are looming larger" (New Bible Commentary, 21st Century Edition).

The record of Jehoiakim is the only one among those of the last four kings of Judah that has a concluding formula (v.8). 2 Kings 24.6 and this verse may imply that he died in Judah but neither says that he was buried. Jeremiah prophesied, "He shall be buried with the burial of an ass, drawn and cast forth beyond the gates of Jerusalem" (22.19). Jeremiah also prophesied other dishonour for the dead body of Jehoiakim (36.30): "his dead body shall be cast out in the day to the heat, and in the night to the frost". That verse also prophesied that, "He shall have none to sit upon the throne of David". His son Jehoiachin did reign, but his brief reign of only three months and ten days does not nullify that prophecy.

The Chronicler does not record any persons carried into captivity at this time but Daniel 1.1-4 tells of some of the king's seed and others taken to Babylon. This was a fulfillment of Isaiah's prophecy to Hezekiah about his descendants becoming eunuchs in the palace of the king of Babylon (Is 39.7; 2 Kings 20.18). This was the first deportation. There are three others recorded in Jeremiah 52.28-30. Possibly the reason this one is not mentioned there is because there was no record of how many were deported with Daniel and his three companions while the other three deportations have the total number recorded.

The "abominations" mentioned in v.8 would include all the abominations Jeremiah wrote about as noted in Jeremiah 22.13-19; 25.1-11; 26.1-24; 36.1-32. They would include the fact that Jehoiakim was guilty of the murder of Urijah the prophet (Jer 26.20-23). It would also include the statement that the king wanted to take Baruch the scribe and Jeremiah the prophet, but the Lord hid them (Jer 36.26).

Jehoiakim's death meant that his son Jehoiachin would have to bear the greater part of Babylon's reaction to Jehoiakim's rebellion. The phrase, "that which was found in him", may include idolatrous practices that he did secretly and were later found out. Of course, God knew all the time. The writer of the Kings, the Chronicler, and Jeremiah all have a similar assessment of Jehoiakim.

Verses 9-10: The Reign of Jehoiachin

2 Kings 24.8 gives the age of Jehoiachin when he began to reign as 18. Since 2 Kings 24.15 tells of Jehoiachin being carried to Babylon with his wives, that would indicate that 18 is the right age rather than 8 as in v.9. There can be no real doubt that Jehoiachin began to reign at 18 years of age as stated in 2 Kings 24.8. Verse 9 says, "he did that which was evil in the sight of the Lord". This verse also records that he reigned three months and ten days, which is more exact than the account in Kings, which simply has three months.

Verse 10 tells of Jehoiachin being brought to Babylon. Jeremiah prophesied of his humiliating defeat (Jer 22.24-30). 2 Kings 24.10-12,15 show that this prophecy was fulfilled. Nebuchadnezzar and his army besieged Jerusalem. Jehoiachin, his mother, and others were taken to Babylon. There was a small deportation (v.7) when Daniel and his companions and others were taken into exile (linking it with Daniel 1.1-4), but v.10 records the first major deportation.

"However, his exile is of considerable importance in 2 Kings 24.10-16 and Jeremiah 22.24-30, and is also reported in the Babylonian chronicle: 'he (Nebuchadnezzar) besieged the city of Judah and...seized the city and captured the king. He appointed there a king of his own choice, received its heavy tribute and brought it to Babylon" (Selman).

Jeconiah or Jehoiachin is recorded as having seven sons (1 Chr 3.17-18). It is likely that most of the seven were born in Babylon. But not one of those sons ever sat on David's throne, as Jeremiah prophesied, "...no man of his seed shall prosper, sitting upon the throne of David, and ruling any more in Judah" (22.30). Jechonias is mentioned in Matthew 1.11 in the genealogy of Joseph who was married to Mary, the mother of the Lord Jesus Christ. Since Joseph was not the biological father of our Lord Jesus, the Lord Jesus inherited the legal right to the throne without inheriting the curse pronounced on Jeconiah. Mary's genealogy is given in Luke 3. Mary was not descended from Solomon but rather from Nathan, another son of David (Lk 3.31).

Verse 10 refers to Zedekiah as the "brother" of Jehoiachin. 2 Kings 24.17 is more accurate when it states that Zedekiah was his (Jehoiachin's) father's brother. The word "brother" can refer to a blood relative. 2 Kings 24.17 states that when Nebuchadnezzar put Zedekiah on the throne, he changed his name from Mattaniah to Zedekiah. Zedekiah signifies "righteousness" or "justice of the Lord". "The latter is interpreted by the rabbis as a warning by Nebuchadnezzar that divine justice would overtake him should he break his oath of allegiance and prove disloyal" (Slotki).

Verses 11-19: The Reign of Zedekiah, his Fall, and the Fall of the Temple

The beginning of Zedekiah's evil reign is recorded in v.11. 2 Kings 23.31 and 24.18 make it clear that Jehoahaz and Zedekiah had the same mother. Jehoiakim had a different mother. Zedekiah was 13 years younger than Jehoahaz. The words in vv.11 and 12a are fewer than 2 Kings, but from vv.12b-16 the Chronicler has a much greater explanation for the exile than 2 Kings 24.20 and Jeremiah 52.3.

Verse 12a shows that Zedekiah was a wicked king, but he was characterized more by weakness than by wickedness. Jeremiah 38.5 especially records how spineless a character he was. He was kind to Jeremiah, but he timidly yielded to Jeremiah's persecutors. Four men complained to the king about the preaching of Jeremiah and wanted to punish him. Zedekiah replied, in the words of Jeremiah 38.5, "Behold, he is in your hand: for the king is not he that can do any thing against you". So the four men put Jeremiah in a dungeon and left him to die of starvation. That was the most severe imprisonment Jeremiah ever had. But Ebed-melech, an Ethiopian, courageously went to Zedekiah and saved Jeremiah's life by getting the king to reverse his decision and have Ebed-melech get him out of the dungeon which he tenderly did (Jer 38.7-13).

Zedekiah asked counsel of Jeremiah a number of times, but he never brought himself to obey God's Word to him through the prophet. Zedekiah lacked the strength of character and courage to stand against the princes who pressured him to follow their advice (which was contrary to Jeremiah's counsel). Edersheim gives an accurate description of Zedekiah: "As for Zedekiah himself, his conduct was characterized by that helpless perplexity and vacillation, which were the outcome of weakness and want of religious conviction".

Verse 12b says that he "humbled not himself before Jeremiah speaking from the mouth of the Lord". This was true of Zedekiah throughout his reign, but especially is seen in Jeremiah 38 when Jeremiah told him (v.17), "Thus saith the Lord, the God of hosts, the God of Israel; if thou wilt assuredly go forth unto the king of Babylon's princes, then thy soul shall live, and this city shall not be burned with fire; and thou shalt live, and thine house". Zedekiah expressed his fear. Jeremiah gave him assurance, but Zedekiah still refused to obey. He feared man more than he feared God. "The fear of man bringeth a snare: but whoso putteth his trust in the Lord shall be safe" (Prov 29.25).

"The king is condemned not for any specific actions...but for his overall rebelliousness towards God and man. This is illustrated by negative versions of the two expressions from 2 Chronicles 7.14 (*did not humble himself...would not turn*), and by other typical phrases which indicate his similarity with the generation which died in the wilderness (*stiff-necked*, cp. Ex 32.9; 33.3,5; Deut 9.6; 2 Chr 30.8) and with the Pharaoh who opposed Moses (*hardened his heart*; cp. Ex 8.15,32). These same attitudes are identified in the New Testament as the cause of unbelief toward Jesus and the gospel (Acts 7.51; Mk 6.52; 8.17; Heb 3.13)" (Selman).

There were very serious consequences for Zedekiah, for Judah, and for Jerusalem because he would not humble himself. How pathetic that his last sight was of his captors murdering his sons before gouging out his eyes. Jeremiah prophesied that Zedekiah's eyes would behold the eyes of the king of Babylon (34.3). Ezekiel prophesied, "I will bring him to Babylon to the land of the Chaldeans; yet shall he not see it, though he shall die there" (12.13). How could both of these prophecies come true? The answer is that after Zedekiah saw the king of Babylon, his enemies put out his eyes. Because he refused to humble himself, Judah was taken captive and the city was burned, including the temple.

Zedekiah rebelled against the Lord (v.12b) and then he rebelled against Babylon (v.13) as his brother Jehoiakim and his nephew Jehoiachin had done before him. 2 Kings 24.20 and Jeremiah 52.3 both record that Zedekiah rebelled against the king of Babylon, but neither one tells about his breaking the oath that he had sworn in the name of the Lord. That is only recorded here and in Ezekiel 17.12-21. It seems likely from Ezekiel 17.12-13 that the king of Babylon made him swear when he first made him king. Leviticus 19.12 states, "ye shall not swear by my name falsely". For

Zedekiah to break his solemn oath and rebel against Nebuchadnezzar was his own undoing and also the undoing of Judah, inviting swift retaliation.

Surely the serious mistake by Zedekiah in breaking his oath and the serious consequences of it is a warning for all time. God wants His people to be persons of integrity and to be true to their word.

Zedekiah was a stark contrast to his father (vv.12b-13) in his pride and the hardness of his heart, a contrast to Josiah whose heart was tender and who humbled himself before God (34.27). When Zedekiah "stiffened his neck, and hardened his heart from turning unto the Lord God of Israel" (v.13), he was again a contrast to Josiah of whom it is recorded in 2 Kings 23.25, "And like unto him was there no king before him, that turned to the Lord with all his heart, and with all his soul, and with all his might, according to all the law of Moses; neither after him arose there any like him". Josiah turned whole-heartedly to the Lord while his son refused to do so. Josiah got the blessing of the promise of 7.14, which has "humble" and "turn" in the conditions, but Zedekiah missed it.

How sad that all the chiefs of the priests who should have opposed idolatry were ring leaders in it (v.14). "The abominations of the heathen" refers especially to idolatry, and all the immorality and perversity that went with it. Ezekiel 8 describes the terrible and abominable idolatries and pollutions of the temple during Zedekiah's reign. This verse shows that the priests and the people were equally guilty along with Zedekiah as a cause for the exile.

Verses 12-14 help to explain the exile, but vv.15-16 especially describe why it took place. These verses are solemn but precious and need not be limited to the reign of Zedekiah. In v.15 where it is stated that "the Lord God of their fathers sent to them by his messengers", the phrase that follows, "rising up early and sending" (RV), is found in various forms 10 times in Jeremiah (7.13,25; 11.7; 25.4; 26.5; 29.19; 32.33; 35.14-15; 44.4). This shows the urgency of God's message. Jeremiah referred to himself once with that phrase (25.3). Verse 15 shows God's care and compassion for His people and His dwelling place. God has still the same care and compassion for all His people today and for His dwelling places. All companies of believers gathered to the name of our Lord Jesus are His dwelling places today. The same verse calls to mind the words of our Lord Jesus when He lamented over the inhabitants of Jerusalem (Lk 13.34): "O Jerusalem, Jerusalem, which killest the prophets, and stonest them that are sent unto thee; how often would I have gathered thy children together, as a hen doth gather her brood under her wings, and ye would not!" How sad to read of the response here (v.16) - evil treatment of God's messengers and despising God's Word, "until the wrath of the Lord rose against his people, till there was no remedy". We read of wrong treatment of Urijah the prophet (Jer 26.20-23) and of Jeremiah (Jer 37.15-16; 38.6). Some recorded instances of mocking God's messengers are found in 1 Kings 22.24; 2 Kings 2.23; 2 Chronicles 30.10; Jeremiah 17.15, and 20.8.

The AV margin and the RV margin both have "Hebrew *healing*" for "remedy" (v.16); there was no humbling, no turning, and consequently no healing. God's people refused the blessing of 7.14. "His people" (v.15) calls to mind "my people" (7.14). So the real reason for their exile and captivity was not simply sinful acts, but rather their refusal to respond properly to the Word of God.

"The theme of intensity and persistence in sin is further emphasized by the statement that the people had refused to be dissuaded from their evil ways even by God's prophets. What constitutes the greatest evil for the Chronicler - and it is a theme taken up elsewhere in the Bible - is not the wrong doing in and of itself, but wrong doing in defiance of the clear knowledge of what is right (Mk 12.1-12; Lk 16.31; Is 1.2-3)" (McConville).

As long as we are open to receive God's Word, there is always a possibility of recovery. But we are warned that once we close ourselves to receiving God's Word, there is no longer any possibility of recovery.

"The statement in these two verses is certainly so very general, that it may apply to all the time of gradually increasing defection of the people from the Lord their God; but the author of the Chronicles had primarily in view only the time of Zedekiah in which the defection reached its highest point" (Keil).

However, there may be some truth in Dillard's comments on these two verses: "Here, however, the Chronicler describes the guilt of Israel as cumulative: rather than each generation or king experiencing weal or woe in terms of its own actions, there is cumulative weight of guilt which ultimately irretrievably provokes the wrath of God and brings the great exile".

Verse 17 significantly begins with the word, "Therefore". This is the conclusion of moral logic. The previous five verses give ample reasons why God brought upon them the king of the Chaldeans. The sword was in the hand of the Chaldeans. It was important for the post-exilic people of God of the Chronicler's day to know those reasons. Keil fittingly writes, "the judgment is brought into definite relationship to the crime: because they had profaned the sanctuary by idolatry (v.14), they themselves were slain in the sanctuary". Selman also becomingly observes, "Because Israel wanted none of God's compassion (v.15), 'no compassion' was received from their conquerors (v.17)". The last phrase, "he gave them all into his hand", emphasizes that this was God's governmental dealing against Judah.

All the vessels and treasures of the house of God and the treasures of the king and of the princes were brought to Babylon (v.18). Verses 17-19 record a thorough destruction. The word "all" is found five times in these three verses. Besides that, "young man…old man", "great and small", and the word "destroyed" deepen the impression of complete destruction. Jerusalem was besieged for 18 months. The famine was so severe that they resorted to cannibalism even as Deuteronomy indicated they would if they forsook God (Deut 28.53-57). Lamentations 4.10 bewails this fact.

Verse 19 records the burning of the house of God and the breaking down of the wall. That was in the year 586 BC. Ezra tells of the rebuilding of the temple in chs.1-6 of his book. Nehemiah records the building of the walls in the first part of his book. "The 586 BC destruction of Judah is also the subject of Biblical prediction that involves more verses than any other direct prophecy that is to be found within Scripture - 608, distributed among 17 different books of the Bible" (Payne). 2 Kings 25.1-21, Jeremiah 39.1-10 and 52.4-27 have greater detail. The city was destroyed 22 or 23 years after the death of Josiah and 5 years after the glory of the Lord had departed from the midst of the city (Ezek 8.4; 11.23). The city was destroyed 136 years after the fall of Samaria.

Verses 20-23: The Hope of Rebuilding the Temple

Verses 20-21 have a little glimpse of restoration, but vv.22-23 have the brightest hope. Verse 20 tells of those who were carried away to Babylon that, "They were servants to him and his sons until the reign of the kingdom of Persia". The words "to him and his sons" refer to Nebuchadnezzar, his son, his grandson, and all his successors. The Babylonian dynasty ended after the third succession. The first part of v.20 adds to the impression of thorough destruction. The men of Judah faced two tragic alternatives - death or deportation. The word "servants" means "slaves". They were used in forced labour. The word "until" shows that the captivity would only be for a limited time. This is the first mention of Persia in the Old Testament.

The references to Jeremiah in v.12 and vv.21-22 indicate that the Chronicler may have been dependent on Jeremiah for this part of his writing. "'Jeremiah the prophet speaking from the mouth of the Lord' (v.12); 'by the mouth of Jeremiah' (vv.21-22). These words illustrate inspiration. The words were from the mouth of Jehovah, that is, the words were God's words; the instrument used for making them known to Israel was Jeremiah's mouth. The words did not originate in Jeremiah's mouth, but in Jehovah's mouth" (Williams). Jeremiah prophesied twice about the length of the captivity (Jer 25.11-12; 29.10-11). It is touching that God adds, after promising a return after 70 years, "For I know the thoughts that I think toward you, saith the Lord, thoughts of peace, and not of evil, to give you an expected end" (Jer 29.11). The RV has for the last words, "to give you hope in your latter end". God's people had to go into captivity because of their departure from God and their refusal to hearken to His Word, but God was gracious in limiting the captivity to seventy years.

Verse 21 records that the land enjoyed her sabbaths for 70 years. Leviticus 25.4-7 states that God's people were not to sow in the land every seventh year. It is not necessary to suppose that the sabbath year was always neglected. We can only legitimately conclude that ever since the time of Moses up to the beginning of the captivity, there had been about 70 years when the sabbath year had been violated (Lev 26.34-35). This verse also gives hope. Since the sabbatical years had been kept now, there was no reason why they could not return to their land.

As already stated, while vv.20-21 give some hope of restoration, the brightest hope is in vv.22-23. "The book ends with the same words as open its sequel in the book of Ezra (36.22-23; Ezra 1.1-3); we may suppose that when the whole work of the Chronicler was divided up, these verses were repeated here so that this book should end on a hopeful note. Indeed, since 1 and 2 Chronicles stand last in the order of the Hebrew Bible, it could be seen to be important that the whole Bible should end with a prospect of salvation. Restoration is to be effected by God's stirring up of Cyrus the Persian to re-establish the temple. The exile is past, but the task of rebuilding both temple and people remains to be traced in the books that follow" (Ackroyd).

The last four verses of 2 Kings also have a note of hope. In the 37th year of the captivity, Jehoiachin was released by Evil-Merodach (Nebuchadnezzar's successor) immediately after the death of Nebuchadnezzar. He was dressed in royal apparel, given a seat at the king's table, and treated with respect by all around. This event reminds us of the kindness that David showed to Mephibosheth in 2 Samuel 9. It is a reminder also that God will yet restore Israel though she will not deserve it in future any more than she did then. We see the kindness of God to the house of David in this incident. There is also a hint in this record that the captivity of the people he represents would also come to an end.

McShane in commenting on these last verses of 2 Kings writes, "At the end of the dismal history of Israel and Judah, with all its revelation of the most favoured people in the world, it is good to see a glimmer of light shining in the midst of darkness". Jeremiah also prophesied of Jehoiachin dying in Babylon (22.26; 52.34).

"The mysterious ways of the Lord are nowhere more plainly seen than in His having raised up a pagan king to provide for the post-exilic redemption for His chosen people. In startling language, Isaiah referred to Cyrus as God's anointed one (Is 45.1). How remarkable that God should display His universal sovereignty by calling a Persian king to be a type of the Saviour of all who will believe, even Jesus Christ" (Dyer & Merrill). Surely the closing words of 2 Chronicles are a reminder that God is in control. He is superintending the events of world history for His glory and the good of mankind (Job 12.23; Ps 76.10; Acts 17.26). Cyrus was an instrument of God's providence and was named by Isaiah over 100 years before he was born (Is 44.28; 45.1). In 2 Chronicles 36.22, the words, "the first year of Cyrus, king of Persia" refer to his first year of rule over Babylon. Daniel may have directed Cyrus to Isaiah 44.28 and 45.1.

"Cyrus of course is thinking only of the house in *Jerusalem*, but in the Chronicler's thought the phrase is inevitably connected with both houses of the Davidic covenant, the dynasty as well as the temple. In the end, therefore, the end is also a fresh start...The final phrase, *let him go up*, which is a single word in Hebrew, breaks off in the middle of Ezra's version of the edict. Its effect is to emphasize that the readers' expected final response to the book is to exercise faith in God's promises" (Selman).

"The Chronicler had the task of relating the eclipse of Israel's nationhood, but the edict of Cyrus heralded the termination of captivity and gave promise of a renewal of the glories of the past" (Slotki).